# MORALITY AND RESPONSIBILITY OF RULERS

# Morality and Responsibility of Rulers

## *European and Chinese Origins of a Rule of Law as Justice for World Order*

Edited by
ANTHONY CARTY
and
JANNE NIJMAN

OXFORD
UNIVERSITY PRESS

OXFORD
UNIVERSITY PRESS

Great Clarendon Street, Oxford, OX2 6DP,
United Kingdom

Oxford University Press is a department of the University of Oxford.
It furthers the University's objective of excellence in research, scholarship, and education by publishing worldwide. Oxford is a registered trade mark of Oxford University Press in the UK and in certain other countries



First Edition published in 2018



Published in the United States of America by Oxford University Press
198 Madison Avenue, New York, NY 10016, United States of America

British Library Cataloguing in Publication Data
Data available

Library of Congress Control Number: 2017947323

ISBN 978–0–19–967005–5

# *Acknowledgements*

The editors first and foremost would like to thank the authors of this volume for the enriching journey across East Asian and Western intellectual traditions of political, moral, and legal thought on which we embarked together. The project has been a true adventure.

We have had the privilege of meeting twice, in Amsterdam and Hong Kong, to exchange and examine rule of law ideas across different traditions of international intellectual history. At these seminars, initial versions of the chapters in this volume were presented and discussed. Not all participants to these seminars have authored a chapter in this volume, but all have contributed significantly to the coming about of this volume. We are grateful to Chad Hansen, James Tracy, Wang Zhong Jiang, Yang Xiaodong, YI Ping, and in particular to Heinhard Steiger, who has been such a committed, knowledgeable, and warm supporter of this project throughout the years.

The editors are grateful to the Amsterdam Center for International Law of the University of Amsterdam's School of Law, the Chiang Ching-Kuo Foundation of Taiwan, the Amsterdam law firm Diepen van der Kroef, the Dutch Royal Academy of Sciences, the Hong Kong University's School of Law, and the Hong Kong Chamber of Commerce in the Netherlands for making these seminars possible. We are grateful also to our home institutions—the University of Amsterdam and Hong Kong University—for their stimulating and intellectual support of the project.

A special acknowledgement moreover is due to the Hong Kong Research Grants Council, whose generous award was fundamental to the Chinese dimension of the book. The project was authorized by the General Research Fund under the title: The Impact of Western International Law on the Disintegration of the late Qing Empire and the Continuing Consequences for Today. The Council not only facilitated contact with Chinese scholars and supported the seminar in Hong Kong, and partially also Amsterdam, but, most vitally, also funded the research students and assistants who make up a very large part of the Chinese section of the book. This project has provided a grounding for their first steps into a scholarly life. The combination of this project with one on a critique of the varieties of Western humanism involved in the construction of Western international law we believe to be uniquely fortunate and enriching.

We are eager to acknowledge the anonymous OUP referees for their helpful and insightful comments on the project.

More generally we would like to thank Anne van Mulligen (University of Amsterdam) and Zhang Xiaoshi (Hong Kong University) for their research assistance. In particular we thank Zhang Xiaoshi for the (simultaneous) translations she provided at the Amsterdam seminar. Only her mastery of the detail of the subject matter made this remarkable feat possible.

At OUP, Merel Alstein, Emma Endean-Mills, and Natasha Flemming have been patient supporters of the project and very helpful in guiding us through the production process.

Tony wishes to acknowledge especially Miss Cui Yan for the vital part she played in the preparation of the HKRGF funding proposal. After the approval of the proposal, she had to take up a position as an assistant professor in the Law Faculty of Shandung University at Weihai. Cui Yan was funded by an internal Hong Kong University grant matched by the Law Faculty. In addition, Tony wishes also to acknowledge that Chapter 12, 'Humane Governance' as the Moral Responsibility of Rulers in East Asian Confucian Political Philosophy by Chun-chieh Huang, was translated by Zhang Longyi, a research assistant supported financially by the Hong Kong Research Grant Council's award. Janne wishes to express special thanks to Catherine Brölmann for her genuine interest in and support of this project.

This volume does not easily fit existing disciplinary categories, nor does it want to. It seeks to serve the study of the history of international legal and political thought, but not solely. The editors hope this volume will be of interest to anyone involved with (reflection on) questions of international law and governance in today's world where the West is significantly engaged with non-Western powers on an equal basis.

Finally, we dedicate this volume to our students, who we hope will engage actively in the much-needed transcultural humanist dialogue on international law and international relations.

*Amsterdam and Beijing*
*May 2017*

# Contents

## II. LAW AND JUSTICE IN CHINESE THOUGHT ON WORLD ORDER

# *List of Contributors*

**Anna Irene Baka** is the Legal Officer at the Greek National Commission for Human Rights

**Joseph Canning** is Affiliated Lecturer in the Faculty of History at the University of Cambridge

**Anthony Carty** is Professor of Law at the School of Law of the Beijing Institute of Technology

**Emily Cheung**, LLB, DLP, Hong Kong University

**Qi Fei** is a PhD candidate at the Chinese University of Hong Kong

**Maranatha Fung**, LLB, DLP, Hong Kong University

**Peter Goodrich** is Professor of Law and Director of the Program in Law and Humanities at Cardozo Law, New York, and Visiting Professor in the School of Social Science, New York University, Abu Dhabi

**Henan Hu** is Assistant Professor in the School of Law of the South China University of Technology in Guangzhou, Guangdong, China, and a PhD graduate of Hong Kong University

**Chun-chieh Huang** is Emeritus Professor, National Taiwan University, Institute of the Humanities

**Patrick Sze-lok Leung** has a PhD in Chinese History and he is a lecturer in the Department of Chinese History at Hong Kong University

**Susan Longfield Karr** is based at the Department of History at the University of Cincinnati

**Janne Nijman** is Professor of History and Theory of International Law at the Faculty of Law, University of Amsterdam; and Member of the Board and Academic Director of the T.M.C. Asser Instituut in The Hague

**Anthony Pagden** is Distinguished Professor of Political Science and History at the University of California, Los Angeles

**Andrew RC Simpson** is Senior Lecturer in Law at the University of Aberdeen

**Christoph Stumpf** is Professor of Law at the Faculty of Law and Economy at the Martin Luther Universität, Halle-Wittenberg

**Jing Tan** is a PhD Candidate at Hong Kong University

**Tian Tao** is Professor of History in the School of History and Culture at Tianjin Normal University

**Xavier Tubau** is Associate Professor at Hamilton College

**Aihe Wang** is Professor of Chinese Studies at Hong Kong University

**John Witte, Jr** is Robert W. Woodruff University Professor of Law; and Director of the Center for the Study of Law and Religion at Emory University

**Bijun Xu** is a Postdoctoral Fellow, Institute for Governance Studies, Tsinghua University

# The Moral Responsibility of Rulers

## Going Back *Beyond* the Liberal Rule of Law for World Order

*Anthony Carty and Janne Nijman*

## 1. General Introduction*

### 1.1 Introduction

It is a generally accepted idea in contemporary international legal scholarship that to think about an international rule of law is a liberal project, the 'sole thinkable principle of organization' for the modern international system. Martti Koskenniemi opened his seminal article 'The Politics of International Law' with the observation that

> [s]ince the publication of Emmerich de Vattel's *Droit des gens ou principes de la loi naturelle appliquées à la conduite et aux affaires des nations et des souverains* (1758), jurists have written about international matters by assuming that the liberal principles of the Enlightenment and their logical corollary, the Rule of Law, could be extended to apply in the organization of international society just as they had been used in the domestic one.[1]

He captures well the general understanding of the international rule of law in contemporary international scholarship. Underlying this common understanding of an international rule of law is the analogy with a liberal domestic society and the idea that it is a thoroughly *modern* legal concept. Both that analogy and the reduction of the rule of law idea to a project of European modernity deprive the international rule of law of a history of its own, as it is understood as merely a part of the liberal model for international society. We take issue with these two underpinnings. First, extending the liberal model from the domestic to the international society is highly problematic as it reifies a fundamental misunderstanding of the nature of international society.[2] It transposes a constitutional set-up claiming the primacy of law over politics to

* The presentation of the chapters in the Contents follows roughly an historical chronology, firstly in the history of ideas, and then in the state practice. It consists of reflections of the editors which are not necessarily shared by the individual authors, and which are certainly less rich.

[1] M Koskenniemi, 'The Politics of International Law' (1990) 1 EJIL 4.

[2] See H Morgenthau, *Scientific Man and Power Politics* (Chicago UP 1946); see also the conclusion to Chapter 6 in this volume (on Richelieu).

*The Moral Responsibility of Rulers: Going Back* Beyond *the Liberal Rule of Law for World Order.* Anthony Carty and Janne Nijman.  Published 2018 by Oxford University Press.

the international level. It supposes moreover that most disputes are comparable to private law disputes—hence Hersch Lauterpacht's famous private law analogy and international law—and that a professional judiciary is in place to settle disputes. Morgenthau argues that liberal internationalists take judicial settlement out of the context of democratic constitutionalism where individuals are equal in strength or weakness before the law, into an international context where States are not remotely equal and have much less clearly defined rights and interests. Additionally, they cannot usually be compelled by international sanctions.[3] Morgenthau prefers to approach international disputes with a theory of prudence and moral judgement by statesmen, which entails recognition of the complexity of the usual disputes. 'The choice is not between legality and illegality but between political wisdom and political stupidity.'[4] To enforce the liberal internationalist principles of international law without relying on prudence and moral judgement—thus denying the political dimension—risks producing chaos rather than peace and justice.[5] In short, the liberal internationalist analogy between the national and international society is unhelpful.

Second, to present *rule of law for world order* ideas as by definition *modern* ideas—'modern' in the Hobbesian variant of 'liberal'—that have developed as a response to the *pre*modern tradition of natural jurisprudence and its subjectivism, is flawed too. This is so because the history of rule of law thinking is much older: in Europe, ever since Greek and Roman antiquity the idea of a rule of law is part of the law-as-justice discourse. While in China the liberal conception of rule of law may be non-existent, ethical thinking about guiding and constraining the power of the emperor dates back even longer. Also, this identification of the rule of law with liberal modernity has in the theory of international law represented by Koskenniemi, cited above, entrapped international law and the rule of law idea in particular in Hobbesian ontology, sociology, and politics.[6] Whence it leaves no room for law grounded on and creating a space for rational argumentation and moral judgement, no room for politics within law as practical reason, within a space of 'rule of law as justice'. It also leaves no escape from politics as the 'furthering [of] subjective desires' pure and simple.[7]

This volume engages with these two interrelated, in our understanding fundamental, misconceptions. The liberal, domestic society-bred, rule of law model cannot simply be transposed to today's international society and 'rule of law for world order'—thinking does not start with Hobbes, nor is it by definition modern/liberal of the Hobbesian persuasion. While this interpretation has come to dominate the discipline, and therefore the choice of Koskenniemi, who most adroitly captures the spirit of this harsher humanism, the present volume is a first attempt to break free. As such, it is both a historical and a modestly philosophical project. In section 1.2, we will briefly pause at the

[3] See Morgenthau (n 2) 108–21. [4] ibid 120.

[5] cf Morgenthau's position against the Vietnam War early on (*NYT Magazine* 1965 'We are deluding ourselves in Vietnam').

[6] See in particular Koskenniemi (n 1).

[7] Koskenniemi (n 1) 5; A Carty, review of M Koskenniemi, *The Politics of International Law* (Hart 2011) (2012) 13(2) Melbourne Journal of International Law 1–20. There are more optimistic versions of the possibility of rationality in modern liberal theories of the rule of law, above all J Habermas, *Between Facts and Norm, Contributions to a Discourse of Law and Democracy* (W Rehg tr, MIT Press 1996).

dual identity of this volume. Section 2 then introduces the alternative intellectual history of early-modern European thought as carved out in this volume, section 4 does the same for the intellectual history of Chinese thought. Section 3 is an interlude to bridge sections 2 and 4. In section 5 we allow ourselves some philosophical reflections inspired by the intellectual histories narrated in this volume. Ultimately, 'going back beyond the liberal rule of law for world order' means that this volume engages in a revisit of natural law jurisprudence. That tradition takes a good look at human nature and when formulating standards of morality, which are considered relevant to (international) law, and it conceives of law as justice, that is, it includes a space for ethics, for moral judgement. Hence, it is likely that the philosophical part of our project—the going back *beyond* modern liberal internationalism—will encounter critiques that are commonly directed against classical natural law theories. These will probably be critical of the hegemonic nature of 'universality', the subjectivity of 'right reason' and justice, and the impossibility of objective values. These considerations will be confronted in section 5; here we will build primarily on the historical inquiry we have undertaken, which explains the turn to *ius gentium et naturae* as a counter-hegemonic force, that is, as a turn to law as justice constituting a source of morality for standards of governance. Hence, rule of law as justice provides a source to draw on for rulers when making moral judgements and a source for the ruled when contesting the authority that binds them.

## 1.2 A dual project: history and philosophy of international law

The present volume aims to offer a two-step critique of the liberal understanding of the idea of a rule of law for world order that dominates international law and international legal thought. It carves out an alternative history of rule of law for world order thinking—'rule of law as justice'—and on the basis of this 'turn to history'[8] it means to point to a philosophical way out.

In the dominant liberal internationalist version, the rule of law is understood to be based upon the consent of the absolutely free and sovereign agent, upon the latter's willingness to follow consensual, agreed procedures to resolve disputes and, more generally, upon a willingness to engage in negotiations in good faith, especially by providing reasoned justifications for one's viewpoint. Liberal internationalism rejects the idea of a system of objective values inherent either in human nature or in a natural world order of Being. On the contrary, it depreciates values and natural principles (of justice) as subjective and highly political, and it puts forward the idea of a very thin international rule of law—ie minimal obligations of States to each other coupled with rather thick obligations of the State towards itself, grounded in an expansionist conception of freedom—as the modern way.

[8] See also eg M Koskenniemi, 'Why History of International Law Today' (2004) 4 Rechtsgeschichte 61–66; A Kemmerer, 'Turning Aside: On International Law and Its History' in R Miller and R Bratspies (eds), *Progress in International Law* (Martinus Nijhoff 2008) 71–93; T Skouteris, 'Engaging History in International Law' in J Beneyto and D Kennedy (eds), *New Approaches to International Law* (T.M.C. Asser 2012) 99–122, 103; G Galindo, 'Martti Koskenniemi and the Historiographical Turn in International Law' (2005) 16 EJIL 539–59; M Craven, 'Theorising the Turn to History in International Law' in A Orford and F Hoffmann (eds), *The Oxford Handbook of the Theory of International Law* (OUP 2016) 21–37.

The liberal rule of law idea came to replace and suppress natural law and justice in international law and international legal thought in (early) modernity. With its appropriation by the liberal tradition the idea was cut off radically from a very long and rich tradition in which, for example, Aristotle and Cicero had defined rule of law, especially in the context of relations among nations, in terms of the 'rule of reason'[9] and the rule of natural law.[10]

As a history project, this volume first turns to early-modern European thought to reconnect to a non-liberal history of the law of nations. While this going back to history may be understood as a critical move emerging from both historiographical dissatisfaction with how the history of the rule of law idea is constructed and political dissatisfaction with the continuous reproduction of liberal internationalist international law and politics, the intellectual history that is carved out in this volume is a true history project in itself, and relevant as such. It aims to unearth alternative understandings of *ius gentium et naturae* and rule of law for world order in early-modern European thought; understandings that have been marginalized by the domination of liberal international thought since Hobbes.

The volume sets out to do this without having defined the rule of law idea beforehand, recognizing the multiplicity of its meanings. As the rule of law is an essentially contested concept, authors and editors discern the concept or idea to operate rather as a jurist's sensibility about the relationship between law and politics, about speaking truth to power, about constraining force and power, about subjecting rulers to standards of a higher normative order (generally rooted in natural law) prescribing them to act responsibly, virtuously, justly, and non-arbitrarily, to the benefit of the people and the common good. In short, our history project on the rule of law idea is neither an essentialist nor a nominalist project.

In Part I 'Law and Justice in Early-Modern European Thought on World Order' the historiographical focus is on how, in the context of the gradual shift from a medieval to a modern Europe, from an empire to sovereign States, the quest for good government and accountability of (newly emerging) sovereign rulers causes early-modern European scholars to turn to *ius gentium et naturae* in lieu of the *dominus mundi* system of emperor and pope, as the higher normative structure to ground, guide, and constrain the conduct of the newly emerging rulers of Europe both within and without the State. It shows how timely rule of law concerns—loosely defined as they may have been—then contributed to the development of the idea of an international or universal rule of law and to the development of the law of nations and nature as such. Indeed, it is a history of the law of nations as a higher *public* law of nature rather than as a model of *private* law such as in Hobbesian or liberal contractarianism. As such, we explore the 'rule of law'-driven, early-modern turn to *ius gentium et naturae* as an *important counter-hegemonic contribution to the development of the law of nations relevant to international jurisprudence today*. The turn to *ius gentium et naturae* as a body of norms to hold rulers to account for their conduct within and

[9] Aristotle, *The Nicomachean Ethics*, Book V.

[10] Cicero, *The Laws*, Book II. 13. See also BZ Tamanaha, *On the Rule of Law History, Politics, Theory* (CUP 2004) 11.

without their State made by many early-modern scholars spurred the development of international law and international legal thought. Of course, this turn also served to justify colonialization and extra-European war and trade. The latter move was a hegemonic one that minimalized the normative power of *ius gentium* by redefining natural law as natural rights. The former move may be taken as *counter*-hegemonic in that it sought a 'symbiotic relationship' for *ius gentium* as universal natural law and justice, so as to make sure *ius gentium* would be normatively substantive enough to fulfil its role as a standard to identify rulers' responsibilities and hold them to account. That is, for the authors of Part I *ius gentium* has a 'rule of law as substantive justice' role, a morally thick or material rule of law.

In Part II our second main historiographical objective unfolds. That is to put these early-modern European ideas into a cross-cultural dialogue with Chinese thought in order to explore anew the foundations for world order today, or at least possible ideational bridges for Europe–China relations. Obviously, both traditions of thought are internally hugely diverse as well as contested. Another element complicating such intercultural dialogue is the fact that the international rule of law is generally understood as a Western project. Indeed, in as far as the idea of a rule of law is linked to the modern State its origins are European, developed within the European discourse. To unpack this understanding above all brings out the particular liberal conception of the (international) rule of law that has come to dominate. This recognized, our first historiographical objective is just that: freeing rule of law for world order thinking from its liberal entrapment and giving it back its 'law as justice' roots so as to make it available for our second historiographical objective, that is the cross-cultural dialogue on pluralist international order. This dialogue comes with the realization that the different cultural understandings of international order and law (as morality, justice or ethics) are not so incommensurable as they are often argued to be.

Section 4 of this chapter explicates the intellectual history as developed in Part II of this volume. It brings to the fore how for centuries the Chinese official ethic was taken to be Confucianism.[11] Confucian thought has several key characteristics, which may amount to an idea of universal order. It is founded on the idea of a universal empire that is all-embracing and indivisible. Thus, there can be neither rivalry nor equality between individuals and States. Hence, a direct comparison with *ius gentium* raises many difficulties. The system of Confucianism proceeded from China as the centre of the world, with others submitted to its greatness in a hierarchical structure. The Tianxia or emperor placed himself at the top of the world order. At the end of the day the system was ethically rather than legally grounded. This way of thinking is sharply opposed to either a Hobbesian or Vattellian model of (sovereign) equality and appears to attach to China a dangerous ideological tool.

This said, the Confucian system of thinking in late-imperial China (1644–1911) imposes considerable restraints upon the conduct of the emperor and includes the idea of a scholar class imbued with the Confucian ethic to advise on responsible

[11] As Henan Hu explains in Chapter 13 this is usually what is regarded as traditional Chinese thinking.

government. The hierarchical social structure also requires moral quality of the emperor to be supreme, his rule is a rule of leading by moral example. A Chinese way of thinking generally more agreeable to the West is the Daoism of Lao Zi. Daoism envisaged a metaphysical order above independent States in the Warring States and the Spring and Autumn periods. This is a primordial theory of law resting on an ontology of the Unnameable, which exists before the coming into being of Heaven and Earth. Unlike the compelling example of Confucian benevolence, the Lao Zi Daoist inspires through restraint and through opening space for others. It has as a government model the self-restraining ruler, and is inherently anti-hegemonic.

Studying both European and Chinese thought within the context of a single volume on morally responsible rulers, no matter how difficult, does provide us with the first leads for further transcultural dialogue about good government, 'rule of law' conceptions, the limits of (international) law, and the need for ethics and political wisdom within the context of international law. A major belief of our work is, in any case, that international law is underdetermined and thus there is always a need for ethical judgement. Our historical project aims to uncover within both Eastern and Western traditions of thought pockets of softer humanism that may assist us in going back beyond a Hobbesian international order.

## 2. An Intellectual History of European 'Law of Nations and Nature' (Part I of this Book)

### 2.1 A tradition of northern humanism

In what became a seminal book, *The Rights of War and Peace: Political Thought and the International Order from Grotius to Kant*, Richard Tuck examines 'the relationship between the modern, liberal political theories of the seventeenth century—the theories which rested on the concept of *natural rights*—and the humanist political theories of the previous century'.[12] With his account of this relationship, he sets out a history of *modern* political and legal thought, centred crucially around Hobbes,[13] that grounds international order on autonomous agents and individuality expressed in rights language and that identifies (early-) modern international thought as *liberal* to its core.

While we take no issue with Tuck's critique of liberal internationalist thought and its—ultimately—predatory nature, nor with his argument that the modern, liberal tradition defined international law into a very thin, sovereign rights (and entitlement) based legal order developed largely to justify conquest and colonization beyond Europe, we do call into question Tuck's reductionist reading of early-modern

[12] R Tuck, *The Rights of War and Peace* (OUP 1999) 1.

[13] See for earlier contributions to the standard account of Hobbes's political and moral theory, eg Th Nagel, 'Hobbes' Concept of Obligation' (1959) 68(1) Philosophical Review 68–83; D Gauthier, *The Logic of Leviathan. The Moral and Political Theory of Thomas Hobbes* (1969); JWN Watkins, *The Hobbes's System of Ideas Ideas* (2nd edn, Hutchinson University Library 1973); J Hampton, *Hobbes and the Social Contract Tradition* (1986).

European humanism—which we argue was crucially ambiguous and diverse. There are various humanist traditions to take into account when reading the early-modern natural law theorists (such as Grotius), which one has to recognize lest their theories on the law of nations and nature might be misunderstood.[14]

Tuck's interpretation of Hugo Grotius is a case in point. This interpretation amounts to a proto-Hobbesian reading that centres around Grotius's redefinition of natural *law* as individual natural *rights* and that marginalizes the concept of natural law as 'law as justice' in Grotius's thought. It builds on a reductionist reading of sixteenth-century humanism as a single monolithic tradition of harsh Italian humanist war jurisprudence and *Ragion di Stato* theory, which then would have come to define seventeenth-century natural law jurisprudence as natural rights theory. Understanding Italian humanist war jurisprudence as '*the* humanist view of international relations',[15] or assuming one school of thought to be *the* Renaissance humanist anthropology and world view, overlooks the richness and crucial ambiguity of early-modern humanism. Underlying the historical inquiries in this volume, however, is a recognition of the multiplicity of early-modern humanisms in general and the distinctiveness of northern humanism in particular. This is crucial since it does not provide egoism and self-interest as grounding notions for the law of nature and nations yet sociability and the human capacities to reason, will freely, and care.

The European tradition of northern humanism defies Tuck's dichotomy between late scholasticism and early-modern humanism crucially on this anthropological unpinning of law and legal thought.[16] Both late scholasticism and early-modern humanism draw on an *imago Dei* anthropology, conceiving of humans as rational animals with an innate, metaphysical *telos*, endowed with intrinsic dignity, worth, and power.[17] Compared to, for example, contemporary reformer Martin Luther, Erasmus minimized the effects of the Fall on humans as *imago Dei*, thus staying closer to the official Thomist line of the Church.[18] The *imago Dei* doctrine within early-modern humanism counterbalanced the Renaissance emphasis on the exploration and cultivation of human individuality with an inherent value and dignity shared by all—a *shared* humanity. Given that all humans are created *in imagine Dei*, there is an ontological basis for the idea of a universally shared humanity and thus for an anthropology with seemingly more faith in human (spiritual) potential than

[14] See also eg B Kingsbury and B Straumann, 'State of Nature versus Commercial Sociability as the Basis of International Law' in S Besson and J Tasioulas (eds), *Philosophy of International Law* (OUP 2010) 31–52.

[15] Tuck (n 12) 9.

[16] Erasmus's hostility towards (Parisian) scholasticism and vice versa has been exaggerated—see MA Gillespie, *The Theological Origins of Modernity* (Chicago UP 2008) 95–96ff. See for Quentin Skinner's qualification of the opposition of humanism and scholasticism for example Q Skinner, *The Foundations of Modern Political Thought, Vol 1 The Renaissance* (CUP 1978) 82, 104.

[17] See for the nominalist movement, which denied humans the capacity to understand the world through reason—as it is only particulars without universals—as well as the metaphysical *telos* inherent in their nature, against scholasticism, Gillespie (n 16) 14–15, 92.

[18] JE Nijman, 'Grotius' *Imago Dei* Anthropology: Grounding *Ius Naturae et Gentium*' in M Koskenniemi, M Garcia-Salmones, and P Amoroso (eds), *International Law and Religion* (OUP 2017).

its liberal counterpart, which arguably had been informed more by the harsh individualism and Machiavellian opportunism of Italian humanism.[19]

With Machiavelli and Erasmus, to stage them as protagonists, Italian and northern humanism developed distinctive responses to the challenge of reconciling Christian piety and virtues with Roman ideas about glory and martial virtues.[20] Notably, northern humanism focused on the morality and piety of the ruler rather than on his or her martial virtues.

Humanism generally downplayed the effects of the Fall and rather than emphasizing the corruption of human nature, creation *in imagine Dei* enabled emphasis on human dignity; in the context of Italian humanism this led to a human's quasi-divine status as co-creator of the world.[21] Thanks to being *imago Dei*—human's rational nature—self-examination could contribute to self-creation, self-mastery, moral self-improvement, and therewith to understanding and realizing one's *telos*.

For Machiavelli however this *telos* did not direct ultimately to God, that is, the *common* good, but to one's '*own* good, and it is good that is always enjoyed at the expense of others'.[22] In Machiavellian humanism, humans are self-interested, and vicious in their pursuit of their own good and glory; the world is 'governed by sin' with all the consequences for social and political life and thus for government. Those who govern are virtuous as they are the legislator and make and maintain 'a well-regulated state'.[23] This may require 'evil', but this does not affect their virtuous rule (*virtu*). In short, Machiavellian humanism 'emphasize[d] martial virtues of the Romans and deemphasize[d] or abandon[ed] both Christian piety and Platonism'.[24] 'Machiavellian humanism is both heroic and tragic [ . . . ] [It] offers a sorry solace to those who seek peace and stability, and only the slightest hope to those who long for glory or hope for wisdom.'[25]

In northern humanism, human nature is conceived as rational, predisposed to virtue, directed towards the common good, towards God, and assigned to participate inherently in the universal order of love. The classical idea of *humanitas* as *vir humanus* is 'subsume[d] under' the *imago Dei* anthropology and therewith the northern humanist political agenda could rest on moral formation and spiritual self-perfection rather than on predatory self-preservation and heroisms.[26] Northern humanism is a holistic moral renaissance of humanity (as *imago Dei*). Compared to Italian humanism, which shows some affinity to medieval nominalism, northern

[19] See eg Tuck (n 12); Gillespie (n 16).

[20] See eg on the contrast between Machiavelli and Erasmus and the difference in content between Italian and northern humanism, Gillespie (n 16); J IJsewijn, 'The Coming of Humanism to the Low Countries' in PO Kristeller, Th Brady, and H Oberman (eds), *Itinerarium Italicum. The Profile of the Italian Renaissance in the Mirror of Its European Transformations* (Brill 1975), 276; B Bradshaw, 'Transalpine Humanism', in JH Burns (ed), *The Cambridge History of Political Thought 1450–1700* (CUP 1991); JD Tracy, *The Politics of Erasmus: A Pacifist Intellectual and His Political Milieu* (University of Toronto Press, 1978); H Lutz, *Ragione di stato und christliche Staatsethik im 16. Jahrhundert* (Aschendorffsche Verlagsbuchhandlung 1961); RT Adams, *The Better Part of Valor: More, Erasmus, Colet, and Vives, on Humanism, War, and Peace, 1496–1535* (University of Washington Press 1962).

[21] Gillespie (n 16), forecasting the seventeenth-century liberal conceptions of dominium.

[22] ibid 92 (emphasis ours). [23] ibid 91. [24] ibid 88. [25] ibid 92.

[26] Bradshaw (n 20) 103–08; hence the mirror-of-princes literature or wisdom literature more generally.

humanism is still closer to the rational and universal of the Thomist tradition of natural law.[27] Be it that northern humanism emphasizes less the *imago dei* capacities of intellect and will and more the spiritual capacity to care—the Christian virtues of *caritas* and *pietas*.[28] Erasmus is celebrated for his reconciliation of Renaissance *humanitas* and Christian *pietas* and for his identification of the moral teachings of the Greek and Roman philosophers with Christian charity.[29] His humanism absorbed elements of the Netherlands movement of *devotio moderna* and centred on the humanity of Jesus and Christ's philosophy, that is, joined together, on the capacity of human beings to imitate Christ in his piety, morality, and justice (the *Imitatio Christi*). Hence, his humanist educational programme for all—clerics and laypeople, princes and subjects—was tailored to reform, pacifism, and the general promotion of moral action.[30] The capacity of language was no guarantee for the promotion of the common good, it could easily be applied to promote self-interest at the expense of the former. (The parallel with international law (as language) is easily made.) So, for Erasmus and other northern humanists, it all came down to (spiritual) self-perfection through the imitation of Christ's *caritas*—his charity or caring—and the human moral autonomy and responsibility to *judge* good from bad, virtue from vice. In short, this humanism was a turn inwards rather than an expansionist turn outwards. A turn from which we took inspiration in section 5.

The writings of northern humanists like Erasmus and More were socially and politically progressive; critical of Augustinian voluntarism and anthropological pessimism. Faith in the human capacity for self-perfection could bring to bear political reform or *renaissance* of both the domestic and 'international' sociopolitical order. Their critique of the elites aimed to end the latter's arbitrary, morally corrupt, and self-serving rule.[31] Rather than *Ragion di Stato* as the basis for a politics of glory and aggrandizement (national and international) and a warrior ethos, the northern humanist agenda aimed to establish a justly governed *respublica* with self-reflective, wise, and morally responsible rulers, who focus on the public good and public welfare—the commonwealth—and who are peacemakers on the international plane.[32] It is a 'conception of government as directed by reason and virtue to the goal of *respublica*, the commonwealth'.[33] Government is not premised on a pessimistic view of human nature, as merely in need of coercion and punishment. It relies also on moral–political education, ethical rule, social justice, the emancipation of the *populus*, and constitutional organization to subject power to morality and law.[34] Similarly at the international level, northern humanists speculate about a *rule of natural reason and virtue* in the interest of the commonwealth—'international relations are conducted on the basis of natural justice, not cynical opportunism'.[35] In *Education of Christian Prince*, Erasmus advocates 'government by consent and

[27] Bradshaw (n 20); Ch Trinkaus, *'In Our Image and Likeness', Humanity and Divinity in Italian Humanist Thought* (Chicago UP 1970).

[28] Bradshaw (n 20); Trinkaus (n 27).

[29] Gillespie (n 16) 95, 99; Bradshaw (n 20); Trinkaus (n 27).

[30] Gillespie (n 16) 96–98.

[31] Bradshaw (n 20) 118.

[32] ibid 104–06, 118, 127.

[33] ibid 115.

[34] ibid 125–31

[35] ibid 119–24, 109–13.

under the law; political liberty based on a common humanity; the heinousness of political corruption and tyranny'.[36] Erasmus argues good government should come from a spiritually and morally well-educated prince, who cultivates virtue and thus is able to make morally responsible and caring (benevolent) judgements—deciding on behalf of the people. A wise ruler never digresses into oppression, yet aims to serve the communal good. Nor is he after territorial expansion. Wise rulers maintain peaceful relations with their neighbours, so as to prevent their people from being subjected to the burdens of war.[37]

Factoring in this softer, northern, or Erasmian humanism is particularly relevant to understanding the international thought of early-modern jurists such as Budé, Grotius, and Leibniz.[38] Part I thus presents interpretations of for example Vitoria, Grotius, and Selden that differ from the interpretations found in liberal international legal history. Taking into consideration northern humanism is moreover crucial in the context of the intercultural dialogue we envisage in this volume. It brings common ground because of a traditionally similar appreciation in the East of the cultivation of moral virtue, the desire to do good (benevolent or charitable) and right to others, over military or martial virtues with its focus on glory and (territorial) expansion.

While a reductionist reading of humanism supports an account of the development of a 'thin' international—moral and legal—order in the context of European expansion and emerging capitalism and therewith a conceptual history of the liberal international rule of law idea, it glosses over alternative understandings of international order, such as inter alia Grotius's or Leibniz's, in which *ius* as objective law and justice is foundational. It contributes moreover to closing off alternative histories of rule of law thinking in which a rule of *ius gentium* does not purport primarily or exclusively to ground individual liberty and natural rights. Instead—as it draws on early-modern natural law thinking that deals with universal natural justice, virtues, and the (moral) responsibility of rulers—it purports to a morally 'thicker' conception of international order. It is a rule of law that draws on the communal and intersubjective dimensions of society and human nature rather than on an ever-present fear of the other, corrupting judgement.

## 2.2 Episodes of an intellectual history: turning to *ius gentium et naturae* as a moral standard for critique and contestation

The history of international legal thought as developed in Part I is narrated largely as an intellectual history centred around individual jurists and their context; *together* the episodes provide, however, a European history of *ius gentium et naturae* in general

[36] ibid 126.

[37] *Erasmus: The Education of a Christian Prince with the Panegyric for Archduke Philip of Austria* (L Jardine ed, CUP 1997) vi–xxiv.

[38] JE Nijman, 'Images of Grotius, or the International Rule of Law beyond Historiographical Oscillation' (2015) 17(1) Journal of the History of International Law 83–137; JE Nijman, 'Grotius' *Imago Dei* Anthropology: Grounding *Ius Naturae et Gentium*' in M Koskennimi, M Garcia-Salmones, and P Amoroso (eds), *International Law and Religion* (OUP 2017) 87–110.

and of the idea of a 'rule of law as justice' in particular, spanning the fourteenth to the early eighteenth century. Going back beyond the *liberal* rule of law means we pick up the history of 'rule of law for world order' thinking in Renaissance Italy with its debate on universal and territorial sovereignty and its frictions between well-established vertical and emerging horizontal power relations. In short, the transition from the medieval to the (early) modern.[39]

In Chapter 1 of Part I, Joseph Canning argues carefully that late medieval jurisprudence of Roman and canon law has 'provided the origins of European notions of a universal rule of law in two senses: a legal order of universal extent and a structure of objective higher legal norms of universal application' (p 00). Obviously—Canning stresses—Italian late medieval jurists did not have a concept of *inter-national* law yet, '[t]he foundational presupposition ... was that there was a universal rule of law, in that there were two universal authorities in one legal world with generally accepted norms—the Roman emperor and the pope' (p 00). That is, Italian late medieval jurists worked to develop a rule of law established by actual universal *authorities* and drawing on many different legal sources. Canning examines this 'foundational presupposition' in four areas of medieval jurisprudence (universal and territorial sovereignty in public law, private international law, general principles, and just war theory). The emerging Italian sovereigns met the emperor's claim to universal sovereignty increasingly with 'non-recognition' and challenged the old, medieval, 'universal rule of law'.

Canning shows how late mediaeval jurists such as Bartolus and Baldus turn to *ius gentium*—that is, the law that is the product of natural reason—to argue the de facto independence of kingdoms and city-republics,[40] while Neapolitan jurists like Caramanico and Oldradus used *ius gentium* to justify their *de jure* independence from the emperor. Through this turn to *ius gentium* the jurists gained access to another source of law—ie natural law or reason. They could thus derive from *ius gentium* a people's right to self-government and argue the need for territorial sovereignty. *Ius gentium* here is the body of law used to *contest* the emperor's universal sovereignty. Understanding *ius gentium* to guarantee the de facto and/or *de jure* independence of emerging States vis à vis the emperor amounts to understanding *ius gentium* as a structure of objective higher legal norms derived from natural reason. Sovereign rulers were breaking free from the old rule of law—the medieval system of emperor and pope—and a new rule of law announced itself: by the end of the Middle Ages, European rulers were understood to be subjected to, and thus had to govern in accordance with, the higher legal norms and principles of *ius divine, ius naturale* and *ius gentium*. The latter are all non-derogable by human law. In Canning's words:

[39] eg R Lesaffer, *European Legal History: A Cultural and Political Perspective* (CUP 2009); Skinner (n 16) vol I.

[40] Aristotelian political thought grounded Baldus's development of the de facto thesis, Canning explains: 'these city-republics attained sovereignty because they were composed of citizens understood as natural, political men' (see Chapter 1, p 58).

> There is no doubt that these jurists made fundamental contributions to the growth of ideas of the universal rule of law [ . . . ] They accorded an elaborate treatment to universally applicable higher legal norms of which the *ius gentium* was the most important in their own works and for later jurists who referred back to their thought. In this respect, the late medieval jurists were setting forth limits on the exercise of power by governments and rulers. They operated with the concept of positive law but saw it as human law limited by divine Law, natural law and the *ius gentium*, itself conceived on two levels—that of a universally valid law produced by natural reason and that of the sum of laws made by mankind.[41]

Canning's chapter on late medieval legal thought also provides grounding to Part I as a whole. Most notably thanks to his discussion of late medieval Roman and canon law in general (see eg Simpson) and of just war theory in particular (see eg Pagden, Stumpf). His short discussion of the concepts of the good (*bonum*) and the equitable (*aequum*) in late medieval thought foreshadows Susan Karr's argument in Chapter 2 on early-modern humanist jurists. Canning briefly explains that medieval scholastic jurists, such as Accursius, Bartolus, and Baldus, distinguished between what is good (defined in terms of civil law) and what is equitable (defined by natural reason) when dealing with 'law as the art of the good and the equitable'. Due to this distinction, justice was not an integrated part of *ius* in the way of civil law. Hence, the move to *ius gentium* conceived of as law produced by natural reason and thus law of which justice did constitute an integral part.

By the early sixteenth century, humanist jurists such as Budé (France), Zasius (Freiburg, Holy Roman Empire), and Alciati (Milan, Italy) found the law in need of thorough reform. In their view, the medieval scholastic tradition had mishandled Roman law to such an extent that civil law and jurisprudence were judged to be in crisis. In a reflection that seems to relate as much to our own project as to the project of these early sixteenth-century humanists, Susan Longfield Karr states:

> In moments when the [(international)] law and justice appear out of joint, when it no longer seems as if everyone (persons and states) is equal before the law, or that the laws themselves are no longer predictable, calls for reform take on a particularly urgent tone. In the early sixteenth century, such a call was made by humanist jurists who held that the rule of law had not simply been replaced by a rule of men, but worse, by a rule by law and lawyers.[42]

These humanist jurists held that this 'rule by law and lawyers' resulting from the scholastic tradition had brought 'endemic corruption', a lack of accountability of political and legal authorities, and unjust laws. In their view, lawyers were 'abus[ing]' the law, 'bend[ing] it to mean whatever suited best their interests or 'the will of their patron' without concern for the common good and justice. They critiqued a rule of law that was a rule of law detached from justice and thus empty and meaningless in the face of the legal and political authorities that needed to be kept in check. They called for reform of both civil law and the legal profession itself for both to be brought back into concord with universal justice. To remedy this crisis and to purge the law from errors and scholastic 'faulty' interpretations, they set out to restore the corpus of Roman law, to rediscover the universal moral principles underlying all law,

[41] See Chapter 1, p 72. [42] See Chapter 2, p 75.

and thus to reconnect civil and universal jurisprudence. Their work was a work of critique and contestation, their methods historical and comparative.

The humanist jurists that Karr discusses set out to reinterpret both *ius* and *ius gentium* and therewith to reattach law and (natural) justice. To start with, they restored *ius* to its objective meaning as captured by the Digest, '*ius* [law] is the art of goodness and fairness', that is, *conjoined*, not split as the scholastics had maintained. They redefined *ius* in its subjective meaning as inherently human, a universal characteristic of human qua human being endowed with dignity, reason, and will.[43] And, subsequently, they gave *ius* the highest moral authority and came to link natural law to *ius gentium* directly.

While medieval (Christian) scholastic jurists had distanced civil and universal jurisprudence and changed the Roman law hierarchy of laws by demoting civil law and *ius gentium* and by promoting natural law (reason), these humanist jurists grounded *ius gentium* in a redefined *ius* and therewith gave it the highest moral authority as an expression of both *ius* and natural law. In their view, *ius gentium* 'provided the moral foundation of all laws'. Being the source of government and of universal rights and obligations of both ruler and subjects, *ius gentium* came to set the standard for good and just government internally and externally; for holding 'civil laws, institutions and authorities accountable to a universal rule of law'. The transformation of *ius gentium* as the highest source of law within the overall legal order secured a 'symbiotic relation' between civil and universal jurisprudence thus creating space for using the latter to critique and reform the former. As a law common to all humankind and binding upon sovereign rulers, it was applicable to their internal and external relations.

These early sixteenth-century humanist jurists moved *ius gentium* to the centre of early-modern political thought and very high up in the hierarchy of laws. They reinterpreted *ius gentium* as directly linked to natural reason and as a source of universal rights and obligations well before Vitoria and Grotius. They did so by the need to confront what Karr captures as a rule of law crisis. Their reinterpretation aimed to replace the rule by law and lawyers with a true and universal 'rule of law and justice', which could assist in holding legal and political authorities to account and reform unjust laws. 'Prior to, within, and between civil societies, *ius gentium* stands as an expression of a universal rule of law precisely because it is an expression of natural law, and thereby, justice' (p 88). The turn to *ius gentium* was also a turn to natural law and justice out of what we have termed a rule of law sensibility.

An exploration of legal arguments of sixteenth-century Scottish humanist jurists, John Leslie and David Chalmers, concerning the laws of royal succession to defend the claim of Mary Queen of Scots to the throne of England yields another example of a turn to Roman law and notably to *ius gentium et naturae* in search for universal legal authority and truth higher than statutory law. The former could set out 'legal frameworks according to which monarchs were expected to govern' and thus also to

[43] See on the importance of imago Dei thinking in early humanist thought, Ch Trinkaus, *'In Our Image and Likeness', Humanity and Divinity in Italian Humanist Thought* (Chicago UP 1970); Gillespie (n 16); Nijman (n 18).

exercise their statutory powers justly. Chapter 3 by Andrew Simpson points to a rule of law sensibility behind these Scottish humanist lawyers' turn to *ius gentium* and to natural law as sources of learned authority on universal justice and truth to guide the interpretation of the laws (of royal succession). Simpson discerns the fundamental idea that the ruler should rule in accordance with justice and legal truth; and this rule of law extends beyond domestic relations into the external realm—albeit only in the case of a Scottish claim to the English throne.

For Leslie, Simpson points out, the higher, binding legal standards of universal justice and legal truth demand the interpretation of statute to subscribe to the standards of reason and equity (this means, Henry's interpretation of statutory powers is judged as irrational, unnatural, and arbitrary, in short, unjust and excessive). If interpretation was not in conformity with the learned law, the statute should be considered void.

For Chalmers, the study of universal history revealed the universal natural order to be infused with the (Aristotelian) end of seeking the divine—Perfection. He explained the successfulness of political rulers and societies by the conformity of their laws, policies and actions to this natural order and therewith by their 'cultivat[ion of] contemplative virtue' which contributed to 'the path to happiness'. History shows, Chalmers argues, that female rule is in full conformity with this universal natural order; many women 'had governed successfully, with great political virtue' (p 108). The *droit de regner* given by the people (modelled on Roman law *lex Regia*) was the legal basis for the ruler to govern. The people's right to self-government was derived from *ius gentium*, the same *ius gentium* that prescribed according to Chalmers the cultivation of the virtuous self in order to produce virtuous rule. Chalmers returns moreover to late medieval jurists interpreting Roman law, such as Oldradus da Ponte,[44] to argue that from *ius gentium*—the dictates of right reason—flows the right to arrange for their own governance; this leads arguably to Queen Mary's legitimated claim of succession to the English throne.

The chapter on these two Scottish jurists focuses on their arguments on the Scottish claim to the English crown and compared to the other chapters moves less into the development of *ius gentium* with respect to external relations more generally.[45] Nonetheless, it seems to confirm a more general turn to *ius gentium* for norms higher than the sovereign ruler. For both Leslie and Chalmers, the (strategic) turn to *ius gentium* consisted in a turn to the dictates of right reason established in *ius gentium*. Neither Leslie nor Chalmers subscribed to Jean Bodin's position that all law depends on sovereign will; rather, they work with a universal natural order and an idea of a 'rule of learned law', that is, an idea of the rule of justice and equity. Ultimately, these conceptions draw on wisdom and prudence, on virtue.

[44] See Chapter 1, p 62.

[45] The true impact of ambassador John Leslie on *ius gentium* may have come only with the case that made him write English diplomatic history: when he was prosecuted as a Scottish ambassador to the English court for having conspired against Queen Elisabeth (1558–1603). Vattel mentions the case in his magnum opus.

In light of our objective to bring out the diversity of early-modern humanism and the relevance of it to international thought, this volume includes one chapter entirely on Desiderius Erasmus, influential contemporary of the legal humanists discussed here (see Chapter 4). Erasmus too attacked scholastic theologians and jurists for corrupting the law, misinterpreting the Bible, propagating a false doctrine of war, and neglecting the common good and justice. He too called for reform, a call that reached beyond the legal profession and the European elites of political and legal advisers busy justifying often unjustifiable acts of European Rulers. His call extended to the reform of some of the Rulers themselves. They, he argued, were in dire need of moral, spiritual, and political (re)education. Xavier Tubau points to Erasmus's profound discomfort with chivalric culture and the cultivation of martial virtues in the contemporary education of the princes. While Erasmus worked with the language of (the pedagogical tradition of) Italian humanism, in substance he produced a particular—Erasmian or northern—humanism.

Erasmus's work is radically political, as both he and Thomas More wrote 'scathing indictment[s] of the political elites of Northern Europe'.[46] He criticizes (European) politics for being based on dynastic interests and quests for glory, while neglecting the common good, understood to include the concerns of the people. He holds 'the philosophy of Christ' as a mirror in front of the Princely faces.[47] As a humanist, Erasmus argues for a historical and contextual reading of the Bible. Such reading is an important element of his attack on the so-called just war theory. The use of force and violence in the Old and New Testaments cannot be read, he finds, as casuistic argument for what is permitted. The philosophy of Christ that emerges from a historical and contextual reading surely 'argues against war'. War may be part of life, but surely it cannot be justified by what Erasmus understood as the philosophy of Christ—no matter what twisted legal basis the scholastic theologians and jurists may argue or construct. To mould theology and universal jurisprudence to justify and even command rather than prohibit and constrain the use of force was utterly unacceptable to Erasmus. War cannot be a means to administrate justice. Natural law and universal jurisprudence should be reinterpreted in Christian philosophical terms. Hence, rather than formulating his critique on the basis of existing (scholastic) natural law theory, he also called for the reform of the latter, on the basis of the Philosophy of Christ. Tubau explains:

> [t]he whole of Erasmus's intellectual project is defined by an unshakeable faith in the possibility of radically transforming contemporary society—both the Christian and the non-Christian—by recuperating the original message of Christ.[48]

Erasmus rejects the just war theory as the appropriate 'international' framework for rulers to use and argues that the 'philosophy of Christ, is the framework within which rulers should be educated and within which they should exercise their power'.[49]

[46] Bradshaw (n 20).

[47] See the Italian mirror-of-princes literature but adapted to the virtues he considered in need of cultivation.

[48] See Chapter 4, p 124.

[49] ibid p 118.

Erasmus's model of the moral education of the princes aims to equip the princes for making sound moral judgements, to assure their rule would be based on (Christian, ie non-martial) virtues, and thus contribute to a new world order in which princes serve the common good, (thus) shy away from war, and are accountable to the people for their actions at home and abroad. Erasmus reinterprets the Italian humanist tradition in the sense that while he proceeds within the (Aristotelian and Ciceronian) virtues tradition, he places Christian virtues at the centre of his political and international thought. In his view, the Christian ruler has to cultivate a profound understanding of Christ's message of peace and justice. Erasmus's political theory thus is a critique of the expansion of military or political power by European rulers, which included the European expansion over sea. It amounts to an anti-imperialist version of European humanism propagated by those 'who saw [no] virtue in military glory' (and rejected bellicose arguments of humanists, like the Spanish Sepúlveda in relation to for example the Turks), and 'who regarded war as an evil which it was every Christian's duty to avoid'.[50] Erasmus calls for self-control and self-cultivation to secure virtuous government. To be sure: being a good—virtuous—ruler is not a privilege of Christian Rulers only; non-Christians can be virtuous too. For Erasmus, not faith but war was the defining factor in the 'civilized'–'barbarian' distinction. This marks his thinking about external relations of sovereigns; rather than defining 'virtuous government' differently for the national and international domain, he expects the same degree of self-control and self-cultivation from the ruler in both realms of action. Bellicose relations with other sovereigns simply do not serve the common good, the welfare of the people, which should guide sovereign actions in all domains.

Being a theologian, not a lawyer, Erasmus seems to have had rather limited expectations of the force of law in guiding and constraining power. After all, in his view, lawyers were abusing the law, even natural law, to justify war and violations of the common good. His moral work is however profoundly political, exactly in its call upon the European princes to cultivate Christian virtues and in drawing on Paul's plea for 'the renewal of the mind'. His argument for a 'rule of Christian morality', as a standard to hold European rulers to account, is a scathing critique of the existing political practices. Underpinning Erasmus's argument against the legitimacy of war is ultimately his understanding of human nature as the *imago Dei*; this is what moreover enables the *imitatio Christi* and thus grounds the duty to the self-cultivation of the (Christian) virtues. In short, Erasmus's humanist position rests on a classical ontological and anthropological understanding that the virtuous human is a possibility. If princes pursue the charted course, their actions and relations will change. Rather than through war, disputes among rulers should be settled by arbitration, which is a practice of *justice* that involves wisdom or prudence to find a settlement based on equity and respect for the common good (including public welfare). We will return to Erasmus's political thought and critique on natural law theory. Here, it suffices to stress that he does not separate the international from the national

[50] A Pagden, *The Fall of Natural Man: The American Indian and the Origins of Comparative Ethnology* (CUP 1986), 114.

legal–political sphere of the *respublica*. For him, government in both spheres should be 'renewed' so as to be guided by the wisdom of (civil, not martial) virtues and to be of service to the well-being of the *populus*, ie the common good. Wars of aggrandizement are a threat to social justice, not a good practice for the Christian prince.[51]

In 1527, Erasmus was faced with an organized attempt to have his works condemned. The Spanish late-scholastic theologian Francisco de Vitoria was one of the hands therein. He had studied with the same theologians in Paris that had taken issue with Erasmus's ideas and had returned with these ideas to Spain. He became one of the founders of the so-called School of Salamanca. Chapter 5 of the volume, written by Anthony Pagden, deals with their ideas—of Francisco de Vitoria and his successors Domingo de Soto and Bartolomé de Las Casas in particular—about *ius gentium* and natural law as frameworks for international relations. This is a school of thought heavily involved in the debate on the legitimacy of European—*in casu*, Spanish—expansion overseas.

Pagden engages with the currently dominant view—set out most famously by Anthony Anghie—that Vitoria's reinterpretation of *ius gentium* grounded on the 'civilized'–'barbarian' distinction aimed at justifying Spanish *occupation* of the Americas. 'Civilized' then for the dominant view meant Christian, and only Christians could have true rights, true *dominium*. Pagden disagrees with this view simply because it comes down to ascribing to Vitoria the view that '*dominium* [derives] from grace not law'. This is a heresy Calvinists may have fallen prey to, but it was unthinkable to neo-Thomists like Vitoria and Soto. Whether Christian and civilized or non-Christian and/or less civilized, all forms of *dominium* (both government and property) derive from natural law, that is, a universally applicable natural law grounded on the *imago Dei* capacities, most notably, natural reason, invested in all humans.

Pagden and Anghie concur on Vitoria's rejection of the 1493 Donation as a lawful way for Spain to establish territorial sovereignty or property rights over the lands of the American Indians. True to the Thomist appropriation of Aristotelian political thought, Vitoria recognized neither pope nor emperor as *dominus mundi*. Hence, he needed to turn elsewhere—to *ius gentium* and to natural law—to assess the legitimacy of Spain's presence in the Americas.

Pagden explains how for Vitoria *ius gentium* was the law of the *whole* world, which was 'in a sense a commonwealth [*respublica*]' or as Soto termed a universal 'human republic'. It was a 'positive law' in the sense that it was stipulated by a 'hypothetical common understanding between all—or most—of the peoples', yet also natural law as it was constructed through natural reason. And '[b]ecause the *ius gentium* as the law of humanity, drives from the *consensio omnium gentium et nationum* or at least the *consensus maioris partis orbis*, rather than the will of individuals, in cases of conflict, [it] will always trump the human or civil law'. This is a hierarchical reordering of laws and one in which *ius gentium* had 'the force of a positive enactment [*lex*]'.[52]

[51] Bradshaw (n 20).

[52] See Chapter 6, p 139.

This universal rule of *ius gentium*—which Pagden compares with what today is called 'a fully evolved "international rule of law" '—finds effectuation through the rulers who are the members of the commonwealth. So, they may act as its agents 'draw[ing] upon the authority of both the law of nations *and* the natural law to act on behalf of the world *respublica*'. This is a line of reasoning present in the debate also today. Pagden shows how this understanding of the law of nations could establish an obligation to protect the innocent American Indians against the *harmful* practices of cannibalism and human sacrifice—violations of both natural law and the law of nations—sanctioned by (the laws of) their native rulers. However, from Spain's overriding obligation as an agent representing the universal commonwealth to 'defend the innocent', no right to occupy the territory of the American Indians nor any legal basis for Spanish sovereignty or property rights could be derived. Once the American Indian rulers and peoples were safe and civilized the former had to withdraw. Vitoria's turn to and reinterpretation of *ius gentium* consisted in an understanding of *ius gentium* as a *universal* rule of law, regulating *equally* relations among Europeans and between European and non-European political communities, laying down universal responsibilities.

With Chapter 6 on Cardinal Richelieu, Anthony Carty shows scholastic theory of natural law and in particular the tradition of just war theory to be continuous into the seventeenth century. Carty takes issue with Koskenniemi's and Jouannet's argument that no form of international law existed in seventeenth-century France, writing off Richelieu's thought on French foreign policy and the law of nations as 'inherently theological', part of 'pre-history', and thus irrelevant for international legal thought today. The traditional claim of Richelieu as an admirer of Machiavelli and his *Ragion di Stato* doctrine to the detriment of the aim of concluding treaties and keeping them (as sacred), is refuted by Carty's careful historical research.

Carty offers a reading of Richelieu's thinking in which there is a role for law to play but it is law as justice, law in the classical natural law tradition. Those who rule are subject of the rule of law as justice, the rule of God or the rule of reason. In Richelieu's world, kings and ministers are rational instruments of the practical implementation of God's will on earth. In other words—and here Carty hints at similar understandings in Chinese thought:

> the king, as God's agent, had a responsibility to discern the opaque complexity of existence in a spirit of humble quest after divine inspiration and guidance, ie in a spirit of prayer. The French religious vision was one of harmony of all under heaven, ie under God's will, where the small would be secure against the large, each having its place.[53]

Such harmony would emerge as an order of reason, thanks to reason imprinted in human nature. The sovereign has moreover the responsibility to give the example of the good spiritual life thus advancing the living law. Richelieu's idea of royal (absolute) government comes close to the Chinese idea of ruling by the 'Mandate of Heaven'. It is the responsibility of the ruler to cultivate knowledge of God, that is, of the higher laws of reason in order to rule justly. Just rule or government requires

[53] ibid p 154.

the maximum application of human reason—that is what Richelieu's interpretation of Machiavelli's *Ragion di Stato* came down to: the rule of reason. Richelieu's rule of reason is an 'intensely personal and private foundation for normative order[: "good conscience and the penetrating judgement of a judicious mind"]' operating within the frame of the higher law of reason (p 156). Hence, even war waged by an absolute king can be unjust. Natural law prescribes that every decision to that end requires scrutiny of the justice of the cause, the proportionality of the means, and of 'what the situation demands'; in short, Carty puts forward Richelieu's understanding of natural law as a 'matter of judgement'. Judgement calls for guidance by the virtues (eg moderation) and thus for the good (spiritual) life of those who rule. Richelieu's thinking on treaties, Carty suggests, roots in this same understanding of the responsibility of the sovereign.

Richelieu's thinking amounts to the idea of a universal rule of law as justice or as reason. Presented here as part of seventeenth-century international thought, this thought points to 'rule of law' conceptions proceeding in a natural law vein, grounded in human capacity to cultivate the self and to develop judgement guided by virtue, and as such alternative to the liberal—Hobbesian—course that would come to dominate modern rule of law thinking. Carty thus moves seemingly into the philosophical project intertwined with our historical project and forecasts a possible twenty-first-century interpretation of classical natural law's right reason(ing) as good judgement and the rule of law as justice and judgement. In the next section, we will develop this thinking further. First, this intellectual history continues with some more seventeenth-century episodes.

With the exploration of the Calvinist jurist, Johannes Althusius, contemporary of the Arminian or Erasmian humanist Hugo Grotius, this volume continues to carve out an intellectual history that complements the now standard narrative of seventeenth-century political and legal history as Italian humanist infused and Hobbesian in its origin. A chapter on Althusius also means recognizing the impact of the Reformation on seventeenth-century European thought and therewith the influence of religious, Protestant thinking on the development of such modern legal notions as human rights, constitutional order, popular sovereignty, liberty, and the rule of law. Being 'modern', for John Witte (Chapter 7) too, is not equivalent to being fully secular as the proto-Hobbesian theories suggest. In fact, 'Protestant theological jurisprudence, Catholic political theory and canon law, and Jewish biblical thought [ . . . ] were just as critical to the modern Western political project.'[54] The bifurcation of modernity comes to the surface here.[55] Hobbes had an impact on moral and political thought such as to put it on a liberal course in which the state of nature is a state of war and natural law is *not* the law of right reason. Instead, there is an alternative tradition with a different view on human nature, subjectivity, human freedom, and the power of right reason and of judgement in the social world developed by rationalists such as Althusius, Grotius, Selden, and Leibniz.

[54] See Chapter 7, p 167. [55] Gillespie (n 16).

In Althusius's universal jurisprudence, both subjects and rulers are bound by law. Underpinning his (interrelated) understanding of both universal and constitutional law is, Witte shows, a lawyer's rule of law sensibility: a ruler's relations both within and without the State are governed by law and justice. Althusius's universal jurisprudence is fundamentally a natural law theory. Natural law as the will of God for men or as right reason is imprinted in every human mind or soul. In his view, the principles of goodness, equity, justice, and the common good are known to the human mind, thanks to reason and conscience. The duty of love is written on every human heart. Natural law or justice was the law to be applied by all for the governance of the self and of the relations with others. In short, Witte explains Althusius's theory of law, politics, and society as a universal jurisprudence that is based on a 'symbiotic theory of human nature' amounting to a Christian social contract theory.

In traditional Calvinist anthropology, humans are created as persons bearing the *imago Dei*, yet their capacities are corrupted completely by the Fall ('total depravity'). Witte's reading of Althusius shows however how he understands postlapsarian humans as 'virtuous' and 'rational' persons, as 'moral, loving, communicative, and social beings, whose lives are most completely fulfilled through symbiotic relationships with others'. His anthropology was thus 'more complex [ ... ] than the bleak Hobbesian view of self-interested individuals driven by an ethic of self-preservation to dangerous and destructive behavior unless coerced into political and social conformity by an all-powerful sovereign' (p 175). Rather, according to Althusius, they are inclined to form associations on the basis of covenants. Any association—ranging from marriages to States and empires—is governed by the general or universal natural law of community, this means it circumscribes the authority that rules.

Althusius moreover does not shy away from the problem of different interpretations given across cultures to what natural law (also called natural justice or natural equity) prescribes, 'How can we determine and distil those features of the natural law that should be part of a universal rule of law?' Althusius discerns common or comparable sets of laws across cultures, different positive laws that were reflections of the same underlying 'natural and divine, immutable equity that is mixed into them, as indications of the common practice of natural law'. Witte explains:

> at a certain level of abstraction, the moral laws of the Bible and common laws of the nations converge, even though they have very different origins, ends, and languages. 'A law is both natural and common', Althusius wrote, 'if the common use of right reason produces it for the necessity and utility of human social life. It, too, can then be called natural law'. 'While some distinguish among common law (*ius commune*), natural law (*ius naturale*), and the law of nations (*ius gentium*), others more properly call each of them forms of the [same] natural law ... Christ himself often called natural law things that are usually called the law of nations.'[56]

Althusius understood natural law or right reason to prescribe to or infuse in every human person across cultures the 'inclinations to piety and justice, to faith and order, to love of God and love of neighbor'. The 'universal rule of [natural] law',

[56] See Chapter 7, p 173.

Althusius discerns, requires any ruler or magistrate to translate natural law into positive laws and to apply the laws with justice and equity. Althusius did not write so much specifically about relations among rulers. Yet, he understands *ius gentium* as natural law; and, together with applicable covenants, it is the law that governs rulers and demand righteous judgement of them in relation to their people and among each other.

With Althusius we moved well into the realm of seventeenth-century natural law theories. This volume's analyses of Althusius and Grotius provide neither a Hobbesian reading of their work nor an interpretation based on the idea that these two jurists were 'profoundly sympath[etic]' to the harsh Italian humanism of the sixteenth century. Rather the analyses bring out a closeness with the Christian humanism of the North.

In the same vein, Christoph Stumpf (Chapter 8) opposes the now predominant liberal, morally minimalist, reading of Grotius. He qualifies the foundational role attributed to the natural right to self-defence and argues that Grotius is not only interested in substantively more developed legal principles but also builds a comprehensive legal system upon them making 'law "rul[e]" through its moral appeal'.

According to Stumpf, Grotius's rule of law conception is rooted in a late-scholastic understanding of objective natural law, in which law and natural justice are intertwined, not in a mere subjective natural rights understanding of natural law. Grotius derives both rights *and* obligations. While Stumpf consistently upholds Grotius's distinction between the legal reality for Christians and non-Christians, the universal natural law framework reaches beyond the 'circle of Christian nations' and embraces the 'wider circle of all nations' united by a universal bond of human natural fellowship. Natural law and justice ground the all-embracing universal—thus, also international—rule of law idea in Grotius's legal thought, ensuring a morally rich law to rule.

Stumpf discusses what this means for relations between government (derived not from grace but from natural and human law) and citizens, as well as for peaceful and bellicose relations among sovereigns. Whether within or without the State: the government is responsible for the common good of its people. But rather than grounding this on a harsh and predatory natural right to self-preservation and therewith on a sharp distinction between the national and the international, Grotius in Stumpf's reading proceeds from an integrated universal legal order within which in times of war as well as peace sovereigns have beyond the care for their own society a general responsibility for the society of humankind as a whole.

Stumpf's interpretation thus rejects a 'liberal' and proto-Hobbesian understanding of Grotius's legal thought in general and of his rule of law conception in particular. Stumpf does not read Grotius as someone who redefined natural law as natural rights and universal justice subsumed in the universal right to self-preservation under the influence of *Ragion di Stato* humanist doctrines. His reading of Grotius brings out a social theory of international society and law that draws on a much more substantive—morally richer—notion of justice and human reason.

While with the death of Erasmus and Budé, northern humanism may have lost much of its 'cultural force', it was not completely lost on a scholar like Grotius who admired his fellow countryman for his irenicism. Situating Grotius in the tradition of Erasmian humanism with its focus on Christian virtues, such as justice and moderation, and on the Aristotelian–Christian notion of 'the common good', which relates justice teleologically to God, the ultimate End and all Perfection, helps better to understand Grotius's arguments on the international society as a state of nature and on the natural law of nations.[57] Christian virtues, the common good, human natural fellowship, the *appetitus societatis*, and justice, are not merely relevant for the national—domain, they are equally normative for the international domain.

Chapter 9 proceeds with Grotius in the sense that Peter Goodrich explores the classic debate on the law of the sea between Hugo Grotius and John Selden. While Grotius and Selden take up different positions, Goodrich shows how both lawyers as legal humanists have more in common than what keeps them apart as a civil law and a common law jurist, respectively. The different positions come down more to different perspectives on the law than to different foundations for the law they develop. Rather than to understand Selden's humanism as imperialist and nationalist,[58] or Grotius as proto-Hobbesian, Goodrich argues that Grotius and Selden share a humanism that draws both on Roman law—Gaius's *Institutes* in particular—and on its local versions. They share a *respublica litteraria* and therewith method, language, and sources, most notably the ancient poets. Goodrich argues that Grotius and Selden share, more than generally acknowledged an understanding of 'common humanity' and friendship, notions which they both use to underpin the commonality of the sea. Sharing this humanist sensibility, the law they carve out to rule the seas and to thus deal with questions of dominion and/or jurisdiction of the seas is not so dissimilar. The role played by the anecdote of King Cnut in Selden's argument is puzzling and a fascinating hook on which Goodrich hangs his argument for an alternative reading of Selden.

Goodrich reads both Grotius and Selden as adhering to a version of humanism that draws on the Pythagorean maxim 'friendship holds all things in common' as present in Gaius's *Institutes*, hence on 'a fundamental though now rather lost tenet of [humanism]'. The new (international) law of the sea Grotius and Selden develop roots in this version of humanism, Goodrich argues. They both develop the law from the *auctoritates poetarum*, the pre-legal sphere of the poets of Antiquity, the sphere of amity, community, and common humanity. This is a version of humanism that Goodrich links up ultimately with Erasmian humanism, equally centred around amity and equity. It is a humanist tradition revolving around the principles of common humanity and mutual trustworthiness (*fidelitas*). The sea is actually approached as unrulable by kings.

Goodrich shows through Selden's use of the anecdote of Cnut and the sea that kings are subjects too, subject to the rule of natural law and justice. Goodrich discerns in the story of Cnut as a king ruling by the pen and not by the sword, a sort of rule of law sensibility that is in tune with the sixteenth-century shift from the rule *by* law and force to the rule *of* (natural) law and the rule *of* the *ratio scripta*. It is a shift

[57] Nijman, 'Images of Grotius' and 'Grotius' *Imago Dei* Anthropology' (both n 38).
[58] Tuck (n 12) 119.

that is intertwined with seventeenth-century natural law thinking about a universal rule of natural law and justice to which even the King (Cnut) is subject. Even without command, when space on earth is unmarkable or undemarcatable, there can be *nomos*: law drawn from *logos* or reason spoken by the sea (nature) and versed by the poets to whom both Grotius and Selden lend their ear. After all, the word is sacred in the Christian world of both. So, while law may be commanded on land and not at sea, there may be a legal order for the seas too. Not a commanded order, but a *common* order founded on commonality and binding for all, including sovereign rulers. Arguably, the anecdote of King Cnut includes the transposition of the idea of a 'rule of law as justice and *aequitas*' (or judgement) to the (high) seas. The rule of law then is transplanted to the international space where there is no command but where kings are subjected equally to the authority of the poets through whom natural law is spoken. It is a small step from the law of oceanic space to a law for the space of the kings, the subjection of the king to the rule of law as justice and *aequitas*. The rule of law conception of Selden that Goodrich thus carves out is indeed close to that of Grotius. Both develop for the seas a (humanist) rule of 'the law of the poets, [as] the nomos of nations'. An international rule of law is grounded in ancient poetry. A rule of law idea is one which requires a sensibility of *aequitas* and poetic justice, a rule of law as poetic judgement, that is, a 'lesbian—which is to say flexible—rule of justice' (p 218).

With the late seventeenth-/early eighteenth-century philosopher and lawyer G. W. Leibniz, the examination of European conceptions of rule of law for world order comes to an end. In Chapter 10, Janne Nijman argues that Leibniz, the last Homo Universalis, developed a theory of universal justice by which he meant to keep a universal moral and political structure in place while accommodating the newly emerging sovereign States. Relations among these States and their rulers were governed by the *ius gentium et naturae*; sovereignty was thus not absolute but relative, ie rulers endowed with sovereignty were bound by universal law and justice. Leibniz's theory of the *ius gentium et naturae* is the last of the early-modern theorists who so clearly embodies the transition from the medieval to the modern. His great interest in China and in Chinese politics and morality influenced his thinking and enabled him to seek philosophical and cultural exchange on the basis of equality and to learn from the Chinese in all areas of knowledge, but above all from their political philosophy and—what he read as—their natural theology in particular. Leibniz's turn to Chinese thought, however imperfect, was a turn to—what he understood as—the moral–legal unity of reason underlying human plurality.

The chapter on Leibniz's universal rule of law encompassing all—China and Europe—rounds up this volume's first historiographical objective: to bring out the diversity of early-modern humanisms.[59] There is a northern—softer—humanism that differed from harsh Italian humanist jurisprudence in ways relevant to this volume on international thought.

When we read seventeenth-century theorists of *ius gentium et naturae* with that difference in mind, a non-liberal history of early-modern *ius gentium et naturae*

[59] See p 225.

thinking becomes visible. The discussions of Part I bring to light conceptions of a universal rule of law in which the national and the international are not separated but conjoined. The latter is not defined in terms of *Ragion di Stato* doctrine, natural *rights*, and an ultra-minimalist normativity, but rather, together with the former, as a sphere in which justice-based law demands rulers to rule wisely, that is, to be guided by practical, moral virtues, to serve the interest of the *populus* and the universal society as a whole. It shows a turn to *ius naturae et gentium* in order to make emerging States and their rulers responsible to standards of law and justice. As such, conceptions of rule of law as justice and equity are at play.

## 3. Interlude

The idea of the order of the world which we, the editors, discern in both Eastern and Western traditions is an ethical order of virtue, which does not seek for legitimacy merely in consent but is concerned with the moral quality of the conduct of rulers. The universal rule of law as justice encompasses us all. Leibniz had a concept of order as harmony based upon a maxim of order and diversity, uniquely pluralist in resisting Eurocentrism. The basic point is that all exercise of power is constrained by natural law and justice—joining both the public and the private. Rulers play cards in private life and play with treaties in public life, Leibniz sneered. Positive law is simply not enough, both the private and the public sphere require the cultivation of virtue—that is, in particular, justice as *caritas* as Leibniz would argue—to move to just order.

What this means is that a universal natural society, that is, society beyond the institution of the individual State, is not without law—which is a fundamental difference from the tradition of Hobbes, Locke, and Kant as described by Tuck. Leibniz's universal jurisprudence makes a crucial distinction about civil and natural law that the latter (ie universal jurisprudence) rules outside the State in a natural world society. Democracy is no guarantee for good, virtuous governance, arbitrary power against reason is also found in national and international assemblies. A plurality of votes (consent of the majority) does not exclude abuse. The natural law tradition argues that international society being a natural society is in need of moral standards and—at the risk of getting ahead of ourselves—a postmodern revisit of this tradition would point to standards that draw on shared humanity, on mutual recognition of the other as similar, and as such generate standards to guide and constrain political leaders in their moral judgements. Government should belong to the wisest. Or, to put it differently, those in government are obliged to cultivate virtue—or, to use an Erasmian word, 'wise integrity'—so as to be the wisest and to rule in accordance with law and justice. It is right reasoning which distinguishes the good from the bad. It rests on the piety of the soul and the habit of living the good. Love or charity signifies converting the happiness of another into one's own happiness, as Leibniz argued. Revisiting northern humanist-influenced early-modern natural law thought brings to the surface that law concerns the internal dimension of human life as much as the external. Natural justice has therefore the personal virtues, charity, wisdom, and goodness at its heart. This will include, a responsibility actively to prevent evil from happening. Justice has a relationship with the principles of equity, because a virtuous reason will perceive how a particular solution will fit the particular circumstances.

## 4. An Intellectual History of the 'Law of Nations and Nature' in the Chinese–European Encounter (Part II of this Book)*

### 4.1 Introduction

This section introduces the Chinese part of the present volume's intellectual history of international thought. It begins by presenting four chapters on the history of Chinese ideas (Chapters 11–14). Confucianism was the dominant ethical system of the Chinese Empire and two expert Chinese Confucian scholars, Chun-Chieh Huang and Aihe Wang discuss its problem place within an absolute monarchical system resting ultimately on military force. Another two chapters by younger Chinese and Hong Kong scholars then reflect on the compatibility or translatability of Chinese and Western legal philosophical ideas, as a matter of historical practice. One chapter stresses the variety of Chinese and Western ideas, some more compatible than others; the other chapter explores directly the possibility of incommensurability. These more abstract and philosophical chapters are followed by three case studies of Western, including Japanese, imperialism in the late nineteenth century, to explore in depth the actual clash of mentalities between Chinese and Western individual figures. The conclusion recommends the avoidance of stereotypes. The final chapter by the leading Chinese historian of the epoch 1860–1911 provides a wider panorama of the place of Western international law in Chinese intellectual culture until the fall of the Empire.

### 4.2 Episodes of an intellectual history: moral standards within the Chinese Cultural Universe

In Chapter 12, Chun-Chieh Huang develops the concept of humane governance, the nurturing of the people in Confucianism, but warns that this will be at the expense of the exploration of the legitimacy of political authority. This legitimacy deficit leads to a rejection of Confucianism by modern constitutionalists in, for example, Taiwan.[60] It also renders suspect a way of thinking which could become a signpost for a country the size of China.[61] Huang calls this ethics of responsibility rather than the ethics of intention. Humane governance points to the humane heart, but does not impose effective controls on political power. It does not appear to assure accountability, which is essential to all variants of the rule of law. Indeed, there is a

* The presentation of the chapters in the Contents follows roughly an historical chronology, firstly in the history of ideas, and then in the state practice. It consists of reflections of the editors which are not necessarily shared by the individual authors, and which are certainly less rich

[60] See Chapter 12, p 284.

[61] See WA Callaghan, Chinese Visions of World Order: Post Hegemonic or a New Hegemony? in *International Studies*, vol 10 (2008) 719–61.

measure of authoritarianism in the compassion the ruler has for his subjects whom he treats as family members.

Confucius brings together, says Huang, ethics from the individual to family to social relationships and finally to national and international politics. The nurturing of character alone grounds an ethocracy. Mencius sees the ruler as having maternal compassion. In this context, the heart is the home of benevolence. Benevolence does not discriminate among all creatures under heaven. The mind–heart connects the individual with the universe itself. One should never harbour anger or a grudge. The individual cultivates him/herself and thereby brings peace and security to his/her fellows to the people, to the State, to Heaven.

But, says Huang, there is no answer for when the ruler does not follow Confucius. There is in this case a nostalgia of the intellectual under authoritarian regimes. The subjectivity of the head and of the people gets no further than the management *for* the people. And, East Asian rulers could easily escape from this ethic, warns Huang. Hence there is a deep opposition between Confucianism and legal, constitutional modernity. In this respect, it is difficult to see any difference between the Confucian ethic and the early-modern northern humanist guidelines for princes.[62] Neither has mechanisms to enforce self-cultivation in order to truly rule on behalf of the people.

However, further reflection may reveal why the issues raised by Huang are not decisive for a moral responsibility of rulers within a global framework of international law. It is argued, by modernists, that liberal contract theory offers relatively precise agreed standards, whereas the language of the good heart does not. But Confucius's famous critique of law applies here and especially to international law, where the issue is anyway whether there is law at all in a state of nature, beyond civil institutions. Confucius says that as soon as a law is made, lawyers can be found to argue any number of meanings of the law and all human ingenuity goes into wriggling out of the law. Therefore, it is an unwise standard to guide people. Ethics are considered far more superior. This Confucian argument does not suppose ethics or morality as a system of rules—except for the one rule which is virtually the same as the Christian rule. Instead, one supposes the wise, prudent, restrained 'other-oriented' person capable of exercising moral judgement (the wise and moral judgement which we have seen Morgenthau calls for).

There is a profound meaning behind the idea that there is a *law* to bind the prince even if he is not subject to any command. The absence of real institutions makes the core issue one of the moral responsibility of the individual ruler. Confucianism has written into its critique, a critical legal studies scepticism about the capacity of law to restrict and bind human ingenuity. It confronts legal positivism on its own ground and says that legal interpretation without a good heart is a hopeless venture.[63]

[62] This goes to the similarity in the sense that rulers are required to cultivate themselves in order to rule well and just, truly on behalf of the people. Erasmus was thus focused on the moral education of the prince, yet it has to be pointed out that Erasmus understood free and willing consent of subjects as part of the legitimacy of government. This was however the basis for demanding the highest moral quality of the ruler to be able to rule truly in the interest of the communal good. Erasmus goes beyond self-restraint as the ruler is obliged to serve God, that is, to pursue the common good. The ruler is educated, has to educate herself, to know the moral standards s/he is obliged to meet.

[63] C Hanson, available at http://philosophy.hku.hk/ch/index.html.

Hence the comparison of early-modern northern humanism and Confucianism addresses a gap at the very centre of public and international law. The comparison offers a programme towards a universal transcultural ethic, which, as Leibniz shows, will not anyway be satisfied with the idea of arbitrary behaviour by assemblies.[64] Leibniz identifies the problem with the expression, princes play at cards at their leisure and play at treaties at their work. But, so do the people. The crisis of Brexit in Europe and the election of Donald Trump as President of the United States show how intense confrontations of globalization can put unbearable stress on individual judgements (see sections 5 and 6).

An alternative to Confucianism within Chinese thinking is suggested by Henan Hu in Chapter 13. She reviews the debate instigated by WA Martins in the late nineteenth century,[65] that there was a style of international law in the ancient Spring and Autumn periods comparable to the West and that a Confucian-style international law could be drawn out of the *Book of Rites*, edited by Confucius. She also considers the reformist Confucianism of Kang You Wei, after the Sino-Japanese War. The difficulty was that Kang 'attempted to incorporate China into the international system but retained its imperial structures'. The contemporary Zhao Ting Yang also has the same tendency in wishing to replace the Western system of nation States, with a Confucian world institution, erasing the internal–external distinction so prominent in Western thinking. However, this modern Confucianism is widely seen as running the risk of imposing Chinese values on others. Hu comes to the conclusion that China's association with Confucianism is always going to be accompanied by its association with the tributary system, where there is a hierarchy of States, however benevolent.

So, Hu offers an alternative way to bridge East and West, through a comparison of Grotius and Laozi. She does so by relativizing the imperial epochs of Chinese history and considers the present international situation of China not completely exceptional. She goes back to the Spring and Autumn periods to Lao Zi, whom she says 'is recognized as the first person in Chinese history to create a primitive theory of natural law and dialectics'.[66] He favoured a divided status quo rather than a restoration of the unity of empire. After reviewing at length Grotius's theory, she concludes that while he accepted a 'superior and objective standard of sociability or common good … he did not accept any superior institutions above States'.[67] Nor was he a realist in the modern international relations theory sense. Instead, he thought world society was regulated 'under moral and ethical standards in which humans were seen as the fundamental underpinnings of the international society'.[68]

Daoism is remarkably close to northern European humanism. Lao Zi was concerned with the welfare of the ruled and the disadvantaged. His primary direction was towards values compatible with the contemporary international values of fairness, equality, and peace. He had a metaphysics, that is the Dao, as the Unnameable is the beginning of Heaven and Earth. Dao is an eternal name, lying beyond the

[64] See section 3. [65] See Chapter 13, p 295. [66] ibid p 299. [67] ibid.
[68] ibid p 304.

everyday human world (and therefore clearly not the Chinese Empire!). There has to be absolute being before there can be the individual beings who make up the actual world. This world view meant that individual humans, all equally contingent and small, were all equally dependent on a larger order of being, just as in Christian and Jewish thought in the West. Henan Hu elaborates this philosophy and concludes that Daoism encourages rulers to be modest.

There is an inherent dialectic in being, between the yin (negative) and the yang (the positive), between Heaven and Earth. Their coming together in communication is the He—harmony. Dialectic is at the core of Daoist cosmology. As Hu puts it, 'everything comes into being through the communication of two opposite essences yin and yang. Therefore, everything has its opposite. The two essences stay in harmony because of their balance' (p 307). If one side goes to extremes, the other will revert. There are invariables and the modest, open, and flexible spirit knows this and is able to appreciate the need to allow the people both to be governed and the space to develop themselves.

Concretely to follow the Dao is to be without arbitrariness, to nourish without control, to give all things the space to be what the 'Unnameable' allows. Dao, as the Way, is not a set of rules, any more than Confucianism, but a spirit of confidence in the face of a world, which is not malign. All are utterly capable of making morally responsible judgements. There are contradictions, the yin and the yang, but they reconcile themselves in a harmony of Being. In any case, too many desires are the root of conflict. Those who want too much, end up with nothing. The sage 'disregards the excessive ... and the extreme'. This Daoist world is almost anti-institutional. The wise ruler is the one who allows the spontaneity of being to respond to its own inner dynamic. As Hu says, 'the rulers of States should refrain from occupying and contending with each other' (p 309). As she says, the Daoist world is cosmological and ontological, ethical, and social. Hu means above all that humans are only a part of the world, of a nature infinitely larger than they are. They have to understand that their place, important as it is, is limited.

Both Grotius and Lao Zi consider the State as only an assistor of the people, to protect them, not an arbitrary force. Humans (ie before States) were destined to live in natural and unrestrained ways. They both understood interstate relations in a spirit of non-hegemony and peaceful coexistence, accepting superior objective standards, not superior political institutions. In particular, Lao Zi preferred the status quo of political divisions to wars of unification, as Confucius wanted to see a unified world order under a superiority. In Hu's view both treat spontaneous movements of peoples as the real foundation of law. This humanism is indigenous in both the West and the East and so, she says, it is universal. Humanism rather than statism is the essential convergence of the two, the natural law system of Grotius and Lao Zi's way of the Dao.

Chapter 14 by Emily Cheung and Maranatha Fung contextualizes the significance of different meanings of 'natural law' in mid-nineteenth-century China. It is part of a sequence of further studies in the volume which highlight a Chinese understanding of Western international law as a form of 'natural law' which was to lead to serious disillusion at the time of the Sino-Japanese War. Fung and

Cheung address the confusions of translation from the perspective that Chinese culture could have accepted a concept of natural law, but could not grasp the tangled nature of Wheaton's work, and indeed nineteenth-century Western international law, which was primarily positivist, resting on State consent. Since the time of Grotius and even Vitoria and Suarez, the notion of general consent could be evidence that a rule or principle was part of natural law, but, by the nineteenth century, empirical evidence of consent was itself the primary ground of legal validity. The Chinese word *gongfa* includes the two meanings of general consent between States and the idea that the general consent is part of natural law.

The idea of 'Tiandao thinking', write Cheung and Fung, is similar to natural law, except the transcendent God is absent. However, Neo-Confucianism 'incorporates the enlightenment of Buddhism/Taoism', while retaining the self-consciousness of Confucianism. Neo-Confucianism, since the Song dynasty, contains the concept 'xingli'. 'Xing' means 'natural instincts and life', while' 'li' means 'reasons'. The authors say '[t]ogether "xingli" also means the principle and discipline of life, emotions and reasons, humanity and justice' (p 322). The authors say '[i]t is the last meaning . . . Qing readers were likely to equate "xing" and "li" in Martin's translation with Neo-Confucian thinking'.[69]

At the same time, the main purpose of our authors is to demonstrate that, overall, the complex mix of positivism and natural law in Western international law at the time, with positivism predominating, meant that insuperable problems of translation arose. They enumerate several examples. 'Quanli' for right, was a combination of the concept of power/'quan' and 'li'/wealth while the whole idea of right was unclear to the Chinese tradition and likely to confuse a Qing reader. Of course, many of the concepts Wheaton is translating, from the contractarian and Hobbesian tradition, are indeed difficult to translate, precisely because this more modern tradition of Western international law is alien to the more traditional Chinese thinking. This is particularly clear in Fung and Cheung's discussion of the key international law concept of 'independence'.

The authors point out that independence is crucial to Vattel. It is translated as 'zizhu'/self-direct. However, they point out that the Chinese are not able to translate the Western notion of 'independent moral being'. The word 'zizhu' is equated to 'state' as well, to give the result that 'an independent moral being' is translated into Chinese as 'the state is self-directed and has righteousness to be observed'. Indeed, the authors point out that 'moral being' as a body politic capable of enjoying rights is not directly translated. They say this shows 'that the Chinese translation fails to translate highly abstract concepts deriving from Western metaphysics such as "moral being", and hence resort to concrete and anthropomorphic expressions' (p 326). Indeed, the concept of 'emperor', remained attached to the individual person and the concept of absolute State, in the sense of 'State with an absolute ruler', remained alien in imperial China.

[69] See Chapter 14, p 322.

The argument becomes even clearer with the difficulties in translating the notion of the absolute, as inherent, sovereign rights of States—the very core of Hobbsianism. Fung and Cheung point out that the Chinese translation 'ziran' means 'the (mother) nature' in modern Chinese. However, in ancient Chinese, according to Lao Zi, 'ziran' 'is a phenomenon that a thing exists according to its own existence and form without any distortion or external coercion'. Fung and Cheung conclude that 'ziran' means in ancient Chinese, 'itself as it is', not having any fixed state or mode. After considering the possibility of using 'ziyou' as a translation of 'absolute—it means 'it itself has or is', Fung and Cheung come to the conclusion there is no Chinese equivalent of the idea of 'absolute' in a proposition about the right of States to independence. They say 'absolute' and 'ziran' or 'ziyou' 'are definitely not equivalent concepts'. So, they conclude 'due to this inability to convey the meaning of "absolute"/"absolute right", the inviolable and inconvertible nature of absolute international rights such as the right of self-preservation is not adequately translated' (p 327). This means the Qing would never have understood the Western inherent (fear-based) fixation—continuing until today—on security, so that an immense discretion will always be left to the State, in any Western concept of order, to defend itself.

Coming onto the more specifically historical chapters, the concern turns to the actual presence or absence of a Chinese ethic, more specifically a Neo-Confucianism in the perspective of the Chinese officials in relation both to the Emperor and to foreign diplomats. Aihe Wang in Chapter 11 is acutely concerned with the contrast between the 'blue-sky' serene world of classical Confucian ethics and the vulnerability of the Confucian scholar in a power structure rooted in a conquering warrior absolute monarchy. In a way, she also raises the liberal, modern challenge that the rule of law requires some kind of institutional constraint on power and not just an individual ethic.

Aihe Wang provides an exhaustive and authoritative history of Confucianism within the history of China and thoroughly reinforces Hu's criticisms of Confucianism in contrast to the Dao, although she does not mention Lao Zi. She portrays how the concept of the Mandate of Heaven was always used by military conquerors to provide legitimacy for their use of force. As Confucianism became the official ideology of the State during the time of Emperor Wu (141–87 BC), she draws a very sharp contrast between the Confucian ideology represented by Dong Zhonshu (the time of Emperor Wu) and the Dao-oriented thinking of the King of Huainan. The former represented an authoritarian institution of centralization and hierarchy, with the Confucian scholar class claiming to interpret a moral cosmology to strengthen the authority of the emperor, and, by implication, that of his scholar advisers. Their task was to interpret the will of an anthropomorphic deity from Zhou theology, attributing to it a heart, intention, and love. Heaven manifests his will in omens as Heaven's speech (p. 261). Only the sage Confucius could understand and interpret the moral consciousness of Heaven. Their recommendation was for wholesale centralization of culture, whether in its political, military, or economic aspects. At the same time, the Chinese Empire was in constant military expansion in all directions. It concluded with a recommendation for the conquest and execution of the Huainan kings, among others. As Wang puts it, 'the ideological unification was essential for building an authoritarian and centralized imperial order. By suppressing different cultural and philosophical traditions, it established universal rules and standards that were themselves the web of the centralized empire.'[70]

In contrast the King of Huainan, Liu An and his consultants submitted a book called *Huainanzi* to the Emperor Wu. They advocate a cosmology of natural law. Cosmological phenomena are the result of resonance (*ganying*), that is, 'the phenomena of the same category and sharing the same *qi* affecting one another spontaneously, free from human intentions'. Wang quotes

> When the *Yang qi* prevails, it scatters to make dew;
> When the *Yin qi* prevails, it freezes to make frost and snow

Wang points out how 'the resonance of things cannot be subject to moral judgement or knowledge'. She observes '[t]he resonance of things belonging to the same category is darkly mysterious and extremely subtle. Knowledge cannot explain it, nor discussion unravel it.'[71]

Not surprisingly, Wang says that the two opposing theories of 'resonance' are 'instrumental of the two models of rulership—the active sovereign of centralized power versus the non-active sovereign of a pluralistic world'.[72] Rejecting sovereign, absolute, and central authority, *Huainanzi* says that resonance has nothing to do with status, but accepts anyone who unites with *Dao*. Persons such as a blind musician, a commoner's daughter, a high official, all reach the *Dao* through perfect sincerity (*jingcheng*). As a result, the ruler, summarizes Wang, 'is not taking action to dominate and control, but rather [is] uniting with Dao through non-action'. In the course of suppressing Daoism, on the advice of his Confucian scholars, the Emperor Wu forced the King of Hainanzi, Liu An, to commit suicide 'and his family, followers, and the people involved with him were killed by the tens of thousands'.

Such violence raises a question comparable to the relevance of the Grotian ethic for the West. How does one bridge the gap between the natural law ethic and the raw politics of international relations? Civic humanism culminating in Kant (Tuck's interpretation) sees the need to overcome the 'unnatural' natural disorder outside the civic community of the State, with an international civic order, resting ultimately on consent, which means a rule of law as a restraint of raw liberty as power, but, still, effectively a self-restraint. Then law becomes something external, public, verifiable—legal contractual commitments.

The paradox of course is that this is not realizable even today. Documents such as the UN Charter and the liberal rule of law principles, such as *pacta sunt servanda*, and non-intervention are also essentially an ethical system, only a hypothetical standard of ethics given a formal semblance of law, because adopted in treaties. In practice, the standards are underdetermined—leaving almost everything to ethical judgement—and often not observed or enforced. For instance, the concepts of peace and security, duties to settle disputes peacefully, and to negotiate in good faith are all as vague in the UN Charter as they are in the Analects of Confucius, the Bible, or the Koran, to

[70] See Chapter 11, p 264. [71] ibid p 262. [72] ibid.

mention just three religious or ethical texts. Therefore, in practice the logical power of the ethical perspective, for example—as it is espoused by Grotius and Laozi—is not weaker than supposedly more rigorous formulations in the law. However, the ethical perspective, that is, of the morally responsible person does not have the ethical–realist dichotomy. It assumes that the crises of disharmony caused by moral failure are precisely the issues which the moral and intellectual discernment of a wise and moderate intellect/heart has to discern, diagnose, and challenge. We have simply the ethical and the unethical. The latter of course disturbs the former, but the solution is the abandonment of the unethical, once it is called by its name. And that is exactly what is necessary. This is no less practicable than the liberal ideology of the rule of law which may be, as we have argued in the Introduction[73] and the chapter on Richelieu, dangerously simplistic when applied to international society.

In the next stage, our comparative study tries to show a way forward. This means a return to a practicable, critical form of historical–political case study. We explore the first interactions of the East and West from the middle of the nineteenth century. In this way, we illustrate how the search for right reason and the good heart can show themselves, perhaps in both Confucianism and in Daoism, but also in a Western diplomacy which has sometimes not completely submitted itself to the harsher humanism absorbed by nineteenth-century international legal positivism. The form of the case studies allows one to grasp how it is that the ethical principle can be governing not simply in the conduct of the rulers—called to moral responsibility—but also how the independent critic can offer insights into the issues at play. In practice beyond the individual restraint of rulers, anyway today under huge pressure of a not always wise press and public opinion (see section 5). There is, at present, as always in the past, little prospect of improving the international conduct of States and their governments. Now, in an age of transparency, everyone has a moral responsibility to be vigilant (see section 5).

The next three chapters (16–18) are concerned with the collapse of the tributary system and the problematic replacement of it by the Western 'Vattelian' system of the sovereign equality of States. They offer many paradoxical features, illustrating all the themes discussed so far in this section 4. They span the years from the late 1870s (the Ryukyu Crisis) to the Gulf of Tonkin Crisis of the mid 1880s to the final collapse of the tributary system with the Sino-Japanese War. The case studies allow a very close observation of the play between the official ethic of Confucianism and the more formal ethos of Western international law. They also allow a comparison of the merits of the two systems.

China posed as the guardian of Ryukyu between 1879 and 1882, as afterwards it was to do for the Kingdom of Annam and Korea. International law, Western style, was supposed to be based on the sovereign equality of independent States. In the first case study of Ryukyu conducted by Anthony Carty and Patrick Leung Japan tried to represent to the world that China's supposed protective role for Ryukyu meant that China considered itself higher in standing than any other country, a threat to

[73] Morgenthau (nn 2 and 4).

everyone's independence. It also used the Western international law argument that China had never effectively occupied the territory of Ryukyu or purported to exercise sovereign jurisdiction over the island. However, Satow saw through this strategy and explained that China was merely benevolently trying to protect the autonomy of Ryukyu from Japanese encroachment. The meaning of the tributary system, which China was defending, meant only that China felt a responsibility to represent Ryukyu in the face of Japanese encroachment. Satow represented Chinese conduct as pure benevolence, but China was to be disappointed that neither Japan nor any Western power would support its efforts on behalf of Ryukyu. In other words, China thought it obvious, and Satow agreed with China, that the Ryukyu people wished to retain their autonomy and also obvious that Western powers should see that this was only fair and just and that they should therefore support China in achieving this objective. However, the West remained indifferent and the only US concern was that its harbouring rights should be preserved under a new Japanese regime.

The limited doctrine of legitimacy or protection of statehood in international law meant that the mere fact of contracting treaties with foreign powers did not guarantee the autonomy of Ryukyu. The US in particular needed only a guarantee from Japan that it would obtain the same benefits under Japanese rule as when Ryukyu had autonomy. However, this is not to say that international law could give no guidance as to whether Japanese initiatives towards Ryukyu were without foundation. The Chinese as well as the Japanese archives show that Japan could not find any way to justify their claims except emphasizing the geographical and cultural features of Ryukyu. They even used Confucian arguments during the negotiation with China, such as claiming a State could not serve two superiors at the same time. As Carty and Leung point out, there was no exclusion of this in Western international law at the time, eg relations between Balkan States, Russia, and Turkey. Even Japan's own Western legal adviser, Boissonade suggested that China, as a State claiming suzerainty over Ryukyu, should not be excluded from the negotiation with Ryukyu. The King of Ryukyu (1878–79) was coerced through an unlawful imprisonment to assent to an incorporation. At the same time, within the Chinese bureaucracy a weakness in the Confucian ethic was exposed. The new Chinese ambassador to Japan, He, recommended that the only way to deal with Japan over the issue was by demands backed by a visible, credible threat to use force. Li Hongzhang considered this view alarmist and the Chinese remained confident that reasoned argument with Japan would be fruitful. The Chinese thought the Japanese would recognize that China's ambition was only for the welfare of the people of Ryukyu who desired to retain the very high degree of autonomy which they enjoyed under the Chinese vassalage and tributary system. In contrast, Japan, was transforming its own traditional feudal law, under which the Ryukyus were also its vassals, into a modern, centralized State, along Western lines. This necessitated Ryukyu being integrated into a unitary Japanese State.

What this chapter shows is a theme which will recur later, especially in the chapter on the Sino-Japanese War. There does not appear to have been any civilizational cleavage between Western and Chinese officials about the importance and meaning of concepts of justice and fair treatment. Western lawyers could see well that

Chinese intentions were constructive and Western legal advisers could also see that the Chinese Tributary system also incorporated these values. Finally, the same advisers could see that even existing Western international law principles could support Ryukyu in its claim to the very high degree of autonomy Vassal States enjoyed. The crucial stumbling block was that the rest of the international community—outside Japan—were not willing to support these principles with the use of force. We will return to this defect in the commentary on the chapter on the Sino-Japanese War.

The next case study (Chapter 17) concerns also an attack on China's tributary system, this time by France. The Kingdom of Annam hovered between treaties of equality with France and its tributary relationship with China. As it came to realize that treaties of protectorate were much more intrusive than the Chinese tributary relationship, it appeared to want to go back to the latter. There followed the most involved legal discussions between France and China where, at least on the French side, the issue of incommensurability was uppermost. The French would attribute no legal significance to the Chinese tributary relation with Annam. However, on the Chinese side, its ambassadors understood very well the nature of international law. It led them to accept in part that they had acquiesced in the loss of Annam, but also their legal understanding enabled them to resist French practices, which they knew contradicted Western international law, in particular the demand for an indemnity. In the end, it is not easy to say that culture played much of a role in the conflict as France and China seemed on a collision course. China wished to help to protect Annam without strings as to its domestic affairs. However, it had an ambition to maintain Annam as a buffer State against France. This ambition was defeated. Annam was, eventually, almost completely incorporated into the French Empire. Again, international law could not defend the personality of its subjects and Confucianism did not bar Chinese officials from understanding the contradictions between French behaviour and international law.

From the legal aspect, the Chinese–French confrontation consisted of a series of very minute treaty negotiations, in which the Chinese conceded virtually everything asked for by the French. The final break came over a disputed interpretation of a Chinese commitment to evacuate 'immediately' all its troops from Tonkin. Some were remaining, unexpectedly for the French, and that led to a clash, where the French were the losers, thereupon demanding revenge. However, the clash was caused by a misunderstanding, which could have been avoided with more calm on the French side. The issue of principle, dear to the French, had been conceded. The Chinese had conceded that Annam had concluded a Western-style protectorate with France, which excluded China completely from Annan.

The very high level of cultural sophistication of Chinese officials in this case, especially Marquis Zeng Jize, one-time Chinese ambassador to Paris, and his intellectual mentor, Guo Songtao, allows the authors to conclude their chapter with important reflections on the relationship of Western international law to Chinese values. As the authors put forward, against the legal positivist exclusion of morality, Confucianists cannot fathom any system of law which is unethical or unreasonable, as one should be reasonable in taking decisions. The liberal exclusion of morality from law—by which is meant what the parties consent to be bound to—could not be accepted by

Confucian officials. The principle of reasonableness had to govern every matter, in a spirit of compromise. The Tianxia system is certainly Sino-centric and hierarchical, but, as the authors say, interpreting Guo Songtao, 'Tian Xia is a dynamic concept as it changes with the expansion of the Chinese Empire and of the world, to the knowledge of China.' When facing up to new systems of law, and particularly the idea of international law, the Empire under Heaven draws instant analogies and simply assumes that, since Heaven is dominated by reason, international law as the law of Heaven, must, by definition, be dominated by reason too. As the law of nations was a form of natural law, it could be conceptualized as a 'nexus of higher moral rules applying to a family of States which had to act reasonably to each other in order to be legitimate under the Mandate of Heaven'. For the Qing literati, 'international law, justice and reasonableness were overlapping concepts' (p 405).

One important and perhaps very significant difference between Chinese and especially French culture concerns the significance of silence in relation to acquiescence. The authors of Chapter 17, Anna Baka and Lucy Qi, argue it is possible to see traces of Daoism, in the sense described in most detail by Hu in her chapter, in Chinese practices. This admittedly clear cultural difference had, and continues to have, great legal significance. As the authors put it 'China's affinity to its vassal States as well as its strong cultural and racist ties to Vietnam were considered proof enough that China's historical titles were incontestable' (p 410). This comes back to the distinction between late modern Western (contractarian: see section 5) law and Chinese ethics, as approximating to natural law, mentioned in the last paragraph. The Chinese considered it reasonable that practices of exchange between China and Vietnam that had existed for centuries would continue in some form, as practically needed. First, that was only reasonable, and, second, the legitimacy of continued exchanges could be assumed, without constant provocative assertion, precisely because it was reasonable. Exchanges would not take place just to make a point, but when appropriate in the circumstances. According to Zeng: 'Even though France concluded a treaty with Vietnam, China's rights over Vietnam still exists. It is France's good intention to protect Vietnam. Yet China also has its right of protection. Protection established later does not invalidate protection established before.' For the French silence, absence of protest, was acquiescence. Yet if they had 'studied more carefully the Chinese administration, they would have noticed that inaction was a natural, inherent characteristic of the Confucian system' (p 410).

Finally, the case of the first Sino-Japanese war over Korea in 1894–95 (Chapter 18), Korea was the death knell for the tributary system. The same considerations appear to apply here as in the other two cases. International law does not protect Korea from eventual incorporation into the Japanese Empire. However, Japan successfully articulates to the West the idea that it wants to favour Korea's definite status as an independent country rather than the much vaguer Chinese idea that it was a benevolent superior able to protect Korea. Japan, China, and Korea concluded numerous treaties, which could have defined their relations with one another, except that the Western doctrine on war meant they could be abrogated where one State, Japan, chose to have recourse to war.

Bijun Xu and Patrick Leung use the case study to highlight the specific questions of whether Western international law was an order with an ethical foundation or whether it should be considered as a purely positive system of law. Such a legal order would be based only on consent, which they could decide, at any time, to let fall away, if the enforcement of the treaties and other consensual obligations did not appear to be of interest to particular States. Surprisingly, Xu and Leung reach the conclusion that the legal order should have been sufficient to save Korea from further encroachment on its freedom by Japan, and to have provided a framework within which Korea could have called upon China to assist it in maintaining domestic order, without unwanted Japanese intrusions which it (Korea) could not dislodge. That is to say, the various treaties concluded by China, Japan, and Korea covered all the disputes that arose in the Sino-Japanese War. It was simply the case that Japan violated these treaties and the international community—governed by Western international law—did not care.

There were various treaties whereby Japan, China, and other countries recognized the independence of Korea. However, there was one key treaty, the Tianjin Convention of 1885, which set out the circumstances under which Japan and China could send troops to Korea. It required mutual notification and withdrawal of troops as soon as the need had passed. Korea itself was not a party to the Treaty or bound by it. The Treaty did not explicitly show that there had to be a request for assistance from Korea, but the authors argue from the *travaux préparatoires* that this was clearly understood by Japan in its negotiations. Also, it is reasonable and just in the nature of the situation that assistance is offered when asked and withdrawn when no longer needed.

The authors show that Korea did request assistance from China in 1894 and not Japan, that Japan forced a treaty upon Korea in 1894, stating they were allies, that there should be no Chinese troops on Korea soil, and that Japan used the pretext of China transporting troops to Korea as a context for starting a war, without any declaration. Furthermore, and most vitally, the authors show that the Western powers were aware of a Japanese strategy of aggression towards China and Korea that had as its object to expel Chinese influence from Korea and establish an exclusive Japanese control over Korea. Russia and England both declared as much to Japan. However, all of the powers decided to remain neutral in the ensuing conflict.

The most important part of Xu and Leung's deliberations is their comparison of Confucian concepts of international order and Western international law to judge the outcome of this conflict. Texts of Confucius and Mencius are analysed to try to draw out a standard of conduct to see whether it could be applied to the late nineteenth century. Striking starting points were that an individual standard of moral behaviour applied to Chinese, whether they were individuals, family leaders, or emperors. However, the very idealist standard of Confucianism assumed that the just person had no reason to live in fear of the other, and, anyway, a doctrine of just war would come up against the fact that States, as equal, would not have authority to punish one another. The right of punishment extended only to a superior over an inferior. The doctrines of Confucius did not rule out self-defence as a lesser of two evils, but the true, lasting foundation of world order would be the example of moral inspiration of the morally perfect leader. Where the enemy was not impressed, the ruler could always displace himself and start a new kingdom elsewhere. This philosophy should dissuade those who see Confucianism as a way to Chinese world hegemony, but the authors do not consider the standards of Confucianism helpful enough for the late nineteenth century of complex treaties and alliances, which were, in any case, not respected by any of the state parties. Confucianism, whether of Confucius or Mencius was bound to appear naive, a fairy tale of ancient kings and rulers. Hence the disastrous impact of the Sino-Japanese War on Chinese cultural self-confidence (of which more from Tian Tao—below).

At the same time, the authors come to the conclusion that international legal standards, while clear enough, existed in some kind of social or community vacuum, in the sense that Western powers did not see an interest in regarding positive international law, expressed in treaties, as something that had to be observed or enforced whether on legal or ethical grounds. The powers were aware of what Japan was doing and called it aggression. They realized that arguments Japan used about Chinese interference in Korean affairs and Japan's role in guaranteeing Korean autonomy, were threadbare—that Japan's underlying strategy was conquest and exclusion. Yet they did not resist and instead acquiesced. In particular the UK was informed by its minister in Korea that the Japanese intended to conquer Korea, and to conquer Formosa, at the same time. The authors conclude that international legal standards, such as the independence of States and the sanctity of treaties, were not standards the States were prepared to uphold. One could say that war was not illegal at the time. That is the general view, but the authors prefer to say that there was a total normative vacuum filled neither by Confucianism, nor by international law.

The final two chapters are more purely historical and tend to confirm the pessimistic note of the conclusion of the above chapter. Chapter 19 on Ernest Satow, Li Hongzhang, and the Russian Manchurian railway by Jing Tan and Anthony Carty takes another twist by approaching the role of ethical education in the lives of the actual diplomats from both the West (England) and China in late Qing China. It deals with both the issues of cultural incommensurability and the divide between the subjective, internal human world and the 'real' world of public affairs. The interchange between these two towering figures occurs in the aftermath of the Boxer Rebellion and during the negotiation of the Boxer Protocol, but concerns the narrower question as to whether the proposed contract or treaty between Russia and the Qing over the Manchurian railway system constituted an effective break-up of Manchuria from China. The chapter explores the similarity of the education of UK officials (in the Greek classics) and the Chinese (in Confucian classics). It explains the more superficial character of the former focusing on linguistic skills, while the latter witnesses the dying Confucian bureaucratic ethic, now submerged in the class interests of the Han Confucian imperial bureaucracy, itself almost as powerful as the weakened Qing monarchy. This bureaucracy repeatedly failed to generate an international vision beyond its own sectional, domestic interests.

In this context, the chapter provides a vision of the supposed inscrutability of Chinese negotiating styles by pitting them against a British Sinologist perfectly capable of penetrating the Chinese political world. While Satow has himself strong traces of the ethic that Grotius and Laozi would commend, he is also himself imprisoned in the Anglo-Russian rivalry for predominance in China. At the same time, Satow is following a British policy since 1860 to maintain the integrity of Qing China, much as Britain tried for a time to maintain the Ottoman Empire intact. Satow was to retire from service in 1906 recommending to the Foreign Secretary, Sir Edward Grey, an 'ethical' treaty policy, based upon mutual advantage and absence of coercion. Railway concessions should be about facilitating infrastructure and not about—as he feared with the contract Li Hongzhang favoured with Russia—handing over territorial control of parts of China to foreign States. To achieve his goal, Satow called up his superior, Sir Edward Grey, to respect the equal dignity of the Chinese Empire. Grey passed the advice onto Satow's successor in Peking, Sir John Jordan, who continued the policy of maintaining the territorial integrity of China.

However, China's Confucian ethic was no longer able to sustain the Empire for the reasons described in the chapter. The self-interests of the senior bureaucrats, of Han origin, who came through the imperial examinations, depended upon the Empire for their survival, as the throne depended upon them. However, it was increasingly difficult for these bureaucrats to engage actively and proactively in relations with the outside world. Survival depended upon supremacy within China. The chapter follows the antics of its supreme figure, Li Hongzhang, who manoeuvred, always from a position of weakness, by trying to play, for example British and Russian diplomats and diplomacy off again one another. In Satow he had a match, who could work fluently with many of Li's rivals within the Chinese bureaucracy. At least that showed there was no incommensurability of cultures.

The broader sweep of Tian Tao's history of the whole period from the 1860s (from the time of the publication of Martin's translation of Wheaton) until the fall of the Empire in 1911–12, indicates just how, by 1900, there was no longer any consensus among the wider community of literati and intellectuals in China in any community of values. (See Chapter 15.)

Tian Tao's very rigorous historical chapter leads on from this by describing how the late nineteenth century began with an overly optimistic view among the Chinese intelligentsia of the power of an ethical Western-style international law to assist China in its relations with foreign powers. However, the shock of the 1894–95 Sino-Japanese War changed everything utterly. A social Darwinism and realism came to permeate Chinese intellectual circles. The conviction was sown—which has probably remained—that the only possible foundation for Chinese security had to be in its own self-strengthening[74]—the rise of the self-strengthening movement focusing on material factors such as technology.[75] This does not lead to an overt challenge to Western international law, but, among intellectuals then and probably today, it is expected that international law will be marginal to the realities of world society. Self-strengthening is definitely not a version of Confucianism (or Daoism for that

[74] S Suzuki, China's Perceptions of International Society in the Nineteenth Century: Learning More about Power Politics? *Asian Perspective* 28(3) (2004) 115–44.

[75] See Chapter 15.

matter). Hence Confucianism came under attack as a source of China's weakness. The latter would now be subordinated to the interests of the State, as a form of soft power.

Tian Tao details through a minute analysis of books, journals, and the press, the extent to which the wider Chinese community distanced itself from any belief that Confucian values could be matched with a Western international law, that could have a simple ethical foundation. There was an enormous and very widespread interest in Western international law. However, the impression of repeated successes of Western military prowess, from the Sino-French War, through the Sino-Japanese War to the final humiliation of the Boxer Rebellion, was that all that counted in international relations, was military power, and the industrial strength which grounded it. Confucian ideals of world order, above all Kang Youwei's, were too idealist. The primary focus of China had to be on material strengthening. The other great intellectual of the turn of the century, Liang Qichao tended to believe, in Tian Tao's words, 'that world politics were dominated by power, not by morality and universal truth. In the cruel competition for existence, the backward countries were faced with the danger of being destroyed.' This fear of extinction might create in the Chinese the sense of danger necessary to promote Chinese self-reformation. In the meantime, 'in imperialist times international law was produced by power, so it was "the convention of the reciprocity of the powers", but not the weaker side's amulet'.[76]

## 5. Going Back *Beyond* Liberal Internationalism: Contours of an Ethocratic 'Rule of Law' for World Order

### 5.1 Introduction

In spite of centuries of Sino-European encounters, the histories of both Part I and II do not present a historical school of international thought that China and Europe developed together. The intellectual traditions of China and Europe share no common roots in that sense. However, what Part I and II do show is that versions of softer humanism, a prominent role for human reason and morality, natural jurisprudence, and virtue ethics are present within both intellectual traditions. Both histories moreover bring to the forefront the limits of international law and therewith the ultimate need for reason, reasonableness, and moral judgement. As such, these historical studies provide foundational elements and leads for a contemporary turn to ethics, to the vision of a shared humanity as the basis for global justice, and to moral personality and responsibility as a prerequisite for political wisdom and for a transcultural dialogue about the moral standards to guide judgement (in governance).[77]

This section aims to contribute to the much-needed development of such a transcultural dialogue between Chinese and European traditions of international thought, and to ground the few philosophical remarks with which we would like to

[76] See Chapter 15, p 352.

[77] cf A Lejbowicz, *Philosophie de droit international* (PUF 1999) 404–12, 413–18.

conclude the introduction to the volume.[78] Both Chinese and European ethical–juridical–political traditions are internally contested and highly complex. As editors, we are fully aware that to bring Chinese and European traditions of thought into dialogue is an exercise almost too complicated to do well. And, yet, we are convinced that it is necessary to engage in such a transcultural dialogue. Revisiting natural jurisprudence is a necessary first step.

We have taken inspiration from both Part I (the reconstruction of early-modern northern humanist thought and its contribution to a non-Hobbesian version of seventeenth-century natural law thinking) and Part II (Chinese humanist anthropologies and moral and political thought) in an attempt to open up this dialogue, and point to a possible shared transcultural humanist anthropology of international law that could warrant a move beyond liberal internationalism.

Dealing with both Confucian and Daoist thought, Part II carves out a humanism that is not about hierarchy and superiority, but about *shared* humanity. As such, it comes remarkably close to European northern humanism and natural law theory as informed by the former and brought out in Part I. In both histories, we find profound concern for the welfare of the ruled and the disadvantaged, as well as a view of rulers as obliged to foster introspection and moral development of the self. Trustworthy rulers are rulers who cultivate their spirit's capacity for morally responsible judgement. Regardless of how Eastern or Western traditions name the Way Inward, the key is moral (self-)education. In our view, the latter is highly significant in the context of today's debate on 'the politics of international law'.[79]

The accepted meaning of the phrase 'the politics of international law' today is the 'indeterminacy of international law'. The indeterminacy of the law requires those who work with the law to make ethical judgements. Judgement requires those who rule to nurture moral character and to practice virtue ethics. Law cannot do without ethics. Either we languish in semi-nihilism or worse, or we allow for a turn to ethics in international law. Should we accept as just whatever our rulers state to be just, as in the Hobbesian world? Is it not more true to say that we all have to make political, ethical choices because the law is indeterminate? We need foundations for such choices. This is what our volume tries to provide, from an East–West humanist perspective. Our claim is that we need a rule of law as justice that draws on the communal and intersubjective dimensions of (international) society and human nature; that may be characterized as 'ethocratic'. Our turn to history is also a return to ethics:[80] Law becomes justice reached through the just judgement. Law is concerned with the justice required by the situation, a measurement of appropriate conduct, especially in relationship.

[78] See A Carty, *Philosophy of International Law*, (1st edn, Edinburgh UP 2007) ch 8; JE Nijman, 'Paul Ricoeur and International Law: Beyond "The End of the Subject". Towards a Reconceptualization of International Legal Personality' (2007) 20 LJIL 25–64.

[79] Brought to the forefront of international legal debate by Martti Koskenniemi's famous *From Apology to Utopia* book (Finnish Lawyers' Publishing Company 1989) and his 1990 EJIL article 'The Politics of International Law'.

[80] M Koskenniemi, '"The Lady Doth Protest Too Much" Kosovo, and the Turn to Ethics in International Law' (2002) 65 MLR 159–75.

Our claim thus builds on the historical explorations of Chinese and European traditions of thought in Part I and II, which have in common two significant applications of moral standards. Law as justice constrains power, while, second, providing, as justice, the basis for a just conclusion. Hence, the maintenance and cultivation of moral character of those who rule—and advise them—is crucial. Our approach in other words is a turn to ethics, that works as a postmodern revisiting of natural jurisprudence. This means we have a lot to explain. How do we conceive of natural law? What do we think about the hegemonic nature of universality, the subjectivity of 'right reason' and justice, and the (im)possibility of objective values? And, how do we jump from the early-modern *ius gentium et naturae* as a counter-hegemonic force in European thought, to the role of virtues in Chinese thought, and then to a transcultural dialogue on postmodern natural law and justice, while at the same time critiquing the liberal assumptions about the trustworthiness of those who govern? The answer to all these self-anguishing questions is very simple. Neither we nor the ancient Chinese sages are asserting a personal authority. Rather, we are inviting a process of critical self-reflection, as Socrates would have done, but without his ironical skills. If international law is actually about making judgements, it is crucial we debate this in order for the political act of judgement to be morally responsible rather than utterly subjective, self-serving, corporatocratic, mediacratic, and/or mobocratic.

Underpinning our claim is a new—transcultural—anthropology of law in international society, which connects (international) law to moral (self-)education, and which, by building on the moral theory of personhood in the natural law tradition, pushes for a move away from an international order of fear and distrust to an international pluralist order of recognition and respect (section 5.3). First, we pause at how the predominant Eastern and Western anthropologies of law in international society have met in the past (section 5.2).

## 5.2 Harsh Western legal modernity meets complacent naivety of nineteenth-century Chinese Confucians

The international law that hit China hard in the nineteenth century consisted in the harsh version of international law produced by Western modernity. It was then—with the historical encounters described in the case studies of Part II—that Chinese socialization into international society and international law started.[81] As pointed out above, this Western liberal perspective on (international) law builds on Hobbesian natural rights theory developed out of early-modern natural law thinking impacted by Italian humanist war jurisprudence.[82] In this tradition, 'modern' natural law broke away from late medieval and late-scholastic thought, while adopting the Renaissance doctrines of individual moral agency, *Ragion di Stato*, self-preservation, and self-defence, and war. In short, the Hobbesian anthropology of international law set us up for a violent international order. International

[81] Suzuki (n 74). [82] Tuck (n 12).

law became geared to a fearful subject living in a (fearful) state of mind incapable of self-reflexivity; it became focused on pre-emption and egoistic conduct (both understood as legitimate because in line with the quest for security and material needs to preserve oneself), and in the same vein came to look at international society as a non-society, amoral and anarchical.

As the authors of chapters in Part II of this volume argue, the nineteenth-century Qing literati and officials saw international law and reasonableness as overlapping concepts comparable to the understandings of natural law thinkers like Grotius and other northern humanists some centuries earlier.[83] The Dao traditionally attacks the very roots of conflict by insisting upon the self-denial and restraint of the ruler. The virtue of modesty is paramount. At the core of Daoism is the idea that the ruler should leave space for others, not seek to occupy all space. Meanwhile, the Confucian doctrine of the world family has no place for the idea of the domestic *versus* the foreign, or indeed for the national. The Chinese rule of reason is to unite moderation and prudence. Again, this is comparable to European thought as discussed in Part I. To be sure, there are profound differences between East and West, for example concerning the metaphysics of good and evil, which in the West ties in with the legal and the illegal. In contrast, the yin and yang of Daoism unites contradictions rather than dividing and rejecting. As the positive and the negative they are both necessary and form a totality in their complexity, as Henan Hu has outlined. The outcome is HE (a Chinese word for Peace) or peace and harmony. Confucian benevolence has an element of universality that is historically associated with imperial China. This has a compelling, hierarchical character and was fully unsuited to confront the Hobbesian outlook of the West. Confucian philosophy of endless negotiation and compromise could only crack and collapse in the face of the determined, conquering spirit of colonialism. Confucianism was as all-embracing as Daoism, encompassing all humanity but as a unity in a single family and not as rivals, equal in fact, but always striving for pre-eminence. Concepts of harmony and benevolence are however present also in European thought—one only has to think of a scholar like GW Leibniz.

Part II provides detailed historical discussions of the interaction between Confucian and other Chinese ideals on the one hand and Western thought on the other, between the 1860s and 1870s and around the time of the final disasters of 1895–1900. This is motivated by the belief that a shared ideational order, bringing together Western, largely northern, humanism and Chinese humanism—not strictly anthropomorphic in its Neo-Confucian and Daoist strains—could have been possible intellectually and culturally. For this reason, the editors of this book consider that it is not hopelessly inappropriate—at a time when more openness exists in China to the values of the ancient Chinese classics—to conclude by exploring the *artificiality* of the Western legal tradition in that it has closed off the values and methods of morality of Northern European humanism when taking its liberal internationalist course. We argue to correct that exclusion, and to bring it into

[83] See for instance, Chapter 15, Part I, and Chapter 17, Part III.

dialogue with Chinese humanist thought. Of course, in the conclusion to an introduction we cannot expound what would be a whole new philosophy of international law—albeit one that merely tries to re-establish the Western traditions' ruptured links with their own past. All we can do is outline the formal steps that could be taken.[84]

The histories of ideas in Part I and II encourage us to rethink the recognition of a shared humanity. Not through the Christian *imago Dei* nor through a hierarchical Confucian vision, but through recognition of the other as similar. A new anthropology of international law, which draws on shared humanity and on cultivation of virtues, takes us away from the individualist to the communal, from the radically subjective to the intersubjective, from anarchy to a pluralist order of mutual recognition and respect.

## 5.3 A new anthropology of international law for a pluralist order of recognition and respect

We would like to argue that a transcultural dialogue can foster a new—transcultural—anthropology of international law out of the intellectual traditions of both East and West. The reappraisal of non-liberal early-modern natural jurisprudence opens up a move beyond Hobbesian and liberal contractarian views. We suggest taking our inspiration from European early-modern natural law theory, with its sharp eye for the moral quality of the person *also* in the state of nature, and from Chinese thought, which has a central place for moral narratives addressed to individual rulers. In order to build a connection to the present, we suggest looking also to Ricoeur and his foundational theory of mutual recognition (preceding all of Hobbes's primitive concerns: competition, mistrust, and desire for glory) so as to carve out a postmodern understanding of human nature: the nature of human selfhood as self-reflexive and intersubjective. We seek to turn away from destructive anthropologies of fear and impotence towards a modestly constructive anthropology of capacity, respect, and care.[85]

In his magisterial *The Course of Recognition*,[86] Ricoeur deconstructs the theory of positive law that views law as grounded in contract and the constitution as a contract. He thus repudiates the ideas of Thomas Hobbes who would not allow for any view of law emanating from man as a moral person, since in his view humankind was immoral, and driven by passions of rivalry, vanity, and fear.[87] He thought humans had to commit to legally binding, ie enforceable contracts of mutual restraint, ultimately resting on the systemic power of the Leviathan. Hobbes thereby abolished

[84] See for a renewed, extended, and certainly not conclusive attempt to set out some stages, A Carty, *Philosophy of International Law* (2nd edn, Edinburgh UP 2017) 300; Nijman, 'Images of Grotius' and 'Grotius' *Imago Dei* Anthropology' (both n 38) and Nijman (n 78).

[85] See A Carty, *Philosophy of International Law* (1st edn, Edinburgh UP 2007) ch 8; Carty (n 84) ch 3; Nijman 'Images of Grotius' and 'Grotius' *Imago Dei* Anthropology' (both n 38).

[86] P Ricoeur, *The Course of Recognition* (Harvard UP 2015).

[87] Th Hobbes, *Leviathan* (1651), ch 13 'Of the Natural Condition of Mankind as Concerning Their Felicity and Misery', Part I 'Of Man'.

all anthropomorphic foundation for moral and/or legal personality, and moral decision. Ricoeur explains that in the Western liberal tradition, as developed from Hobbes, no relationship exists between one person and another, which is why moral personality as such is irrelevant to a purely positivist contractual approach to law.

Ricoeur gives himself the task of reintroducing moral personality and responsibility.[88] This leads us on to a central proposition of the present volume, which is that the formulation of critical reflections on the actual practice of decision makers against a standard of moral responsibility, is a primary task of legal doctrine. That is to say, it is part and parcel of the international law profession to discuss and assess, with the help of moral standards of mutual recognition, restraint, prudence, and moderation, the shortcomings of behaviour driven by passions of jealousy and anger—a measuring of the actual practice of statesmen against natural law in the classical sense. Moral courage to speak truth to power, to explicate and account for the ethics guiding judgement, then becomes a primary burden of legal *doctrine*. Judgement and decision-making require foundations, which we seek here in a cross-cultural, East–West, humanist perspective.

Ricoeur offers a postmodern return to a classical tradition of humanism, which can be universal. He was careful to exclude the ontological in his foundational anthropology of the capable and vulnerable human being in need of the other to understand herself and the world.[89] One has to depart from the fiction of the self-foundation of the contractual, isolated individual (human or State) to move into the dialogic and social dimension marked by ethics. Ricoeur says there is no way the constitutional experience of a community can be understood except through the history of its self-constituting. This applies equally to the interactive experience of various communities—States in East and West—in the present international relations context. Bilateral acts, such as promises, contracts, and treaties, are generally directed at others and as such make up aspects of international life in which States strive to relate to and conflict with one another.

The method for the exercise of critical reflection upon State practice—the original idea of legal doctrine—in this book is phenomenological, following Ricoeur's philosophy. Attaching to the content of that approach, the historical studies of Part II show a clear absence of mutual respect and recognition and thus of relationship in State practice. They point to rivalry, inequality, and vanity in the concrete relations of statesmen with one another. The Western will to dominate, repeatedly evidenced, also by Japan in imitation, is the fundamental phenomenological distortion of any relationship.[90] The chapters point also to incomprehension at the cultural and linguistic levels. While the Hobbesian tradition denies moral personality as a possible starting point for constitution and international order (we have seen how both have origins in fear and violence, distrust, and domination), Ricoeur finds the possibility of moral personhood for responsible relations in intersubjective recognition.

[88] P Ricoeur, *Oneself as Another* (Chicago UP 1992) and, *The Just* (Chicago UP 2000); see also Nijman (n 78) 25–64.

[89] eg P Ricoeur *Oneself as Another* and *The Just* (both n 88).

[90] See Carty (n 85) ch 8; Carty (n 84) ch 3.

Recognition is 'a vital human need',[91] and mutual recognition is a natural basis for normative intersubjectivity. Contrary to Hobbes, Ricoeur argues for mutual recognition to be present in the state of nature and to explain political association preceding formal law and rule.[92] There is ethics in the state of nature, to sum up Ricoeur, which explains the move towards political association. Mutual recognition as a moral foundation for political society and the struggle for recognition may account for the possibility of peace. Recognition springs then from humans' natural capacity to love or care a capacity rooted in turn in human intersubjectivity. The possible—(mutual) recognition and thus peace—depends however on responsibility in all human relations.

The chapters in the volume confirm the proposition, forwarded by Ricoeur and shared by the present editors, that in today's world, (mutual) recognition and respect is the issue at stake. His humanist account of recognition rooted in an understanding of human nature captured in terms of intersubjectivity and capacities works well, we suggest, as a transcultural anthropological foundation in international relations. It is speculative in the sense that the possible depends on human initiative, on independent—natural and unprompted—rather than responsive action. But as a possibility it is philosophically sound, the ethical as present in international order—analogous to the state of nature—may produce relations of recognition and subsequently peace. With the possibility of moral personhood, responsibility and responsible relations become possible.

Part II of the volume exemplifies moments in history where international law and institutions have failed to be an order of mutual recognition (as equal) and mutual respect. Distrust is sown through denial of recognition and respect. We claim there is a responsibility on statespersons to maintain international law and institutions as 'orders of recognition',[93] especially since within the idea of positive law is encapsulated an anthropology and philosophy of international law as a 'structure of trust'.[94] Failure of political leaders to live up to this responsibility has the international legal order, or the 'international rule of law' collapse like a house of cards—to honour Leibniz's metaphor.

## 6. Epilogue

As editors, we have set up this research project and edited volume to contribute to a more global intellectual history of international legal thought, which means we want to be careful not to overstretch the initially historical research project into a more theoretical argument on contemporary international law. Yet we do think it is fair to be explicit about our own philosophical motivations and to explain how

[91] C Taylor, 'The Politics of Recognition' in A Gutmann (ed), *Multiculturalism: Examining the Politics of Recognition* (Princeton UP 1992) pp 25–73, 26.

[92] Ricoeur (n 86) 168–69 draws on Grotius and Suarez here. See for Grotius's similar understanding of the state of nature, Nijman, 'Images of Grotius' (n 38).

[93] Ricoeur *The Just* (n 88) 6–7 draws here on Jean-Marc Ferry.

[94] ibid 7–8.

we situate our (brief, more philosophical) argument within the complexity of modern national societies in interaction with one another. In an attempt to respect our authors and the initial set-up of our research project, we opt here for an epilogue.

Mainstream international law proceeds from the assumption that States have a legal conscience, but it has no workable or operational way to explain how this is supposed to work.[95] How precisely one presents Confucian moral narratives to modern Leviathans or where and how mutual recognition, as called for by Ricoeur, is to take place between superpower giants may be obviously urgent, but needs more concrete explanation.

In short, thanks to the desire of mutual recognition and mutual understanding, humans constitute themselves in relations with others, through oneself as another, through interpersonal otherness (the immediate other close by), and through institutional otherness (the faraway other who's recognition is mediated through institutions (including law).[96] The sovereign subject parallels the human subject. The (sovereign) self is no longer defined by fear and an inclination to attack in order to be secure or to expand (economically); it enters the realm of recognition—receiving and dispatching it—and therewith the realm of intersubjectivity, of relations between moral persons. Hence, the phenomenon of law and justice as part of Being becomes visible. Ricoeur thus points to a move away from misrecognition and domination through mutual recognition as equally valuable and an absolute (not of service to the self) and through institutional structures (including law) channelling the struggle for recognition and respect.[97]

When following the standard of Ricoeur's ethical phenomenology of the person, the person—in our context, the men and women of State (and their (legal) advisers)—reveals a new dimension of herself, a critical self-reflection, as she seeks to understand a world other than her own; an exercise comparable to learning another language—an appropriate analogy for an ethic of international relations. Translation of the language worlds of one another is essential for a person to recognize herself as a figure of passage from one national or ethnic society of peoples to another. The critical observer—the role for doctrine—can assess from a more detached perspective how far these patterns of translation through empathy are in fact present phenomenologically, or can be reasonably anticipated at any point. Ricoeur's message for lawyers is that the true dynamic of international legal argument comes from recognizing that the foundation of all deontology stems from the desire to live well with norms and the ethics of discursive argument.

But how can 'generalities on the borderline between legal theory and political theory', ie early-modern humanism and ancient Chinese moral narratives, be connected to the contemporary world of interacting nation States? Underpinning our

[95] A Carty 'Doctrine versus State Practice' in B Fassbender and A Peters (eds), *The Oxford Handbook of the History of International Law* (OUP 2012) 972–96. One need only consider and wonder at the impatience of much of the doctrine with the subjective element of custom, the psychological element, and the desire to 'simplify things by abandoning it in favour of "objective criteria" '.

[96] For us, this is the potential basis of a critique of international organizations as part of these institutions. But we will not develop this further here.

[97] Ricoeur (n 86).

view is not merely a rejection of the contractarian theory of law as a myth and ideology—we also confront one of its many offshoots, the corporate theory of the State, which is often the foundation of international legal personality, shielding off individual decision-making and the responsibility for the choices made. In fact, legal method is preoccupied only with competences; as such it leaves legal responsibility rooted in theories of legal will of the State. Where is the way to the moral person *inside* the Leviathan of the State, which is for the modern lawyer a corporate formal entity, a hierarchy of competences, with each level of the hierarchy free of direction, moral or otherwise, as long as it remains within its legal boundaries?[98]

If one pierces the corporate, formal veil of legal personality, one can easily locate the actual individuals who are taking the decisions and who can be and should be challenged by the critical, ethical phenomenology and humanist theory of recognition, which this volume ultimately expounds. One returns to the Confucian pyramid of personal responsibility, which begins with the individual, extends to the family, then onto the State and finally to the world— personal responsibility every stage of this Confucian way. These are the legal subjects to be addressed by this volume. This is why the intellectual history of Part I and the concrete, archive-based, historical studies making up Part II, are particularly appropriate. They represent ethics concretely lived and denied. Brought together, or, rather, put into a conversation, the (alternative) early-modern natural law thinking, defined by a softer, northern humanism, as carved out in Part I, and the concrete Sino-Western encounters of Part II, have pushed our turn to history into a turn to personal ethics. A turn to ethical judgement in this age of existential anxiety and uncertainty risks however to be a turn to the self-alienated human being.

In other words, piercing the formal veil of the stateperson in search for moral individuals making the choices in which the will of the State will consist, requires a discussion of the contemporary context, that is to say, a discussion of the fierce social, cultural, and economic pressures under which the individual has to try to preserve some moral integrity. It is becoming increasingly clear that Western-style formalist democracy, based on the idea of political contract, is put to the test in an era of 'post-truth' politics, where politicians can sway the public with blatantly untrue statements, about which veracity that same public does not appear to care. China's political system produces a will of the party not the people, so the capacity to promise within the international (legal) order is to a significant extent disconnected from the will of the people too.

This theme is developed radically by Bernard Stiegler in *Dans la disruption* (2016).[99] People's identities are now completely colonized by a consumer culture and industry. This phenomenon was first explained in chapter 2 of Adorno and Horkheimer's *Dialectic of the Enlightenment*, in 1944.[100] Stiegler explains further that the basic condition of democracy, that promises made for elections can be trusted and will be kept,

[98] See Carty (n 84) ch 2; Carty (n 85) ch 3.

[99] B Stiegler, *Dans la disruption. Comment ne pas devenir fou?* (Les Liens qui Libèrent 2016).

[100] M Horkheimer and TW Adorno, *Dialectic of Enlightenment: Philosophical Fragments* (ed G Schmid Noerr, tr E Jephcott, Stanford UP 2002).

is frequently broken. With Adorno and Horkheimer in mind the idea that humanity is 'sinking into a new kind of barbarism' is hard to suppress.[101]

The consistency of moral intention and imagination necessary to make considered political commitments seems often lacking. Ultimately, this points to a fundamental objective of our work. The meta-question—before all law—has to be the restoration of the moral identity of the individual. This comes prior to all talk of the techniques of formal democracy and the rule of law.

The connections which Stiegler makes point to a deeper analysis of today's total loss of faith in the political order. His own solution, after analysis of such phenomena as Dominique Strauss-Kahn and the French political society at large—as driven by corrupt politicians unrestrained in their pursuit of pleasure, wealth, and power—is a return to the message of Aristotle and other ancient Greek philosophers. This is to recognize phenomenologically the absence of the Aristotelian virtues of moderation, prudence, fairness, and justice in today's politics; while in public life each and every person has to show restraint and understanding of limits as an absolute precondition of morally responsible politics. There is however also a complicity of the general public in the unrestrained life of the politicians and underlying the philosophical remarks made in conclusion of the Introduction, is an attempt to detect a window of opportunity not just for legal doctrine but for a wider public, with access not just to traditional media, but also the modern social media, to engage instantly in an effective, impactful critical debate about contemporary events. In practice, this comes down to access to information about contemporary international affairs. The individual needs to exist morally, reclaim moral identity, within his/her networked life in the information and technology age.

In practice whether laws are followed or maintained in force depends in modern societies on public opinion and the apparent acquiescence of people. Political society depends upon the continuing acquiescence (rather than consent) and also engagement of an incalculably large variety of individuals and groups. Given the huge importance of the media's impact in determining political choices, the task of exercising morally responsible judgement applies to everyone. In democracy, the ideology is that we all are rulers. So, we have to show awareness of what Stiegler warns is the nature of the public space afforded by the culture industry in for instance the United States and the one political party in China. In the US, the relationship of the new Trump administration with the media is only another low point in case.

James Der Derian provides an illustration of how this critique could be brought to the heart of international law and relations. This inevitably is presented in America by an American about America, but the concern here is with form and technique which are globally applicable. In *Virtuous War* (2009: ch 5, 'The Virtual Enemy'), he argues 'that as States dematerialize and deconstruct, as national identities become more fluid, as simulations and scenarios reach for a credible threat, the public image

101 Admittedly, the editors are finishing this introduction in the first days of Trump's presidency.

of the foreign enemy is only reducible to a wanted poster'.[102] This is a description of a primarily media-driven, one-dimensional international scene and the question is how to decipher it.

Der Derian does call for a close reading of technical data, which is hardly available in any society which is not as open as America.[103] He thinks it points to sectional interests which have an interest in fomenting domestic insecurity with paranoid pictures of the foreign. He calls this 'Infoterror' (ie terror spread through false information).[104]

Der Derian introduces a metaphysical argument crucial for our study. 'With bipolarity gone, or, worse, internalized by the US into a purely psychological state of manic heights of liberal internationalism and melancholic lows of neo-isolationism, *the sobering neutralizing effects of reciprocity have been lost.*'[105] Here he is perhaps talking of the absence of a 'reality check' on American ambitions since the end of the Cold War and the effects of solipsism which that could induce. Of course now there is the rising spectre of China. Der Derian goes on to consider Paul Virilio's argument that the media-driven acceleration produces an anaesthetic of disappearances in which the political subject is diminished and finally engulfed in a growing infosphere. 'This is not to say images speak for themselves. There is a continuous political and rhetorical struggle to anchor the free floating meanings of images with captions of one kind or another.'[106] These captions have the aim to distinguish friends (ourselves) and enemies (our rivals). This rather complex world is what we have now to fathom. However, any nightly review of the entries of fellow international lawyers and other friends on Facebook or WeChat will show that the struggle against infoterror has long started.

This is the context in which Der Derian offers a counter strategy of '*infopeace*, by which [he] mean[s] the production, application and analysis of information by peaceful means for peaceful ends'.[107] He explains: 'It draws on a long tradition of peace-thinking, exemplified in early Christian pacifism and Eastern philosophies, in which the need for peace begins internally and proceeds outwardly. It starts by embracing a wholeness of the individual and expands to families, communities, countries, and beyond.'[108] This brings him right alongside the humanism of this book. Infopeace 'seeks to make a difference through a difference in the quality of thinking about the global contest of will, goods and might'.[109] There is a need to measure information by quality rather than quantity in terms of its contribution to reducing personal and structural violence.[110] Infopeace aims to oppose a natural state of war with accounts of past and future possibilities of peace.[111] What Der Derian wishes is this infoterror to be countered by infopeace, information disseminated by reasonable people to help encourage moderation in judgement. As such, infopeace 'relates to internal States of being. It seeks to prevent, mediate and resolve States of war by the actualization of a mindful state of peace.'[112] This could not be

[102] J Der Derian, *Virtuous War. Mapping the Military–Industrial–Media–Entertainment–Network* (2nd edn, Routledge, 2009) ch 5.
[103] ibid 103–15. [104] ibid ch 11, 249, 250, 254. [105] ibid 115 (emphasis ours).
[106] ibid 252. [107] ibid 256. [108] ibid. [109] ibid. [110] ibid.
[111] ibid. [112] ibid.

more elementary and even banal sounding. However, what is encouraging for the studies of ancient thought in which we engaged in this volume is his clear invocation of ancient thought and the meeting of East and West. The Eastern thinking Der Derian has in mind is Confucianism, which he associates with early Christian pacifism and Erasmus in particular, that is, the northern European humanism of our volume.

In China, different rules for the media apply. There is a famous firewall, which does not generally block foreign news as such, but will endeavour to control any news thought critical of China. There is a powerful social media, but not with the bite that Der Derian can describe and recommend, despite widespread use of VPN (an an internet system which can jump the Chinese electronic firewall which blocks Google, Facebook, etc). The Chinese are planning to put an end to VPN. What Der Derian's thinking enables us to address, from a Western perspective, are some structural questions about modern China where we may recognize and address some connections with our histories. Any direct apparent connection between ancient Chinese thought and the government will raise anxieties about Confucianism as a State ideology as Henan Hu discusses in her chapter. However, it is possible to engage in critical reflection of certain aspects of Chinese State policies in the light of sections 4 and 5 of this chapter. China has since the Republican era (the 1920s) aspired to be a nation state in the Western style, which means it is structurally inevitably caught up in all the Hobbesian-style interstate rivalries as is the West. Its relations with the US and Japan are particularly fraught as are its relations with its neighbours in the South China Seas. Carty and Lone have suggested that with Western-style interstate rivalry China has little hope of bringing peace with its neighbours in the South and East China Seas.[113] A return to ancient Chinese thought could be more promising.

At the same time China claims that it is trying to redress the economic injustices of history in developing countries with its new equality-based partnerships, especially in Africa.[114] The Institute of Development Studies is a UK Overseas Development Ministry funded institute which engages critically with Chinese counterparts about the economic history of colonialism and present developments. It is a critical forum for examining whether China also develops patterns of economic imperialism and exploits African countries for its own advantage in new unequal treaties, whether China exports its own authoritarian government styles and encourages disregard for human rights.

Our volume has implicitly attempted to address these questions by trying also to provide a fair and objective account of one of the more intense periods in the history of China and Western imperialism. It does provide some context for anxieties about Chinese nationalist revisionism and indeed for the wider question

[113] A Carty and FN Lone, 'A New Haven Perspective on the Eastphalia System' (2011) 19(1) Asia Pacific Law Review 95.

[114] eg J Gu and A Carty, 'China and African Development: Partnership Not Mentoring' *IDS Bulletin, Institute of Development Studies*, Sussex; Y Zhang J Gu, and Y Chen, China's Engagement in International Development Cooperation: The State of the Debate, *IDS Evidence Report* 2014.

of whether China might wish to restore the ideological aspect of Confucianism which was an integral part of imperial China. Here, it is possible to engage again critically with Chinese scholars about what the concept of 'Rising Powers' means? For instance, again, the Institute of Development Studies has produced such joint UK–Chinese studies as 'The BRICs in International Development'.[115] Does China, as a leader of the BRICs have a constructive goal, especially for world economic order and from where might it find the intellectual resources for such a project? Or is it merely ambitious to replace the US as a world economic hegemon?

Finally, there is a constant exchange on international law within China at domestically hosted international conferences. One such forum was the CASS (Chinese Academy of Social Sciences) International Law Forum in December 2016 (after the finalization of the present collection of chapters), where two papers by Chinese scholars addressed ancient Chinese thought and even the importance of reviving natural law thinking from the time of Grotius to redress the institutional deficiencies and substantive law gaps of positive law. In particular, Li Zan from the CASS International Law Institute presented 'Doctrine of International Law to Construct the Community of the Common Destiny of Mankind'. He proposed that to realize substantive and not just formal justice it is necessary to go beyond sovereignty and to search for a basis to the justice of international society. Positive international law and institutions are not producing peace and harmony. Specifically, positivist institutional regimes, such as Kant's contractual system of sovereign-based federalism ignores the necessity of a philosophical method of inner peace. The inner peace of human beings must come first. Then there is second a possibility of adjusting predatory economic relations with a substantive principle of 'compensatory inequality'. Beyond that, the foundation for peace can only be the human awareness of the evil of war at a spiritual level. Chinese traditional culture can help fortify this spiritual dimension for world order.

The second paper in the same spirit came from HE Zhiping (Jilin University), called 'The Relative Natural Law in International Relations'. This presentation is more explicitly and easily recognized by a westerner. Natural law provides the ethical foundation which positive law cannot, as is seen from the tragedies of the twentieth century and the revival of natural law at Nuremberg and Tokyo. Natural law is not a system of rules but an ethic of good behaviour. It is above States and peoples, who have to strive to find in it the source for the ideals they wish to share, in feedback, with other States and peoples. Despite its vagueness, natural law is quickly recognized when States go beyond the basic limits of tolerance in bad behaviour. It then emerges as a standard of restraint. He (i.e. HE Zhiping) equates natural law with ethics and says that without its presence among States and peoples, serious disharmony, conflict, and even abyss will follow. Positive law has to find its way based upon natural law.

[115] J Gu, R Caret, A Shankland, and A Chenoy, *The BRICs in International Development* (Palgrave 2016).

It is the latter which enables States and peoples to understand their own concrete situations and position themselves accordingly in their relations with one another.

It is believed that in dialogue with Chinese and Western development economists, as well was with Chinese and Western philosophers of international law, we have a credible intellectual forum in which to present and receive feedback with respect to the ideas of international legal history and philosophy in this book.

# PART I

# LAW AND JUSTICE IN EARLY-MODERN EUROPEAN THOUGHT ON WORLD ORDER

# 1

# The Universal Rule of Law in the Thought of the Late Medieval Jurists of Roman and Canon Law

*Joseph Canning*

## 1. Introduction

The jurisprudence of Roman and canon law of the thirteenth, fourteenth, and fifteenth centuries provided the origins of European notions of a universal rule of law in two senses: a legal order of universal extent and a structure of objective higher legal norms of universal application. Roman law and canon law came to be studied together. Modern legal historians have applied the term *ius commune* or 'common law' to describe this form of legal scholarship as a Europe-wide system of law within the context of Western Latin Christendom.[1] From the 1220s, the scholarship of Roman law also came to include fundamental norms of feudal law through study of the *Libri feudorum* which was added as a tenth collation to the *Authenticum*, the form in which the Novels of Justinian were known. This had considerable implications. Susan Reynolds has famously argued that the whole notion of 'feudalism' was a legal construct of sixteenth-century jurists commenting on the *Libri feudorum*.[2] The most important exponents of this Roman and canon law juristic discourse were the Italians, Bartolus of Sassoferrato (1313/14–57) and Baldus de Ubaldis of Perugia (1327–1400). I have myself previously used the concept of the *ius commune* but now have reservations about employing it. The term *ius utrumque* to describe both Roman and canon law is unproblematic because it was a medieval usage. There are two problems however in using the notion of the *ius commune* to describe the jurisprudence of late medieval Roman and canon law. It is a modern category which has come into prominence from the middle of the twentieth century. Bartolus and

[1] See, for instance, F Calasso, *Introduzione al diritto comune* (Giuffrè 1951); M Bellomo, *L'Europa del diritto comune* (Il Cigno Galileo Galilei, Edizioni di Arte e Scienza 1989). Kenneth Pennington has used the *ius commune* as an operating principle in his studies of late medieval jurisprudence as, for instance, in his *The Prince and the Law, 1200–1600: Sovereignty and Rights in the Western Legal Tradition* (University of California Press 1993).

[2] S Reynolds, *Fiefs and Vassals: The Medieval Evidence Reinterpreted* (OUP 1994) 1–14.

Baldus, for instance, used the term *ius commune* as a description of the Roman law as the law common to the Roman Empire, whereas, in the *Corpus iuris civilis* itself, the *ius gentium* was described as the *ius commune* of all mankind.[3] Furthermore, to designate the *ius commune* as a system in the way its modern users do could be misleading. It would be better to think of it as a form of legal order because it was not so articulated as modern systems of law. It should also be remembered that, although jurists had knowledge of both Roman and canon law, they tended to be predominantly civilians or canonists and certainly to write commentaries on one body of law or the other. Thus, Bartolus was overwhelmingly a Roman law jurist. Baldus was highly unusual in that he wrote commentaries on Roman law, canon law, and feudal law. Indeed, the integration of Roman and canon law is notable to a high degree in Baldus's work: his commentaries on the Roman law abound with references to canon law and his commentary on the *Liber extra decretalium* is full of Roman law references.

The foundational presupposition of medieval Roman and canon law scholarship was that there was a universal rule of law, in that there were two universal authorities in one legal world with generally accepted norms—the Roman emperor and the pope. This was easily perceived to be the case as regards the pope: canon law applied as the universal law for Catholic Christendom—it was valid everywhere. The case of Roman law was more complicated. The late medieval Commentators sought to accommodate that law to their contemporary political and social reality. In the *Corpus iuris civilis*, the emperor was indeed described as lord of the world (*mundi dominus*)[4] and was the model for sovereignty but jurists had to cope with the problems of the actual geographical extent of the empire and the relationship of the emperor's power to that of other rulers. In short, they had to address questions of universal and territorial sovereignty. The co-existence of both laws as the twin pillars of the *ius utrumque* also meant that an enduring problem within it was that of the relationship between temporal and spiritual power—in broad brush terms, that between church and state. In medieval Roman and canon law jurisprudence, there was a sense of a Europe-wide community characterized by common legal norms and forms of universal power and authority within it.

But it is more problematic to maintain that medieval Roman and canon law scholarship was the origin of international law. Medievalists would tend to be loath to use the term 'international' in interpreting the Middle Ages. It seems on the face of it to be a modern term suited to a world in which there is a multiplicity of nation States. But such caution may be out of place in that there were political entities which may reasonably be termed States in the late Middle Ages and there were certainly nations in one form or another. Nationalism there was not. Within the broad spectrum of the term 'state' it is reasonable to maintain that late medieval jurists operated with ideas of state.[5] The pioneering historian of early diplomacy,

[3] See *Institutiones* 1.2.1; *Digestum* 1.1.9.

[4] *Digestum* 14.2.9 (Venice edn 1498, fol 234r)—I have used this edition of the *Corpus iuris civilis* because it is derived from the medieval Vulgate version (*littera Bononiensis*). The phrase in the original Greek is 'tou kosmou kurios'.

[5] See J Canning, *Ideas of Power in the Late Middle Ages, 1296–1417* (CUP 2011) 153–57.

Garett Mattingley, did consider that the term 'international' could be applied to the jurisprudence of the late Middle Ages and to Roman and canon law scholarship in particular.[6] These jurists certainly considered internal and external sovereignty but the question is whether they gave attention to the staple problem of modern international relations—the relations between States. Bartolus was concerned with the relationship between Italian city-republics and the emperor; Baldus with the relationship between the emperor and cities, kingdoms, and Italian *signori*. In other words, whereas the international relations between States are viewed horizontally, these jurists were primarily concerned with a vertical relationship between universal and territorial powers. So long as one bears this in mind, it may not be misleading to say that medieval jurists both addressed questions which may be classified as belonging to the field of international law, and were sources for early-modern treatments of the subject. Hugo Grotius, for instance, made considerable use of their works.[7]

## 2. Universal and Territorial Sovereignty: A Public Law Problem

In terms of public law, the fundamental question addressed by medieval Roman and canon law jurists was indeed that of the relationship between universal and territorial sovereignty. The problem arose because there was a glaring discrepancy between the claim in Roman law that the emperor was lord of the world and his relative lack of power in reality. Only in central Europe did he have any form of political power, and a highly attenuated one at that. In Italy north of the papal States he was the nominal legal overlord, but because of prolonged imperial absences from the peninsula, many city-republics were moving from practical autonomy to outright sovereignty. In addition, in the kingdoms of France, England, and the Iberian peninsula, any claims to imperial superiority were rejected. How was it possible for Roman law jurists to reconcile the universal sovereignty of the emperor with the fact of the territorial sovereignty of kingdoms and Italian city-republics?

This was specifically a problem for Roman law—canon law incorporated the principle of territorial sovereignty. In his decretal *Per venerabilem* in 1202 Innocent III had famously said, 'the king of France does not recognize a superior in temporal matters'.[8] Furthermore, Clement V in his constitution *Pastoralis cura* of March 1314 had treated the Roman Empire as being territorially limited: it did not include the lands of the church (*terrae ecclesiae*) in Italy—the papal States and the kingdom of Sicily.[9] The *locus classicus* for the discussion of the problem in Roman law was the law *Cunctos populos*, the first few words of which were, 'All peoples whom the

[6] See G Mattingley, *Renaissance Diplomacy* (Penguin repr 1973) 19–22.

[7] See copious references to the works of medieval jurists in the *marginalia* of his *De iure belli et pacis*. For a useful English translation including Grotius's *marginalia*, see H Grotius, *The Rights of War and Peace* (edited with an introduction by R Tuck, from the edition by J Barbeyrac, 3 vols, Liberty Fund 2005).

[8] 'Quum rex ipse [Francorum] superiorem in temporalibus minime recognoscat' (*Liber extra decretalium* 4.17.13), E Friedberg (ed) (Akademische Druck- und Verlagsanstalt repr 1959 col 715).

[9] *Clementinae* 2.11.2 (Friedberg edn, cols 1151–53).

sovereign authority of our clemency rules'.[10] To whom did 'quos' apply? Was 'quos' to be understood declaratively, and thus as signifying that all peoples were under the emperor's rule, or was it to be interpreted restrictively, and thus as indicating only those peoples who were actually subject to him?

A solution to the problem in Roman law terms was reached by Bartolus and Baldus who made ingenious use of the *de iure*–de facto distinction. For them, the emperor remained *de iure* lord of the world but they accorded full legitimacy to the de facto sovereignty of city-republics and, in the case of Baldus, of kings as well. Bartolus's justification of this move was a progressive elaboration of the theme of consent. Building on the work of previous jurists he distinguished between custom as tacit consent and statute as express consent. He maintained that the element of consent common to both forms of law meant that they were of equal force (*paris potentiae*). It was recognized that custom did not require the authorization of a superior—neither therefore did a city's statutes need such authorization. Bartolus then took the next step: the lack of a need for a superior's authorization led on to non-recognition of a superior—the clearest sign of sovereignty. He described such a city as a 'free people' (*populus liber*). He next took a decisive step by declaring that a city of this kind was its own emperor (*civitas sibi princeps*). This was an audacious argument to say the least.[11] The English canonist Alanus Anglicus (*fl. c.*1190–*c.*1210), who worked at Bologna, and the Italian civilian Azo (d.1220) had provided the foundations for the prevalent argument, developed by English, French, Spanish, and Neapolitan jurists during the thirteenth century that a king who did not recognize a superior was emperor in his kingdom (*rex in regno suo est imperator regni sui*).[12] Bartolus was transposing this essentially personal idea of sovereignty to the corporate bodies of city-republics. This may be described as an idea of genius but it was a somewhat clumsy and problematic formulation because a city was not actually the emperor and it could always be objected within terms of Roman law that ultimate sovereignty lay with the *princeps*. Thirteenth-century canonists in their treatments of *Per venerabilem* had discussed whether the king of France's non-recognition of a superior in temporal matters existed *de iure* or de facto. Civilians and canonists before Bartolus had used the *de iure*–de facto distinction in discussing non-recognition of a superior by kings and city-republics, but he was the first jurist, civilian or canonist, to accord full legitimacy to de facto claims to sovereignty. Baldus followed Bartolus's argument but he avoided using the formulation, *civitas sibi princeps*, preferring to describe the city as being in the emperor's place (*vice principis*), maybe because of the reservations expressed above. But Baldus went far beyond Bartolus's essentially legal arguments by providing an underpinning in political philosophy for the de facto thesis. He overtly turned to Aristotelian political thought: these city-republics attained sovereignty because they were composed of citizens understood as natural, political men.

[10] 'Cunctos populos quos clementie nostre regit imperium' *Codex* 1.1.1 (Venice edn 1498) fol 4r.

[11] For a full discussion of Bartolus's thesis, see J Canning, *The Political Thought of Baldus de Ubaldis* (CUP 1987) vol 4 Cambridge Studies in Medieval Life and Thought 96–97.

[12] See J Canning, *A History of Medieval Political Thought, 300–1450* (repr with new introduction Routledge 2005) 124–25, for how these two formulas became combined. For Alanus Anglicus, see the biography by J Canning in *Oxford Dictionary of National Biography* (OUP 2004).

Bartolus in contrast had made little use of Aristotle considering that the works of the philosopher were not to the taste of jurists. Baldus also made a highly distinctive contribution through his treatment of city-*populi* and kingdoms as corporations, enabling him to distinguish between the abstract and perpetual elements of these entities and the human beings who composed them or ruled over them. Bartolus had focused on city-republics—Baldus went beyond him in extending the de facto argument to include kingdoms. Most importantly, Baldus also expressed the de facto argument in terms of the Roman law category of the *ius gentium* as a means of justifying the sovereignty of both city-*populi* and kingdoms—*Digest*, 1.1.5 (the law, *Ex hoc iure*) stated that kingdoms were founded by the *ius gentium*.[13]

In his commentary on *Digest*, 1.1.9,[14] Baldus derived both the existence of a people and its power of government from the *ius gentium*:

> Peoples are from the *ius gentium*, and therefore a people's government is from the *ius gentium*, as above [D.1.1.5]. But government cannot exist without laws and statutes. A people, therefore, for the very reason that it has existence, consequently has governmental power as part of that existence, just as every animal is ruled by its own spirit and soul.[15]

The people's power of self-government was inherent—it did not derive from an external superior. Furthermore, Baldus consolidated his argument by applying the principle of self-preservation to the people in the context of justifying the people's indigenous lawmaking capacity as an expression of its autonomous power of self-government:

> Moreover in as much as anything has an essential form it also has a capacity to act. But the people derives its form from itself, and therefore also the exercise of self-preservation as regards its existence and proper form. For it is natural and allowed that anything should strive after the conservation of its existence.[16]

The overall meaning of Baldus's lengthy commentary on *Digest* 1.1.9 was that peoples possessed an autonomous capacity to legislate through the exercise of their own consent, a capacity which was an aspect of their power of jurisdiction derived from the *ius gentium* itself; that this capacity could be obscured where the hierarchical structures of the *ius commune* (in the sense of the Roman law) were operative; but that wherever a people was freed from the restrictions of the *ius commune* its rights of self-government under the *ius gentium* re-emerged, partly when its autonomy

[13] 'Ex hoc iure gentium introducta sunt bella, discrete gentes, regna condita, dominia distincta' (Venice edn 1498) fol 4v.

[14] 'Omnes populi, qui legibus et moribus reguntur, partim suo proprio, partim communi hominum omnium iure utuntur, nam quod quisque populus ipse sibi ius constituit, id ipsius proprium civitatis est vocaturque ius civile, quasi ius proprium ipsius civitatis: quod vero naturalis ratio inter omnes homines constituit, id apud omnes gentes pereque custoditur vocaturque ius gentium, quasi quo iure omnes gentes utuntur' (Venice edn 1498) fol 5r.

[15] 'Populi sunt de iure gentium ergo regimen populi est de iure gentium, ut supra [D.1.1.5]. Sed regimen non potest esse sine legibus et statutis, ergo eoipso quod populus habet esse habet per consequens regimen in suo esse, sicut omne animal regitur a suo spiritu proprio et anima' ([Lyon] edn 1498) fol 9r.

[16] 'Preterea quantum unumquodque habet de forma essentiali tantum habet de virtute activa; sed populus habet formam ex se, ergo et exercitium conservandi se in esse suo, et in forma propria; nam hoc est naturale et permissum quod unumquodque studeat conservationi sui esse' ([Lyon] edn 1498) fol 9r.

existed *de iure* (by imperial or papal concession), fully when it existed by custom (*de consuetudine*) and thus de facto. In his commentary on *Digest* 1.1.9, Baldus was dealing with non-confirmation by a superior. But he went on to justify the sovereignty of city-*populi* by accepting that they had made the crucial step to non-recognition of a superior through the exercise of the popular will. This was the logical extension of his basic *ius gentium* argument. Their sovereignty was the product of de facto popular consent, a capability deriving from the *ius gentium*, itself a product of human reason. In the case of kingdoms, Baldus, like all jurists, held that before the creation of legal systems all peoples could elect their kings on the basis of the *ius gentium*; but he also maintained that a kingdom's inhabitants by virtue of the *ius gentium* still continued to possess the right to elect their kings in his own day. This meant that peoples, deriving their origin from the *ius gentium*, could on this basis through natural reason establish a republican (in the case of cities) or monarchical form of government (in the case of kingdoms).

Bartolus's and Baldus's *de iure*–de facto thesis was a truly ingenious example of juristic logic. But their solution to the problem of the relationship between universal and territorial sovereignty did involve fundamental problems. It could well be objected that their full acceptance of de facto power would mean that any form of government which actually existed was legitimate. The rule of a tyrant for instance could be justified on this basis. This was the question of the hour in fourteenth-century Italy. There was in full swing a political process whereby communal or republican regimes were more and more being replaced by lordships, rule by *signori* who were described by their republican opponents as tyrants or despots. Bartolus himself was opposed to these *signori* and in this sense could be understood as a republican theorist. Both jurists intended that their thesis of de facto power should apply to legitimate regimes within the overall context of the achievement of justice, a fundamental presupposition of Roman law. Baldus was much more sympathetic to *signori*, spending the last ten years of his life in the service of the greatest of them all, Giangaleazzo Visconti, lord and then from 1395 Duke of Milan. Baldus retained both *de iure* (through imperial or papal vicariates) and de facto justifications for signorial rule but always rejected lords who actually ruled in a tyrannical way. There was also a more deep-rooted problem: the sheer legal strength of the *de iure* position underlying the power of the emperor or the pope. The world view of both jurists involved a Roman empire understood in its widest sense as Catholic Christendom. Within this, the powers of emperor and pope were divinely sanctioned and therefore could not be changed. Jurists did not have the option to tinker with this arrangement. Bartolus's line of argument, brilliant though it was, was always something of a struggle within a system centred on monarchy. Within such a system, in which *de iure* power lay with the *princeps*, any claim to sovereignty based on will (as in the pro-active non-recognition of a superior) would have to be expressed in de facto terms. There could always be the lingering thought that such a claim was not quite as good as a *de iure* one: the argument could appear somewhat artificial. It is noteworthy that neither Bartolus nor Baldus based their arguments for the sovereignty of Italian city-republics on the *lex regia*—according to Bartolus, this had been a grant of sovereign authority from the Roman people to the emperor which had become irrevocable with time; according to Baldus it had been irrevocable from the start. The *lex regia* had been the mechanism in terms of Roman law for the establishment of the Roman Empire whose legitimacy had then been confirmed by Christ. The Roman emperor and the pope were the twin pillars of Bartolus's and Baldus's world. A full recognition of the power of popular consent was the basis for both jurists' thesis which in Roman law terms had to be expressed by means of a creative interpretation of the *de iure*–de facto distinction.

Bartolus and Baldus had produced a justification for a plurality of sovereign States within the context of an overall universal legal structure. It was a brilliant legal *tour de force* which would only convince like-minded fellow lawyers but it did have its flaws. Bartolus and Baldus only had to go to the lengths that they did because of the *de iure* sovereignty accorded to the emperor as *princeps* within Roman law. The structure of political authority which they developed in their works set forth a form of hierarchy of sovereignty: it was a kind of pyramid with the universal sovereignty of the emperor at its apex but with the territorial sovereignty of kingdoms and city-republics accepted below that. There is really no way of describing this thoroughly medieval view other than as a hierarchy of sovereignty.

But there was another way of approaching the problem of universal and territorial sovereignty. Some civilians, notably from the Neapolitan school of jurists, rejected the universal authority of the emperor. Neapolitan jurists had also used the concept of the *ius gentium* as a foundation for their arguments for the sovereignty of the kings of Sicily. The characteristic pro-Neapolitan view was that of a political world in which the emperor did not enjoy universal sovereignty but only territorial dominion over the areas where he could exercise actual political power; elsewhere the *ius gentium* provided the legal title for monarchies. The pro-Neapolitan *ius gentium* argument envisaged a world of a plurality of kingdoms where the empire was only one territorial body among several. Marinus da Caramanico (d.1288) was a notable example: using the *ius gentium* to justify the independence of kings (especially the king of Sicily) from the emperor, he maintained that the Roman Empire, having been founded on force, existed 'in fact rather than in law' (*de facto potius quam de iure*).[17] Another Neapolitan jurist, Andreas de Isernia (d. *c*.1316) maintained that in his day the world had returned to its pristine condition before the conquests of Rome.[18] Oldradus de Ponte (d.1335), who taught at Padua (and probably Bologna and Siena) and served the *curia* at Avignon, also produced a well-known exposition of the pro-Neapolitan view in his *Consilium* 69 in which he justified King Robert of Naples's rejection of imperial overlordship in the latter's dispute with Emperor Henry VII who sought to try him for treason. Oldradus denied that the Roman emperor was *de iure* lord of the world on the grounds that the Roman people, themselves lacking any just title to dominion over other nations, could not through the *lex regia* legally transfer any such authority to the emperor.[19] The *de iure* independence

[17] M da Caramanico, *Super libro constitutionum* Proem, 3–7 and 17 in F Calasso (ed), *I Glossatori e la teoria della sovranità* (3rd edn, Giuffrè 1957) 180–86 and 196–97.

[18] See A de Isernia to *Libri Feudorum* 2.56, n 2 (Lyon edn 1579) fol 286r.

[19] Lyon edn 1550 (n 7) (fol 24v) and (n 12) (fol 24v–25r).

of kingdoms (and indeed cities) was based on the fundamental *ius gentium*, and was thus anterior to and stronger than any claims of the Roman emperors to rulership over them, because imperial jurisdiction was a product solely of the *ius civile* of the Romans, whereas other peoples were free in their *ius civile* to deny any subjection to the emperor.[20] The independence of the kingdom of Sicily was thus guaranteed by the *ius gentium*, and indeed like that of Spain was reinforced by the argument that its inhabitants had conquered it with their own blood.[21]

## 3. Private International Law

It has long been recognized that medieval jurists of Roman and canon law made important contributions to the origins of private international law. Bartolus's role in this respect is well known and EM Meijers highlighted Baldus's treatment of this area.[22] Bartolus and Baldus were particularly interested in conflict of laws. In the forefront of their minds were conflicts between the statutes of Italian city-States. This reflected the political and legal developments whereby city-States had developed autonomy and then territorial sovereignty, although some remained at the lower level. The fundamental point was that when a citizen of one city moved to another or, for instance, did business there, he remained as much a foreigner as was someone from England, France, or Germany, for instance. Another area of conflict concerned complications about the citizen status of women, since there were grades of citizen—an example would be the problems involved in the status of a woman who married a citizen of another city and went to live there with him (or indeed elsewhere). The Roman law was used by jurists and courts to provide general principles of law to help solve such questions of conflicts of laws between different city-statutes. The range of disputes was wide reflecting all aspects of medieval life which came under law: commercial contracts, for instance, financial transactions and the fraught issue of dowries. A particularly rich source of information for legal, political, and social historians is provided by the large number of jurists' legal opinions (*consilia*) surviving from the early fourteenth century onwards.[23] The earliest extant collection of a jurist's *consilia* is that of Oldradus de Ponte. But the most extensive is that of Baldus who has left us well over 3,000 known *consilia*.[24] These juristic

[20] nn 5–6 (fol 24r–24v).

[21] nn 8–9 (fol 24v). See also G Montagu, 'Roman Law and the Emperor—the Rationale of "Written Reason" in Some *consilia* of Oldradus da Ponte' (1994) 15 History of Political Thought 4–23.

[22] See EM Meijers, 'Balde et le droit international privé' in R Feenstra and HFWD Fischer (eds), *Etudes d'histoire du droit* (IV Universitaire Pers Leiden 1966) 132–41.

[23] For *consilia* dealing with cases of the citizenship of women born elsewhere, see J Kirshner, 'Mulier alibi nupta' in I Baumgartner (ed), *Consilia im späten Mittelalter. Zum historischen Aussagewert einer Quellengattung* (Jan Thorbeke Verlag 1995) Schriftenreihe des Deutschen Studienzentrums in Venedig vol 13 147–76.

[24] See H Lange, *Consilien des Baldus (†1400)* (Verlag der Akademie der Wissenschaften und der Literatur 1973) Akademie der Wissenschaften und der Literatur. Abhandlungen der Geistes- und Sozialwissenschaftlichen Klasse vol 12. For more recent discussions of Baldus's *consilia*, see K Pennington, 'Allegationes, solutiones, and dubitationes: Baldus de Ubaldis' revisions of his *consilia*' in M Bellomo (ed), *Die Kunst der Disputation. Probleme der Rechtsauslegung und Rechtsanwendung im 13.*

opinions provide a rich treasury of information about the application of Roman and canon law to everyday life and, since they deal with individual cases, open wide a window on the lives of people in the past.

## 4. Generally Applicable Legal Norms

But the most important, and the most long-lasting contribution of the medieval scholarship of Roman and canon law was to the development of the notion of generally applicable norms of law, the categories of natural law and the law of peoples (*ius gentium*). In according such a fundamental normative role to natural law these medieval jurists were going far beyond anything to be found in the *Corpus iuris civilis* itself—they were clearly influenced by developments in medieval theology in this respect. Natural law did feature in the *Corpus iuris civilis* but there was no extensive discussion of it—it in no sense appeared as a norm against which positive law could be judged (and if necessary found wanting). Confusion could arise because two completely different strands of interpretation coexisted in the codification. It included the definition of the classical Roman jurist, Ulpian, that natural law was that which we shared with the animals, including procreation and the education of children. This was a truly basic and hardly normative approach. On the other hand, it also included a definition by a later Roman jurist, Gaius, who widened the notion of natural law and identified it with the *ius gentium* as a product of human beings' natural reason. Late medieval jurists developed this insight, treating natural law and the *ius gentium* as legal norms derived from reason. This status gave these laws general application.[25] But the crucial category of the *ius gentium* posed a problem. At one level, it was seen as a product of natural reason and at another as laws which human beings had created, that is a form of positive law. This was why Bartolus introduced a distinction unknown in the *Corpus iuris civilis*: he distinguished between *ius gentium primaevum*, the product of reason belonging to natural law, and *ius gentium secundarium*, the assembled customs of all peoples of the world and thus pertaining to positive law. The works of Baldus in particular gave extensive treatment to natural law and the *ius gentium* as higher norms. The whole question of derogations from natural law by positive law was discussed at length in a way that is not to be found in ancient Roman jurisprudence. The category which is crucial for the development of international law is clearly the *ius gentium*. But there is a crucial difference between the late medieval *ius gentium* and the early-modern *ius inter gentes*.[26] Medieval *ius*

*und 14. Jahrhundert* (Oldenbourg 1997) Schriften des Historischen Kollegs, Kolloquien vol 38, 29–72; K Pennington, 'Was Baldus an Absolutist? The Evidence of His *consilia*' in C Frova and others (eds), *VI Centenario della morte di Baldo degli Ubaldi, 1400–2000* (Università degli Studi 2005) 1–16.

[25] For the juristic treatment of natural law and the *ius gentium*, see B Tierney, *The Idea of Natural Rights. Studies on Natural Rights, Natural Law and Church Law, 1150–1625* (Eerdmans 1997) Emory University Studies in Law and Religion vol 5, 43–77 and 135–57; and the profound study by AS Brett, *Changes of State: Nature and the Limits of the City in Early Modern Natural Law* (Princeton UP 2011) 62–89.

[26] See, for instance, DR Kelley, 'Law' in *The Cambridge History of Political Thought 1450–1700* (CUP 1991) 92.

*gentium* did not govern the relationships between territorial States which, of course, the *ius inter gentes* did—it was not international law in the early-modern sense. But there may be a sense in which it was a form of international law because it applied generally in human affairs.

Bartolus and Baldus like other late medieval jurists saw Roman law as an expression of reason—that is why it was described as a 'true philosophy' and jurists were its priests.[27] It provided a whole mental and legal world. Increasingly, reason of law (*ratio iuris*) and the law as 'written reason' (*ratio scripta*) became operating legal principles. But the real future of this approach lay somewhat later—in the sixteenth century and beyond as Roman law developed into a system more articulated than anything known in the Middle Ages and increasingly detached from the Roman Empire in any institutional form.

A fundamental problem, indeed weakness, of modern international law is of course the difficulty of enforcing any of its norms on sovereign States or rulers. A similar problem applied in the late Middle Ages—how to ensure that rulers acted according to the higher norms of natural law or the *ius gentium*. Jurists maintained that such fundamental norms provided a structure limiting the actions of the emperor, kings, and cities. Divine Law also served the same function. But could rulers and governments actually be controlled? Did such norms have actual bite? Who was there to enforce them on a recalcitrant ruler or government?

In theory, even an absolute monarch was limited by such norms. The concept of absolute power (*potestas absoluta*) was an invention of thirteenth-century canonists. The formulation is not to be found in the *Corpus iuris civilis*. The term did not mean absolute power in a literal or modern sense. It meant that the *princeps* was freed from the laws (*legibus solutus*) only in the sense of freedom from human laws not from higher norms. Using a form of argument developed in theology, a distinction was made between the ruler's absolute power and his ordinary power (*potestas ordinaria* or *ordinata*): since his power was legal, he normally worked within the constraints of the laws which he had made. The *locus classicus* in this respect was the law *Digna vox* (*Codex* 1.14.4) which stated that it befitted the *princeps* to profess that he was bound by the laws, because his authority depended on the authority of the law.

The notion that the ruler's power was subject to higher norms was the overwhelming orthodoxy of late medieval jurists. Yet there was of course an elaborate legal casuistry concerning derogation from higher norms and presumptions about the justice of the actions of the *princeps*. The *princeps* could derogate from higher norms *ex causa*—when applying these norms in practice to particular cases, he could interpret them extremely freely and in such a way that he might appear to have denied their specific effects without being understood to have thereby abolished their general principles, a process analogous to casuistry in theological terms. A classic juristic distinction was made between the Mosaic law's prohibition of killing and the validity of judicial execution. This capacity for derogation was accorded to monarchs and sovereign peoples (by those jurists who accepted this latter concept). There were

[27] *Digestum* 1.1.1: 'Ius est ars boni et equi cuius merito quis nos sacerdotes appellat: iusticiam namque colimus . . . veram, nisi fallor, philosophiam, non simulatam affectantes' (Venice edn 1498) fol 4r.

limits, however, to this process: Bartolus's teacher, Cynus de Pistoia (1270–1336/37), for instance, had said that some parts of the *ius divinum*, such as the prohibition of the marriage between a man and his mother simply could not be the subject of derogation.[28] It was, however, possible to accept that such derogation did not infringe the integrity of higher norms by seeing the *causa* involved in it as the practical application of reason. Yet the initiative in assessing the validity of the *causa* lay with the ruler.

Similarly, the jurists were willing to give great scope to the presumption of the good faith of the *princeps*. Yet, the presumption of a just cause on the part of the *princeps*, as when imperial rescripts infringed the general provisions of higher norms, did not absolve the *princeps* from actually having a just cause. The *princeps* was presumed to be willing what was objectively just: it was not considered that what he willed was automatically just simply because he willed it. Thus, when Cynus maintained that imperial rescripts contrary to the mutable part of the *ius divinum*, the natural law, and the *ius gentium* made without specified just cause were valid 'quoad observantiam', he did not mean that such rescripts necessarily constituted valid derogations from such higher norms, but only that his subjects must presume that their superior was acting with just cause and obey. Cynus made it clear that this only applied when there could be a just cause: an obviously unjust rescript would be a different matter.[29] Although there was thus a strong presumption in favour of the *princeps*, which meant that his freedom of action and will was thereby considerably enhanced, the jurists maintained as their general position that the *princeps* through his will alone and without just cause could not derogate from higher norms. It was only positive law that he could change without needing any cause or reason save his own will.

The vexed question of the ruler's alienation of his subjects' private property was particularly at issue. The vast majority of jurists maintained that a subject's private property could not be taken away by the *princeps* without just cause: property rights were guaranteed by the *ius gentium*. Bartolus adhered very clearly to this opinion. But there was a growing recognition among jurists from the end of the thirteenth century and in the fourteenth that in reality the *princeps* did remove his subjects' property at will. The French jurist, Jacobus de Ravannis held that the *princeps* could without cause remove his subjects' property through his plenitude of power but that he sinned in so doing. Similarly, Cynus maintained that the emperor could remove an individual's property 'without any cause in the world' (*sine aliqua causa de mundo*) but that he could not do this *de iure*, because he sinned in so doing.[30] But a deviant opinion began to develop among some jurists. Jacobus Butrigarius, one of Bartolus's teachers in the 1330s, made no mention of sin when he said that the emperor could remove his subjects' property without cause. This trend culminated in the extreme opinion expressed by Baldus and his brother Angelus—they held that the *princeps* (understood as the emperor or, in Angelus's case, the pope) could remove a subject's property without just cause. As Baldus said, 'Whatever reason

[28] To *Codex* 1.19.7 (n 10) (Frankfurt edn 1578) fol 36r.
[29] To *Codex* 1.22.6 (n 7) (Frankfurt edn 1578) fol 40r.
[30] To *Codex* 1.19.7 (n 12) (Frankfurt edn 1578) fol 36v.

motivates the *princeps* himself is considered cause enough'[31]—the emperor's will was all that was required to take away a subject's property. Baldus was making use of the notion of the emperor's absolute power: 'The goods of the individual do not belong to the *princeps* ... the emperor can however dispose of these through his absolute power, as if they were his own ... and, especially, if he has a cause'.[32]

It was implied that such a cause was not essential. Absolute power was clearly not limited by the higher norm of the *ius gentium*. Angelus took the same line: 'The *princeps* by his absolute power can remove the rights of individuals'.[33] Furthermore, 'the emperor by his plenitude of power can remove our property from us even with no cause urging him to do so'.[34] Angelus actually had the pope in mind. Plenitude of power, originally a papal attribute, was extended to the emperor as Baldus also maintained: 'It is a privilege of the emperor alone to take away the rights of one person and give them to another through his plenitude of power.'[35]

The capacity of higher norms to limit the power of the ruler was also undermined in late medieval jurisprudence in another way: the prevalence of the doctrine that the will of the *princeps* served as sufficient reason (*pro ratione voluntas*). Thus, there was a trend in late medieval jurisprudence towards elevating the power of the monarch. But in the case of cities higher norms continued to be seen to have a more restricting authority. Thus, for instance, Baldus in the immediate continuation of the passage quoted above from C.1.19.7, said: 'It is otherwise with a statute of the people, because this should not contain such motivation as its cause, but rather a cause which is credible and suitable; otherwise it is not valid.'[36] His fundamental position was the traditional one among jurists: the people's laws must adhere to the general principles of the higher norms of the *ius divinum, ius naturale* and *ius gentium*, which provided overall guidelines; but in the detailed application of these general principles to specific cases, a people's customs and statutes might severely modify the general provisions which were of their nature expressed in very broad terms. As an example, civil law (including the law of cities) could in particular cases, such as in the technicalities surrounding the making of a will, infringe the simple precepts of the *ius gentium*.[37] Human law could not abolish the precepts of Divine Law, natural law and the *ius gentium*: these remained immutable as standards according to which mutable human laws were to be judged and interpreted, but

[31] 'Habetur pro causa quelibet ratio motiva ipsius principis' (to *Codex* 1.19.7 [Lyon edn 1498] fol 63r).

[32] 'Bona vero singularium personarum non sunt principis ... de his tamen imperator disponere potest ex potestate absoluta ut de propriis ... et maxime causa subsistente' (to *Codex* 7.37.3 [Lyon edn 1498] fol 201v).

[33] 'Princeps ex absoluta potestate tollere potest iura singularium personarum' (to *Digestum* 8.4.13,1 (Lyon edn 1520)).

[34] 'Imperator de plenitudine potestatis auferre potest nobis dominium etiam nulla causa suadente' (to *Digestum* 6.1.15,2, fol 180r (Lyon edn 1520)).

[35] 'Solius enim principis privilegium est iura unius auferre et alteri dare ex plenitudine potestatis' (to *Codex* 3.34.2 [Lyon edn 1498] fol 190v).

[36] 'Secus est in statuto populi, quia non debet inesse causa motiva, sed debet inesse causa probabilis et condigna, alias non valet.'

[37] To *Codex* 4.35.10 [Lyon edn 1498] fol 295v and *Digestum* 17.1.29,4 (Additio) [Lyon edn 1498] fol 111v.

which in practical application might be subject to rational distinctions according to particular circumstances.

There was, however, another form of law which in effect performed the role of a fundamental norm of legal life: feudal law. At one level, of course, feudal law was customary and, therefore, positive law. But medieval jurists had come to see that feudal relationships, unknown in the *Corpus iuris civilis*, were the product of nature as the force for change in human life. Feudal customs had become so ingrained in the structure of life that they were seen as expressing the way the world was. As Baldus, in his commentary on the *Libri feudorum* said, 'The *princeps* is subject to feudal customs as if they were latterly discovered natural law, because natural law is born every day'[38]—feudal custom amounted to nothing less than a day-to-day revelation of the natural law. Jurists had long described custom as second nature (a derivation ultimately from Aristotle and Cicero).[39] The civilian, Guido de Suzaria (d. *c.*1290), in a famous *quaestio*, now lost but reported by Cynus, had established what became the *communis opinio*, that the *princeps* was bound by his contracts and privileges which were guaranteed by the natural law and the *ius gentium*.[40] All jurists saw the feudal bond as being based on contract, the most fundamental legal relationship without which human intercourse and society would be impossible. The sanctity of contract, and the *fides* involved in keeping it, were so fundamental that they were seen as the product of the *ius naturale* and the *ius gentium* and were prior to any positive law power possessed by the emperor, and limited him as well as anyone else. Among the Commentators, the prime form that such contracts and privileges took was feudal: as Baldus said of the emperor in this connection, 'God has subjected the laws to him, but he has not subjected contracts to him.'[41] Furthermore the *princeps* was bound by his predecessors' feudal contracts and privileges, because these were not purely personal but made by virtue of the imperial office.[42] Feudal custom thus performed its function of protecting the rights of the subject against the ruler's whim: Baldus most notably accorded to the subjects' feudal rights a protection which he denied to their property rights. Feudal custom therefore appeared as a fundamental ethical norm which severely limited the sovereignty of the *princeps*.

But for universal norms of law such as Divine Law, natural law and the *ius gentium* to have genuine bite throughout late medieval Europe there would have to have been some form of international court of justice. There was no such court in terms of civil law but there was in terms of canon law. The papacy had come to serve as a court of appeal in spiritual matters throughout Europe. But many spiritual matters had secular aspects and implications. An example of a true international law contribution by the papacy was Pope Alexander VI's bull *Inter caetera* of 1493 which divided the

[38] 'Nam princeps est subiectus consuetudinibus feudorum tanquam sit ius naturale istius posterioris inventionis, quia ius naturale quotidie nascitur' (to *Libri Feudorum* 2.7 (Pavia edn 1495) fol 36r).

[39] See Baldus to *Liber Sextus Decretalium* 2.2 (MS: Cod. Vat. Lat. 5925) fol 8v, 'Consuetudo est altera natura'; Aristotle, *Nicomachean Ethics* 1152a; and Cicero, *De finibus bonorum et malorum* 5.74.

[40] See Cynus to *Codex* 1.14.4 (n 7) (Frankfurt edn 1578) fol 26r.

[41] 'Deus subiecit ei leges, sed non subiecit ei contractus' (to *Libri Feudorum* 1.7, fol 17v).

[42] To *Digestum* 1.14.1 (fol 20v).

world into geographically defined Spanish and Portuguese spheres of influence—a division modified by the Treaty of Tordesillas (1494) between Spain and Portugal.

There was a remaining feature of late medieval juristic treatment of higher norms which deserves mention not least because early-modern humanist jurists were to take issue with it. At the very beginning of the *Digest*, law was described as the art of the good and equitable ('*ius est ars boni et aequi*').[43] Logically this could mean that *bonum* was joined with *aequum* or that there was an antithesis between the two. In the context of the *Corpus iuris civilis* the notion of an antithesis could scarcely be inferred and humanist jurists tended to stress the unity between the two concepts.[44] Accursius, however, had introduced a distinction between *bonum* and *aequum*: 'Note that good is one thing and equitable is another as here. For something is good and equitable. ... For it is good and not equitable, like *usucapio*. ... Thirdly something is equitable and not good.'[45]

Accursius's Gloss on the *Corpus iuris civilis* was the culmination of the work of the school of the Glossators. Subsequent medieval jurists used and elaborated his distinction. It permitted a distinction between positive law, what was *bonum* in terms of *ius civile* (like prescription for instance), and norms of equity based on the exercise of natural reason applied to interpret the letter of the law in individual cases. Jurists produced elaborate discussions which both preserved the distinction and sought to reconcile the two categories.[46]

## 5. Just War Theory

Fourteenth-century jurists of the Roman and canon law made a further contribution to the notion of the universal rule of law in the area of just war theory. That is to say, they explored what they considered to be universally valid criteria for determining whether wars were justified or not. They were part of a medieval theological and juristic tradition, the legacy of which still exists in modern jurisprudence. Indeed, medieval writers laid the foundations for all later theories of just war. The key idea of medieval just war theory was that wars, if they were to be legitimate, had to be justified in moral terms. There was no question of simply accepting war as a fact of life. Indeed, in the Middle Ages just war theory went even further to include the notion of holy war, that is one of which God was the author—it was waged *deo auctore*. All holy wars were just wars but not all just wars were holy ones.

Behind medieval juristic treatments of warfare lay the arguments of theologians because society was Christian in its presuppositions. In terms of Western Latin Europe, the classic exposition of just war theory was produced by St Augustine of Hippo (354–430)—despite his reservations about the justice of the Roman

[43] *Digestum* 1.1.1. See text to n 27. [44] See Chapter 2 in this volume.

[45] 'Et nota quod aliud est bonum et aliud est equum ut hic. Est enim quoddam bonum et equum ... est enim bonum et non equum, ut usucapio ... est tertium equum et non bonum' (gloss to *Digest* 1.1.1, (Venice edn 1498) fol 4r).

[46] See, for instance, N Horn *Aequitas in den Lehren des Baldus* (Böhlau 1968) Forschungen zur neueren Privatrechtsgeschichte vol 11, 18–24.

Empire and its wars.[47] His ideas remained fundamental for all medieval treatments of warfare. According to Augustine, the purpose of just wars was to avenge injuries: defence was *a*, but not *the* motive. He drew on the Roman notion of *bellum iustum*, as expressed notably by Cicero: war was justified by the restitution of goods or rights, that is to say the *status quo ante bellum*. Augustine, in contrast, saw war as a punishment for sin (which could be unconnected with the *casus belli*). War was a consequence of sin and a remedy for it. He made a distinction between the internal mental attitude of the soldier and the external act (of killing). For warfare to be just, a charitable inward disposition towards the enemy must be maintained: paradoxically, killing could be an act of love towards the enemy, a divinely approved punishment for his sins. The aim of such charitable warfare was peace: lust for rule and domination (*libido dominandi*) was ruled out. Furthermore, just war could only be carried on at the command of public authority (in Augustine's case, the emperor). The requirements of public authority and a charitable inward disposition in warfare were necessarily connected because Augustine considered that it was only possible to maintain such a detachment if the soldier was acting on superior authority—that private wars did not permit such an attitude. Augustine also taught that clergy could not participate in warfare—it was solely for laymen, and soldiers at that. Augustine's just war theory thus confronted the question of whether Christians could opt out of the fallen world in which they found themselves. He pointed out that pacifism served to encourage the triumph of evil.

In the twelfth century, jurists made important contributions to the development of just war theory. This was in the context of the take-off of Roman law and canon law scholarship from the later eleventh century onwards. Canonists in particular were concerned with the problems associated with warfare. Most influential was the work of Gratian whose *Decretum* (finalized *c.*1140)[48] became the standard handbook of canon law. Gratian conveniently assembled the relevant texts on warfare and came down on the side of the Augustinian solution, quoting many excerpts from Augustine's writings.[49] Gratian's treatment was not original but he provided an easily remembered and extremely useful summary of legal questions associated with war. He included the basic Roman law description of war as a product of the *ius gentium*.[50] Following Augustine, he stressed the requirements of requisite authority and the avenging of injuries. Gratian produced a legal definition of just war: it

[47] The classic treatment of Augustine's and medieval theories of just war remains FH Russell, *The Just War in the Middle Ages* (CUP 1975) Cambridge Studies in Medieval Life and Thought 3rd series vol 8. See also J Turner Johnson, *Ideology, Reason and the Limitation of War: Religious and Secular Concepts, 1200–1740* (Princeton UP 1975); J Barnes, 'The Just War' in N Kretzmann, A Kenny, and J Pinborg (eds), *The Cambridge History of Later Medieval Philosophy, 1100–1600* (CUP 1982) 771–84.

[48] See A Winroth, *The Making of Gratian's* Decretum (CUP 2000) Cambridge Studies in Medieval Life and Thought vol 49.

[49] See for instance *Decretum Gratiani, Causa* 23 *quaestiones* 1 and 2, E Friedberg (ed) (Akademische Druck- und Verlagsanstalt repr 1959) cols 889–95.

[50] 'Ius gentium est sedium occupatio, edificatio, munitio, bella, captivitates, servitutes, postliminia, federa pacis, induciae, legatorum non violandorum religio, conubia inter alienigenas prohibita. hoc inde ius gentium appellatur, quia eo iure omnes fere gentes utuntur' (*Decretum Gratiani, Distinctio* 1, *c.*9, Friedberg edn col 3).

could have three purposes—to repel invasion, recover property and avenge prior injuries. He also addressed the question of the church's role in warfare. Clerics were forbidden to shed blood (an ancient prohibition in terms of canon law) and could not therefore directly participate in warfare but the church could initiate and direct wars against its enemies. Just cause would be defence of the faith against heretics and infidels. Bishops with temporal estates could send troops for their secular lords' wars and accompany an army with papal consent, although they could not actually fight themselves.

Theologians in the thirteenth century continued to address the question of the just war. Thomas Aquinas (1224/25–1274), for instance, did not innovate in his treatment of just war but, following Augustine, produced an easily memorable formula for the assessment of whether a war was just and, indeed, his statements were very influential into the modern period. For a war to be just three things were required—the authority of the ruler, a just cause and right intention (that either good might be accomplished or evil avoided).[51] Just cause included defence and the avenging of injuries received. The aim of war was peace and it could be made illicit by cruelty and the lust for domination. Aquinas articulated a common good argument: the aim was to preserve the state. But he added the Augustinian element of the punishment of sin. War applied where law could not be enforced—in the external relations with other rulers and States. Augustine, Gratian, and Aquinas defined the overall contours of just war theory. In other writers, there were different emphases. The theologian, Alexander of Hales (*c.*1185–1245), for instance, produced a more complicated definition of the justifications for war—according to authority (*auctoritas*), state of mind (*affectus*), intention (*intentio*), condition (*conditio*), desert (*meritum*), and cause (*causa*).

Among thirteenth-century jurists, canonists further developed questions relating to ideas of just war. There was disagreement on the prime question of which secular authorities could conduct just war. Alanus Anglicus and Hostiensis (*c.*1200–71) maintained that solely the emperor and the pope could do so. But most Decretalists, including Innocent IV (d.1254), extended this capacity to all rulers not recognizing a superior. The cumulative effect of Decretalist and Thomist doctrine was that it became accepted that territorially sovereign powers could justly wage war. Since each ruler was judge in his own case, just war became an instrument of statecraft—princes would never consider that they fought unjust wars. Two deficiencies in medieval just war theory are worth noting. Any war, to be just, depended on the war guilt of the opposing party—there was no place for a war where there was justice on both sides. There was also an inadequate treatment of non-combatants, perhaps because war seen as a punishment for sins, including those unconnected with the *casus belli*. Since everyone was perceived to be a sinner, this would dull sensitivity to the plight of those not participating in the fighting.

[51] *Summa theologiae* 2a2ae.40.1, Blackfriars (ed) (Eyre & Spottiswoode 1972) 81–85. For Aquinas's just war theory, see JD Tooke, *The Just War in Aquinas and Grotius* (SPCK 1965); G Beestermöller *Thomas von Aquin und der gerechte Krieg: Friedensethik im theologischen Kontext der Summa Theologiae* (Bachem 1990) Theologie und Frieden vol 4.

Fourteenth-century jurists further developed just war theory. Two were particularly of note in this respect. The civilian, Johannes de Legnano (*c.*1320–82/83), who was of great renown in his lifetime, wrote a tract specifically devoted to war (*Tractatus de bello*).[52] Baldus himself wrote an important *consilium* on the question of just war.[53] Drawing on the existing tradition, he identified five conditions for a just war. The first, under the heading of *persona*, addressed which persons could legitimately be involved in a just war. Such a person had to be a layman and not a cleric because ecclesiastical persons were not allowed to shed blood (that is, as he said, unless the shedding of blood was an inevitable necessity). The pope could however declare a just war. Clerics could not fight themselves but could authorize military action and provide support for it. Under the second heading of *res*—the matter of the war—he mentioned the restitution of goods and defence of one's homeland. He expressly referred to the *ius gentium* as a justification for wars of this kind. The third condition, under the heading of *causa*, specified that the war must be fought out of necessity and to gain peace. Motive (*animus*) was the fourth category: hate and greed were ruled out; charity, justice, and obedience justified war to gain security. Fifth, he referred to *auctoritas*: the authoritization by the *princeps* was required for a just war. If any of these five conditions were absent, then the war was not just. He widened his discussion by referring to Augustine's *Civitas dei* as support for the observation that war was a necessary condition in this world because peace could not exist in its fullness so long as vices ruled. He concluded by saying that the pope can give permission for a cleric to take up arms but not to shed blood, to protect the standing of the church, the faith, and the safety of his homeland. These were traditional views but they do show how categories of scholastic discussion of just war were deeply embedded in juristic language.

Medieval treatments of just war theory were very detailed but they by no means exhausted the subject. Medieval theologians and jurists did however lay firm foundations for the elaboration of just war theory in the Second Scholastic of the sixteenth and seventeenth centuries[54] and by Grotius[55] in his *De iure belli et pacis*—he, for instance, made considerable use of Baldus's writings, as his marginal references attested.

## 6. Conclusion

In considering the works of the late medieval jurists of Roman and canon law, a distinction has to be drawn between the senses in which they participated in developing notions of the universal rule of law and the question of whether they contributed in any way to the emergence of what can be identified as the early stages of international law.

[52] See J de Legnano, *Tractatus de bello, de represaliis et de duello*, in TE Holland (ed) (OUP 1917).
[53] *Consilium* 5.439 (Venice edn 1580) fols 116v–117r.
[54] See Chapter 5.
[55] See Chapter 8.

There is no doubt that these jurists made fundamental contributions to the growth of ideas of the universal rule of law, but in two specific ways. They accorded an elaborate treatment to universally applicable higher legal norms of which the *ius gentium* was the most important in their own works and for later jurists who referred back to their thought. In this respect, the late medieval jurists were setting forth limits on the exercise of power by governments and rulers. They operated with the concept of positive law but saw it as human law limited by divine Law, natural law, and the *ius gentium*, itself conceived on two levels—that of a universally valid law produced by natural reason and that of the sum of laws made by mankind.

The fundamental orientation of these late medieval Commentators on the Roman and canon law was to produce a law valid for their own day. They had to confront the particular problem of accommodating the claims of the emperor in the *Corpus iuris civilis* to the reality of emerging territorial States in the late Middle Ages. They therefore concentrated on the question of the relationship between universal and territorial sovereignty—a vertical relationship. These jurists were at the first stage of the considered response to the emergence of territorial States. The second stage was the development of jurisprudence focusing on the relations between such territorial States. This would be the beginnings of what can be understood as international law in the conventional modern sense—a law concerned with the horizontal relations between territorial States, although with due attention given to the problem of universal legal norms and the status of bodies such as the United Nations Security Council and the International Criminal Court. The late medieval jurists did consider matters relating to this second stage, especially questions of private international law and notions of just war. But their prime focus was on the vertical relationships of the first stage, that is to say, a problem of hierarchy.

I am therefore very cautious about claiming that these late medieval jurists contributed to the development of early international law as normally understood. On the other hand, there is clear evidence that early-modern theorists of international law did refer back to these jurists. It is a challenge to address the juristic thought of the late Middle Ages in terms of international law. But it is the kind of challenge which opens up new possibilities of interpretation. At the beginning of this chapter, I expressed some of the reservations a medievalist might feel in applying the term international to the late Middle Ages. From consideration of the topics that I have touched upon, it is clear that there may be something useful to be gained from using the category 'international' as a research question when studying the jurists of this period. But it seems to me that, because these are the very early days of such an enquiry, more thought and research is required in this direction. But whatever conclusions one may reach about the applicability of the term 'international', it is already crystal clear that a historical enquiry into the origins of ideas of the universal rule of law must include the contributions of the late medieval Roman and canon law jurists.

# 2

# 'The Law of Nations Is Common to All Mankind'[1]

## *Jus gentium* in Humanist Jurisprudence

*Susan Longfield Karr*

### 1. Introduction

If medieval or scholastic jurisprudence provided the origins of European notions of universal law—religious and secular—over the course of the thirteenth, fourteenth, and fifteenth centuries,[2] the new or humanist jurisprudence that began to emerge in the early sixteenth century fundamentally reinterpreted it. Why and how humanist jurists did so has significant implications for our understanding of the history, development, and transformation of *ius gentium*, not only as a fount of universal rights, natural and civic, but also in terms of its relation to *ius inter gentes* which, although primarily concerned with positive international law, nevertheless embodies and invokes an idea of universal justice that enables us to make claims and set expectations that go beyond the mere realpolitik or *raison d'état* motives often associated with the history and development of international law.[3]

Understanding *ius gentium*—as something more than a precursor of *ius inter gentes*—also enables us to see that rather than merely consisting of a steady stream of examples of 'might makes right' between competing empires and national States, the history and development of international law is steeped quite centrally in civil jurisprudence, especially in attempts by lawyers and jurists to limit political and legal authority of rulers over their subjects. The attempt to limit authority within States, as the history and development of the natural rights tradition in the West clearly shows, has direct and significant implications for attempts to limit authority

[1] U Zasius, '*De Iustitia et Iure*, lecture' in *Opera Omnia* 7 vols (Lugundi 1550 repr Aalen 1964) col 258.

[2] See Chapter 1 in this volume.

[3] C Schmidt, *The Nomos of the Earth in the International Law of Jus Publicum Europaeum* (Telos 2003); R Tuck, *Rights of War and Peace: Political Thought and the International Order from Grotius to Kant* (OUP 1999); M Koskenniemi, *The Gentle Civilizer of Nations: The Rise and Fall of International Law* 1890–1960 (CUP 2001).

between States. Thus, although the endeavour to use civil law to limit civil authority may appear to be detached from concerns with universal jurisprudence, and the international order that it eventually underpins, it is not.

Indeed, one cannot invoke a higher principle of justice to limit the authority of a ruler, or convince a ruler that it is not only necessary, but also right, for him to do so, unless one establishes first how civil and universal jurisprudence are conjoined. Nor can one persuade subjects, who may question reforms and changes in the law, that such changes are making the realm more stable and just, unless these changes are rooted in universal jurisprudence. As to do otherwise, in either case, is to assume that legal authority and civil order rest on force and power, not justice, and as such that law itself is unpredictable and arbitrary. In other words, unless civil and universal jurisprudence are in concord, there can be no rule of law, there can only be a rule of men.

In the context of holding rulers, civic institutions, and civil laws to a higher criterion of justice—in accordance with a rule of law—*ius gentium* was transformed at the hands of early-sixteenth-century humanist jurists from a relatively insignificant category of law among the scholastics to a fundamental and foundational category that could be invoked not only to reform and transform civil jurisprudence within a specific nation in Europe, but also to address questions associated with conquest, colonization, commerce, and war between nations across the globe. In its simplest terms, what enabled jurists and theorists to use the idea and category of *ius gentium* to address *regional* and *transnational* problems across and beyond Europe from the mid-sixteenth century was the reinterpretation of *ius gentium* as the source of rights, natural and civil, in *local* contexts within civil jurisprudence in early sixteenth century. Without attention to humanist jurisprudence Francisco de Vitoria (1492–1546), Alberico Gentili (1552–1608), and Hugo Grotius (1583–1645) look to be entirely out of joint with the scholastic traditions that came before them, whereas with careful attention to humanist jurisprudence, their innovations especially in terms of the junctions between justice and right, *ius gentium* and *ius*, and natural law and *ius gentium*, come into focus as part of juristic tradition, rather than a rapid—and revolutionary—departure from it.

Given this fundamental link between civil and universal jurisprudence via *ius gentium*, it should be no surprise that the humanist jurists' understanding of the former fundamentally affected how they interpreted the latter and vice versa. Moreover, moral claims that rely on universal conceptions of justice can no sooner be confined to a particular legal case than moral claims within civil jurisprudence can be confined to a single context; claims based in universal justice become precedents, and these precedents become a fundamental part of civil jurisprudence, which is turn can shape how universal jurisprudence is understood more generally. There is, in other words, a symbiotic relation between civil and universal jurisprudence. What is more that relationship is expressed, transformed, and reimagined through the language of the law, always shifting and changing whenever adapted to a new context or country. The sixteenth-century humanist jurists' understanding of *ius gentium* might well have been closer to the Chinese understanding of the same term in the nineteenth century, than either shared with the meaning that Grotius employed to distinguish *ius gentium* from *ius inter gentes* in the seventeenth. Only careful attention to civil jurisprudence, in both contexts, will tell. In any case, the symbiotic and linguistic relationship between universal and civil jurisprudence is what distinguishes the history of *ius gentium* as well as *ius inter gentes* as more than a mere progression from one kind of state of affairs to another, as more than merely the emergence of an interstate system in Europe—and the expansion of that system across the globe—from the sixteenth to the nineteenth centuries.

The fundamental link between civil jurisprudence and universal jurisprudence becomes even more apparent in times when *ius inter gentes* falls out of joint with the universal principles of justice and right, as it has done on several occasions throughout the twentieth and now twenty-first centuries. Each time *ius inter gentes* is at odds with justice and right, we are invited to re-examine, reassess, and reinterpret the history and development of civil jurisprudence in the West as much as international law around the globe. In each case, there is an effort to restore something perceived as lost, namely, a universal rule of law that not only treats rulers and subjects alike, but also entails a sense of fairness and predictability between and among them. In moments when the law and justice appear out of joint, when it no longer seems as if everyone (persons and States) is equal before the law, or that the laws themselves are no longer predictable, calls for reform take on a particularly urgent tone. In the early sixteenth century such a call was made by humanist jurists who held that the rule of law had not simply been replaced by a rule of men, but worse, by a rule by law and lawyers. They amplified that call by making another: they called for the reform and restoration of civil jurisprudence across Europe—at once anticipating and echoing the calls of secular rulers to decouple civil and ecclesiastical law—in order to restore the principles of justice and right that had been corrupted as a result of traditional jurisprudence.

Unlike a rule by men, which is often characterized as those who use the law to pursue their own self-interests at the cost of the common good, the rule by law and lawyers appears to serve a common good—but looks can be deceiving. As even while the rule by law and lawyers is ensconced in what appears to be a rational and ordered system of rules and procedures that protects it from being abused, it is prone to endemic corruption. Armed with the ability and expertise to bend the law to the will of their patron—or even to their own will—the very jurists who create and manage civil law and civic institutions could place themselves outside and above it. As such the rule by lawyers created by traditional jurists effectively buffered whomever wielded the power to rule a kingdom, republic, State, or empire—and those who were charged to administer it—from being subject or accountable to the laws they were creating and sanctioning.

By the early sixteenth century this state of affairs increasingly had the potential to create civic strife and discord because it had effectively enabled a regime not only of 'might makes right', but also as professional administrators and jurists to exercise authority that was above and beyond their station. Moreover, courts of law, civil institutions, and legislative bodies that were permeated with disputes had the potential to set societies—already embroiled in wars and conflicts—ablaze. Indeed, from at least the outset of the Italian Wars in 1494 to the end of the War of Spanish

Succession in 1714 the whole of Europe was locked in internal and international conflicts—political, legal, commercial, and religious. Each of these conflicts were part and parcel of longer process of State- and empire-state formation within and beyond Europe; and each were as significant for the development of an international order between States as they were for the reinterpretation of civil jurisprudence within States.

## 2. Humanist jurisprudence

In the opening decades of the sixteenth century humanist jurists such as Guillaume Budé (1467–1540) in France, Ulrich Zasius (1461–1536) in Germany, and Andrea Alciati (1492–1550) in Italy and France deliberately set out to offer an alternative interpretation of Roman law, and thereby civil jurisprudence, from their scholastic predecessors and contemporaries.[4] It was necessary to do so, they held, because law and justice had fallen out of joint; lawyers and jurists had managed to corrupt the law and legal interpretation not only as a result of their own ambitions and the desires of their patrons, but also as a consequence of what Budé, Zasius, and Alciati held as a grave and grievous error at the very foundations of scholastic jurisprudence: the misinterpretation—and thereby misunderstanding—of the underlying relationship between justice and right, as expressed in law—customary, natural, and civil—over time. These errors, they held, extended directly from the *Gloss* of Accursius (1182–1263), whereby definitions of the basic categories within Roman law, such as *ius* (right), as well as explanations concerning the relation between natural law, *ius gentium*, and civil law, had set the parameters for legal interpretation and practice for centuries.

Because the original errors in the *Gloss* had led to additional errors and faulty interpretations across Europe, Budé, Zasius, and Alciati held that in order to bring civil laws and civil customs back into accordance with universal justice, a thoroughgoing restoration of the *corpus* of Roman law was necessary. Approaching Roman law and traditional jurisprudence by returning to its sources, and thereby exploring it through a historical and comparative perspective, not only enabled Budé, Zasius, and Alciati to show where and how the law had been corrupted, but also to argue that the foundational and fundamental principles that underpinned the *corpus* of Roman law, principles that were embodied and expressed by the language of the law itself, underpinned all bodies of laws, written and unwritten, across time and space.

In an era already rife with calls for legal reform, most notably those initiated by Maximilian I in 1495 in the Empire and by Louis XII in 1499 in France, Budé, Zasius, and Alciati set out—albeit in different ways and to differing degrees—to provide tools, resources, and training for lawyers and jurists across the continent to draw upon in the ongoing process of purging errors and corruptions from civil

[4] S Longfield Karr, 'Nature, Self, and History in the Works of Guillaume Budé, Andrea Alciati, and Ulrich Zasius: A Study of the Role of Legal Humanism in Western Natural Law' (PhD diss, University of Chicago 2008).

jurisprudence.[5] Given that so many of the corruptions that needed to be addressed extended from misinterpretations and misunderstandings—and even the intentional twisting—of foundational principles and categories of Roman law by scholastic jurists, it should be no surprise that a common feature among their works was a full-scale attack on the traditional lawyers. Their attacks were quite bitter, brutally direct, and in some cases exaggerated to the point of diminishing the import of their own arguments. Nevertheless, their works left little doubt how dangerous they regarded the errors within scholastic jurisprudence to be.

Their attacks also reflect their concern, in the middle of an opportunity to bring the law and justice back into concord, that those who created the mess in the first place would be given the authority to fix it. Hence their calls for reform in legal education, interpretation, and practice were urgent: if the errors of the scholastics were sanctioned by being reproduced and extended, the opportunity to improve the laws more generally, and thereby restore justice, might have been lost altogether. If faulty interpretations were confirmed and extended through the process of systemization and codification, then customary practices and universal rights that stood at the very basis of social, civil, economic, and political institutions across Europe could be further diminished, violated, and even demolished. If left in the hands of traditional jurists, the already dangerous rule by lawyers could be extended. Rather than restoring civil jurisprudence, and thereby a rule of law based in universal jurisprudence, these jurists might continue to use their expertise to extend power, rather than ensure justice. This could magnify the very kinds of legal and political authority that Budé, Zasius, and Alciati were explicitly questioning, critiquing, and attempting to limit through their restoration—and redefinition—of such fundamental terms, such as justice (*iustitia*) and right (*ius*), within Roman law.

While deeply concerned with the meaning and significance of words in context, restoring the language of Roman law was no mere academic exercise. In a world in which Roman law served as the common denominator that tied jurists and lawyers together across Europe, and as the foundational text of civil law, restoring the basic terms and categories within Roman law would provide those charged to reform unjust laws as well as codification with an understanding of civil jurisprudence based in universal jurisprudence, rather than repeated errors or political interests. However, through the application of their humanist methods, Budé, Zasius, and Alciati ultimately reinterpreted the law that they set out to restore. In the process, they used the categories of *ius* and *ius gentium* to defend universal rights and obligations in the face of the creation of new forms—and the expansion of older forms—of legal and political authority.

They did so in their capacity as councillors and advisers, as lawyers and jurists, as well as, and most important, in their capacity as professors in the universities,[6]

[5] The call for reform was not limited to jurisprudence, see B Bradshaw, 'Transalpine Humanism' *The Cambridge History of Political Thought 1450–1700* (CUP 1991) 95–131; WJ Bouwsma (ed), *The Waning of the Renaissance 1550–1640* (Yale UP 2000); CG Nauert, *Humanism and the Culture of Renaissance Europe* (CUP 2006).

[6] J Neff, *Ulrich Zasius: Ein freiburger Humanist* (1890); PE Viard, *André Alciat, 1492–1550* (1926); HJ Berman, *Law and Revolution: The Formation of the Western Legal Tradition* (Harvard UP 1983);

wherein they were training those who would be responsible for administering and reforming local laws in Germany, France, and northern Italy. Only through careful attention to changes in the meaning, language, and interpretation of Roman law, in relation to particular contexts, in response to particular problems, and even to promote particular interests, would it be possible to observe the universal principles such as justice, good, and equity, and right that underlie it. Thus, rather than study Roman law as normative and attempt to abstract universal principles from it as the scholastic civil jurists had done,[7] Budé, Zasius, and Alciati historicized law and its sources in order to observe the moral principles on which it was based.

## 3. Restoring the Rule of Law to Restore Justice

Crucial to acquiring a proper understanding of Roman law—and thereby the universal jurisprudence that underlies it—was an appreciation of the link between natural law, *ius gentium*, and civil law, which Budé, Zasius, and Alciati investigated in respect to their origins, their extent, and their history. They turned to the origins of law and the origins of society—historical and moral—in order to explore when, how, and why these categories of law diverged and even conflicted with one another, as well as when, how, and why they intersected and agreed. And in so doing, they fundamentally broke with traditional scholastic civil jurisprudence in the first decades of the sixteenth century, not only in regard to their interpretation of *ius gentium,* but also in their definitions of *ius*. They did so in three interrelated ways.

First, in defining *ius* and its relation to justice and law, Budé, Zasius, and Alciati rejected the split between equity and good introduced by Accursius (1182–1263) in the thirteenth century,[8] and maintained by Bartolus de Saxoferrato (1313–57) and Baldus de Ubaldis (1327–1400) in the fourteenth century, as well as by those who followed them.[9] Departing from Accursius, Bartolus, and Baldus, they restored the definition of *ius*, in its objective aspect, in accordance with the definition provided within the first lines of the *Digest* itself, namely, '*ius* is the art of goodness and fairness'[10]—which they interpreted as '*ius* is the art of what is good and what is fair, conjoined'.[11] Second, they redefined *ius* in its subjective aspect, they argued that *ius*

DR Kelley, *Foundations of Modern Historical Scholarship: Language, Law, and History in the French Renaissance* (Columbia UP 1970); S Rowan, *Ulrich Zasius: A Jurist in the German Renaissance, 1461–1535* (1987).

[7] JW Baldwin, *The Scholastic Culture of the Middle Ages, 1000–1300* (D. C. Heath & Company 1971); NW Gilbert, *Renaissance Concepts of Method* (Columbia UP 1960); N Kretzmann, A Kenny, and J Pinborg (eds), *The Cambridge History of Later Medieval Philosophy: From the Rediscovery of Aristotle to the Disintegration of Scholasticism, 1100–1600* (Klostermann 1981).

[8] Accursius, *Digestum vetus sive pandectarum iuris civilis totus primus ex pandectis Florentinis* (1566) fo II.

[9] MP Gilmore, *Argument from Roman Law Argument from Roman Law in Political Thought, 1200–1600* (Harvard UP 1967); Berman (n 6); J Canning, *The Political Thought of Baldus de Ubaldis* (CUP 1987); C Fasolt, *Limits of History* (University of Chicago Press 2004); F Maiolo, *Medieval Sovereignty: Marsilius of Padua and Bartolus of Saxoferrato* (Eburon Academic 2007).

[10] Digest. Book 1. Title 1. Section 1.

[11] U Zasius, 'De iustitia et iure, praefatio' in *Opera Omnia* (Scientia Verlag 1964) col 15.

was as an intrinsic and inherent characteristic of man qua man, shared by all, universally throughout time and across geographical space, without distinction.[12] Third, to ground their moral discussion of *ius*—the moral authority of which extended directly from man's fundamental attributes of dignity, reason, and will—within civil jurisprudence, they linked natural law directly to *ius gentium*, which they held encapsulated customs in common within communities and between communities from the origins of mutual company itself.[13]

*Jus gentium* (extending from a combination of *ius* and natural law) provided the moral foundation of all laws—written and unwritten—for the legal humanists. This was the case because they held that *ius gentium* was the substance from which all civil laws were made. Furthermore, because they held that *ius gentium* was historically prior to civil law, if civil authorities (jurists and lawyers in particular, but also rulers) attempted to diminish or demolish universal obligations and rights through civil laws *ius gentium* could be invoked as a means to limit their ability to do so. Here, Budé, Zasius, and Alciati departed from those scholastic jurists who held that *ius gentium* and natural law had altogether different origins—that natural law was the creation of God, whereas *ius gentium* was the creation of man—and from the Romans, when they argued that *ius gentium* could hold civil laws, institutions, and authorities accountable to a universal rule of law.

Moreover, they held that *ius gentium* had within it a 'history' of society, in so far as it encompassed customs, rights, and obligations that were common among members of a specific community from its origins. Thus, *ius gentium* also encompassed common practices, rights, and obligations that all people shared—across time and space. It was the common denominator of all peoples, tied the community of men together, and regulated relationships within communities across the globe. As a body of customs observed by man over time, *ius gentium* stood at the basis of political and legal authority itself, and at the foundation of *ius gentium* stood *ius*.

Here there are two crucial and interrelated aspects to highlight. First, in relation to *ius*: Budé focused on *ius* as a characteristic of man qua man,[14] Zasius stressed *ius* as that which ultimately concerned relations between men within society and between societies,[15] and finally Alciati concentrated on *ius* as that which primarily concerned the relation between individuals on the one hand, and rulers on the other.[16] Second, although each shared the same definitions of *ius* as the art of good and equity conjoined and held it to be a distinguishing characteristic of man, they each focused

[12] G Budé, *Annotationes* (Ex officina Ascensiana, 1508) fo X–XI; Zasius, 'De iustitia et iure, praefatio 1550' cols 14–15 and 'De iustitia et iure, lecture, 1550' (n 11) cols 243–44; cols 252–55; A Alciati, 'De iustitia et iure, lecture' in *Opera Omnia* (Isingrinius 1546), 1–2.

[13] Budé, *Annotationes* (n 12) fo X–XI; Zasius, 'Praefatio, De Origine Legibus' 1–4; Zasius, 'De iustitia et iure, lecture' (n 11) cols 249–51; Alciati, 'Oratio in Laudem Iuri Civilis, Principio Studii Cum Avenione Profiteretur [1518]' (n 12) 506–11; 'Oratio Andreae Alciati, Dum Bononiam [1537]' (n 12) 1051/52, 1055/56; 'Bona Fides' in *De verborum significatione* (Sebastianus Gryphius, 1535) cols 305–13; 'De iustitia et iure, lecture' (n 12) 1–6.

[14] Budé, *Annotationes* (n 12) fo X–XI.

[15] Zasius, 'De iustitia et iure, lecture' (n 11) cols 249–56.

[16] Alciati, 'De iustitia et iure, lecture' (n 12) 1–14.

on—and indeed combined—different definitions of *ius gentium* provided within the first title of the *Digest* within their theories of universal and civil jurisprudence.

Budé focused primarily on Gaius's definition of *ius gentium* as the law all men shared by virtue of natural reason.[17] In his discussion of *ius gentium*, Budé linked man's dignity and reason to *ius* and law, with the result that *ius* was a distinguishing characteristic of all mankind, by nature.[18] As such *ius* was the fundamental criterion for determining the justice of civil law, what distinguished man from animals, and that which all mankind held in common.[19] In addition to Gaius's definition, Zasius paired the obligations one has from *ius gentium*,[20] such as the obligation to obey God, one's parents, and one's fatherland as explained by Pomponius,[21] to the definition provided by Florentinus that explained a basic feature of *ius gentium* was the right to repel violent injuries to one's body and property,[22] which Zasius further linked to the definition of force (*vim*) in the *Digest*.[23] Alciati's discussion encompassed all of the above, but focused centrally on Hermogenian's definition,[24] which stressed the consequences of *ius gentium* including war, the founding of nations and kingdoms, individuated property, and the establishment of commerce. In his discussion, just as Zasius, Alciati directly linked *ius gentium* to the definition of force.[25]

As one would expect, the definitions or aspects of *ius gentium* that they emphasized informed how they discussed its relation to *ius*. For example, whereas Budé emphasized the link between *ius* and *ius gentium* within man and Zasius primarily focused on the relation between *ius* and *ius gentium* between men, Alciati emphasized the relation between *ius* and *ius gentium* within man, between men, and between rulers. Through their discussions of *ius*, and the relation between *ius* and *ius gentium*, Budé, Zasius, and Alciati not only restored fundamental categories of Roman law, they also introduced a new order of the laws into early-modern legal thought. And it was in this process that they brought *ius gentium*—as the source and protector of rights and obligations—from the sidelines into the core of early-modern political thought. Only by placing them within a broader context—in comparison with the Romans and the scholastic Doctors—is it possible to articulate how fundamentally different their interpretations were from those who preceded them. Only by placing them in context is it possible to see that by reordering the law, they effectively fused universal and civil jurisprudence through their reinterpretation of *ius gentium* as both an extension of natural law and as the source of universal rights.

## 4. The Order of the Laws

Nearly every aspect of the *corpus* of Roman law—as codified by Justinian in the sixth century—focused on concrete principles and the applied practice of civil law.

17 D.1.1.9. 18 Budé, *Annotationes* (n 12) fo XI; cf Cicero, *De Legibus* I 28.
19 ibid fo X–XI.
20 Zasius, 'De iustitia et iure, praefatio' cols 14–15, and 'De iustitia et iure, lecture' (n 11) cols 243–44; cols 252–55.
21 D.1.1.2. 22 D.1.1.3. 23 D.43.16.1. 24 D.1.1.5.
25 Alciati, 'De iustitae et iure, lecture' (n 12) 1–2.

Civil law was the rule of law, that is, the highest, most important, most authoritative, and most just law precisely because it was the civil law.[26] Although followed by *ius gentium*, the importance of *ius gentium* paled in comparison, as it concerned the relation between societies, and disputes between citizens and non-citizens under Roman rule.[27] While *ius gentium* served an important function and thus had some importance to Roman lawyers and jurists, natural law was of little significance. It concerned such basics as reproduction and preservation shared by both man and animals, but was not particularly important in terms of the application and practice of civil law.[28] Thus, even though *ius gentium* was significant in terms of war and conflict, and natural law was part of the hierarchy of Roman law, neither was as central as civil law. In short, the order of the laws in the *corpus*, from highest and most perfect, to the lowest and most general, was: first, Roman civil law, second *ius gentium*, and distinctly third in degree of importance, natural law.

That the *corpus* of Roman law was primarily practical in nature helps to account for the centrality of specific kinds and principles of civil law within it. It also accounts for its form: it is a collection of laws from the *Twelve Tables* onward, with little or no jurisprudence framing or accompanying it. Because the laws within *corpus* developed over time, in light of particular problems in particular contexts, it is full of contradictions and inconsistencies that were left unresolved by the compilation under the direction of Tribonian (485–542). Nevertheless, upon the 'rediscovery' of the Roman *Digest* in the eleventh century, those who studied and taught it attempted to bring the contradictions within the text into concord.[29] They did so in order to use it to rationalize, expand, and change customary practices within Europe; to support and question the expansion of political and legal authority; and to address contests and conflicts between individuals and groups as well as between competing claims for power by kings, popes, and emperors.

In this context of rapid change and contested authority the medieval jurists, through the methods of logic, reconciliation, and abstraction, for lack of a better term, invented—or created—civil jurisprudence as distinct from, but still related to, universal jurisprudence.[30] In the process, they changed the hierarchy or order of the laws. In the context of Universal Latin Christendom, the highest law was not man's creation (civil law) but rather God's will or plan (eternal law). Generally, God's will or plan, the eternal law, was revealed in part to man through divine law (the Decalogue) and in part through reason (natural law).[31] As civil law was a creation of man, it had the potential to be in accordance with divine law and to embody the

[26] The *corpus* consists of the *Code*, the *Pandects* or *Digest*, the *Institutes*, and the *Novellae*.

[27] Before Emperor Caracalla extended citizenship to all freeborn men within the Empire in 212 CE.

[28] D.1.1.3. [29] Berman (n 6) 120–64.

[30] P Vinogradoff, *Roman Law in Medieval Europe* (OUP 1929); Gilmore (n 9); S Kuttner, 'Revival of Jurisprudence' in RL Benson and G Constable (eds), *Renaissance and Renewal in the Twelfth Century* (Harvard UP 1982) 299–323; M Bellemo, *The Common Legal Past of Europe: 1000–1800* (Catholic University of America Press 1995); P Stein *Roman Law in European History* (CUP 1999).

[31] See A Thompson and J Gordley (tr), *Gratian, The Treaty on Laws* (Catholic University of America Press 1993); T Aquinas, ch II 'Law and Chapter IV: Right, Justice and Judgment' in RW Dyson (ed), *The Political Writing of Thomas Aquinas* (CUP 2002) 58–204.

principles of natural law. It also had the potential to depart from both, or, stated differently, it simultaneously reflected man's better nature and his baser nature. In addition to eternal law, canon law was also introduced to the hierarchy of laws. The latter was sometimes in accord with civil law, and sometimes in direct conflict with it. *Jus gentium* was considered the lowest order of the law because it resulted from man's interests and failings. In this account of the order and importance of the categories or types of law, natural law was promoted, while the medieval jurists demoted both civil law and *ius gentium*.

Despite being the most corrupt form of law, *ius gentium* nevertheless remained significant because it explained and accounted for the origin of practices, such as property, slavery, and war, which looked to be at odds with and even in direct contradiction to divine and natural law. Because these institutions appeared to be in contradiction with both divine law and natural law on the one hand, but were sanctioned by civil laws on the other, there had to be a means to justify their existence. The category of *ius gentium* provided just such a means: jurists could use it to explain why these institutions and conditions existed in the first place, that is, why man needed them. Very broadly, *ius gentium* was identified as the law that emerged postlapsarian and thus extended directly from man's wickedness.

However, because the Fall of Man was part of God's will and plan, *ius gentium* was not entirely unjust. It therefore needed to be logically and theologically accounted for as a part of and reconciled into a normative system based on its relation—as distant as it was—to eternal law, divine law, and natural law. Indeed, a key aspect of justifying practices that fell under the rubric of *ius gentium* was to split equity from good in the definition of *ius*, and thereby in the definition of justice. And it is this split that corresponds with the split within *ius gentium* between a higher (more just) and lower (least just) form, between primary *ius gentium* and secondary *ius gentium*.

Primary *ius gentium*, although corrupt, was a necessary form of law because from it property, jurisdictions, kingdoms, territories, and commerce originated. The lowest, least just, most corruptible form of law in this system was secondary *ius gentium*. This is the case because war and slavery originated from it. Yet, although secondary *ius gentium* was the lowest form of law, it did not lack moral authority entirely. Again, because it was part of the normative system, despite its depravity, its existence and necessity could be justified with reference to higher forms of law, and further, it could be logically reconciled with them by means of scholastic methods. Through the application of dialectics, the species (*ius gentium*) could be shown to logically follow from the genus (eternal law); the premise (man's wickedness) could be shown to be a fundamental part of the syllogism (the eternal plan or will of God). The order of the law reflected the Great Chain of Being, with each kind of law fulfilling a particular function—and thereby occupying a particular place—within universal jurisprudence, as such civil law and *ius gentium* occupied different links in the chain—or invoking another image, different rungs in the ladder.

This ordering was for the most part consistent in the scholastic tradition of legal thought—canonist and civilian—throughout the medieval and late-medieval periods. The order changed significantly, or rather, *ius gentium* became grounded differently and therefore gained moral authority when Budé, Alciati, and Zasius reinterpreted *ius gentium* in light of the problems and processes of early-modern State formation. In the process, they departed from the traditional hierarchy and put forward another in which *ius gentium* was central. They did so decades before Vitoria reinterpreted *ius gentium* within the context of European expansion and about half a century before the so-called fathers of international law, Gentili and Grotius, reinterpreted *ius gentium*, as part of—and yet distinct from—*ius inter gentes*, in order to address problems attendant upon religious, political, and commercial wars within and beyond Europe.[32] Indeed, one might argue that it is precisely because *ius gentium* gained moral authority at the hands of the humanist jurist, that it gained significance in civil jurisprudence on the one hand and became the lingua franca of universal jurisprudence on the other.

Yet it must be remembered that Budé, Zasius, and Alciati's reinterpretation of *ius gentium* in the early sixteenth century resulted from their attempts to fuse civil and universal jurisprudence in order to bring about legal and social reform within early sixteenth-century Italy, France, and the Holy Roman Empire. Thus, although they presented a fundamentally different order of the laws, wherein the emphasis on the rule of law as opposed to a rule by lawyers was central, it is paramount to recognize the limits of their gaze: they were distinctly focused on local and regional issues. In other words, they used *ius gentium* to demarcate the limits of political and legal authority on two levels—within States and between States—and as a result *ius gentium* took on two different, albeit related, characteristics depending on what level Budé, Zasius, and Alciati were focusing on.

On its most basic (primary) level civil jurisprudence—as an extension of *ius gentium*—holds all legal and political authorities accountable to a universal criterion of justice, making it impossible (ideally) for the rule of law to be subverted by power and interests. Although hierarchies continue to exist in society based on status, the civil rule of law requires that no one stand outside or above the law itself. Within civil society, if civil jurisprudence is in perfect accordance with universal jurisprudence, everyone would be equally subject to and restrained by a rule of law. However, when these same principles of justice and right are extended beyond the civil sphere, to the level (secondary) of a universal rule of law—which also extends from *ius gentium*—all States, kingdoms, and empires are equally free from restraint. That is, States are not equal because they are subject to a single positive law as subjects are, *but rather because they all stand as equals in the absence of one.* In this respect *ius gentium* enables all nations to be equal to one another, rather than subjected to or clients of an imperial power, whereas something along the lines of *ius inter gentes* mapped onto the early sixteenth century would have surely reaffirmed and reified the very hierarchies that were increasingly called into question as dynastic and territorial wars began to reshape the continent on the eve of European expansion and European Reformations. That all nations were free from legal restraints and political subjection, however, did not mean that they were free to do whatever they pleased to one another; might did not make right. Rather, just as the moral

[32] See Chapters 5 and 8 in this volume.

authority of *ius gentium* entails moral obligations within civil society, *ius gentium* entails moral obligations beyond civil society. Indeed, that it does both—whether it is through *ius* or through natural law—is precisely what makes *ius gentium* common among all mankind.

## 5. The Moral Authority of *jus*: Budé

Despite the fact that Budé did not have formal legal training, nor a nuanced understanding of legal or juridical practice, with the publication of his *Annotationes* in 1508 he launched a systematic and unrelenting attack against professional and university-based jurisprudence—an attack that helped lay the foundations for a reinterpretation of the relation between justice, right, and law, and thereby the source and extent of legal and political authority. Focused on restoring fundamental terms within Roman law, Budé's purpose in his *Annotationes* was not to reform scholastic jurisprudence, so much as to eviscerate it. Within this text Budé attempted to offer a direct alternative to the interpretations found in the *Gloss* of Accursius, the standard *Gloss* used to teach and interpret Roman law in the universities since the thirteenth century. Moreover, throughout this polemic Budé criticized lawyers and jurists for using their expertise in jurisprudence to augment their own reputations and positions in society

But that was not the worst of it. Bude also held that armed with their methods and knowledge, scholastic lawyers and jurists could exceed the bounds of propriety and block an edict to reform or diminish their place in administering justice and law. Moreover, as specialists they could exchange their expertise for profit, patronage, and glory to those who wished to use the law to their own benefit, especially those who desired to limit the power of King Louis XII. To protect against this, it was imperative that those who administered the law had a nuanced understanding of the principles that underpinned it; they required a proper understanding of the meaning, significance, and fundamental characteristics of justice. Understanding justice and law properly, would in turn enable lawyers and jurists to better understand their place as those who administer justice, rather than create laws. Hoping to provide jurists with that understanding, Budé dedicated the *Annotationes* to the newly appointed chancellor of France whose task was to ameliorate errors introduced into civil laws and procedures by traditional jurisprudence, and thereby to bring French customs and laws back into accordance with universal justice.[33]

Budé simply opened his *Annotationes* by asserting that according to the first words of the *Digest* '*ius* is what is good and what is fair conjoined'.[34] Yet, he continued, Accursius had 'separated equity and good in an improper and ignorant fashion'.[35] By misinterpreting *ius* the guardians and ministers of the law—the

[33] See F Simone, *Culture et politique en France à l'époque de l'humanisme et de la renaissance* (Accademia delle Scienze 1974); F Baumgartner, *France in the Sixteenth Century* (St Martin's Press 1995); J Garrisson, *A History of Sixteenth Century France, 1483–1598* (R Tuck tr, Macmillan 1995).

[34] Budé, *Annotationes* (n 12) fo 1. [35] ibid.

professors, the lawyers, and the judges—had corrupted the law itself. Without a proper understanding of *ius*, nothing was stable, nothing was secure; the civil law had the potential to become a mere plaything; all that the law enforced and protected had the potential to become relative. In addition to their misunderstanding of *ius*, professional lawyers and jurists had allowed the law to be bent by influence, shattered by power, and corrupted by wealth to serve their own interests. Budé's critique, however, did not stop there—it was not simply that the definition of *ius* had been corrupted, and thereby the law, but justice itself had been violated. Not only was *ius* the art of what is good and fair conjoined, it was also for Budé, drawing on Cicero's *On the Laws*, the fundamental distinguishing characteristic of man qua man due to its connection to reason:

> Reason is attributed to all by nature: to these same [people] right reason is given also. And therefore so too has *lex* been given [by nature]: which is right reason in ordering and forbidding. If *lex*, so too *ius*: to all reason has been given. Therefore *ius* has been given to all.[36]

By corrupting *ius*, the jurists not only corrupted the law and abandoned justice, but they also affronted man's dignity—for profit, for glory, for fame, and for applause. As such, Budé held civil law as the lowest form of law because it served interest and power rather than justice. In his account of the order of the laws, natural law although universal was not the highest law precisely because it was the law shared by man and animals, whereas *ius gentium* was the highest law precisely because it was not shared with animals. Moreover, *ius gentium* was the highest law based on its relation to *ius*:[37] because just as all men possessed natural reason, all men possessed *ius*, and therefore all men possessed *ius gentium*.[38]

Indeed, for Budé, it was *ius gentium* (not natural law), which linked all men to one another across time and space, without distinction. Quoting from *Book I* of Cicero's *De legibus* almost word for word, Budé argued that this was the case because *ius gentium* was the law that spread throughout the globe and structured relations between men as they pursued justice and the common good in tandem from the origins of mankind itself.[39] For Budé's *ius gentium* had moral authority above and beyond civil law precisely because it was based in *ius*, the distinguishing characteristic of man qua man from his origins.[40] All of this marked a radical departure from the scholastic understanding of *ius*, the relation between natural law and *ius gentium*, and the relation between civil and universal jurisprudence.

## 6. The Moral Authority of *jus gentium* I: Zasius

Zasius did not simply reject the definition of *ius* in the *Gloss* in favour of Budé's interpretation, he went beyond it: he set out to show that *ius*—as an attribute of universal justice as well as a distinguishing characteristic of man qua man—was

36 ibid fo XI; Cicero, *On the Laws* book I, s [22].
37 Budé, *Annotationes* fo IX–XI.
38 ibid fo X.
39 ibid fo IX–XI; Cicero, *De legibus* book I, especially ss [22]–[28].
40 Budé, *Annotationes* fo XI.

justice in action.[41] As such, careful attention to the actions of man—demonstrated in customs and legal texts—over time revealed the fundamental and foundational principles of law shared between all.[42] For Zasius, *ius gentium* was a higher order of law than civil law because it was based in *ius* and because it was historically prior to civil law. Moreover, civil law was a lower order of law because it had the potential to embody *ius gentium* as well as substantially depart from it. Just civil laws were those that extended from *ius gentium—primary* and *secondary*—which in turn extended from natural law, and thus had at their very basis *ius*, that is, equity and good conjoined.[43] Whereas civil laws that violated *ius*, laws that were either good or equitable (or neither), were unjust and therefore needed to be carefully reformed.[44]

*Ius gentium*, as an expression of natural law, and a record of justice or objective *ius*, for Zasius, was also a higher order than civil law because it was the source of universal obligations and rights.[45] Man had universal rights and obligations because he had an innate sense of justice; man needed universal rights and obligations because he was subject to his reason as much as his passions.[46] Man created customs and laws, over time, to help balance his two natures in mutual company. As the creation of man, however, these customs and laws had the capacity to reflect man's baser nature, and as such departed from a universal rule of law when used to advance the interests of some, without concern for equity and good conjoined; without concern for universal justice. In these cases, *ius* (subjective) could hold civil law to a higher standard of justice (objective *ius*), through the category of *ius gentium*. Here is Zasius's innovation: *ius gentium* could be used as a criterion of justice to effect legal reform because it was a quality of natural law, and thereby an expression of *ius* (subjective and objective). *Ius gentium* had moral authority precisely because it was natural law in action. Through *ius*, natural law and *ius gentium* were joined, as such *ius gentium* was an expression of universal jurisprudence that was also the substance from which just civil laws (civil jurisprudence) extended.

As a professor at the University of Freiburg as well as city and imperial councillor, Zasius was charged with the task of training students who would play a significant role in the reform of the laws and administration of justice throughout Germany and he was called upon to effect legal reforms himself. Indeed, his most notable contribution to this process—informed by his reinterpretation of the relation between *ius* and *ius gentium*—was the creation of the Freiburg *Code*. As one of the earliest local civil codes within the Empire, it would serve as a model for many other sixteenth-century German cities and principalities engaged in rationalizing and transforming their laws from customary unwritten traditions into a written one through the process of creating codes that would not only reflect local customs but also customs in common across the Empire.[47]

41 Zasius, '1518 Preface' 2 and 'De iustitia et iure, lecture' cols 251–52 (n 11).

42 Zasius, 'In Laudem Legum Oratio' 112.

43 ibid 'De iustitia et iure, lecture' cols 252–55.

44 ibid '1518 Preface' 3 and 'De iustitia et iure, lecture' col 265.

45 Zasius, '1518 Preface' 2–3 and 'De iustitia et iure, lecture' cols 252–55; col 267.

46 Zasius, 'De iustitia et iure, lecture' col 250.

47 Zasius, *Neue Stadtrechte und Statuten der Stadt Freiburg im Breisgau* [1520] (Scientia Verlag 1968); HJ Knoche, *Ulrich Zasius und das Freiburger Stadtrecht von 1520* (Müller 1957); Rowan (n 6).

In the context of legal reforms, especially given the role his students would play in serving as advisers, creating civil codes, and administering them, the practical importance of joining universal and civil jurisprudence via *ius gentium* is clear: in the absence of a single legal structure or single 'national' law, understanding the origins and development of *ius gentium* could provide students with a criterion by which they could compare various laws with one another. Recognizing why 'The Law of Nations is Common Among All Mankind'[48] would enable them to understand what was at the base of—and what regulated—relations among, between, and within societies since the origins of mutual company itself and thus to bring the customs and laws of different communities within Germany into concord with one another. Understanding *ius gentium* would also enable students to observe how specific civil laws had diminished, violated, or demolished customary rights and obligations. Armed with a substantive understanding as to how *ius, ius gentium*, and natural law were related, conceptually and historically, students could bring various civil laws that missed the mark of justice back into agreement with it.

The moral authority of *ius gentium* was not, for Zasius, limited to embodying the universal rights and obligations of man, but extended also to the rights and obligations of communities.[49] As a result of the progress of life, communities were transformed naturally into civil societies. Although civil societies were governed by specific civil laws, the rights and obligations that extended from *primary* and *secondary ius gentium* transcended these civil laws, and indeed could hold them accountable. This was the case because all bodies of civil law, no matter what community created them, embodied aspects of *ius gentium*.[50] Further, for Zasius, not only were all men equal in relation to *ius gentium*, but so too all communities. In this respect, *ius gentium* was at the basis of *just* war between societies, in so far as it enabled one community to vindicate its rights and to protect its boundaries against another—and it was at the basis of the exercise of *just* force by individuals within civil society, in so far as it enabled man to protect himself, his family, and his property against threats by another.[51]

The protection and vindication of these rights and obligations was at the basis of just civil laws within civil society. Just laws balanced the rights and obligations of all through a civil rule of law that promoted the common good and justice. Those who administer civil laws, moreover, must have the authority to punish, but that authority must be limited by the law itself; civil authorities cannot be above the civil law, they too must be subject to just punishment when they violate it. In essence, those who administer and interpret the civil laws must be held accountable to the civil rule of law and by extension to a universal rule of law.

[48] Zasius, '*De Iustitia et Iure*, lecture' (n 11) col 258. [49] ibid cols 249–54.
[50] ibid col 254. [51] ibid cols 252–55.

But not all civil law and not all civil authorities are just. Over time the power of those who rule and punish has been augmented at the cost of the universal obligations and rights of those subject to their authority. Even if this authority was extended through civil laws, and thereby legally, it was still unjust. That the civil laws could be used in such a way as to legitimate unjust authority on behalf of rulers and lawyers—violating rights and obligations that stood at the basis of civil society itself—was precisely why *ius gentium* had greater moral authority than civil law for Zasius. Because not all civil laws were just, there had to be a higher law that could be appealed to when they missed the mark of justice as otherwise there would be no means to reform them, and thus no checks against the creation of unlimited power.

*Ius gentium* served this purpose for Zasius because it was the fourth quality of natural law and because of its relation to *ius* in terms of the art of good and equity conjoined, as a distinguishing characteristic of man, and because it embodied universal obligations such as promise keeping, fearing God, and obeying one's parents, as well as the universal rights to repel violent injuries to one's body, property, and fatherland in the face of immediate danger. Within civil society these universal rights and obligations enabled the pursuit of a common good, beyond civil society they enabled the pursuit of peace and security. Prior to, within, and between civil societies, *ius gentium* stood as an expression of a universal rule of law precisely because it was an expression of natural law, and thereby, justice.

In restoring the Roman tripartite, Budé and Zasius reinterpreted *ius gentium* in such a way that it could be used as a criterion to reform unjust civil laws, and in the process conjoined civil and universal jurisprudence. This was possible because each held that *ius gentium* was a form of natural law, the knowledge and practice of which distinguished man from animals. Further, they each held that *ius gentium* had moral authority on account of its relation to *ius*, as a distinguishing characteristic of man qua man and as universal criterion of justice. However, despite these fundamental departures from traditional scholastic and Roman jurisprudence both Budé and Zasius presented the relation between the different categories of law in terms of a hierarchy. Nevertheless, the source of the authority of each kind of law was not dependent on moral theology or the Great Chain of Being as with the scholastic jurists, or civil authority as with the Roman *corpus*, but rather it was dependent on *from* whence each type of law originated and *when* it originated—*ius gentium* was a higher form of law because it extended from *ius* and existed from the very origins of man qua man, and thus, from the origins of mutual company. *Ius gentium* was, in other words, an expression of universal jurisprudence and thus the universal rule of law.

## 7. The Moral Authority of *jus gentium* II: Alciati

Alciati not only departed from the Roman *corpus* and scholastic Doctors, but also from his fellow legal humanists. Caught in the context of instability and insecurity wrought by the Italian Wars, including the destruction of his own home in Milan, the call for legal reform and the centrality of *ius* and *ius gentium* was even more urgent for Alciati.[52] Under the patronage of conflicting rulers in and beyond Italy, most notably Francis I and the Dukes of Milan, it should be no surprise that Alciati did not place natural law, *ius gentium*, or civil law in a hierarchal order; that he did not reproduce contested hierarchies between superior and inferior rulers in his order of the laws, but instead tried to find an alternative to them.

Just as no one ruler was above another in the realm of *ius gentium*, no one category of law was above another, even as the laws differed in scope. As such, Alciati's order of the laws is best represented in terms of a series of concentric circles wherein all of the categories of law are on an equal plan. At the centre of the circle is man, who is called upon to follow all the laws, even when they are in conflict. Exploring questions of justice and right, Alciati moved from the most extensive category of law (natural law) to the least inclusive category (civil law). In each instance, however, the link between universal and civil jurisprudence remained intact via the centrality of *ius* as both a characteristic of man qua man and universal justice.

Natural law was the most extensive category of law, for Alciati, because it encompassed natural relations between individuals, such as marriage and friendship as well as artificial relations governed by civil laws between rulers and their subjects. The category of *ius gentium* was less extensive because while it encompassed relations between individuals that existed prior to civil society and relations between rulers vis-à-vis one another after the advent of civil society, it did not concern relations within discreet societies—unless civil laws attempted to restrain *ius*. As such, both natural law and *ius gentium* were far more extensive than the civil law, despite the fact that they departed from one another in terms of their scope. In this order of the law, *ius gentium* linked natural law and civil law to one another on the basis of its relation to *ius*, objective and subjective. Subjective *ius*, as encompassing the universal rights and obligations of all, stood at the basis of the moral authority of *ius gentium*, whereas objective *ius*, as the art of equity and good conjoined, stood at the basis of the moral authority of natural law. Universal and civil jurisprudence were—just as with Budé and Zasius—linked via *ius*. But for Alciati, more so than his humanist contemporaries, *ius* worked on two levels.

Within civil society, natural law on account of *ius* held civil law—the least inclusive category of law and potentially the least just—to a higher standard of justice. If civil law violated natural justice (objective *ius*) it needed to be reformed.[53] Moreover, it was morally justifiable for one to refuse to yield to an unjust civil law.[54] This was the case, as Alciati explained in his 1518 'Oration in Praise of the Law' delivered at Avignon,[55] because in nature all men were equal in force, whereas in civil society all men were equal before the law. As such, they must restrain their *ius* or right to meet force with force and agree to settle their disputes in courts, which in turn promotes the security of society as a whole and provides moral legitimacy to those who administer and

[52] A Grimaldi, *Grimaldi's Funeral Oration January 19, 1550, for Andrea Alciati* (H Green tr, A Brothers 1871); Viard (n 6); R Abbondanza, 'Jurisprudence: The Methodology of Andrea Alciato'; R Abbondanza, 'La Vie et les œuvres d'Andre Alciat' in *Pédagogues et juristes* (Vrin 1963)

[53] Alciati, 'De iustitia et iure, lecture'; 'Oratio Andreae Alciati, dum Bononiam'; 'Bona Fides' (n 12).

[54] Alciati, 'Bona Fides' in *De verborum significtione* (n 13) cols 305–08.

[55] Alciati, 'Oratio in laudem iuris civilis, principio studii cum Avenione profiteretur' (n 12) 507.

approve the laws in society. If a specific civil law is unjust, if it has the capacity to place one under the unlimited power of another, then the condition man lives in is not one of peace, but of uncertainty and insecurity.

Although man agreed to restrain his right to meet force with force in civil society, by placing his neck under the laws, it is significant that he did not alienate his *ius* altogether. Man restrained his right to use force in exchange for justice, thus if and when civil laws violate objective *ius* (justice), man still has recourse to subjective *ius* (force).[56] If civil law became arbitrary, if those who administered the laws attempted to diminish or demolish universal obligations and rights by splitting good from equity to advance their own interests or those of their patrons, then the entire artifice of civil society could come into question. Alciati did not argue, however, that it would be morally justifiable to violently resist an unjust law, but rather that if it conflicted with natural law or *ius gentium* it would be unjust to yield to it. Beyond civil society—on the level of dukes, princes, kings, and emperors—force, *not justice*, was the main criterion of analysis for Alciati.[57] This was the case because lacking a single positive or single authority that stood above them, there was no means of determining the justice of their actions vis-à-vis another.[58] Thus, the only means by which this question could be settled was through *ius gentium*, which included the right of war and the conditions of peace.

Disputes between rulers must be settled in accordance with *ius gentium*, because they have the right of war in accordance with *ius gentium* and thus stand in relation to one another as equals with no one above them.[59] Further, all wars are just according to Alciati, because all enemies are just. To engage another in war (defensive or offensive) was to recognize them as an enemy, and thereby recognize them as an equal. Those who were not equals were deemed as bands of brigands, robbers, and pirates. In conditions of peace, all rulers likewise stood as equals: none were subject to the power of one another. Only if one conquered or vanquished another completely would their equal status as just enemy change. Even in contracting peace, superior and inferior princes were equals in relation to *ius gentium*. Or, in the terms of another humanist jurist Jean Bodin (1530–92): a ruler or State that is not an equal to other rulers and States is not sovereign.[60]

The relation between rulers, in this respect, mirrored the condition man lived in before he entered civil society. Indeed, Alciati directly linked the right of man to defend himself and his property to the right of rulers to defend their possessions and their subjects in his discussion of the first title of the *Digest*: 'For wars are started in order to ward off injustice and protect ourselves and our property.'[61] Furthermore, in both cases *ius*—here in its narrowest meaning as the right to meet force with force—'originated from *ius gentium*. For such *ius* permitted anyone to ward off an injustice.'[62]

[56] Alciati, *Emblem* 13, '*One Ought Not Yield, Even under Torture*' in W Barker and J Chadwick (tr), *Alciato's Book of Emblems: The Memorial Web Edition in Latin and English* <http://www.mun.ca/alciato/index.html> (October 2015).

[57] Compare Alciati, 'De iustitia et iure, lecture' 1–4 and 'Oratio Andreae Alciati, dum Bononiam' 1053/54 with 'Oratio in laudem iuris civilis, principio studii cum Avenione profiteretur' 507 (n 12).

[58] Alciati, 'De iustitia et iure, lecture' (n 12) 5–10.

[59] ibid 6.

[60] J Bodin, *Six Books on the Commonwealth* (1572).

[61] Alciati, 'De iustitia et iure, lecture' (n 12) 2.

[62] ibid.

Yet, this image was not without significant distortions in so far as man was only morally justified in exercising force in matters of defence, whereas rulers were morally justified in exercising force offensively and defensively.[63] In the former case, civil courts made the determination as to whether or not an action was justified after the fact, in the latter case there were no formal mechanisms of arbitration, and hence actions could only be justified in accordance with *ius gentium*. Might did not make right in either case, only the rule of law—civil or universal—could determine whether the exercise of *ius* was just.

Yet, a crucial distinction remained in terms of the exercise of just force. Because man was persuaded to abandon his unsociable condition to pursue justice, he agreed to become equal under civil law and to settle disputes according to it to gain security. In restricting his rights, man took on the obligation to follow the civil law, to defend the fatherland, and to contribute to a common good. In exchange, rulers took on the obligation to administer justice among their subjects: to protect them from one another as well as from external threats. Kings, emperors, princes, free cities, or republics could not restrain their *ius* to meet force with force in order to submit to a political or legal world order that would place their subjects' persons and property in the power of another ruler. If they were to do so, they would stand in danger of becoming subject to the power and rule of another and thereby they would lose their status as equals before *ius gentium*.

For Alciati, only if rulers retained the right to meet force with force would it be possible for them to protect the rights, obligations, liberty, and property of their subjects against internal and external threats.[64] Without it, rulers or States could not ensure the security and the common good, and those who lived under their authority would have no stability. This right to meet force with force within civil society concerned punishing those who broke the civil laws, beyond civil society it concerned relations of war and peace with those who were beyond civil laws. Without just civil laws, there would be no gain for man to enter civil society; there would be no stability. Without limits placed on rulers (civil laws), as well as restraints (treaties and alliances) between rulers, there would be no security. Without just laws and just force, expressed in and by a universal rule of law, there could be no society—civil or international. Thus, for Alciati, the legitimacy of political and legal authority squarely depended upon the ability of civil laws and civil authorities to protect and secure *ius* by restricting power within society and the ability to exercise *ius* beyond it. Although *ius gentium* primarily concerned relations between rulers above civil society and natural law primarily concerned relations between individuals within civil society, this did not sever the fundamental connection between civil and universal jurisprudence. Nevertheless, the fact that *ius gentium* could not hold civil laws directly accountable to universal jurisprudence accounts for why Alciati does not quite fit with his humanists' contemporaries. At the same time, however, his discussion of *ius gentium* as realm of rights rather than obligations also distinguishes him from the likes of Gentili and Grotius.

[63] ibid 3. [64] ibid 4–6.

## 8. Conclusions

Alciati's jurisprudence as exemplified in his order of the laws went beyond Budé and Zasius's understanding of *ius gentium* because when it came to the relation between princes he seemed to be anticipating what will later develop into *ius inter gentes* and he might even have been on the cusp of putting forth a theory that would accommodate the more modern understanding of an international or world order. But he stopped short, in part perhaps because he had pushed the discussion to its limits, especially in terms of his own safety. Given the fact that his own fortunes and stability were so often threatened by the instability of the Italian Wars, and by the end of his life the early stages of the Reformation, it is rather astounding how far he advanced his theory in the early sixteenth century. In that respect, it should not be forgotten that Budé and Zasius likewise promoted their new interpretations of *ius gentium* in the middle of conflict and political and religious instability in France and the Holy Roman Empire.

What is even more remarkable, in the case of Zasius and Alciati in particular, was that they did so in the universities. That is, at the same time they were training students to become lawyers, jurists, and ministers they were also training students to recognize the limits of civil laws and civil authorities. At the same time as they were training their students how to codify and rationalize new laws, and change existing ones through reform, they were setting out a theory of jurisprudence that effectively argued that the moral authority of States was dependent on rulers and subjects fulfilling obligations to one another, first and foremost among them, to live in accordance with justice and right. In so doing they appealed to a universal rule of law, which entailed the recognition and preservation of universal obligations and universal rights among persons, between subjects and rulers, and among rulers vis-à-vis one another; a universal rule of law that could be used to hold specific civil laws and particular civil authorities accountable to a higher criterion of justice. In each case, their understanding of *ius gentium*—as the basis of civil and universal jurisprudence—held that there was (ideally) no situation in which 'might made right' within or beyond civil society. By reinterpreting the legal tradition that they inherited from their scholastic predecessors and contemporaries, Budé, Zasius, and Alciati, in their own ways, transformed *ius gentium* so thoroughly that it became the source of universal rights. Rights that rulers were morally obligated to secure, protect, and vindicate within their jurisdictions, as well as rights that rulers were morally obligated to respect vis-à-vis the subjects of another. In so doing they contributed to a juristic tradition that Vitoria would draw on when he later set out a series of rights that he asserted were common among all mankind, and thus were fundamentally related to *ius gentium*, in his discussion of the limits of Spanish political and legal authority vis-à-vis their own subjects as well as other nations.

# 3

# 'Cleare as Is the Summers Sunne'?*

## Scottish Perspectives on Legal Learning, Parliamentary Power, and the English Royal Succession

*Andrew RC Simpson*

### 1. Introduction

In sixteenth-century Europe, the laws of royal succession were frequently presented as inviolable and unalterable. Perhaps the most famous example was the French Salic law.[1] These rules supposedly constituted guarantees of political order and stability, which expressed elements of the legal frameworks according to which monarchs were expected to govern. Those who sought to circumvent them were sometimes fiercely resisted.

Nonetheless, monarchs occasionally attempted to alter the laws of royal succession.[2] Frequently those who were opposed to such changes argued that they were illegal, or—more subtly—that their application to disinherit particular individuals would be illegal. But, in order to make such arguments, they first had to establish that there was a framework of legal authority according to which one could judge, or at least authoritatively interpret, the offending enactment or statute. On some occasions, it was possible to do this simply by making reference to the existing law of the jurisdiction in question.[3] But where this was not the case, it was necessary to

* The quotation in the title is taken from *Henry V* Act I, Scene 1, line 233 (C Hinman (ed), *The Norton Facsimile. The First Folio of Shakespeare* (Norton 1968)). I am grateful to Professor John Ford and Dr Mátyás Bódig of the University of Aberdeen and to Eddie Simpson for their comments on earlier drafts of this chapter. The WM Tapp Studentship at Gonville and Caius College, Cambridge, and the Clark Foundation for Legal Education generously funded my doctoral research, on which this chapter draws. I am also grateful to Professor Peter Thanisch of the University of Tampere, Finland, for first suggesting to me that I might write a chapter on this topic as a contribution to this project. Any errors remain my own.

[1] See Q Skinner, *The Foundations of Modern Political Thought*, vol 2 (CUP 1978) 260–61, 293–97; FJ Baumgartner, *Radical Reactionaries: The Political Thought of the French Catholic League* (Libraire Droz 1975) 53–81; RE Giesey, 'The Juristic Basis of the Dynastic Right to the French Throne' (1961) 40(51) Transactions of the American Philosophical Society 3.

[2] Consider, for example, M Levine, *The Early Elizabethan Succession Question 1558–1568* (Stanford UP 1966) 11, 147–62.

[3] See Giesey (n 1) 17–22, 25–38.

look beyond that law for other sources of legal authority that might command some force in the dispute.

In attempting to identify authority relevant to such questions, many jurists drew upon their learning in Roman law and canon law as if it possessed some sort of general applicability. Joseph Canning's contribution to the present volume has already outlined why they might do this in other contexts, and it is helpful here to reiterate several of the points advanced in his chapter (see Chapter 1). In the medieval period, students of the *ius utrumque* developed the idea that there were 'generally applicable norms of law, the categories of natural law and the law of peoples (*ius gentium*)'. The general applicability of these laws was thought to arise from their status as 'legal norms derived from reason'.[4] As Canning also notes, a distinction could be drawn between the *ius gentium* that constituted the 'product of reason belonging to natural law', on the one hand, and the *ius gentium*, on the other, as the 'assembled customs of all peoples of the world . . . pertaining to positive law'.[5]

Canning's contribution also helpfully illustrates how many jurists attempted to identify the substantive content of what they believed to be the generally applicable standards of natural law and the *ius gentium*. Of course, these standards were not simply conflated with Roman law and canon law. Nonetheless, because Roman law and canon law were treated as authoritative expressions of reason, it followed that they were of great relevance to the attempt to identify natural law and the *ius gentium*, which were seen as 'legal norms derived from reason'.[6]

This last point could be further unpacked. Obviously, the intrinsic reason and legal 'truth' within the texts had to be discovered and interpreted. This task was entrusted to expert students of those texts—that is to say, to jurists. They disputed among themselves how best to interpret the learned laws. Over time, expert consensus would emerge concerning the meaning and scope of particular texts. Such consensus could, in turn, be trusted to reveal the extent to which the texts expressed intrinsic justice or reason. The binding force of law could be attributed to legal truth that had been discerned in this manner. Such truth could then, in turn, be used to interpret the scope and force of positive laws and statutes made by individual monarchs and polities—Bartolus employed such an approach.[7] Where individual statutes were inconsistent with legal 'truth', many jurists thought it was legitimate to construe them narrowly, sometimes to the point of depriving them of much potential effect.[8]

[4] See Chapter 1, p 63. [5] ibid. [6] ibid.

[7] On Bartolus's approach, see JA Clarence Smith, 'Bartolo on the Conflict of Laws' (1970) 14 American Journal of Legal History 157, 247, particularly at 163–74; P Stein, 'Bartolus, the Conflict of Laws and the Roman Law' in P Feuerstein and C Parry (eds), *Multum Non Multa. Festschrift für Kurt Lipstein Aus Anlass Seines 70. Geburtstages* (Muller 1980) 251; P Stein, 'Civil Law Reports and the Case of San Marino' in O Behrends, M Diesselhorst, and W Eckart Voss (eds), *Römisches Recht in der europäischen Tradition. Symposion aus Anlaß des 75. Geburtstages von Franz Wieacker* (R Gremer 1985) 323, at 331–32; P Stein, *Roman Law in European History* (CUP 1999) 71–4; JD Ford, *Law and Opinion in Scotland during the Seventeenth Century* (Hart 2007) 310–12.

[8] The formulation of this argument owes much to Ford (n 7); on learned authority, see 1–59, 181–246 in particular. Of course, Ford does not advance the claims made here about the royal succession in early-modern England. I have also attempted to outline the understanding of learned authority presented here in more detail in A RC Simpson, 'Legislation and Authority in Early-Modern Scotland' in Mark Godfrey

It will be argued below that Scottish lawyers relied upon similar assumptions in one early-modern dispute concerning the laws of royal succession to the throne of England.[9] Various Scots sought to defend the rights of their monarchs, first Mary, Queen of Scots, and then her son, James VI, to succeed to the English Crown on the death of Elizabeth I. In order to achieve this end, they had to overcome the claim that Henry VIII, Elizabeth's father, had lawfully exercised a statutory power to alter the succession so as to bar the Scottish claim.[10] As will be explained below, the Scots relied upon legal learning, including the learning of Roman law and canon law, and the English common law itself, to demonstrate how this statutory power ought to have been interpreted so as to be exercised justly, in accordance with legal truth, and what they termed 'natural law' and the '*ius gentium*'. They concluded, rather unsurprisingly, that such a just interpretation would have resulted in the preservation of the Scottish claim to the English throne.

In the process, these Scots lawyers consistently sought to persuade their English counterparts that bodies of authoritative legal learning beyond the English common law could and should be used to guide the just interpretation of English statutes. In so doing, they arguably drew on the idea that this authoritative learning could be trusted to reveal generally applicable norms of law comparable to those mentioned in Canning's contribution to the present volume. Yet Canning's caveats to his arguments concerning such norms must also be borne in mind here. Scots lawyers were not necessarily appealing to a fully articulate 'system' of higher norms. They were appealing to vaguer legal orders, and indeed to a method of discovering generally applicable legal truth, so as to demonstrate how the exercise of English statutory power should be interpreted and constrained.[11] Furthermore, the sources considered here do not seem to reveal any anticipation of the later *ius inter gentes*.[12] For example, there is not really any sense that the dispute was seen as one between the Scottish and English polities as such. Rather, the dispute concerned the principles to be used in guiding the correct interpretation of an English statutory power to alter the laws of royal succession. It will also be shown that the Scots lawyers considered here did not only seek to discern those principles through reliance on Roman law and canon law. They embraced a broader understanding of the 'learning' that could be used to facilitate the interpretation of statutes in a manner that would be consistent with legal truth. This chapter will consider the legal arguments advanced by two Scottish jurists in defence of the claim of Mary, Queen of Scots to be recognized as the heir to the English throne. The lawyers in question were Bishop John Leslie of Ross and David Chalmers of Ormond. The decision to focus on these writers arises from the fact that they were probably among the first in Scotland to advance in print a detailed series of legal arguments in favour of the right of the Scottish Queen to succeed Elizabeth I of England. Constraints of space do not make it possible

(ed), *Law and Authority in British Legal History 1200–1900* (CUP 2016) 85–119. See also A RC Simpson and A LM Wilson, *Scottish Legal History Volume One: 1000–1707* (EUP 2017) 103–218.

[9] Giesey (n 1) examines various ways in which the learned laws could influence such discussions in medieval and early-modern France.

[10] Levine (n 2) 147–62. [11] See Chapter 1, p 63–4. [12] ibid.

to consider how later Scottish jurists, such as Thomas Craig of Riccarton, developed their views.[13] Furthermore, the reconstruction of the thoughts of Leslie and Chalmers is necessarily preliminary, and requires further development in a lengthier treatment. Yet it is hoped that this chapter will provide a foundation for the future exploration of the questions raised here.

## 2. Leslie's *Defence*

A former professor of canon law at King's College, Aberdeen, Bishop John Leslie had sat in the College of Justice, the supreme Scottish court in civil matters, during the personal reign of Mary. He had also served as a member of the Privy Council.[14] In 1569 he published, anonymously, a short treatise defending the honour of Mary, Queen of Scots, and her right to succeed to the throne of England.[15] Hereafter this will be referred to as Leslie's *Defence*. Originally it was expressly written for an English audience.[16] An amended version of the treatise was completed in 1570, and published the following year.[17] While the work was published in the name of Morgan Philippes, a Catholic who had left England when Elizabeth became Queen, by October 1571 Leslie had acknowledged that he was the author.[18] A further English edition of the section of the *Defence* dealing with the succession was printed in 1584, and on this occasion Leslie put his name to the work.[19] Leslie's book was divided into three parts. The first defended Mary from accusations of adultery and involvement in the death of her husband;[20] the second examined her claim to the English throne;[21] and the third defended the lawfulness of rule by women in general. Only the second book will be considered in any detail here.

[13] On Craig's views here, see Thomas Craig, *The Right of Succession to the Kingdom of England* (London 1703).

[14] See Leslie's entry in the *Oxford Dictionary of National Biography* <http://www.oxforddnb.com> (15 January 2014): Rosalind K Marshall, 'Lesley [Leslie], John (1527–1596), Bishop of Ross, Historian, and Conspirator'.

[15] John Leslie, *A Defence of the Honour of the Righte Highe, Mightye and Noble Princesse Marie Quene of Scotlande* ... (1569). Contractions in quotations from this work have generally been expanded below.

[16] Consider Leslie (n 15) sig A2$^r$–A6$^r$.

[17] John Leslie, *Concerning the Defence of the Honour of the Right High, Mightie and Noble Princesse, Marie Quene of Scotland* ... (1571).

[18] Geoffrey C de Parmiter, 'Edmund Plowden as Advocate for Mary, Queen of Scots' (1979) 30 Innes Review 35, 41–42, 50–51.

[19] John Leslie, *A Treatise Towching the Right, Title and Interest of the Most Excellent Princesse Marie, Queene of Scotland* ... (1584). Two other editions (of 1580 and 1587) were also printed, one in Latin and the other in French (see Marie Axton, 'The Influence of Edmund Plowden's Succession Treatise' (1974) 37 Huntingdon Library Quarterly 209, 213 n 11).

[20] On this, see Gordon Donaldson, *Scotland James V—James VII* (1971) 107–31; on Leslie's first book, see also Andrew RC Simpson, 'Power, Reason and Equity: Two Juristic Accounts of Royal Authority in Sixteenth-Century Scotland' in Jørn Øyrehagen Sunde (ed), *Constitutionalism before 1789: Constitutional Arrangements from the High Middle Ages to the French Revolution* (Pax Forlag A/S 2014) 128, 137–44.

[21] There is some debate as to whether or not Leslie actually wrote the second section of the *Defence* that he published. For this debate, see Levine (n 2) 94–95; Axton (n 19) 210–11; Parmiter (n 18) 41–50; JH Baker, 'Browne, Sir Anthony (1509/10–1567), Judge' ODNB (n 14). Three manuscripts of the second section of the text are in existence; two are attributed to Sir Anthony Browne, and the third to

## 2.1 Legal learning and the just construction of statutory powers

As was noted above, Leslie's argument considered at length the question of how Henry VIII ought to have interpreted a statutory power granted to him by Parliament in 1536.[22] This allowed him to regulate the English royal succession by his last will and testament. The question of whether or not Henry VIII had actually exercised the right Parliament conferred upon him was open to debate. Nonetheless, it was believed by some that the Tudor king had executed a will altering the succession, and that in so doing he had disinherited the heirs of his older sister Margaret, and also, apparently, one of the daughters of his younger sister Mary. Among the disinherited descendants of Margaret Tudor were the Stuart monarchs of Scotland, including Mary, Queen of Scots. Of course, Mary herself was determined to pursue her claim to be recognized as the heir to the English throne.[23] Thus lawyers who supported her cause were faced with the task of demonstrating that the will—assuming it had indeed been executed by Henry—did not operate to bar her claim.

Leslie commenced his arguments by stating that even if Henry had validly executed the will in question, 'the iustice and ēquitie of [Mary's] cause, and the invincible force of trewthe' showed that even the king's will could not 'beare and beate yt downe'.[24] What exactly Leslie meant by justice, equity, and the 'invincible force

Sir Nicholas Bacon (Parmiter (n 18) 41). The second section of the 1571 edition of Leslie's *Defence* is attributed to 'Morgan Philippes, Bachelar of Diuinitie, [Leslie's pseudonym] assisted with the aduise of Antonie Broune Knight, one of the Iustices of the Common Place. An. 1567.' Levine and Axton have assumed that Sir Anthony Browne was the true author of the second section of the *Defence*, and that Leslie simply published the work. Against this view, Parmiter argues that Leslie's own claim that he wrote the treatise with Browne's help is the most plausible explanation for its composition. Parmiter notes that the evidence of the three manuscripts mentioned already is open to question; certainly, Sir Nicholas Bacon was not the author of the tract, as he was not in favour of Mary's right to succeed. Other treatises were wrongly attributed; Browne was credited with writing a treatise undoubtedly written by Edmund Plowden. This confusion probably resulted from Queen Elizabeth's treatment of those who dared to speculate on the succession; she sent one, John Hales, to the Tower, for his temerity in commenting on the matter. Parmiter also points out that Plowden's treatise was written in the winter of 1566–67, at which point in time he believed that he was the only common lawyer who had written in Mary's favour; furthermore, he and Browne worked closely together, and so Plowden would probably have been aware of any work written by his colleague. He did note that there was another work that lacked knowledge of English law, which cannot have been the treatise attributed to Browne. Axton suggested that Browne wrote the treatise after reading Plowden's work, but this theory too is problematic; Parmiter points out Browne would have had very little time to write in this scenario—he was dead five months after the completion of Plowden's treatise. For these points, see Parmiter (n 18). Interestingly, the author of the treatise attributed variously to Browne and Leslie also relied very heavily on argumentation from the learned laws, as will be shown shortly. As I have argued elsewhere, he did so in a manner that is perhaps more indicative of the work of a Scots lawyer trained in the learned laws rather than an English lawyer whose primary training was in the common law. See Andrew RC Simpson, 'Early Modern Studies of the Scottish Legal Past' (PhD thesis, Cambridge University 2011) 231–35. In any event, Leslie adopted a slightly edited version of the treatise as his own in 1584, indicating that he endorsed its conclusions (see Leslie (n 19)). Here the second section of the *Defence* will be treated as Leslie's own work, which he wrote with the assistance of Sir Anthony Browne—as Leslie himself claimed in 1571. Nonetheless, it is clear that further work should be done to establish the precise history of the treatise; the manuscript evidence may be of particular help in this regard.

22 Leslie (n 15) f 106$^{r}$–19$^{r}$; see also f 85$^{v}$–106$^{r}$; for the power, see 28 Hen 8 c 7 and 35 Hen 8 c 1, as found in *The Statutes of the Realm*, vol 3 (11 vols, London 1810–28) 655–62, 955–58.

23 See Levine (n 2) 5–12, 147–62, 210–11; Leslie (n 15) f 110$^{r}$–11$^{r}$.

24 Leslie (n 15) f 106$^{v}$.

of trewthe' here will be considered in more detail below. It might be thought that he was simply using strong rhetoric to defend his monarch's claim. But an alternative reading of his comments would place more emphasis on their literal meaning. This would imply that Leslie thought the standards of truth, equity, and justice had greater force in law in matters concerning the royal succession than the will attributed to Henry VIII, which had ostensibly been executed in accordance with a statutory power. The question of whether either reading of his comments is correct will be examined further below.

Immediately after making these points, Leslie made it clear that his attention was limited to the proper interpretation of the power granted by Parliament; he expressly refused to comment on whether or not Parliament actually had the right to regulate the succession.[25] Rather, he began by asking whether or not the words of the statute had given Henry VIII a general and arbitrary power to dispose of the English Crown in whatever manner he pleased.[26] Leslie pointed out that the 'generaletie of the wordes' of the statute permitted the kingdom to be 'set ouer to a furious, or a made man, or to an ideot, or to some forraine, and Machometicall Prince'.[27] However, he argued that

> the good mynde and purpose of the parliamente, and mans reason do in no wise beare yt. Yf ye graunte that theis wordes muste nedes haue some good and honeste construction and interpretation (as reason doth force you to graũnte it).[28]

Thus, Leslie argued that the words of the statute had to be interpreted in light of the intention of Parliament, and with some 'honeste construction', as was dictated by reason. Otherwise, the words of the statute would be general enough to permit Henry VIII to pass the Crown to a mad man—which Leslie thought was clearly an absurd interpretation. Yet this raised an obvious question. Were there any legal standards according to which one could interpret the statute attributed to Henry VIII, so as to confer upon it a rational and honest construction?

Leslie went some way towards answering this question in the arguments that followed. First, he explained what he thought the aims of the legislature must have been in promulgating the statute. These had been to avoid all 'ambiguities, dowbtes, and diuisions towchinge the succession'. Parliament had trusted Henry to 'mynde the wealthe of the realme' and to 'moste prudentlie consider and weighe the matter of the succession, and prouide for the same accordinglye'.[29] Consequently, if Henry's will had not 'plainlye and euidentlye' tended to this 'ende and scope', and

> yf a zelous mynde to the common welthe, yf prudence and wisdom did not rule and measure all theys doings: but … yf this arbitremente puttethe not awaye all contentions and striffes … yf this be not a testamente and laste will, suche as Modestinus definethe: *testamentum est iusta voluntatis nostrae sententia, de eo quod quis post mortem suam fieri velit*. Then thowghe the kinges hande were put to yt, the matter goeth not altogether so well and so smothe.[30]

[25] ibid f 106$^{v}$. [26] ibid f 106$^{v}$–07$^{r}$. [27] ibid f 107$^{r}$–07$^{v}$. [28] ibid f 107$^{v}$.
[29] ibid f 108$^{r}$. [30] ibid f 108$^{r}$–08$^{v}$.

Thus, if it was obvious that Henry's will had not been written with the concerns listed in mind, then lawyers could question the extent to which it constituted a competent expression of the statutory power granted to him to alter the succession. Furthermore, Leslie argued that if the will did not conform to the definition of a 'testamente and laste will' outlined by Modestinus in the *Digest* of Roman law,[31] then whether or not it was a will for the purposes of the statutory power conferred upon Henry could be questioned. This was the first instance of his use of the learned laws to interpret the scope of Henry's authority to regulate the succession to the English throne. In so doing, Leslie appealed to a tradition of legal ideas that was not specific or particular to the English jurisdiction. He clearly thought that those ideas were of use in giving a statute an honest construction, as was required by reason. But how exactly he conceptualized the authority of that tradition of ideas in an English context is not yet clear.

In the arguments that followed, Leslie continued by outlining various standards according to which the validity of the will attributed to Henry VIII might be judged. He noted that the will altered the order of succession laid down by the natural law, the *ius gentium*, and the English common law. Aside from making brief references to the injury the kings of England would feel if disinherited from the royal lines of succession in other nations, he essentially elaborated on this point by stating that the will constituted an 'vnnaturall acte'. The lack of detail provided perhaps makes it dangerous to make too much here of his reliance on the *ius gentium* and natural law.[32] But shortly afterwards he returned to explore the question of the proper construction of the statutory power granted to Henry by Parliament. In order to commence the next stage in his argument, he began by introducing some further information concerning the effects of the will attributed to Henry. This had apparently not only disinherited the heirs of his older sister Margaret Tudor, but also the Lady Frances, the daughter of Henry's younger sister Mary. Leslie pointed out that even if Englishmen could find some reason for excluding Mary of Scotland from the succession because of her foreign birth, they surely could not accept that Lady Frances's disinheritance was just.[33] Pointing to this apparent irrationality in the will, Leslie commented

> yt ys to be considered, whether yt standethe with reason and iustice, with the honour of the kinge, and the whole realme, or with the mynde, purpose, and intente of the said parliamente, that the kinge shoulde not onlie frustrate and exclude suche, whose right by the common lawe ys moste evidente and notorious, but call and substitute suche other, as by the same lawe are plainelie excluded.[34]

Here Leslie seems to have drawn attention to 'reason and iustice' as valid standards according to which one might interpret the scope of the statutory power conferred upon Henry VIII. This resembled his earlier claim that the rights of Mary, Queen of

[31] The reference is to *Digest* 28.1.1; I have used T Mommsen, P Kruger, and A Watson (eds), *The Digest of Justinian* (University of Pennsylvania Press 1985) 4 vols.

[32] Leslie (n 15) f 109$^{r}$–09$^{v}$ (the pagination in the original is misprinted as '107').

[33] ibid f 110$^{r}$–11$^{r}$.

[34] ibid f 111$^{r}$–11$^{v}$.

Scots, were consistent with equity, justice, and the 'invincible force of trewthe', and this called into question the legal force of the will.

Yet Leslie still had to make apparent exactly what he meant by the standards of reason, equity, and justice. The last quotation made above seems to imply that he thought the 'common lawe'—which he had earlier referred to as the *English* common law—revealed standards that were consistent with justice and equity, when compared with the provisions of the will.[35] This will be considered in more detail below. Nonetheless, when trying to establish whether or not it was consistent 'with reason and iustice' that Henry VIII should have exercised his power to 'frustrate and exclude' Lady Frances, and Mary, Queen of Scots, Leslie also encouraged his readers to consider 'manie notable rules of the cyuill lawe'.[36] This reveals that he thought that the relevant standards of reason according to which Henry VIII ought to have interpreted his statutory power could be discerned through the study of Roman law. In other words, here Leslie was evidently treating Roman law as a body of learning concerning justice. While this learning was not specific or particular to the English jurisdiction, it could nonetheless be used to interpret English statute so as to construe it in light of equity. Leslie had already begun to rely on this approach when he argued that Modestinus's definition of a testament could be used to determine whether or not the purported will of Henry VIII was truly the sort of 'will' Parliament had empowered the king to make.

The specific rules of the 'cyuill lawe' that Leslie cited to interpret the power conferred upon Henry VIII all tended to support the view that the English monarch would have exceeded his authority had he executed the will that disinherited the Lady Frances. First, Leslie argued that a grant of general authority—like that given to Henry to regulate the succession—permitted the grantee to do no more than the granter would have been permitted had he been 'speciallie asked and required'.[37] Leslie cited an opinion from Marcellus and two opinions from Ulpian to this effect.[38] For example, Ulpian had said that a debtor's grant of a general real security over present and future assets would not be presumed to have covered 'household equipment, clothing' and slaves whose services were essential to the debtor. A reasonable debtor could be presumed to have excluded such things from the security. So, a general grant, such as a general grant of authority, had to be read and interpreted in light of what was reasonable.[39] Second, Leslie argued that 'generall wordes … of the testatours' had to be 'restrained and referred to hable, mete, and capable persons onlie'.[40] He referred to an opinion of the jurist Modestinus, who had held that the Roman *cursus honorum* could be altered, allowing people to advance to higher social rank more quickly than would normally have been permitted.[41] Nonetheless, this

[35] See ibid f 109$^{r}$ (wrongly numbered in the original as f 107). That Leslie meant here the English common law, and not the *ius commune*, is also evident from the fact that elsewhere in his book he used the term 'civil law' to refer to *ius commune* learning, and 'common law' to refer to English law. To name a few examples, see ibid 31$^{r}$–31$^{v}$; 75$^{r}$–111$^{v}$ (civil law); 56$^{v}$–57$^{r}$, 75$^{v}$ (common law).

[36] ibid f 111$^{v}$. [37] ibid. [38] *Digest* (n 31) 42.8.12; 39.5.7; 20.1.6.

[39] ibid 20.1.6. [40] Leslie (n 15) f 111$^{v}$.

[41] *Digest* (n 31) 50.4.11.pr-1; cf Peter Garnsey, *Social Status and Legal Privilege in the Roman Empire* (Clarendon Press 1970) 254 n 2.

was only permissible in favour of 'suitable' people. Clearly Leslie's claim was that Henry VIII—assuming he had made the disputed will—had not taken into account who was in fact 'hable, mete, and capable' to wear the Crown of England. Thus, his actions, in breaking the normal order of royal succession, were as irrational as an arbitrary breach of the *cursus honorum* would have been in ancient Rome.

So far, Leslie had claimed that any power granted by Parliament in statute had to be interpreted and exercised in accordance with the standards of reason revealed in legal learning. He had specifically referred to the learning of Roman law, which was not particular to the English jurisdiction. But he had also indicated that the learning of the English common law had a role to perform here too. Furthermore, he had appealed to the standards of the *ius gentium* and natural law, albeit that he did not flesh out his comments in that regard in much detail. What he had not done was to explain what would happen when statutory powers were *not* interpreted and exercised according to the standards he outlined. His views in this regard became apparent during the course of his next argument, which was also drawn—ultimately—from Roman law.

## 2.2 The consequence of exceeding justly construed statutory powers

Leslie commenced the next stage of his argument essentially by summarizing the points made above. He explained that 'statutes must be ruled measured and interpreted accordinge to the minde and direction of the generall and common lawe'.[42] Here he was actually alluding to a maxim familiar to both English civilians and common lawyers.[43] This was *statutum contra ius commune stricte interpretandum est*. Of course, in civilian hands, this simply represented the basic Bartolist position, outlined in the introduction to this chapter. Bartolus had claimed that the learned laws (the '*ius commune*' referred to in the maxim just quoted) expressed the standard of learning according to which the equity and reason of the laws in each jurisdiction were to be judged. If these local laws were found wanting according to this standard, they could legitimately be construed narrowly and applied to as few cases as possible.[44] But in the hands of English common lawyers, the maxim had long been handled rather differently. For them, the relevant standard of reason and justice was expressed in the English common law. Their reading of the maxim just cited indicated that statutes which departed from *that* standard were to be interpreted strictly.[45] On the other hand, as Baker puts it, statutes 'which "enlarged" the common law … were to be taken broadly, by the equity'.[46] Sometimes common lawyers were even prepared to argue that Parliament could not have willed anything irrational, with the relevant standard of rationality being that found in the English common law. As a result, judges were occasionally prepared to interpret a statute 'contrary to the text to make it agree with reason'.[47]

42 Leslie (n 15) f 111$^{v}$.

43 Richard Helmholz, *Roman Canon Law in Reformation England* (CUP 1990) 167–68.

44 See also text accompanying (n 7).

45 Helmholz (n 40) 167–68.

46 John H Baker, *The Oxford History of the Laws of England*, vol 6 (OUP 2003) 77–78.

47 See Baker (n 46) 80–81; the text in quotation marks is found at 81 n 194, and is quoted by Baker from *Fulmerston v Steward* (1554), found in *Les Comentaires, ou Reports de Edmund Plowden* (1613), 102 at 109$^{v}$.

Elsewhere in his *Defence* Leslie used the term 'common law' to refer to the English common law,[48] and there seems little reason to doubt here that he meant to appeal to that standard here too. Nonetheless, he had also made clear his belief that the learning of the 'cyuill lawe' should also be used to interpret English statutory powers in light of reason and legal truth. That might well have made some of his readers think he was alluding to the more Bartolist approach. The possibility that Leslie would in fact have been content with either of these two readings of his arguments will be considered further below.

All this still does not address the question of what Leslie believed would happen when statute conferred a power that was used in a manner that was inconsistent with the learned standards he mentioned. He addressed this question in the following passage:

> in testamentes, contractes, and namelie in statutes, the generalitie of wordes muste be gentilie and cyvilie moderated and mesured by the common lawe, and restrained, when so euer any man shoulde by that generalitie take any dōmage and hurte vndeservinglie. Yea the Statute shall rather in that case cease and quaile, and be taken as voyde. As for example yt appeareth by the ciuill lawe, that yf yt be enacted by Statute in some cities, that no man shall pleade againste an instrument, no not the executors: Yet this not withstandinge, yf the executour make a trewe and perfecte inuentorie of the goodes of the testatour, yf he deale feaithfullie and trewlie, rather then he shoulde wrongfullye and with oute cause paye the testatours debte of his owne, he maye come and pleade againste the instrumente.[49]

In support of his argument, Leslie cited the *De Verborum Significatione* written by the great humanist scholar Andrea Alciato.[50] In that work, Alciato showed that while he opposed the methods of study promoted by Bartolus when seeking the true historical meaning of the texts of Roman law,[51] he endorsed the use of those methods in court. He began by stating his general view that 'statutes ought not to be counteracted by the *ius commune*'. But then he pointed out that

> if someone is unjustly laid open to loss due to the generality of the statute [*ex generalitate statuti*], I was always [in the habit of] making a restriction to the *ius commune* [*semper restrictionem ad ius commune faciebam*].[52]

Consequently, if it were thought that a party would suffer loss through the general or broad reading of a statute that was inconsistent with the equitable and rational *ius commune*—here meaning the learned laws—then the matter would simply be judged according to the provisions of the *ius commune*. Put another way, the statute would be construed narrowly so that it did not affect the outcome of the dispute. It was thought this would prevent injustice. Alciato then gave an example of this practice, making reference to Justinian's *Code*.[53] He noted that the Italian States

[48] See (n 35) and the accompanying text.

[49] Leslie (n 15) f 112$^r$.

[50] Andrea Alciato, *De Verborum Significatione Libri IIII* (1572) 27.

[51] For Alciato's views in this regard, see Stein, *Roman Law in European History* (n 7) 76–77.

[52] Alciato (n 50) 27. I am grateful to Alison Simpson for discussing this translation with me.

[53] *Code* 6.30.22.9; reference can be made to the version of the *Code* available at < http://droitromain.upmf-grenoble.fr> (15 January 2014).

had prohibited anyone from relying upon any defence to plead against certain legal instruments. However, this could seriously undermine the position of an heir. Under ancient Roman law, an heir was potentially liable for the debts of the deceased, regardless of whether or not the deceased's estate was large enough to cover them. Justinian amended this law to allow the heir to escape such potentially ruinous liability by permitting him to make an inventory of the deceased's estate within a certain period after his death. If the heir did this, he would only be liable for the deceased's debts up to the value of the inventoried goods. Thus, the position in the learned laws was that an heir could rely on such an inventory as a defence to claims made against him personally by creditors of the deceased.[54] However, as Alciato pointed out, if the creditors were in one of the Italian city States, and they relied upon one of the privileged instruments against which no one could raise a defence, then the heir would lose the protection given him by Justinian's law. He might become personally liable for huge debts, due to a statutory departure from the apparently just and rational position in the learned laws. Consequently, Alciato commented

> Wherefore, let there be this interpretation, that a law of this kind [ie the statute found in some Italian city States] should rather be invalidated, than any injustice be tolerated. For it must be generally acknowledged that every arrangement in the laws, rescripts, testaments and contracts is abridged, in case any injustice is introduced.[55]

Leslie clearly paraphrased Alciato closely. To some extent, he endorsed his central argument. This was that where a judge saw that a statute departed from the standards of equity and reason found in the learned laws, and where he saw that this would cause loss to a party before him, then the judge was permitted to 'interpret' the statute so as to deprive it of effect in that case. But Leslie did not follow Alciato slavishly. For Alciato, the crucial standard of learning was found in the *ius commune*. But, as has been explained, here Leslie drew attention to the English common law. He claimed that the 'generalitie of wordes' in statutes had to be 'gentilie and cyvilie moderated and mesured by the *common lawe*, and restrained, when so euer any man shoulde by that generalitie take any dōmage and hurte vndeservinglie' [emphasis added].[56] Leslie treated both the English common law and the learned laws as repositories of legal learning that could be used in the authoritative interpretation of English statutes. Both could be used when seeking to identify the standards of 'reason' and 'equity' according to which statutes could legitimately be interpreted.

Leslie's point was that statutory powers had to be interpreted and exercised in conformity with the legal learning he had identified. This revealed what would happen if anyone attempted to rely on the 'generalitie' of statutory words in order to exercise a power that was inconsistent with such learning. In that case, the statute would, as Leslie put it, 'cease and quaile, and be taken as voyde'. That did not mean that in all cases the statute would 'quaile'. Rather, any attempt to use its powers in

[54] See WW Buckland, *A Text-Book of Roman Law from Augustus to Justinian* (3rd edn, rev Peter Stein, CUP 1963) 304–19, particularly at 316–17.

[55] Alciato (n 50) 27.

[56] Leslie (n 15) f 112$^r$.

an unjust manner would be 'voyde', as it would be assumed that Parliament had not intended statutory authority to be used in such an arbitrary and irrational manner.[57]

Leslie concluded with the claim that if Henry VIII had indeed exercised his powers by writing the will that excluded the heirs of his sister Margaret and Lady Frances from the line of royal succession, then the will would be invalid. This exercise of statutory power was irrational and 'vnnaturall', when judged according to the legal learning of the English common law and the learned laws. Therefore, if he had written the disputed will, it followed that Henry had clearly exceeded the statutory powers granted him by Parliament to regulate the succession. This was because it could be assumed that Parliament would have wanted him to exercise those powers in a manner consistent with justice and reason.[58]

## 2.3 Conclusion

Thus, Leslie believed that legal learning that was neither specific nor particular to the English jurisdiction could be relied upon to reveal the standards according to which one could judge the justice of an interpretation of a power granted by an English statute. Leslie also considered what would happen where an individual who was granted a statutory power interpreted and used it in a manner that was subsequently found to be unjust and irrational, according to these standards of legal learning. In that case, the attempt to use the power would have no legal force or effect.

This is evidently what Leslie meant when he said that the claim of Mary, Queen of Scots was equitable, and could not be defeated, because it rested upon the 'invincible force of trewthe'. The justice or legal truth that Leslie identified through his legal learning revealed how Henry VIII ought to have exercised the power to regulate the succession. The will attributed to him exceeded his authority thus defined, and consequently did not operate to bar Queen Mary's claim to the English throne. It should be noted that Leslie evidently hoped to persuade his English counterparts that his arguments were correct. His own opinion in this regard would obviously not have possessed any real authority in England. But he may well have believed—as did at least some of his near-contemporaries in Scotland—that where the legal experts within a particular jurisdiction reached consensus that a particular legal proposition expressed legal truth and justice, then that proposition acquired the binding force of law. Hence Leslie may have believed that if his English counterparts recognized the accuracy of his views, then they might thereafter have gained force in England.[59]

[57] ibid f 112$^r$. [58] ibid f 112$^r$–12$^v$.

[59] On the role of expert consensus in shaping near-contemporary Scots law, see the discussion in Ford (n 7) 1–59, 181–246; see also Simpson (n 8) for a study of this topic in the context of mid-sixteenth-century Scots law. Again, Ford does not comment here on Leslie's work or the question of the succession to the English throne in the terms discussed here. As regards the question of whether or not English lawyers would have found Leslie's argument persuasive, it may be worth noting that English common lawyers who wrote during the early seventeenth century were prepared to rely upon Roman law in order to analyse the scope of various royal powers. For this, see RH Helmholz, 'Continental Law and Common Law: Historical Strangers or Companions?' (1990) Duke Law Journal 1207, 1216. It is my intention to test the thesis presented here by exploring, in another publication, the attitudes to the question of the succession that were held by those English lawyers with whom Leslie was evidently

Taken together, these points support the line of argument outlined in the introduction. Leslie believed that there existed bodies of learning concerning binding legal truth that were not particular to the English jurisdiction, or any other jurisdiction. These possessed general applicability and probable authority in interpretation of the rules of many, if not all, such legal systems. Consequently, he thought that English legal experts could use such learning to interpret the scope of statutory powers, and so constrain their exercise in practice.

Thus, in some ways, Leslie's approach to the relationship between legal learning and statutory interpretation closely resembled that of Bartolus. Nonetheless, as has also been seen, he treated the English common law as a body of learning that could disclose the standards required to interpret specific rules in light of justice and truth. It might be argued that he did this simply to please his English readers, and that in reality Leslie was simply writing as a Bartolist. And yet this is unlikely, because elsewhere Leslie expressed the view that one could find a rich source of legal learning in another tradition of legal thought that was, unlike the learned laws, particular to a specific jurisdiction. This was, perhaps unsurprisingly, Scots law. Constraints of space make it impossible to go into this point in detail, but in 1578 Leslie described Scots law as rooted in the ancient *Leges Kenethi Regis*, which expressed 'the entire universal law', and which was to the Scots 'an image of the Twelve Tables' of Roman law.[60] He claimed that Scots law had been produced through reliance upon the wisdom of the Scottish nobility and clergy.[61] And yet, at the same time, Leslie accepted that both the local Scottish tradition of learning and the learning of the learned laws had considerable authority in the augmentation of Scots law. In a famous passage, he commented that 'if a case reveals that is entangled by many controversies (as often happens) which cannot be resolved by our native laws, immediately whatsoever is deemed to be necessary for the purpose of settling this controversy, is brought forth from the civil laws of the Romans'.[62] In other words, Roman law was not only authoritative where no local materials were available. Rather, it was authoritative where the local learning could not adequately address the problem in itself.

Leslie's approach to the relationship between the learning of Scots law and that of the learned laws seems to resemble his attitude to the same relationship between those laws and the English common law. In both a Scottish and an English context, Leslie expected lawyers to rely on their own local learning, and also on more eclectic and generally applicable learning that was not necessarily specific to their own jurisdictions, so as to resolve cases that were 'entangled by many controversies' in light of justice and equity. He encouraged English lawyers to recognize that the legal learning of the learned laws could illumine the position at common law, in order to

engaging in argument. This is of course necessary to render the general line of argument presented here convincing. I am grateful to Professor Ford for discussing this point with me.

[60] John Leslie, *De Origine, Moribus & Rebus gestis Scotorum Libri Decem* . . . (Rome 1578) 71. I have also made reference to EG Cody (ed), *Leslie's Historie of Scotland* (Blackwood 1888) Scottish Text Society Series One vols 5, 14, 19, 34. See also Simpson and Wilson (n 8) 182–84.

[61] Leslie (n 60) 62–70, 73–75.

[62] ibid 71; I am grateful to Professor Ford for discussing the translation of this passage with me.

reveal the true extent of a statutory power. Such legal learning revealed the 'invincible force of trewthe' which the king could not overcome in the exercise of a statutory power. Once the English recognized this—and this was clearly also important—Leslie presumably thought that they would be legally bound by the 'trewthe' to recognize Mary, Queen of Scots, as the next in line to their throne.

Thus Leslie at least believed that generally applicable norms, akin to those described by Canning (Chapter 1 in this volume), could in principle be derived from the study of the learned laws. By using such norms in the interpretation of statute, legal experts might legitimately seek to constrain the exercise of power within their individual jurisdictions.

## 3. Chalmers's *Discours*

David Chalmers of Ormond adopted a different approach to the question of how one could respond to the impediment to Queen Mary's succession that arose from the will attributed to Henry VIII. Like Leslie, Chalmers had served as a judge in the College of Justice during Mary's personal reign. He went into exile sometime after Mary's downfall in 1568, and spent the next fourteen years on the continent, engaged in the twin pursuits of espionage and scholarship. As Goodare notes, he spied for so many major European powers that it is no longer clear which of them it was that he was double-crossing.[63]

In 1579, Chalmers used three Parisian publishing houses[64] to print a volume containing three scholarly tracts. One was his *Histoire Abregee*, which contained brief accounts of the lives and deeds of all the emperors and popes, and of all the monarchs who (it was believed) had reigned in France, England, and Scotland.[65] The second, his *Discours*, constituted a defence of the rights of women to inherit both the goods of their parents, and also the rule of kingdoms.[66] In this treatise, as will be considered shortly, he examined the validity of Henry VIII's will. The third tract, Chalmers's *Recerche*, explored the institutions and structure of the Scottish commonweal. In dedicating the *Recerche* to Mary, Queen of Scots, Chalmers presented all three tracts as works of political counsel.[67] Why did he associate the study of history with the

[63] Julian Goodare, 'Chalmers [Chambers], David, of Ormond (*c*1533–1592), Historian and Judge' ODNB (n 14).

[64] I have consulted the following volumes: Cambridge University Library (CUL) Shelfmark R*.14.18.F; Aberdeen University Library (AUL) Shelfmarks pi9(4) Cha 1 and pi9(4) Cha 2. The CUL volume was printed by Michel Gadoulleau, the first AUL volume was printed by Jean Feurier and the second AUL volume was printed by Robert Coulombel. For the purposes of this chapter, the Feurier edition has been used; no substantial differences have been noted between the three volumes. I discuss these matters and Chalmers's French works more generally in Andrew RC Simpson, 'Counsel and the Crown: History, Law and Politics in the Thought of David Chalmers of Ormond' (2015) 36 Journal of Legal History 3.

[65] David Chalmers, *Histoire Abregee* (Paris 1579).

[66] David Chalmers, *Discours de la legitime succession des femmes aux possessions de leurs parens: & du gouuernement des princesses aux Empires & Royaumes* (Paris 1579).

[67] David Chalmers, *La Recerche des Singularitez Plus Remarquables, concernant l'estat d'Escosse* (Paris 1579) Sig A2$^r$–A3$^r$.

provision of sound political advice? It is helpful to answer this question before considering his arguments concerning Henry VIII's last testament. This is because in that context too he drew upon his assumptions about historical learning in order to articulate standards that could be used to judge the legal validity of the will.[68]

## 3.1 The foundations of Chalmers's juristic thought

The key to understanding the link Chalmers drew between historical learning and good political counsel lies in some general assumptions that he held, together with many other thinkers of the time. In a passage paraphrased from Jean Bodin's *Six Livres*,[69] which was in turn ultimately dependent on Aristotelian beliefs,[70] Chalmers made clear his belief that the purpose of a commonweal was to facilitate human happiness. The 'happiness' in question lay in the contemplation of matters human, natural, and divine.[71] Put another way, it lay in exploring the universal order of causes and effects of earthly and heavenly things. Through such contemplation, man would ultimately be led to God, who was the final cause of all creation. This universal order of causes and effects infused the whole of creation with its *telos* or goal of seeking out the divine. Any human action or political policy that was inconsistent with that order would lead to ruin; such actions and policies were, for Chalmers, 'sinful'. On the contrary, any policy that was consistent with that order would lead to success.

Drawing on these beliefs, Chalmers explained how the study of history could reveal which political policies and human laws conformed to the divine order that he mentioned. Since he believed that that order infused all of creation, he could also rationally believe that history tried and tested human actions and ordinances against the natural order. This revealed the extent to which such policies and statutes enabled men to live in societies that were politically successful—meaning societies that provided them with the securities and necessities of life that then freed them to cultivate contemplative virtue. The chronicles and texts that recorded this historical trial and testing were fallible, but by adopting sound historical method one could discern the true record of the past. It seems that he believed that this, in turn, would show men the path to happiness.[72]

[68] For a more detailed account of the arguments outlined here, see Simpson (n 64). I am grateful to Dr David Porter for his advice concerning the correct translation of Chalmers's French works. Any errors remain my own.

[69] Chalmers (n 67) sig A4ʳ–A4ᵛ, paraphrasing Jean Bodin, *Six Livres de la Republique* (Paris 1577) 5. I am grateful to Dr Porter for first pointing out to me Chalmers's close dependence on Bodin's work here.

[70] Earlier in his argument, at Bodin (n 69) 3–4, Bodin cited Bk VII Chs 3 and 15 of Aristotle's *Politics*. Aristotle's reasons for coming to this conclusion are helpfully summarized in Jill Kraye, 'Moral Philosophy' in Charles B Schmitt and Quentin Skinner (eds), *The Cambridge History of Renaissance Philosophy* (CUP 1988) 303, 334–35.

[71] For the political and the contemplative virtues, and for the range of medieval and renaissance views on the relative merits of devoting human life to these ends, see Kraye (n 70) at 330–39; Richard Tuck, 'Humanism and Political Thought' in Anthony Goodman and Angus MacKay (eds), *The Impact of Humanism on Western Europe* (Longman 1990) 43–65.

[72] Chalmers (n 67) sig A3ᵛ–A4ᵛ.

## 3.2 Historical learning and legal truth

Chalmers showed how this eclectic learning of universal history could be applied to address an important political question of the day. Was rule of a commonwealth by a woman consistent with divine law and natural law? John Knox had famously argued that, in general, it was not.[73] In his *Discours*, Chalmers sought to refute such arguments, and this helped to underpin his own defence of Queen Mary's right to succeed Elizabeth I, regardless of Henry VIII's will.

Chalmers rigorously applied his historical learning to show that women throughout history had governed successfully, with great political virtue. He advanced these arguments based on the *ius naturale*, the *ius gentium*, and the divine positive law, and also based on human positive laws.[74] Chalmers endorsed commonplace definitions of these different types of law; for example, he described the *ius gentium* as that which natural reason had established, and which all nations universally observed.[75] Yet in identifying the content of those laws concerning who had the capacity to govern in each case, Chalmers relied heavily on historical learning. So, his title concerning human positive law was in reality a list of those women who, since antiquity, had ruled commonwealths successfully[76]—presumably meaning that they had maintained the political peace and stability required to facilitate the pursuit of contemplative virtue. In Chalmers's thinking, this demonstrated the conformity of female rule with the great divine order that infused the universe. He repeated this pattern of argument elsewhere.[77]

Thus, Chalmers drew upon historical learning in order to draw an important legal conclusion. This was that a woman had the lawful right to rule a kingdom, if she were called to the succession thereof by right of inheritance.[78] Like Leslie, Chalmers seemed to move seamlessly from the recognition of legal 'truth' to making claims about which precepts could enjoy the binding force of law. In his juristic arguments, Leslie drew primarily on the learning of the learned laws, while Chalmers drew heavily on the legal learning revealed by the eclectic study of universal history. Yet both men seem to have associated the identification of binding law with some prior recognition of legal truth.

That Chalmers was relying on learned authority to identify precepts that possessed the force of law at this juncture can be further illustrated by examining an important passage found towards the end of his *Discours*, where he examined the validity of the will of Henry VIII.[79] Here Chalmers claimed that he was essentially following Leslie's arguments,[80] but in fact he made a few important modifications to the Bishop's claims. Like Leslie, he considered the possibility that the document had in fact been properly executed, and expressed the will of the king, acting on the

[73] John Knox, *The First Blast of the Trumpet against the Monstrous Regiment of Women* (Geneva 1558).

[74] Chalmers (n 66) f 3$^{v}$–4$^{v}$.

[75] ibid f 3$^{v}$–4$^{r}$.

[76] ibid f 22$^{v}$–27$^{v}$.

[77] ibid generally; see in particular f 16$^{v}$–20$^{v}$.

[78] Obviously, this had consequences for the French Salic law, which Chalmers described as an 'ancient custom'. Its political value had been undermined by historical trial and testing, in his eyes—see Chalmers (n 62) f 24$^{v}$–27$^{v}$. Note that Jordan presents an intriguing analysis of Chalmers's views concerning the right of women to rule in elective monarchies (these views were subsequently commented on in Simpson (n 64) 19); I intend to consider this in more detail elsewhere. See Constance Jordan, *Renaissance Feminism. Literary Texts and Political Models* (Ithaca and London 1990) 245–46.

[79] Chalmers (n 66) f 30$^{r}$–31$^{r}$.

[80] See ibid f 3$^{r}$, 27$^{v}$–32$^{v}$.

authority of a statute promulgated by Parliament. In response Chalmers constructed an argument to the effect that such an act could not, of itself, alter the succession. He made it clear he thought this followed in a realm like England, where, he said, the people had given the *droit de regner* to their first monarch, and to his legitimate heirs. Chalmers then claimed that this settlement had endured for centuries. Consequently, it was impossible to disinherit a particular heir from the line of royal succession unless it was shown that he or she had committed some grievous offence; and Parliament acting alone did not have the authority to do this.[81]

These arguments require some unpacking. In this passage, Chalmers was drawing on ideas found in the learned laws. The notion that the English *droit de regner* had been established through a transfer of power by the people to their kings was, of course, modelled on the Roman *lex Regia*. Ulpian had famously claimed that the Roman emperor possessed power to make laws because of the *lex Regia*, through which the populace committed to him its entire *imperium* and *potestas*.[82] Yet one cannot understand the full meaning of Chalmers's comments here simply by looking at Ulpian. In the medieval period some jurists, such as Bartolus, had claimed that only one *lex Regia* had been validly enacted—the *lex Regia* of the Romans. They, having conquered all peoples, transferred this universal power to their emperor. Consequently, Bartolus was able to make the claim that, *de iure*, the emperor remained in full power and authority as the sole *dominus mundi*, in accordance with the text of the *Digest* that declared him to be such.[83] But other medieval jurists, such as Oldradus da Ponte, had questioned this view. They had argued that all peoples had once had the right to provide for their own governance, a right that flowed from the *ius gentium*. That right had temporarily and unlawfully been removed by Roman force. Those peoples who had since thrown off the imperial yoke, and who had thereafter refused to recognize any superiors, had recovered the right recognized in the *ius gentium* to govern themselves. But this only followed if they had, by Oldradus's time, recognized no superiors for many centuries. The refusal to recognize any superiors was thus confirmed, *de iure*, by long acquisitive prescription.[84]

Elsewhere, Chalmers described the foundational act in the establishment of the Scottish kingdom in terms that make it clear he thought of this as a *lex regia*,[85] and here he was evidently thinking in similar categories when analysing the English *droit de regner*.[86] By implying that the English polity had been established by a *lex regia* that had been confirmed by long prescriptive use, Chalmers was arguably alluding to and relying upon the authoritative discourse mentioned above,

[81] ibid f 30v–31r. [82] *Digest* (n 31) 1.4.1.pr.

[83] Joseph Canning, *The Political Thought of Baldus de Ubaldis* (CUP 1987) 23–30; see also *Digest* (n 31) 14.2.9.

[84] Canning (n 83) 68–70; see also G Motagu, 'Roman Law and the Emperor—The Rationale of "Written Reason" in some *Consilia* of Oldradus da Ponte' (1994) 15 History of Political Thought 1.

[85] Chalmers (n 67) f 1v, 9r.

[86] In another chapter I hope to explore the extent to which English or French readers might have found Chalmers's analysis here convincing. For some near-contemporary attitudes of civilians operating in England towards both the *lex Regia* and the idea that it represented the foundational law of the English polity, see Brian Levack, *The Civil Lawyers in England 1603–1641* (OUP 1973) 88–95.

which was drawn from the learned laws. The assumptions were, first, that the English had recognized the dictates of right reason and legal truth found in the *ius gentium*, that they should provide some form of government for themselves; and, second, that they had then done just that, by creating the English monarchy. At an earlier stage in his argument, Chalmers had accepted that the constitution of magistrates—and so, it would seem, individual governments—flowed directly from the recognition of the dictates of right reason established in the *ius gentium*.[87] Having made these points, Chalmers indicated that the English *lex regia* had established a fixed line of royal succession. Perhaps he meant to imply that this was revealed through the exercise of the *droit de regner* over an exceptionally long period of time.[88]

Having relied upon the learned laws to aid him to recognize the foundational laws of the English, Chalmers then indicated that there was some need to apply those laws to the question of whether or not Mary, Queen of Scots should be allowed to succeed. He had already established that the legal learning he had amassed through his historical researches permitted female rule. But did the laws permit the exclusion of an individual from the line of royal succession if he or she had committed some particularly grievous offence? And who had the right to determine whether or not such an offence had been committed? In considering these questions, Chalmers was obviously examining the possibility that the English Parliament might possess some right to disinherit Mary, Queen of Scots, on the grounds of her alleged crimes of murder and adultery.

In responding to these questions, Chalmers was prepared to go much further than Bishop Leslie. He argued that the greatest power that Parliament held, following the provisions of all laws, 'both human and divine', was to show the crimes committed by a delinquent, 'to his competent judge, and to demand justice'. Otherwise, if Parliament were to wield greater power, all order would be destroyed, and all superiors deposed at the whim of their subjects. This had been revealed by the 'experience of such disorder' which had been felt many times in England. Chalmers cited the recent example of the conflict between the Houses of York and Lancaster for the throne, during which the claims of the House of York had initially been ignored in favour of those of the House of Lancaster. This had led to disastrous civil war.[89]

So, who was the 'competent judge' of monarchs? Who did have the power to declare an individual unworthy to wear a crown? Chalmers did not expressly answer this question. But he did proceed to note that it was impossible to defraud monarchs of their crowns, who recognized no superiors other than 'God, and his church'. It is just possible that Chalmers thought that there was vested in the Roman Catholic Church some universal authority to remove a 'delinquent' from the line of royal succession;[90] such thinking would have been consistent with the Papal Bull *Regnans in excelsis* (1570).[91]

87 Chalmers (n 66) f 4$^{v}$, 5$^{v}$–6$^{r}$. 88 ibid f 30$^{v}$. 89 ibid f 30$^{v}$–31$^{r}$.
90 See ibid f 31$^{r}$.
91 For a translation of *Regnans in excelsis*, see Claire Cross, *The Royal Supremacy in the Elizabethan Church* (Allen & Unwin 1969) 152–54.

What is certain is that Chalmers relied heavily on his legal learning in order to enable him to recognize and analyse the foundational English *droit de regner*, which he probably thought had been established through long prescriptive use. Chalmers's legal learning revealed that these laws should be interpreted to allow female succession to the English Crown. Chalmers also relied upon his learning to demonstrate the inability of Parliament to circumvent such laws. He seems to have accepted that the normal laws of succession that he had examined allowed delinquents to be disinherited. But he also argued that legal learning showed that such delinquency had to be established by due process.[92] He then claimed that Parliament's supreme power within such a process affecting the royal succession was simply to establish that an individual had committed crimes, and to ask a superior power for redress.

## 3.3 Conclusion—Chalmers on history, learning, and law

Consequently, Chalmers drew upon his learning to establish a framework that had legal force capable of challenging even the authority of Parliament to act in certain ways. Importantly for the purposes of this chapter, the learning Chalmers called upon was, like Leslie's, not specific or particular to any one jurisdiction. It drew upon both the learned laws and Chalmers's eclectic historical research, which apparently revealed which human ordinances conformed to the divine order that governed the universe. In the process, it revealed norms that might be expected to be recognized as generally applicable in practice. Yet, again like Leslie, and again importantly for this chapter, Chalmers drew upon learning that was necessarily local too. Chalmers drew upon ordinances promulgated in many jurisdictions across Christendom as guides to legal truth when attempting to establish the legitimacy of female rule. He could do this precisely because he believed that *all* local laws had been open to trial and testing by history itself against the great divine order of causes and effects that infused and governed the universe. In addition, when he turned to examine the foundational laws of the English in light of the learned laws, again Chalmers assumed that the English had recognized the dictates of right reason found in the *ius gentium* for themselves. In other words, Chalmers, like Leslie, seems to have thought of the law of England as possessed of the same sort of learning that could be found in the learned laws. Local frameworks of legal learning overlapped and interacted with bodies of learning that were not specific to any jurisdiction so as to help lawyers to recognize laws with binding force. It seems Chalmers believed that where parliaments promulgated individual statutes that were inconsistent with such laws, then the statutes could be construed narrowly so as to be virtually deprived of much of their potential effect. Indeed, Chalmers seems to have gone further as regards the English statute that purported to confer power on Henry VIII to alter the line of royal succession. As far as Chalmers was concerned, that statute attempted to achieve something that was simply beyond the power of a parliament acting alone.

[92] Chalmers (n 66) f 30$^{v}$–31$^{r}$.

## 4. Conclusion

This chapter has sought to show that Scots lawyers believed that justice, as legal truth, had a legal authority of its own, and they also thought that this authority could be discerned through reliance on legal learning. In the attempt to recognize laws with the 'invincible force of trewthe', to quote Leslie, lawyers in any jurisdiction could draw upon learning that was neither specific nor particular to their own jurisdiction. So, in an English context, Leslie relied upon the traditional learning of Roman law to establish legally binding constraints on the exercise of a statutory power. Similarly, Chalmers relied upon the eclectic learning of human history to discover what natural reason revealed about the right of women to rule. He also deployed such legal learning to establish limits on the power of parliaments to act in certain ways, and indeed to make laws. This makes it clear that neither jurist would have agreed with Jean Bodin's claim in contemporary France, that all law making was dependent upon an exercise of sovereign will.[93] Furthermore, their respective discourses did not focus upon any idea that the relevant norms to be used in the resolution of the dispute over the succession flowed from binding obligations imposed by agreements between England and Scotland as sovereign States. Their approach did not presume the operation of a *ius inter gentes* in a more modern sense. It has been argued in the past that one Scot writing in the 1560s—William Maitland of Lethington—did adopt something akin to this approach, and that he made use of various treaties between England and Scotland in advancing his claims.[94] But this seems to be absent from the works considered here.

So, were the assumptions of these Scottish jurists concerning the authority of law simply those held two centuries earlier by Bartolus, elements of which were outlined by Canning above? It has been argued here that they were not. Both Leslie and Chalmers had a broader concept of 'learning' than Bartolus. Both were prepared to draw upon a wider range of traditions of ideas as authoritative guides to legal truth, some of which were particular to their own jurisdictions, and some of which were not. The authoritative learning that revealed justice and truth was already found in the jurisdictions of Scotland and England to some extent, and also across Christendom. In the opinion of Leslie and Chalmers, it seems that all such generally applicable learning could be used by legal experts in individual jurisdictions to augment their understanding of the justice and reason that could have binding force. They thought that it might also be employed by jurists in one jurisdiction—such as Scotland—who sought to persuade their counterparts in another—for example, England—that their laws should be interpreted in a particular manner. The Scottish jurists evidently hoped that their English counterparts would endorse

[93] See Skinner (n 1) 297–301; JH Franklin, 'Sovereignty and the Mixed Constitution: Bodin and His Critics' in JH Burns and Mark Goldie (eds), *The Cambridge History of Political Thought 1450–1700* (CUP 1991) 307–09.

[94] Kirsten Post Walton, *Mary Queen of Scots and the Politics of Gender and Religion* (Palgrave Macmillan 2007) 56, 63–66.

this interpretative approach. They also hoped that their readers would recognize the learning they had identified as being generally applicable and possessed of probable force in the resolution of the legal dispute at hand, regardless of the particular territorial boundaries involved. In this way, they sought to resolve the questions raised over the English royal succession.

# 4

# Humanism, the Bible, and Erasmus's Moral World Order

*Xavier Tubau*

## 1. Introduction

Erasmus's thoughts about the morality of rulers in their relations with each other have not received the careful scholarly attention they deserve. Among the ideas that have hindered a proper assessment of his thinking on this subject is the widespread view that humanists were simply a group of learned experts in rhetoric who defended their masters' ideas and whose works were politically inconsistent.[1] The projection of contemporary ideas onto Erasmus's texts—like those of liberal Catholicism subsequent to the Second Vatican Council,[2] or the so-called realist conception of international relations that prevails today[3]—have had the same negative effect. In this chapter, Erasmus's ideas about the morality of rulers in their

[1] For the view of humanists as experts in rhetoric, not as philosophers, see PO Kristeller, 'Humanism and Scholasticism in the Italian Renaissance' (1944–45) 3 Byzantion: International Journal of Byzantine Studies 346–74, reprinted in his *Studies in Renaissance Thought and Letters* (Edizioni di Storia e Letteratura 1956). The consequences of this interpretation in the context of political history can be seen, for example, in J Hankins, 'Humanism and the Origins of Modern Political Thought' in J Kraye (ed), *The Cambridge Companion to Renaissance Humanism* (CUP 1996) 118–22. The first important revision of Kristeller's thesis in the context of political history was put forward by Q Skinner in *The Foundations of Modern Political Thought*, vol 1 (CUP 1978) 101–12.

[2] For the influence of Vatican Council II on some interpretations of Erasmus's political thought, see B Mansfield, *Erasmus in the Twentieth Century: Interpretations c 1920–2000* (University of Toronto Press 2003) 83, 119–21, 130, 150, and 204.

[3] R Tuck, *The Rights of War and Peace: Political Thought and the International Order from Grotius to Kant* (OUP 1999) argues that for 'Grotius, Hobbes, and their followers, self-preservation was a paramount principle, and the basis for whatever universal morality there was' (5). This 'radically simplified and 'minimalist' universal morality' was a development of 'the humanist view of international relations' (9), which would in turn have been constituted using the ideas of Cicero and Tacitus on wars 'for glory and dominion, including pre-emptive-strikes' (31). According to Tuck, in spite of the apparent pacifism of Erasmus's works, his defence of a war against the Turks reflected a 'humanist view of international relations', for, in essence, he was defending the integrity of the *respublica christiana* in the same way as Cicero defended that of the *civitas romana* (29–31). Tuck's interpretation concerning Grotius has been rejected by B Straumann, *Roman Law in the State of Nature: The Classical Foundations of Hugo Grotius' Natural Law* (CUP 2015) 95–119, 130–42. See also J Nijman, 'Images of Grotius, or the International Rule of Law beyond Historiographical Oscillation' (2015) 17 Journal of the History of International Law 83–137 (esp 121–30).

relations with each other will be placed in context to show that they are both consistent and coherent with the rest of his philosophy. In the first section, I shall analyse Erasmus's criticism of the moral and legal justifications for wars at the time. In the second, I shall examine his ideas about the moral order in which the ruler should be educated and in which political power should be exercised, with the role of arbitration as the way to resolve conflicts between rulers. As I develop these two closely related questions, I shall show the links between Erasmus's thought and Italian political humanism prior to Machiavelli, but I shall also highlight those aspects that are specific to his intellectual project for reforming contemporary religious life.

## 2. The Early Sixteenth Century

From the Late Middle Ages and during the first century of modern Europe, dynastic norms and practices dominated European politics.[4] 'Rulers and would-be rulers competed to extend not only their own honor, prestige, and territory, but also that of their dynastic line.'[5] Marriage, conquest, inheritance, and succession within the framework of dynastic rivalry were the fundamental means employed to shape a significant part of European politics over several centuries: 'the survival or extinction of the dynasty was the difference between peace and war, and the accidents of inheritance shaped the power blocs of Europe as a whole'.[6] Rulers did not act in the name of a *raison d'état* or national interest, but mainly in the name of dynastic interests. The loyalty of the subjects to their ruler and his dynasty was the basis of political stability. Rulers' decisions, however, were not taken in an environment devoid of norms. Despite the different nature of the political entities that formed medieval and Renaissance Europe, 'ranging from large dynastic monarchies to small fiefs and free cities', it was considered that they all took part 'in a greater hierarchical and juridical *continuum* under the supreme, if theoretical, leadership of the pope and the emperor'. Thus, 'the powerful system of norms and rules derived from natural law, customary law, ancient Roman law, feudal law, and canon law', known as *ius commune*,[7] 'provided a framework of juridical concepts and political ideals that was common to the whole of the Latin West'.[8] In this context, the figure of the

[4] See H Koenigsberger, *Estates and Revolutions: Essays in Early Modern European History* (Cornell UP 1971); H Rowen, *The King's State, Proprietary Dynasticism in Early Modern France* (Rutgers UP 1980); R Bonney, *The European Dynastic States, 1494–1660* (OUP 1991); JH Elliott, 'A Europe of Composite Monarchies' (1992) 137 Past and Present 48–71; GC Gibbs, R Oresko, and HM Scott, *Royal and Republican Sovereignty in Early Modern Europe: Essays in Memory of Ragnhild Hatton* (CUP 2004).

[5] DH Nexon, *The Struggle for Power in Early Modern Europe: Religious Conflict, Dynastic Empires, and International Change* (Princeton UP 2008) 6.

[6] R Mackenney, *Sixteenth Century Europe: Expansion and Conflict* (Macmillan 1993) 219.

[7] K Pennington, *The Prince and the Law 1200–1600: Sovereignty and Rights in the Western Legal Tradition* (University of California Press 1993) 1. See also M Bellomo, *The Common Legal Past of Europe 1000–1800* (Catholic University of America Press 1995) 55–111.

[8] R Lesaffer, 'Peace Treaties from Lodi to Westphalia' in R Lesaffer (ed), *Peace Treaties and International Law in European History: From the Late Middle Ages to World War One* (CUP 2004) 11.

jurist, trained in the *ius commune* and familiar with the rules of legal argumentation, became indispensable for legitimizing the political action of rulers.[9]

There were people who showed their disagreement with the premises and dynamics that shaped European politics, a substantial number of whom had been educated in the pedagogical tradition of Italian humanism. Erasmus was undoubtedly one of the humanists most committed to this critical discourse during the first decades of the sixteenth century. He describes and gives his opinion on contemporary politics in works such as his treatise *The Education of a Christian Prince* (Institutio principis christiani 1516), in the declamation entitled *Complaint of Peace* (Querela pacis 1517) and in his *Discussion concerning proposals for war against the Turks* (Consultatio de bello Turcico inferendo 1530) and in his commentaries to the adages *One ought to be born a king or a fool* (*Aut regem aut fatuum nasci oportere*), *Sparta is your portion; do your best for her* (*Spartam nactus es, hanc orna*), *The Sileni of Alcibiades* (*Sileni Alcibiadis*) and *War is sweet for those who have not tried it* (*Dulce bellum inexpertis*), among others.[10] In these works, he points out that the actions of contemporary rulers are generally guided by dynastic interests and the quest for honour that a military victory brings; treaties between rulers are signed on the understanding that they can be broken in the event of an unfavourable situation arising for one of the parties; moreover, wars have become the continuation of politics by other means, with the aggravating factor that they are now waged principally by mercenaries.[11] Erasmus generalizes in his observations, he occasionally makes mistakes through a lack of information and sometimes manipulates what information he does have in his own interests.[12] Nevertheless, the diplomatic and military history of the early years of the sixteenth century confirms in large measure this analysis of what motivated and guided contemporary political action.

As far as Erasmus was concerned, the problem had two sources: the jurists and theologians who worked as counsellors to the rulers and the chivalric culture that prevailed in European courts. He was critical of the fact that contemporary wars

[9] L Martines, *Lawyers and Statecraft in Renaissance Florence* (Princeton UP 1968); J Brundage, *The Medieval Origins of the Legal Profession: Canonists, Civilians, and Courts* (University of Chicago Press 2008); R Lesaffer, *European Legal History: A Cultural and Political Perspective* (CUP 2009); J Black, *Absolutism in Renaissance Milan: Plenitude of Power under the Visconti and the Sforza, 1329–1535* (OUP 2009); L Armstrong and J Kirshner (eds), *The Politics of Law in Late Medieval and Renaissance Italy* (University of Toronto Press 2011).

[10] Quotations from Erasmus in English translation are taken from *Collected Works of Erasmus* (CWE) (University of Toronto Press Toronto 1974–). In the case of the *Adages*, I quote from the selection made by W Barker (University of Toronto Press 2001) from the translations of the *Adages* published in CWE 31–34. With regard to the translation of the *Paraclesis*, Erasmus's preface to his edition of the New Testament, I quote from J Olin's translation included in *Christian Humanism and the Reformation: Selected Writings* (Harper & Row 1965) 92–106.

[11] See, for example, *Education of a Prince* (CWE 27) 277–79, 284. *Adages* 335–37: 'War is sweet for those who have not tried it'; *Adages* 56, 58: 'One ought to be born a king or a fool'; *Adages* 186–88: 'Sparta is your portion; do your best for her'; *Adages* 253, 262: 'The Sileni of Alcibiades'.

[12] The best study on the 'political thought' and 'political opinions' of Erasmus is by J Tracy, *The Politics of Erasmus: A Pacifist Intellectual and His Political Milieu* (University of Toronto Press 1978). See also his *Erasmus of the Low Countries* (University of California Press 1996) 94–97; M Van Gelderen 'The Low Countries' in HA Lloyd G Burgess and S Hodson (eds), *European Political Thought 1450–1700: Religion, Law and Philosophy* (Yale UP 2007) 379–84.

had been started by young rulers 'inflamed by the bad examples of their forbears and of stories which fools have spread from foolish books' and 'encouraged by the calls of flatterers, goaded by lawyers and theologians, with the consent or connivance of bishops, perhaps even at their demand'.[13] According to Erasmus, medieval chivalric literature had become the source of models of behaviour and future rulers were, therefore, being educated in a culture that privileged arms over letters.[14] Contemporary theology and law similarly endorsed and even encouraged the development of this warlike behaviour: 'We have heard bellicose sermons of this sort from monks, theologians, and bishops.'[15] Erasmus keeps quiet about humanist literature's own role in this exaltation of honour and military glory and no doubt exaggerates the part allegedly played by counsellors as warmongers.[16] Nonetheless, the crucial role of chivalric culture in the education of rulers and the influence wielded by jurists and theologians over their decisions are two amply documented realities in the cultural and intellectual history of the sixteenth century.[17]

The problem of the legal and moral justification of wars and the education of rulers are the two areas that Erasmus's discourse about contemporary European politics concentrates on. The framework within which Erasmus develops this analysis of contemporary politics is the same one on which the whole of the intellectual project of Renaissance humanism is founded. As a Renaissance humanist, Erasmus understood the recuperation and assimilation of the Greek and Roman legacy as the point of departure for a reform of the whole of civilization. So, on the basis of a sound knowledge of Latin and Greek and with an acute awareness of the historical dimension of words, things, and people, the disciplines were ripe for revision and correction by means of new editions and philological commentaries on their foundational texts; that meant every discipline without exception, including canon law and theology and, therefore, their foundational texts, the Old and the New Testaments.[18]

[13] 'War is sweet' *Adages* 350. Throughout the article I speak of 'theologians' and 'jurists' (canonists), but it should be remembered that the dividing line between these professions was not clear-cut; see B Tierney, 'Introduction to this Edition' in his *Foundations of the Conciliar Theory: The Contribution of the Medieval Canonists from Gratian to the Great Schism* (Brill 1995) xv–xx.

[14] Tracy 1978 (n 12) 59 points out, for example, Erasmus's discontent with the influence exercised by Guillaume de Croy, 'scion of a family long prominent in the chivalric culture of the Burgundian court', on the education of the future Charles V. See, for example, *Education of a Prince* (CWE 27) 272–73; *Adages* 55, 61: 'One ought to be born'; *Adages* 185: 'Sparta is your portion'; *Adages* 338–39: 'War is sweet'.

[15] *Adages* 328: 'War is sweet'; see also 319; *Adages* 252, 255: 'The Sileni'; *Adages* 214–15: 'As warts grow on the eye'.

[16] Skinner (n 1) 244–48.

[17] J Huizinga, *The Waning of the Middle Ages: A Study of the Forms of Life, Thought and Art in France and the Netherlands in the XIVth and XVth centuries* (Arnold 1924); AB Ferguson, *The Indian Summer of English Chivalry* (Duke UP 1960); G Weise, *L'ideale eroico del Rinascimento e le sue premesse umanistiche* (Edizioni Scientifiche Italiane 1961); A Scaglione, *Knights at Court: Courtliness, Chivalry, and Courtesy from Ottonian Germany to the Italian Renaissance* (University of California Press 1992); DJB Trim (ed), *The Chivalric Ethos and the Development of Military Professionalism* (Brill 2002).

[18] Recent bibliography on this topic includes: R Witt, *In the Footsteps of the Ancients: The Origins of Italian Humanism 1250–1420* (Brill 2000); *The Two Latin Cultures and the Foundation of Renaissance Humanism in Medieval Italy* (CUP 2012); A Moss, *Renaissance Truth and the Latin Language Turn* (OUP 2003); C Celenza, *The Lost Italian Renaissance: Humanists, Historians, and Latin's Legacy* (Johns Hopkins UP 2004); A Mazzocco (ed), *Interpretations of Renaissance Humanism* (Brill 2006); GM Cappelli,

The educational model for rulers that Erasmus proposes as well as his point of view on war are inseparable from his historical reading of the New Testament. Christ's message, he points out, is opposed to any type of violence. Medieval jurists and theologians have misinterpreted Christ's words in order to be able to justify Christians taking part in war. It is necessary, he goes on, to recuperate the original message of Christ in the New Testament. Christ's message, which Erasmus always presents as the 'philosophy of Christ' is the framework within which rulers should be educated and within which they should exercise their power. Using the political language of fifteenth-century Italian humanism, the practices of governance in his own native land and his project to restore the true teaching of Christ as his basis, Erasmus proposes a new moral order for European political life in which the political legitimacy of the ruler and the behaviour proper to a Christian prince are two sides of the same coin. In the following pages, I shall examine how Erasmus articulates this thought.

## 3. The Just War Theory

The eloquence and vehemence of Erasmus's texts against wars made his own contemporaries think that Erasmus totally rejected the use of force and the legal and moral arguments that supported it. The Faculty of Theology at the Sorbonne accused him for this reason of putting the very foundations of political power at risk:

> Although wars and conflicts among Christians are to be avoided as much as possible, nevertheless this proposition, as it stands, alleging that a war against the violence of wicked men is never licit, as if there could never be a just cause for a war to defend one's self, even if one observed the due process of law, undermines the whole government and is at odds with both natural and divine law.[19]

Erasmus, however, does not censure all wars. As he himself makes clear:

> I simply admit that I have written some rather distasteful things for the purpose of frightening Christians away from the insanity of war ... but when I discuss seriously the question of whether war is permissible for Christians under any circumstance, I declare that it should be allowed either if terrible necessity requires it or if a notable benefit, a commendable one, suggests it.[20]

This explanation, in any case, opened the door to accusations of inconsistency, given that Erasmus would be justifying the use of force—for example, when he accepts a defensive action in the face of a hypothetical attack by the Turks—at the same

*L'umanesimo italiano da Petrarca a Valla* (Carocci 2007). For biblical philology, in particular, see JH Bentley, *Humanists and Holy Writ. New Testament Scholarship in the Renaissance* (Princeton UP 1983); E Rummel, *Biblical Humanism and Scholasticism in the Age of Erasmus* (Brill 2008).

[19] *Clarifications concerning the censures published at Paris in the name of the Theology Faculty there* (CWE 82) 61.

[20] *Apology against the patchworks of Alberto Pio* (CWE 84) 345. See also *Education of a Prince* (CWE 27) 282; *Clarifications* (CWE 82) 62.

time as he was presenting the doctrine of Christ as being opposed to any kind of violence.[21]

To understand Erasmus's position on war, it is important to distinguish the different levels of analysis on which he deals with the subject: that is, in philosophical terms, within the tradition of the theological anthropology of Christianity, and in historical terms. From the philosophical standpoint, Erasmus describes the physical and psychic nature of man to underline the extent to which he was created for peace rather than war. This description is the legacy of theological commentaries on the Old Testament on the well-known passage in Genesis (1:27), which had been enriched by the Italian humanists with ideas and concepts taken from Stoic philosophy:[22]

> [Nature] had placed certain seeds of peace in our souls, by which we are borne towards love and concord. For if we all studiously follow the impulses of nature, we are eager for living together in companionship, we pursue friendships, we love nearness and the need for others, and we rejoice in familiar society.[23]

In short, war is contrary to human nature, he says, because man, created by God in his image and likeness, is a social being born for friendship.[24] Those who take part in wars, therefore, end up destroying 'every bond and covenant of Nature and of Christ'.[25]

More significant is Erasmus's analysis of war in historical terms. The target of his attacks in this context is the so-called theory of the just war. This theory developed by theologians and jurists (canonists) indicated that some wars could be just if they

[21] Erasmian bibliography analysed this apparent contradiction in a host of studies throughout the last century; see Mansfield (n 2). This contradiction was interpreted by some as proof of inconsistent thinking. See for instance P Brachin, '*Vox clamantis in deserto*: Réflexions sur le pacifisme d'Erasme' in JC Margolin, *Colloquia Erasmiana Turonensia*, vol 1 (University of Toronto Press 1972). The distinction between the original message of Christ and the historical circumstances of the sixteenth century, which formed the basis of Erasmus's thought on war, opened the way for a reconsideration of the problem. Authors who have examined this point in some depth are JA Fernández, 'Erasmus on the Just War' (1973) 34 Journal of the History of Ideas 209–26; JC Margolin, 'Érasme et la guerre contre les Turcs' (1980) 13 Il Pensiero Politico 3–38; RG Musto, 'Just Wars and Evil Empires: Erasmus and the Turks' in RG Musto and J Monfasani (eds), *Renaissance Society and Culture: Essays in Honor of Eugene F. Rice* (Italica Press 1991); AG Weiler, 'The Turkish Argument and Christian Piety' in J Sperna Weiland and WThM Frijhoff (eds), *Erasmus of Rotterdam: The Man and the Scholar* (Leiden 1988). R Dealy's study, 'The Dynamics of Erasmus' Thought on War' (1984) 4 Erasmus of Rotterdam Society Yearbook 53–67, is the best analysis of the topic.

[22] For speeches on the dignity and misery of man in the Renaissance, see C Trinkaus, *'In Our Image and Likeness': Humanity and Divinity in Italian Humanist Thought* (Constable 1970) 2 vols; PO Kristeller, *Renaissance Concepts of Man and Other Essays* (Harper & Row 1972); C Stark, 'Renaissance Anthropologies and the Conception of Man' in A Moudarres and C Purdy Moudarres (eds), *New Worlds and the Italian Renaissance: Contributions to the History of Intellectual European Culture* (Brill 2012).

[23] A passage from his *Speech on Peace and Discord* (*Oratio de pace et discordia*), taken from the translation by J Tracy, *Erasmus: The Growth of a Mind* (Droz Genève 1972) 42, who cites the Stoic sources of Cicero (*Tusculanae* III.2) and Seneca (*Ep.* 73:15–16) in a note.

[24] 'War is sweet' *Adages* 319–21. For the Stoic ideas in this passage, see RP Adams, *The Better Part of Valor: More, Erasmus, Colet, and Vives on Humanism, War, and Peace, 1496–1536* (University of Washington Press 1962) 94–99.

[25] *Complaint of Peace* (CWE 27) 305.

were declared and waged under particular circumstances.[26] For understandable reasons, Erasmus did not write any text concerning the problem of the theory of war. There is, however, a constant dialogue with this tradition within the framework of his attacks on contemporary wars. It is important to emphasize that Erasmus did not take issue with the effectiveness of some of the tenets of this theory as a matter of principle. In the adage *Dulce bellum inexpertis* he had already recognized the legitimacy of a defensive war against the Turks, and in the *Consultatio de bello Turcico inferendo* he articulated an analysis of a hypothetical war against the Turks with elements of this tradition: legitimate authority, just cause and last resort.[27] Erasmus's intention was to demonstrate that the theory was based on a distortion of Christ's original message in the New Testament.[28] From his point of view, it was one thing to recognize the existence of just wars in the contemporary world and quite another to argue that Christ's message endorsed the justice of those wars.

As far as Erasmus is concerned, Christ's message in the New Testament is unambiguous: 'The whole philosophy of Christ argues against war.'[29] Christ commands us to love our enemies, turn the other cheek, not offer resistance, not seek revenge.[30] Erasmus repeats these ideas insistently in his texts because for him they represent the essence of Christianity: 'Christ wanted his teaching to be as simple, easy and obvious as possible, even for labourers, and this is expressed in a few clear words: You shall love your God with all your heart and you shall love your neighbour as yourself.'[31] Christ's message, however, must be understood in its historical context, which is not the same as the context of the Old Testament or of the contemporary world either. So, for example, according to the theologians in Paris, Erasmus was wrong to interpret Jesus's request to Peter to put his sword away (Lk 22:49–51) as prohibiting Christians from using force under any circumstances. Erasmus responds that the theologians seek to transfer 'what is spoken in the person of Luke in the paraphrase and is rightly spoken in those times ... to my person and apply it to these times'. Erasmus concludes that he is not prohibiting contemporary Christians from using force under any circumstances, but simply that Luke prohibited 'the evangelists

[26] The best history of reflections on the legal and moral aspects of war can be read in the anthology of texts compiled by GM Reichberg, H Syse, and E Begby (eds), *The Ethics of War: Classic and Contemporary Readings* (Blackwell 2006). See also S Niditch, *War in the Hebrew Bible: A Study in the Ethics of Violence* (OUP 1995); W Harris, *War and Imperialism in Republican Rome 327–70BC* (OUP 1979) 166–75; F Russell, *The Just War in the Middle Ages* (CUP 1977); JT Johnson, *Ideology, Reason and the Limitation of War: Religious and Secular Concepts 1200–1740* (Princeton UP 1975); J Muldoon, *Popes, Lawyers, and Infidels: The Church and the Non-Christian World, 1250–1550* (Liverpool UP 1979); P Haggenmacher, *Grotius et la doctrine de la guerre juste* (PUF 1983); Tuck (n 2).

[27] *Adages* 349: 'War is sweet'; *On the Turkish War* (CWE 64) 246, 264–65.

[28] M Isnardi Parente, '*L'Educazione del principe cristiano* di Erasmo da Rotterdam' in D Quaglioni and P Carta (eds), M Isnardi Parente *Rinascimento politico in Europa* (Antonio Milani 2008) 50.

[29] *Education of a Prince* (CWE 27) 284, and also 286. See HM Pabel, 'The Peaceful People of Christ: The Irenic Ecclesiology of Erasmus of Rotterdam' in HM Pabel (ed), *Erasmus' Vision of the Church* (Sixteenth Century Journal Publishers 1995).

[30] Mt 5:3–11, 17–18, 39, 42–44; Lk 6:27–35. See, for example, *Adagia* 342: 'War is sweet'.

[31] 'Christus suam doctrinam simplicissimam atque ipsis etiam agricolis facilem et obviam esse voluerit, quam paucis ac dilucidis verbis explicat: Diliges dominum deum tuum ex toto corde et proximum tuum sicut te ipsum' *Ratio vera theologiae* in GB Winkler (ed) *Erasmus von Rotterdam In Novum Testamentum praefationes* (Wissenschaftliche Buchgesellschaft 1967) 476.

of his time' from using force under any circumstances.[32] The consequences of this historical reading that Erasmus proposes, as I shall go on to explain, are crucial for understanding his views on war and violence in general.[33]

## 3.1 The Old and New Testaments

Two of the most significant issues in his analysis of this problem are, first, the use of the Old Testament as a doctrinal source to justify the use of military force, and, second, the assimilation by canon law and theology of concepts associated with the use of force that originated in Roman law. St Ambrose and St Augustine took passages in the Old Testament to justify Christians taking part in war.[34] The whole of later tradition would follow their example, as Erasmus himself recalls: 'If it were always a sin to make a war, we are told, God would not have commanded the Jews to fight against their enemies.'[35] For Erasmus, this line of argument is historically untenable. The wars in the Old Testament, Erasmus points out, took place in a particular historical and religious context. They were wars ordained by God against strangers and idolaters in the context of a divine mission.[36] Nonetheless, 'after Christ ordered the sword to be put away, it is not proper for Christians to fight'[37] Erasmus's analysis of a passage from the Sermon on the Mount (Mt 5:43–44) is an example of his desire to question the justification of violence in historical terms on the basis of the wars in the Old Testament. In his *Paraphrase on Matthew* he writes:

> Take now also this precept that is regarded as the chief one in the Law: 'You shall love your neighbour [Lev 19:18] and hate your enemy', it says. It demands kindness, but only towards those who are kind and well deserving, whereas it allows us to bear ill will towards those who injure us. You see how I do not take anything away from this precept, but how much I add to it. . . . I require you, the followers of my teaching, to love your enemies as well.[38]

[32] *Clarifications* (CWE 82) 62, 66.

[33] For Erasmus's historical approach to the New Testament, see MO Boyle, *Erasmus on Language and Method in Theology* (University of Toronto Press 1977); C Augustijn, *Erasmus: His Life, Works, and Influence* (University of Toronto Press 1991) 84–86; F Rico, *El sueño del humanismo: de Petrarca a Erasmo* (Alianza 1993) 113–25; I Bejczy, *Erasmus and the Middle Ages: The Historical Consciousness of a Christian Humanist* (Brill 2001) 18–24; C Christ-Von Wedel, *Erasmus of Rotterdam: Advocate of a New Christianity* (University of Toronto Press 2013).

[34] Russell (n 26) 12–26.

[35] *Adages* 339: 'War is sweet' (Num 25:16; Judg 4:6–7). Modern historiography on the theory of war has reconstructed its beginnings in philosophy, historiography, and Greek and Roman law, but the fact remains that for the medieval and Renaissance world the father of the theory of the just war was St Augustine. That was also Erasmus's point of view, as can be deduced from a comment in his *Adages* 335–36: 'War is sweet'. See also *Education of a Prince* (CWE 27) 283–84, as well as the article by R Padberg, 'Erasmus contra Augustinum. Das Problem des bellum justum in der erasmischen Friedensethik' in *Colloque Érasmien de Liège* (Les Belles Lettres 1987) 279–96. For Erasmus's opinion of St Augustine as a bishop (positive) and as a writer (negative), see A Visser, 'Reading Augustine through Erasmus' Eyes: Humanist Scholarship and Paratextual Guidance in the Wake of the Reformation' (2008) 28 Erasmus of Rotterdam Society Yearbook 67–90.

[36] *Education of a Prince* (CWE 27) 286; *Complaint of Peace* (CWE 27) 300, 305. See Christ-Von Wedel (n 33) 234.

[37] *Adages* 340: 'War is sweet'. See also *Education of a Prince* (CWE 27) 286.

[38] *Paraphrase on Matthew* (CWE 45) 110.

According to Erasmus's interpretation, the Jews were allowed to hate their enemies, whereas the Christians were required to love them. The Faculty of Theology in Paris censured this interpretation because Erasmus was stating that morals were not the same in both Testaments, which meant questioning the Augustinian principle that 'what pertains to morals remains unchanged in both laws'.[39] Erasmus does not renounce his historical reading of the passage and retorts defiantly that 'there are thousands of places in the books of the orthodox Fathers which would have to be condemned if they were measured by that exact standard, "morality is the same in both testaments" '.[40] By denying that the Old and the New Testaments reflect the same point of view on violence, Erasmus was establishing that Christians could not justify a war on the basis of the Old Testament. He concludes that to extract a moral teaching from the episodes of war in the Old Testament, the Christian reader should read them in allegorical terms, as examples of spiritual struggles against the devil.[41]

## 3.2 The Gospels and Roman law

Erasmus also censures the use of the principles of Roman law by the theologians and jurists who articulated the theory of the just war. As I have already mentioned, Erasmus does not question the fact that these principles may hold in particular instances: 'We have also accepted some things from Roman law because of their obvious fairness.' What he criticizes is that, with the intention of reconciling Roman law with the Gospels, 'we have twisted gospel teaching as far as we could to fit them'.[42] The most important principle of Roman law for Erasmus in this context is the right to self-defence (*vim vi repellere licet*). The principle of personal defence in the face of aggression was a basic principle of Roman law ('vim vi defendere omnes leges omniaque iura permittunt', Dig. 9.2.45.4), and from ancient times it had been perceived as a principle of natural law—the UN Charter, Ch VII, Art 51 still recognizes the right of States to legitimate self-defence against an armed attack. This link between the right of legitimate self-defence and natural law had already been established, for example, by St Isidore (*Etymologies* 4.1–2), a passage that Gratian had included in the first distinction of the *Decretum* when he presents the different types of law and defines natural law (D. 1 *c*.7).[43] Erasmus does not dispute that this principle of Roman law is operational in the contemporary world, as was highlighted with respect to a hypothetical invasion by the Turks. Nor is he interested in analysing the links between this principle of Roman law and natural law, although his occasional comments about the law of nature (*lex naturae*)—'a kind of spark of perfect nature existing in imperfect man'—suggest that he did not consider this principle as belonging to natural law.[44] In reality, the object of his criticism is the projection of

[39] *Clarifications* (CWE 82) 98.

[40] ibid 101.

[41] *Complaint of Peace* (CWE 27) 299–300. See S Markish, *Erasmus and the Jews* (University of Chicago Press 1986) 27–47.

[42] *Adages* 336: 'War is sweet'.

[43] Russell (n 26) 56.

[44] I am quoting C Douglas McCullough, 'The Concept of Law in the Thought of Erasmus' (1981) 1 Erasmus of Rotterdam Society Yearbook 93. See also O Schottenloher, '*Lex naturae* und *lex Christi*' in J Coppens (ed), *Scrinium Erasmianum*, vol 2 (Brill 1969). Erasmus recognizes that natural law may

this principle that belongs to Roman civil law onto the law of the Gospels, in other words, the philosophy of Christ:

What if the words 'it is allowed to repel force with force' belong to the law of the emperor, not to the law of the gospel? ... For what right do they have to use force to repel the force of wicked men when they have been commanded to love even their enemies, to do good to those who do evil to them, to pray for their persecutors [Mt 5:54], and when they have been told 'do not offer any resistance at all to evil' [Mt 5:39]?[45]

According to Erasmus, instead of interpreting the original text correctly, theologians and jurists were twisting the sense of it to adapt it to the needs of their own times. So, for example, faced with the impossibility of reconciling the principle of *vim vi repellere licet* with the principle of not putting up resistance, medieval commentators like Nicholas of Lyra were indicating that it was not a matter of precepts but counsels.[46] Erasmus reproached these interpretations of Christ's words by saying that 'we defend war with the words of Christ ... we make Christ our authority for it, twisting his words to the point that it seems he commanded, not tolerated, the practices he had previously forbidden'.[47]

## 3.3 The philosophy of Christ and the Contemporary Era

Erasmus questions the link between Christianity and war because he wants to recuperate for his contemporaries what he considers to be the original message of Christ. This does not mean that he seeks to lay the foundations of a society based literally on the New Testament. The New Testament contains what Erasmus called the philosophy of Christ expressed in precepts and examples, but it also contains a set of norms and customs that were relevant only to the times of the Apostles and not to earlier or later periods. Erasmus points out that the New Testament asks for tolerance to be shown towards heretics and false prophets until the Day of Final Judgment (Mt 13:24–30, 36–43), the faithful are recommended to be moderate in their treatment of Jews and pagans, and the 'beatitude' of those who castrate themselves for 'the realm of God' (Mt 19:12) is mentioned.[48] For Erasmus, none of these three things makes sense in the contemporary world. The philosophy of Christ, on the other hand, represents an 'eternal wisdom' that defines the essence of a Christian.[49] According to Erasmus, the life of Christ offered an 'absolute archetype' of what

have normative value but stresses that treating natural law as part of scholastic thought on war involves a departure from the message of Christ; Erasmus's view was that it was in fact Christ who restored the true nature of Man, so that all natural law ought by definition to be identified with Christ's law: 'Indeed, this philosophy easily penetrates into the minds of all, an action in especial accord with human nature. Moreover, what else is the philosophy of Christ, which He himself calls a rebirth, than the restoration of human nature originally well reformed?' (*Paraclesis*, 100).

45 *Clarifications* (CWE 82) 65 and 64.

46 *Adages* 341: 'War is sweet'. For the texts of Nicholas of Lyra in his Biblical *Postilla*, see S Seidel Menchi, *Adagia: Sei saggi politici in forma di proverbi* (Einaudi Torino 1980) 363.

47 *Adages* 341: 'War is sweet'.

48 Bejczy (n 33) 20–22; Christ-Von Wedel (n 33) 41.

49 *Paraclesis* 95. Augustijn (n 33) 84.

Christian behaviour should be:[50] 'Our Lord came not merely to tell us what was allowed—how far we might fall below perfection—but what goal we must strive for with all our might.'[51] In this way, the reader, whether Christian or not, should 'drink in the teaching of Christ', think and read constantly about his life 'with the intention of becoming better than he was before, not of adapting the Gospel text to fit his own affections but of correcting his way of life and his desires to match the rule that it lays down'.[52]

It is as well to remember, though, that it is not always possible to act in accordance with this 'archetype'. On occasions, the determination to act in accordance with Christ's example may jeopardize peace in the Christian republic; the failure to defend oneself from an attack by the Turks would be an example of this. At the time when the Apostles were writing, repelling force with force was not allowed; to accept the contrary would have been to debase the glory of the victories won by the Apostles and the martyrs; nevertheless, 'although it was fitting that the church should arise initially from such foundations, there is no necessity for things to remain permanently the same'.[53] For Erasmus, given the social, political and religious circumstances of his time, it was permissible to repel force with force 'as long as you add not only the restraint of a blameless defence but also a regard for Christian gentleness—a model which it is fitting we should emulate as well as we can'.[54] This tolerance of war, of course, is circumstantial. The whole of Erasmus's intellectual project is defined by an unshakeable faith in the possibility of radically transforming contemporary society—both the Christian and the non-Christian—by recuperating the original message of Christ.[55] Tolerance of war depends on where society finds itself on the road towards full assimilation of the philosophy of Christ, because in the end 'if all Christians were such as Christ wanted them to be, there would be no war among them, not even a quarrel'.[56]

## 4. The Moral Education of Rulers

Erasmus questions the legitimacy of the just war for the Christian on the basis of his historical reading of the New Testament. In doing so, he took issue with a doctrinal tradition that went back more than a thousand years and called into question the foundations of the just war theory, namely, the framework of concepts and ideas used by rulers, on the advice of the jurists and theologians of the courts of Europe, to declare war. From this radical perspective of the problem, we realize that Erasmus did not see natural law or the law of nations (*ius gentium*) as jurists and

[50] *Clarifications* (CWE 82) 67. 'He is the sole archetype, and whoever departs from it even in the slightest deviates from what is right and runs outside the true path', *The Handbook of the Christian Soldier* (CWE 66) 84.

[51] *Adages* 341: 'War is sweet'.

[52] *Paraclesis* 105; *Paraphrase on Matthew* (CWE 45) 6.

[53] *On the Turkish War* (CWE 64) 236.

[54] *Clarifications* (CWE 82) 65. See Bejczy (n 33) 22–23.

[55] Bejczy (n 33) 194. See *Adages* 346–50: 'War is sweet' (about the 'war against Turks' 346).

[56] *Apology* (CWE 84) 349. See Dealy (n 21) 62.

theologians—from Innocent IV to Francisco de Vitoria, for example—saw them, that is, as sources from which to extract principles that enabled wars between rulers to be regulated. The solutions to the problems of the contemporary world could not be found in the theoretical edifice of medieval scholasticism, which had been corrupted, according to the humanist Erasmus, by its erroneous and self-serving interpretations of the ancient texts. The only way to reform European politics was to educate rulers, and the political class in general, in a new moral order, which Erasmus conceived of as outside the scholastic tradition.

The principles that should guide this education are set out in his works on political themes. With regard to the moral education of rulers, two important principles that go hand in hand in Erasmus's political thought involve them having a degree of responsibility that includes accountability for their political actions. A ruler's political decisions are controlled and approved by the citizens and so should be oriented to the common good, not to private interest. Otherwise, the ruler is a tyrant. Based on this premise, which is consistent with the political theory of fifteenth-century Italian humanism and the tradition of government in the Netherlands, Erasmus articulates his thoughts on the politics of domestic government as well as foreign policy.

## 4.1 Responsibility of rulers

As was the case with other humanists in northern Europe, Erasmus's political theory represented 'an extension and consolidation of a range of arguments originally discussed in *quattrocento* Italy'.[57] In the turbulent Italy of the Late Middle Ages, the external and internal legitimacy of a ruler was no longer grounded in hereditary rights. The families that ruled in Milan, Florence, and Naples in the mid-fifteenth century had scarcely been in power for two decades. On the other hand, it was difficult for 'the divinely sanctioned powers of the emperor and the pope', who represented 'the two perennial foundations of the legal order of the *ius commune*',[58] to continue carrying out effectively the legitimizing function that they had held. The Empire was immersed in a process of political 'disintegration'.[59] After the Great Schism and the conciliar movement, the pope was starting to be considered as just another political leader in the context of European politics.[60] Before this political crisis, the humanists articulated a theory of political power in which legitimacy was founded neither on hereditary rights nor on papal or imperial investitures. Political legitimacy was founded exclusively on exercising the virtues appropriate to the good

[57] Skinner (n 1) 244. See, for example, *Education of a Prince* (CWE 27) 206, 218–19; *Adages* 57: 'One ought to be born'; *Adages* 251: 'The Sileni'.

[58] J Canning, *Ideas of Power in the Late Middle Ages 1296–1417* (CUP 2011) 137.

[59] J Whaley, *Germany and the Holy Roman Empire I: Maximilian I to the Peace of Westphalia 1493–1648* (CUP 2012) 40. See also Bonney (n 4) 92–99.

[60] For the growing importance of the papal states after the conciliar movement, see P Prodi, *Il sovrano pontefice. Un corpo e due anime: la monarchia papale nella prima età moderna* (il Mulino 1982), and AD Wright, *The Early Modern Papacy: From the Council of Trent to the French Revolution, 1564–1789* (Routledge 2000).

ruler, whether the regime was a republic or a monarchy: 'for a person to be a prince it is not enough to be born, to have ancestral statues, the sceptre, and the crown'.[61] These humanists appropriated both the Aristotelian and Ciceronian traditions of political virtue, as well as concepts arising from the political theory developed in the medieval legal tradition, but did so by severing the ties 'with theology and, above all, with feudal reality'.[62] Within this framework, the citizens are the only ones who concede political power to the ruler on the basis that he is acting in the common interest, and, consequently, they may lawfully take it away from him if the ruler behaves like a tyrant. Erasmus himself summarizes it as: 'A prince's duty ... is to rule; whereas in truth to be a prince is nothing but to organize the common good ... For power that is not united with wisdom and goodness is tyranny and not power, and the public will, which gave it to him, can equally take it away.'[63] The political language of Erasmus is to a large extent the language of Italian political humanism prior to Machiavelli, an author unknown to Erasmus and whose work was actually an attempt to destroy the theory of virtue politics articulated by the fifteenth-century Italian humanists.[64]

As a subject of the Burgundian-Habsburg Netherlands, Erasmus had been educated in a political environment that made him particularly receptive to the ideas of fifteenth-century Italian political humanism. James D Tracy has pointed out that the: 'Netherlanders were accustomed to think of the prince as being restrained by contractual agreements with Estates.'[65] Neither his general observations on political theory nor his opinions on contemporary politics can be separated from this

[61] *Adages* 59: 'One ought to be born'. In an age when hereditary succession predominated, Erasmus argues that the election of rulers by their own subjects would be the most intelligent option. Reality is, however, what it is. In this context, the education of future rulers, important in any political regime, becomes an urgent necessity (58). See also *Education of a Prince* (CWE 27) 206–7. For these passages, see Tracy 1978 (n 12) 36–39.

[62] GM Cappelli, 'Il castigo del Re. Bartolo, Pontano, e il problema della disubbidienza' (2014) 34 Studi Umanistici Piceni 91–104 (103).

[63] 'The Sileni' *Adages* 253, 252; 'among Christians supreme rule means administration of the state, and not dominion', in *Adages* 59: 'One ought to be born'; see also *Education of a Prince* (CWE 27) 222. 'Civil laws can not only depose an emperor for misgovernment, but even sentence him to death', *Julius excluded* (CWE 27) 179. In *Education of a Prince* this law is mentioned, but it is pointed out that it is no longer in force (CWE 27) 231. Aristotle had already referred to the idea of the ruler as administrator, not tyrant, in *Politics* 1315b. The humanists—from Petrarch onwards—take up the idea again for the political context of the fifteenth century. See *Adages* 344: 'War is sweet'. For tyranny and tyrannicide in Erasmus, see Isnardi Parente (n 28) 37–40; M Turchetti, *Tyrannie et tyrannicide de l'antiquité à nos jours* (PUF 2001) 337–43. See also M Hörnqvist, *Machiavelli and Empire* (CUP 2004) 194–227.

[64] For fifteenth-century political humanism, see GM Cappelli, 'Petrarca e l'umanesimo politico del Quattrocento' (2005) 7 Verbum 153–75; '*Corpus est res publica*. La struttura della comunità secondo l'umanesimo politico' in L Geri (ed), *Principi prima del Principe* (Bulzoni 2012) 117–31; 'Machiavelli, l'umanesimo e l'amore politico' (March 2016) 134 *Engramma* (online); and his edition of Giovanni Pontano's *De principe* (Salerno 2003). See also R Esposito, 'La fondazione etica della politica. Il mito del tirano tra Antico e Rinascimento' in his *Ordine e conflitto. Machiavelli e la letteratura politica del Rinascimento italiano* (Liguori 1984); R Fubini, *Italia Quattrocentesca: Politica e diplomazia nell'età di Lorenzo il Magnifico* (Franco Angeli 1992); J Hankins, 'Machiavelli, Civic Humanism and the Humanist Politics of Virtue' (2014) 32 Italian Culture 98–109. For the critical reassessment of so-called Florentine civic republicanism (which I take into consideration in this section), see J Hankins (ed), *Civic Renaissance Humanism: Reappraisals and Reflections* (CUP 2004); GM Cappelli, 'Conceptos transversales. República y monarquía en el humanismo político' (2009) 21 Res Publica 51–69.

[65] Tracy 1978 (n 12) 46.

context; so when Erasmus privately gives his opinion about the conflicts between the Seventeen Provinces and the Habsburg dynasty, his 'comments reflect a decidedly urban and States perspective, despite his connections to the court'.[66] Similarly, when he takes stock of the loss of the people's freedoms and the increased political power of the princes, he is thinking specifically, as Tracy himself States, of his own native land:

> If you compare the present with the state of things seventy years ago, as our forefathers describe it, it is unbelievable how much the freedom of the people, the status of the towns, the authority of parliaments, and respect for the church's hierarchy have all declined; conversely, how much the power of princes—and their demands—has grown and, in a word, how much more applicable is that too-famous maxim, 'what pleases the prince, that is the law'.[67]

Despite the fact that the political context was different from that of the Italian States, Erasmus must have seen a direct correlation between the institutional traditions of his own country and the political theory developed in the works of fifteenth-century Italian humanism. The *Panegyric for Archduke Philip of Austria* (1504) and, in particular, *The Education of a Christian Prince* (1516) are obvious examples of this correlation; written in the language of Italian political humanism, the two works were, among other things, moral and political guides for the two titular heads of the Duchy of Burgundy, Philip IV (1481–1506), and Charles II (1506–56), the future Holy Roman Emperor. Speaking through the voice of the 'native land', which is irritated by Philip's journey to Castile in 1502, Erasmus pointed out:

> Spain, it is true, once gave your sister a husband, and more recently gave you a wife, but I gave you life. You were crowned for her, but born for me: I admit I owe everything to you, but in return you owe yourself to me. That is a bold thing to say, but it is true. I know I address no tyrant, but my prince.[68]

## 4.2 The Christian prince

The responsibility of the ruler for his actions and control of his political action by the citizens are, therefore, two key principles in the political thought of Erasmus. He, however, like other humanists from northern Europe, reinterprets this tradition from the moment when he places the person of Jesus Christ at the centre of his

[66] Tracy 1997 (n 12) 97, where several examples of this political position of Erasmus are remarked upon in relation to Maximilian's actions. See also Tracy (n 23) 20.

[67] *On the Turkish War* (CWE 64) 261 (Institutes 1.2.6; Dig. 1.4.1). See also *Adages* 60: 'One ought to be born'. This increase in power moves the Christian rulers closer to the political customs of the Turks: 'But what shall I say about their system of government? Where is the rule of law among them? Whatever pleases the tyrant, that is the law' (CWE 64) 258.

[68] *Panegyric for Archduke Philip of Austria* (CWE 27) 17. 'A state, even if it lacks a prince, will be a state', asserts Erasmus, because 'a prince simply cannot exist without a state, and in fact the state takes in the prince, rather than the reverse. What makes a prince a great man, except the consent of his subjects' *The Education of a Prince* (CWE 27) 272; 'Government depends to a large extent on the consent of the people, which was what created kings in the first place' (284; and also 215). See *Adages* 186: 'Sparta is your portion' and *Adages* 213: 'As warts grow'. Tracy 1978 (n 12) 5, 35, has indicated the importance of political *consensus* for Erasmus.

political theory.[69] For him, the virtues of the good prince in the political tradition of the fifteenth-century Italian humanism are in harmony with the message and example of Christ: 'If the prince attains complete virtue, this will make him fully a Christian, and if he becomes fully a Christian, this will enable him to lay the foundations of a perfect commonwealth.'[70] The central role of Christ in the education of the ruler is the core idea dealt with in the treatise *The Education of a Christian Prince*: 'What must be implanted deeply and before all else in the mind of the prince is the best possible understanding of Christ.'[71] It is however in his paraphrases of the Gospels where the exemplary nature of Christ as a model for the rulers of the time was made explicit.

Erasmus published his paraphrase of the New Testament in small volumes between 1517 and 1524. The dedications in these paraphrases are significant; the four Gospels and the Acts of the Apostles were dedicated to the five people with most political power in Europe at the time: the paraphrase of Matthew was dedicated to Charles V (1522); John to the Archduke Ferdinand (1523), who was Charles's brother, and Regent of the Empire since 1521; the paraphrase of Luke to Henry VIII (1523); Mark to Francis 1 (1524); and the Acts of the Apostles to the recently elected Pope Clement VII (1524). These paraphrases of the texts of the Apostles were free of the erudition that normally accompanied this sort of commentary: no authorities in the margins nor any of the habitual accumulation of patristic and scholastic loci to illustrate the meaning of a biblical passage.[72] The objective of placing these volumes among the readings of the emperor, the pope, the monarchs mentioned and the ruler of the empire was to engineer it so that the political and moral action of these men drew inspiration from the accounts of the life of Christ as transmitted by the Apostles. Religion, of course, was omnipresent in the daily lives of the rulers, but Erasmus thought that it was a purely ritual religiosity and that their moral education was, in fact, supplied by the culture of chivalry that held sway in European courts.[73]

In these prologues, Erasmus reflects on the relationship between reading the Gospels and political action: 'What business has a lay prince, what business has a young man, with the gospel?',[74] bearing in mind, he observes, that a paraphrase of the Gospels might appear to be more appropriate reading matter for 'abbots or bishops'.[75] Erasmus goes on to say that the 'philosophy of the Gospel . . . is more needed by the world's most powerful monarchs than by anyone', because 'if they go wrong, it is the whole world that suffers'. He acknowledges the difficulty of guiding political action on the basis of the message of Christ: 'It may be that a secular prince, absorbed

69 Adams (n 24); Skinner (n 1) 230–36; B Bradshaw, 'Transalpine Humanism' in J Burns (ed), *The Cambridge History of Political Thought 1450–1700* (CUP 1991).

70 Skinner (n 1) 232–33. See *Education of a Prince* (CWE 27) 214.

71 *Education of a Prince* (CWE 27) 212.

72 For the paraphrases of New Testament texts, see J Coppens, 'Les idées réformistes d'Érasme dans les préfaces aux Paraphrases du Nouveau Testament' (1961) 3 Analecta Lovaniensia Biblica et Orientalia 34; J Chomarat *Grammaire et rhétorique chez Érasme*, vol 1 (Les Belles Lettres 1981) 587–710; HM Pabel and M Vessey (eds), *Holy Scripture Speaks: The Production and Reception of Erasmus' Paraphrases on the New Testament* (Toronto UP 2002).

73 See simply Augustijn (n 33) 43–88.

74 *Paraphrase on John* (CWE 46) 5.

75 *Paraphrase on Matthew* (CWE 45) 5.

as he must be for the most part in grosser business and in his duty to defend the public peace, cannot always achieve the results he clearly perceives to be the most just.' Nonetheless, the mere assimilation of these 'solid principles of philosophy' would guarantee that 'he will always strive for what is nearest to the commands of Christ and will be deflected as little as possible from his aim'.[76]

In practical terms, according to Erasmus, the good Christian ruler will be the one who renounces any policy of expansion, whether through military alliances and action or matrimonial alliances. Any military action that imposes political power on a new territory entails raising taxes to pay for mercenary troops, as well as calamities for the civilian population.[77] In point of fact, a ruler should be content with the 'province' that he has been entrusted to govern and should work towards reaching a good understanding with neighbouring regions in order to promote trade and cooperation.[78] Erasmus criticized the eagerness of European rulers to expand their political power via alliances and military actions: 'you will hardly find one ... who is content with the authority he has and does not attempt to add something to the extent of his dominions'.[79] So, for example, he considered that Pope Julius II was the instigator of the League of Cambrai as well as the Holy League: 'Today there is not one Christian king whom I have not incited to battle, after breaking, tearing, and shattering all the treaties by which they had painstakingly come to agreement among themselves', the pope boasts in *Julius exclusus*;[80] he also reproached King James IV of Scotland for his alliance with Louis XII and his attempted invasion of England, which brought him nothing but his own death at the Battle of Flodden (1513);[81] finally, he rebuked Louis XII of France for his military actions in Italy as being damaging to the kingdom of France: 'The kingdom of France is by far and in every way the most prosperous of all, but she would have been still more prosperous had she refrained from invading Italy.'[82]

Furthermore, for Erasmus, any attempt to use marriage to extend political power meant subordinating the general interest to the private interests of a particular dynasty: 'the fortunes of princes may be improved by alliances of this kind, but the fortunes of the people suffer and are diminished'.[83] Rulers should always marry men or women from their own kingdom to guarantee the loyalty of the people towards their own rulers;[84] in this respect, the political consequences of the marriage of the Duke of Burgundy, Philip IV, to Joanna of Castile must have been uppermost in Erasmus's mind.[85] Despite the fact that these marriage alliances often formed part of the agreement in peace treaties between two rulers, Erasmus denounced the extraordinary fragility of the peace, given that it could be broken on the death

76 *Paraphrase on John* (CWE 46) 5–7.
77 *Education of a Prince* (CWE 27) 282–83, 284, 285. See Tracy (n 12) 88–90.
78 *Education of a Prince* (CWE 27) 279, 276 and *Adages* 183–91: 'Sparta is your portion'.
79 *Adages* 184: 'Sparta is your portion'; *Adages* 344: 'War is sweet'.
80 *Julius excluded* (CWE 27) 173. See Tracy (n 12) 31.
81 *Education of a Prince* (CWE 27) 278; *Adages* 187–88: 'Sparta is your portion'.
82 *Education of a Prince* (CWE 27) 277, 282; *Adages* 187: 'Sparta is your portion'.
83 *Education of a Prince* (CWE 27) 278.
84 ibid 277–78.
85 *Adages* 186: 'Sparta is your portion'; see also *Education of a Prince* (CWE 27) 256, 278–79.

of one of the spouses or the betrothed.[86] A 'stable and lasting' peace could only be achieved by rulers who acted in accordance with the 'true principles' of a moral order based on the teachings of Christ, control of themselves and their passions and the consequent exercise of the virtues of the good ruler.[87] In the face of a chivalric culture that extolled the sword above the pen, and in the context of his call to recuperate the original piety of Christianity, Erasmus defends the duty to cultivate one's soul and to exert self-control.

## 4.3 Arbitration

Besides the moral education and guidance of rulers, Erasmus proposes arbitration as a means of peacefully resolving territorial and diplomatic conflicts between them: 'If some dispute arises between princes, why do they not take it to arbitration instead?'[88] The figure of the arbiter, already described in Roman law, had a place in the practice of justice at the time.[89] The arbiter was a man of honest reputation hired by two parties in dispute who was delegated—by means of the so-called *compromissum*—to resolve a conflict. He knew all aspects of the question at the heart of the conflict between the parties and had to apply the laws in a strict way in order to formulate the final ruling. Judicially speaking, the arbiter (*arbiter*) and the judge (*iudex*) proceeded in the same way, but differed in two important respects: the arbiter, unlike the judge, was chosen by both parties and could be hired at any stage of the dispute; in the same way, the arbiter, given his private character, did not have jurisdiction, so that his ruling could not affect the rights of anyone who had not hired him. A third category was that of the *arbitrator*, a sort of friendly mediator who did not judge the case according to the written law, but on the basis of equity (*aequitas*).

Erasmus's idea of arbiters corresponds more to the figure of the *arbitrator* than to the *arbiter*. He talks of 'earnest and learned bishops', 'venerable abbots', 'nobles of great age with the wisdom of long experience', but not specifically of individuals with legal training.[90] Erasmus assumes that arbitrators will go through the process of formulating a ruling on any dynastic conflict guided by that *aequitas*,

[86] *Education of a Prince* (CWE 27) 278.

[87] 'But if a peace were to be based on true principles, it would be stable and lasting' *Education of a Prince* (CWE 27) 278; 'the qualities of a king: namely wisdom, a sense of justice, personal restraint, foresight, and concern for the public well-being' 206 (see also 256).

[88] *Education of a Prince* (CWE 27) 284.

[89] L Fowler, 'Forms of Arbitration' in S Kuttner (ed), *Proceedings of the Fourth International Congress of Medieval Canon Law* (Biblioteca Apostolica Vaticana 1976) 133–47; L Martone, *Arbiter-Arbitrator: Forme di giustizia privata nell'età del diritto comune* (Jovene 1984); MS Anderson, *The Rise of Modern Diplomacy 1450–1919* (Longman 1993) 204–8, and the entries 'Arbitrage', 'Arbitration', and 'Arbitre' written by A Amanieu, in R Naz (ed), *Dictionnaire de droit canonique*, vol 1 (Librairie Letouzey et Ané 1935–65) cols 862–901, with the basic sources on this particular in both canon and civil law.

[90] *Adages* 346: 'War is sweet'. See also *Education of a Prince* (CWE 27) 284 and *Complaint of Peace* (CWE 27) 310. For arbitration in Erasmus, see O Schottenloher, 'Érasme et la *respublica christiana*' in JC Margolin (ed), *Colloquia Erasmiana Turonensia*, vol 2 (University of Toronto Press 1972) 675–76; X Tubau, *Erasmo mediador: Política y religión en los primeros años de la Reforma* (Universidad de Valladolid 2012) 79–92.

which in this context means 'a tempering of the law out of feelings of humanity'.[91] Thus, led by the same criteria that should guide the political actions of rulers, the common good and peace of the Christian republic, these arbitrators will seek the best possible solution for the two parties in dispute. This flexible approach to the law—because extreme right is extreme wrong—ensures that the circumstances and the overall benefits will be taken into consideration when issuing the ruling.[92] As Erasmus himself succinctly puts it: 'An unjust peace is preferable by far to a just war.'[93]

## 5. Conclusion

Erasmus argues that there is a moral order within which rulers need to be educated and on the basis of which power should be exercised. Up until Erasmus's time, the moral order had been regulated by the Church by means of canon law; Erasmus's complaint was that canon law had not regulated this order efficiently, in particular, because it had distorted the message of Christ by creating a theory of just war that promoted rather than curbed warfare. Consequently, Erasmus argues for the recuperation of Christ's original message and calls for the gradual subjection of sovereigns to the philosophy of Christ, as well as to the theory of virtue politics developed by fifteenth-century Italian humanism. So, according to Erasmus, the ruler should be satisfied with the territory that has been entrusted to him, should not use marriage as a tool for extending his political power over other regions, should endeavour to maintain good relations with rulers of neighbouring territories, and should take every political decision with the common good of the community that he has been entrusted to govern in mind. Furthermore, the political legitimacy of a ruler is no longer founded on a papal or imperial investiture or on hereditary right, but exclusively on the exercise of the virtues appropriate to a ruler, which in practical terms would mean, for example, developing a foreign policy in accord with the guidelines indicated by Erasmus for European rulers of the period. If the ruler did not comply with those guidelines, the citizens who granted him political power could, in the same way, take it away from him. In this respect, Erasmus's challenge is that the enforcement of a moral world order no longer depends on the Church, but on the morality and responsibility of the rulers themselves, or else, they should settle their differences through arbitration. The true message of Christ, which can be accessed through Erasmus's paraphrases of the New Testament for example, equips rulers to act appropriately in the political sphere. Hence, the moral formation of rulers, grounded in Christ's message and the virtue politics of fifteenth-century Italian humanism, is the keystone of the moral world order that Erasmus proposes for his contemporaries.

[91] Ep 2126 (CWE 15) 149. The central place occupied by *aequitas* in Erasmus's thought was already made clear by G Kish, *Erasmus un die Jurisprudenz seiner Zeit: Studien zum humanistischen Rechtsdenken* (Helbing and Lichtenhahn 1960) 55–68, 108–32. See also Isnardi Parente (n 28) 48–49.

[92] *Adages* 129–30: 'Extreme right is extreme wrong'.

[93] *Adages* 345: 'War is sweet'.

# 5

# Legislating for the 'Whole World That Is, in a Sense, a Commonwealth'

## Conquest, Occupation, and 'the Defence of the Innocent'

*Anthony Pagden*

## 1. Defending the Innocent

'It is difficult for us in the present age', wrote Sir Travers Twiss, former Queen's Advocate General, and salaried champion of Leopold II's occupation of the Congo in 1856

> to measure the degree of courage and noble principle which impelled these excellent monks to vindicate the right of the oppressed against the authority of the Church, the ambitions of the Crown, the avarice and pride of their countrymen, and the prejudices of their own Order. These were the early streaks of dawn the earnest of the coming day.[1]

The 'excellent monks' were Francisco de Vitoria who held the Prime Chair of Theology at the University of Salamanca between 1526 and his death in 1546, and his successor Domingo de Soto. Both were members—and Vitoria has some claim to being the founder—of what has subsequently come to be called the 'School of Salamanca'. The oppressed whose rights they had supposedly vindicated were the native peoples of the Americas. Ever since at least the early twentieth century it has become a commonplace to refer to Vitoria, and the 'school' in general, along with Hugo Grotius, as the 'fathers of international law'.[2] What was clearly significant for Twiss about both Vitoria and Soto was not, however, that they had somehow invented 'international law', but that what they had to say about the law of nations, the *ius gentium* had been prompted by their indignation at the abuse by the papacy of any acceptable notion of territorial sovereignty. It had, in Twiss's words, been the

[1] *Two Introductory Lectures on the Science of International Law* (1856) 6–88, and see M Koskenniemi, *The Gentle Civilizer of Nations: The Rise and Fall of International Law 1870–1960* (CUP 2001) 78.

[2] See eg J Brown Scott, *The Spanish Origin of International Law: Lectures on Francisco de Vitoria (1480–1546) and Francisco Suarez (1548–1617)* (School of Foreign Service, Georgetown University 1928).

'scandal given by [the] extreme reach of the authority on the part of the See of Rome coupled with the cruel and rapacious abuse of the Donation made by the Spaniards' which had 'provoked' a 'champion from amongst the ranks of the theological casuists to step forth in [sic] behalf of the native inhabitants of the newly discovered countries'.

For Twiss and a later generation of international lawyers, in particular those associated with the *Institut de droit international* (of which Twiss was a member), the members of the School of Salamanca became the champions of a certain kind of moral insistence upon the obligations which European rulers had necessarily incurred in their, usually brutal, dealings with non-European peoples. 'Reading these pages', wrote another member of the *Institut*, the Belgian jurist Ernst Nys, of Vitoria's *De Indis*, in 1894 'that breathe with the love of humanity, from which emerges a truly independent spirit, and where each line is witness to a profound knowledge of the texts' made him regret that Vitoria and his 'illustrious disciples' had not been able to exercise a greater influence over the 'science of the law of peoples'. It was, he believed, now up to him, and to his generation, to rectify this error.[3]

More recent scholarship, however, has tended to cast Vitoria and his successors in a rather different light.[4] Beneath the School of Salamanca's seemingly emancipatory and anti-imperial claims there lurked the assumption that Europeans as 'civilized' (and Christian) peoples had a natural, and hence universal, right to exercise sovereignty over non-civilized and inevitably non-Christian peoples. Typically, Antony Anghie has argued that for Vitoria 'the Indian is excluded from the realm of sovereignty ... [and] exists only as the object against which the powers of sovereignty may be exercised in the most extreme ways' and that 'Vitoria bases his conclusion that the Indians are not sovereign on the simple assertion that they are pagan'.[5]

Anghie's project, and that of most of his followers, is to demonstrate that the 'civilized'/'barbarian' distinction which plays a central role in nineteenth-century conceptions of international law—and against which so many members of the *Institut de droit international*, had fought—could be found in Vitoria's reformulation of the law of nations. By implication, therefore the entire project of a universal law had not merely been a response to what the German jurist Carl Schmitt in 1951 called

[3] *Les Origines du droit international* (1894), 129 and see A Fitzmaurice, *Sovereignty, Property and Empire, 1500–2000* (CUP 2105) 255. True to his word, in 1914, Nys arranged for the publication of Vitoria's works by the Carnegie Endowment for International Peace.

[4] See, eg, L Nuzzo, *Il linguaggio giuridico della conquista. Strategie di controllo nelle Indie spagnole* (Jovene 2004); J Thuo Gathii, *War, Commerce and International Law* (OUP 2010); JM Barreto (ed), *Human Rights from a Third World Perspective: Critique, History and International Law* (Cambridge Scholars 2013); for an analysis of this literature, and the legitimacy of 'anachronistic' readings of Vitoria (and others), see M Koskenniemi, 'Vitoria and Us. Thoughts on Critical Histories of International Law' (2014) 22 Journal of the Max-Planck Institute for European Legal History 119–38.

[5] *Imperialism, Sovereignty and the Making of International Law* (CUP 2005) 27, 29. Anghie's assumption that Vitoria was trying to work out a theory of sovereignty in 'the shifting political conditions of Renaissance Europe' is also mistaken. Vitoria's use of 'public and private *dominium*'—the closest he comes to any modern notion of sovereignty—is perfectly in keeping with Roman law usages of these terms. Anghie also attributes an uncertainty to Vitoria on the distinctions between Divine, natural, and civil law which appears to be entirely his own.

'European land-appropriation'; it had also been entirely corrupted by it.[6] I believe this to be wrong. Not because it is anachronistic—I have no objection to that —nor even because it is tendentious; but because it attributes to Vitoria things which he did not say, could not have said, and which none of his subsequent readers from the sixteenth to the twentieth centuries supposed him to have said. It is certainly true that Vitoria, in common with probably all Europeans before about the middle of the twentieth century, accepted a broad distinction between 'civilized' and non-civilized peoples, and he clearly associated 'civilization' closely with 'Christianity'. But had he held the view that Anghie attributes to him he would, on his own account, have fallen prey to the heresy, espoused most strikingly in his day by the Calvinists (and thus, and not incidentally, by the British) of deriving *dominium* from grace not law. For all the members of the School of Salamanca, all of whom were neo-Thomists, the civil law—and therefore all matters of government—derived not from divine dispensation, much less from Divine Law, but from the natural law; and the natural law was, by definition, the same for all peoples everywhere. In the words of the much-cited verse from the Gospel of St Mathew (5:45) 'he maketh his sun to rise on the evil and on the good, and sendeth rain on the just and on the unjust'. Unbelievers could not, therefore, be deprived of their rights or their goods by believers merely on the grounds that they were unbelievers for, as Vitoria phrased it: 'unbelief does not cancel out either natural or human (civil) law, but all forms of *dominium* derive from natural or human law; therefore they cannot be annulled by lack of faith'.[7] It is true that there is a sense in the writings of nearly all the School of Salamanca that 'civilized', and more importantly Christian, Europeans bear some kind of moral duty towards non-Christians. But these are more in the nature of Kantian 'imperfect duties' and they certainly do not convey any legal or political *rights*, much less constitute grounds for sovereignty. The claim that non-Christians—even the 'Saracens' who had indeed proved to be the 'perpetual enemies' of Christianity for than more a century—in fact, enjoyed precisely the same legal and political status, and thus the same legal and political rights, as non-Christians was, as we shall see, a central part of Vitoria's main argument.[8]

[6] C Schmitt, *The Nomos of the Earth in the International Law of the Jus Publicum Europaeum* (GL Umen tr and ed, Telos 2003) 69.

[7] 'On the American Indians' 1. 3, in A Pagden and J Lawrance (eds), *Vitoria Political Writings* (CUP 1991) 244.

[8] Anghie also claims that 'the Indians could be characterized as Saracens, as heathens, and their rights and duties determined accordingly' (*Imperialism, Sovereignty and the Making of International Law* 17). But the 'Saracens'—ie the Turks—are the 'perpetual enemies' of all Christians not because they are unbelievers, but because they occupy the lands—in particular the 'Holy Land'—which rightfully belongs to Christendom. The Indians are also, although this would not alter the structure of Vitoria's argument 'invincibly ignorant'—that is they had never, and through no obvious fault of their own, heard the Gospel, whereas all Muslims (and Jews) are 'vincibly ignorant' in having heard and rejected it. There were some who argued that had the Indians been more 'worthy' God would have sent Christian preachers to them before 1492, and this argument is supported by Aquinas's assertion that 'If a man born among barbarian nations, does what he can, God Himself will show him what is necessary for salvation, either by inspiration or sending a teacher to him' (Sent. II, 28, Q. 1, A. 4, ad 4). But for the neo-Thomist, such as Vitoria, even the most unworthy is still capable of exercising *dominium*.

All the members of the School of Salamanca also rarely lost an opportunity to emphasize the fact that the laws which governed the relationships, bellicose or otherwise, between the Spanish and the Indians, belonged to the law of nations, and they applied equally to the relationship between the Spanish and the French or any other European power. If, for instance, the Spanish possessed a natural right of access to the Americas, as Vitoria claimed they did, because by the terms of what he called 'the right of natural partnership and communication' (*ius naturalis societas et communicationis*) every man had a right 'to visit and travel through any land he wished' it followed that, by the same right, the French could not lawfully 'prevent the Spaniards from traveling to or even living in France and vice versa'.[9] Since, of course Castilian civil law forbade the subjects of the King of France from doing just that, this would have given the French as perfect a right to wage war against Charles V as he had to make war on the Indians. As another member of the *Institut*, Gaston Jèze observed in 1896 'As Vitoria already said in the sixteenth century, civilized powers have no more right to seize the territories of savages than savages have to occupy the European continent.'[10]

Anghie is right about one thing, however. Vitoria's attempt to refute the claim that the Spanish could be in possession of any a priori sovereignty in the American, begins with his rejection of the so-called papal Donation of 1493. This was made up of five bulls issued by Pope Alexander VI in 1493 granting to the Catholic Monarchs, Ferdinand and Isabella, in perpetuity, 'to you and to your successors' all territorial rights over all those lands 'as you have discovered or are about to discover', which were not already occupied by another Christian prince.[11] They were the most assertive, and the most persistent of the claims made by a European power to exercise sovereignty and property rights over the 'newly-discovered' peoples of the Americas, and they launched what Schmitt described as a 'legendary and unforeseen ... and unrepeatable historical event', which, in turn, had given rise to 'the traditional Eurocentric order of international law'.[12] For the conquest and occupation of America presented the jurists and theologians of Christian Europe with a truly novel problem: how to legitimate the appropriation of lands and peoples of whose existence the Europeans had previously had no prior knowledge. Before the 'discovery' of America—and in this sense it really was a 'discovery'—the only legal claims for 'land appropriation' had been made in territories which, like the Holy Land, had once formed part of the Roman Empire and were therefore supposedly a part of the *respublica Christianorum*. If America, was, however, in Vitoria's words 'previously

[9] 'On the American Indians' 3. 1. *Vitoria Political Writings* 280. For a more detailed account of the *ius naturalis societas et communicationis*, see A Pagden, *The Burdens of Empire: 1500 to the Present* (CUP 2015) 53–56.

[10] *Étude théorique et pratique sur l'occupation* (1896) 103; Fitzmaurice (n 3) 294–95.

[11] They are printed in J Gil and JM Maestre (eds), *Bulas Alejandrinas de 1493 texto y traducción, Humanismo latino y descrubrimiento* (Universidad de Sevilla and Universidad de Cadiz 1992) 16. And see H-J Prien, 'Las Bulas Alejandrinas de 1493' in B Schröter and K Schüller (eds), *Tordesillas y sus consequencias. La política de las grandes potencias europeas respecto a América Latina (1494–1898)* (Vervuet Iberoamericana 1995) 12–28.

[12] Schmitt (n 6) 69.

unknown to our world' and no one except a few with peculiar axes of their own to grind, doubted that that it was, then some new mode of legitimation for its acquisition would have to be found.[13]

All Alexander's bulls, and in particular *Dudum siquidem* of 25 September which extended the claim as far as the 'Western as well as Eastern regions and those that exist in India' relied upon an assumption, generally upheld by the canonists, but dismissed by almost everyone else, that the pope possessed *dominium* over both spiritual and secular matters, and that this could be exercised over both Christians and non-Christians. This, in turn, supposedly conferred upon the papacy the right to distribute the goods of its subjects as it so wished. Only the most committed champions of papal supremacy were prepared to uphold such a claim. It was, said Soto bluntly, nothing other than a prescription for tyranny, the kind of assertion to rights over the private property—and the persons—of the subjects of a prince that was acceptable only to Turks. Christian princes, by contrast, whose rule might be absolute but was never arbitrary, could not make use of the goods (*bona*)—and still less of the persons—of their subjects 'except where it is necessary for the defence and government of the community'.[14]

Both Vitoria and Soto were prepared to concede to the papacy some degree of instrumental authority in securing 'spiritual ends' and that, under certain circumstances, that authority could be said to extend to the 'power to make new princes, to unmake others, to divide empires and many other such things'. But in what Vitoria somewhat elusively described as the 'ordinary course of events': 'the pope has no power at least to judge the case of princes or the title of jurisdictions or realms'.[15] And it was clear to him that the conquest of the Americas belonged to the 'ordinary course of events'. It was also obvious that even if the pope did have such a power 'he could not give it to secular princes' for it would necessarily be held by the papacy and not by an individual pontiff, and could not therefore be alienated, any more than any wholly secular ruler could give away any part of his realm which was not also his own personal private property.[16] Furthermore although the pope clearly had some standing as a moral arbiter between Christian princes he 'has no dominion in the lands of the infidel', for precisely the reason that, as we have seen, *dominium* was taken to derive from nature not grace.[17] From this it must follow that, if the pope's universal authority derives from his status as Vicar of Christ, it cannot possibly extend to those who do not believe in Christ.

Vitoria was convinced, as indeed were most of his successors, that although the papal Donation clearly imposed an unequivocal moral obligation on the Spanish monarchs to make every attempt to evangelize the Indians—something emphasized

[13] 'On the American Indians' I, Introduction, *Vitoria Political Writings* 233. The same applied, *mutatis mutandis*, to the west coast of Africa, in which the Portuguese had also resorted to a papal donation. and Alexander VI's bulls in many respects follow closely that made by Pope Nicholas V the 1454 in to Afonso V of Portugal.

[14] *De iustitia et iure, libri decem* IV. IV. i. (Salamanca 1556) 301.

[15] 'On the Power of the Church' I. 5.8. and 5.3, *Vitoria Political Writings* 92 and 87.

[16] 'On the American Indians' 2. 2, *Vitoria Political Writings* 261.

[17] 'On the Power of the Church' I. 5.1, *Vitoria Political Writings* 84.

in *Pius Fidelium* of 25 June 1493—it could not be used as grounds for any right to exercise sovereignty or property rights, despite the fact that that is precisely what all five bulls claimed to be doing. Vitoria is, furthermore, insistent that the Spanish cannot wage war on the 'barbarians'—as he habitually calls them—in order to enable the Spanish to convert them as at least some of the canonists had also claimed. Since 'the right of natural partnership and communication' is a natural one, the Indians are under an obligation to allow the Spanish to enter their territories freely so long as they do so peacefully and, in their capacity as 'ambassadors of Christendom'.[18] However, the right to preach (*ius predicandi*) like the right to trade, has no standing of its own. Both are merely the consequences of 'the right of natural partnership and communication', and what Kant would later call the universal right of hospitality. Any attempt to violate that right would constitute grounds for a just war. So long, however, as the Indians 'permit the Spaniards to preach the gospel freely and without hindrance' they may not 'impose anything on them by war', whether or not the Indians chose to believe what they hear.[19] Assuming it to be the case that the 'Christian faith is set before them in a probable manner'—which means 'with provable and rational arguments and accompanied by manners both decent and observant of the law of nature' (which, however, Vitoria is certain has not been the case in America), then the 'barbarians' are obliged to accept the 'faith of Christ under pain of mortal sin'. But they are only obliged to do so under pain of mortal sin, and no secular power has the authority to wage war on mortal sinners merely because they are sinners.[20] Even if their rulers were to convert to Christianity these, although they can dismantle the trappings of the old faith and outlaw the 'unnatural' practices that had accompanied it, cannot force their subjects 'to believe or to accept baptism'.[21] Conversion must be a free choice, and, if it is to be valid, must be done out of sincere conviction. It would, therefore, Vitoria added, be 'the height of absurdity to claim ... that the barbarians may refuse Christ with impunity, but are obliged to accept Christ's vicar on pain of war and the plunder of all their goods'.[22]

America was clearly terra incognita. It had never formed a part of the Christian *oikumene*. The claim of the pope to exercise jurisdiction of any kind beyond the limits of Christendom was invalid (so too was the even flimsier claim of the Roman jurist Bartolus that the Roman Emperor was *de iure*, 'lord and monarch of all the world' which Vitoria dismissed in a few lines). It was therefore obvious, Vitoria concluded, 'that from what I have said the Spaniards when they first sailed to the land of the barbarians, carried with them no right at all to occupy their countries'. Since, however the Spanish clearly were now in occupation and since, or so he claimed to believe, Ferdinand and Isabella, 'Most Catholic Monarchs' and Charles V, officially entitled 'Most Righteous and Christian Prince', could not have failed 'to make the most careful and meticulous inquiries' into a matter of such concern to both their security and their conscience, the only possible argument which could justify the

[18] 'On the American Indians' 3. 1, *Vitoria Political Writings* 283.
[19] *Vitoria Political Writings* 285. [20] ibid 271.
[21] 'On Dietary laws, or Self-Restraint' 1. 5, *Vitoria Political Writings* 221.
[22] 'On the American Indians' 2. 2, *Vitoria Political Writings* 263.

Spanish presence must derive from some other source; not from canon law, but from the law of nations.[23]

Although they are never very explicit on the subject, for Vitoria and most of the School of Salamanca the law of nations, the *ius gentium* is essentially a positive law arrived at by a hypothetical common understanding between all—or most—of the peoples of the globe. In this respect it was believed to govern what Christoph Stumpf describes here as a 'wider circle of nations [beyond that is those belonging to the *respublica Christianorum*] … united by a universal human fellowship amongst human beings, which disregards religious persuasions or specific philosophical inclinations of individual members'.[24] And although for Vitoria civil power derives from the natural law directly, and not from the *ius gentium*, as it did for Baldus,[25] the *ius gentium* is closer to the natural law than it is to the civil (or human) law. (It is not, however, as it will later become for Gentili and Grotius, essentially identical with it.)[26] Underlying this assumption is the claim that the whole world is, as Vitoria phrased it, 'in a sense a commonwealth [*respublica*]'. This has something in common with the familiar Stoic circles, with the individual at the centre and humanity at the periphery, and with what Susan Longfield Karr, describes here as Andrea Alciati's 'ordering of the laws'.[27] Vitoria, however was not a Stoic (although Cicero who was his source in this as in much else was). The Stoic circles moved outwards from the individual to the family to the community to the city and finally to humanity itself. On this understanding, the civil law (the law of individual families and cities) although it must be in accordance with natural law and compatible with the *ius gentium*, in cases of conflict with the latter must take precedence over it. Vitoria, reversed this relationship. Because the *ius gentium*, as the law of humanity, derives from the *consensus omnium gentium et nationum* or at least the *consensus maioris partis orbis*, rather than the will of individuals, in cases of conflict, it will always trump the human or civil law. This view was dismissed by Samuel Pufendorf (who was a self-professed Stoic) as 'crude indeed', but then for Pufendorf the *ius gentium* was not, as it was for Vitoria, a universal law for all humankind, but a law among nations, a *ius inter gentes*.[28]

Most of the 'School' alluded to some similar conception of an international, or at least supranational, legal community: what Cicero had described as a 'human society' bound by a 'common human law'.[29] Soto, for instance, speaks of the 'human republic' and the great Jesuit metaphysician Francisco Suárez, of 'the quasi political and moral unity of the human race' although he ascribed no legislative powers, actual or potential, to it.[30] For Vitoria, the world *respublica* took the form of a single legal person, with *de iure* at least, full powers of enactment—the *vis legis*—so that,

[23] *Vitoria Political Writings* 264. [24] See Chapter 8. [25] See Chapter 1.

[26] 'On Civil Power' 1. 2–3, *Vitoria Political Writings* 9–11. [27] See Chapter 2.

[28] *De iure naturae et gentium libri octo*, CH Oldfather and WA Oldfather (tr) (Clarendon Press 1934) II, 364–66. For a more detailed discussion of this point, see Pagden (n 9) 64–66.

[29] *De Re Publica* II, 26.

[30] L Pereña (ed), *Tractatus de legibus ac deo legislatore*, vol IV (Consejo Superior de Investigaciones Científicas 1971–81) 135 and cf the comments in R Tuck, *The Rights of War and Peace: Political Thought and the International Order from Grotius to Kant* (OUP 1999) 77.

in Vitoria's words: 'the law of nations does not have the force merely of pacts or agreements between men, but has the force of a positive enactment (*lex*)'.[31] This makes it—to use the modern description—a fully evolved 'international rule of law'. But although the world *respublica* does possess *de iure* the 'power to enact laws' (*potestas ferendi leges*) there clearly exists no institutions that could transform this into a de facto authority.[32] For Vitoria, as for the medieval jurists of the Roman and canon law to whom he was indebted, the *auctoritas* of a justly ordained *princeps* was required in order to wage a just war.[33] The question then arose: who, in the absence of some analogue of the United Nations, has the power to assume the authority for 'the whole world'? Vitoria's answer is that since the 'efficient cause' of that power is the natural law, any legally established ruler, although his authority can only derive from a purely domestic source, is entitled to assume the legislative authority of the entire world for the 'powers [of the *ius gentium*] can only exist if exercised though the princes of the commonwealth'.

'It should be noted', he wrote

> That the prince has the authority not only over his own people, but also over foreigners to force them to abstain from harming others; this is his right by the law of nations and the authority of the whole world. Indeed, *it seems he has this right by natural law*: the world could not exist unless some men had the power and authority to deter the wicked by force from doing harm to the good and the innocent.

Under the appropriate conditions then, it would appear that any sovereign was in a position to draw upon the authority of both the law of nations *and* the natural law to act on behalf of the world *respublica.*[34] It might, therefore be argued, that in the case of the Americas the Spanish are merely acting as the agents, and by the authority, of a supposed international community, the universal *respublica*. They are in America by historical contingency, or, as some would argue because of their virtue, and, as a consequence the task of deterring 'the wicked by force from doing harm' has fallen to them. But their role could just as easily have been assumed by any other ruler, Christian or—since unbelievers have just as much right to *dominium* as unbelievers—non-Christian.[35]

[31] 'On Civil Power' 3. 4, *Vitoria Political Writings* 40. See also V Beltrán de Heredia (ed), *Comentarios a la Secunda Secundae de Santo Tomás*, vol III (Biblioteca de teólogos españoles 1934) 89–90. For a more detailed account, see D Deckers, *Gerechtigkeit und Recht. Eine historisch-kritische Untersuchung der Gerechtigkeitslehre des Francisco de Vitoria (1483–1546)* (Universitätsverlag Freiburg 1991) 345–94.

[32] 'On Civil Power' 3. 4, *Vitoria Political Writings*, 40 and see A Miaja de la Muela, 'El derecho *totius orbis* en el pensamiento de Francisco de Vitoria' (1965) 18 Revista española de derecho internacional 341, 348–52.

[33] See Chapter 1. Vitoria allowed that private citizens might be able to 'declare and wage defensive war' but this was very constrained and did not extend to the crucial right to punish the aggressor, or to seek retribution from him, 'On the Law of War' 1.2, *Vitoria Political Writings* 299. For Grotius's very different use of the 'private war' argument see Tuck (n 30) 81–83.

[34] 'On the Law of War' 1.4. 19, *Vitoria Political Writings* 305.

[35] Richard Tuck calls this the 'the Vitorian compromise' and claims that it 'became the most popular official defence of the conquest'. But it is not clear how it qualifies as a compromise as it does not give the Crown any right of occupation and possession, nor, for this reason, was Vitoria's argument ever used in any official sources as a 'defence'. Tuck (n 30) 75.

This in itself would not, of course, have provided the Spanish Crown with sovereign rights in the Americas. But if it could be shown that the Indians had persistently violated (and the violation would have had to be persistent) the juridical order observed by all the other members of the world commonwealth, this would impose on the Spanish an *obligation* to intervene, 'either on account of the personal tyranny of the barbarians' masters towards their subjects or because of their tyrannical and oppressive laws against the innocent'. Unsurprisingly, Vitoria is prepared to accept the claim that the American Indians had been forced by their native rulers to live under 'tyrannical and oppressive laws' might indeed be true. The principal evidence for this was the much-discussed practices of human sacrifice and, cannibalism. (This, however, as another of Vitoria's colleagues, Diego de Covarrubias pointed out, could only apply to those Indian societies where such crimes were actually practised, which, in effect meant only New Spain.)[36] The fact that both human sacrifice and cannibalism were manifestly contrary to natural law was not the issue since it was also the case that such things as adultery and theft—widely practised by Christians—are also contrary to natural law. 'But the princes of unbelievers cannot wage war against Christians even though they are adulterers and thieves; conversely, therefore, Christian princes cannot wage war on them [the Indians] either.' And, he warned, an 'untoward consequence of accepting that they could punish crimes against nature would be that the king of France has a perfect right to invade Italy'.[37] The truly significant difference between 'unnatural' activities practised among individuals in Christian States and the cannibalism and human sacrifice practised in the Americas is that whereas the former are forbidden by civil, as well as natural law, the latter were sanctioned by the State. The justice of the law does not derive from the moral authority of the lawmaker, but from the quality of the laws themselves. Even the laws of tyrants are binding 'since utility and respect are better served by obedience to a tyrant's will than by disobedience to all law', so long, however, and only so long, as those laws 'serve the purposes of the commonwealth'.[38] Since ordering your subjects to sacrifice and eat each other could not possibly be described as fulfilling the purposes of any true *respublica*, such laws could not be 'binding in conscience', and the tyrants responsible for enforcing them, might legitimately be overthrown. It was the *harm* which the rulers of the 'barbarians' were prepared to inflict upon their own subjects that constituted a breach not only of the natural law but also of the *ius gentium*. And that would seem to provide grounds for the agents of the 'world commonwealth' to intervene on their behalf. We have here, in embryonic form a version of the modern concept of 'the Responsibility to Protect' which argues that 'Where a population is suffering serious harm, as a result of internal war, insurgency, repression or state failure, and the state in question is unwilling or unable to halt or avert it, the principle of

[36] 'De Justitia belli adversus indos' in L Pereña Vicente (ed), *Misión de España en América 1540-1560* (Consejo Superior de Investigaciones Científicas 1961) 222–23.

[37] 'On Dietary laws, or Self-Restraint' 1. 5, *Vitoria Political Writings* 219.

[38] 'On Civil Power' 3. 6, *Vitoria Political Writings* 43.

non-intervention yields to the international responsibility to protect.'[39] And just as R2P—as it has come to be called—cannot confer any right of occupancy or sovereignty on the intervening power, neither can Vitoria's 'defence of the innocent'.

Vitoria was also prepared to accept that, although the Spanish may not use force in their attempts at evangelization, conversion to Christianity is of such importance for the Indians themselves, that any ruler who actively prevented them from converting would, in effect, be inflicting unacceptable harm upon them. And if that were the case then, 'the Spaniards could wage war on behalf of their subjects for the oppressions and wrongs which they were suffering'. Once again, however, all the Spanish would be doing in this case would be fulfilling an obligation to the world on behalf of an oppressed people from which they could claim to derive no benefit whatsoever for themselves.

The duty to defend the innocent applied (and in this respect it differs markedly from R2P) even if the 'barbarians' themselves should resist, as they clearly had done, their putative saviours, for: 'It makes no difference that all the barbarians consent to these kinds of rites and sacrifices, or that they refuse to accept the Spaniards as their liberators in this matter.' It was an accepted fact that prolonged habit is capable of distorting every human being's understanding of the natural law, and by implication the law of nations. 'For sometimes', wrote Vitoria, 'due to bad customs, and in those who have fallen profoundly into evil, the knowledge of the natural law may be changed', or as Soto phrased it, 'that which nature teaches is not within the reach of everyone, but only those who have serene reason and are free from all obscurity (*nebula*)'.[40] It might, therefore, be 'lawful to defend an innocent man even if he does not ask us to do so, or even refuses our help, especially when he is suffering an injustice (*iuria*) in a matter where he cannot renounce his rights, as in the present case'.[41]

From all of this it clearly followed that if the rulers of the 'barbarians' refuse to abandon their crimes against their own peoples: 'their masters may be changed and new princes set up'.[42] It is obvious from the context of the argument, however, that since the issue for Vitoria is one of universal justice, there can be no grounds for claiming that these new princes, even if placed there by the Spanish, have themselves to be Spanish, or even Christian. They are acting here as the agents of the civil power, and 'the final cause for civil power' is not belief or even 'civility', but 'natural necessity'.[43]

Vitoria applies a somewhat similar argument to what he calls 'the protection of converts'. Although the whole world might be one *respublica*, it is nevertheless divided into different nations and societies, some of which are constituted by belief.

[39] Described by the International Commission on Intervention and State Sovereignty, as the 'Responsibility to Protect' (International Development Research Centre 2001) and see in general, A Orford, *International Authority and the Responsibility to Protect* (CUP 2011) which although it mentions briefly Vitoria's refutation of the papal bulls says nothing about the 'defence of the innocent'.

[40] F Puy and L Núñez (tr) (eds), *De legibus. Comentarios al tratado de la ley* (Universidad de Granada 1965) 94; Domingo de Soto, *De iustitia et iure* III I ii (195).

[41] 'On Dietary laws, or Self-Restraint' 1. 5, *Vitoria Political Writings* 225.

[42] 'On the American Indians' 3.5.15 *Vitoria Political Writings* 287–88. This is the fifth 'just title'.

[43] 'On Civil Power' 1. 2, *Vitoria Political Writings* 6–10.

If the Indians convert to Christianity, and their rulers 'try to call them back to their idolatry by force or fear', the Spanish have a perfect right, which also amounts, to a duty to

> wage war on them and to compel the barbarians to stop committing this wrong, not only because of the right that every man must have to be allowed to accept the true faith but because those Indians have been converted, they are now bound to the Spanish by ties of friendship (*amicia*) and partnership (*societas*).

They have, so to speak become part of the *respublica Christianorum* which the Spanish now have a clear obligation to defend.[44] But, although Vitoria is silent on the issue, even that would not confer either sovereign or property rights on the Spanish. Once the wrong had been righted, they would have no other legal option but to withdraw. 'If necessity and the requirements of war demand that the greater part of enemy territory or a large number of cities be occupied', he argued elsewhere, 'they ought to be returned once the war is over and peace has been made, only keeping so much as may be considered fair in equity and humanity for the reparation of losses and expenses and the punishment of injustice'.[45] However this might be interpreted, it clearly did not constitute a licence for occupation and the *de iure* annihilation of what were recognized as being entire political communities.

It was also the case that any war fought on behalf of third parties—and in particular on behalf of innocent third parties—must constitute the fulfilment of a duty. The Spanish in the Americas have incurred this obligation towards the Indians because, even though they were not bound to them by formal ties of *amicia* or *societas*, there were nevertheless their neighbours (*proximi*), and therefore common denizens of the world commonwealth, and 'as is shown by the parable of the Samaritan (Luke 10:29–37); ... [all men] are obliged to love their neighbors as themselves', and vice versa, and this love carries with it a corresponding duty to assist each other in times of crisis.

Most of Vitoria's successors were prepared to accept some version of this argument, although the theologian Melchor Cano protested that any actions performed on behalf of the good of others could only ever be acts of 'charity not justice' and could not, therefore involve force. If the Indians were to ask for assistance in order to 'expel the tyrants' then the Spanish might intervene, but not if they were, as the Indians appeared to be, perfectly satisfied with their 'barbarous customs'. Any other kind of intervention, 'in defence of the innocent', would have to be limited to assistance of the kind that, for instance, the French might offer the Spanish in times of conflict, and this clearly would not give the Spanish any more right 'to occupy [the Indians'] territories' than it would give the French the right to occupy Spain.[46] Once again the point is being made that any principle in the law of nations that applies to Spanish relations with the Indians must, if it is to have any *universal* value, apply equally to relations between any other European, or non-European people.

[44] 'On the American Indians' 3.2, *Vitoria Political Writings* 285–86.

[45] 'On the Law of War' 3. 7, *Vitoria Political Writings* 324.

[46] 'De dominio indorum' in Pereña Vicente (n 36) 106–07.

The only possible grounds that the Spanish might claim to possess a right to a presence in America in anything but a purely defensive posture is therefore inextricably linked to a moral obligation to offer assistance to the oppressed. The same also applied to the always subversive question as to whether the American Indians might be incapable of self-government. Vitoria and all his successors routinely denied the suggestion that the Indians might be Aristotle's 'natural slaves' and that even if they were, in fact, 'as foolish and slow-witted as people say they are' this would not, in itself, deprive the Indians of their natural right to 'true *dominium*'.[47] Vitoria was, however, prepared to concede 'for the sake of argument although certainly not asserted with confidence' that the Indians might be, like 'natural slaves' in that by all accounts they were 'unsuited to setting up or administering a commonwealth (*respublica*) both legitimate and ordered in human and civil terms'. If that were the case then the 'princes would be bound to take change of them as if they were simply children'. Such 'princes'—who although they are in actual fact the kings of Spain, might, by implication, be drawn from any people with the necessary abilities to act as guardians—would, however, be acting, not in in their own interests and not pressing any claim on their own behalf, but acting, once again, as agents of the world commonwealth, 'for the benefit and good of the barbarians'. And on this he concluded, 'The whole pitfall of souls and salvation is found to lie'.[48]

It was not the case, as Hugo Grotius later supposed, that what he called, 'bringing the gentiles against their will to a more civil kind of behaviour' was, 'thought wicked and impious of all the divines, but especially the Spaniards'[49] What was, was the supposition that this process of 'civilizing' might confer upon the civilizer any significant rights over the person or properties of the person to be civilized. For as any war made in 'defence of the innocent', had necessarily to be limited to exercising what are, in effect, moral duties, they cannot be used to provide the basis for any kind of occupation. The only kind of war the Spanish could make in retaliation against such a people could, therefore, only be a purely defensive one. But as the Indians cannot be supposed to be fully aware of the justice of the Spanish cause (always supposing it to exist)—Vitoria had nothing but contempt for the famous *Requerimiento*—there is 'right on one side and ignorance' on the other meant that it 'may be just on both'. The analogy here is once again with the condition not between a European and a 'barbarian' power, but between two European powers. The king of France occupies 'Burgundy in the mistaken but colourable belief that it belongs to them [the French]', rather than to Charles V, as a fief of the Holy Roman Empire. Charles then, 'has a certain right to the province and may seek to recover it by war; but the French may defend it'. In the case of the Indians, even if they could be said to have waged an entirely unjustified war against the Spanish, they had done so in all probability because they are 'understandably fearful of men whose customs seem so strange and whom they can see are armed and much stronger than themselves'.

[47] 'On the American Indians' 1. Conclusion, *Vitoria Political Writings* 251. On the Indians as natural slaves, see Pagden (n 9) 87–92.

[48] 'On the American Indians' 1. Conclusion, *Vitoria Political Writings* 290–91.

[49] D Armitage (ed) R Hakluyt (tr), *The Free Sea* [*Mare Liberum*] (Liberty Fund 2004) 15.

This fear would then be 'just' and consequently it 'made them innocent'. It could not, therefore, grant the Spanish the usual rights covered by the *ius post bello* which included, crucially, 'occupying their communities'.[50]

It is a very strong statement indeed, for although he does not say so explicitly, all that Vitoria would seem to have left his king was a series of obligations under the law of nations to help the 'barbarians' to escape from the consequences of their barbarism but no sovereign or property rights whatsoever.

## 2. Conquest and the Responsibility to Civilize

Vitoria and his successor would seem to have successfully discredited the Bulls of Donation as anything other than an encouragement to evangelize. For the Spanish monarchy itself, however, the bulls remained the principal, and the only undisputable, claim to sovereignty in the Americas until the final demise of the 'Kingdoms of the Indies' in the nineteenth century. They are, for instance, the only justification for the Spanish presence in America offered by the historiographer royal, Antonio de Herrera, in his massive official history of the conquest of the Americas, *Historia general de los hechos de los Castellanos en las islas y tierra firme del Mar Océano* of 1601–15, and the *Recopilación de leyes de los reynos de Indias* composed in 1680 by the jurist Juan de Solórzano y Pereira which constituted a distinct code of law for the Americas, States, echoing the terms of *Inter caetera*, that

> By donation of the Holy Apostolic See and other just and legitimate titles We [the King of Spain] are Lord of the Western Indies and the Mainland of the Ocean Sea, which has been discovered or is still to be discovered, and has been incorporated into our Royal Crown of Castile.[51]

It was also with the true meaning of the bulls and the various theological, and scriptural problems that they raised, which the famous 'debate' (although in fact the two men never met) between Bartolomé de Las Casas, official, 'Defender of the Indians', and the humanist historian, royal chaplain, and translator of Aristotle, Juan Ginés de Sepúlveda in Valladolid in 1550–01, was overwhelmingly concerned. To judge from Domingo de Soto's wry account of the event, it was something of a shambles. Sepúlveda provided only a summary of his arguments and kept pretty much to the question under debate. Las Casas, however, went on at very great length in an 'attempt to reply to everything the doctor had ever written and everything, that in his view it was possible to oppose'.[52] Between them Las Casas and Sepúlveda, as Soto makes clear, hijacked a meeting whose original purpose had been to discover, 'by what manner and

[50] 'On the American Indians' 3.5, *Vitoria Political Writings* 282.

[51] Quoted in Francisco A Ortega Martínez, 'Entre "constitución" y "colonia", el estatuto ambiguo de las Indias en la monarquía hispánica' in *Conceptos fundamentales de la cultura política de la Independencia* (Universidad Nacional de Colombia 2012) 61–91, 64. On Antonio de Herrera, see D Brading, *The First America, The Spanish Monarchy, Creole Patriots and the Liberal State, 1492–1867* (CUP 1991) 205–10.

[52] *Aquí se contiene una controversia* in Bartolomé de las Casas *Obras completas* (Alianza 1988–98) X, 106.

under what laws our Holy Catholic Faith could be preached and promulgated' and how the Indians might be 'subjected to the majesty of the Emperor our lord, without harming the royal conscience in conformity with the Bulls of Alexander'. In other words, the issue at stake had been intended to be not a legal but a purely moral one. It had also been one which studiously avoided any consideration of the still highly contentious issue of the legal status of the Spanish occupation of the Americas. Instead, remarked Soto, 'these gentlemen' rather than discuss this question, 'in the manner of a consultation' had 'treated and debated another' namely: was it

> licit for His Majesty the Emperor to make war on these Indians before preaching to them the faith, in order to submit them to his authority so that they might be more easily and more comfortably instructed and enlightened by the evangelical doctrine, and in the understanding of their errors and in the Christian faith.[53]

Sepúlveda argued that the war 'was not only licit but also convenient'. Las Casas, of course, maintained the contrary. Neither man, however, questioned the legitimacy of the Spanish presence in the Americas nor of the lasting validity of the Alexandrine donation. It was on this, Las Casas insisted, and on this alone, that the 'juridical and fundamental basis' of the Castilian title to the Indies was based.[54] Las Casas's prime concern was not with the legitimacy of the occupation, about which, as he said again and again, and even reiterated in the preamble to his will, he was never in any doubt, but with the behaviour of the occupiers. What was at stake was the legitimacy of the *means* by which the Indians had been, as Las Casas expressed it elsewhere, 'brought into history', so as to become, as both the pope and God had intended them to become, Christians and subjects of the Spanish Crown. On Las Casas's reading of history, sacred and profane, America was unique, a true donation, not only of Pope Alexander VI, but of God. It had been for this reason, he claimed, that God had provided their discoverer with a first name—'Christopher'—which meant in Latin 'Christ-bearer'—and a second ('Colón' in Spanish) which could be glossed as 'Colonizer'. For Las Casas, the entire course of the Spanish overseas empire had been a part of God's design to bring these 'countless peoples' into the narrative of the history of Christianity, and it had been Columbus's voyages that had 'broken the locks that had held the Ocean Sea fast ever since the Flood'.[55] The same rules which applied to the conversion and settlement of America also applied, *mutatis mutandis*, to the conversion and settlement of Africa and Asia. But because the *rights* which the Spanish Crown claimed in America were dependent upon a unique historical event, they were consequently entirely *sui generis*, and thus, for Las Casas, confined to one time and one place. They could never, therefore, be defended in terms of any kind of universal *law*, other than the canon law which underpinned the pope's right

[53] ibid.

[54] *Tratado comprobatorio del imperio soberano y principado universal que los reyes de Castilla y León tienen sobre las Indias* [1552] in *Tratados de Fray Bartolomé de las Casas* (Fondo de Cultura Económica 1965) II, 925.

[55] *Las Casas on Columbus: Background and Second and Fourth Voyages, Repertorium Columbianum* (Brepols 1999) VII, 23–28.

to make the Donation in the first place. Nor, of course does Las Casas make any appeal to anything resembling Vitoria's world commonwealth. For him there could only exist one such *respublica*, and that was the *respublica Christianorum*. It is little wonder that Soto, so obviously chaffing at the limits his commission had imposed upon him, not 'to give or make known my own opinion, or to add any argument or judgment on the one or the other, but to report faithfully the substance of their and to resume their arguments', protested that had he not been so constrained he would have considered the entire matter from quite 'another position'.[56]

Las Casas had, however, another reason for insisting on the validity of the bulls. For if Vitoria—whom he rarely mentions by name—was right in his refutations of the pope's claims to universal jurisdiction then the only rights which the Castilian Crown could claim in America would have to have been acquired as the outcome of a just war or, as he put it, they would have to have been grounded 'in arms and in power'. If that were the case, then the Kingdoms of the Indies could only have been founded, 'as that great Alexander and the Romans and all those who were famous tyrants, as today the Turk harries and oppresses Christendom' had founded their empires.[57] And that would have been a blatant denial of his image of the Spanish empire as the means of fulfilling God's not-so-hidden plans for humankind. Las Casas's objective throughout all of his voluminous writings on the subject was to demonstrate that while the Spanish occupation of the Americas was fully justified by the Donation it served only one end: namely the conversion of the Indians. The wars of conquest, which he denounced at every turn, were an aberration brought about by the rapacious, unprincipled, and un-Christian behaviour of the conquistadores. Since the Indians were, on his account, docile and rational beings, and Christianity was a docile and rational faith, the conquests should never have taken place at all. For this same reason Las Casas replied, to Sepúlveda's use of a version of Vitoria's 'defence of the innocent' as grounds for depriving the Indians of their sovereignty and their goods, that while the protection of the subjects of a State from the tyranny of its ruler was clearly a moral obligation, and that the papacy was bound to defend the innocent even if they were pagans, 'because they belong potentially (*in potentia*) to the Church', this could not be achieved through conquest.[58] If war were the only means available then, 'it would be better to relinquish that protection' for when compared with all the evils of warfare, even human sacrifice was the lesser of the two.[59]

The same would also apply to the claim which Sepúlveda had made repeatedly that the Indians were incapable of self-government. Las Casas was of course eager

[56] *Aquí se contiene una controversia* 105.

[57] *Tratado comprobatorio del imperio soberano* 921.

[58] *Argumentum apologiae adversus Genesium Sepulvedam theologum cordubensem* in A Losada (ed), *Obras completas* (Alianza 1988) IX, 361. And see N Capedevila, *La Controverse entre Las Casas et Sepúlveda* (Vrin 2007) 183–87. The *Apologia* was the initial text which Las Casas had presented at the 'debate'.

[59] *Aquí se contiene una controversia*, 121. Sepulveda's reply was that from all that he had heard 'more than 20,000 persons were sacrificed each year' in New Spain and that 'multiplying that by the thirty years since the conquest makes 60,000 [sic]' in addition 'that war prevented the loss of an infinity of souls' (ibid 143).

to demonstrate that this was in itself flawed. The Indians were as advanced, as sophisticated, and as civil as any of the societies of the pre or non-Christian world, and he wrote a massive rambling tome, the *Apologética historia sumaria*, to prove the point.[60] True the Indians still 'suffer from many and great defects in their societies', an inescapable consequence, as he understood it, of their paganism, which would be remedied once they had all been converted to the true faith—something which, in his view, would require a radical reform of the present colonial administration.[61] Vitoria, as we have seen, had taken a similar position. Although the Indians were certainly not 'natural slaves', they did nevertheless 'seem to us insensate and slow-witted'. But this could only be due 'mainly to their evil and barbarous education'.[62] Once exposed to Christianity and the civilizing ways of the Spanish, they would be transformed into true civil beings. For those who, like Las Casas, accepted the validity of the papal bulls, the ultimate objective of this civilizing process could only be full incorporation into the Spanish monarchy. If the Americas had indeed been ceded legitimately to the Spanish Crown by the papacy, the fully civilized Indians would never be in a position to claim anything resembling a right to 'self-determination'. On the other hand, neither could there be any grounds for treating them any differently from any of the other subjects of the Spanish monarchy. The earliest attempt to create an independent body of legislation for the new American dependencies, the Laws of Burgos of 1513, had made this clear.

> Whereas it may so happen that in the course of time ... the Indians will become so apt and ready to become Christians, and so civilized and educated, that they will be capable of governing themselves and leading the kind of life that the said Christians lead ... [they] shall be allowed to live by themselves and shall be obliged to serve in those things in which our vassals in Spain are accustomed to serve.[63]

For Las Casas, and on this point he was fully in agreement with Sepúlveda, the polities which had existed prior to the arrival of the Spanish had been dissolved by papal decree in 1494, and a new entity which this act had created, the 'Kingdoms of the Indies' had been incorporated into the Crown of Castile by royal decree in 1519. The 'Spanish Monarchy' was a God-ordained, papally sanctioned state which would continue in its present course until the end of time. No part of it could legally at any time be detached from the whole. This, of course, was in stark contrast to Vitoria's position. For, as all the members of the School of Salamanca claimed the initial Spanish occupation had only been intended to create—as Vitoria had his successors had insisted it had—a regime which would guarantee the continuing protection and possible improvement, of the innocent, this would have to cease once those

[60] For more extensive account of this text and its place in the 'debate', see A Pagden, *The Fall of Natural Man: The American Indian and the origins of comparative ethnology* (CUP 1982) 119–45.

[61] *Tratado comprobatorio del imperio soberano* 1137.

[62] 'On the American Indians' 1. Conclusion, *Vitoria Political Writings* 250.

[63] Art 4 of an appendix of 28 July 1513. Text in Charles Gibson, *The Spanish Tradition in America* (Norton 1968) 81.

objectives had been achieved. At that point he concluded, the Spanish would have to withdraw, and the 'whole Indian expedition and trade would cease'.[64]

The same logic dogged all the European empires which based their claims to occupation on some kind of moral responsibility to protect and improve the lot of the colonized in the name of a code of universal justice. For if this 'civilizing', as it came to be called, was indeed the mission of the colonizing powers, then their political and legal status could only ever be temporary. True, in practice, occupation might last a very long time. But the conclusion that it had to be abandoned at some time was inescapable. Over three centuries later, in July 1833, when Thomas Babbington Macaulay made his speech before the House of Commons on the renewal of the charter of the East India Company he declared that

> by good government we may educate our subjects into a capacity for better government; that having become instructed in European knowledge they may, in some future age, demand European institutions. ... Whenever it comes, it will be the proudest day in English history. To have found a great people sunk in the lowest depths of slavery and superstition, to have so ruled them as to have made them desirous and capable of all the privileges of citizens would indeed be a title to glory all our own.[65]

The road from this perception of the ultimate limits of empire to Woodrow Wilson's insistence in 1918 upon the right of the colonized peoples of the world to 'self-determination' was relatively direct one. The subsequent incorporation of that claim into the Universal Declaration of Human Rights of 1948, the International Covenant on Civil and Political Rights, and the International Covenant on Economic and Cultural Rights of 1976, although presented as the moral initiative of non-colonizing powers was, in fact, the outcome of an historical perception of the legal—and moral—relationship between colonizer and the colonized, and the possible implications of any concept of a universal or transnational rule of law, which reached back to the sixteenth century.

[64] Vitoria, however denies that the *trade* would have to cease since, 'the Portuguese ... carry on a great and profitable trade with similar sorts of peoples without conquering them'. 'On the American Indians' 3. Conclusion, *Vitoria Political Writings* 291–92.

[65] *Hansard. House of Commons Debate*, 10 July 1833, cc 479–550 in <http://hansard.millbank-systems.com/commons/1833/jul/10/east-india-companys-charter> (18 August 2016). See also TR Metcalf, *Ideologies of the Raj*, vol II.4 (1994) *The New Cambridge History of India* 34.

# 6

# Cardinal Richelieu between Vattel and Machiavelli

*Anthony Carty*

## 1. Introduction, the Contested Nature of the History of International Law

A central feature of our East Asian–European dialogue is that Richard Tuck believes the scholastic, humanist ethic was marginalized by a 'tougher' humanism modelled on a resurrected vision of Roman civilization.[1] This counts widely as a significant contribution to the intellectual history of international law. It does not necessarily contradict Tuck's dichotomy to say that he should not have overlooked Cardinal Richelieu completely, since he can reply that, in so far as Richelieu was influenced by scholasticism, he will merely have prolonged the place of just war theory and natural law for a century without preventing the eventual triumph of the predatory liberal internationalism, which is the main focus of his book. The difficulty remains, as has already been argued extensively by the author, in another place,[2] that it is very difficult to define what are the issues for debate concerning any book on the history of international law.

As a part of 'Western civilization' the history is influenced by all the normative sources of that civilization, Greco-Roman philosophy and law, Christian natural law and canon law, Renaissance humanism in various forms, the Enlightenment, and Western modernity. All of these traditions may appear from a distance (to an outsider perhaps) to harmonize into a systematic view of 'Western civilization', but in fact their relationships to one another are bitterly contested. In particular, there is no authoritative or convincing account of how these various normative sources can ground a coherent picture of the history of international law. There is a tendency among writers to favour one particular element or building block of Western legal civilization: the differences within early-modern Western humanism. The

[1] R Tuck, *The Rights of War and Peace* (OUP 1999) esp 227, where he contrasts the humanist Gentile for whom the survival of the State overrode moral constraints, while the scholastic Molina thought the State had to be seen as involved in a network of moral obligation grounded in natural law.

[2] A Carty, 'A Book Review' (2013) 26(2) Leiden Journal of International Law 487–92, B Kingsbury and B Straumann, *The Roman Foundations of the Law of Nations* (OUP 2010).

book reviewed by the author, *The Roman Foundations of the Law of Nations* places great weight on the significance of Roman law, not precisely because it contained rules favourable to a lack of moral restraint in international affairs, but more loosely because of the association of that legal order with an empire in constant expansion.[3]

Whatever the difficulty of questioning the usefulness of Tuck's dichotomy between humanism and scholasticism, there is a more serious charge raised more specifically by historians of international law, such as Koskenniemi and Jouannet, that there is simply not a rigorous discipline of international law, going back to the sixteenth century and beyond, of which either humanists such as Gentili or scholastics such as Molina—or for that matter Richelieu—could be said to be a part. This judgement can only signify that the so-called international law profession cannot expect to find anything of more than esoteric interest in returning to these people.

Such a position is vigorously asserted at length by Koskenniemi in his contribution to *The Roman Foundations of the Law of Nations*, entitled 'International Law and *raison d'état*: Rethinking the Prehistory of International Law', a forty-page piece which is, in principle, relevant to any claim of the Roman foundations of international law, the overall purpose of the book. Koskenniemi begins by noting that 'The mythical origin of modern international law is often found in Alberico Gentili's famous diatribe against the theologians.'[4] What Koskenniemi may mean is to question whether 'in some relevant respect today's international lawyers are involved in the same pursuit as lawyers such as Gentili four centuries ago'.[5] Koskenniemi's criticism exposes the fact that the editors of the book have not the ambition to offer an authoritative conception of either the nature or the historical structural development of international law. Despite the title *The Roman Foundations of the Law of Nations*, the book merely 'adds' Roman law as a building block without explaining whether other usually supposed building blocks, such as the Catholic Church's tradition of canon law, had been or continued to be of some importance to the international law tradition.

However, the main interest here is Koskenniemi's treatment of seventeenth-century France. To take only one part of his chapter, 'International Law in Enlightenment France',[6] Koskenniemi says there was no law in the seventeenth century. He argues that in France there was an express turn against law and lawyers as possessors of the knowledge of statehood.[7] *Raison d'état* was understood as derogation from the common law. It is probable that what he is describing is the declining function of lawyers in French constitutional law. Yet Koskenniemi makes the remarkable statement that 'concentration on the extraordinary moments of great policy, linked with utmost secrecy in diplomacy and political decision-making, notoriously prevented the emergence of any coherent French foreign policy for most of the 17th century'. He explains that this is because only in 1688 did the French foreign ministry set up an archive. Yet foreign affairs in an absolute monarchy will hardly be the exclusive prerogative of a foreign minister.

[3] Carty (n 2). [4] Kingsbury and Straumann (n 2) 297. [5] ibid.
[6] ibid 305–20. [7] ibid 310.

Koskenniemi argues further that there was no significant French international law tradition at all in pre-revolutionary France. French-language work was produced by Protestant diaspora such as Jean Barbeyrac, who translated Grotius in Berlin.[8] Koskenniemi appears here to equate French observance of the law of nations (however understood) with the presence or absence of a distinctive creativity and hence influence of French legal doctrinal writing.

This very unsure grasp of seventeenth-century French diplomatic history leads to a bizarre dismissal of Richelieu, Mazarin, and Louis XIV as not 'coherent' because there were no foreign ministry archives in an absolutist State. Whatever the value of Koskenniemi's judgement about the importance of the French foreign ministry for any of the above figures, the more fundamental point is Koskenniemi's implicit assumption that if the leading figures of France were guided by or listening to theologians and not lawyers, then they cannot have been 'doing international law'. Koskenniemi does not consider it appropriate to consider the place of theology. He talks instead, disdainfully, of the difficulty of exorcizing theology, shown by the continuing messianic teleology evidencing what he calls an 'inherently theological disposition'.[9]

Jouannet holds a similar, if more briefly and moderately expressed view, perhaps influenced by a laic, republican, and secular French perspective, that religion should remain a private matter. Indeed, she castigates Richelieu as an admirer of Machiavelli, and thereby, given his undoubted prominence in his time, she considers she has provided a proof that no form of international law could have existed in his epoch. In her *Liberal-Welfarist Law of Nations: A History of International Law* she attributes to Richelieu admiration for Machiavelli's precept that 'There is no dishonor in breaking conventions by which the nation has been committed to a course of action.'[10] She argues that no one could write this in the eighteenth century where *pacta sunt servanda* had become a legal rule binding on States—for all of which assertions she provides no references. In other words, in the secular, liberal worlds of Koskenniemi and Jouannet, Richelieu is as alien to modern Western international law imagination as the Ming and Qing dynasties, which were his contemporaries.

In fact there appears to be a widespread consensus that the medieval scholastic tradition of the just war tradition, going back ultimately to Augustine, continued to dominate in the ultra-Catholic France of Cardinal Richelieu and Louis XIII. Cornette, a French historian, demonstrates that Richelieu followed precisely this in the 19 May 1635 Declaration of War against Spain.[11] Cornette finds, in any case, plenty of use of lawyers among the councillors and advisers who defended and propagated Richelieu's policy against the Spanish Hapsburgs. Lesaffer, a Flemish legal historian, confirms the same view in his massive sixty pages of text on the same Declaration of War.[12] Equally, Lesaffer finds plenty of roles for lawyers. He

[8] ibid 313–14. [9] ibid 297.

[10] E Jouannet, *Liberal-Welfarist Law of Nations: A History of International Law* (CUP 2012) 24.

[11] J Cornette, *Le roi de guerre: Essai sur le souveraineté dans la France du grand siècle* (Payot 1993) 123–28.

[12] R Lesaffer, 'Defensive Warfare, Prevention and Hegemony: The Justifications for the Franco-Spanish War of 1635 (Part I)' (2006) 8 Journal of the History of International Law 91; R Lesaffer,

explains the care with which Richelieu built legal arguments around a common interest that France had in preserving the sovereign equality of other smaller States and its own desire to restrain Spain. Arguments about the justice of war were essential for Richelieu to retain support at home in public opinion, as well as to sway allies and cause sedition among enemies. Finally, the American historian Church, while completely in line with the above analysis, places the primary emphasis on the role of theologians. Basing his argument on the *Testament politique*, he shows how Richelieu says no war should be undertaken until judged as to its equity by theologians 'of the requisite capacity and honesty'.[13]

## 2. Cardinal Richelieu and the Divinely Rational Rule of the World versus the Rule of the Beast

Indisputably Richelieu's world does appear strange to the twenty-first-century mind. He pursues a doctrine which brings together religious faith and reason in a divine right of kings, a royal absolutism. This attributed to Louis XIII an authority which not merely came from God, but was actually about the implementation of God's will on earth. This was not to be incompatible with reason, but reason was concerned with the practical implementation of divine will. This is a way of thinking about international society which it is very difficult for Europeans to understand now, but if one goes back to Machiavelli's rejection of the Christian medieval tradition at the time of the Italian Renaissance, at the end of the fifteenth century, one may see that the humanism of which Tuck treats as becoming predominant in Western European culture, had an ontological as well as ethical aspect.

The question was not simply how individuals or princes treated one another, but also how they were 'compelled' to treat one another by the nature of 'reality'. There was a part of 'reality' which man could not know, predict, or control. It was described as blind fate or *Fortuna.* It recognized existence as constantly threatening, requiring drastic measures not merely of pre-emption against the other, but a constant need to reconfigure the contours of relations in constantly changing circumstances. Drawing on the interpretation of Machiavelli in his *Thoughts on Machiavelli*,[14] Leo Strauss also stresses a dichotomy. The imitation of God is replaced by the imitation of the beast, the God-Christ-Man gives way to the Beast-Man Chiron. Chiron is the centaur of Greek mythology who reared Achilles. The beast is the fox and the lion. Strikingly Machiavelli considers humanism is not enough, as man is half human and half beast.[15]

'Defensive Warfare, Prevention and Hegemony: The Justifications for the Franco-Spanish War of 1635 (Part II)' (2006) 8 Journal of the History of International Law 141.

[13] W Church, *Richelieu and Reason of State* (Princeton UP 1972) 501–2.

[14] L Strauss, *Thoughts on Machiavelli* (Free Press Glencoe Illinois 1958/University of Chicago Press 1978).

[15] ibid 78.

Machiavelli also contrasted Christianity and Rome. The former preaches weakness and humility, a lack of esteem for the world. While Rome honours the world and valour. It sees a harmony between truth and worldly strength.[16] Self-reliance in striving for excellence has to take the place of the consciousness of guilt or sin.[17] In terms of international law, this means the following. In Strauss's words:

> Given the instability of human things, States cannot choose the true way or the right mean which consists in keeping what one has and in not taking away from others what belongs to them; one is forced to choose one of the extremes: either to allow others to take away from one what one has or else to take away from others what belongs to them; honor, worldly honor, dictate the choice of the latter.[18]

Behind these musings lies an ontology of a threatening Being. Strauss goes on to address Machiavelli's assertoric quasi-theology. Drawing on Livy's concept of *Fortuna*, rather than God,[19] Fortune and Heaven are used synonymously.[20] The end which Fortune pursues is unknown, and so are her ways to that end.[21] However, the fact that well-being depends upon vanquishing fortune means it is the enemy. Like a woman, 'if one wishes to keep her down, it is necessary to beat her and to pound her'. She is changeable and unreliable and to put one's hopes in her is madness.[22]

Machiavelli always comes back to the instability of things. So Strauss on Machiavelli:

> Yet since all human things are in flux, one cannot always do what reason suggests but must sometimes do what necessity demands: a consistent policy limited to preservation is impossible. One must choose between losing to others what one possesses or taking away from others what they possess. But the latter course is more honorable than the former. One cannot leave it then at sacrificing the virtue of giving; one must choose the vice of rapacity.[23]

Machiavelli disputes the anthropology on which classical natural law, with Plato and Aristotle appeared to rest. Their imagined republics are based on the premise that most men are good; but if most are bad, the ruler cannot possibly rule his subjects if he does not adapt himself in considerable measure to their badness. Aristotle also thought most men desire wealth and honour, but this leads him to the conclusion that the best men should rule the many bad ones by coercing them, while remaining immune to badness themselves.[24] Morality is only possible after its condition has been created and the condition cannot be created morally. Aristotle thinks that man is worst of all if he lives without the law of right, which depends upon political society. Men become virtuous by habitation, which requires laws, customs, which arise in political society. However, for Machiavelli if virtue presupposes political society, political society is preceded by pre-moral or sub-moral men and founded by such men. There cannot be a mortal law of unconditional validity; hence morality is possible only when created outside of morality. One might suppose men good—in which case they do not need political society, or one can suppose civil society is founded by men of heroic virtue—of a kind of moral virtue which is not derived by

[16] ibid 178–79. [17] ibid 190. [18] ibid 191. [19] ibid 213.
[20] ibid 214. [21] ibid 215. [22] ibid 216. [23] ibid 240. [24] ibid 254.

habitation. He thinks this is an unwarranted belief in the goodness of which men are capable.[25]

Machiavelli concludes that instead of semi-divine or divinely inspired benefactors, men like Cesare Borgia or especially the criminal Emperor Severus reveal the true features of the first founders of society. So:

> The situation in which the foundation took place recurs whenever society as a whole is in grave danger from within or without. In all such situations, the modes used by the original founder must be used again if there is to be society and its offspring, morality. Morality can only exist on an island created or at any rate protected by immorality.[26]

For the religious spirit of Richelieu this 'reality' of radical uncertainty and instability was also present but he gave it a different name, the struggle between God and Satan. As an avid reader of the Spanish mystics such as Teresa of Avila, the phenomenal world recognizable in Machiavelli's work called instead for a recognition of God's mysterious command of the universe. Man's unequal partnership with God signified that the king, as God's agent, had a responsibility to discern the opaque complexity of existence in a spirit of humble quest after divine inspiration and guidance, ie in a spirit of prayer. The French religious vision was one of harmony of all under heaven, ie under God's will, where the small would be secure against the large, each having its place. Even the idea of law itself, in the narrower sense of dynastic title—claims of the French Crown to patrimonial lands—had to be moderated and presented only in the context of the possibilities of the overall harmony of Europe.

If one returns to the question whether one can only speak of a rule of international law, or law of nations after Vattel and into the nineteenth century, this will help one to focus inquiry concerning Richelieu more sharply on the closeness of the relationship in his mind between the rule of God, the rule of reason, and the rule of law. That is to say, the focus will be much more on the role of method of normative order, before considering the specific content, particularly with respect to treaties and the question of war. Richelieu begins the second part of his *Political Testament* with the words:

> The Reign of God is the Principle of the Government of States; and, indeed it is a thing so absolutely necessary that without that Foundation it is impossible for any Prince to rule well, or for any State to be happy ... But all Men are so sensible by their own Reason, that their Origin does not proceed from themselves, but that a God is their creator, and, consequently, their Director that they all feel that Nature has imprinted that Truth in their hearts with indefaceable characters ...
>
> And so many Princes have been leaden with Blessings in submitting their Authority to that from whom it was derived, for having only sought their Grandeur in that of their Creator and for having taken more care of his Reign than of their own.[27]

[25] ibid 254–55. [26] ibid 255.

[27] Political Testament ch 1, p 2, see the online edition of the *Second Part of the Political Testament of the Famous Cardinal, Duke de Richelieu* <http://quod.lib.umich.edu/e/eebo/A57249.0001.001/1:4.3?rgn=div2;view=fulltext> (2 September 2016).

Church comments that in this passage Richelieu seems to be groping for words to express how central were the religious qualities and purposes of royal government.[28] Hence the personal example of the sovereign himself, the good life of the prince is a living law and more effectively compelling than all the laws that they might make to coerce towards the good that they wish to procure. The converse of the reign of God is clear where Richelieu continues:

> So many Princes have undone themselves and their States, by laying the foundation of their conduct upon a judgment contrary to their knowledge (of God) and so many have been filled with benedictions for having subjected their authority to that from which it was derived.[29]

So, Church notes that here Richelieu is speaking of government according to a higher law.[30] Nothing could be clearer than that Richelieu considered this dimension to be essential for the rulers of Christian States. The same standard applied to ministers as to princes. The law of God requires precepts beyond the standards of honesty among men. The ideal minister should be versed in both, but if there is any question of deficiency it should be in earthly wisdom, because knowledge of God's law is fundamental and without it, the minister cannot be expected to understand more ordinary matters. 'In a word, the statesman must be faithful to God, the Statesmen and himself, in that order.'

Nonetheless, the chief resource for Richelieu in fulfilling these obligations was reason. In his words, in the *Political Testament*

> Natural knowledge convinces us that Man being created reasonable, Reason ought to be the Ground of all his Actions, since otherwise he would act against his Nature, and consequently against Him who is the Author of it.[31]

There is an exact correspondence of absolute reason, rule, and obedience. Richelieu clearly excludes all that is arbitrary or unreasonable:

> That as we ought never to will anything, but that which is just and reasonable, so we must never will anything without putting it into execution and without exacting an intire Obedience to our commands; since otherwise Reason would not reign sovereignly.[32]
>
> The practice of that Rule is easier in that Love is the most powerful Motive to oblige Men to obey, and that it is impossible for Subjects not to love the Prince, when they are sensible that Reason is the Guide to all his Actions.[33]

Church summarizes Richelieu's reasoning as signifying effective government is procured through following the precepts of Divine Law through maximum application of human reason. The successful pursuit of State goals is simultaneously reasonable and for the purpose of achieving religiously defined objectives.[34]

Church goes on to consider how Richelieu understood the notion, usually attributed to Machiavelli, of reason of state. For Richelieu it signified the rule of reason in political affairs. Kings and ministers, being men of superior intellect and power,

[28] Church (n 13) 493. [29] ibid 493–94, Church quoting from the *Political Testament.*
[30] ibid 494. [31] Political Testament (n 27) 5. [32] ibid. [33] ibid 6.
[34] ibid 495.

as well as being divinely bestowed with reason, should invariably act in accordance with reason. At the same time, there is also the issue of a means–end rationality, also predicated on the legitimacy of a higher morality of State policy at the expense of traditional legal and moral values. In matters of domestic security Richelieu, notes Church, had a doctrine of emergency, in recognition of the fact that conspiracies against the public welfare are usually conducted with such cleverness and secrecy that one has no clear proof of them until they happen, which is when they cannot be undone.[35]

However, it was an essential part of his religious faith that Richelieu did not give such a large space for conjecture in public affairs as to undermine any possibility of public order, national or international. Instead, as Church quotes him, 'good conscience and the penetrating judgment of a judicious mind, being learned in the course of affairs, discerns the future through the present . . . and shields this practice from a bad outcome'.[36]

This very intensely personal and private foundation for normative order can only make any external review of the conduct of States under absolutism very problematic. The element of accountability attaching to the rule of law appears impossible to realize. As Church explains, divine absolutism means that Richelieu has been chosen by God to guide France, through the 'royal majesty which is the second majesty after the divine (and which) found in his mind, (Richelieu's), the means of solving all these problems.' Drawing here from the *Memoires*, Church remarks how the Cardinal is supposed to enable his majesty, his master, to emerge gloriously from challenges because of God's grace.[37]

It is not simply the intimacy of this relationship which is impenetrable. It is also the ontological foundation of the wider reality the relationship is confronting. This brings one back to the fear of uncertainty, also in the face of international conspiracies. It is stated in the *Memoires* that it is the prayer of the king which is rewarded by the Divine Benevolence, where the end and purpose of the war (now in 1638) is the peace of Christendom, that God has rewarded the king with the birth of a boy (the future Louis XIV). This is taken as a sign of divine aid in the many good fortunes of France.

In any case, Church draws upon a huge repository of publicists, among others, Duplex, whose work indicates just how obscure the decision-making was. Decisions between the prince and the director as matters of State are such as not to discuss with other ministers and the secret may not be divulged. Church quotes Duplex:

> After all, since political government is organized after the model of the celestial hierarchy no criticism of it can be made. For as God established an intelligence in each celestial sphere to activate it and cause it to revolve according to its natural course, so that which guides the movement of the primary body gives an impulse to all others and forces them to rotate every twenty four hours, so also each of our inferior ministers should carry out his particular function and daily account to the first Minister with a full and punctual report.[38]

[35] ibid 496. [36] ibid 499. [37] ibid 474. [38] ibid 466.

This religious faith is the frame encompassing the dangerous and unpredictable world of politics, national and international. This world was in the safe hands chosen by Louis XIII, his minister Cardinal Richelieu. Louis's greatest achievement was to choose a minister who combined loyalty to Christian principles with knowledge of the secrets of State. Church quotes another of Richelieu's intellectual messengers and interpreters, de Run (p 412), that 'Kings have certain obscure designs which resemble prophecies and can be best understood only after their fulfilment'. Church comments on this typical structure of absolutist thought: unquestioning reverence by the subjects for the superior knowledge of kings and ministers of the secrets of State, all within a religious frame of reference.[39]

Church provides ample evidence that the *Political Testament* represents an authentic account of Richelieu's thinking, if also in the sense that he supervised its composition, even if it was written by his secretaries. It reflects his profoundly religious, and conservatively hierarchical view of French society. The French people were volatile, did not respect either rules or authority and put their own interests before the polity. Only the absolute authority of the monarch could discipline such a fractious society.[40] This was not a licence for arbitrary rule. Instead, Richelieu followed a classical sense of the qualities a minister needed to guide the realm: 'judgment rather than audacity, prudence in all things, honesty before God and man, willingness to endure great responsibility and criticism, courage and firmness'.[41] This rationality, combined with steadfastness, had to be itself rooted in even more radical constraints. Government had to be according to higher law coming from God. The minister needed not only earthly wisdom but also knowledge of God's law. If he is to be deficient in one of these it should be the former, because without knowledge of the later he will not understand more mundane matters. Religious belief and rationality went together because man was created rational. To do something contrary to reason would be to go against one's nature and hence against one's Creator.[42]

Clearly, this vision was thoroughly illiberal. The task of the king and his ministers was to establish the reign of God in their kingdom, through the maximum application of reason, to assure policies that were reasonable and just, ensuring that through following the precepts of Divine Law, with the maximum application of human reason, State goals could be fulfilled, which were for the purpose of attaining religiously defined goals.[43]

## 3. Cardinal Richelieu and the Construction of International Law

A much more secular but equally sympathetic picture of Richelieu is presented by Fritz Dickmann almost ten years earlier. This study focuses primarily on the specific role of law in Richelieu's diplomacy from 1624 to December 1642, but also, and more especially, to the influence of his sole-authored Instructions to French

[39] ibid 412.
[40] ibid 480–89. On authority for the authenticity of the *Political Testament*, see esp 481–83.
[41] ibid 491–92. [42] ibid 494. [43] ibid 494–95.

Ambassadors for the Westphalia Peace, which determined French policy in the years running up to the Peace Congress.[44]

The concept of law, in the international context, which Dickmann recognizes Richelieu as following is the validity of religious ethical principles. Despite the doctrine of absolutism in monarchical rule, he does not accept the doctrine of Balthazar de Ayala that it is for the king, as sovereign ruler, to decide if it is just to wage war. The scholastic doctrine required that, beyond the question of the king's competence as sovereign, he must have a just cause.[45] Dickmann meticulously outlines what such 'Natural law' thinking meant. It was a matter of reaching just and appropriate goals in so far as was possible in the circumstances, taking into account all relevant considerations, including legal–historical titles of his monarch to territory, the reason of state, ie the continued well-being of the State, existing treaties and, above all, the possibility of a guaranteed international security, resting not merely on treaties but also on material, physical guarantees backing them up. In other words, the well-being of the State depended upon the security of its frontiers and, therefore, the quality of the relations with its neighbours. How these could be stabilized was a matter of judgement taking into account all relevant factors. The outcome should be a series of multilateral treaties, which would assure lasting international peace.

The actual context for Richelieu had a very large number of elements. Austria and Spain had become united under one royal family, the Hapsburgs. They were, in his eyes, searching to turn the Holy Roman Empire, with its seat in Vienna, into a further national State, which would add the whole of Germany, most of Italy, and the Lowlands (now Holland and Belgium) into one State, whose size would threaten the liberties of the rest of Europe and especially France.

France had a tradition of opposing such a strategy on grounds of historical, legal title, ostensibly going back to the time of Charlemagne, when the leftovers of the Roman Empire were briefly under the control of one Frankish king. French legal scholarship endeavoured to argue for a recovering of as much as possible of these lands, that the lands of the French kings were inalienable French domain, whatever treaty or cession a French king made either voluntarily or by ceding way to a conquest. Richelieu encouraged legal scholarship in this area and took very seriously, as a matter of personal legal conviction, his duty to protect, as far as possible, the domain of his master.

A second strand of legal right of which Richelieu was aware and would employ is the traditional right of resistance of lords against kings who were not historically

[44] F Dickmann, 'Rechtsgedanke und Machtpolitik bei Richelieu: Studien an neu enteckten Quellen' (1963) Bd 196 H 2 *Historische Zeitschrift* 265–319; also republished in Fritz Dickmann, *Friedensrecht und Friedenssicherung, Studien zum Friedensproblem in der Geschichte* (Vandenhoeck & Ruprecht 1971) 36–78. The new sources are *Acta Pacis Westphalicae*, im Auftrage der Vereinigung zur Erforschung der neuen Geschichte, Max Braubach und Konrad Repgen (hrsg) Serie I Instruktionen Bd I: Frankreich, Schweden, Kaiser, Münster 1962. Dickmann is insistent that, while the *Political Testament* carries a strong impression of being Richelieu's genuine thinking, there is no conclusive proof that he was the author himself, or even that the work was made under his supervision. In contrast the Instructions to the French Ambassadors are in his own handwriting and can be definitely taken to be his own exact understanding of law and international diplomacy.

[45] Dickmann (n 44) 46–47.

absolute monarchs, such as the Holy Roman Emperor and the king of Spain. So he was prepared to support German princes who were subject to the Holy Roman Empire's attempt to turn itself into a modern nation state. Equally, he supported the Portuguese and the Catalans against the Spanish king's attempts to absorb them into an integral State. There was a particularly decisive case of the Prince of Trier which was not a case of resistance. He had made a treaty of neutrality with France and Sweden and was treated as a traitor by the Holy Roman Emperor. This was for Richelieu (ie in his instructions to his ambassadors) a particularly clear case of imperial arbitrariness, as the emperor had already refused the prince's appeal for help. Here Richelieu justified intervention on the grounds of natural law and religion.

At the same time, Richelieu considered he had to reach some form of stable peace with Austria–Spain. He could not just aim to drive these powers to distraction. There had to be a compromise which would also appear reasonable to his enemies. The Instructions show that Richelieu debated long and hard about France abandoning Navarre, the traditional homeland of the Bourbons, now kings of France, for the sake of a secure Pyrenees border. In the east he did not push for a Rhine frontier for France and thought claims to some cities such as Verdun were much stronger than to others such as Metz. However strong he thought the French claims to Milan, he considered compromise with Spain was a higher goal. In other words, the classical Thomist doctrine of the just war applied. It was not simply a matter of the justness of the ends but also the appropriateness of the means which had to be considered. Relatively stronger legal claims might justify more physical insistence, but the overall aim had to be the possibility of a general peace.

According to Dickmann's readings of Richelieu's Instructions to French Ambassadors, the fundamental principle guiding him was there had to be a just moderation on the part of the king, not pushing through his rights at any price. This was especially clear in the case of French rights to Milan.[46] Ironically, reason of state called for moderation. Historical legal titles called for an intransigence of conviction.[47] Richelieu's thinking concerned a very close consideration of the importance of concluding treaties. The French lawyers, whom Richelieu readily employed, had devised a doctrine, frequently used by French kings, that any treaty concluded by a king in violation of French historical legal claims, was void as a violation of the domain of France. Richelieu had to wrestle with this idea. He could see that it was subversive of all possible international order based on treaty and he wanted to conclude a series of treaties. So, he anguished around a doctrine that land could not be ceded, for example, to redeem a king from captivity. That could be bought with money. However, the greater security of the State could be purchased with a cession of land, provided the most rigorous care was taken to assure that it was appropriate. Once the decision was made it should be binding.[48] Richelieu had to represent a credible doctrine of binding treaties. In the

[46] ibid 65. [47] ibid 66. [48] ibid 68.

Instructions to French Ambassadors, he insisted a treaty had to be accompanied by collective guarantees. Far from being indifferent to treaties where reason of state demanded, he thought the whole future of Europe had to lie in interlocking treaties of security and guarantee.[49]

Nothing could be more important than the care taken in concluding treaties, and here Church's use of the *Political Testament* reinforces Dickmann's argument when it comes to the legal force of treaties. For instance, Richelieu sees the treaty obligation as resting in the honour and reputation attaching to the good faith of the Prince. Indeed, he sees the greater prince as more vulnerable than the smaller prince, because, being already so advantaged, his reputation will mean more than for a weaker prince, whose advantage will matter more than his honour, eg infidelity to an ally will matter much less to the smaller.[50] In Richelieu's exact words, in the *Political Testament*:

> Kings must take a great care what Treaties they make: but when they are made they must keep them Religiously.
>
> I am sensible that many Politicians teach the contrary; but without considering in their Place what the Christian Faith affords us against those Maxims; I maintain that since loss of honor is greater than the loss of life a great Prince should sooner venture his Life and even the Interest of his State, than to break his word, which he can never violate without losing his Reputation, and consequently the greatest Force of Sovereigns.[51]

As Church also explains, Richelieu thought reputation so important—a good opinion for whose loss they should risk sacrificing fate and grandeur. Richelieu went so far as to insist that rulers should reject all gains that conflicted with their honour.[52] Church remarks further that treaty relations, for Richelieu, were a matter of relations with fellow princes, where the interests of the State were of less moment than the principles of princely honour.[53]

It is the idea of law as justice, as proportionality, reasonableness in all the concrete circumstances, which infuses Richelieu's approach to the classical Thomist concept of the justice of war. Legal competence of the sovereign must be combined with the justice of the ends and with the justice or appropriateness of the means. Do the means justify the ends rather than do the ends justify the means, is at the heart of the natural law doctrine of just war.

There is an anguishing process of reflection on what the situation demands rather than resort to some abstract, predetermined (democratically agreed) rule, as modern law would be understood. Church outlines the general principles of this idea of law in Richelieu, while Dickmann amasses an immense amount of detail from the Instructions to French Ambassadors. There could be war for the national good.[54] War is sometimes inevitable and necessary for such purposes as to regain lost territory, avenge an insult, protect one's allies, stem the progress and pride of a conqueror, and to forestall ills that threaten and cannot otherwise be met. But before undertaking any such war those in charge of State policy must determine its justice according

[49] ibid 70–71. [50] *Political Testament* (n 27) 30. [51] ibid 31.
[52] Church (n 13) 500. [53] ibid 501. [54] ibid.

to the most fundamental precepts of Christian morality. In the *Political Testament* Richelieu himself writes:

> that there can be no successful war unless it is just, because if it is not, even though the occasion for it may be favorable according to worldly precepts, it will be necessary to render an account for it before the tribunal of God.[55]

Therefore a thorough examination of the equity of the war has to be made by theologians of requisite capacity. The anti-Spanish policy against a fellow Catholic State was believed to be justified by Christian morality. Church notes how Richelieu concludes his *Political Testament* by emphasizing the obligation of kings and ministers to rule justly in the sight of God.[56] So Richelieu affirms:

> If they (kings and ministers) use their power to commit some injustice or injury that they cannot do as private persons they commit a sin as prince or magistrate that has its origin solely in their authorship and for which the King of Kings will demand a most exact accounting at Judgment Day.[57]

Dickmann devotes, quantitatively most of his researches to how Richelieu deliberated back and forth the considerations which justified continued war and could make up a just peace. The most difficult issue was Navarre, as the homeland of the Bourbons. He debated the advantage of giving Spain the security of the Pyrenees, despite the clear French legal title, but what persuaded him against was his deep distrust of Spanish ambitions. The king, with the consent of the General Estates, could renounce his title for the good of the State, but in this case, as a matter of judgement, Richelieu thought it better to look for a system of general guarantees to secure Spain at peace. Dickmann stresses that the decision—to retain the legal claim—was not made as a matter of principle but in the light of the concrete situation.[58]

Demands to recover French lands would have to be based upon grounds similar to private law, that a kingly cession was followed by non-fulfilment of a commitment from the other side, that a gift was treated with ingratitude, eg by following up with an aggressive war. He preferred such type of reasoning to an absolute appeal to the inalienability of the French king's domain. However, the judgement of the statesman was necessary to decide what might achieve the possibility of a permanent peace, where a cession is to acquire the repose of all of the rest of the land,[59] again a matter of judgement as to whether the means were appropriate to the end.

Richelieu had the larger aim to secure the position of France in Europe. Higher than any right of conquest had to be the goal of winning a leadership role in Europe based upon trust and good reputation, which France did have in the later Middle Ages, before the unification of Austria and Spain. Within this frame a policy of limitless conquest and thoughtless pursuit of one's own claims—however legally justified in a particular case—would not always be compatible with this goal.[60]

[55] ibid 382. [56] Church (n 13) 503. [57] ibid 452.
[58] Dickmann (n 44) 69–70. [59] ibid 68–69. [60] ibid 52–54.

There is a lot of controversy whether any of these territorial claims, going back as far as Charlemagne, had any justification. However, Dickmann considers Richelieu could have grounds for distinguishing more or less just claims, where, eg issues of disposition by will, violation of a monarchical title, conquest in a just war—each case had to be considered closely.[61] However, it is precisely the treaty-making power of the king which has to be preserved, in his exercise of discretion as a statesman. The experience of Francis I of France renouncing a treaty with Spain in 1555 on the grounds that it violated an inalienable right of the French Crown, must threaten the security of all treaties.[62]

For the modernist international law, returning to Koskenniemi and Jouannet's characterization of the seventeenth century, the question arises whether the language of statesmanlike judicious discretion belongs in legal or political discourse. Dickmann reviews the historian's debates where he rejects Mommsen's claim that while Richelieu was not an unrestrained Machiavelli still all he aimed for was a mere gut instinct for the interest of State—even if pursed in a moderate way—without any theoretical justification of the State. This would make Richelieu merely an opportunistic politician, since not overstretching power is also a goal that Machiavelli would recommend. Dickmann claims in contrast that Richelieu was a theologian and that he never ceased to think theologically.[63]

Basing himself also on the correspondence between Richelieu and the king, Dickmann is insistent that Richelieu was always concerned to reach the 'right' political solution, that there were overriding principles for the 'right decision'. This is in the context of the 'divine right of kings' which doctrine Richelieu fostered. However much the content of decisions might have come from him—a matter which Dickmann says remains ambiguous—there is no doubt that he was insistent that all substantive decisions were taken by the king, as the final authority. The king, for his part, was not content that Richelieu would merely list options for decision but would actually indicate his choice clearly. The crucial issues of declaration of war and preparations of the peace even weeks before Richelieu's death in December 1642, were always cleared with the king.[64] It was the king's divine responsibility to do what was 'right' as it was Richelieu's responsibility to lead him there. That sense of right was, however, not a following of rules, but a just appreciation of what was most appropriate in the circumstances.

[61] ibid. [62] ibid 66. [63] ibid 73–74.

[64] ibid 74–78. For an interpretation within the most authoritative recent French scholarship which corresponds to Dickmann's assessment of Richelieu, see Lucien Bély, 'La construction hésitante et fragile d'une puissance modern' in *Histoire de la Diplomatie Française* (Perrin 2005) 253–308. Bély does not stress Richelieu's attachment to law as such, but confirms his desire to ensure the security of all European States and smaller entities within a system of collective security. In contrast to Louis XIV, there was absent a strategy of aggression by France. Dickmann may well be seen as part of a movement of German scholarship to revise the picture of Richelieu as a person who sought to keep Germany permanently disunited. Bély specifically counters this thesis. See also A Carty, 'State and Nation in the International Law Tradition: A History of French–German Antagonisms and Possible Responses in the Spanish Late Medieval Tradition' in M Stolleis and M Yanagihara (eds), *East Asian and European Perspectives in the History of International Law* (Nomos Verlag 2004) 215–42.

## 4. Conclusion: Liberalism, the Rule of Law, and the Other

Now it is proposed to conclude by considering Richelieu's views, not just in the light of Tuck's critique of liberal thought, but also in the face of the second major problematic of our dialogue in this book, the Western belief that there is, or should be, a universal rule of law. The idea of the rule of law may contain within it the idea that all States are encompassed by it, but it may also imply the challenge that there are States whose ethos is to work against it. For critics such as Morgenthau, international law is a liberal construct, which applies to international relations, the logic of domestic relations among individuals. States are treated as individuals and their relations with one another have to be marked by a mutual respect of freedom and equality. This equality has implicit in it that the international community is plural and that relations are marked by a secular, rational logic of equality. This thinking is a response to the apparent actual plurality of international relations from a European perspective.[65]

It is this apparently innocuous, liberal, humanist perspective which confronts and then violently crushes the Qing, Confucian Chinese international order in the French and British attacks on Peking in 1860, the burning of the Old Summer Palace and the imposition of the liberal order on China in the Treaties of Tienstin and Peking (1858, 1860).[66] There is much that postmodernism has written on the manner in which the so-called Enlightenment excludes the 'barbarous Other' in its definition of rationality and civility, for which Vattel is most reputed. Fitzpatrick has set this out in his study: '"The Desperate Vacuum" Imperialism and Law in the Experience of Enlightenment'.[67] Fitzpatrick's arguments are perhaps a variant of Tuck's, that Enlightenment's liberal, rationalism cannot project the universal, but has to define itself against the 'Other'. The universalist project contains an anti-universalist contradiction. The affirmation of the universal has to include the exclusion of what is not recognized as worthy to be part of the universal. Tuck, perhaps in contrast, recognizes that a new humanist vision of Roman-inspired greatness was more crudely conflictual and did not have to conceal its brutality beneath an ideology.

Morgenthau's account of the rule of law ideology as applied to international society is inevitable somewhat diffuse. Since the seventeenth century, the West has become dominated by rationalism, the belief that the intellect triumphed over biology and emotion, to discern logical principles or causal laws which explained the

[65] HJ Morgenthau, *Scientific Man vs. Power Politics* (University of Chicago Press 1946).

[66] WC Costin, *Great Britain and China 1833–1860* (Clarendon Press 1937); B Brizay, *Le Sac du Palais d'été. L'expédition anglo-française de Chine en 1860* (Editions de Rocher 2011) 503.

[67] Peter Fitzpatrick, '"The Desperate Vacuum" Imperialism and Law in the Experience of Enlightenment' in A Carty (ed), *Post-Modern Law* (Edinburgh UP 1990) 90. Although the text of the rest of this chapter was written originally in January and February 2016, the Fitzpatrick text and most of the following text directly from Morgenthau are now also published in Anthony Carty, *Philosophy of International Law* (2nd edn, Edinburgh UP 2017) 219–22 in a slightly fuller form, with additional content, but without mention of Richelieu. The final three paragraphs of this chapter are unique to it.

operation of the world. Grotius and Leibniz are the founders of this movement. The belief that humans use unequal resources to strive to dominate one another is replaced by the belief that certain social systems, eg feudalism and aristocracy *cause* war, while others such as liberalism appreciate the soundness of rational exploitation of resources, free exchange and communication, and the regulation of disputes through compromise—based upon free communication—and through impartial adjudication.[68]

It remains to elaborate how these starting principles apply to international relations and what Morgenthau calls 'the Science of Peace'.[69] Domestic regimes based upon democracy, free consent of the ruled to their rulers, and free exchange of labour, goods, and capital signify a public space free of violence and in which disputes can be resolved through negotiation or arbitration. The projection of this domestic image on international society signifies that nations are as individuals, autonomous, entitled to freedom from interference, and with no obvious reason to want to dominate and absorb one another. Rivalries need not be destructive, beyond the spirit of robust competition and striving for maximum individual autonomy.

This is all in sharp contrast to Richelieu's vision of an anarchy of many States, fatally unequal in size, hugely diverse in religious, cultural, ethic, geographical, and other characteristics—especially unequal distribution of resources—which face one another in an environment of constant change and instability. One does not have to agree with Morgenthau's essentially classical vision of human nature and society, to realize the force of the argument of Jouannet and Koskenniemi that the world of Richelieu is not remotely like that of the 'Men of 1873' whom Koskenniemi describes in chapter one of *The Gentle Civilizer of Nations.*[70] Morgenthau is not here arguing a realist thesis that such liberal principles do not govern world society. Quite the contrary, liberal powers such as the USA, Britain, and other European powers enjoy military ascendency in the world and are capable repeatedly of enforcing such principles and making them an effective reality. Instead, he is objecting that such principles of liberal internationalism ought not to be enforced because they involve a fundamental metaphysical misunderstanding of the nature of social reality, and thereby increase the havoc and chaos of international society.

The fundamental reason is precisely that the international rule of law distorts social reality.[71] This is in a number of precise respects. Given that the liberal model of world society is too simplistic it is inevitable that the characterization of clashes among States in legal terms will have the effect that:

> The legal decision, by its very nature, is concerned with an isolated case. The facts of life to be dealt with by the legal decision are artificially separated from the facts which precede,

[68] Morgenthau (n 65) esp ch 2 'The Age of Science and the Social World' and ch 3 'The Repudiation of Politics'.

[69] ibid ch 4.

[70] M Koskenniemi *The Gentle Civilizer of Nation: The Rise and Fall of International Law 1870–1960* (CUP 2002).

[71] Morgenthau (n 65) 108–21.

accompany, and follow them and are thus transformed into a 'case' of which the law disposes 'on the merits'.

A political situation presenting itself for a decision according to international law is always one particular phase of a much larger situation, rooted in the historic past and ramifying far beyond the issue under legal consideration.[72]

The social reality of international society is of power seeking. For Morgenthau this dangerous world calls for what he calls political evaluation:

The test to which political decisions in the international sphere must be subject refers, therefore, to the measure in which those decisions affect the distribution of power. ... The question which Richelieu, Hamilton ... or Disraeli would ask before they acted ... was: Does this decision increase or decrease the power of this and other nations?[73]

However, it is important to understand what precisely Morgenthau means by 'political evaluation'. Morgenthau quotes the speeches of Edmund Burke at the time that the American colonies were struggling for independence. Lawyers and sheriffs cannot but follow the law, but 'legislators ... have no other rules to go by, but the great principles of reason and equity, and the general sense of mankind'.[74] Even in domestic society, peace and order depend not upon the victory of the law with the aid of the sheriff and of the police 'but upon that approximation to justice which true statecraft discovers in, and imposes upon, the clash of hostile interests'. This requires not 'the legal acumen of the judge but ... the political wisdom of the legislator and of the chief executive'.[75]

Morgenthau is not attempting to save a wider concept of law than the one with which he is familiar, the liberal rule of law. However, if one revisits the concept of natural law, not in its rationalist form as in his view expounded by Grotius, Leibniz, and Vattel,[76] but in its classical medieval form, as still inhabited by Richelieu, then it becomes clear that Morgenthau is searching for an idea of law which has been lost. To return to the language of the defence of Richelieu by Dickmann, Morgenthau is not calling for opportunistic calculations which individual politicians may resort to for their own polity, but a vision of balance and moderation, which can bring harmony, always only for a time in constantly changing circumstances, to the conflicts among all the polities which affect his own. Law is therefore a just measure and proportion of relations among things, then in the seventeenth century as now in the twenty-first century.

This notion of law has a long pedigree in the pre-rationalist tradition of natural law, which is not so much a system of rules deduced from principles, eg the rule of non-intervention deduced from the principle of sovereign equality, as it is a theory of judgement. The entire weight of this notion of law is placed in the powers of discernment of the State official, in this case, Richelieu. No attempt is made to downplay the incommensurability of Richelieu's world view with the present.

However, there is one further element to be mentioned which grounds the priority of discretion and judgement over rules defined and determined by a formal

[72] ibid 118. [73] ibid 101. [74] ibid. [75] ibid 121.

[76] In this volume we argue against this view.

procedure to assure widespread, if not universal consent. This element is the ontological. Morgenthau does not articulate it in these religious or philosophical terms as starkly as Strauss in his commentary on Machiavelli. However, it is increasingly recognized by scholars sometimes thought postmodernist such as David Campbell, as well as moral theologians such as Oliver O'Donovan.[77] The former attributes the radical insecurity of supposedly liberal societies, since the onset of modernity, precisely to their abandonment or loss of any ontological foundations. Campbell says that a culture which has erased the ontological conditions for certainty—which is the essence of the liberal culture defended by the anti-theological Koskenniemi—has to find discourses of external and even internal danger to ground a State project of national security. Likewise, O'Donovan sees precisely in the ontological vacuity of liberal contractarianism—the idea that a society founds itself out of nothing through a contract—the insecurity which drives and compels democracies such as above all the Anglo-Saxons and the French, to impose their formal visions of democracy and the rule of law on the whole world. Identity comes for O'Donovan from divine recognition. Without this recognition, societies live in perpetual fear of one another, a fear which they endeavour to overcome by trying to force others to become like themselves, and therefore familiar and unthreatening.

To enter the world of Richelieu is to enter a world created by reason, and which can only be governed according to reason. However, for Richelieu, this reason can only be discerned 'through a glass darkly' and, as Strauss has so brilliantly shown and Morgenthau lucidly repeated, Richelieu could have had no more worthy an opponent than Machiavelli in his search for European peace and serenity.

[77] The former is discussed in A Carty, *Philosophy of International Law* (Edinburgh UP 2007) at 140–43 and the latter in A Carty, 'The Moral Theologian, Oliver O'Donovan and International Law' (2008) 9(3) Political Theology 339–62.

# 7

# The Universal Rule of Natural Law and Written Constitutions in the Thought of Johannes Althusius[1]

*John Witte, Jr*

## 1. Introduction

In *The Hebrew Republic: Jewish Sources and the Transformation of European Political Thought*, Harvard historian Eric Nelson sharply criticizes the 'standard narrative' of seventeenth-century political history. The standard narrative describes this as a century devoted to the separation of religion and politics and to the construction of a secular order built on 'pagan classical' learning, Machiavellian politics, and early Enlightenment liberalism. This is largely a 'myth', Nelson argues, propounded by postmodern secularists. The reality is that the seventeenth century saw 'the full fervor of the Reformation unleashed', and 'political theology' made very much part of 'the mainstream of European intellectual life'. It was in this overtly religious milieu that the West built many of its cardinal institutions of confederation, human rights, constitutional order, popular sovereignty, democratic politics, and rule of law. Protestant theological jurisprudence, Catholic political theory and canon law, and Jewish biblical thought, says Nelson, were just as critical to the modern Western political project as the purportedly secular theories of Machiavelli or Hobbes.[2]

My interest has been to excavate some of the early-modern Protestant foundations of modern law, politics, and society, and to show their enduring influence on the Western legal and political tradition.[3] In this chapter, I focus on the contributions of Calvinist jurist, Johannes Althusius (1557–1638), who served as professor

[1] This chapter is drawn in part from my *The Reformation of Rights: Law, Religion, and Human Rights in Early Modern Calvinism* (CUP 2007), ch 3 [hereafter RR], with permission of the publisher.

[2] (Harvard UP 2010), 2–3. For context, see Eric Gregory, 'The Jewish Roots of the Modern Republic' (2012) 105 Harvard Theological Review 372–80.

[3] See J Witte, *Law and Protestantism: The Legal Teachings of the Lutheran Reformation* (CUP 2002); J Witte, *God's Joust, God's Justice: Law and Religion in the Western Tradition* (Eerdmans 2006); J Witte, *From Sacrament to Contract: Marriage, Religion, and Law in the Western Tradition* (2nd edn, Westminster John Knox Press 2011); J Witte and JA Nichols, *Religion and the American Constitutional Experiment* (4th edn, OUP 2016).

and rector at the Herborn Academy, a new Calvinist college, from 1586 to 1604 before moving to Emden, an important seaport near the border of the Holy Roman Empire and the newly united Netherlands and a major Calvinist intellectual centre. There he served as leader of church, State, and society for the rest of his life, while continuing to write voluminously.[4] He was legal counsel for the city (*Stadtsyndicus*) and was deeply involved in the city's multiple legal, commercial, and diplomatic negotiations.[5] He played a leading role in helping Emden wrest greater independence from the local territorial count and nobles, which gave him a small taste of international diplomacy, but nothing on the order of jurists like Hugo Grotius.

Althusius was 'the clearest and most profound thinker which Calvinism has produced in the realm of political science and jurisprudence'.[6] Unlike other figures covered in this volume, and other Calvinists of his day, Althusius wrote little that was original about the moral character of the good ruler or the nature of international law, and he said almost nothing about China or Asia. What commends his work for this volume is that he wrote a great deal about a 'universal law' rooted in divine commandments and natural laws that were binding on rulers and subjects alike. This universal law, he further argued, was to be adapted and adopted in written constitutions forged for each political community. Such constitutions, he argued, were to be detailed and popularly ratified documents that separated and enumerated the executive, legislative, and judicial powers of cities, provinces, nations, and empires alike and that guaranteed and enumerated the natural rights and liberties of all subjects. It was the universal law of God and nature together with the written constitutions of each community that constituted the 'rule of law' for Althusius.

These themes come through in many of his two dozen books,[7] but are especially prominent in his two most famous titles. His massive *Politics* of 1603 (revised in 1610 and 1614) set forth a comprehensive theory of social, political, and legal order and activity, and the forms and norms of sovereignty, authority, and liberty that obtain within each sphere.[8] His three-volume *Theory of Justice* (1617, 1618) laid the groundwork for a comprehensive theory of law and justice.[9] Althusius presented these two tracts as 'comprehensive', 'total', and 'universal' accounts of law and politics. Each tract drew on hundreds of scholarly sources—sundry ancient Greeks and Romans, various apostolic and patristic writers, numerous medieval theologians, philosophers, and civilians, a few canonists, various Protestant jurists, all manner of

[4] See E Wolf, *Grosse Rechtsdenker der deutschen Geistesgeschichte* (4th edn, Mohr 1963) 177–219.

[5] See, eg, *Recess vnd Accord-buch, das ist, Zusamen Verfassung aller Ordnung[en], Decreten, Recessen, Accorden, und Verträgen, so zwischen … Herrn Edtzarden vnd Herrn Johan … Herrn vnd Graffen zu Ostfrieszlandt* (Emden Kallenbach 1612, 1656).

[6] CJ Friedrich, 'Introductory Remarks' in CJ Friedrich (ed), *Politica Methodice Digesta of Johannes Althusius (Althaus)* (Harvard UP 1932 [1614]) xviii.

[7] See D Wyduckel, 'Einleitung, Literaturverzeichnis' in D Wyduckel (ed), H Janssen (tr), *Johannes Althusius, Politik* (Duncker & Humblot 2003) vii–lxxxii.

[8] I have used the 1614 Friedrich edition and adapted the English translation: *Politica Johannes Althusius*, FS Carney (ed) (tr) (Liberty Fund 1995) [hereafter Pol]. See further Johannes Althusius, *Civilis conversationis libri duo recogniti et aucti. Methodice digesti et exemplis sacris et profanis passim illustrati* (Hanau Hanoviae Antonius 1601) [hereafter Civ Conv].

[9] Johannes Althusius, *Dicaeologicae libri tres, totum et universum Jus, quo utimur, methodice complectentes* (Apud Christophorum Corvinum 1618) [hereafter Dic].

contemporary Catholic and Protestant political writers, especially from Salamanca, and several collections of civil, imperial, feudal, and urban law. There was good reason for this intense eclecticism. Althusius was writing for the ages, not just for his own age. By copiously combing and combining the insights of sundry Jewish, Greek, Roman, and Christian sources, he sought to create what he called a 'total' and 'universal' theory that would appeal not only to fellow Calvinists and countrymen but to anyone in his world of Christendom who was serious about faith and order, authority and liberty.

Althusius built his system on two main foundations, which I take up in the next two sections: (1) a 'demonstrative theory' of universal natural law that focused on the concordance between Christian and classical, biblical, and rational teachings of law, authority, and rights; and (2) 'a symbiotic theory of human nature' that focused on the natural and necessary attachments of the person to God, neighbour, and society, including especially the role of covenantal political associations in maintaining human liberty and community.[10]

## 2. Demonstrative Theory of Natural Law

In working out his legal theory, Althusius sought to demonstrate the ultimate concordance between biblical and rational, Christian and classical teachings on the nature and purpose of law. Civil law and canon law jurists of his day typically distinguished three main types of law: (1) the natural law or law of nature (*ius naturale, lex naturae*), the set of immutable principles of reason and conscience that are supreme in authority and divinity; (2) the law of nations or common law (*ius gentium, ius commune, lex communis*), the legal principles and procedures that are common to multiple political communities and often the basis for treaties and other diplomatic conventions; and (3) the civil law or positive law (*ius civile, ius positivum*), the statutes, customs, and cases of various States, churches, fiefdoms, manors, and other local political communities.[11] Theologians and moralists, in turn, generally distinguished three main types of biblical law: (1) moral law (*lex moralis*), the enduring moral teachings of the Decalogue and the New Testament; (2) juridical or forensic law (*lex juridicales, ius forensi*), the rules and procedures by which ancient Israelites and apostolic Christians governed their religious and civil communities; and (3) ceremonial law (*lex ceremonialis*), the Mosaic laws of personal diet, ritual sacrifice, priestly life, and the like that governed the religious life of the ancient Israelites. Some theologians saw parallels between these three ancient types of biblical law and the three layers of modern Catholic and Protestant church law that governed, respectively, the essentials of doctrine and morality, the commonplaces of ecclesiastical polity and property, and the discretionary aspects (the *adiaphora*) of local church life.[12]

[10] See Pol Preface; Dic I.25–26.
[11] Dic 1.13.6, 10.
[12] Pol XXI.35–40; Pol XXII.1–12. See also Pol, Preface (1603, 1610, and 1614 edn) for Althusius's discussion of the relationships among the disciplines of theology, law, ethics, and political science.

Althusius's mature legal theory collapsed these sundry hierarchies of law into two main types: natural laws and positive laws. And he subsumed most of the other traditional types of law within these two categories. He treated the moral laws of the Bible and the common laws of nations as two visible forms of the same invisible natural law hidden within each person's reason and conscience. And, he regarded the laws of ancient Israelites and of modern churches as two types of positive law that stood alongside the positive laws of historical and modern States. The modern validity of all these positive laws turned on their concordance with the natural law. Their modern utility for any polity turned on their compliance with the fundamental law (*lex fundamentalis*) of the community.

Natural law is 'the will of God for men', Althusius argued. God has 'written this natural law' on the hearts, souls, minds, and consciences of all persons, as Romans 2:15 and sundry other biblical and classical sources make clear. Everyone, by his or her very nature, thus has the 'ideas (*notitiae*) and inclinations (*inclinationes*) of this natural law' born within them. Some of these 'natural inclinations' are common to humans and animals. Like animals, humans by nature are inclined to 'preserve their lives and to procure the necessities to remain alive'. They are inclined to defend themselves against force and *force majeure*. They are inclined to ally themselves with others and to rally around natural leaders to aid them in their self-defence. They are inclined to 'procreate by the union of male and female and to educate their natural-born children'. They are inclined to care for themselves and for their loved ones when they are sick, hurt, or ailing. Self-preservation, self-protection, and self-perpetuation are 'natural inclinations' that the natural law teaches to persons and animals alike.[13]

The natural law also teaches persons higher ideas that appeal uniquely to human reason and conscience, Althusius argued. By them, 'a man understands what justice is, and is impelled by this hidden natural instinct to do what is just and to avoid what is unjust'. Through the natural law, God commands all persons to 'live a life that is at once pious and holy, just and proper'. God teaches them the natural 'duties of love that are to be performed towards God and one's neighbor'. He sets out the basic 'rules of living, obeying, and administering' that must govern all persons and associations. He sets forth 'general principles of goodness and equity, evil and sinfulness' that every man must know in order to live with himself and with others. He teaches the 'actions and omissions that are appropriate to maintaining the public good of human society' as well as the private good of households and families. By the natural law, Althusius wrote in final summary of his position, 'God teaches and writes on human hearts the general principles of goodness, equity, evil, and sin, and He instructs, induces, and incites all persons to do good and avoid evil. He likewise condemns the conscience of those who ignore these things and excuses those who do them. He thereby directs them to goodness and dissuades them from evil. If they follow the path of goodness, he excuses them. If they do not, he condemns them.'[14]

This natural law has had many names in the classical and Christian traditions, Althusius recognized—Godly law, Divine Law, moral law, natural law, natural

[13] Dic I.13.10–18; Pol I.32–39; Pol IX.21; Pol XVIII.22; Pol XXI.16–19; Pol XXXVIII.37.
[14] Dic I.13.1, 14–15; Pol XXX.16, 19–20.

justice, natural equity, the law of conscience, of the mind, of reason, or of right reason, the law inside people, the immutable law, the supreme law, the general law, the common law, and others. Parsing the names for the natural law was not so important to Althusius. He regarded them mostly as synonyms and used them interchangeably.[15]

Knowing the norms that the natural law teaches, and applying them responsibly for the governance of self and others was the more important and the more difficult task. Althusius knew the traditional formula taught by the medieval scholastics and by the neo-scholastics of his day: that the natural law gives all persons an innate or natural knowledge of good and evil (called *synderesis*); that by exercising their reason persons can come to understand the norms of this natural law; and that by exercising their conscience they can learn to apply these norms equitably to concrete circumstances. But Althusius also recognized that, throughout history, persons and peoples have reached different formulations and applications of the natural law. Even in avowed Christian societies today, he wrote, persons have 'different degrees of this [natural] knowledge and inclination. This law is not evidently inscribed equally on the hearts of all. The knowledge of it is communicated more abundantly to some and more sparingly to others, according to the will and judgment of God.' So, given this reality, how can we really know 'the nature of the norms of the law that are implanted in us by nature?' How can we be absolutely certain that we as individuals, or as the leaders of our communities, have 'a true perception' of the contents of the natural law? How can we even know which person's or community's formulations of the natural law are better than another's? How can we determine and distil those features of the natural law that should be part of a universal rule of law? Persons are fallible creatures who perceive natural law only 'indirectly', 'circumstantially', 'through a glass darkly', through 'flickering shadows' emitting from distant caves of light. Communities have widely variant 'customs, natures, attitudes, and viewpoints' that are affected by the 'age, condition, circumstances, and education' of their members. There is no universal code of written natural law to consult. So, how can we be sure of the natural law's norms and contents?[16]

We can know the norms of the natural law if we study both Scripture and tradition, revelation, and reason very carefully, Althusius argued. We know that God has given a fuller revelation of his law in the Bible, particularly in the Ten Commandments and in the moral teachings of Moses and the Prophets, Jesus, and St Paul. This cannot be a new form of natural law, for God would not and could not contradict the natural law that he already revealed to us in and through our human nature. Biblical moral law is rather a more perfect conformation and elaboration of the natural law ideas and inclinations that are already inscribed on the hearts and minds of everyone, believers and non-believers alike. Through Moses, God rewrote on stone what was already written on our hearts. Through Jesus, God rewrote this law anew by fulfilling its commandments and promises and by teaching his followers how to discern

[15] Dic 1.13.13–18; Dic I.14; Pol XXI.1–20.

[16] Dic I.6.4–6, 26; Dic I.13.16–18; Pol XXI.20–21; Pol XXIII.1–20.

its 'weightier matters'. To be sure, Althusius acknowledged, biblical moral law has clearer precepts and higher purposes than any other form of natural law. It provides a more certain knowledge of the will of God for our lives. It sets out a pathway to salvation for those who can abide by its letter and a pathway to sanctification for those who can live by its spirit. But the Bible's moral law only rewrites more copiously the natural law that is already written cryptically on the hearts of everyone.[17]

While God and Scripture have rewritten the natural law for believers to discern, reason and experience have rewritten this natural law for non-believers to discover. In every major civilization, Althusius argued, enlightened leaders and magistrates have emerged who have used their natural reason to translate the general principles of natural law in their minds into specific positive or proper laws (*leges positivum, leges propriae*) for their communities. These enlightened leaders have inevitably tailored these positive laws to 'the customs, nature, needs, attitudes, conditions, and other special circumstances' of the people ruling and being ruled. This has produced widely variant positive laws over time and across cultures, particularly when these local laws are viewed in their details. But these enlightened leaders have also inevitably positioned these laws to reflect some of the natural light within their hearts, and have maintained these laws because they have proved to be both right and useful. This has produced laws that are common, even universal, to many peoples and polities, even those that have had no interaction with each other. Every major civilization, said Althusius, has developed comparable sets of law to govern religious worship and observance, to honour marriage and the family, to obey authorities and to respect traditions, to protect human lives, properties, and reputations, to care for relatives, widows, orphans, and the poor, to speak respectfully to others, to testify truthfully, to honour promises, contracts, and agreements, to vindicate wrongs and to punish wrongdoers, to fight wars and repel attacks, to give to each and everyone what is due. These common laws, independently developed by different peoples and polities over time and across cultures, must be regarded as 'visible expressions of the same invisible natural law' within all persons, Althusius argued. They must be taken as reflections of 'the natural and divine immutable equity that is mixed into them', as indications 'of the common practice of natural law'.[18]

These common laws (*iura commune)* or general laws of nations (*iura gentium*)—gathered from the commonplaces of sundry positive laws and the common practices of sundry legal communities—stand alongside biblical moral laws as a second form and forum of natural law. Indeed, at a certain level of abstraction, the moral laws of the Bible and common laws of the nations converge, even though they have very different origins, ends, and languages. 'A law is both natural and common', Althusius wrote, 'if the common use of right reason produces it for the necessity and utility of human social life. It, too, can then be called natural law.'

[17] Pol VII.7–12; Pol X.3–12; Pol XVIII.32–44; Pol XXI.22–29.

[18] Dic 1.13.4–18; Dic 1.14.1–14; Dic I.35.22–23; Pol VII.7–12; Pol IX.20–21; Pol X.3–12; Pol XVIII.32–44; Pol XXI.22–29; Pol XXII.1–10.

While some distinguish among common law (*ius commune*), natural law (*ius naturale*), and the law of nations (*ius gentium*), others more properly call each of them forms of the [same] natural law. ... Christ himself often called natural law things that are usually called the law of nations.[19]

Althusius rested his case on the contents of the universal natural law most firmly on the confluence between the Commandments of the Decalogue and the moral teachings of sundry classical traditions. For him, the Decalogue was the clearest and most comprehensive confirmation and codification of the natural law, of every person's inner natural inclinations to piety and justice, to faith and order, to love of God and love of neighbour. As such, 'the Decalogue has been prescribed for all people to the extent that it agrees with and explains the common law of nature for all peoples'. 'The precepts of the Decalogue ... infuse a vital spirit into the association and symbiotic life that we teach'.

They carry a torch to guide the kind of social life that we desire; they prescribe and constitute a way, rule, guiding star, and boundary for human society. If anyone would take them out of politics, he would destroy it; indeed, he would destroy all symbiosis and social life among men. For what would human life be without the piety of the First Table and the justice of the Second [Table of the Decalogue]? What would a commonwealth be without the communion and communication of things useful and necessary to human life?[20]

Every serious legal community thus has comparable positive laws dealing with spiritual matters, worship, holiness, blasphemy, rest days, family, household, property, crime, fidelity, contracts, evidence, and procedure that are reflected in the Ten Commandments.

But beyond the Decalogue, not all biblical law should be taken as natural law, Althusius insisted, nor considered mandatory or even useful for modern times. Many of the Mosaic laws are simply the positive laws of the ancient Jewish people. Many of the legal actions and admonitions of the patriarchs, judges, and kings of ancient Israel are simply evidence of one positive law system in action. Particularly the Mosaic 'ceremonial' laws and customs respecting diet, dress, sacrifice, ritual, levitical life, temple rules, and more, even though if they may have been authored by God, have no place in modern Christian or secular communities. At best, they serve as an illustration of how one legally sophisticated ancient community exercised its natural inclinations and obligations to religious worship and ritual life. While a modern-day Christian magistrate would do well to develop a comparable set of ceremonial laws tailored to the needs of the local community, and perhaps even emulate some of the ancient biblical prototypes, he or she cannot simply 'impose these Jewish positive laws, which by their nature are changeable and obsolete'. That would be to 'destroy Christian liberty'.[21]

[19] Dic I.13.11, 18–19.

[20] Pol, Preface (1610 and 1614 edn); Pol XXI.29. See also Pol VII.7–12; Pol X.3–12; Pol XVIII.32–44; Pol XXI.22–29, 41; Dic I.13.10–18; Dic 1.14.1–3.

[21] Pol XXI.33–40; Pol XXII.3–4; Dic I.14.5–11; Dic I.16.9–10; Dic I.101.43; Dic 115.1–36.

More useful in our day, for Christian and non-Christian polities alike, are the 'juridical laws' of Moses. These are the many detailed laws and procedures set out in the Bible to govern crime and tort, marriage and family, property and commerce, procedure and evidence, and more. These provisions, and the examples of their application by biblical kings and judges, are more useful and probative because they give more specific content, context, and coherence to the Decalogue and other statements of natural law. '[T]he moral commandments of the Decalogue are general', Althusius wrote. 'They have no certain, special, and fixed punishment attached to them', let alone procedural mechanisms for how they should be justly and equitably interpreted and applied. The juridical law of Moses 'makes more specific determinations, which it relates to the circumstances of the act'. So, while the natural law commands 'that evildoers ought to be punished', it 'proposes nothing concerning the punishment', save the bald commandment, 'thou shalt not kill', which cannot be just in all circumstances. The juridical law 'works out specifically that adulterers, murderers, and the like are to be punished by death, unless the punishment should be mitigated on account of other circumstances. The Mosaic law has various punishments for these crimes', and prescribes a number of useful procedures to weigh the evidence of the crime and to determine a just punishment.[22] Similarly, the Mosaic juridical law offers a number of useful legal rules and procedures for the acquisition, use, and maintenance of public and private property, for the litigation and settlement of private disputes, and for the proper interactions between husband and wife, parent and child, master and servant, creditor and debtor, seller and buyer. None of these juridical positive laws of Moses should be considered binding upon modern day Christians just because they happen to be in the Bible. But in so far as they are parts and products of the natural law, these juridical laws are edifying for our day, and can be appropriated as apt in the construction of modern positive laws.[23]

What underscored the natural validity and modern utility of the juridical laws of Moses was that they often had parallels in other legal systems, most notably in the classical Roman law distilled in the *Corpus Iuris Civilis* of Justinian. 'Virtually all Europeans still use' the classical Roman law, wrote Althusius, because its detailed laws have also proved to be 'both right and useful'.[24] To be sure, some ancient Roman law provisions betrayed the natural law more than illustrated it. Think of the many old laws celebrating the pagan imperial cult, the domestic laws that permitted infanticide, sex with slaves, and prostitution, the commercial laws that countenanced exploitation of orphans, captives, and slaves, and others. Such laws that openly contradict the Decalogue and other natural law principles cannot be viewed as binding on anyone, said Althusius. But the classical Roman law texts also hold numerous more enlightened legal teachings, many parallel to those in Mosaic juridical law, that are 'consistent with the natural law and that cater to public utility and the common good'. Some of these Roman laws have also been adopted and adapted into the canon laws of the medieval church and the civil laws of early-modern European

22 Pol XXI.33; Dic 1.14.5; Dic I.16.9–18.
23 Pol VIII.72–91; Pol XXI.32–33; Dic 1.14.20; Dic I.15.18–21.
24 Dic 1.14.1–14; Pol VIII.72–86; Pol XXI.30–40; Pol XXII.1–3, 10.

nations. When these ancient Roman law texts and their later legal adaptations are interpreted and applied 'naturally, equitably, and justly', they, too, can be taken as reflections and illustrations of the universal natural law in action.[25]

This was the method that Althusius used to work out an elaborate system of public, private, criminal, and procedural law for his day. He started with the natural law principles of Scripture and tradition. He then cited the elaboration of these principles in the precepts and procedures of various legal systems with an eye to discovering and demonstrating what they held in common. He combed very carefully through biblical law and classical Roman law. He rummaged more freely and selectively through medieval and early-modern civil law, canon law, feudal law, manorial law, and urban law. The more frequently he found a legal principle, precept, procedure, or practice repeated in diverse sources, the more readily he held this up as a feature of a universal rule of law. Althusius did not take the next step that other early-modern figures like Grotius and Pufendorf took in arguing for international and interstate laws, treaties, and conventions based on these universal legal principles. He was content to demonstrate which laws were 'universal rules' and left it others to work them into the machinery of international law and interstate diplomacy.

## 3. A Symbiotic Theory of Society and Politics

Althusius started his theory of society and politics, like his theory of law, with an account of the state of nature—now human nature, and more particularly the nature of persons as creatures and image bearers of God. God created humans as moral creatures, Althusius argued, with a natural law written on their hearts and consciences and 'an innate inclination', 'hidden impulse', and 'natural instinct' to be 'just and law-abiding'. God created persons as natural rights holders, vested with a natural sovereignty rooted in the supernatural sovereignty of God, whose image each person bears from birth. God created persons as resilient creatures, with a natural capacity to preserve, protect, and reproduce themselves. God created humans as 'virtuous' and 'rational creatures', who are called to pursue a 'holy, just, comfortable, and happy' life. God created persons as social creatures with a 'symbiotic impulse for community', 'an instinct to live together with others and to establish civil society'. God created persons as loving creatures, who naturally need to give and to receive love in order to be fully human and to abide fully by the most primal command of the natural law: to love God, neighbour, and self. And God created persons as 'language-bearers', as 'creatures of communication', equipped to learn, teach, and develop the complex norms, habits, and gestures of proper communication and interaction in the home, church, State, school, business, and other associations.[26] This was a far more complex anthropology than the bleak Hobbesian view of self-interested individuals driven by an ethic of self-preservation to dangerous

[25] Dic I.14.16–20; Dic I.15.1–21; Dic I.16.8.

[26] Pol I.1–35; Pol XX.19–28; Dic I.7; Civ Conv I.1, 7–11; Civ Conv II.2–6, 9–10.

and destructive behaviour unless coerced into political and social conformity by an all-powerful sovereign.

Althusius distinguished three main types of associations that exist in most advanced civilizations: (1) private natural associations anchored in marriage and family ties; (2) private voluntary associations (*collegia*), such as corporations, guilds, businesses, charities, and more formed by related or unrelated parties; and (3) public or political associations—whether local (villages, towns, and cities), regional (duchies, provinces, and territories), or 'universal' (nations or empires). Each of these associations, he argued, is formed by a 'tacit or explicit' contract or covenant—a 'bond of association and common agreement' about the 'property, work, and rights in common' among the members of each association. By this 'bond', 'contract', or 'covenant', the members agree to 'communicate and share' a portion of their property, work, and rights with other members of that association, 'each fairly and properly according to his ability'. By so doing, each person's multiple and unique needs are met so far as possible in the context of creating a community and common life. Althusius called these voluntary social contracts the 'founding charters' or 'consensual constitutions' of the natural, voluntary, and political associations that together form a commonwealth.[27]

Each of these founding agreements, he continued, is governed by a 'general law of community, association, or symbiosis' (*lex communis, lex consociationis, lex symbiosis*).[28] This universal law of community teaches that in any such contractual association, some must be ruling authorities, others must be obedient subjects. The 'right to rule' (*ius majestatis*) is assigned according to natural and intellectual ability, the duty to obey is accepted in accordance with individual and social need. Structures of authority and obedience are 'unnatural', Althusius believed, but they are 'necessary' for personal flourishing and social order. 'By the natural law all men are equal and subject to the jurisdiction of no one, unless they subject themselves to another's authority by their own consent and voluntary act, and transfer to another their rights.' Most people agree, however, to transfer their rights and subject themselves to these 'unnatural' structures and strictures of authority, for they realize that without them even their most elementary associations will not long survive, and even their most basic rights will mean little.[29]

The general law of association, however, puts basic limits on the activities of every authority—whether in the home, church, State, or other association. Every authority must rule 'for the sake' of his or her subjects—for the purpose of allowing them to seek their ultimate end of attaining a 'holy, just, comfortable, and happy' life. Every authority must care for the soul and the body of his or her subjects. Every authority must ensure that the 'moral law' is applied 'equitably and justly' within that association, always striving to balance firmness and fairness, rule and right, justice and mercy in accordance with the teachings of 'natural equity' (*aequitas naturalis*). Every authority must develop a body of proper internal laws (*leges propriae*) of the association tailored to 'the nature, utility, condition, and other special circumstances' of the

[27] Pol I.1–10, 19, 25, 27, 29–35; Pol II.1–6; Dic I.7, 90.
[28] Pol XXI.19; Dic 1.14.
[29] Pol I.10–18; Pol XVIII.18.

association and its members. Every authority must put into 'practice the common natural law' that governs all persons, and must 'indicate how individual members of that association are able to seek and attain the natural equity' to which they are entitled.[30] For Althusius, familial, private, and political associations alike were distinct spheres of law and love, justice, and equity. Each association was grounded in the natural law and governed by the general law of associations. Each association, in turn, was a source of positive or proper law. Each made specific laws for the sake of achieving justice and equity for that association and protecting the rights and liberties of its members.

*Political associations.* In his full social theory, Althusius analysed the private natural and voluntary associations in great detail, but let's focus on the public political associations that are formed by covenants among these private (natural or voluntary) associations. The simplest such public political associations, and the earliest to develop, are hamlets and villages, then larger towns, counties, and cities. These small local associations eventually covenant together to form larger public associations—duchies, provinces, territories, or prince-bishoprics. Not uncommonly, these intermediate public associations conjoin to form commonwealths, nations, or empires—'universal public associations', as Althusius called them.[31] While he did not call this 'interstate' or 'international law' per se, these layers of 'political covenants' among independent sovereign political peers functioned in effect as international agreements.

While this political evolution from private to public political associations can be seen in the history of many peoples, for Althusius the 'earliest', 'best', 'wisest', and 'most perfect example' was recorded in the political history of biblical Israel.[32] The Israelite people moved from the marital household of Abraham and Sarah to the extended families of Isaac and Jacob, then to the twelve tribes founded by Jacob's twelve children, then to the towns and cities led by Joshua and the later Judges, and finally to a single nation of Israel ruled by kings. As Althusius read the Bible, each step in this political evolution of Israel was forged by a 'consensual covenant' between the rulers and the people, with God presiding as third party governor and guarantor. When the people and their families and tribes needed judges to govern their new cities, God commanded them: 'You shall establish judges and moderators in all your gates that the Lord gave you through your tribes, who shall judge the people with righteous judgment' (Deuteronomy 16:18). When the tribes later came together to form the nation of Israel, they entered into covenant with King David. The Bible recorded this critical final step of Israel's political evolution as follows:

> Then all the tribes of Israel came to David at Hebron, and said, 'Behold, we are your flesh and bone. In times past, when Saul was king over us, it was you that led out and brought in Israel; and the Lord said to you, You shall be shepherd of my people Israel, and you shall be prince over Israel.' So all the elders of Israel came to the king at Hebron; and King David made a

[30] Pol I.3, 10–18; Pol IX.1–8; Pol XX.24–30; Dic I.13.
[31] Pol VI.1; Pol XVIII; Pol XXXVIII.84–86; Dic I.32, 81.
[32] Pol Preface (1610 and 1614 edns); Pol XVIII.18–40; Pol XIX.79; Pol XXII.15–19.

covenant with them at Hebron before the Lord, and they anointed David king over Israel. (II Samuel 5:1–3; Deuteronomy 17:14–15)

These same political covenant ceremonies were repeated anew with King Solomon, King Rehoboam, and others (1 Kings 1:34–40, 12:1–20).

Althusius recited this biblical history and sundry other political histories to draw out enduring lessons for the development of a just and stable legal and political order for his day, filled as it was with domestic and international turmoil. One lesson was that both biblical and natural law condone the doctrine of popular sovereignty, which he defined as the natural right and power of the people to rule themselves or to elect representatives to rule on their behalf. 'God has formed in all peoples by the natural law itself the free power to constitute princes, kings, and magistrates for themselves', he wrote.

This means that, insofar as any commonwealth that is divinely instructed by the law of nature has civil power, it can transfer this power to another or others, who, under the title of kings, princes, consuls, or other magistrates, assume the direction of its common life.

This natural right to self-rule is so powerful and universal that even God Himself respected this right when the ancient Israelites insisted on its vindication. 'God marvelously governed this people for about four hundred years as if he himself were their king', wrote Althusius. And God had the perfect natural right, as the Creator of the law of nature, to rule the Israelites permanently as their king. But 'the people requested their own king. God was at first indignant and gave them Saul, whom God designated and immediately chose himself' and whom he crowned through the services of his prophet Samuel. But the people did not welcome Saul. They wanted another king, David, to serve in his stead. God yielded to their choice. 'By his word, he established the descendants of David in the control of the realm. But God performed these actions in such a way that the people were not excluded from giving their consent and approval.' While God helped to coronate these earthly kings to rule in his stead, 'the kings were considered to be chosen by the people as well, and to receive from them the right to rule as king (*ius regis*)' on behalf of the people.[33]

If even God yielded to the natural right of the people to select their own political rulers, then surely every earthly ruler must yield to this natural right as well. 'Rulers are made for the people, not people for the rulers', Althusius wrote. 'The people can exist without the ruler, but the ruler cannot exist without the people.' 'By nature and circumstance the people are prior to, and more important than, and superior to their rulers.' The people elect rulers for the sake of delegating to them the administration of laws that they cannot manage easily on their own. These rulers must act on the people's behalf, and with the interest of the people in mind. They can exercise no more authority over the people than the people can exercise over themselves, and no more authority than the people have explicitly delegated to these rulers. In particular, rulers may not trespass natural laws or natural rights any more than the people can. And they may never convert their political office into an instrument for 'their

[33] Pol IX.3–4; Pol XVIII.8, 18–20, 58–59; Pol XIX.8–10, 15–18, 73; Dic 1.32.15–19.

personal and private benefit rather than for the common utility and welfare'. As a precaution against such abuse, Althusius insisted that no atheist, heretic, or bastard, and nobody who was impious, impish, or immoral be allowed to serve in political office.[34]

A second lesson Althusius drew from this biblical story was that political associations, like natural and private associations, must be formed by voluntary covenants or contracts sworn by the people and their rulers before God. Althusius described these political covenants as mutual promises by the people and their rulers to uphold the laws of God and nature, the natural rights and liberties of the people, and the faith and order of the community. The rulers swear an oath of office before the people and before God to 'administer the realm or commonwealth according to laws prescribed by God, right reason, and the body of the commonwealth'. They swear to 'bear and represent the person of the entire realm, of all subjects thereof, and of God from whom all power derives'. They swear to maintain the soul and body, piety and justice, faith and order of the people and the community. The people, in turn, by 'common consent', promise to 'bind themselves to obey and comply with the supreme magistrate who administers the commonwealth according to prescribed laws' so long as those positive laws 'do not conflict with the law of God and the right of the realm'. They further promise to accord legitimate magistrates their 'trust, compliance, service, aid, and counsel', to pray for the magistrates' survival, wisdom, flourishing, and happiness, to pay their taxes, to register their properties, to answer their conscriptions, and to oblige all other just laws and orders that cater to the peace, order, and happiness of the commonwealth.[35]

Althusius distinguished various types, phases, or dimensions of the political covenant. The first was the agreement among the people themselves who, directly or through their representatives, chose to form a political association regardless of its type of government. The second was between the rulers and the people, by which each side defined the forms and norms of government of the political association, and their respective duties and rights, powers and privileges therein. The third was between the ruler and God to maintain a godly commonwealth that served to the glory of God and secured the blessings of liberty for the people and their associations. The fourth was between the chief magistrate and the lower magistrates, by which each side agreed to check and balance the other as a safeguard against tyranny. For Althusius all these agreements together served as the 'fundamental law', 'founding constitution', and 'contractual mandate' of the political community.[36]

Althusius regarded political covenants—at the urban, provincial, and national levels alike—as the best guarantee of the 'ultimate rule of laws (*leges*) and rights (*iura*) in human society'. 'Rule by law' and 'rules of law' grounded in the law of nature and enumerated and bounded by the political covenant, he thought, provided the commonwealth with 'a guiding light of civil life, a scale of justice, a preserver of liberty, a bulwark of public peace and discipline, a refuge for the weak, a bridle for

[34] See analysis in RR 169–76.

[35] Pol VI.30–31; Pol VII.4–12; Pol XVIII.18; Pol XIX.6–7, 14, 98; Pol XX.1–2; Pol XXVIII.30–32.

[36] Pol X.4; Pol XIX.6, 15, 23, 29, 49; Pol XX.18; Pol XXVIII.30–32; Dic I.13.3, 6–8.

the powerful, a norm and straightener of rulership'. For Althusius, these political covenants were not just mythical, metaphysical, or metaphorical constructs. They were to be written charters and constitutions, to which the rulers and the people solemnly swore their allegiance before God. They specified in detail the mutual rights and duties of the people, the powers and prerogatives of the rulers, and the principles and procedures for the creation and enforcement of positive laws. 'Written constitutions', he wrote, provide the best 'fences, walls, guards, or boundaries of our life, guiding us along the appointed way for achieving wisdom, happiness, and peace in human society'.[37]

These written constitutions must make clear that, at every level of government, the people remain sovereign and supreme; they retain their fundamental rights as persons and as members of private associations. Even the 'right of national sovereignty' belongs ultimately to the people as a whole, not to any person within it—especially not to any king or other supreme ruler who happens to occupy their political office. All the people who constitute the nation are literally, said Althusius, the 'owners of the nation's rights of sovereignty'. Through the creation of the national covenant, or constitution, the people as a whole may agree to delegate the administration of their power to a national or royal office. Because of this delegation, 'the king represents the people, not the people the king'. The king must be responsible to the people, represented in their various associations.

> The right of a king consists in the faithful and diligent care and administration of the commonwealth entrusted to him by the people. . . . The king holds, uses, and enjoys these riches . . . as a usufructuary [a leaseholder]. When the king dies, or is denied the royal throne by legitimate means, these rights of the king return to the people, the owner [of these rights]. The people then reassign them as it thinks best for the good of the commonwealth. Therefore the right of the king is one thing, the right of the people another. The former is temporary and personal; the latter is permanent. The former is lesser, the latter greater. The former is a loan given by contract to the authorized king, the latter is an indivisible property [owned by the people].[38]

Not only do the people retain their fundamental sovereignty and rights; the lower political associations also retain their fundamental identity and sovereignty as parts of these broader political structures. Each local political association retains its own 'right of sovereignty' (*ius majestatis*), its own 'rights, privileges, benefits, and prerogatives' that the people have delegated to them. This is the political power to exercise personal and subject matter jurisdiction within that political association, to undertake legal actions on behalf of and for the sake of the members, to 'dispose, prescribe, ordain, administer everything necessary and useful' for the maintenance and flourishing of the political association and the people. Of course, a city's right of sovereignty is subject to that of the higher provinces and nation, just as a province's right of sovereignty is subject to the highest sovereignty of the nation. But these local political rights of sovereignty remain in place and must be respected so far as

[37] ibid.
[38] Pol Preface; Pol IX.4, 15–24; Pol XVIII.102–4; Pol XXIV.29–50; Pol XXXVIII.31, 39–40.

possible, Althusius argued. For the more local the administration of authority, the more 'individualized the care that is given to the individuals and groups'. The agreement of a city to join a province, or of a city and province to join a larger national republic, does not end their political identity or sovereignty, but confirms it. It guarantees representation of their local interests in higher politics and assures them of protection and support in the event of attack or emergency. It further confirms that the higher political associations are created by and composed of these smaller associations, and ultimately dependent upon them for their survival. Lower political associations are the essential foundations of higher political associations, without which a province or nation state would crumble.[39]

Althusius's insistence on preserving local political sovereignty, even while defending the rights and powers of a sovereign nation state, was a critical argument in the defence of the Dutch confederacy of his day, and eventually in the development of the modern theory of political federalism. It also had strong implications for sorting out the complex political relationships of various polities in the Holy Roman Empire of his day, not least the city of Emden, and various interstate and international relations, too. His views stood in marked contrast with the theories of royal absolutism and nationalist sovereignty propounded by Jean Bodin, James I, and others whom Althusius roundly dismissed as misguided. For Althusius, sovereignty was a universal blessing vested in all the people in their particular associations, not an indivisible prerogative vested exclusively in a hereditary monarch. Federalism was an essential guarantee of the sovereignty of the people, and the lower private and political associations that they inhabited, a buffer against the inevitable tendencies of higher magistrates towards political tyranny and nationalist absolutism.

Federalism was not the only such safeguard. Separation of powers served that function as well. Althusius called for a 'mixed government' that combined monarchical, aristocratic, and democratic elements but that separated executive, legislative, and judicial powers. Each power should enjoy a measure of control over and dependence on the other, said Althusius, and all powers are subordinate to the law of the State itself, particularly the fundamental law that brings these powers into being. All powers and authorities should exercise 'moderation' 'so that the right of each member of the commonwealth is conserved, and neither diminished nor increased to the detriment of another'. It is especially important to ensure 'that the power of the king is not so enhanced that the liberty of the people is suppressed'.[40] Althusius worked out in detail the layers of urban, provincial, and national offices that discharged these powers, and the particular procedures, purposes, and prerogatives that attached to each. He devoted a good deal of his *Politics* to this huge analytical task, focusing especially on the respective powers of the executive and legislative offices over religion and morality, rights and liberties, education and welfare, war and crime, property and contracts, taxation and commerce, money and titles, diplomacy and negotiation, and more.[41] His *Theory of Justice* added several long chapters

[39] Pol VI.39–44; Pol VIII.3, 40, 50–67; Pol XVII.24–31; Dic I.33.1–8, 24, 31–35.
[40] Pol XXIX.2; Pol XXXVIII.1–16; Dic I.32.20–22.
[41] Pol VII–XXXVII.

on the judicial power and the rules of evidence and procedures, pleading and appeal, representation and advocacy that obtain therein.[42]

Checks and balances were yet another safeguard against political excesses at the local, provincial, and national levels. Particularly noteworthy were the heightened powers and roles that Althusius assigned to the 'ephors' in ensuring the separation and cooperation of powers and the effective and efficient administration of the republic. The ephors were no longer the vaguely defined 'inferior magistrates' and 'emergency officers' that John Calvin had introduced into reformed political thought in his 1536 *Institutes of the Christian Religion*. Althusius's ephors were critical officers called to exercise a range of legislative and executive powers at the urban, provincial, and national levels of government. Reflecting some of the political complexities of the Holy Roman Empire in his day, Althusius distinguished among various types of ephors and the responsibilities of each. Some ephors were hereditary and permanent, some elected and temporary. Some were clerical appointees with assigned ecclesiastical roles, others lay delegates with assigned temporal roles. Some ephors had general power over the whole national realm, others had power only over local provinces and cities. The most important common task of all the ephors was to 'administer, govern, and conserve the body and rights' of the individual provinces and of the individual cities, guilds, estates, and private associations that constituted the provinces. Althusius thus called ephors the 'rectors, governors, directors, administrators, regents, pastors, leaders, deliverers, and fathers' of the realm. The ephors with national jurisdiction were also called to elect and constitute the nation's supreme magistrate. They were to advise the supreme magistrate and give their consent to all his general laws. They were to stand in for him if and as needed. They were to defend him when he was unjustly attacked. They were to contain and control him—'restraining and impeding his freedom in undertakings that are wicked and ruinous to the commonwealth, in containing him within the limits of his office, and finally in fully providing and caring for the commonwealth'. They were to resist and depose him if he became a tyrant.[43]

*Tyranny*. Althusius's detailed account of law, rights, society, and politics made the definition of tyranny rather straightforward to him. A tyrant, he said, is one who 'violates, changes, overthrows, or destroys' 'the fundamental law and rights' (*lex et jura fundamentalis*) of the commonwealth or 'the natural laws and rights' (*leges et iura naturali*) on which the fundamental laws and rights are based.[44] Althusius dutifully recited the familiar arguments for resistance to tyranny that earlier Protestant and Catholic writers had offered. The Bible's calls to obey 'the powers ordained by God' always presuppose that these rulers are legitimate representatives of God. Tyrants who offend God and defy true religion are no longer God's agents, and must be removed both for God's sake and for the people's sake. Tyrants forfeit their political offices and become private persons against whom the natural rights of self-defence can apply. The people must always consent to their rulers, and they would not and could not consent to a tyrant. Tyrants are those who violate the people's

[42] Dic I.33.7; Dic I.81–82; Dic III.1–5.

[43] Pol XVIII.2–9, 48–49, 63–91, 107–110.

[44] Pol IX.21; Pol XXXVIII.5–7, 37; Dic I.113.1–3.

ancient charters and privileges, which charters sometimes condition a ruler's legitimacy on compliance with its terms and stipulate a right to resist if those conditions are breached. No tyrant can be tolerated who threatens to smash the ship of state on the rocks. History is full of examples of courageous leaders who have stood up to tyrants.

Althusius also recited the traditional rules and rationales for leaving the judgement and execution of resistance to designated ephors and other officers rather than to the crowd. Wild insurrection will ensue if private persons are left free to judge and resist tyrants on their own. We must leave these judgements to constitutional authorities who can judge both whether an official has become tyrannical and what remedies are apt for a ruler judged to be tyrannical—reprimand, restriction, removal, revolt, or regicide. All these and other arguments were well known in contemporary Protestant and Catholic circles, and Althusius peppered his account with citations from all manner of authorities in support.[45]

Althusius's more distinct contribution was to show that tyranny is in its essence a 'constitutional violation'—a violation of the political covenant by which the polity itself was constituted, a violation of the constitutional duties of the rulers and the fundamental rights of the people as set out in this political covenant, and even more fundamentally a violation of the natural law and natural rights that undergird and empower all constitutions and covenants. For Althusius, a tyrant was a magistrate who acted 'illegally and unnaturally' (*contra legem et naturam*) in breach of the contractual and covenantal duties that he or she swore to God and to the people. Tyranny existed wherever there was any 'egregious', 'chronic', 'persistent', 'pervasive', 'willful', 'intentional', and 'widespread' breach of a ruler's constitutional duties, abuse of constitutional powers, neglect of constitutional offices, usurpation of another's constitutional office, or violation of the people's constitutional rights. Of course, 'not every such misdeed by a magistrate deprives him of his scepter', Althusius cautioned. 'A marriage is not dissolved by a misdeed committed by one mate against another—unless it is a misdeed like adultery, which runs directly contrary to the very nature of marriage.' Likewise, a political association is not dissolved just by any official misstep. But dissolution may well occur when the magistrate's tyrannical conduct runs 'contrary to the fundamentals and essence of the human association', 'begins to shake the foundation and loosen the bonds of the associated body of the commonwealth', or 'destroys civil or political life ... and the most important goods of the commonwealth, such as its peace, order, virtue, law, and nobility'. 'Is there not equal reason for conceding divorce between a king and a commonwealth because of the intolerable and incurable cruelty of a king by which all honest cohabitation and association with him are destroyed?'[46]

With that formula in hand, Althusius worked through all the essential constitutional powers and duties that each executive, legislative, and judicial authority at each level of government had to discharge. He focused especially on government

[45] Pol VIII.91–92; Pol XVIII.69–86; Pol XIX.35–37; Pol XX.12–21; Pol XXXVIII.30, 36–40, 43–76; Dic I.113.25.

[46] Dic I.113.9–17; Pol XVIII.105; Pol XXXVIII.3–27.

powers relating to peace and order, war and diplomacy, crime and delicts, taxation and commerce, property and money, banking and commerce, religion and morality, education and welfare. Egregious, chronic, persistent, pervasive, and intentional abuse, misuse, or neglect of these powers to the 'grave detriment' of the commonwealth were all potential cases of tyranny to Althusius. Such magisterial conduct must, at minimum, empower private subjects to engage in non-violent disobedience and public ephors to institute constitutional remedies.[47] In more serious cases, it allowed for sanctions, restrictions, or removal of the offending magistrates, even revolutionary revamping of the government as a whole.

Another egregious form of tyranny was the systematic 'violation or abridgement of the rights of the members of the community and their associations'. Althusius singled out for special emphasis governmental conduct that violated the people's natural rights—that 'impeded orthodox religious exercise', that abolished schools and education, that 'chronically neglected the sick, poor, and innocent', or that 'consistently abused private individuals' in their lives and bodies, their lands and goods, their standing and reputations, their homes and relatives, their contracts and associations. All of these 'rights and duties given by God are older and more powerful' than any of those set out in the written constitution or political covenant. 'Even if they are not made explicit in the constitution', or given adequate procedural interpretation, these natural rights 'must be understood to be in effect. God is superior to and master of both the rulers and the people', and the rights and duties set out in the natural law must take precedence over all others. Moreover, the political covenant 'between the people and their ruler does not create duties that are superior to those which exist between . . . a wife and a husband, children and parents, master and servant, patron and client', and other such natural associations. With respect to these private associations, the law of the State serves only to 'deter and punish dishonest, immoral, or unholy people . . . who subvert these existing structures of authority or [legitimate] holders of power within them'. When State authorities themselves subvert these social structures, resistance is both natural and necessary.[48]

Althusius also focused on violations of the procedural rights of the people. He listed violations of a number of important criminal procedural rights—false arrests, accusations, indictments, and sentences of innocent parties; false imprisonment or protracted pretrial incarceration, torture, starvation, or enslavement of prisoners; use of anonymous indictments and untested evidence; denial of rights to defend oneself, to have counsel, to examine hostile witness, to introduce exculpatory evidence, or even to have one's day in court following prescribed procedures; imposition of extraordinary tribunals or *ex post facto* laws; use of biased, bribed, or incompetent judges; imposition of unjust, inequitable, or widely variant punishments; failure to grant appeals of motions, judgements, or sentences; excessive fines, cruel punishments, and more. Each of these abuses and violations of procedural rights should give individual victims constitutional redress, Althusius argued, and a persistent

[47] Pol XXXVIII.10–28; Dic I.36.38, Dic I.113.17–21.
[48] Dic I.113.8–9 12, 18; Pol X.5–10; Pol XXXVII.21–22, 33–34, 36.

pattern of such abuses to several victims at once is prima facie evidence of judicial tyranny that requires a more systemic response.[49]

## 4. Summary and Conclusions

Drawing on a vast array of biblical, classical, Catholic, and Protestant sources, Althusius systematized and greatly expanded many of the core political and legal teachings of the Calvinist tradition of which he was a leading member—that the republic is formed by a covenant between the rulers and the people before God, that the foundation of this covenant is the law of God and nature, that the Decalogue is the best expression of this higher law, that church and State are separate in form but conjoined in function, that families, churches, and States alike must protect the rights and liberties of the people, and that violations of these rights and liberties, or of the divine and natural laws that inform and empower them, are instances of tyranny that must trigger organized constitutional resistance.

Althusius added a number of other core ideas to this Calvinist inheritance. He developed a natural law theory that still treated the Decalogue as the best source and summary of natural law but layered its Commandments with all manner of new biblical, classical, and Christian teachings. He developed a theory of positive law that judged the validity and utility of any human law, including the positive laws of Moses and the canon laws of the church, against both the natural law of Scripture and tradition and the fundamental law of the State. He called for a detailed written constitution as the fundamental law of the community and called for perennial protection of 'the rule of law' and 'rule of rights' in every political community. He developed an expansive theory of popular sovereignty as an expression of the divine sovereignty that each person reflects as an image bearer of God. He developed a detailed and refined theory of natural rights—religious and social, public and private, substantive and procedural, contractual and proprietary.

More striking still was Althusius's 'symbiotic theory' of human nature and 'covenantal theory' of society and politics. While acknowledging the traditional Calvinist teaching of the total depravity of persons, Althusius emphasized that God has created all persons as moral, loving, communicative, and social beings, whose lives are most completely fulfilled through symbiotic relationships with others in which they can appropriately share their bodies and souls, their lives and spirits, their belongings and rights. Thus, while persons are born free, equal, and individual, they are by nature and necessity inclined to form associations—marriages and families, clubs and corporations, cities and provinces, nation States and empires. Each of these associations, from the tiniest household to the vastest empire, is formed by a mutually consensual covenant or contract sworn by all members of that association before each other and God. Each association is a locus of authority and liberty that binds both rulers and subjects to the terms of their founding contract and to the

[49] Dic I.113.20–83; Pol XXIX.47–60.

commands of the foundational laws of God and nature. Each association confirms and protects the sovereignty and identity of its constituent members as well as their natural rights and liberties.

Althusius applied this Christian social contract theory most fully in his description of the State. Using the political history of ancient Israel as his best example, he showed historically and philosophically how nation States develop gradually from families to tribes to cities to provinces to nations to empires. Each new layer of political sovereignty is formed by covenants sworn before God by representatives of the smaller units, and these covenants eventually become the written constitutions of the polity. The constitutions define and divide the executive, legislative, and judicial offices within that polity, and govern the relations of its rulers and subjects, clerics and magistrates, associations and individuals. They determine the relations between and among nations, provinces, and cities, and between and among private and public associations—all of which Althusius called a form of 'federalism' (from '*foedus*', the Latin term for covenant). The constitutions also make clear the political acts and omissions that constitute tyranny and the procedures and remedies available to those who are abused. Althusius produced the most comprehensive Calvinist legal and political theory of law, and many of his insights anticipated teachings that would become axiomatic for Western constitutionalism and human rights.

# 8

# Hugo Grotius and the Universal Rule of Law

*Christoph Stumpf*

## 1. Introduction

In the context of his critique of subjectivism, Alasdair MacIntyre scathingly remarks that '[t]he lawyers, not the philosophers, are the clergy of liberalism'.[1] MacIntyre here directs his main criticism at the concept of 'justice in procedure', meaning that any procedure that complies with certain 'fair' standards will by necessity result in a 'just' outcome, without this outcome being subject to any further scrutiny in terms of a 'substantive justice'. In other words: one needs a lawyer to determine the essence of justice, not a philosopher.

There is a strong tradition of reading Hugo Grotius's works in this 'liberal' sense as a protagonist of a supposedly 'modern' sense of international law, severing the ties between morality and law that had accompanied much of traditional jurisprudence, and delineating rules of international law out of certain principles of self-defence—and ultimately self-interest. The argument inherent in this tradition is that Grotius is not so much interested in the substantive moral quality of legal principles, but rather argues in favour of a minimalist standard of natural law, which any government could assert on an international level by waging war against those that infringed this moral standard.[2]

If one reads the entire body of Grotius's major work on international law, the *De Iure Belli ac Pacis* and cross-checks it with those of his works which focus on theological matters, such as the *Meletius sive de Iis Quae inter Christianos Conveniunt Epistola*, and his treatment of the relationship between the spheres of spiritual and temporal laws, such as in the *De Ordinum Hollandiae ac Westfrisiae Pietas Vindicata* and the *De Imperio Summarum Potestatum circa sacra*, a rather different outlook on Grotius and his views on the substance of law and justice emerges: the political theorist Martin Wight describes Grotius's concept of international law as relying on a

[1] A MacIntyre, *Whose Justice? Which Rationality* (Duckworth 1988) 344.

[2] On this see for example R Tuck, *The Rights of War and Peace* (Clarendon Press 1999) 94–102; on the broader traditions of interpreting Grotius as 'prophet of peace' or as 'war hawk', see JE Nijman, 'Images of Grotius, or the International Rule of Law beyond Historiographical Oscillation' (2015) 17 Journal of the History of International Law 83–187.

'dual' or 'concentric' system of international relations.[3] According to this interpretation, the inner circle of nations follows the ideal of a society of Christian nations, the *respublica Christiana*. Yet this inner circle of nations is embedded in a wider circle of nations. This wider circle of nations is united by a universal human fellowship among human beings, which disregards religious persuasions or specific philosophical inclinations of individual members, an idea that had been put forward already by the scholars of the Salamancan school such as Francisco de Vitoria and Francisco Suarez. Consequently, the outer circle encompasses both Christian and non-Christian nations. This community of Christian and non-Christian nations is seen as a worldwide family of nations, bound together simply by the common bond of human fellowship. This common bond of human fellowship also implies certain legal standards to be observed by any human being in interactions with other human beings.

The following analysis of Grotius's concept of an international rule of law will start by identifying the place of law in society: any adequate grasp of Grotius's idea of the rule of law is dependent upon an understanding of his definition of 'law' and its different subcategories as well as the obligatory effect of different kind of laws to individuals. Given that the rule of law in modern terminology primarily focuses on the individual State governance, the establishment of the State and its operation under an overarching internationally applicable set of laws will be dealt with on a second step. Finally, any idea of a rule of law needs to prove itself in situations of conflict, which then necessitates an analysis of Grotius's views on the law of war, the law to war, and the law in war.

Overall, it will be argued that Wight's interpretation of Grotius corresponds more to what can be identified with a particular 'Grotian system of international law' than the aforementioned 'liberal' perception of Grotius as moral minimalist, and that Grotius's system of international law is informed by a profound concept of a 'rule of law' in the sense of several sets of legal obligations binding any human being, members of governments and citizens alike, in any conduct. While the legitimacy of self-defence is certainly of great interest for Grotius, especially in his treatment of the laws of war, the central aim of Grotius, as to be shown in the following, is to highlight certain legal standards which are valid for any human being, at any time and any place. However, the enforcement or even merely the enforceability of such legal standards, eg by way of self-defence, is not a requirement for such standards to be deemed as 'law': for Grotius, law 'rules' through its moral appeal, not so much through its susceptibility of being asserted through the use of force. One could even go as far to say that Grotius does not even strictly distinguish between 'obligatory' legal rules on the one hand and 'commendable' moral principles on the other.

## 2. The Place of Law in Society

Any concept of a rule of law cannot do without defining as its basis the term 'law' itself. Here Grotius displays himself on the one hand as adherent to a scholastic

[3] M Wight, *Systems of States* (Leicester UP 1977) 125–28.

strand of jurisprudence, but at the same time goes beyond it in presenting a system of law as personal obligations established by divine or human will.[4]

For Grotius, there are two major categories of law: the first major category is Divine Law. Divine Law can either be entailed already in the creation of the world itself in the sense of 'natural law'. Such natural law is binding upon any human being by God's act of creation. Also Divine Law can be promulgated by God subsequently to creation by a separate act of divine legislation. This subcategory of Divine Law Grotius calls 'arbitrary divine law'. Arbitrary Divine Law is made known by God to human beings through revelation.[5] As arbitrary Divine Law needs to be notified to human beings in order to create any obligatory effect on them, it will not bind any human being that remains ignorant of it; but even if it is made known to someone, it will not necessarily be enforceable, because its acceptance will require the secret assistance of the Holy Spirit, which God could grant or withhold as according to his own discretion.[6] Given that God is the creator and supreme legislator, Divine Law provides a truly international framework to 'rule' anything within its remit, even if it will not necessarily be enforceable vis-à-vis all human beings in the same degree.

The second major category of law for Grotius is human law. Human law can either be national law, set into force by a human legislator; or it can be international law, as agreed upon between several or all nations.[7] National law is human law which is only applicable in one particular State or parts of it. The law of nations is human law which governs relations between States.[8] As such, the law of nations provides a second layer of legal obligations subject to an international rule of law.

For Grotius, both natural law and arbitrary Divine Law provide the legal framework for all human social life on the international as well as on the domestic level. Natural law and—to those to whom it has been made known—arbitrary Divine Law obligate human beings directly and individually. Thus, Grotius regards human beings as personally responsible agents in international relations, in particular when shaping human international law by agreement between several nations.[9] In this we can perceive a key aspect of the rule of law in Grotius's concept: natural law, being obligatory for all human beings, will always be the main criterion for evaluating the validity of human law. For those human beings bound by arbitrary Divine Law, meaning those to whom arbitrary Divine Law has been revealed, it will be an additional moral and legal standard to comply with in any human conduct.

The principles of the law of nations derive their obligatory nature from an act of will of all or of several nations, and thus—quite similar to modern public international law[10]—are established by way of a consensus among the nations concerned.[11]

[4] For a comparison between Grotius and Gentili, see P Haggenmacher, 'Grotius and Gentili: A Reassessment of Thomas E. Holland's Inaugural Lecture' in H Bull, B Kingsbury, and A Roberts (eds), *Hugo Grotius and International Relations* (Clarendon Press 1990) 133–76.

[5] H Grotius, *De Iure Belli ac Pacis*, I.I.xv.1; the English translation of the original Latin text here follows my interpretation in C Stumpf, *The Grotian Theology of International Law* (de Gruyter 2006).

[6] Grotius, *De Iure Belli ac Pacis*, II.XX.xlviii.1. [7] ibid I.I.xiv. [8] ibid I.I.xiv.

[9] Stumpf (n 9) 157–61.

[10] W Graf Vitzthum, 'Begriff, Geschichte und Quellen des Völkerrechts' in W Graf Vitzthum and A Proelss (eds), *Völkerrecht* (de Gruyter 2016) 1–10.

[11] Stumpf (n 9) 105–7.

Grotius points out that only few rules of the law of nations are acknowledged as binding in every part of the world, whereas most rules of the law of nations are only acknowledged in certain regions. European nations might employ other paradigms when agreeing on a particular set of principles governing the relationships with their respective neighbours than Asian States might among themselves. Differences in climate and in the geographical situation might also result in distinct regulations: for example, in densely populated lands, such as of Europe, the human law of nations is more likely to produce detailed provisions for the determination of borderlines than in scarcely populated deserts or archipelagos.[12] The only truly universally applicable type of law—and therefore the core element of a universal 'rule of law'—is in Grotius's opinion natural law, while even the applicability of arbitrary Divine Law is narrower, obligating only those who have received support from the Holy Ghost in accepting it, or who have at least been notified of its existence and content.[13]

However, for Grotius arbitrary Divine Law in the shape of a distinct law of the Gospel will have a general binding force upon Christians in addition to the more general natural law: this can be illustrated by Grotius's observation that there is a general obligation of Christians to join together to resist non-Christian opponents, as according to Grotius all Christians belong to one body, individually and jointly, as nations. Therefore, any Christian has to serve Christ not only with one's personal means, but also with the power entrusted to one.[14] This means that among Christians, Christian governments and citizens alike, there will be a rule also of arbitrary Divine Law.

In consequence, Grotius treats basically any interrelation among human beings as well as interrelations between human beings and God in legal terms. At the outset it is striking that, even though much of Grotius's work is devoted to identifying the standards under Divine Law, Grotius nevertheless puts greater interest in human law than many of the theological and moral scholars dealing with international law before him, given that he views the laws of nations as human law, whereas for example Gentili, as one of his most important predecessors, had equated it with a Divine Law of nature:[15] like Gentili, the canon lawyers and also the Scholastics of the School of Salamanca had dealt with international law mainly in terms of a framework of principles of Divine Law, and in consequence had accorded relatively limited importance to human law for matters of international relations.[16] Furthermore, medieval Christian authors—quite similarly to modern 'classic' legal authors—had viewed the temporal governments of people as the only relevant participants in international relations, whereas States or nations had not yet been fully recognized as legal subjects in their own

[12] ibid 106. [13] Grotius, *De Iure Belli ac Pacis*, II.XX.xlviii.1. [14] ibid II.XV.xii.

[15] Haggenmacher (n 4) 170–72; on this see also JE Nijman, Grotius' *Imago Dei* Anthropology: Grounding *Ius Naturae et Gentium* in M Koskenniemi, M Garcia-Salmones, and P Amoroso (eds), *International Law and Religion* (OUP 2017) 87–110).

[16] HF Köck, *Der Beitrag der Schule von Salamanca zur Entwicklung der Lehre von den Grundrechten* (Duncker & Humblot 1987) 29–31; H Dreier, 'Kanonistik und Konfessionalisierung: Meilensteine auf dem Weg zum Staat' (2002) 57 Juristenzeitung 3–5; C Stumpf, 'Völkerrecht unter Kreuz und Halbmond: Muhammad al-Shaybani und Hugo Grotius als Exponenten religiöser Völkerrechtstradition' (2003) 41 Archiv des Völkerrechts 90–92.

right and subjective 'human rights' had not yet emerged as relevant legal category,[17] whereas, as we shall see in the further course, Grotius is interested in the individual's responsibility, as government or as citizen, under divine and human law. Grotius in this respect also differs from many medieval and early-modern moral theologians who had maintained only Christians could hold rightful authority, whereas the authority of non-Christians could not be fully acknowledged from a Christian legal perspective.[18] While Grotius never hides away his particular Christian outlook on law, he is nevertheless keen on identifying a common legal ground for Christians and non-Christians alike, which then can ensure an effective and all-embracing, truly international rule of law.

## 3. The Establishment of the Government and Its Place under the Rule of Divine Law

The idea of a rule of law is dependent not only upon certain legal standards, but also upon an institution which at the same time implements law into practice and in so doing still acknowledges law as a limitation of its own conduct. Seeing that the establishment of a State and its government by necessity limits the space for previously legitimate self-defence by a monopolization of the legitimate use of force within the government's authority, Grotius's perception of the nature and the legal implications of the establishment of States and their government will be decisive in determining whether his system of international law can truly be viewed as minimal and positivist, as claimed by some authors, or rather propagates a profound concept of a substantive rule of law, as suggested above.

Grotius's strictly distinguishes between a natural 'pre-state' situation, in which self-defence is permissible to anyone and anywhere under natural law, and the subsequent establishment of the State's authority under human law, which in the pursuit of the common interest of its citizens curtails the former general legitimacy of self-defence.[19] For Grotius, natural law as well as arbitrary Divine Law directly apply to all human beings, without any restatement of such legal principles by human law being necessary. There are various remarks in *De Iure Belli ac Pacis* on a *status ante republicam conditam* as an abstract projection that illustrate the relationship between natural law and human law, as an exception in the case of political breakdown, or as a description for regions that are in principle uninhabited, such as the high seas.[20] So there still may be instances, in which no State power is present, in which human laws are absent, and therefore recourse has to be sought to principles of Divine Law. However, for most practical purposes there are now States in existence, and Grotius here is interested in the interplay between human law and Divine Law in the practical operation of its government.

[17] C Stumpf and PR Melot de Beauregard, 'Die Entwicklung der staatlichen Souveränität im Spiegel der kanonistischen Völkerrechtslehre' (2003) 42 Der Staat 459–61.

[18] Dreier (n 16) 3–5.

[19] Grotius, *De Iure Belli ac Pacis*, I.III.i. and ii.

[20] Stumpf (n 9) 120.

In Grotius's opinion, human beings have a 'social appetite' which induces them to live in communities, a desire that is one of the core elements of human nature.[21] Grotius believes that natural law provides for human beings to be social in the sense of an obligation for human beings to seek each other's company.[22] This becomes clear in Grotius's examination of the original acquisition of rights, in which he elaborates on various forms of personal relationships, starting with the rights of parents over their offspring,[23] before dealing with the right of the husband over his wife and the law of marriage,[24] before finally arriving at further associations, which could either have a private or a public character.[25] The latter could be formed by one single nation or be formed out of several nations.[26] This means that the establishment of States and the institution of government are acts under human law and not divinely prescribed, but nevertheless consequences of natural human instincts.

Already in the pre-state condition of society, Grotius believes certain legal principles to govern the relationships among its members. One of such legal principles under natural law is that of representation: according to Grotius, it follows from natural law that in a common matter all or the majority of the members of an association could oblige all members personally, meaning that the minority will have to submit to the will of the majority.[27] As any human association is established through explicit or tacit consent of its members, all members will have to honour the promise given within the act of the establishment.[28] Apart from this, human society is not yet legally differentiated.[29] Neither is there yet any legally relevant hierarchy within human society other than the natural hierarchy among family members.[30] Moreover, there is not yet any legitimate rule to be exercised by some members of society over others. Additional requirements under arbitrary Divine Law seem to be absent.[31]

According to Grotius, the State and the authority of its government emerge out of the natural institution of human society. As already mentioned above, for Grotius the establishment of the State is not strictly necessary or even commanded by Divine Law, but nevertheless legitimate and even a logical consequence of human inclinations. Grotius thereby refutes the notion of a divine establishment of the government's position, which had been argued in favour of by the majority of medieval Christian jurists.[32] For Grotius, the organization of common affairs and the protection of individuals is the chief motivation for human beings when establishing a State.[33] The State for Grotius hence presents a particular connection of human beings which also, by virtue of its establishment, creates eminent powers of the State's government over the citizens.[34] Grotius views such powers as rights acquired

[21] Grotius, *De Iure Belli ac Pacis*, Prolegomena 6, 14, 16; Stumpf (n 9) 116.

[22] Grotius, *De Iure Belli ac Pacis*, Prolegomena 6, 14, 16.

[23] Grotius, *De Iure Belli ac Pacis*, II.V.i.–vii; Stumpf (n 9) 117.

[24] Grotius, *De Iure Belli ac Pacis*, II.V.viii–xvi.

[25] ibid II.V.xvii–xviii.

[26] Stumpf (n 9) 117.

[27] Grotius, *De Iure Belli ac Pacis*, II.V.xvii; Stumpf (n 9) 117–18.

[28] Stumpf (n 9) 118.

[29] C Link, *Hugo Grotius als Staatsdenker* (Mohr Siebeck 1983) 22–24.

[30] Grotius, *De Iure Belli ac Pacis*, II.V.xxi.

[31] Stumpf (n 9) 118.

[32] HG Walther, *Imperiales Königtum, Konziliarismus und Volkssouveränität: Studien zu den Grenzen des mittelalterlichen Souveränitätsgedankens* (Fink 1976) 29–31; Stumpf (n 9) 118–21.

[33] Grotius, *De Iure Belli ac Pacis*, I.I.xiv.1.

[34] ibid II.V.xxiii–xxv.

by the State by virtue of the citizens' acts of subjection. The purpose of the State is the administration of common affairs and the well-being of its citizens, in particular in relation to the citizens' security. In consequence, the State will enact laws to govern the interrelation among citizens which will impose certain limitations on the freedom of the individual citizens.[35] This also includes the upholding of the rule of law in domestic affairs.

While the gathering of human beings constituting human society is a result of respective implications of natural law, the establishment of the State out of human society results from a voluntary human act.[36] Consequently, the establishment of the State for Grotius belongs to the sphere of human law, although it is certainly covered by and dependent upon the principles of natural law. Hence any obligations or rights which are conferred on or established by the founding of a State as aspects of the government's authority rely on a respective expression of human will. Such rights and obligations, to be sure, have to be in compliance with natural law and are even supported by natural law, but are not a consequence of it. Furthermore, once the State and the government's authority have been established, it is a consequence of natural law that the rights and obligations of the government's against the citizens and vice versa will have to be honoured. In this sense, Grotius's concept of natural law also supports the idea of a rule of law within the State's establishment.

As regards arbitrary Divine Law, Grotius holds that Christian citizens have a duty of obedience to their governments, which is a consequence of their submission to the governments' authority. However, he establishes no precept of the law of the Gospel as arbitrary Divine Law to the effect that a Christian society has in any case to appoint governments and submit itself to them.[37] Grotius explains St Paul's statement of the State being a divine institution in his letter to the Romans with God's approval to its establishment.[38] Nevertheless, Grotius does not see any immediate role which divine revelation could assume in this context: While States are not required by arbitrary Divine Law to exist, arbitrary Divine Law certainly shapes the functioning of the State in general and the exercising of rule in particular. In this sense, we can see a particular Christian rule of law in application in Christian States.

A rule of law needs an absence of conflicts between its individual legal components: for Grotius, human law and, consequently, also any act of human government, can therefore only be legitimate as far as it does not contravene Divine Law, natural law as well as arbitrary Divine Law. There are several areas in which the reaches of Divine Law and human law overlap in Grotius's concept: first, for Grotius, human law is necessarily subordinate to Divine Law, meaning that human law may not contradict Divine Law.[39] Second, provisions of human law may according to Grotius entail certain consequences under Divine Law: for example, while Divine Law does not provide for a concept of proprietary rights, the fact that human law introduces a system of proprietary rights results in offences against such proprietary rights being

[35] D Willoweit, *Rechtsgrundlagen der Territorialgewalt: Landesobrigkeit, Herrschaftsrechte und Territorium in der Rechtswissenschaft der Neuzeit* (1975) 248–50.

[36] Stumpf (n 9) 120. [37] ibid 121. [38] Grotius, *De Iure Belli ac Pacis*, I.IV.vii.3.

[39] Stumpf (n 9) 125.

deemed as contravention against the principles of justice under natural law as well.[40] Consequently, it is a breach of natural law not to render alien property to the person to whom it is due. If human law provides a law of loans, it is against natural law not to perform the obligation under a loan.[41] Third, human law can regulate areas left unregulated by natural law and arbitrary Divine Law: for example, by establishing State authorities the previous legitimacy of self-defence under natural law is severely curtailed, and only survives as far as no State authority is available for defending individuals on their behalf. This is possible as Grotius does not understand any freedoms of natural law or arbitrary Divine Law to grant positive rights; natural law and arbitrary Divine Law merely allow certain ways of conduct through the absence of commands or prohibitions to the contrary.[42] The use of force is thus monopolized with the State authority. However, the initial freedom survives wherever State authorities do not exist or are not available.[43]

While, Grotius is rather indifferent as far as particular forms of a State's constitutional arrangements—for example monarchy, aristocracy, or democracy—are concerned, he insists that once a form of government has been established, the governments as well as the citizens will be bound by that agreement until such agreement is altered by way of consent. While any constitutional arrangement in essence belongs to the sphere of human law, it is an obligation under natural law and arbitrary Divine Law to abide by them—or in other words: the rule of law binds governments and citizens alike. Interestingly, the establishment of a court system for Grotius probably presents the most severe limitation of the original situation prior to the establishment of the State. As far as courts are available, the previous freedom of self-defence is restricted in consequence;[44] on the other hand, self-defence is still legitimate as far as no courts are not available, for example in times of emergency or in waste lands.[45]

Connected to the establishment of the State are obligations of the citizens vis-à-vis the government's authority. While Grotius does not engage in detail on this topic in the *De Iure Belli ac Pacis*, some insights may be gained from his views on the question of whether or not citizens are under an obligation to obey unjust or incompetent governments. Grotius here notes that some authors hold the view that kings are only to be obeyed as far as they govern their people in a good manner.[46] While Grotius concedes that no one has to carry out manifestly unjust commands, he is doubtful if it could be really for any citizen to determine the quality of an order of government. For Grotius, the evaluation of State acts is too complicated to leave this task for any individual citizen to determine.[47] However, for Grotius this is not only a matter of practicality: he claims that citizens are under a general obligation to obey the government because of the government's political authority. However, the government's political authority may not be trumped by an external moral authority, as otherwise the submission of the citizens to the government would be thwarted:[48] according

[40] Grotius, *De Iure Belli ac Pacis*, I.I.x.4. [41] Stumpf (n 9) 126. [42] ibid.
[43] Grotius, *De Iure Belli ac Pacis*, I.III.i.; Grotius, *De Imperio*, III.
[44] Grotius, *De Iure Belli ac Pacis*, I.III.i.2. [45] ibid I.III.ii.1. [46] ibid I.III.ix.1.
[47] ibid I.III.ix.2. [48] ibid I.III.viii.1.

to Grotius, human beings are free to decide whether or not to join together in a State, but once they submit to the authority of a State's government they may no longer unilaterally revoke their submission. For Grotius, this is even more relevant for Christians, as a higher degree of obedience could be expected from them under arbitrary Divine Law than from people who were not bound by arbitrary Divine Law.[49] In this context, Grotius does not present us with an explicit treatment of the State's obligations vis-à-vis its citizens in any of his works. In particular, he does not put forward any concept of subjective human rights which the citizens might raise against the State.[50] Nevertheless, we may draw inferences on his views on the State's responsibilities for its citizens from Grotius's comments on a potential legitimacy of civil resistance of the citizens against the State. Obviously, civil resistance can present a challenge as much as a safeguard to the rule of law, so the question in which case it can be legitimate is important for the concept of rule of law as such. Given that any human beings' original freedom of self-defence is severely curtailed upon the establishment of the State, the use of force is, in principle, monopolized with the State.[51] Grotius applies this principle also to the question whether any citizens could ever legitimately engage in self-defence against the State's authorities. Indeed, as Grotius notes, many States regard it as a grave legal offence to disrespect the State's authorities by resisting it.[52] Similar principles apply also under arbitrary Divine Law, as Grotius notes that Jewish law had ruled out disobedience against the High Priest or other authorities,[53] and that Christ had commanded to render to the emperor what is due to him in the Gospel; in this sense, the Gospel had expected even more obedience to the State from Christians than Jewish law or any other law had done.[54] Grotius in this context also points to St Paul, who had stated that anyone who resists the government's commandments resists the commandments of God, and had consequently demanded from Christians not to disrespect the government, as God had approved of its appointment for the benefit of human beings.[55] While Grotius acknowledges that there may be instances of governments that do not govern well, he claims that such instances will always present exceptions from the rule. Not even minor State authorities were allowed to resist injustices committed against them by their superiors.[56]

Nonetheless, while Grotius consistently stresses the duty of citizens to pay respect to the State authorities as a principle, he also concedes that Divine Law allows for certain exceptions:[57] though God could certainly demand unlimited observance of his laws, even at the cost of one's own life, God rarely required such extreme sacrifices.[58] In this context Grotius claims that laws in general have to take into account the weakness of human beings. Moreover, since the institution of the State is essentially shaped by the will of its founders, Grotius claims that it will have to be asked if the State founders had chosen rather to sacrifice the life of a large number of people for the benefit of the State's authority: here Grotius assumes that the States' founders would have allowed resistance at least in extreme cases.[59] There

[49] Stumpf (n 9) 125. [50] ibid 151. [51] Grotius, *De Iure Belli ac Pacis*, I.IV.ii.2.
[52] ibid I.IV.ii.3. [53] ibid I.IV.iii. [54] ibid I.IV.iv.1. [55] ibid I.IV.iv.
[56] ibid I.IV.vi.1. [57] ibid I.IV.vii.1. [58] ibid I.IV.vii.2. [59] ibid.

remains, however, the question whether such general legitimacy of resistance in extreme cases, which may be permissible under natural law and human law, could also be upheld for Christians under the arbitrary Divine Law of the Gospel. As already explained above, Grotius believes that Christians are expected to display a higher degree of obedience and patience than other people not bound by the law of the Gospel. Therefore, Christians are normally required rather to suffer injustice than to engage in active resistance. Notwithstanding this, Grotius still acknowledges that Christians may resort to passive resistance, for example by escaping in cases in which their life is threatened by the State's authorities,[60] which is not a completely surprising statement from Grotius, when we consider his own biography.[61] However, Grotius is not willing to concede any form of resistance beyond the passive avoidance of life-threatening situations: Christians could be expected to suffer as martyrs to injustice. Yet, active resistance against legitimate State authorities will not normally be an option for Christians according to Grotius.[62] Nevertheless he is willing—albeit unenthusiastically[63]—to accept active resistance even by Christians at least in certain cases of usurped power.[64]

A brief comparison between the views of Thomas Hobbes and Hugo Grotius will help to see how distant Grotius is, in his view on government, and consequently also of the rule of law, is from contractual concepts of statehood which shaped the mainstream thought of the seventeenth century, and which still influence modern social and legal theories. First of all, Grotius takes a more positive view towards the nature of human beings and the function of the State than Hobbes: for Grotius it is not the curse of freedom which induces or even forces human beings to assemble in human society and to organize themselves in a State by way of submission, but a more positive desire for an intensified human fellowship to be secured and defended institutionally within a State.[65] In contrast to Hobbes, Grotius still holds the State to be bound by extrinsic legal rules, such as the natural rules on expletive justice and attributive justice, while Hobbes denied any such limitations to be applicable to his Leviathan.[66] A further important difference between Grotius and Hobbes can be seen in their different views on the impact that the States' establishment has in relation to the authority of governments: while Hobbes thought of a social contract as a mutual vow of the citizens in relation to each other with respect to their unconditional submission to the State,[67] Grotius claims that the government as well as the ruled can all be party to certain obligations that could be characterized as contractual.[68] The government can therefore accept obligations towards the ruled people in return for their submission.[69] In so doing, the government is bound by human law as well as natural law to honour such obligations, for natural law requires the honouring of promises as part of expletive justice.[70] As it were, the government also is subject to the rule of law. In Grotius's concept of sovereignty the State is by no means the terrifying monster

[60] ibid I.IV.vii.8. [61] Stumpf (n 9) 155.
[62] Grotius, *De Iure Belli ac Pacis*, I.IV.vii.15. [63] ibid I.IV.xv.1.
[64] ibid I.IV.xvi–xviii. [65] Stumpf (n 9) 118–19. [66] ibid 119.
[67] Hobbes, *De Cive*, cap V. [68] Grotius, *De Iure Belli ac Pacis*, Prolegomena 15–16.
[69] ibid I.III.ix, xvi, xviii; I.IV.viii. [70] Stumpf (n 9) 120.

of the Hobbesian blend: it is no Leviathan that is to replace God,[71] but rather an application of the universal fellowship of all human beings to a specifically defined group of people, subordinated in its entirety to God. Grotius's concept of sovereignty is therefore wholly embedded in and derived from his legal theory.[72]

In consequence, Grotius holds that that all human beings, citizens and those holding authority alike, are bound by a common legal framework. Any human being, be it a ruler, a State servant, or a citizen, is bound by natural law and arbitrary Divine Law prior and subsequent to the establishment of a State. While natural law and arbitrary Divine Law do not require the establishment of States, they support and govern the State's authority upon its establishment: natural law as well as arbitrary Divine Law require the State's authorities to foster the common good for the benefit of the citizens, and natural law and arbitrary Divine Law also require obedience of the citizens vis-à-vis the State's authorities. In this sense, for Grotius the overarching legal categories of natural law and arbitrary Divine Law safeguard the general rule of law within a State.

## 4. The Rule of Law in War

As we have seen, Grotius perceives interaction among human beings along legal terms: this is true already for the legal obligations of individuals within a State, including citizens and officers of the State. But it is also true on the international level, on which legal relations in Grotius's concept present the fabric holding together the human fellowship. This becomes apparent, in particular, in Grotius's analysis of the law of war and the law in war. Here again the relationship between Divine Law, comprising natural law as well as arbitrary Divine Law, and human law, in particular the human law of nations, are of major interest for Grotius. While this is obvious in peace, it also holds true in situations of war. One might even claim that in war Grotius's idea of a rule of law proves itself more evidently than in times of peace, given that war for Grotius, as it were, presents itself as an enforcement of law.

For Grotius, war is a legitimate instrument for the restoration of justice. However, he strictly distinguishes between legitimate reasons for waging war and legitimate conduct in warfare on the one hand, and, on the other hand, the practice of a right to go to war and the law in war at his time, which was quite far removed from what he deemed to be legitimate. Indeed, a large part of the *De Iure Belli ac Pacis* is devoted to a critical examination on what war at his time was in comparison to what it should be under the principles of law heralded by him.[73]

As regards the requirements for waging a just war, Grotius adheres for the greater part to the traditional just war doctrine, requiring a just authority, an adequacy of the means of war deployed, and a just cause.[74] The concept of a rule of law in

[71] H Welzel, *Naturrecht und materiale Gerechtigkeit* (Vandenhoeck & Ruprecht 1962) 120.

[72] Stumpf (n 9) 119.

[73] FH Russell, *The Just War in the Middle Ages* (CUP 1975) 155–57.

[74] C Stumpf, 'Hugo Grotius: Just War Thinking between Theology and International Law' in HG Justenhoven and WA Barbieri (eds), *From Just War to Modern Peace Ethics* (de Gruyter 2012) 197–216; 206–13.

Grotius's treatment of the law relating to a right to war is here visible in systematizing the just reasons for waging war in accordance with potential legal actions in court: according to Grotius, just causes for waging a war could be the defence of rights, the enforcement of claims, and the punishment of offences.[75]

The defence of our lives against attacks warrants the killing of the attacker. While this is already true for individuals defending themselves against personal attacks in a situation where no recourse to State authorities is available, it also applies to States in their defence against attacks by other States[76] The differentiated concept of a rule of law in Grotius's system becomes apparent in his discussion of the proportionality of the measures of defence in relation to the aim of the defence. Grotius here distinguishes between the principles of natural law on the one hand and of arbitrary Divine Law on the other, which both arrive at different results respectively: for example, minor injuries, such as insults or the like, could justify the killing of a human being under natural law provided that justice could not be restored otherwise. However, the killing of human beings could only be justified in rather exceptional cases under the law of the Gospel as arbitrary Divine Law.[77] The situation is similar for Grotius as far as proprietary rights are concerned: according to Grotius, natural law allows the killing of a thief if this should prove necessary for the protection of one's property.[78] However, Jewish law as old arbitrary Divine Law had, according to Grotius, differentiated between defence during the night on the one hand and defence during daytime on the other: the killing of a thief was therefore permissible if the thief was detected in the night, as the absence of witnesses at night-time made it more difficult to identify the thief later and to subsequently recover one's stolen property.[79] However, it was impermissible to kill a thief if he was detected during daylight or if there were witnesses.[80] The situation under the law of the Gospel as new arbitrary Divine Law is even more difficult: while Grotius claims that many authors were rather generous in this respect, he himself displays a much stricter outlook:[81] thus, human beings are only allowed to defend their property at the cost of another human being's life if the property is needed to sustain life. As God had created human beings in his image the life of any human being had to be regarded as much more valuable than any property whatsoever.[82] The rule of Divine Law in the sense of a standard for human law becomes also apparent in Grotius's answer to the question if it is sufficient if a merely human law allows a private individual to kill a thief: for Grotius, this is impossible, for human laws could never claim power over life and death on any type of offence, but only on such offences that required the death of the offender; moreover, human laws could not allow private executions, except in extreme situations.[83]

The second potential legitimate cause for a war is the enforcement of a claim. A violent enforcement of a claim is, however, only admissible if there is no other legitimate authority that might enforce the claim for the claimant.[84] If a State has

[75] Grotius, *De Iure Belli ac Pacis*, I.II.ii. [76] ibid I.II.iii. [77] ibid I.II.x.
[78] ibid I.II.xi. [79] Stumpf (n 74) 208–09.
[80] Grotius, *De Iure Belli ac Pacis*, I.II.xii. [81] ibid I.II.xiii.
[82] Stumpf (n 74) 208–09. [83] Grotius, *De Iure Belli ac Pacis*, I.II.xvi.
[84] ibid I.IV.ii and ff.

been established and it has authority over the obligor, the enforcement of claims will be monopolized with the State. As there is, however, no such authority over sovereign States, they may enforce claims against other States for themselves or for their citizens.

A third potential cause for a just war, in relation to which Grotius's concept of a rule of law becomes most apparent, is the punishment of offences against law. For Grotius, punishment is an objective retribution for individual guilt of an offender according to the principle of attributive justice under natural law.[85] Just as anyone is bound by natural law, anyone can also punish someone who has offended against law, provided that the punisher has not committed the same offence.[86] Again, upon the establishment of a State, the authority for executing punishments is monopolized with the State's authority and delegated to courts.[87] According to Grotius, the punishment of human beings always requires a reason,[88] and the degree of punishment needs to correspond to the advantages which the offender has gained from the offence, the interest of those for the benefit of whom the offence is prohibited, and the interest of anyone else.[89]

Grotius's treatment of the law in war follows a two-step approach. First, he attempts to present the law in war as it is in the practice of his times and under the human law of nations, but then he engages in a painstaking critique of the contemporary law and presents it as in his opinion it should be under natural law and arbitrary Divine Law.

Grotius describes three basic principles which apply to the means to be used in a war: the first principle may be summarized as 'the means serve the cause'. This implies that, in general, anything serving the aim of war is allowed.[90] If a war is just, then in principle any mean is justified too. While just warfare will certainly require a proportionality of the means employed to the cause of the war, Grotius believes that a just war can—and should—be undertaken effectively.[91] This means that the justified party may use hidden tactics, ambushes, and tricks.[92] However, the warfaring parties will still have to adhere to general principles of law, for example the honouring of promises and the compliance with agreements met with the opponent as required under natural law, as natural law will bind anyone in times of war as much as in times of peace.[93] Under Grotius's second principle, the legal evaluation of the situation in a war is to be continuously reviewed.[94] Grotius's third principle concerns what might be called the acceptability of 'collateral damages' in modern military parlance: effects of warfare which might not be acceptable in themselves, may become acceptable if viewed within the context of the cause for a war This includes, for instance, the killing of women and children on a ship, as far as the ship itself is a legitimate military target under natural law.[95] However, this is to be judged differently from the perspective of Christians bound by the law of the Gospel, as

[85] Stumpf (n 74) 210. [86] Grotius, *De Iure Belli ac Pacis*, II.XX.iii.
[87] Stumpf (n 74) 210. [88] Grotius, *De Iure Belli ac Pacis*, II.XX.iv.
[89] ibid II.XX.vi–vii. [90] ibid III.I.ii. [91] Stumpf (n 74) 213.
[92] Grotius, *De Iure Belli ac Pacis*, III.I.vi and ff. [93] ibid III.XIX. [94] ibid III.I.iii.
[95] ibid III.I.iv.

the essence of arbitrary Divine Law: under the law of the Gospel, Christians will be expected rather to waive a rightful legal position than to bring harm upon innocent human beings.[96]

Beyond the establishment of general principles of the law of war, a major purpose of Grotius in the *De Iure Belli ac Pacis* is the analysis and critique of the practice of warfare of his time.[97] Grotius in this respect concentrates on the legal term 'licence'. 'Licence' in the sense applied by him means an absence of punishment, but not in the sense of a positive justification or a permission of the relevant conduct.[98] In consequence, Grotius discusses which licences the human law of nations grants in relation to the conduct of war-faring parties: first, he appears to treat such licences in a rather detached manner, but ultimately it becomes clear that he finds the practice observed by him immoral in the extreme and illegal.[99] In this way, Grotius analyses what he believes natural law and arbitrary Divine Law require for the law of war. Hence, after having described the licences under human international law, for example concerning the killing and enslaving of opponents,[100] Grotius argues in favour of a limitation of such licences under natural law and arbitrary Divine Law.[101] In the same way, after having dealt with the licences granted by human international law on the destruction and removal of things,[102] he judges these licences to be unsustainable under natural law and arbitrary Divine Law.[103] The same manner of description under human international law and curtailment under natural law and arbitrary Divine Law is also applied to the acquisition of property,[104] the right in relation to prisoners of war,[105] the fate of the State authority of the defeated party,[106] and the return of goods.[107] By this we see that Grotius does argue in favour of rule of substantive law even in warfare, which is dominated by a law not subject to any alteration by way of an agreement among human beings, but instead generated by overarching principles of natural justice, which demand unconditional application regardless of the political or religious convictions of the individual.

## 5. Conclusion

In summary, Grotius presents quite the opposite of the liberal position as referenced above by MacIntyre: while Grotius is not really concerned with procedures, he is keen to point out that the true law is rooted in justice that has a worldwide scope, even though still a higher standard is provided by arbitrary Divine Law. In this respect, it is certainly justified to view Grotius as a proponent of a universal rule of law, propagating an individual responsibility of any human being in its respective position. Just as much as a citizen is required to pay due respect to the State's government, any State's government is bound to pursue the common good for the people entrusted to its responsibility.

[96] Stumpf (n 74) 213–15. [97] Grotius, *De Iure Belli ac Pacis*, III.X.
[98] Stumpf (n 74) 215. [99] ibid. [100] Grotius, *De Iure Belli ac Pacis*, III.IV.
[101] ibid III.XI. [102] ibid III.V. [103] ibid III.XII. [104] ibid III.VI.; III.XIII.
[105] ibid III.VII.; III.XIV. [106] ibid III.VIII.; III.XV. [107] ibid III.IX.; III.XVI.

# 9

# *Aquatopia*

## Lines of Amity and Laws of the Sea

*Peter Goodrich*

### 1. Introduction

In matters juristical, and even in relation to the idiosyncratic and local concerns of early-modern Anglican common law's interpretation of the closure of the sea, the starting point is not Grotius but *Gaius noster* and the *Institutes*. This is in part because it has recently and persuasively been argued by Caspar Hirschi that nationalism is a late medieval product of Roman imperialism: 'nationalism is a political discourse constructed by chronically failing would-be-empires stuck in a battle to keep each other at bay'.[1] It is also, and perhaps in larger part, in recognition of the importance of legal humanism, the reception of the myriad classical texts and disciplines, the *Respublica litteraria*, in the formation of the various traditions, the *mores* of *ius commune* or local Roman law. The civilian law flourished throughout the West and was more joined by its parochial differences than it was separated by regional variances. The rules of law, the *regulae iuris*, were a shared collocation of *mores* and 'maximes' that owed as much to fiction and literature, to the *topoi* of adages and the inventions of history, as they did to any putatively more juridical and autonomous science.

My particular concern will be the *mos britannicus*, English *ius commune*, if such a neologistic improvisation is permissible, that peculiar mixture of classical mythology, historical fiction and literary endeavour that makes up the Latin tradition of common law. My example will be John Selden and we can note immediately that in *Mare clausum*, the work in which he supposedly announces England's right to annex an empire, he begins with a thoroughly indicative internationalism in his frontispiece emblem and the motto *non solus*, not alone, and below this *iuxta exemplar [Romanum]*, close to the example of the Roman law.[2] To understand Selden and fully appreciate his expansive and interdisciplinary sense of the rule of law at sea, or

[1] C Hirschi, *The Origins of Nationalism. An Alternative History from Ancient Rome to Early Modern Germany* (CUP 2012) 3.

[2] J Selden, *Mare clausum seu Dominio maris libri duo* (Stansby 1636) frontispiece. Where possible, I have used the 1652 translation by Marchamont Nedham: J Selden, *Of the Dominion, or Ownership of the Sea* (Du Gard 1652) 273–74.

to borrow from Hirschi, literally, which is to say litorally, 'at bay' it is necessary to apprehend the full extent and significance of Selden's legal humanism, his understanding of common law as a tradition shared with the continentals, and common to all humanist legal scholars:

> there are many common Lawyers of other States (for every State in Christendom is governed by its own common Laws and Customs, and hath truly its Common Lawiers ...) so farre from being strangers to Her that they all are to be reputed of her Chiefest Darlings, and some of them are hardly equalled among any other Professors, witness Budé, Cuiacius, Brisson, Savaron ... and the like elsewhere ... For these all were or are practicers of the various common or secular Laws of their own Nations.[3]

Law, for Selden, the offspring of philology and legal learning, is married to Mercury, the God of hermeneutics, and not to any singular nation, jurisdiction or discipline. The lawyers of the various *mores* of Roman law, from the *mos italicus* to the more recently designated *mos hispanicus* and *mos britannicus*, all share their civilian learning and their humanist credentials.[4] It is the *respublica litteraria* that is shared and that plays a role in fabricating a historical style, a fabulation of antiquity that is distinct in content but expresses a method that is common to all. If we turn then to Gaius, the argument that follows, that common lawyers shared their method, language, and hermeneutic principles with their apparent antagonists, the continentals, can find an originary textual support in the early institutional theory of alluvial accession. The commonality of knowledge and of law, divine and human, had an exemplar, I will suggest, in the commonality of the seas. The *oceanus philosophiae* was reflected in the boundless freedom of the seas. For Gaius, and this is seldom recognized, but is rather usually referred to as Erasmus's conception of the common learning of the adages, the sea and the air, by natural law, belong to nobody but rather are common to all—*nullius essent, qualia sunt omnia.*[5] Then, in an example to which we must return, 'if an island arises in the middle of a river, it is shared by all (*omnia communis est*)'.[6] The principle that friends hold all things in common would appear to have its juristic roots as early and as authoritatively as in the *Institutes of Gaius*.

In the discussion which follows I will argue, contrary to now conventional declamations of Selden's imperialism and the fervent nationalism of *Mare clausum*, that in fact his erudite interdisciplinary exposition of the *mos britannicus* is much closer in method and in content to the positions that he ostensibly attacks but in fact simply holds at bay from the shores, the coast line that he intends to protect.[7] It will be my

[3] J Selden, *The Historie of Tithes* (London 1618) xix–xx.

[4] For recent development of the various *mores* of reception, see S Byrne, *Law and History in Cervantes' Don Quixote* (Toronto UP 2012) on the *mos hispanicus*; B Cormack, *A Power to Do Justice: Jurisdiction, English Literature, and the Rise of Common Law, 1509–1625* (Chicago UP 2007) on the jurisdiction of the literary within the *mos britannicus*. Explicitly on the *mos britannicus*, see P Goodrich, 'Intellection and Indiscipline' (2009) 36 Journal of Law and Society 460.

[5] F de Zuluetta (ed), *Institutes of Gaius* (Clarendon Press 1946) Bk II 66.

[6] ibid Bk II 72.

[7] See R Tuck, *The Rights of War and Peace* (1999) 119 referencing Selden as the author of 'the most extreme defence of war for aggrandizement which had yet been presented by any European theorist'; M Somos, 'Selden's *Mare Clausum*: The Secularisation of International Law and the Rise of Soft Imperialism' (2012) Journal of the History of International Law 287, who takes a similar stance, even

argument that Selden shares his historicism, his political theology and literary learning and leaning with his opponent, the practitioner of the *mos gallicus*, humanist and poet Grotius. In synoptic guise, I will suggest that not only does Selden, in his debate with the learned author of *Mare liberum*, share the precious jewels of civilian learning, the *iuxta exemplar* of his frontispiece, but more profoundly he shares a humanistic sensibility and a conception of an interdisciplinary and international *nomos* that exceeds the illiberal learning and fragmentary confusion of those who are trapped in their 'beaten Rode', meaning locked in a single harbour, trapped in one discipline and afraid to venture out.[8] Borrowing liberally from the brilliant work of Bradin Cormack and latterly Susan Byrne, respectively on the literary in the legal, and on the *mos hispanicus,* I will suggest that it is the authority of poetry, what the lawyers term *auctoritates poetarum*, the shared exegetical and normative face and frame of government, antiquity triumphing over novelty, that joins Selden to a shared tradition of European law much more than it separates him according to any specific jurisdiction and parochial doctrine of the 'beaten Rode' of England.

## 2. King Cnut and the *auctoritates poetarum*

Close to one-third of the way through Book 2 of his polemic against Grotius, John Selden makes curious use of an anecdote about King Cnut taken from the twelfth-century *Chronicle* of Henry of Huntingdon. The narrative is well known but bears detailed recuperation. Book 1 of Selden's *Mare clausum* was concerned with law, Book 2 with fact. The context for the Cnutist narrative is thus that of discussion of facts, and specifically the relay of testimonies—the numerous assertions—concerning royal dominion over the sea. It follows on in the same chapter which reproduces, for example, the preamble to a charter of King Edgar's stating that: 'By the abundant goodness of almighty God who is the King of Kings, I Edgar, King of England (*Anglorum Basileus*), and of the Kings Islands, and of the Ocean lying around about Britain (*Oceanique Britanniani*)' thank the divinity for the grace of his supremacy and the dominion of the oceans. This is but one of a fairly interminable but representative set of documentary claims, commissions, charters, warrants, statutes, and other promulgations that assert in varying honorific, acclamatory, and incidental ways the rights of ownership of the sovereign over the waters either in general or more usually such as surround the island. Then comes 'King *Canutus* (or *Cnute*)'.

Said Cnut, we are informed, left a testimony, whereby 'he most expressly asserts the Sea to bee a part of his Dominion'. An assertion of fact. Then follows the well-known story, the empirical proof, in which, in response to his flatterers, and to demonstrate

arguing that Selden is the propagator of the view that 'The whole world is private property from the beginning, and land, sea and air are capable of being privately owned' (323). For further discussion in similar vein, see James Muldoon, 'Is the Sea Open or Closed? The Grotius–Selden Debate Renewed' in K Pennington and M Eichbauer, *Law as Profession and Practice in Medieval Europe* (Ashgate 2012).

[8] Selden (n 3) xxii.

that kings are but men, he is reported by Huntingdon, and by Florilegus, to have had himself carried to the sea and there 'to have made trial of the obedience of the Sea (it being flood) after this manner: "Thou, O Sea, art under my dominion. . . . And there never was any that disobeyed my Command without punishment. Therefore I command thee not to ascend up upon my Land, nor do thou presume to wet the feet or garments of thy Sovereign."' But, as we know, the tide came in and 'did very unmannerly wet not onely the feet, but legs of his Majestie'.[9] Cnut then declares that God alone commands the Sea, as also the heavens and the earth and from then on, the story goes, he refused to wear his crown of gold but rather consecrated it to a crucifix.[10] What is intriguing about the relaying of the anecdote is the strange reasoning that Selden uncharacteristically infers from the story. It is proof positive he states, that Cnut 'professed himself to bee the Soveraign of the Sea'. The most that can be said for this inference is that it rhymes, that it could make bad doggerel and so dubiously join the *auctoritates poetarum* that I will discuss later. But to claim that a king demonstrating vividly and in person that he has no power over the sea, and can neither control the tide nor otherwise order the waters back is proof of ownership and dominion, is without question to gild the lily. There is no logical link between the anecdote and the conclusion that Selden wishes to draw and so the question arises as to why this unnecessary non sequitur emerges momentarily to enliven the rather tedious recitation of document after document purporting to prove the fact that English kings and others have frequently asserted dominion over the waters as if saying it often enough would make it true.

The anecdote is not only wayward in failing to further Selden's argument but is also an outlier in that such a curious and opaque incident is pretty much unique in a work that otherwise is an exhaustive compilation of poetic, historical, and legal documents designed to refute Grotius's civilian arguments for a free sea in his brief and originally unsigned treatise *Mare liberum*.[11] At this particular point Selden protests too much or simply slips and in using this fabled figure of Cnut's aquatic impotence in the face of the oceanic betrays a contrary desire, and most significantly a covert agreement with 'the Verses of the most excellent Hugo Grotius . . . which were very elegantly written' upon the inauguration of King James.[12] Selden, in sum, shares much more with Grotius than he differs. The Cnutist episode is evidence of Selden's argument going awry, an instance of affective slippage, and in the end of his proximity to and agreement with Grotius despite the apparently marked difference in their interpretations and in their express conclusions.

Begin with this Cnutist symptom of Selden's hidden desire, this glimpse of covert motive in which he indicates the opposite of what he purports to argue. The anecdote provides an explicit reference to the fact that these two works share the status

[9] Selden (n 2) 279 (pagination awry). I discuss the literary significance of this anecdote in Goodrich, 'A Fragment on Cnutism with Brief Divagations on the Philosophy of the Near Miss' in P Hanafin and others (eds), *Law and Literature* (Blackwell 2004) 131.

[10] Selden (n 2) 280.

[11] H Grotius, *Mare liberum* (Elsevier 1609); I have used in the main Grotius *The Free Sea* (Liberty Fund 2004).

[12] Selden (n 2) 457.

of inaugural treatises addressing an admittedly vague and dubious question. They are both alike inquiries into what Coke terms doubtful points (*quaeras de dubiis*), and so, despite the apparent idiosyncrasy of *mos britannicus*, common law method, both parties to the dispute end up adopting the same exegetical recourse to poetical, Roman, and scriptural sources.[13] Both polemicists endeavour to draw 'imaginarie lines' upon a recalcitrant sea, and both, I will suggest pay far greater attention and show much stronger affection for the humanistic roots of the new law, than for the ephemeral and incidental putative object of disputation, the dominion of the sea with respect in essence to the protection of mercantile passage and navigation about which neither party is really in disagreement beyond each seeking to keep the other's nation at bay.

There is more at stake in charting the relation of law to the heterotopia of the oceanic, to *aquatopia*, to the unmarked and unimpressionable sea than at first meets the eye. This is an instance, at the very least, of law being made anew, a moment of a humanistic irruption in the juridical, of the poetic in the normative, and of the common law merging with the civilian by virtue of their shared roots. I will argue finally, that it is precisely humanism and more specifically a fundamental though now rather lost tenet of that tradition, the Pythagorean maxim that 'friends hold all things in common', a version of which is relayed as we saw by Gaius, that both Selden and Grotius are struggling to express in accord.

The Cnutist anecdote is a pacific and conciliatory one. The king shows that he is not really so much above the people, that he is not the dominator that the phenomenology of power would like to make him, and in Shakespeare's terms, he bleeds, as well as getting wet. This is significant and can take us back to the very beginning of the English edition of the treatise where, in a remarkable dedicatory epistle to the 1652 translation, Marchamont Nedham praises Selden for wielding the pen to such good effect: 'It is a gallant sight to see the Sword and Pen in victorious equipage together; For, this subdue's the souls of men by Reason, that onely their bodies by force. The Pen it is which manifests the Right of Things.'[14] The body is the prisoner of the soul, the pen, the text will inscribe and control both right and law, norm and force, but the reference is more classically legal than purely theological. It is a citation to the opening of Justinian's *Institutes*, and to the frequently relayed statement that the emperor should not only 'be decorated with arms but also armed with laws'.[15] At one level the reference is conventional, emblematic even, and we find it, for example, early in the first part of Coke's *Institutes* in an image of crossed sword and rod of office laid upon an open book, with the rubric, in Latin, 'For God, for Fatherland, and for you'.[16] A stirring if ornamental rallying call, you might think, but here it performs a different function, and one which Ernst Kantorowicz has usefully remarked,

[13] Here I draw upon S Jones, 'The Poetic Ocean in *Mare Liberum*' in O Ben-Dor (ed), *Law and Art: Justice, Ethics and Aesthetics* (Routledge 2011) 188.

[14] Selden (n 2) fol b1 (facing).

[15] P Birks (ed), *Justinian's Institutes* (Duckworth 1987) dedication (In Nomine Domini nostri) 'Imperatoriam maiestatem non solum armis decoratam, sed etiam legibus oportet esse armatam'.

[16] E Coke, *First Part of the Institutes of the Lawes of England* (Society of Stationers 1618) preface (*Deo, Patriae, Tibi*).

namely that of expressing the priority of the pen, the precedence of written law over the force of the sword, and so the transition from the lexical priority of arms over laws, to the new dominion of the 'Pen militant'.[17]

The shift or better hierarchy to which Selden refers is of course towards the literary, the book in its myriad forms, from the rule of war, classically the law of the bow, to the lyre, and in the early-modern period from the law of the sword to *ratio scripta* understood by the *prudentes*, the wise, as the rule of the arts. Underlying and shared by all these various modes of militant written assertion was Selden's belief in the priority of philology, the primacy of the text, in the order of the disciplines. In the *History of Tithes*, philology is 'the great Lady of Learning with her attendants' who stands over the disciplines and, more importantly for our purposes, all jurisdictions, liberal and legal, indifferently. The queen of the arts and sciences, philology is 'as fit for a student of the Common Laws of England, as for any other pretending what facultie soeverr'.[18] The shift, which is strikingly visible in the legal emblems of the era, is from force to law, from sword to quill, from military to literary.[19] Ernst Kantorowicz, in his essay on arms and laws thus traces a shift in the representation of sovereignty. The *symbola heroica* of the mid-sixteenth century depict the sovereign, in accordance with the preface of Justinian's *Institutes*, as decorated with arms and armed with laws. The sword has the dominant role, in the right hand, and the book, the laws, a secondary place on the left, often, according to the doctrine of two swords, themselves requiring force for their implementation. In the second half of the sixteenth century, however, the sovereign starts to be depicted looking away from the sword and towards the book and at the same time the emphasis of the motto and explanation turns from arms that kill to laws that govern. Where early legal and political emblems show the sword above the book or in front of the law tables, by the 1650s the sword is more usually either obscured by the book or the tip of the sword is actually disarmed, which is to say immobilized and blunted by a book.[20] The new era of print thrusts the book before the sword and thus moveable type turns the law of the sea into a question of printing, a clash of writings, a war of texts: letters and arts 'become the lodestar of humanistic dreams and princely ambitions, the Renaissance variety of Plato's philosopher-king'.[21] The legal emblem books provide ample evidence of the shift to writing, to the arts of bookish litigations and pontifications, a sea of ink to contest the dominion of the oceanic. It seems at root, for all our authors, for Selden and Grotius, our exemplars here, to be a grammatological question, a matter of scribble, of writing power, of finding an arche-writing, a structural

[17] E Kantorowicz, 'On Transformations of Apolline Ethics' in *Selected Studies* (Augustin 1965) 399. See further P Goodrich, 'The Evidence of Things Not Seen' in P Goodrich and V Hayaert (eds), *Genealogies of Legal Vision* (Routledge 2015). Generally, see P Goodrich, *Legal Emblems and the Art of Law* (CUP 2014).

[18] Selden (n 3) xix.

[19] See P Goodrich, 'The Evidence of Things Not Seen' in Goodrich and Hayaert (n 17).

[20] An early example of this shift, more or less contemporary with the first edition of *Mare clausum*, can be found in J Bruck, *Emblemata poltica* (Heyden 1618) 29. See also, for a different but comparable emblem of a sword encircled by a vine, W Julius Zincgref, *Emblematum ethico-politicorum* (Merian 1619) 66.

[21] Kantorowicz (n 17) 408.

inscription that will decide for us the question of whether the seas are open or closed, *mare apertum* or *mare clausum*, in Selden's dichotomous diction.[22]

Selden's choice of the word *aperio*—rather than *libero*—is usefully indicative. It connotes opening in the sense of uncovering, revealing, making visible and has ceremonial religious connotations. The Benedictines in particular symbolized mystic birth as entry into the word, and into speech, which they enacted through a rite of *apertio oris*, of opening the mouth. Cardinals too were invested through a similar ritual of instituting speech and the pope would open the mouth of the neophyte while saying *Nos aperimus tibi os*—we open your mouth.[23] In the same vein, in the context of religious art, the image had to be opened, the mode of viewing being termed *aperire imagines*, and the subject would thereby be insufflated with the living and breathing flesh of the icon unveiled.[24] The question of whether the sea could be opened, *mare apertum*, was thus initially a question of making it speak, of bringing forth its *logos*, of reviving it, and from that inferring—illating—its being as its law.

The first dimension and perhaps the most intriguing facet of the indeterminate status of the sea, for both Selden and Grotius, is semiotic. The problem with any closure of the sea is not simply that of its oceanic unboundedness, of immensity, of its limitless and chaotic character, but also and perhaps more significantly its impermeability, its resistance to any marks or signs. How can the arts be inscribed on the sea, what bounds, limits, notes, plough-lines, *reja*, or other signs can set out and express a distribution and division of the sea? Is the notion of marking or restricting the sea, of *nomos* and dominion, not contrary to the unwritten and un-inscribable being of the sea? The question is fundamental to our authors. It may also, as Miéville suggests, be preposterous.[25] Such a polemical comment, however, should not deter analysis but rather can be treated as its own kind of closure. The preposterous and the juridical, the 'as if' and the normative are common bedfellows. The point that Grotius and Selden share is a concern with the impossibility of reading and interpreting the sea, this *perpetuum mobile*, this vanishing sign, this site of shipwrecks and storms that rough hew the best laid of human plans.[26] Grotius thus, in the introduction to *De Iure praedae*, which is properly of course the introduction to *Mare liberum*, writes of the dependence of distributive justice on the measure of proportionality in allotments: 'The Universe is order in consonance with this same justice by God himself, called by Plato "the Geometer", precisely because He administers law and equity according to a certain principle of proportion.'[27] The problem according to Grotius, however, is that no such mapping and limiting of the sea is possible, no lines

[22] Selden (n 2) at f2r and ff.

[23] There is a useful discussion in P Legendre, *Le Désir politique de Dieu* (Fayard Paris 1988) 156.

[24] On which, see G Didi-Huberman, *L'Image ouverte* (Gallimard 2007) 42ff.

[25] A passing remark in C Miéville, *Between Equal Rights: A Marxist Theory of International Law* (Haymarket 2006) 211, which Grotius himself, in his 'Defense of Chapter V of *Mare Liberum*', also discounts: 'Therefore the proximate reason why the sea can not be possessed is neither its fluid nature nor its "continually flowing to and fro" (which Welwood brings up)'.

[26] The key reference here is H Blumenberg, *Shipwreck with Spectator: Paradigm for a Metaphor of Existence* (MIT 1997) where the human discomfort with the 'unreckonable and lawless sea' is elegantly traced.

[27] H Grotius, *Commentary on the Law of Prize and Booty* (Liberty Fund 2006) 29.

are visible or constant and Selden is to the same effect when he early in his treatise cites St Ambrose as commenting that he has never heard of a nautical Geometrician, namely 'a Thalassometrician, one that could measure the Bounds in the Sea'.[28]

It is because the sea is *sui generis*, without marks, notes, or allotments, and is viewed as a threatening and untamed space that recourse has to be made next to an invisible law, a hidden *nomos* that requires an Augustinian reading by means of faith.[29] God has inscribed the law of the sea by 'tacit indication' and it is for the faithful to unveil that law through scriptural study and through appreciating the various levels of the text. Selden too refers soon to the Divine Law and oracles of the Holy Scriptures as the proper starting point and draws some inferences of a marginal kind without resolving very much either from *Genesis* and its gift of dominion over fish, or from later instances of battles at sea. All are agreed that the question is doubtful and so the aid of the poets has to be called in, or, as Grotius puts it in his opening page, 'we hear the poets speaking'. This is the antique *nomos*, the classical diction of the philosophers, the Pythagorean and Platonic muses who provide the answers to the conundrums of hidden truths and dubious points of law. When matters are opaque and texts enigmatic then the cure is reference to the poets, the first *nomikoi* in humanistic method and knowledge. These then are primary sources, the *auctoritates poetarum* which, as adverted, in Sir Edward Coke's diction and in early-modern legal practice generally answer foundational and other dubious points of law: 'verses were invented for the helpe of memorie and it standeth well with gravitie of our lawyer to cite them'.[30] Selden and others are equally clear that poetic *formulae* found the law in the mode of maxims, proverbs and other mysteries that convey the dogmatic starting point of scriptural arguments. It is in all events initially the poet who makes nature speak, and dictates the divine intendments that nature signifies and transmits. The poets stipulate the original *nomos*, the first order, method and rhythm of law, its inscription and custody in impermanent and changeable words. Abraham Fraunce, who devotes an entire book to expounding the 'logike' of law, begins symptomatically with a prefatory poem and then in his introductory epistle 'To the Learned Lawyers of England', cites Horace on questions of style:

> Woordes are lyke leaves, as Horace reporteth: leaves spring before Summer, and fall before Winter; and the same inconstancy is in words. Let us therefore use that phrase whiche is most usuall; and though in knowledge and conceipt we contend to bee singular, yet in uttering our thoughtes, let all bee partakers.[31]

This adumbration of the shared knowledge that survives the impermanence of words and the mutability of modes of expression is precisely the poetic. It is poetry that survives and continues, the poetic that houses the adages, epigrams, aphorisms,

[28] Selden (n 2) 5.

[29] DW Robertson (tr), Augustine, *De doctrina Christiana, On Christian Doctrine* (1958) 31, discussing how 'we walk by faith and not by sight' through the text, the scriptures, thus providing at least a possible method for an unmarked regimen of the sea.

[30] Coke (n 16) 237r.

[31] A Fraunce, *The Lawiers Logike, Exemplifying the Præcepts of Logike by the Practise of the Common Lawe* (How 1588) fol qq 2.

*regulae*, and maxims that make up what Bacon termed *Philosophia prima*, the law of laws (*legum leges*) that underpins all particular and merely contemporary rules and assignments. It is thus the poets who can potentially open the mouth of the sea and make it signify.

Grotius turns first to Homer, Ovid, Vergil, Horace, and more to lay the grounds of a humanistic argument against private appropriation of the sea, which 'oweth its common use to men'. As Stephanie Jones articulates it:

> Gathered together, Grotius' uses of the poets may be read as articulating a resistance to a Hobbesian resolution to the question of obligation. The poets signify ... a space that is filled by a sensibility of the ocean and the residue of a non-proprietorial sensibility that has otherwise been lost.[32]

She interprets this as a mythic, Arcadian past preserved by the poets and prior to law—*usus facti, non juris.* Grotius's notion of the incomprehensibility of the sea requires poetic resolution, a measure of the hieroglyphic and indexical. Selden is to precisely the same effect, and even before responding to Grotius had already relied heavily upon the poets in his history of the mythographic sources of common law, *Jani Anglorum*.[33] He opens by acknowledging 'the Lady *Muse* who is the Governess of Antiquities' and moves swiftly to justify a method that begins with poetry and story as the support of the history, custom and use that become common Anglican law. Citing the Latin poet Ennius, Selden treats these sources as stories that only serious scholarship can recuperate:

> Antique, buried in rubbish, old and musty,
> Which make one verst in customs old and new,
> And of Laws, Gods and Men giving a view,
> Render the careful Student skill'd and trusty.[34]

The foundation of law is necessarily figurative, a matter of receiving and interpreting the inspirations of the muses not simply as a declaration of method but as a substantive practice necessary to the relay of those norms that found the law: 'For time to Laws themselves gives Law full oft'.[35] The history of English law thus begins with a discussion of the plays of Sophocles and then turns to Plutarch writing 'in a Poetick strain' who gives us an authoritative verse on the judicial function of the Furies (the *Eumenides*) as the exemplar of an early and feminine rule:

> But ye with eye of Justice, and a face
> Of Majesty survey all humane race,
> Judges commission'd to all time and place.[36]

The poem founds and supports Selden's argument that the *Semnai theai* were the originary lawgivers and the model for the venerable goddesses of English law. That work evidently provides the exemplary method that *Mare clausum* follows and is fully

32 Jones (n 13) 199.

33 J Selden, *Jani Anglorum facies altera* (1610) in R Westcot (tr and ed), *Tracts Written by John Selden* (Basset 1683).

34 Selden (n 33) preface, fol a2 verso.

35 ibid fol b1 recto.

36 Selden (n 33) 4.

suggestive of the primary role that the *auctoritates poetarum*, the norms of an antique poetic tradition, a humanistic erudition that is shared by all genuine scholars, will play in delineating the commonality and uses of the sea. In the later work, however, the argument is taken further and is articulated in terms of historical fables and that early history that is obscured under 'a fabulous Representation'. Acknowledging that the 'fabulous Age' is not a direct source of argument, Selden goes on to specify that 'wee manifest Historical Truth out of the most antient Historians, though wrapp't in the mysteries of Heathen Priests and Poëts. For, (as Lactantius saith well) even Those things which the Poëts speak are true, but cover'd under a certain veil or Figure'.[37] Fiction is the figure of truth, as one maxim has it, and it is useful not least because fable is necessary to carry the common belief, to persuade and move to action.

Even here the position of the lawyers is not far from that of the poets nor from Sydney's famous defence of 'poesy' in which poetry elicits both the opaque obscurities of nature and the hidden state of origins, of sacred sources and divine signs.[38] The poets precede the lawyers, which is evident in the order of progression of both Grotius's and Selden's texts. The poetic is the starting point because it alone can address the invisible and ineffable. Poetry is the augur and inaugurates. It establishes the hierarchy of signs which starts, in Selden's elegant and detailed schema, with 'Obligatorie law' natural or divine. This is universal 'Common Law written throughout the whole world, in the very Books of nature … set down in those Divine Oracles that have been committed to writing' and has the 'autoritie of the father of nature'. It is immutable and so to be distinguished from permissive laws and those alterations and additions that constitute the 'intervenient' positive law of diverse nations. What is important for the purposes of tracing the emergence of the law of the sea, the law of that which cannot be inscribed, marked, or written upon, is that the order of law is an order of significations that moves from the figurative to the literal, from symbolic to the scriptural, and from poetry to proverb, maxim to law.

The authority of the poets is the expression of law in cases of doubt, and nothing could be more dubious than the question of origins and specifically the origin of *imperium* and *dominium* over a space as uncertain as that of the sea. It requires *poesis*, invention, the making of an original symbolization and naming that can in the first place mirror the mythological and ceremonial status of the point of exit from discourse into faith, the *quoad non ultra* that juristically frames the maxim as a dogma, and as a mystery and vision of law.[39] The poetic is also pliable, it is in Selden's scheme obligatory but it is also open to interpretation through its signs and its practices, through scripture and custom. The point to be stressed, however, is a more blatant and simple one. Grotius and Selden share a humanistic concern with the primary texts of the tradition, and these texts descend from the poetic to the juristic. Selden, to take the home example, the antiquary common lawyer, occupies the bulk

[37] Selden (n 2) 47.

[38] P Sidney, *An Apologie for Poetrie* (Olney 1595) 3–4, noting that the earliest philosophers, Thales, Empedocles, Parmenides, Pythagoras, were poets and 'sange their naturall Phylosophie in verses', and so too the famous Greek lawmaker Solon is also deemed a poet.

[39] E Whitehouse, Fortescutus illustratus, *or a Commentary on that Nervous Treatise* De Laudibus Legum Angliae (Roycroft 1663) 136.

of Book 1, the legal part of the argument, prior to the factual, with poets, fables, customs, and maxims. Only once what could be coined the sovereign arguments have been relayed and addressed, the poetic, historical and theological analysed, is it necessary to turn to law: 'And therefore in the last place, let us take such opinions of the Lawyers into consideration'.[40] It is here that Selden directly addresses Grotius's arguments and offers a different interpretation of the classical philosophers and the Roman law sources that had been arrayed to support the argument that the sea is held in common and belongs to all. For Selden, the sources are correct, but the civilian interpretation is at least in part erroneous.

The general shared inheritance, the universal wealth of knowledge and law is reflected in the amicable community of humanity which from the beginning, as Gaius noted, held all things in common. That origin was shared in 'a state of Communitie, in that Divine Act of Donation whereby Noah and his three sons, Shem, Cham and Japhet (who represented as it were the person of Adam) became Joint Lords of the whole world'.[41] All things are held in common according to Selden, 'in a figurative sense after the manner of the Poëts', in the sense of scholarship and spiritual similitude that identify the human and the legal as universal. Sharing more than they differ, it is only in a secondary and borrowed sense that what God gave is separated and subjected to the tellurian *nomos* of the plough and demarcation into territory and specific *leges terrae*. It is by accretion and use, through marking and mapping that the land has been occupied and dominion established and this trajectory of cartographic and territorial passion is used by Selden to make a limited claim whereby, according to the common law of prescription, of custom and use, the sovereign can obtain dominion of such part of the sea as can be mapped, demarcated, and protected around the sovereign territory. It is thus by analogy, by proceeding *ad similia* that Selden excises a small part of the sea, but a little portion of Grotius's 'immense (infinit) ocean', to the use, possession, and protection of the adjoining shores of the kingdom. This is precisely the argument from Roman law that *accessio* can justify ownership in certain circumstances, namely when land washes up on the banks of another's property, then the owner of that property can claim the additional land which now abuts their domain. In Selden, this argument is illustrated expansively by the actual production of a map that marks the spaces between coastal promontories and isthmuses as English 'Rodes' (harbours), *vestibulas*, otherwise termed 'Regias cameras' or *camerae*, the king's chambers, the royal ports.[42] There is an *oeconomy* of the sea, coded according to a computation of '*Promontorium series, Rumbi, Leucae*' which is to say promontories, rhumb lines, and nautical miles between the projected coastal points of the map.[43] It is by accession that the waters are measured, by reference to the coast and the land that dominion, the 'sea coast' is demarcated and that the limits and bounds of the realm of England are demonstrated.

The point to be pursued is that, whatever the differences of interpretation, it is the pen, the ink, the arts and letters, the chorography and cartography and not the

[40] Selden (n 2) 150. [41] ibid 17–18. [42] ibid 367.
[43] For an excellent expansion of this point, see Cormack (n 4) 259–65.

sword that are the determinant features and measure of the question. It could be argued that this is because not much hangs on what the lawyers say. They are, after all, consulted last and dismissed quickest. The better answer, however, is that the relative insignificance or secondary place of the lawyers' opinions rests upon the fact that where the question is that of the origin of dominion and so directly a matter of the source of law, then there can be no direct apprehension of the relevant *nomos* and prescriptive rule. What lies at the beginning, the lawyers consistently claim, is variously too distant from the eye, too ancient and hidden, too masked by fable and figure, too veiled to be directly apprehended. It requires not law, but authority, which in turn is based upon skill in history, nature, philosophy, and poetics to address the origin of dominion as against the autonomy and commonality of the oceanic. It also requires a scriptural method, meaning the techniques of theological exegesis to compose and present the relevant arguments. The lawyers write in the style of the theologians, they amass texts, compound scriptural authorities, collate edicts, warrants, commissions, and other epistles and promulgations in voluminous support of what is at first appearance a quantitative argument in favour of the position proposed. In looking to the question of originals and in seeking the support of the poets and philosophers, the lawyer here cannot avoid being an interdisciplinarian, a practitioner of hermeneutics, a humanist concerned with the transmission of classical letters and only latterly with civil or common law as it reflects those prior authorities and legitimations, the *mens emblematica* as transmitted by the Roman sources of all common law.

## 3. Lines of Amity

Returning momentarily to the narrative of Cnut's inability to command the sea, it ends with the king being carried back to the land and with the sea being left to divine rather than human dominion. The golden crown is hung up, free of incumbency, condign for its overreaching of jurisdiction. Cnut, and this despite Selden's best efforts, is with Grotius in treating the ocean as outside of human dominion and sovereign command. There can be no 'pourpresture', seizure or enclosure of the sea, not so much because it is boundless but because it is everywhere, because it touches all, because it is unmarked except by those rhumb lines necessary to chart the 'King's Chambers, havens, or ports' and so keep the piratical and foreign at bay. This is the *prima philosophia* that the poets and humanist scholars have generally relayed, and which Gaius confirms through the doctrine of *accessio*, the juristic version of metonymy that allows dominion and so also protection of everything that adjoins the sea coast and litoral vestibules of the kingdom.[44] The latter point can confirm the shared method and common purposes of the apparently opposed authors. The

[44] On which see the preface to the second edition of J Selden, *Titles of Honor* (Stansby 1531) where he likens knowledge first to precious jewels, the exempla of humanist learning, and then to disciplines as islands which are always connected to other islands—the continent itself being no more than a large island.

essentially theological method of argument is concerned initially not simply with finding the earliest and so most authoritative texts in support of any particular position, but beyond that the goal is to locate and authorize an originary nomination, a noting and naming of the law and here that of the sea.

Common law method differs only slightly from that of the civilians. Grotius in his introduction to *De Iure praedae* follows the Roman hierarchy and defines law as 'the unerring mind of God'. Within that definition, the word law is derived from *Iovis*—Jove—and from *iurare*—to swear—an etymology that places the oath, the ritual word at the heart of law. God as oracle, through nature names things, *bios* with *logos*, and humanity by the same token is from the beginning bound by their own *logos*, the classical *sacramentum* or action in law that instils good faith, compact, and so the indissoluble tie between what is said and what is done. The medium of speech, unique via nature to humanity, is a divine gift and is 'so sacred and inviolable an instrument for the interchange of blessings and the reciprocal intimation of human will that, in the eyes of all men, there is no more grievous disgrace than that attached to lying'.[45] It is the word, nomination, and by extension agreement, the exchange of words and the holding true to such words that founds community and commonality, the love and amity that constitutes and binds the group. It is from these first principles that community is derived and it has the sanctity of the word at its root, because faith in language is at the origin of being human and of being together. What defines community is thus what is shared, language and faith, justice as *fidelitas*, adherence to what has been agreed. The *ius gentium* is the law intimated by nature and is 'a species of covenant binding upon all', and directed at the common good.[46]

It is from these first principles, variously extracted from the Bible, from Aristotle and Plato, from Justinian's compilations, that the freedom of the sea can be inferred. *Mare liberum* is an expression of that which is common to all, that touches all, and so is sacred according to the early legal sources. The *Institutes* defines things held in common as those that pertain to the community as a whole, and these are not and cannot be owned by individuals, they can neither be goods nor possessions because they are given to all and by that token are sacred. The word sanction indeed derives from the sanctity of what has been violated, the communal compact, the will of the whole.[47] The ocean is sacred because it is subject to divine right (*divini iuris*) and then by extension because it is held in common by all, and finally because it is unmarked and so not subject to division according to the law of things. It is from these first principles that Grotius arrives at the conclusion that the seas are a space of amity, a fact of human friendship, and that in belonging to all they must logically be shared in common. This fact is manifest by the Roman lawyers when they 'published those noble sentences against private avarice'.[48] King Cnut would agree but would frame the limitation upon dominion not in terms of avarice but in those of the more

[45] Grotius (n 27) 35. [46] ibid 36.
[47] Justinian, *Institutes* 2.1. The theme too comes of course from Gaius, and is reprised in *Digest* 1.8.
[48] Grotius (n 11) at 32.

basic constraint of jurisdiction and the boundaries of merely human powers that render avarice in the end both inappropriate and ineffective.

Selden is more pragmatic but his thesis is not ultimately so different. It is often pointed out that Grotius's work on the freedom of the sea was motivated by a political desire to justify Dutch attacks upon Portuguese and Spanish vessels in the East Indies. While that is the case, it does not speak to the medium, the commonality of the sea and the freedom of navigation, but rather to the warring state of two nations, wherever they happen to encounter. The hostility is directed at the enemy and not at the sea. Cnut who originated the 'Danegeld', a tax to pay for the king's expenses in protecting his subjects from the depredations of pirates, would not dispute this particular interpretation. Again, incrementally, the question is that of why Selden uses the example of Cnut and how this strange slip, this non sequitur, this image of what law cannot command, can resolve the supposed difference with Grotius and so bring the purportedly antithetical texts into a fundamental agreement, a textual compact with critical possibilities for our understanding of international law.

The civilian method, as exemplified in the 'prolegomena' to *Praedae* involved argument from general principles of scripture and philosophy to adumbration of specific rules and for purposes of the law of the sea, the acknowledgement that here, to borrow a phrase, the law was the wind. For Selden, the legal authorities are only briefly mentioned because the real source of common law is *lex terrae*, the custom and use of the land, the commons of Anglican law. The thesis that Selden wishes to avoid, that of the common character of the sea is only briefly mentioned by way of reference to Ulpian and *Digest* 1.8. The assertion of the common law adoption of the rule that the sea is shared and so free is even briefer. We find this citation to common law sources in Book 2, chapter 2, page 383. About as far as one can get from the main argument and primary narrative as is possible without actually escaping the covers of the work entirely. Bracton is cited on *res communes*, the words coming directly from the *Digest* and we are told that by natural law running water, air and the sea are common to all—*communia sunt omnes*.[49] Slightly later, Selden goes further and cites Sir John Cowell as blindly following Bracton. His *Institutiones* are compiled 'in too careless a manner, (while they have set down the Institutions of our English law) have unadvisedly utter'd by the way touching that antient communitie of the sea'.[50] These views are for Selden, quite humorously, 'reliques of Ulpian, or of the School of Imperiall Law, too slightly and carelessly added by the way in writing'.

For Selden, royal promulgations, common law custom, and 'the known Law of the Land' displace and override the views of the contemporary civilians. In countless documents, statutes, charters, warrants, commissions, instaurations, and gifts, the sovereign is declared to have dominion over the sea and the seas are named by reference to the territories that they surround and so become, by contiguity, part of the territory. They are named and it seems that in the naming they become annexed

[49] H de Bracton, *De Legibus et consuetudinibus Angliae* 1.12.5–6.

[50] Selden (n 2) 391–92. J Cowell, *Institutes of the Lawes of England Digested into the Method of the Civill or Imperiall Institutions* (Roycroft 1651) 53: 'By natural right these things are to be esteemed as common. Running water, the Air and Sea'.

to the territory that names them and then custom, the continued use of the name attaches the space named to the dominion of those that most consistently name it. It is what Bentham would later, no doubt, have termed the jurisprudence of approbative acquisitive appellation. This is the primary argument of Book 2 and the forms of naming are expanded from textual sources to inscriptions upon coins, showing Britannia seated over the seas, to the map of Britain which, as discussed, shows the surrounding waters marked by lines of sight, and so owned as far as the local geometer, the lawyer cartographer can see the sea. Time and again it is the simple yet emphatic assertion of names of dominion, images of possession, borders and boundaries, imaginary lines and compass projections that provide the graphic support for the arguments and principles drawn from the antique poets, philosophers, and lawyers. These Selden chooses to reinterpret as recognizing that the freedom and commonality of the sea is extinguished by the needs and dominion of the territory and the shore.

Selden's argument is in essence that the notes of dignities (*notitia dignitatum*) that display military and administrative offices and that name the seas as adjoining and included in the command of the sovereign or other official notes of administrative dignity and disposition, provides proof of dominion. These notes then limit the commonality of the common but of course they do so only to the extent that the sea is an incident and adjunct of the territory occupied and indeed can be seen from it. These adjoining waters are part of the royal household and so termed 'sea closets' or 'Royal Chambers' (*Regias Cameras*) and these include all the water that can be included in a direct line from one such closet or port to another along the coast about the realm.[51] These are the vestibules of the territory, the safe points of passage and entry and belong to the household, the *oeconomy*, the suite and court of the sovereign and its territory. It is also the case, however, that these spaces are shared. They are spaces of amity in the classical sense of kinship and filiation, of belonging to the brotherhood, the community, the commons, and what can be seen from the commons. It is not accidental in this respect that Selden's map of the sea is in fact simply a map of Britain with lines drawn as stated along the coast to provide a buffer between the shore and the open—and free—sea. There is no map of the sea, only of the land, of what is encompassed by the unmarked and unseen waters.

Turning finally to Ulpian and the other classical legal and rhetorical sources of the phrase *naturali iure communia sunt omnia haec . . . mare* and its numerous variations we can move to the resolution of the dilemma that the debate proposes and elaborates.[52] There is most crucially and obviously a difference of interpretation, a literary dispute, a war of books. In respect to the question of perspective, Selden starts on the land and views the sea from the territory. The sea is for him the space of the other, of threat, of things invisible and unseen that emanate and most likely irrupt and infest from the beyond, a domain of chaos, of pirates, piracy, and Norwegians. Be that as it may, the sea is conceived by way of analogy to the land and *leges terrae* and thus the map shows the maritime boundaries of the territory, the litoral law, while

[51] Selden (n 2) 370.

[52] Translates as 'by natural law the sea is common to all'.

what cannot be seen, what extends beyond the visible waters, is deemed elsewhere and other, unmarked and excluded. Grotius by contrast views the land from the sea, beginning in the divine and in the friendship and commonality of an 'ocean wherewith God hath encompassed the Earth'. Trade, passage, navigation, and arrival from elsewhere upon the shores dictate, for Grotius, 'that most sacred law of hospitality'. War is thus described as invariably the consequence of shutting shores to travellers and trade and so it is the exclusion of the sea, the failure to recognize the limitations of the positive and merely tellurian that generates conflict, arms not laws. From this perspective, the common precedes the territorial, and collective belonging has precedence over proprietary claims and private dominion.

By way of method and the distance between common law and Roman law, the above differences should not obscure the common starting point and method, the humanistic *lex amicitiae* from which shared space dispute descends. Grotius begins with the principles, Selden, despite the claim to start with law, starts with custom and moves much later to principle. Thus, Selden analogizes the shared sea to the sovereign dominion of the territorial State, whereas Grotius views the commonality of the sea as the principle through which to address the limited dominion of the common and exclusive territory. Both jurists, however, tacitly agree upon the humanistic principle of common humanity, the friendship of faith and law, the fidelity to words, and in a surprising reference to Heraclitus, Grotius asserts that 'the common word is the best criterion, for what seems best to all is the most trustworthy'.[53] The common word is here the law of the poets, the *nomos* of nations, the freedom of the sea asserted over time. Behind that assertion, however, and quite express, though parenthetical in Selden, is a reference to the philosophical root of the claim to commons, recently and lengthily expounded by Erasmus in his essay on the adage *amicorum omnia sunt communia*, friends hold all things in common.[54] Selden views the thesis as 'unadvised' but nonetheless makes reference to 'the Laws of friendship (wherein Philosophers say all things are common)'.[55] Amity and enmity, in Grotius and Selden are the criterion for mapping and division, avarice and commonality, land and sea.

At the root of the entire debate over the freedom of the sea, visible in a variety of references to *lex amicitiae*, and to friendly bonds, is a philosophical maxim that has its juristic transmission via Gaius, but which Erasmus traces back directly to Pythagoras. At the root of the tradition is a maxim that the Christians picked up: 'For as many as were admitted of him into the fellowship and companie of his doctrine, all the money and substaunce of what they had: they laide it together, which thinge not only in worde, but also in deede was *cœnobium*'.[56] The root of the cenobitic is the undivided, and it is precisely amity that precludes division and expresses the justice of the commons. It is in the law of nature that the sea is trackless,

[53] Grotius (n 11) 85.

[54] R Taverner, *Proverbes or Adagies, Gathered out of the Chiliades of Erasmus* (William How 1569) 65v. For a modern translation of a revised and expanded version of the essay, see W Barker (ed), *The Adages of Erasmus* (Toronto UP 2001). The definitive recent study is K Eden, *Friends Hold All Things in Common: Tradition, Intellectual Property, and the Adages of Erasmus* (YUP 2001).

[55] Selden (n 2) 148.

[56] Erasmus (n 54) 66r.

that vessels passing through it leave no trace, and hence both the absence of memory and the impossibility of division must be its principal lessons. Erasmus, again, in the adage *Siculus mare*, captures the point: a shipwrecked Sicilian sits staring at a tranquil sea and considers repeating the voyage on which he had lost his cargo of figs. He says to himself 'I know what you want: you want some more figs'.[57] The ocean is enlaced in desire and purpose, in the possibility of passage and pleasure, commerce and jointure. Most importantly, it must be befriended, its law recognized and its providential character admitted and embraced.

Remaining with the Pythagorean maxim, the Erasmian interpretation of the amicable injunction to commonality of all things is one which portends a law of amity and of the undivided that surpasses and potentially overrides the merely territorial and positive. The object of the cenobitic is spiritual union, amity with the divinity being recognized as the greatest and in pure theory the only real friendship.[58] As for humans, like the ocean itself, they should be trackless, each an amicable other self, common in doctrine and belief. Friendship is, in another Erasmian adage, the greatest necessity—*amicus magis necessarius*—and should be itself an unbroken law. The sea indeed becomes in Erasmus at various points a metaphor for amity and by a similar token, in Grotius and Selden, any attempt to mark the sea or divide the oceans is done according to 'lines of amity'. These can be interpreted according to the sources as 'imaginarie lines' or as in essence trackless courses, like the path of a ship over which the waters rapidly close up again. It is an angelological space, a purely imagistic and vanishing domain over which signs have but a limited and evanescent hold because in the end it is not law but theology, not the administrative order but the hierarchy of honour and in modern terms of diplomatic and political protocol that governs the ungovernable, because unmarked and yet indelibly shared seas.

The ocean is the domain of dignities and honours, of the *ius imaginum* and the status of persons, rather than of any more obvious or directly juridical schemata. The law of amity is historically the law of the sea. This is a voluntary jurisdiction, a poetic and epigrammatic space and thus the importance of Gaius's tacit reference to Pythagoras. The poetic roots of *nomos* here come to the fore, and the rhythmic method of custom and its unwritten inscriptions, its patterns and paths is not uncommon in common law and it suggests at root that all of the references to the sea being held in common are attempts to return to a founding maxim, a philosophical and poetic proverb that founds the humanist tradition in the sharing of ideas, in the commonality of intellectual heritage, doctrine, and faith. The law of amity is a spiritual law, a *nomos* written on water and so *ius non scriptum* in the ancient tongue, and even today, in our argot, this is still called common law. Taking it further, the law of amity is the law of a strange proximity, a law of togetherness, of the sharing of being. It is a law without law, which the Renaissance named *Fortuna*, fate as chance that

[57] Barker (n 54) 170.

[58] W Fulbecke, *A Booke of Christian Ehicks or Moral Philosophie* (Company of Stationers 1586). See also P Goodrich, '*Amici curiae*: Lawful Manhood and Other Juristic Performances in Renaissance England' in E Sheen and L Hutson (eds), *Literature, Politics and Law in Renaissance England* (Macmillan 2005).

writes us all. The law of the sea is the *nomos* of fate and it gains its usual representation in sails and winds that blow the ship to foreign shores. In respect to amity, and specifically the powerlessness of law at sea, another principle inheres to fate and that is the priority of amity over governance, and of justice, of agreement, over law. Such an order, as stated, is honorific and poetic, common but not commanded.

The invocation of the maxim that friends hold all things in common is, as Kathy Eden dexterously evinces, from early on a legal reference and so a complicated imbrication of poetry, philosophy, and law in which it is the jurisdiction of the poetic that holds sway. Here the choice between arms and laws is one that returns to a distinction between law and love, between judgement and compact as the poets have described it and as the humanist lawyers have followed. The proverb is here but one instance of a philosophical ocean (*oceanus philosophiae*) that mirrors the immensity of the sea. Law can never comprehend that infinity and so must follow its poetic expression, its philosophical maxims, the trackless path of amity and the lesbian—which is to say flexible—rule of justice. *Aequitas*, to coin a phrase, is the law of the aquatic, or, to attempt a maxim of my own, *in mare semper est aequitas*—equity is the essence of the sea because like equity, the sea expands and contracts, insufflates and exhales, opens and closes according to a temporality, a lunacy, all its own. That was the lesson of Cnut.

## 4. Conclusion

My argument has been that underlying the war of books, the polemical scribblings, the scholarly impugnations, the erudite juristic exchange between Grotius and Selden is expressive of a certain *ius honorarium*, a law of amity, embodied in shared verses, in a common poetic that only seems to divide them. The war of books is in truth a hedonistic embrace, an expression of a common erudition, a sharing of adages and apothegms, of the figures that found the commonalities and so also the communicative possibilities of the law of honour and the tracking of the sea. Specifically, our two authors, common and civilian both, are agreed that the sea is variously free or subject to the trackless dominion of an amicable justice. Law belongs to the land, it is common to the *nomos* of territory and the markings of the plough. The sea has no law, but such a statement begs the question now of what we mean, what we practise, by way of law. How are we to deal with an *aquatopia*, which is precisely neither utopia nor heterotopia, nor even Miéville's dystopia but rather its own and ever-adjoining space? That will be my last point and, loyalist that I am, I will take it again from Selden.

The strange story about Cnut once more. It deserves unpicking further because in its very strangeness it is symptomatic of what is at stake in the war of books over the law of the sea. There is only a law of amity in books, a humanist commonality of ideas that is strong enough a bond to incorporate both love and hate, friend and enemy within the cenobitic principle of mutual recognition and adherence to what is held in common, namely language, compact and faith. The more imaginative of the legal philosophers have often acknowledged such a view. Barthèlemy

Chasseneuz, for example, who places law under the aegis of *doctrina*, that is to say, philosophy and the code of honour, the equity of meanings that it makes possible.[59] That is a fair starting point for rethinking the story of Cnut. It was as sovereign, most precisely as lawgiver that he insisted on being carried down to the seashore. He wanted to show, so Huntingdon tells us and the record relays, that he, the king, the great, the law, was merely human and so more common than different. Cnut shared everything in common with those who carried him down to the sea because he was mortal, because he could not but acknowledge that the ocean was greater than kingship, enthronement, sovereignty, and law. Such is a tickly point and as such it needs to be flattened.

In some portraits of Cnut, the king is shown with a peculiar device on his head (see Figure 9.1). It is not a crown. That is the first point and a salient one for an image entitled 'K. Canute the Great'. He is wearing on his head a machine for rolling things flat. This roller is obviously ironic in the context of our little history because the waves are precisely what can neither be rolled away, nor flattened out. More than that, on the side of his head, above the ear, a wave is depicted, water that obviously enough has slipped under and past the roller and is making its course past the king. The image, and images are everything, is thus one of recognition and symbolizes the fact that neither sovereignty nor machine will stop the waters, nor make a road across the water. Another Pythagorean symbol cited by Erasmus can here advertise our point: *per publicam viam ne ambules*, avoid the formulaic and overused path.[60] More explicitly, the image must be opened because it symbolizes the necessity for being to open to the waves, to the greater force, to the oceanic—*aperire imagines* also means to open the person, to show the face, to join rather than to confront. The waves, in other words, are flowing over Cnut, the king is submitting to the *aquatopic*, to a force greater than he the Great, but not the Greatest, to justice as the nature of being as such. In sharing being we are extant together and indivisibly in common.

In attempting to rule the waves, Cnut symbolizes the failure of rules and the limits of law. Here we can refer precisely to the subject form of law and to the magnificent depiction of law being subsumed, drowned by both *aqua* and *aequitas*. The chronicle tells that Cnut was carried to the waterline as the tide was rising. His story, his vision is thus quite directly of bodies, borders, and boundaries, of the literary in the litoral, and the point is not so much their difference as their proximity and commonality. It is his body that the sovereign places on the waterline, the *corpus iuris* face to face with the *oceanus philosophicus*, as also with the source of life and with a greater power and justice than sovereignty can ever embody. Cnut enters the sea, he lets the waters wet him, he evinces the boundary and the limit between land and sea, between law and commons, rule and justice. The principal point may well be a certain priority of justice over law, of commonality over division, but the image is of their proximity, of the point at which in fluid and changeable form they meet.

To go to sea, you need both a machine and desire. You have to want more figs. And you have to take your chances, which is to say that you have to submit to the justice

[59] B Chasseneuz, *Catologus gloriæ mundi* (Valgrissi 1572) 183.

[60] Taverner (n 54) 68v.

**Figure 9.1** King Canute by James Smith courtesy of P. Goodrich

of fate, to the course of the waves, to the being of the oceanic. That is what Cnut endeavoured to evince and that is what Selden covertly relays in repeating the story. The moment of proximity, of the body meeting the waves, of the sovereign losing his power, of being confronting the beingness of the oceanic is the liminal instance and litoral space where law merges with justice, where norm fuses with and succumbs to an affect and affinity that is greater even than Cnut the Great. The image shows his submission to the waters, to feeling, to a proximity that cannot be controlled. And as his subjects carry him back, himself subjectified, I like to imagine that he is a little less of a lawgiver and a little more of a philosopher, less distant and more in common. He has listened to the sea, it still rolls past his ears, and he has shown that there are things that the sovereign cannot control, elements that command the king, and being beyond beings. It is a hermeneutic and humanistic lesson that there are laws of the land but they are not everything, and indeed they are not much. And, last neologism, final *aquatopic* sentiment, a maxim for future consideration, salient to both Grotius and Selden, *in mare veritas*.

# 10

# A Universal Rule of Law for a Pluralist World Order

## Leibniz's Universal Jurisprudence and His Praise of the Chinese Ruler

*Janne Nijman*

Arbitrary power is what is directly opposed to the empire of reason.[1]

Qu'on soit Européen, Chinois, mondain en somme,
La magnanimité n'y regarde que l'homme.[2]

## 1. Preface

Beyond doubt, Leibniz is most famous as the professor of 'metaphysico-theologo-cosmolonigology', Master Doctor Pangloss, in Voltaire's satire *Candide, ou l'optimisme* (1759). In *Candide*, he is ridiculed for his proposition that 'men are born to assist one another' and that 'all is for the best in the best of all possible worlds'.[3] Centuries later, Leibniz appears again in a work of fiction. In Chan Koonchung's science fiction novel, *The Fat Years—China 2013* (2009), party official He Dongsheng recalls Leibniz when he defends the political establishment to which he belongs: '[Leibniz] proposed that, although the world is indeed not perfect, a better world is an impossibility because God had created the best possible world he could. If God can't even do it, how can China?'[4] In this novel, China moves from a Hobbesian period of violent anarchy, fear, and distrust to a Leibnizian order of unity and social harmony thanks to xtc-infused drinking water which brings out man's Leibnizian—'loving and compassionate'—nature.

[1] GW Leibniz, 'Letters to Thomas Burnett' in P Riley (ed), *Leibniz Political Writings*, Cambridge Texts in the History of Political Thought (2nd edn, CUP 1988) 193 (hereafter: LPW).

[2] Leibniz in a 'Letter to Mlle De Scudery' (1697) in Acad Ed I, 14, 752.

[3] Voltaire, *Candide, ou l'optimisme* (1759).

[4] Ch Koonchung, *The Fat Years* (Black Swan edn 2012) 281.

*A Universal Rule of Law for a Pluralist World Order: Leibniz's Universal Jurisprudence and His Praise of the Chinese Ruler*. Janne Nijman.  Published 2018 by Oxford University Press.

Leibniz would have difficulty accepting both Voltaire's and Koonchung's characterization. For Leibniz, the issue at stake was '[Europe] slipping ... into ever greater corruption'.[5] His proposed cure was not xtc, but self-cultivation or self-perfection of rulers and ruled. Corruption, or rather any arbitrary use of power, needed to be fought. Leibniz was committed to the idea of a rule of natural law that governed sovereign powers and he argued that (the newly emerging) European rulers should learn from Chinese moral and political philosophy and from the Chinese emperor, who was the more successful in being the moral and responsible political ruler the law required.

## 2. Introduction

Leibniz studies is not only marked by Voltaire's depreciatory caricature of the eternal optimist. With *A Critical Exposition of the Philosophy of Leibniz* (1900), Bertrand Russell established a rather negative image of Leibniz and his philosophy. To be sure, Russell admired the latter's 'philosophical excellence' in logic and the realm of mathematics, but he rejected Leibniz's moral and political philosophy. Russel's study is scattered with *ad hominem* statements that mean to argue that Leibniz's personality—his need of 'fame and money' and the 'admiration of Princes and (even more) of Princesses'—prevented him from presenting publicly the 'shocking' ideas he held privately and from bequeathing us his philosophy as one coherent and consistent whole neatly put down in a magnum opus.[6] This accusation of dishonesty and lack of intellectual courage returns in Russell's treatment of Leibniz's ethics:[7] '[Leibniz] preferred to support Sin and Hell, and to remain, in what concerned the Church, the champion of ignorance and obscurantism'.[8] A year after the publication of his own book, Russell saw his reading of Leibniz confirmed by Louis Couturat's *La Logique de Leibniz* (1901).[9] Together they influenced the perception of Leibniz decisively for most of the twentieth century.

Nicholas Rescher, however, came to a different—essentially opposite—conclusion at the end of *The Philosophy of Leibniz* (1967). Leibniz may have been eager to persuade and influence, but rather than attributing this to ambition and vanity, Rescher relates it to the political and religious context in which Leibniz worked. He refers to Leibniz's ultimate agenda of

> healing the theological strifes and political discords in Europe of his day. Had fame been his prime goal he would have written more books and fewer letters [ ... ] [T]he aspirations which actuated him were, in the main, not those of selfishness but of public spirit.[10]

[5] GW Leibniz, 'Novissima Sinica' in *Writings on China*, translated, with an introduction, notes, and commentaries by DJ Cook and H RosemontJr (Open Court 1994) §10 (hereafter: NS).

[6] B Russell, *A Critical Exposition of the Philosophy of Leibniz* (2nd edn 1937, CUP 1900) vi, 2–3.

[7] ibid 199, 196. [8] ibid 202.

[9] L Couturat, *La Logique de Leibniz. D'après des documents inédits* (Georg Olms Verlagsbuchhandlung 1961).

[10] N Rescher, *The Philosophy of Leibniz* (Prentice-Hall 1967) 160.

With her highly praised intellectual biography of Leibniz, Maria Rosa Antognazza has now provided a new standard account of Leibniz's intellectual development.[11] She convincingly rejects the 'reductionistic interpretations' of Leibniz's work, among which those advanced by Russell and Couturat. Building on decades of scholarly recontextualization of Leibniz's work, Antognazza presents an alternative interpretation which takes into account both work and life. Ultimately, this was a philosopher

> who, more than anything else, wanted to *do* certain things. If he perceived that some of his most striking philosophical views would have bred disagreement and misunderstanding rather than contributing to his main objectives, he preferred to keep them to himself.[12]

I concur with Antognazza, Rescher, and others that Leibniz's thought, including his legal thought, cannot be understood separately from the political and religious context in which he lived.[13] As the last great advocate of the universal normative structures of the Holy Roman Empire (HRE), he sought certainty, security, and stability in Europe—necessary conditions for improving human lives. As Antognazza shows, all Leibniz's activities centre around this final aim, it shapes his reconciliatory ideas and actions into an 'all-embracing synthetic project'. It is this vision that gives unity to his thought.[14]

Neither Rescher nor Russell nor Couturat took Leibniz's work on China into account. In Needman's second volume of *Science and Civilisation in China* (1956), it is suggested that it 'would [ ... ] be worth examining whether something of that originality which enabled him to make contributions radically new to European thought was Chinese in inspiration?'.[15] More recently, Cook and Rosemont have refuted Needham's claim that Chinese thought would have directly inspired Leibniz's metaphysics:

> [n]evertheless, in finding views approximating his own in a culture 3,000 years and 8,000 miles distant from him, Leibniz could not but be interested in, stimulated by, and sympathetic to early Chinese thought as he had come to understand it.[16]

Drawing on Cook and Rosemont, Franklin Perkins, and Hans Poser, Antognazza takes Leibniz's interest in China and its civilization serious as part of his international and multicultural outlook on the world:

[11] MR Antognazza, *Leibniz: An Intellectual Biography* (CUP 2009). I leave the rather fundamental discussion on whether Leibniz engaged so actively in cultural exchange 'in spite of his philosophical system [or] because of it' aside here. See F Perkins, *Leibniz and China: A Commerce of Light* (CUP 2004) ch 2, 45–107.

[12] Antognazza (n 11) 4–5.

[13] JE Nijman, *The Concept of International Legal Personality: An Inquiry into the History and Theory of International Law* (T.M.C. Asser Press 2004) ch 2.

[14] Antognazza (n 11) 8, 9–10.

[15] J Needham, *Science and Civilisation in China*, vol II (1956) 291–92.

[16] Introduction to Leibniz *Writings on China* (n 5) 2–3; D Mungello, 'How Central to Leibniz's Philosophy Was China?' in W Li and H Poser (eds), *Das Neueste über China. G.W. Leibnizens* Novissima Sinica *von 1697* (Franz Steiner Verlag 2000) 57–67.

> Leibniz's 'Preface' to the *Novissima Sinica* was a hymn to a multiculturalism in which the international community learns and profits from the treasures of different cultures—a view which placed him at the forefront of a non-Eurocentric interest in other civilisations [ . . . ] Leibniz's multiculturalism was yet another manifestation of his outlook on reality as an ordered system ultimately governed by a universal harmony in which diversity was not to be feared or denied but celebrated as richness and fecundity.[17]

Leibniz's quest for universal harmony underlying (religious and cultural) diversity made him exceptionally well disposed to study and appreciate Chinese philosophy and politics as a particular variation of human universality.[18] Philosophical, scientific, cultural, and natural theological exchange would advance humanity at large. Leibniz's (legal and political) philosophy aimed to know and serve God without claiming that God was European.

This chapter argues that Leibniz's work confronts the legal–political crisis in Europe with the ideal of a rule of universal law and justice and setting the Chinese emperor as an example of a just ruler. For Leibniz, this ideal naturally included the world beyond the European continent and surely the Chinese Empire—equal to Europe in 'human cultivation and refinement'.[19] The next section thus deals briefly with the practical political and intellectual context within which Leibniz worked and developed an interest in China. Section 3 deals with Leibniz's 'universal jurisprudence',[20] his theory of law and justice that spans all societies, including the natural society of God and humanity. It shows moreover how much Leibniz's legal philosophy is embedded in his ideas of metaphysics and natural or rational theology. Section 4 connects Leibniz's Christian-bred yet universal agenda of law and governance with his interest in China and Chinese moral and political philosophy. His universal jurisprudence accommodates European and non-European culture, thought, and normativity by conceiving of the two civilizations as different expressions of a deeper structure of 'pre-established' harmony. Leibniz's conception of a universal rule of law and justice and the knowledge of China (as handed on to him by mainly Jesuit missionaries) brought him to perceive the contemporary Chinese ruler and his politics as more evolved than his counterparts in Europe. Leibniz thought European rulers should learn from the wisdom of Emperor Kangxi, whose enlightened, tolerant, and respectful spirit seemed to enable him to avoid war and to settle disputes peacefully, and also from the (ancient) knowledge of natural theology and natural law preserved in Chinese thought as such.[21] Section 5 links up the idea of universal rule of law in the work of Leibniz with the present book's overall argument on the enduring existence of a strand of thought on international law and

[17] Antognazza (n 11) 360.

[18] Leibniz's student Wolff had a similar interest in China. His lecture on Chinese philosophy and the sympathy expressed therein was received badly. He fled Halle. R Tuck, *The Rights of War and Peace: Political Thought and the International Order from Grotius to Kant* (OUP 1999) 191. Kanamori 'Christian Wolff's Speech on Confucianism: Confucius Compared with Wolff' (1997) 4 European Journal of Law and Economics 299–304.

[19] NS §1.

[20] See eg GW Leibniz 'Opinion on the Principles of Pufendorf' (1706) LPW 69 (hereafter: Opinion).

[21] Antognazza (n 11) 360.

politics alternative to the Hobbesian outlook on world society in terms of anarchy, war, and lawlessness.

## 3. A Legal and Political Adviser with a Universal Yet Multicultural Outlook

Gottfried Wilhelm Leibniz was born in Leipzig on 1 July 1646. Leipzig was one of the main cities of conservative Saxony, the Electorate where Luther and the Lutheran Reformation were born. The Electorate supported both. Leibniz grew up Lutheran in the aftermath of the Thirty Years War under the constellation of the Westphalian Treaties (1648), which first and foremost had been meant to end (religious) conflicts within the HRE. He studied philosophy and law at the university of Leipzig and Jena from 1661 to 1663. In 1663, he defended his philosophy thesis 'Metaphysical Disputation on the Principle of Individuation' in Leipzig. In 1666, Leibniz received his doctorate in law from Altdorf University by defending a dissertation entitled '*Disputatio de casibus perplexis in jure*' which connected philosophy and law. 'Hard cases', he argued, should be resolved by drawing on the principles of natural law and justice and the law of nations.[22] His thorough formal education together with independent reading from an early age onwards in the library of his father, a professor of moral philosophy, laid the basis for his distinctive vision:

> By the time he had completed his formal education, Leibniz's vision had been born. He had decided what to do with his life. Born into a fragmented world lacerated by religious, political, and intellectual crisis, 'Wilhelmus Pacidius', alias Gottfried Wilhelm Leibniz, was going to put the pieces together to achieve a universal synthesis for the glory of God and the happiness of mankind. This synthesis would be designed to restore unity in multiplicity, unveiling the universal harmony which despite apparently unbridgeable divisions, governed reality at both the metaphysical and epistemological level.[23]

Hence her conclusion that Leibniz—one of the last *Universalgenies*—was first and foremost 'a philosopher of the Holy Roman Empire'.[24] He argued for the reconciliation of Christendom and defended the reunification of the HRE. In defence of his ecumenical agenda, the religious humanist Leibniz drew on both Erasmus and Grotius.[25]

That said, Leibniz was far from Euro-myopic. His ecumenism meant to transcend both Western and non-Western thought and beliefs.[26] Early on he developed a keen interest in China. Leibniz grew up in a world in which Europeans travelled overseas frequently, developed intensive trade relations across the globe, and had numerous encounters with non-European—non-Christian—people. Cultural diversity was an issue in European philosophy of the time.

[22] ibid 65–66. On the German humanist legal tradition, see Chapter 2 in this volume.

[23] Antognazza (n 11) 66–67.

[24] ibid 9–10; Nijman (n 13).

[25] See eg for Erasmus, P Riley, *Leibniz' Universal Jurisprudence: Justice as the Charity of the Wise* (Harvard University Press 1996) 132; for references to Grotius, see hereafter section 4.

[26] See eg D Mungello, *Leibniz and Confucianism: The Search for Accord* (University Press of Hawaii 1977).

In his early twenties, Leibniz compared Chinese and European medicine ('theirs is better than ours')[27] and referred to the Chinese language in his *Dissertatio de arte combinatoria*—a first step in his quest for a universal language (the *characteristica universalis* or 'universal system of characters').[28] Whether his interest in China was kindled by the commercial interest of Europeans in Chinese goods, Chinese philosophy, or their mathematics and graphic language, the fact is that before long his interest was profound, incessant, and all-inclusive. Never, however, did he develop an argument to colonize China nor did the Duke of Braunschweig-Lüneburg-Hannover, whom Leibniz served from 1676 until his death in 1716 have ambitions in that direction.

Although Leibniz travelled a lot within Europe—the Duke of Hannover actually complained about it—he never visited China. All he knew about China he learned from his mostly Jesuit correspondents[29] and from his reading of all significant sources on China available in Europe at the time.[30] Hence, Leibniz learned about China through a Jesuit lens. The Jesuit missionaries were held in high esteem for their scientific knowledge (in matters such as astronomy, hydraulics, logic, and mathematics) and were accepted in the high circles of Confucian *literati* and at the Kangxi Court.[31] From 1689 onwards, Leibniz corresponds with Jesuit Claudio Filippo Grimaldi (1638–1712) whom he had met that year in Rome. Upon Grimaldi's return to Beijing, where he was president to the Mathematical Tribunal, Leibniz started to write to him to inquire about numerous issues, most notably the Chinese language and Fuxi's *Yi Jing* (Book of Changes) in which Leibniz thought to find a confirmation of his binary numeral system.[32] For Leibniz, the *Yi Jing* thus gave credibility to ancient Chinese thought in general.[33] The *Yi Jing* supported (or so he thought) his quest for a formal or mathematical universal language through which all peoples of the world, irrespective of their religion or culture, would be able to communicate and '*reason* together' and thus to understand each other truly.[34]

Both Grimaldi, who was profoundly influenced by the founder of the Jesuit mission in Beijing, Matteo Ricci (1552–1610), and Flemish astronomer Ferdinand Verbiest (1623–88), another of Leibniz's correspondents, were influential advisers to Emperor Kangxi. Joachim Bouvet (1656–1730), a French mathematician, well versed in Chinese and Manchu, studied the Confucian classics and tutored

[27] Cited in Cook and Rosemont (n 5) 11.

[28] Perkins (n 11) 109; China is mentioned in Leibniz work as early as 1668. By 1679 he had a clear interest in the Chinese language (Cook and Rosemont (n 5) 11; Leibniz (n 5) 11).

[29] Leibniz's correspondence on China is vast. See Rita Widmaier, *Leibniz korrespondiert mit China. Der Briefwechsel mit den Jesuitenmissionaren* (1689–1714).

[30] Perkins (n 11) 108.

[31] ibid 15: 'The Jesuit missionaries associated primarily with the class of Confucian scholar officials, the *ru*, or '"literati", and these served as their main source on Chinese thought.'

[32] Antognazza (n 11) 302, 358.

[33] See eg *Remarks* §9: Sage king Fuxi 'had understood the origin of things from unity and nothing, i.e. his mysterious figures reveal something of an analogy to Creation, containing the binary arithmetic (and yet hinting at greater things) that I rediscovered after so many thousands of years, where all numbers are written by only two notations, 0 and 1' (Mungello (n 26) 72–75).

[34] S Toulmin, *Cosmopolis: The Hidden Agenda of Modernity* (University of Chicago Press 1990) 101.

Emperor Kangxi's children. The Jesuits travelled all over China. The books they sent to Leibniz and the intellectual exchanges they engaged in with Leibniz enabled the latter to study China and to publish on China.

Leibniz's *Praefatio*[35] to the collection of papers *Novissima Sinica* ('Recent News from China', 1697/99) shows a great appreciation of Chinese philosophy, ethics, and politics. As early as 1672, he read Confucius in a translation by the Jesuit Prospero Intercetta. His understanding of Confucianism and Neo-Confucianism became equally 'Jesuit'.[36] Leibniz admired Matteo Ricci and his take on how Christianity could relate to Confucianism.[37] This is not the place to go deeply into the Rites and Terms Controversies, the debate about the religious nature of Confucianism and the compatibility of Confucian rites and practices with Christianity. Since it was 'one of the leading intellectual debates in Europe during Leibniz's lifetime',[38] it is relevant to note here that Leibniz did intervene in the debates—hence his writings on China—and that he followed the position of most Jesuits, that is to accommodate Confucian Rites as well as Terms (assuming that the terms *tian* and *Shang Di* found in the early Chinese classics indicate that Chinese held a conception of God).[39] An interpretation most respectful to the Chinese, yet also most favourable to the latter's gradual acceptance of Christianity. The so-called accommodationist approach best suited Leibniz's own outlook on the diversity of the universe and his ecumenical agenda. '[F]or the Jesuits entering China', 'natural theology became the guiding approach'.[40] Leibniz subscribed to the Jesuit attacks on a Eurocentric understanding of religion and to their view of 'China as a part of God's plan for salvation'. The Jesuits upheld that in fact '[t]he Chinese have preserved knowledge of the true God from more than two thousand years before the birth of Jesus Christ'.[41] Leibniz held that both European and Chinese culture incorporate traditions of natural theology:

> [w]hat we call the light of reason in man, they call commandment and law of Heaven. What we call the inner satisfaction of obeying justice and our fear of acting contrary to it, all this is called by the Chinese (and by us as well) inspirations sent by the Xangti (that is, by the true God).[42]

Through the lens of rationality or natural reason, the traditions of the East and West could meet and develop mutual understanding. The exchange of experiences and

[35] A translation of the preface is included in Cook and Rosemont (n 5) 45–59; Leibniz (n 5).

[36] Perkins (n 11) 13.

[37] eg *Discourse on the Natural Theology of the Chinese* (1716) in Cook and Rosemont (n 5) 75–76; Leibniz (n 5). Hereafter *Discourse on NTC*.

[38] Perkins (n 11) 26, 31. To be sure, it was a debate within the Roman Catholic Church.

[39] ibid 26–29. See eg *On the Civil Cult of Confucius* (1700/01), in Cook and Rosemont Jr, or Leibniz (both n 5) 61–65; *Remarks on Chinese Rites and Religion* (1708), Cook and Rosemont (n 5) 67–74, 70: 'their customs should not be judged by ours'; Leibniz (n 5).

[40] Perkins (n 11) 4–5.

[41] Cited ibid (n 11) 30. They link up Chinese ancient tradition of wisdom with the (ancient) Jewish wisdom tradition. For all kinds of creative solutions to establish this link, see ibid 25.

[42] *Discourse on NTC* §31. For Leibniz, reason was not subordinate to revelation. Leibniz's praise of Grotius's natural theology concerned the latter's argument of the inverse. Grotius coordinated the authority of the revelation of the Bible and the authority of the *ratio* such that the former was subordinated to the latter. AH Haentjes, *Hugo de Groot als godsdienstig denker* (Ploegsma 1946) 27.

knowledge about the shared world would 'bring [humanity] together' and purports to moral convergence too.[43]

I leave aside the discussion on whether Leibniz engaged so actively in cultural exchange 'in spite of his philosophical system [or] because of it'.[44] It suffices to recall that, contrary to contemporary rationalists such as Descartes and Spinoza, who valued and trusted (the universality of) reason to an extent that they considered the study of cultures irrelevant for finding truth, Leibniz valued the study of different cultures and religions, that were for him different applications of the universal capacity of reason. Like Montaigne, Leibniz discerns in the study of cultural diversity also a possibility of *European self-criticism*. Unlike Montaigne, however, Leibniz did not derive a sceptic attitude from the study of human diversity (the differences in cultural, moral, and religious views). Nor did he come to accept, like Locke did, that cultural diversity points to the absence of universal innate principles and ideas and thus to the impossibility of universal consent on truth (or God).[45] Locke and Leibniz did agree however on toleration, (Christian) ideas should not be forced on other cultures.[46]

For Leibniz, in conclusion, a foreign culture or religion was not to be excluded, ignored, or depreciated, but studied and valued as yet another individuation of the same universal. As such, it offered a perspective through which one could study and criticize oneself.[47] Leibniz's metaphysics, the so-called *Monadology*, provided him with an epistemic framework for appreciating and engaging in cultural exchange: '*all individual created substances are different expressions of the same universe* and different expressions of the same universal cause, namely God'.[48] This outlook on order and diversity—'harmony as a maximization of order and diversity'[49]—made Leibniz less susceptible to forces of Eurocentrism, racism, and colonialism. Rather, Leibniz's unique pluralist outlook enabled him to criticize Europe and most notably its rulers on the basis of Chinese moral and political philosophy and practice.[50] Cultural diversity then constituted a source of humanity's potential for *perfection*. Leibniz's interest in China and everything Chinese thus was not driven by a drive for military or harsh commercial expansion, but by a vision of universal enlightenment; and to that end exchange of knowledge and science was essential. On 2 December 1697, Leibniz wrote to the Jesuit missionary Antoine Verjus about the China–European encounter:

> I judge that this mission is *the greatest affair of our time*, as much for the glory of God and the propagation of the Christian religion as for the general good of men and the growth of the arts and sciences, among us as well as among the Chinese. For this is *a commerce of light*, which could give to us at once their work of thousands of years and render ours to them, and

[43] Perkins (n 11). [44] See eg ibid ch 2, 45–107. [45] ibid 12, 38, 32–42.
[46] ibid 41–42. [47] ibid 46; see section 5.
[48] GW Leibniz, 'Primary Truths (1689)' in R Ariew and D Garber (tr) (eds), *Philosophical Essays* (Hackett 1989) 33 emphasis in original; *Monadology* §§56–60 in GW Leibniz, *Discourse on Metaphysics and the Monadology* GR Montgomery (tr) (Prometheus Books 1992), hereafter: *Discourse on Metaphysics* and *Monadology*.
[49] Perkins (n 11) 48. [50] eg NS §§10 and 17.

double so to speak our true wealth for one and the other. This is something greater than one imagines.[51]

## 4. Leibniz's Universal Jurisprudence: a Universal Rule of Law and Justice

While the old European political and legal order fell prey to fragmentation, Leibniz as an adviser on legal and political issues became heavily involved in the German imperial and international (be it mostly intra-European) politics of his days. Elsewhere, I have argued that it is his confrontation with the religious, legal–political context that explains Leibniz's introduction of two important legal concepts—relative sovereignty and international legal personality.[52] Both concepts were necessary to bind all European powers—old and new, major and minor—to the law of nations and nature (*ius gentium et naturae*).

In the *Praefatio* to the *Codex Iuris Gentium Diplomaticus* (1693) Leibniz builds on a rather original argument on relative sovereignty which he posited in *De Suprematu Principum Germaniae* or *Caesarinus Fürstenerius* ('Prince-as-Emperor') (1677);[53] he complements this with the more technical, legal notion of international legal personality (*persona iuris gentium*) that institutes the subjection of all relatively sovereign rulers (bearers of *ius suprematus*) to the law of nature and nations.[54] In 1693, more than in 1677, Leibniz accepts the development of modern, independent sovereign States (the so-called Westphalian order). Consequently, what he is *doing* in the *Praefatio* of the *Codex* with the introduction of *persona juris gentium* is to mitigate the legal and political crisis of his time: to prevent arbitrary and unjust use of power by a reconstruction of the legal *constraint* of sovereigns.[55]

Here, I would like to point to the power of the underlying ideal. Arguably, Leibniz foresaw the implications of the political order following the Westphalian Peace in conjunction with a Hobbesian or Pufendorfian outlook on sovereignty; that is, the

[51] Translation by Franklin Perkins, cited in Antognazza (n 11) 378, fn 198 (emphasis added); *Novissima Sinica* §§22, 59.

[52] Nijman (n 13) ch 2; H Steiger 'Supremat—Außenpolitik und Völkerrecht bei Leibniz' in F Beiderbeck, I Dingel, and W Li (eds), *Umwelt Und Weltgestaltung: Leibniz' Politisches Denken in Seiner Zeit* (Vandenhoeck & Ruprecht 2015) 135–206.

[53] In *Caesarinus Fürstenerius*, Leibniz explains that he values the imperial, constitutional legal structures of the HRE: '*to constrain, by a greater authority, those turbulent men* who, without regard of what is permitted and what is not, are disposed to sacrifice the blood of the innocent to their particular ambition, and often push [them] into criminal actions: *to constrain them*, by the authority which I believe resides somehow in the universal Church, and in the Holy Empire, and in its two heads, the Emperor and a legitimate Pope, using his power legitimately' (LPW 112, emphasis added).

[54] LPW 175.

[55] *Portrait of the Prince* (1679), LPW 98: 'sovereigns and peoples must be restrained by respect for the laws, and since the peace of States with neighbours is ordinarily maintained by the motive of mutual fear, it is necessary that princes rule equally by [justice] and by laws, like Your Most Serene Highness, who has so much solicitude for justice that he wishes that it be rendered without exception of persons and without drawing a distinction between subjects and foreigners'.

absence of a body of law ruling the many sovereign powers. This chapter claims that for Leibniz, being a trained and practising lawyer, the question was: how to preserve a universal rule of law in this newly emerging society of sovereign States? His introduction of both *ius suprematus* and *persona iuris gentium* results from a lawyerly sensibility to the proverbial 'horizontal' structure of the post-Westphalian international society. Both conceptions serve to ensure that all exercise of power, internal as well as external, is constrained and guided by (natural) law and justice. Leibniz was driven by the ideal of a world governed by a universal rule of natural law and justice.[56]

Leibniz developed this ideal as an integral part of his 'universal jurisprudence', an all-embracing philosophy of universal law and justice. It unites theology, moral–political philosophy and even a metaphysical perspective on the natural world into a jurisprudence for humanity. As such, it exceeds the scope of this chapter. Here focus is on three elements: (1) Leibniz follows Hugo Grotius—rather than Thomas Hobbes—and defends natural law and justice as true *law*, applicable within the state of nature, and thus binding on sovereign rulers and States; (2) natural law and justice concern also the *inner* life of human beings; (3) Leibniz's universal jurisprudence has implications for sovereign rulers and States around the world.

First, Leibniz's universal jurisprudence is a theory of law and justice common to God and humans (or, rather, to all rational substances).[57] Put differently, it is a cosmological theory of law: 'Leibniz's legal thought emerges from his all-encompassing understanding of law (*ius*) as the right and rational order of the world. *Ius* is not simply humanly made law (*lex*); on the contrary, *ius* embraces the entirety of divine and human relations.'[58] His writings moreover deal extensively with the relationship between *lex* and *ius*, as already found in his dissertation.[59] From the *Praefatio* to the *Codex Juris Gentium*, which deliberately includes in its title *iuris gentium* and not, for example, *iuris inter gentes*,[60] we learn about Leibniz's cautious view on the positive law of nations—'rulers play cards in private life and with treaties in public affairs'—[61] and its relation with natural law. Putting positive international law in perspective, Leibniz conveys that a purely legal–positivistic approach to international relations does not suffice. His ultimate objective in the *Praefatio* to the *Codex* is to enhance the understanding of the law of nations and its relation with natural law.[62] He argues that a law of nations based solely on the sovereign will of the powerful is unlikely to establish peace, to advance the common good, and to promote universal justice. To reach these goals, a universal legal order that guides and constrains the sovereign rulers in exercising their wills justly is required: that is, a 'true law of nature and of nations'.[63] The positive law of nations may 'chang[e] to time and place'.[64] What Indian or Chinese rulers voluntarily consent to be law in their regions may differ

[56] See (n 54).
[57] Introduction by Riley, LPW 2; *Opinion of the Principles of Pufendorf*; *Monadology*.
[58] R Berkowitz, *The Gift of Science: Leibniz and the Modern Legal Tradition* (Harvard UP 2005) 13.
[59] See text to (n 22). [60] *Codex* 170. [61] ibid 165–69. [62] ibid 170.
[63] ibid 165. [64] See citation in (n 54).

from the law of nations agreed to in Europe.[65] However, universal natural law and justice rules them all.

Thus, for Leibniz, the universal natural society was neither without justice nor without law. He refuted the legal–positivistic position of Hobbes and Pufendorf,[66] who argued that

> there is no obligation at all in the state of nature, and outside of government; for obligations by pacts having to form the right of government itself, according to the author of these principles [Hobbes], it is manifest that the obligation is anterior to the government which it must form.[67]

Leibniz forcefully rejected the Pufendorfian (and Hobbesian) doctrine that law and also justice have their 'efficient cause' in the command of a superior:

> [i]f we admit this, no one will do his duty spontaneously; also, there will be no duty when there is no superior to compel its observance; *nor will there be any duties for those who do not have a superior*. … to deny to the state of nature, that is [a condition] in which there are no superiors, all *binding justice* whatsoever … is a view to which I am astonished that anyone could have adhered.[68]

Here the astonishment points to a lawyer's 'rule of law' sensibility. Leibniz moreover points out that no 'voluntary law of nations' (or Hobbes's own 'social contract', for that matter) would be possible, since there would be no authority to render it valid and binding upon sovereigns.[69] For law to exist independent from the arbitrary will and command of a sovereign (God included) and thus to guide and constrain the sovereign will (for example, in the creation of just voluntary law (of nations) or in exercising executive power), its source or efficient cause has to lie outside the realm of the sovereign will and within rational nature.[70] Leibniz's universal jurisprudence thus reveals a 'rule of law' ideal for the inter-sovereign level of the post-Westphalian world.[71] Like Grotius,[72] Leibniz claimed that natural law and justice govern the

[65] *Codex* 174: '[in] the sphere of the voluntary law of nations, originating in the tacit consent of peoples. It is not necessary that this be the agreement of all peoples or of all times; for there have been many cases in which one thing was considered right in India and another in Europe'; see also ibid 175 and 170. For Chinese international legal relations, Leibniz focused on China's relations with Russia. He narrates how Chinese and Muscovite ambassadors negotiated a peace treaty through mediation of two Jesuit fathers—the Treaty of Nerchinsk (1689)—and included the treaty as well as excerpts of letters from these Jesuit mediators on the peace negotiations in *Novissima Sinica*. NS §§15, 54

[66] eg both the *Praefatio* to the *Codex* (1693) and *Opinion of the Principles of Pufendorf* (1706) hold a critique of the legal positivism of Hobbes and Pufendorf.

[67] Remarks on Shaftesbury's Characteristics (1712) LPW 196; see also Leibniz's reference to Hobbes's characterization of the relations of States and peoples in terms of 'perpetual war' (*Codex* 166).

[68] Opinion 70 (emphasis added).

[69] *Codex* 170.

[70] In his critique of Pufendorf and Hobbes, Leibniz concurs with Grotius's famous '*etiamsi daremus*' statement in the *Prolegomena* to *De jure belli ac pacis* (1625) that claims that natural law would exist even if God would not (eg Opinion 71).

[71] Opinion 70: 'Now, then, will he who is invested with supreme power do nothing against justice if he proceeds tyrannically against his subjects; who arbitrarily despoils his subjects, torments them, and kills them under torture; who makes war on others without cause?' Leibniz could not disagree more.

[72] JE Nijman, 'Images of Grotius, or the International Rule of Law beyond Historiographical Oscillation' 17(1) (2015) Journal of the History of International Law 83.

natural society in which sovereign rulers and States act and maintain relations. The ideal of a universal rule of natural law and justice can be said to define Leibniz's work:

> Arbitrary power is what is directly opposed to the empire of reason. But one must realize that this arbitrary power is found not only in kings, but also in assemblies. ... The remedy of a plurality of votes ... is not sufficient to curb these abuses. [ ... ] Thus one must think in this world of laws which can serve to restrain not only kings, but also the deputies of the people, and judges.[73]

And, thus, for the realization of the rule of natural law and justice: 'government [should] belon[g] to the wisest'.[74]

The second element of Leibniz's universal jurisprudence addressed here for its significance in the context of Leibniz's interest in Chinese political and philosophical thought, is the relation between natural law and justice and the human soul. The system of universal law and justice that God and humans share, included a moral and metaphysical anthropology; this was Leibniz's *Monadology* (1714), which centres on the (novel) concept of 'monad'. Monads are rational or spiritual substances which God (the Supreme Monad also called Supreme Intelligence or Reason) creates by transforming essence into existence, while conjoining it with matter or body in the process.[75] Monads are independent, unsplittable, and interconnected; they tend to the good and the just. Monads exist in degree; the highest monad (next to God and Angels) is the mind, soul, entelechy, or spirit that exists within humans as they are all created in *imago Dei*—'minds are ... images of the Deity himself'.[76] The human mind or soul—being created in the image of God, which is Supreme Reason/Understanding/Knowledge, Will, and Power[77]—possesses these faculties to a lesser degree. The human soul (monads as 'little gods') enables human beings to love God (or Supreme Reason) and know Divine Justice and Goodness. Being intelligent, free, wilful, and capable beings, humans are able to 'imitat[e] [ ... ] divine justice'.[78] With the *Monadology*, partly built on Christian *imago Dei* anthropology,[79] Leibniz provided a foundation for the moral personality and responsibility of human beings.

This goes to the central idea of Leibniz's universal jurisprudence that the 'efficient cause' of natural law and justice consists in rational nature: 'in us is the light of eternal reason, kindled in our minds by the divinity'.[80] Natural law and justice are not a product of divine or human will, but part of God's and humans' understanding of

[73] Excerpts from three Letters to Thomas Burnett (1699–1712) (n 1) 193.

[74] ibid 192.

[75] *Monadology* §62

[76] See eg ibid §83; *Discourse on Metaphysics* XXVIII, 47; Opinion 71;

[77] *Monadology* §§47–48.

[78] Opinion 72; Meditation on the Common Concept of Justice (*c.* 1702–03), LPW 57–58.

[79] *Monadology* §§28–29, 83–84; JE Nijman, 'Grotius's *Imago Dei* Anthropology: Grounding *Ius Naturae et Gentium*' in M Garcia-Salmones Rovira, MA Koskenniemi, and P Amorosa (eds), *International Law and Religion: Historical and Contemporary Perspectives* (OUP 2017); for the different anthropologies of Leibniz and Pufendorf, see I Hunter, 'The Love of a Sage or the Command of a Superior' in TJ Hochstrasser and P Schröder (eds), *Early Modern Natural Law Theories* (Springer 2003) 169–94, 174–78. Hunter explains how Pufendorf means to deny the *imago Dei*, moral or rational being in the individual while for Leibniz each individual is a metaphysical moral person, bearer of the *imago Dei*.

[80] Opinion 75.

eternal moral truths—'the precepts of right reason'. The intelligence of the highest monads involves the faculty of 'perception', which means humans have the capacity to know or love 'perfections'. As such, the human 'mind' or 'soul', with its innate knowledge of natural law and justice, enables humans to 'right reason[ing]' and, subsequently, to distinguish between good and bad, right and wrong. As moral action is a freely chosen action commanded by reason, much depends on the piety of the soul that commands reason and action. A pious soul loves God and means to imitate divine justice and goodness. Piety is in 'the habit of loving or willing the good. Love then signifies [ . . . ] converting the happiness of another into one's own'.[81] Leibniz explains piety as 'the disposition [ . . . ] to contribute to the public good [which is] the same thing [as to contribute to the glory of God'.[82] A pious soul cultivates probity and just actions.

So, while for Pufendorf natural law and jurisprudence relate only to 'external human actions', for Leibniz, natural jurisprudence 'concern[s] itself with what is internal'[83]—that is, with the human rational soul. His universal jurisprudence unites natural or rational religion and theology (ie not dependent on revelation) and natural law and jurisprudence within one and the same system (and 'science') that originates in right reason. A Christian humanist, indebted to Aristotle and the Scholastics, Leibniz conjoins natural law and natural religion to prescribe to *every* human person, subject and sovereign, the (moral and legal) *obligation to cultivate the piety of the soul*.[84]

As such, natural law and jurisprudence dictate a natural law responsibility to cultivate 'spiritual perfection' and to strengthen 'the inclination of [the] soul' to act justly. This is a bearing doctrine of Leibniz's universal natural jurisprudence, it unites spirituality and politics. While somewhat running ahead of things: it means that sovereign rulers bear the responsibility to maintain and cultivate their piety—ie wisdom—actively so as to realize justice and goodness on earth.

The third aspect of the universal jurisprudence discussed here concerns its implications for sovereign rulers. What does the theory of 'the perfect governance of all

[81] *Codex* 171. This refers to an issue Leibniz and Bossuet corresponded on: 'in what way disinterested love is possible, independent of hope, of fear, and of regard for any question of utility'. See also, Leibniz in a letter to Sophie (25 September 1708), L Strickland (tr and ed) *Leibniz and the Two Sophies: The Philosophical Correspondence* (Inter 2011) 356–94, 367 in which he reflects on the book *L'art de connoistre les hommes* (1702).

[82] Letters to Thomas Burnett (n 1), LPW 191; 'The True Piety (before 1710?)' in Lloyd Strickland, *The Shorter Leibniz Essays: A Collection of New Translations* (Continuum 2006) 164–65. Without God—without this characteristic of man to seek God by natural inclination—it is impossible to reconcile altruism with egoism. It is more convincing that man seeks God than that he is by nature inclined to aim for the happiness of others, as, after all, man is also a natural egoist, as Leibniz conceded. See also *Memoir for Enlightened Persons* (mid 1690s) LPW 105: 'to contribute to the glory of God, or (what is the same thing) to the common good'; *Codex* 171.

[83] Opinion 69: Leibniz states that 'nobody can deny that law, duty, sins in relation to God, and good actions are also naturally located in the interior, where—I ask them—shall we consider these topics, which certainly pertain to law and natural justice, if not in the science of natural law?'.

[84] See also Opinion 75. The natural legal obligations of piety rest on 'the immortality of the soul, and God as ruler of the universe' who awards and punishes upon judgement. In Leibniz's view, these are not so much Christian as universal concepts and doctrines established by rational or natural theology (eg LPW (n 1) 225–40). For treatment in relation to Chinese thought, see *Discourse on NTC* §65.

human relations through "wise charity" and "universal benevolence"[85] require from them? What does it mean to conduct international relations in accordance with the *ius naturae et gentium* that flows from natural justice?

Leibniz's conception of natural justice as '*caritas sapientis seu benevolentia universalis*'—ie 'charity which follows the dictates of wisdom' or 'universal benevolence'[86]—conjoins Platonic and Pauline Christian ethics.[87] According to Leibniz, God and humans share in reason and in the understanding of justice: justice consists in wisdom (which results from right reason) and goodness (which results from the free will guided by right reason towards willing the good) conjoined.[88] Wisely charitable acts are those that portion love rationally (or wisely) to the degree of Perfection:

> A good man is one who loves everybody, in so far reason permits. Justice, then, which is the virtue regulates that affection which the Greeks call φιλανθρωπία [philanthropy] will be most conveniently defined, if I am not in error, as the charity of the wise man, that is, charity which follows the dictates of wisdom [...] Charity is universal benevolence, and benevolence the habit of loving or of willing the good. Love then rejoices in the happiness of another.[89]

On this conception of justice, Leibniz grounds his theory of *ius naturae et gentium*. He derives three fundamental principles of natural law (*ius naturae*) from three degrees of justice: '*unde neminem laedere, suum cuique tribuere, honestè (vel popotius piè) vivere*' (ie to injure no one, to give each his due, and to live honestly or rather piously).[90] Strict law or right (*ius strictum*) applies to relations caused by injury or deprivation of possession, this means commutative justice rules. The natural law obligation to give each his due—including to actively 'prevent evil from happening'—is a relation of equity (or charity in a narrow sense). It is an obligation to do good as is fitting. This is determined by 'the rule of reason' or the golden rule.[91] It concerns distributive justice. The natural law principle of piety belongs to universal justice or wise charity in the wider sense of the term.[92] The duty to live piously supplements, or perfects, the previous obligations. To practise universal justice, ie to live piously and imitate divinity, whether as subject or sovereign, obliges to care for the O/other and to aid where necessary and possible.[93]

[85] P Riley, *Leibniz' Universal Jurisprudence: Justice as Charity of the Wise* (Harvard UP 1996) vii.

[86] *Codex* 171.

[87] *Leibniz' Universal Jurisprudence* (n 85) 4ff; P Riley, 'Leibniz's Political and Moral Philosophy in the Novissima Sinica, 1699–1999' (1999) 60 Journal of the History of Ideas 217.

[88] Meditation on the Common Concept of Justice (n 78) 50; Opinion 69: 'In the science of law ... it is best to derive human justice, as from a spring, from the divine, to make it complete. Surely the idea of the just, no less than that of the true and the good, relates to God, and above all to God, who is the measure of all things. And the rules which are common [to divine and human justice] certainly enter into the science [of natural law], and ought to be considered in a universal jurisprudence, whose precepts natural theology will use as well.'

[89] *Codex* 171.

[90] *Codex*, in M-L Babin and G van den Heuvel (eds), *Schriften und Briefe zur Geschichte. Bearbeitet, kommentiert und herausgegeben* (Hahnsche Buchhandlung 2004) 168.

[91] LPW 56.

[92] *Codex* 171–72.

[93] Meditation on the Common Concept of Justice (n78) 53–54, 57: contrary to Hobbes, Leibniz writes '*homo homini deus, homo homini lupis*'.

In the *Praefatio* to *Codex Juris Gentium*, Leibniz elaborated what the three fundamental principles mean for the law of nations and nature. The first principle is to prevent a *legal* claim, or *facultas* (Leibniz builds on Grotius's distinctions of right and his use of Roman law), from arising. It thus is the principle that aims to prevent at the international level (a right to) war. '[A] sovereign of a state has these [three aforementioned natural law] obligations', Leibniz argues, 'the first in relation to all the others in a given situation, and the second in relation to his subjects'.[94] The second principle puts forward the notion of aptitude (*aptitudo*).[95] It belongs to the realm of distributive justice, which concerns a legal but non-enforceable duty 'to do good to everyone; but only so far as befits each one or as much as he deserves; for it is impossible to favor everyone'. However, for those who rule it is not enough to avoid evil, they have 'to procure the good' and 'to improve people's condition'.[96] In Leibniz's view the duty to give each his due obliges a government to develop a system of redistribution. Such a scheme organized by law, would 'make it possible that those who had a merely moral claim acquire a legal claim; that is, that they become able to demand what is equitable for others to perform'.[97] The State thus provides citizens with a legal claim to what is reasonable to take from the public good. Unfortunately, Leibniz himself does not explore in the *Praefatio* the implications of the idea of (re) distribution of public goods within 'the common republic of Christian nations' or international society at large. The principle of natural law that flows from the third degree of justice as wise charity—to life piously or virtuously—is applicable to rulers as much as to their people. This means that sovereign rulers bear the responsibility to cultivate their piety, ie to enhance their rational capacity to imitate divine justice through their actions: they must know the perfections of justice and goodness, study it and meditate on it, and engage actively in the spiritual perfection of the self so that they act justly in both domestic and international affairs.

While *legality* (strict law) means to establish a peaceful, secure, and stable order, and *equity* aims to promote well-being, prosperity, and happiness in a society, *piety* means to lead a ruler to the morally most perfect course of action.[98] Leibniz's focus on piety and therewith on the virtuous inner life of the ruler is part and parcel of his thinking about international relations, international law, and justice. For Leibniz, the main question in international relations and international law is not merely 'what has been done', but 'in what spirit it has been done'.[99] A pious, virtuous sovereign is more likely to comply with the laws of right reason, to act with 'good intention', wisely and charitably, and to work for the common good of humanity.[100] The sovereign is obliged to perfect her spirit, 'whether through liberal education or a noble way of living, or the discipline of life or a sect'.[101] The wisest should govern, according to Leibniz, but rulers also have the obligation to *become* the wisest.

[94] Meditation on the Common Concept of Justice (n 78) 54 and 60–61. [95] *Codex* 172.
[96] Meditation on the Common Concept of Justice (n 78) 53–54. [97] *Codex* 172.
[98] *Discourse on Metaphysics* §13. [99] *Codex* 167.
[100] eg *Memoir for Enlightened Persons of Good Intention* (mid 1690s) LPW 103–10.
[101] *Codex* 173.

Conceived as such, the universal rule of *ius naturae et gentium* confronts the abusive,[102] impassioned, and arbitrary use of power which Leibniz saw widespread in Europe.[103] Rulers are to maintain and promote a just (domestic and world) order and contribute to the global common good—'to make the empire of reason flourish'.[104] As the servants of the universal rule of natural law and justice, they have to 'enlighten the[ir] understanding, [to] perfect the art of reasoning, that is, the method of judging and inventing which is that true logic that is the source of all objects of knowledge'.[105]

## 5. Leibniz's Engagement with China: on Good Government, Just Rule, and Self-Cultivation

Leibniz's study of Chinese moral and political philosophy and politics is an integral part of his universal jurisprudence. In his quest for universal harmony, Leibniz discerned a general correspondence and compatibility of ancient Chinese and Confucian thought with ancient European and Christian thought. This section discusses the three elements of the universal jurisprudence singled out in section 3 in reverse order and links them to elements of Chinese thought as understood by Leibniz. First, the recognition of emperor Kangxi as a living example of what the Universal Jurisprudence implies for sovereign rulers. Second, Leibniz understood Chinese moral and political thought to be founded on universal, natural reason and a conception of rational substances very similar to the moral and metaphysical anthropology of his monadology. Third, for Leibniz the Chinese and European peoples were different, but equal. The universal jurisprudence—with its rule of law conception—was valid for them both. To be sure, neither this section nor this chapter will examine whether Leibniz's understanding of (neo-)Confucianism was actually correct.[106] Leibniz himself was well aware that '[w]hat the ancient priests and philosophers of China thought [wa]s not easy to determine' and that in Europe too disputes about the precise meaning of ancient Greek and Roman philosophers often mount.[107] He decided not to judge 'their customs ... by ours' and to 'think well of the ancient doctrines'.[108] Rightly or wrongly,[109] however, Leibniz was convinced that Chinese thought and European thought were compatible as long as the 'scholastic prejudice' often used by (non-accommodationist) Europeans was set

[102] ibid 174–75: It is prohibited 'to abuse [their] property' and their office.

[103] See eg *Portrait of the Prince* (1679) LPW 85: 'princes must be above their subjects by their virtue, and by their natural qualities, as they are above them by the authority which the laws give them to reign according to natural law and civil law'. See also concerns expressed in the *Codex*.

[104] Letters to Thomas Burnett (n 1) 193.

[105] (n 100) 106.

[106] See eg Mungello (n 26) 13ff.

[107] *Remarks* §§4–5.

[108] ibid.

[109] Obviously, the knowledge of China and Chinese thought that was handed to Leibniz by his missionary friends and correspondents came 'through the filter of their own [European knowledge]' (Cook and Rosemont (n 5) 18).

aside while examining and interpreting the former,[110] and that communication and mutual understanding was possible.

First, Leibniz presented Kangxi Emperor as the personification of the ideal of the wise and charitable ruler the Universal Jurisprudence entailed. That is, the embodiment of the sage king in the best of both Chinese and Platonic–Christian traditions:[111] a true example for European rulers in both internal and external relations. Under his rule the Chinese were living in peace, while in Europe the peoples were scourged by (civil) war.[112] Leibniz considered the well-ordered, civilized, and respectful Chinese society to be the upshot of Kangxi's reign. This is an image that also emerged from the (mostly) Jesuit sources Leibniz studied[113] and it is one that Kangxi himself promoted.[114] Kangxi features prominently in the *Praefatio* to the *Novissima Sinica* (1697/99).[115] The 1699 edition includes Kangxi's portrait in its opening pages and excerpts from Bouvet's prepossessing description in *Portrait historique de l'Empereur de la Chine.*[116] Leibniz explained the high esteem in which the Chinese hold Kangxi in terms of his wisdom, virtuousness, and his respect for the laws:

> Who indeed does not marvel at the monarch of such an empire? His grandeur almost exceeds human stature, and he is held by some to be a mortal god. His very nod is obeyed. Yet *he is educated according to custom in virtue and wisdom* and *rules his subjects with an extraordinary respect for the laws* and with reverence for the advice of wise men. Endowed with such eminence he seems fit indeed to judge.[117]

Leibniz recalls Father Grimaldi praising 'the virtue and wisdom of this prince', 'his love of justice', 'his charity to the populace, his moderate manner of living', and 'his marvellous desire for knowledge'.[118] Leibniz emphasizes moreover that the emperor's reputation as 'a very accurate judge' in the Mandarin civil service examination system that tests knowledge of the Confucian classics reinforces his 'authority'.[119]

For Leibniz's own assessment Kangxi's passion for scientific knowledge and reasoning—mathematics and geometry, in particular—is crucial.[120] Leibniz upholds the Platonic insight that geometry belongs to 'the sphere of [ . . . ] philosophers' and provides an entrance to what is true and wise: 'for, since virtue flows from wisdom, and the spirit of wisdom is truth, those who thoroughly investigate the

110 *Discourse on NTC* §39; on accommodationist position in Rites and Texts Controversies, see text to (n 40); see Mungello on Leibniz understanding of the correspondences between Western and Chinese philosophy (n 26) 116–17 and book in general.

111 NS §§7–9; see eg Riley (n 87).

112 In 1689, for example, Kangxi had managed to solve the controversies with the Muscovites diplomatically, with the assistance of Jesuit Missionaries, and thus to avoid war with Russia. See also (n 65).

113 NS §§7–9; see also section 3.

114 JD Spence, 'The K'ang-His Reign' in *The Cambridge History of China Volume 9, Part 1: The Ch'ing Empire to 1800* (CUP 2002) 157.

115 See also *Discourse on NTC* in Cook and Rosemont (n 5) 75–138.

116 'Introduction' Cook and Rosemont (n 5) 16; NS §§6–7.

117 NS §6 (emphasis added); NS §§7–9: characterizations such as 'a prince of almost unparalleled merit' and 'the highest erudition'.

118 ibid §§8, 49.

119 ibid §7.

120 Riley (n 87).

demonstrations of geometers have perceived the nature of eternal truth, and are able to tell the certain from the uncertain'.[121]

Leibniz ascribes Kangxi's 'superior judgement' to his knowledge of both Chinese and European arts and sciences.[122] Leibniz thus builds his case of Kangxi as a wisely charitable ruler in Platonic–Christian terms, an emperor who ruled in accordance with the laws of Heaven (that is, the laws of rational nature) and who could teach Europeans about good and just government.[123]

An important case in point was, in Leibniz's view, Kangxi's Edict of Toleration of 1692, that is, seven years after the revocation of the Edict of Nantes. European knowledge of geometry gave credibility to European thought more generally to an emperor fascinated by the sciences: 'he easily came to believe that those who had learned thus to reason might teach correctly in other things [ie Christian beliefs]'.[124] Leibniz nonetheless calls for caution and Christian prudence in their work.[125] The Edict 'sanctioned the Christian faith by public law' and 'permitted' its practice in China. As such, Leibniz includes it in the *Novissima Sinica*. Leibniz seems to suggest that the 'wisely charitable' approach Kangxi takes to the Christians in his country is mandated (unsurprisingly) by universal natural law since the 'emperor consulted the "will of heaven"' before he adopted the Edict.[126] The reference reads to suggest that the Edict is sanctioned by Heaven or, in Leibniz's terms, the eternal precepts of (rational) nature. Kangxi thus ruled in accordance with Heaven and stood in a long Chinese tradition of political and moral thought: 'the Monarch [Kangxi emperor] ... is the leader of all sages and the living embodiment of the law, [he] appears to reveal rational expressions of ancient doctrines'.[127]

Leibniz's recognition of Kangxi as an exemplar of the wise and charitable ruler propagated in his universal jurisprudence was reinforced by his study of Chinese ancient and Confucian moral and political theory. Leibniz felt Kangxi's practice of good and just government to be the upshot of a tradition dating back to the Sage Kings of Chinese antiquity (twenty-ninth–twelfth century BC),[128] who are discussed

[121] NS §9; Opinion. [122] NS §7.

[123] ibid §§7–8. See also Riley's comment that Leibniz recognizes in Kangxi the qualities he emphasizes in *Lettre sur l'éducation l'un prince*, Riley (n 87) (final page).

[124] NS §13. [125] ibid. [126] ibid. [127] *Discourse on NTC* §1.

[128] Leibniz follows the traditional periodization of Chinese intellectual history in 'three discontinuous ages'. First, 'ancient' refers to the era of the Sage Kings (twenty-ninth–twelfth century BC) which is the era of such legendary kings as Fuxi, Yao, and Shun, who—history goes—all ruled long and wisely. Second, the era of Confucius (551–479 BC) and his classical successors, such as, eg Mensius and Xunzi (sixth–third century BC). This period is also called the 'period of the philosophers'. Characteristic of their philosophical thinking was however a deep respect for and active engagement with ancient (political) thought. Third, the era of modern, neo-Confucian thought (beginning in the eleventh century), which lasted still during Leibniz's days. The latter included criticism of Buddhism and in Leibniz's view it was atheist. Hence, his argument that the Confucian *literati* should reconnect to their ancient doctrines and beliefs. C&R at 19–20 See eg *Discourse on the natural theology of the Chinese* §§62–65a. There are no written sources of the reign and philosophy of the sage kings. Leibniz however accepted the historicity of these kings (Fuxi's *Yi Jing* plays an important role in this acceptance) and considered the Confucian discussions historically accurate in the depiction of these 'most ancient philosophers' as 'highly intelligent' and 'moral[ly] exemplars' who served their people and thereto used the scientific insights available. He thus follows the picture that emerges from the available (Confucian) literature on this period that Leibniz studied: notably the classic *Shu Jing*, the *Book of History*, or *Book of Documents*, of which some parts were written as early as the eleventh century BC while others were added during

in classical Confucian texts (sixth to third century BC) as wise and charitable rulers whose moral *self-governance* was a source of their wise and just rule.[129] Moreover, Kangxi was reported to take ancient Chinese thought (which Leibniz understood to be *not* atheist contrary to Chinese thought of his days) seriously.[130] Leibniz studied the Chinese classics, among which the *Shu Jing*,[131] the *Book of History* or *Book of Documents*, which deals extensively with the sage king age and conveys the ideal of the Confucian State and government that Leibniz must have appreciated and recognized:

Those in positions of authority were commanded to: *a*) work for the welfare of the people; *b*) maintain the rites and ritual observances of their ancestors; *c*) be frugal; *d*) view their position as a trust conferred by Heaven (tian 天), which was not so much a symbol of deity as it was a reflection of the natural order; *e*) obtain and keep harmony within the social order, and between the social and natural order.[132]

The ideal of the sage king and, for example, the concept of government based on the will or 'Mandate of Heaven' (*Tian ming*) are crucial to Leibniz's engagement with Chinese moral and political thought. The latter concept dates back to the early days of the Zhou dynasty when King Wén and King Wǔ needed to justify their succession of the Shang dynasty. Shang rulers had lost the Mandate of Heaven because of their vicious deeds. The rulers of the Zhou dynasty were successful, virtuous rulers who cared for their people.[133] They ruled in accordance with Heaven's wisdom and justice, in accordance with the eternal rules of Heaven, that is, in accordance with the 'eternal law of rational nature'—the laws of natural reason. They were servants of the law of Heaven, which Leibniz understood to be comparable to the universal rule of natural law and justice.[134]

As to the second aspect, Leibniz saw his monadological ideas confirmed in Chinese metaphysics and attributed Chinese superiority in ethics and politics to the long tradition of natural religion and theology.[135] The Chinese had done well 'in comprehending the precepts of civil life' without Christian revealed theology.

[C]ertainly they surpass [Europe] in practical philosophy, that is, in the precepts of ethics and politics adapted to the present life and use of mortals. Indeed, it is difficult to describe how beautifully all the laws of the Chinese, in contrast to those of other peoples, are directed to the achievement of public tranquillity and the establishment of social order, so that men shall be disrupted in their relations as little as possible. [While Europe is] slipping [ . . . ] into greater corruption [. . . it] needs missionaries from the Chinese who might teach [ . . . ] the use and practice of natural religion.[136]

and after the days of Confucius. It deals with sage kings Yao, Shun, and Yu, and with rulers of the Xia Dynasty (2205–1766 BC), the Shang dynasty (1766–1050 BC), and the Zhou dynasty (1050–256 BC). Cook and Rosemont (n5) 23.

129 *Discourse on NTC* §§45 and 68;

130 ibid §1. Leibniz considered the contemporary, neo-Confucian *literati* to be atheists (eg *Remarks* §§1 and 6) but not the older Confucians and the ancient Chinese.

131 eg *Discourse on NTC* §§16, 17, 45, and 59.

132 Cook and Rosemont (n 5) 23.

133 Confucianism dates back to the days of the Zhou dynasty's decline, the 'Warring States period', and generally saw the Zhou dynasty as the 'golden age'. Perkins (n 11) 16.

134 See text to (n 105).

135 Perkins (n 11) 146.

136 NS §§3 and 10; *Discourse on NTC* §3: China 'surpasses [Europe] in . . . orderly government . . . and public morality'.

In *Discourse on the Natural Theology of the Chinese* (1716), Leibniz transmitted Chinese philosophical and religious concepts into the European discourse and into his own philosophy in particular. Immediately after the opening paragraph Leibniz started to examine Chinese metaphysics and submitted that 'the Chinese do recognize, or have recognized, spiritual substances' too and that 'their Li . . . corresponds to our Divinity'.[137] In both Chinese and Christian thought, God or—according to Leibniz in Chinese thought—*Li* and the human rational soul are intimately connected. For Leibniz, *Li* was 'the foundation stone for ecumenical accord between China and the West'.[138] The perceived correspondence between the higher Leibnizian monad called 'spirit' and the Chinese *li* in human beings and the relationship with God or *Li*, or Supreme Reason, provided Leibniz with a commonality that grounds both traditions of natural theology.[139]

Like the Jesuits, Leibniz thus approaches Chinese thought through natural theology and finds unity in natural reason:

> [the] first principle of the Chinese . . . called Li, that is, *Reason* or the foundation of all nature, the most universal reason and substance; there is nothing greater nor better than the Li. This great and universal cause is pure, motionless, rarified, without body or shape, and can be comprehended only through the understanding. From the Li qua Li emanate five virtues: piety, justice, religion, prudence, and faith.[140]

Although he did not use the term 'monad' as such in the *Discourse on the Natural Theology of the Chinese*, Leibniz described the Chinese *Li* (the first, ordering principle of the universe) and *Qi* (material force or 'primitive ether') in monadic terms: the great *Li* is described in terms of Supreme Intelligence or Reason, the individual *li*'s correspond to the Christian conception of 'spiritual substance or entelechy' that animate matter or bodies.[141] The *Li* has in Leibniz understanding produced the *Qi*. The *li* needs the *qi*, like the monad needs the body. Ultimately, there is the supreme monad: God, Supreme Intelligence or Reason, supreme *Li* or *Xiangti* (sometimes called *tian/tien-chu*).[142] In Aristotelian terms: the monad, the entelechy or spirit or individual *li* seeks perfection.[143]

Leaving the complexities of the monadology and the Chinese *Li–li* aside here, it suffices to stress that in Leibniz's interpretation the connection between the great *Li* and the individual *li*'s corresponds to the relationship between the individual monad and God. Therewith spiritual perfectibility for both Chinese and Christians was grounded in natural reason (and pre-established harmony secured). Around the world, the human person is able to know the commands of justice (as wise charity) and concomitant ethico-legal duties.

[137] *Discourse on NTC* §2, also §9. [138] Mungello (n 26) 75–76.

[139] In the *Discourse on the Natural Theology of the Chinese*, Leibniz deals extensively with the arguments made by the anti-accommodationist Longobardi who argued inter alia that the Chinese *Li* (ie Reason or Order) should be equated with prime matter rather than with active power or Intelligent Nature, in short, with the Christian notion of God (§§3–23).

[140] *Discourse on NTC* §4; *Remarks on Chinese Rites and Religion* (n 39) 68;

[141] *Discourse on NTC* §§14, 19, 21, 38; *Monadology* §62.

[142] *Discourse on NTC* §§28–29. [143] ibid §§21–22.

Leibniz recognizes, or should we say projects, his own idea that spiritual perfection is a rational exercise: '[k]nowledge of reasons perfects us because it teaches us universal and eternal truths, which are manifested in the perfect Being'.[144] Acquiring knowledge of the perfect ideas of morality and justice contributes to the rational governance and perfection of the self and subsequently to acting well and just. Whether perceived as *imago Dei* or the *li*, Leibniz conceives of human beings as realizing themselves as well as the universal rational moral order through spiritual (ie rational) practice that produces knowledge of Perfection. 'What we call the light of reason in man, they call commandment and law of Heaven.'[145] In both traditions of thought, from *understanding* God (or Perfection) or *Li* (to which the Chinese attribute 'Truth and Goodness par excellence' and 'all manner of perfections') emanates moral and spiritual perfection and thus virtuous behaviour.[146]

Leibniz understood spiritual perfectibility to be central to both Confucian ethics and Christian thought and crucial for maintaining virtuous relations, among sovereign rulers and surely between a ruler and her/his people. While in Christian thought the practice of piety—loving God and His proxy: one's human neighbour—was crucial to spiritual perfectibility, Leibniz recognized the spiritual practice ('contemplation of nature' meditation of perfect truth and goodness) in the Chinese practices aimed at reaching knowledge of Heaven. Leibniz thus found an equivalent duty to spiritual and moral self-cultivation in Confucian thought. The objective was that the self be educated in such a way that it would not become corrupted, but rather would proceed by cultivating wise charity. The duty to moral and spiritual self-cultivation of a ruler then was about becoming more conscious and enlightened, about perfecting one's intellect and becoming an ever more virtuous and truthful ruler. Through spiritual exercise, the philosopher-king would identify the laws he needed to enact and the governmental acts he needed to adopt. The Confucian premise behind the notions of the Mandate of Heaven and of the sage king is that human beings can govern well, can be virtuous, do good, and can govern in accordance with Heaven's Laws:

> To offend Heaven is to act against reason, to ask pardon of Heaven is to reform oneself and to make a sincere return in word and deed in the submission one owes to this very law of reason. For me I find all this quite excellent and quite in accord with natural theology.[147]

A third and final point to address is that for Leibniz, as reflected in his universal jurisprudence, Chinese and Europeans were different, but equal. The universal order of natural law and justice governed them all—rulers and subjects, Chinese and Europeans. As such, we are back where we started. In Leibniz's view, both traditions subscribe to the idea of a cosmic or universal natural legal order with Reason (*Li*) as the governing principle.[148] Both Europeans and Chinese, subjects and rulers, are

[144] Opinion 83–84. [145] *Discourse on NTC* §31.

[146] ibid §§8–8a; 'Chinese philosophy more closely approaches Christian theology than the philosophy of the ancient Greeks' (ibid §24a).

[147] ibid §31.

[148] ibid §§26, 29 '<u>Li</u> [as] <u>the natural order of Heaven</u>' also called '<u>Tien-Tao</u>'.

governed by the universal rule of natural law and justice. Within Leibniz's universal jurisprudence, the natural law obligation to perfect the intellect and the moral self is incumbent upon all sovereign rulers.[149] Natural law is found and applied through the inner life of the human (rational) person. It is thus a moral duty of the sage king to practise spiritual cultivation of the self so as to govern and legislate in conformity with wise charity and the laws of the universal natural order. Whether Leibniz was idealizing China or not, importantly he used Chinese moral and political thought as well as the image of the Chinese ruler to set out what wise and charitable rule in conformity with the law of nature and nations would entail and to hold up a mirror to the European rulers of his time.

## 6. A Universal Rule of Law for a Pluralist World Order

Leibniz's universal jurisprudence is not a plea for universal uniformity. Leibniz's universal rule of natural law and justice is an ideal for a pluralist world. In his writings on China, there is no civilizational inferiority–superiority language nor suggestions of incommensurability. China and Europe are different yet equal and they need each other to critically assess and perfect themselves and humanity as a whole. For Leibniz, the world's diversity is a requirement to move towards universal harmony and in fact the Eurocentrism of which Enlightenment philosophers are so often accused is not characteristic of Leibniz's work. On the contrary, his universal jurisprudence celebrates both plurality and harmony, it manifests an at the time rather rare pluralism and non-essentialist universalism.

While Leibniz's perspective on China may have orientalist overtones, we cannot take him as an apologist for European imperialism and colonialism, nor his jurisprudence as centred on Europe.[150] Leibniz recognized regional differences in the practice of international law and he moreover suggested that Chinese—superior—understanding of natural law and justice preceded the European understanding by centuries. This chapter has given a contextual reading of his writings.[151] If we wish to go beyond this immediate context (as such, a legitimate aim),[152] the question would be how this chapter's history of the 'international rule of law' concept and its relation to Chinese political and moral philosophy might contribute to this volume's project as a whole. Leibniz's interest in Chinese moral and political thought testifies to his conviction that natural law—grounded on justice as 'wise charity'—is universal

[149] Perkins (n 11) 20: 'In politics, the primary Confucian advice to rulers was to seek virtue rather than profit and to control the people through virtue rather than violence.'

[150] A Becker Lorca, 'Eurocentrism in the History of International Law' in A Peters and B Fassbender (eds), *Oxford Handbook on the History of International Law* (OUP 2012) 1034–57.

[151] See eg Q Skinner *Visions of Politics, Volume I Regarding Method* (CUP 2002); see on complexity of determining what is the right context, eg M Koskenniemi, 'Vitoria and Us. Thoughts on Critical Histories of International Law' *Rechtsgeschichte* (2014) 119–39.

[152] See eg writings by Anne Orford and Martti Koskenniemi and the interview with both: Alexandra Kemmerer, 'A Conversation with Koskenniemi and Orford' (2015) 17 Journal of the History of International Law 1.

and that it moreover governs the inner life of human beings, whether sovereign or subject. As such, if internalized through a rational practice of self-cultivation or self-perfection, it guides and constrains acts towards the perfection of the individual self as well as to the realization of 'the empire of reason', that is, a political order ruled by natural law and justice—in short, a universal rule of natural law and justice.

To end on a *critical* historical note: with Leibniz's ideas having faded into the background of international legal thought, today's deep structure of international law has taken hold. This chapter has touched upon an available alternative that was lost: ie an international law based on justice as wise charity rather than on self-interest. A strand of thought that draws on a more positive anthropology of law and society, and that pursues the development of the law of nations and world order on the basis of recognition, respect, and benevolence for others rather than on fear and violence.

# PART II

# LAW AND JUSTICE IN CHINESE THOUGHT ON WORLD ORDER

# 11

# Moral Rulership and World Order in Ancient Chinese Cosmology

*Aihe Wang*

## 1. Introduction

Chinese civilization is a rare continuous ancient civilization, in contrast to ancient Egypt, ancient Greece, or Mesopotamia. It had lasted for 5,000 years before it was directly confronted by European modernity in the nineteenth century. Crushed by Western aggression through gunboat 'diplomacy', the ancient Chinese conception of the world order nonetheless has survived as a cultural resource, as chapters in this book show, both for the Western rethinking of international law and order and for the Chinese search to remake itself and reassert its position in the modern international world. Scholars East and West identify a Chinese ideal world order based on Confucianism, centred on the moral superiority of a ruler, who presides over 'All Under Heaven' through moral authority rather than coercion. They see this ideal as a challenge to the dominant Eurocentric world order and an alternative to it.[1]

One problem with this view is its divorce of the ideal from history, and of the concept from practice. If no ruler has ever succeeded in actualizing this ideal moral authority, how could the ancient Chinese ideal persuade the modern international community? Another problem is its divorce of moral authority from the cosmological foundation and social bases in which it was rooted. Since the first aim of this book is to uncover the history of the concept of international rule of law, it is equally important, when engaging the Chinese view of world order in this discussion, to treat it also as a historical realm of contestation rather than a singular, quintessential 'Chinese concept'. To further reduce the 'Chinese' concept of the world to that of 'Confucian', and the 'Confucian' to the 'Neo-Confucian', would empty its rich meaning and reduce it to an oriental cultural label severed from its actual political functions in history.

This chapter examines the Chinese concepts of a moral ruler and of the human world order as an integral part of a cosmology. It reconstructs how this cosmology

[1] Representative scholars who advocate this ideal include Zhao Tingang, Yan Xuetong, and Daniel Bell.

was formed and transformed during historical shift from the hegemonic States of Shang and Zhou (1700–771 BC) to the first unified empires of Qin and Han (221 BC– AD 220). The transitional period in between (771–221 BC) was the time when the Hundred Schools of Thought, including Confucianism, all appeared in response to the most dramatic change in Chinese history. During this historical transition, the idea that Heaven gives its Mandate (*tianming*) to the Son of Heaven (*tianzi*) to rule All Under Heaven (*tianxia*) was contested and the cosmology of Four Quarters was transformed first into five natural forces and then into a moralized cosmology manifesting the will of Heaven. In this history, I will identify the social forces behind this prolonged symbolic and ideological competition, and the impact of these cosmological ideas on the actual political practice that shaped and reshaped the human world. I argue three points. First, Confucianism was just one of many competing theories of how to order the human world, and only by recovering the disputes among these competing theories can we understand the political implications behind the beautiful concepts. Second, the idea of a moral ruler was not an independent moral ideal but part of a larger cosmology that encompassed the divine, natural, and human domains under an overarching universal moral authority. It was constructive of authoritarianism and social hierarchy. It is highly questionable if this idea can be cut off from the religious source from which moral authority originated or from its social and institutional foundations. Third, the Confucian concepts of rulership and the world, which are idealized in texts, actually took shape through centuries of political contestation, inseparable from political and social practice. The same ideas served both as an ideology for autocracy and as a critique of its military and coercive power. Thus, the so-called 'Chinese world view' has never been a single, quintessentially Confucian ideal but a heterogeneous field of constant reinvention. Only by viewing this field holistically can we engage it in the discussion of contemporary world order—not just international relations, but also the holistic context of modernity itself.

## 2. Ruler and the World in the Ancient Cosmology of Four Quarters

The earliest Chinese concept of rulership and the world is found in the cosmology of the Shang period (*c.*1700–1045 BC), which is structured on *Sifang* (Four Quarters) and a centre. In Shang oracle bone inscriptions, *fang* is primarily a concept of political geography, most often describing alien polities, referred to either as 'x *fang*', indicating a specific polity, or simply as '*fang*' or 'many *fang*' (*duofang*), as opposed to 'us' (*wo*)—that is, the Shang ruling clan. The political centre of the Shang was surrounded and thus defined by these alien polities. The domain of the Shang was composed of an 'inner area' and an 'outer area'. The former was called the 'Zhong Shang' or '*zhong tu*'—the Central Shang or central land, including the ancestral capital, the political capital of the living king, and the royal hunting area. The 'outer area' included four lands (*si tu*)—the Eastern, Northern, Western, and Southern lands—and all the Shang lord. Both the centre and its outer domain were further

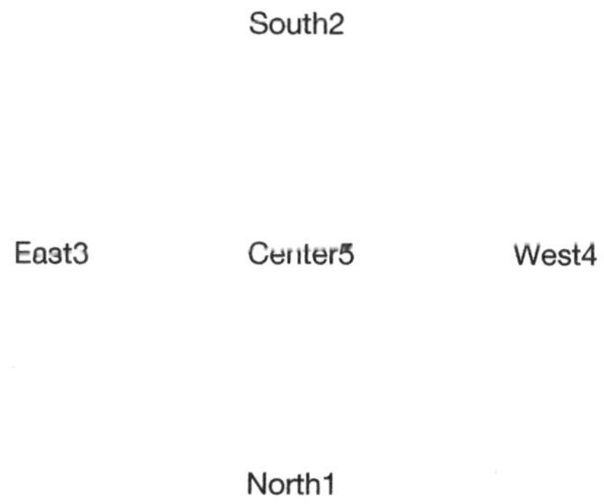


**Figure 11.1**

defined by many *fang* who lived outside of the four lands, and who were most often alien to the Shang.[2] In this context, *fang* represented heterogeneous 'otherness' at the periphery defining the centrality of the homogeneous 'us' (see Figure 11.1). The boundary between the alien polities and the Shang was not marked by fixed territories, but was constantly defined and redefined through dynamic interaction, including invading or raiding each other's territories and livestock; forming alliances or dominant–subordinate relationships; giving blessings or cursings to one another; and trading and giving tribute, where 'x *fang*' sent in shells or other goods. The Shang usually had the upper hand in these interactions, and its domination, while challenged, was not undermined until the end of the Shang period.[3]

While *fang* represents the foreign and the periphery in political geography, the meaning of *Sifang* (Four *fang* or Four Quarters) extends to a comprehensive spatial structure of cosmology, which encompassed political geography. *Sifang* classified all forces of the universe, including spirits, beings, and natural powers, as well as alien polities, on the basis of the four cardinal directions. In Shang theology, all these forces, alien and unknown, were commanded by the high god *Di*, who used them to determine the well-being of the Shang. These forces and spirits were not randomly sent by the unpredictable will of the high god, but rather sent through the *Sifang* structure, ordered in time and space. In other words, rain, clouds, spirits, harvest, disaster, illness, and raids from alien groups and forces arrived from the four *fang* upon the centre—Shang—serving as the mediators between *Di* and Shang. *Sifang* cosmology, consequently, became a primary structure of Shang ritual and political action. It was through *Sifang* that the Shang kings inquired about, made offerings

[2] The political and economic structure of the Shang State as well as its relationship to other polities has been extensively described and debated. See D Keightley, 'The Late Shang State: When, Where, and What?' in D Keightley (ed), *The Origins of Chinese Civilization* (University of California Press 1983) 523–64; Kwang-chih Chang, *Shang Civilization* (Yale UP 1980) 210–60; Aihe Wang, *Cosmology and Political Culture in Early China* (CUP 2000).

[3] For relations between Shang and the many *fang*, see Shima Kunio, *Inkyo bokuji kenkyû* (Hirosaki daigaku Chûgoku gaku kenkyûkai 1958); Hu Houxuan, 'Gong fang kao', in *Jiaguxue Shangshi luncong chuji*, vol 1 (Qilu daxue 1944); Chen Mengjia, *Yinxu buci zongshu* (Kexue chubanshe 1956).

to, prayed to, and negotiated with divine powers. None of the sacrifices was offered directly to the high god *Di*, because the high god did not interact directly with human beings but rather sent forces and spirits as his mediators through the *Sifang* structure. Therefore, the highest of the Shang sacrificial rites, the *di*-sacrifice, was offered primarily to *Sifang*.

*Sifang* as four cardinal directions points to a centre, the human ruler. At the centre, the king derived his political power and monopolized access to the world of the gods and divine knowledge through divination and ritual. Monopolizing access to the world of *Di* meant winning divine assistance and manipulating cosmological forces, as well as dominating political power. The Shang kings achieved this monopoly by way of ancestor worship.[4] Only the ancestors of the king could pass messages directly to the high god, and only the king could communicate with the ancestors. The king's authority and ability to perform sacrifices and to pray to his ancestors thus became the source of his political power and the legitimization of the Shang State. As Keightley has best summarized: 'The king's ability to determine through divination, and influence through prayer and sacrifice, the will of the ancestral spirits legitimized the concentration of political power in his person.'[5]

The *Sifang*-centre cosmology of the Shang thus functioned as a cultural totality, which legitimized rulership of the Shang by constructing the world around it. Based on the conceptions of time, space, and hierarchy in this cosmology, power was exercised in the rituals of everyday life, constructed in a world of cities, temples, and tombs, and implemented in calendars and geography. This cosmology conceptualized power relations, with the centre occupied by the king—his clan and domains—and the periphery inhabited by the alien and subordinate 'others', with time defined by the ritual cycles of royal ancestor worship, and with knowledge of the universe monopolized and reproduced by the ruling clan. In short, it was through this cosmology that the rulership and the world order were defined.

## 3. The Invention of 'Son of Heaven', 'Heaven's Mandate', and 'All Under Heaven'

During the conquest of the Shang, the concepts of rulership and the world changed, and the new concepts of the 'Son of Heaven' and 'All Under Heaven' were invented. The new hegemon that replaced Shang was Zhou—a group living at the periphery of the Shang civilization who had settled to the west of Shang around the twelfth century BC.[6] To the Shang, the Zhou were one of the many *fang*, seen in oracle bone inscriptions as 'Zhoufang'. King Wu Ding of Shang had ordered his lords to attack

[4] In Shang theology, *Di* did not receive prayers from human beings directly; all prayers had to be made to the ancestors, who transmitted the messages to the high god. See Hu Houxuan, 'Yin buci zhong de Shangdi he wangdi' *Lishi yanjiu* 9–10 (1959), 23–50, 89–110.

[5] See D Keightley, 'The Religious Commitment: Shang Theology and the Genesis of Chinese Political Culture' (1978) 17 History of Religions 211–25.

[6] E Shaughnessy, 'Western Zhou History' in M Loewe and E Shaughnessy (eds), *The Cambridge History of Ancient China* (CUP 1999) 209–351, 306.

the Zhou frequently, and the Zhou had at one point become a subordinate polity to the Shang—paying tribute to the Shang, worshipping Shang's founding ancestors, and intermarrying with the Shang.[7] But during the eleventh century BC, after conquering many *fang* and allying with many Shang lords, King Wu of Zhou led a coalition of lords to attack the Shang capital, ending the Shang hegemony.

It was to legitimize this military conquest that the Zhou people invented the concept of Heaven, Heaven's Mandate, and the Son of Heaven. To actually take over a political and ritual centre that had lasted nearly a millennium, and to legitimize such a seizure by a former peripheral *fang* or lord, posed a much greater challenge to the Zhou conquerors than the task of military conquest itself. To do so, the Zhou conquerors did not abandon Shang tradition but continued most of the Shang's religious ideas and practices—including the worship of ancestors, the notion of the high god, and the concept of *Sifang*—as the basis for their political legitimacy.[8] Above all the continuities, however, the Zhou added their innovations. The Zhou claimed that 'Heaven', the high god that Zhou people worshipped, had shifted its Mandate away from the Shang and given it to the Zhou king, the Son of Heaven, and that the Zhou's conquering of the Shang only served to realize this intention of Heaven. In making this claim, the Zhou invented an abstract and absolute supreme universal Heaven, which absorbed the Shang concept of the high god *Di* and provided the foundation for the Zhou's legitimization in replacing Shang.

Another invention was reading omens. Heaven's intention was not obscure, but had its clear manifestation through omens in the celestial and natural world, as demonstrated by the gathering of five planets in the constellation *Yugui* (Cancer) on 28 May of 1059 BC[9] and the uprooting of a giant tree.[10]

Why did Heaven shift its Mandate from one dynasty to another? The Zhou explained the shift in terms of the ruler's *De*—a concept invented by the Zhou to mean the 'power' or 'potency' accumulated over time by the ruler.[11] The very concept of *De* today is interpreted as the Confucian concept of morality, contrasting with coercion or law, such as in the pairing of '*de zhi*' (rule by virtue) versus '*fa zhi*' (rule by law). But at its origin the term indiscriminately included political, symbolic, religious, and moral powers. This all-inclusive concept of *De* was also inherited by legalist and Daoist philosophies. By attributing the shift of the Mandate of Heaven

[7] Zhouyuan, pit number 11, piece numbers 1, 82, 84, 112. See Xu Xitai, *Zhouyuan jiaguwen zongshu* (Sanqin chubanshe 1987) 129–37, 175; Chen Quanfang, *Zhouyuan yu Zhou wenhua* (Shanghai Renmin chubanshe 1988) 150–51.

[8] Based on archaeological evidence and oracle and bronze inscriptions, Kwang-chih Chang asserts that the Zhou continued most of the Shang political and cultural traditions and therefore the Shang and Zhou constitute a continuous Bronze Age of China, rather than a sharp break, as claimed by Wang Guowei and Hsu Cho-yun. See Kwang-chih Chang, 'Shang Zhou guanxi de zai jiantao' CYYY 51 (1980) 305–10; 'Xia Shang Zhou sandai duzhi yu sandai wenhua yitong' CYYY 55(1) (1984) 51–71.

[9] D Pankenier suggests that, rather than being a Zhou innovation, the concept of Heaven's Mandate—the correlation between celestial or natural signs and the changing of dynasties—existed long before Zhou conquered Shang. D Pankenier, 'Cosmo-Political Background of Heaven's Mandate' (1995) 20 Early China 121–76, 172.

[10] Hsu Cho-yun and Katheryn Linduff, *Western Zhou Civilization* (Yale UP 1988) 104.

[11] For a summary of scholarship on *De*, see C Cook, 'Scribes, Cooks, and Artisans: Breaking Zhou Tradition' (1995) 20 Early China 241–78.

to the living king's 'Power'—what he had accumulated through his own action—the Zhou undermined the Shang king's monopoly on access to the divine world through his ancestors, since the living king could lose his *De* or Power and thus lose the Mandate to another lineage. This initiated a long process leading to the concept of a universal sovereignty based on some kind of universal standards rather than on a particular ancestral line.

The Zhou concept of the Mandate of Heaven also changed the perception of the world order. The Zhou king had to occupy and redefine the centre where the Shang king had formerly resided, the centre of the divine world where royal ancestors ascended and descended, and the centre of the multilayered cosmos where the living king communicated with the divine world through rituals. Without possessing such a political, religious, and cosmological centre, the Zhou did not truly possess the Mandate of Heaven. To do so, they had to move from the West to the centre. At the time of the conquest, the Zhou had an identity as 'men of the West', and addressed their own lord as the 'the lord of the western *fang* (*Xifang Bo*)'.[12] Even after the conquest, the Zhou believed that the Mandate was shifting westward onto the Zhou.[13] To transform from lord of the West into the holder of Heaven's Mandate at the centre was an endeavour that involved demographic movement, political organization, military campaigns, and ritual reforms, all of which took generations of Zhou kings to fulfil. Demographically, the Zhou conquerors immediately moved major Shang lords and loyalties to the West, in groups of entire lineages. They also planned to occupy the central region themselves by constructing a new capital, Luo, in the central region. The construction was strategically significant for military and political control of the central plain and the remaining old Shang lineage groups.[14] It was also of cosmological, religious, and symbolic importance for the Zhou's dominance of *Sifang* or 'All Under Heaven' *tianxia*. It was from this new capital in the central region that the Zhou kings fully received the Mandate of Heaven in commanding the *Sifang*. King Cheng, presiding over the new capital, announced that his role from then on was to 'display a brilliant merit like that of King Wen and King Wu, reverently respond to the Mandate of Heaven, harmonize and long preserve the people of the Four Quarters (*Sifang*), and settle their multitudes here'.[15] King Cheng thus declared a threefold definition of kingship—its source from the Zhou ancestors, its authority from the Mandate of Heaven, and its ultimate function of governing the Four Quarters from the centre. The Zhou thus transformed the *Sifang* cosmology into a political geography of 'All Under Heaven ', where the Zhou's Mandate prevailed.

This conceptual innovation of transforming the Four Quarters into All Under Heaven (*tianxia*) was paired with an actual change of world order effected through military conquest and political subjugation that transformed the alien polities

[12] Oracle bone inscriptions from Zhouyuan, pit number 11, piece number 82. For the transcription, see Xu Xitai (n 7) 175.

[13] Tu Cheng-sheng, *Gudai shehui* (Yunzhen wenhua shiye kufen youxian gongsi 1992) 322–30.

[14] Hsu and Linduff (n 10); Cheng-sheng (n 13) 352–94, 509–42.

[15] 'Luo gao' in the *Book of Documents*; see James Legge (tr), *The Chinese Classics*, vol 4: *The Shoo King* (repr, Hong Kong UP 1960) 434–52.

of *Sifang* into subjects of the Zhou king. The Zhou campaigned throughout the *Sifang*, and extended their political order (called the *fengjian* system) to those areas they conquered. By entrusting newly conquered groups to members of the Zhou clan through ritual contracts, the Zhou created a multilayered hierarchy of power that incorporated the Shang nobility, the native populace, and themselves in a tripartite coalition in which a small number of Zhou royal kinsmen ruled over the much larger population of the conquered.[16] The lords maintained the authority of the Zhou clan by their constant military presence as vassals keeping *Sifang* in subjection. Thus, the *Sifang* that was heterogeneous and alien to the centre in Shang cosmology became homogeneous and subject to the centre in the political ideal of the Zhou.

The Son of Heaven actually possessed and ruled All Under Heaven first and foremost through military campaigns and military presence. Like the Shang, the Zhou defined the absolute superiority of the centre—the king and his ruling clan—through the inferiority and peripheral nature of *Sifang*. But the Zhou redefined centrality as the absorption and subjugation of the Four Quarters, rather than their alienation. The Zhou claimed that their ancestor King Wen had received the Mandate to 'possess the Four Quarters' and that he had such a great power that 'throughout the Four Quarters none dared to insult him'; 'throughout the Four Quarters none dared to oppose him';[17] 'in the Four Quarters men are influenced by his power'; and 'all in the Four Quarters of the state render obedient homage'.[18] This total subjugation of the formerly foreign and unpredictable *Sifang* reinforced the absolute dominance and superiority of the centre.

These Zhou inventions included key concepts that became the core of Confucianism, which Confucius himself acknowledged, saying 'I follow the Zhou'. The concepts of Heaven as a universal deity and the Son of Heaven as a universal sovereign undermined the ancestral theology of a particular clan, the Shang, and it was such a revolution of ideas that Confucius inherited from the Zhou. But history also reveals that the first Son of Heaven, the Zhou King, was a military conqueror who continued to rule by the Zhou's own lineage system, whose legitimacy remained problematic even after a millennium's effort of justification. The Zhou invented the concept of Heaven as the supreme and universal moral authority to justify its military conquest and claimed that Heaven's Mandate shifts according to the ruler's *De*. *De* would become a key concept in later Confucianism as morality, but in Zhou theory, as in the Daoist and legalist philosophies that competed with Confucianism, *De* did not preclude coercive force or military might. The new concept of All Under Heaven, in both theory and practice, was achieved through military campaigns and maintained primarily by military presence. After all, the notion that 'Heaven gives his Mandate to the Son of Heaven to rule All Under Heaven' was invented to justify a military conquest and a coercive hegemonic power.

16 Hsu and Linduff (n 10) 147–85; Cheng-sheng (n 13) 479–508.
17 'Da ya' and 'Huang yi' in the *Book of Poetry*; see Legge (n 15) vol 4 451, 455.
18 'Da ya' and 'Yi' in the *Book of Poetry* (ibid 511).

## 4. Five Conquering Forces of the Cosmos

The Zhou theology of Heaven's Mandate was undermined once the Zhou king's possession of 'All Under Heaven' was lost during the Warring States period (the fifth century BC to 221 BC). Both the institution of rulership and the actual world order went through unprecedented and comprehensive changes. The Zhou court was driven from its capital by the invaders from the West in 771 BC and the lingering symbolic existence of the 'Son of Heaven' was ended at the hands of rising local rulers who were previous Zhou lords. The wars for a new hegemony were constantly being waged between States, while within each State civil wars frequently broke out when the rising ministers or military leaders overturned the hereditary lords of the former Zhou ruling clan. Non-kin political relations were formed to break the political order (*fengjian* system) based on Zhou lineage.[19] The constant warfare replaced the chariots of aristocracy with infantry armies of common peasantry, and this created new mechanisms of mass mobilization and control that soon were used to control the civil population as a whole, and thereby changed the basic units and bonds of society. These control mechanisms included taxation on land, registration of the population, reranking the population according to military merit, growing bureaucratic administration, and the absorption of the defeated States into 'districts' (*xian*) of the central government of the territorial State.[20] With the growth of local administration, a class of civil servants emerged, seeking employment from the new autocratic rulers. Eventually, a social hierarchy based on the lineage system of the Zhou was replaced by territorial States administrated by a body of salaried civil servants. It was into this age that Confucian and the hundred school thinkers were born.

The changes in actual world order were facilitated by changes its conception. A new correlative cosmology of five transformative powers was invented to sabotage the idea of a Zhou centre possessing the Four Quarters, and to construct a new type of rulership. It transformed hereditary kingship sanctioned by ancestor worship into territorial rulership sanctioned by cosmic patterns.

Four major rising social forces were responsible for the rise of this new cosmology. (1) Religious and natural experts—ritualists, diviners, astrologers, musicians, physicians, calendar makers—served the new patrons of local power with their expertise.[21] (2) The bureaucratic class was the most powerful in applying the new correlative cosmology to implement and control the new political order.[22] (3) Military specialists invented military treatises as expressions of 'divine patterns inherent in the

[19] Blood covenants during the late Spring and Autumn period formed an early non-kin political relationship. See ME Lewis, *Sanctioned Violence in Early China* (State University of New York Press 1990) 43–52.

[20] ibid.

[21] AC Graham, *Yin-Yang and the Nature of Correlative Thinking* (Institute of East Asian Philosophies 1986) 91–92; D Harper, 'Warring States Natural Philosophy and Occult Thought' in M Loewe and E Shaughnessy (eds), *The Cambridge History of Ancient China* (CUP 1999) 813–84.

[22] R Yates, 'State Control of Bureaucrats under the Qin: Techniques and Procedures' (1995) 20 Early China 331–66.

cosmos' and used such a 'textual vision of warfare' to attack the hereditary nobility, by transforming warfare from a form of service to ancestral cults into an expression of cosmological patterns.[23] (4) And scholars of the hundred schools—masters and students engaged in private learning and seeking employment at various levels as advisers, educators, and civic servants—elevated the assault on the ruling clan's hereditary monopoly to a theoretical level, advocating the superiority of achieving connection with the divine through education. They adopted correlative cosmology into their philosophical texts in the third century BC and synthesized it into a coherent system.[24]

From texts used by these social forces—calendars, astronomical treatises, military treatises, medical treatises, bureaucratic records, and philosophical texts—emerged a system of Five Powers or Phases (*Wuxing*) that took primacy in reconstructing cosmology and the world order. The system of Five redefined the hierarchical system of Four Quarters and a centre into five equal spatial units, thus totally rejecting the supremacy of the centre, the Zhou king. Technically, the imposition of Five Quarters on the original Four Quarters involved correlating the Quarters to numbers and counting the four cardinal directions—beginning from the throne in the North from which the ruler faces South and proceeding to East and West—and adding the central position representing the fifth Quarter, mediating the binary oppositions of North–South and East–West. Chinese diagrams represent the five Quarters in the way as depicted in Figure 11.1.[25]

These five Quarters or directions were further correlated with what became known as the Five Elements, which were conceived simultaneously as essential material substances of the physical world, powers of conquest, and phases of cosmic movement. Correlating the Five Elements to the spatial and numerical structure created a transformative configuration of the Five Powers or Five Phases in the sequence Water–Fire–Wood–Metal–Earth. This order is called the '*Hongfan*' order, since it is found in the '*Hongfan*' chapter of the first Confucian canon, the *Book of Documents*. By continuing the numerical sequence into a second cycle of movement or transformation, the correlative system appears as shown in Figure 11.2.

With further elaboration, people turned this diagram into the so-called 'river chart' (*Hetu*).[26] First, reading from Earth to Metal and then proceeding clockwise produces a generation or birth cycle of the Five Powers: Earth–Metal–Water–Wood–Fire–Earth. By reversing Fire and Metal and reading through Wood, people produced a conquest cycle—Earth–Wood–Metal–Fire–Water—shown in Figure 11.3.

Extending Figure 11.3 from the cardinal to the intermediate points and filling those points with even numbers forms the diagram of *Loshu* (*Lo* document),

[23] Lewis (n 19) 97–114.

[24] AC Graham, *Disputers of the Tao* (Open Court 1989) 313–82.

[25] This technical account is based on Graham's structural analysis with minor alterations (*Disputers of the Tao*, see n 24).

[26] For *Hetu, Luoshu*, and the magic square, see J Major, 'The Five Phases, Magic Squares, and Schematic Cosmography' in H Rosemcord, Jr (ed), *Exploration in Early Chinese Cosmology* Journal of American Academy of Religion Studies, Thematic Studies 50(2) (Scholars Press 1984) 133–66.

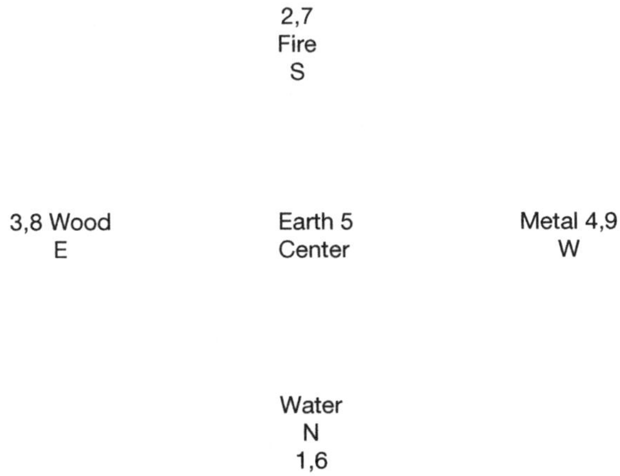


**Figure 11.2**

**Figure 11.3**

the magic square in which numbers add up to fifteen in every direction, shown in Figure 11.4.

While the innovation of this system was achieved primarily by technical professionals such as diviners and physicians, philosophers helped to theorize it. For example, the representation of the earliest order of Five Elements (Figure 11.1) is found in the canonical Confucian text 'Hongfan' and the first records of the 'river chart' and '*lo* document' were found in the *Analects* and commentary on the *Book of Change*, both Confucian canons.

All these transformative orders of mutual conquest and generation facilitated actual changes happening at the time. The diagrams in Figures 11.3 and 11.4 show that the core of this cosmology is a system of Five Powers or Phases, namely Wood,

**Figure 11.4**

Fire, Earth, Metal, and Water, as presented in Figures 11.2–11.4. More than being five elements of substance, they form a cosmology correlating all beings and phenomena in the universe into interactive cycles, including the human body, astronomical phenomena, seasons and directions, animals and plants, and ways of government. There are two major kinds of interactive cycles that have been used to build such correlations—the cycle of conquest and the cycle of birth–generation. In the conquest cycle, Fire conquers Metal by melting it, Metal conquers Wood because metal axes cut down trees, Wood conquers Earth since wooden tools are used to plough the fields, Earth conquers Water by damning it, and Water conquers Fire by extinguishing it. Similarly, in the generation cycle, Fire generates Earth by producing ashes, Earth generates Metal by producing minerals, Metal melts into liquid producing Water, Water irrigates trees to produce Wood, and Wood burns to produce Fire.

Redefining *Sifang*-centre cosmology, the Five Powers provided a new conception of time and space. Time in this system became the rhythm of the dynamic cosmic movement of conquest and generation, rather than the eternal repetition of ancestor worship of Shang and Zhou. Space, once redefined as five cosmic forces, reduced the centre from the 'zone of the sacred'[27] into an equal of the other four, and the five equal units existed in ceaseless interaction of conquest and generation. What remained eternal and permanent was no longer a centre but change itself and the patterns of change. Centre/Earth can be conquered by East/Wood, just as West/Metal is conquered by South/Fire.

This transformation of cosmology fundamentally changed the conception of rulership by separating divine knowledge from kingship, ie the king's body and his ancestral line. Knowledge of the new cosmology was no longer monopolized by the king, but was possessed and reproduced by the rising political and social forces. By using correlative cosmology as the ultimate authority for their professions and guidance of practice, these forces usurped the hereditary king's monopoly of divine knowledge through ancestor worship, thereby sabotaging the divine foundation of

[27] The term is borrowed from M Eliade, *The Myth of the Eternal Return* (Routledge & Kegan Paul 1955).

rulership. Their new cosmology created a direct connection between Heaven and Man, sanctioning and regulating the new territorial political rulers as well as ordering the daily practices of the populace.

The new cosmology also redefined the world order. By reducing the sacred centre to the fifth *fang*, as one of the five interactive powers in a dynamic system, the cosmic cycles of constant interaction denied the absolute and sacred centrality of the former ruling clan, and subjected it to the dynamic conquest and generation cycles of the Five Powers. Such a dynamic cosmology provided a logical pattern and rationale for change in world order, forming a symbolic structure for power competition and ratifying the drastic change in power relations.

This transformation of cosmology was an intrinsic component of the social–political transition. It was destructive of the old world order and of the way power and cosmology had connected, and at the same time constructive of new type of rulership, conceptions of social order, and a new conjunction between knowledge and power.

## 5. The Cosmology of Conquest and the World of the Conquerors

When China finally unified, the first empire of Qin (221–206 BC) actualized this new world order and new type of rulership, using the conquest cycle of Five Powers as the cosmological justification for them. Following the logic of the conquest cycle, the Qin adopted Water as its dynastic symbol, because Water conquers Fire and Fire was the symbol of the Zhou whom the Qin conquered. Water was also associated with violence, killing, and punishment. The First Emperor of Qin adopted the Power of Water (*shui De*) soon after he conquered the other six States, using it to justify the transmission of power by force and to justify imperial sovereignty based on military accomplishment, discipline, and punishment. In the *Records of the Historian (Shiji)*, a history of China completed in the 1st century BC by Sima Qian, we find the following account of the Qin's adoption of this cosmological symbol:[28]

> The First Emperor held that Zhou had the Power of Fire, and Qin was replacing the Power/*De* of Zhou and should follow Water, the Power/*De* that conquers Fire ... Let the beginning of the year be changed and all tributes to the court start at the eleventh month; let robes, garments, feathers, fur, stakes, and flags all be in black; let the number six be used for regulations ... Let the [Yellow] River be re-named the *De* Water, symbolizing the beginning of the Power of Water. [Let policies] be harsh, firm, perverse, and occult, with all affairs determined by penal law. Be severe and strict rather than benevolent (*ren*), kind (*en*), harmonic (*he*), and righteous (*yi*). Only then will it be in accordance with the number of the Five Powers.

The mutual conquests among Five Powers, five *De*, represent an immanent, unintentional, and natural cosmology. The concept of *De* continued to mean power and potency of the ruler as in Zhou theology, primarily referring to the power of conquest. Symbolizing death and punishment, the *De* of Water justified military

[28] Sima Qian, *Shiji* (Zhonghua shuju 1959) 237–38.

force and violence. The colour and number associated with Water—black and six—were used in ceremonies confirming the new political order. Changing the calendar implied the accordance of the dynasty with the temporal order of the cosmos, and changing the name of the Yellow River was a way of claiming imperial sovereignty on earth.

When the first emperor adopted the Five Powers system, he discarded the moral authority of Heaven in Zhou theology and never bothered to look for good omens to prove Heaven's Mandate. Instead, he used the Five Powers to justify his despotic rule of All Under Heaven based on force and violence. He invented the new title—'Huangdi' (the august emperor)—to replace the old title of King in order to claim his supreme sovereignty. In his enthroning edict, he claimed that the new title 'Huangdi' glorifies his personal military achievements:[29]

> I with my single body raised the troops to put down the revolt and disorder. [Thanks to the help of ancestral spirits,] I convicted the six kings for their crimes, and put All Under Heaven in order. Without changing the title of the throne, there would be no way to glorify these achievements and pass them on to later generations.

To the First Emperor, such absolute political power had to be free from the control of any other authorities. While using scholars in his courts, he never submitted himself to the moral authority they claimed to have. When the scholars used antiquity and Heaven to criticize the regime, the emperor ordered a large-scale burning of books and burying of scholars.[30] He also dismissed scholars from his grand *feng* and *shan* rituals, keeping the documents secret between him and heaven,[31] and he turned his frequent ritual journeys into eulogies to his personal power and achievement.[32] He thus used Five Phases cosmology to justify a totalitarian sovereignty gained by force and based on economic strength, military expansion, extravagant rituals, and discipline by reward and punishment. This cosmological justification, however, also predicted its end, since the Power of Water was doomed to be conquered eventually by the Power of Earth.

The Han continued the cosmology of conquest and the Qin type of rulership. Replacing the Qin dynasty after its short life of fifteen years, the founding Han emperor Gao conquered the world with troops, just like the Qin emperor. He also continued most Qin policies and rituals and kept Water as the Han dynastic symbol, sustaining the conquest cycle as State ideology. Scholar-officials tried to constrain the Han emperors by recalling the fall of the Qin. Lu Jia (*c.*206–180 BC), a

[29] ibid 236. [30] ibid 254–58.

[31] In order to perform the grand *Feng* and *Shan* sacrifices to claim the mandate, the first emperor of Qin summoned seventy Confucian masters and scholars from Qi and Chu to meet with him at the foot of Mount Tai. But these scholars talked about how in ancient times the *Feng* and *Shan* sacrifices were kept humble and easy, even 'the wheels of the carriages were wrapped in rushes to avoid doing any injury to the earth and grass of the mountain'. The First Emperor was surely repelled by these restrictions. He therefore dismissed all the scholars, had a carriage road opened up, ascended to the summit, and set up a stone marker 'extolling his own achievement as the First Emperor'. He also kept the documents used in the sacrifices strictly secret, and no men of the time were able to record these ceremonies (ibid 1366–67).

[32] Six eulogies as such were inscribed on stone during the First Emperor's regime and were recorded (ibid 242–62).

scholar-official, repeatedly advised Emperor Gao to follow the classical texts of the *Book of Poetry* and the *Book of Documents*. But Emperor Gao scolded him, saying: 'It [All Under Heaven] was what I myself won from riding on the warhorse, and what has it to do with the *Book of Poetry* and the *Book of Documents*!'[33] The emperor was known to have insulted scholars by urinating in their ritual caps.[34] Jia Yi [201–168 BC], a scholar-adviser to Emperor Wen in the 2nd century BC, attributed the Qin's downfall to its rule by force and its lack of morality, arguing that, while seizing power depended on violence, maintaining power depended on rule by morality. He proposed breaking away from the Qin model by changing the dynastic symbol from Water to Earth, which would again entail an entire series of ritual and institutional reforms.[35] His suggestion implied a criticism of the current policies of rule by law and it was not accepted in his lifetime. Only in 104 BC, sixty years after Jia Yi's death, did Emperor Wu (141–87 BC) install Earth as the dynastic symbol. While this represented a break from Qin, it perpetuated the cosmological logic of the conquest cycle, a cycle of violent upheavals.[36]

## 6. Heaven's Mandate, Son of Heaven, and Confucian Scholars

While the Qin and early Han emperors were using the cosmic cycles of conquest to justify their military conquest and rule by law, Han Confucian scholars used the same system to re-establish Heaven's Mandate and their exclusive authority as Heaven's interpreters. Since this cosmology correlated the myriad of things and phenomena in the universe into a single correlative system of Five Phases, it offered signs from the natural world that could be read as omens. These could be good omens, such as the Zhou used to justify its receiving the Mandate, or bad omens that reproached the bad behaviour of the ruler or even predicted the fall of the dynasty. The underlying principle was that human behaviour that violated the cosmic–social order would cause abnormal phenomena in both the natural and human worlds as signs of an imbalance in cosmic energies. Confucian scholars designated the Son of Heaven as the sole agent who connected Heaven to Man and was responsible for the total cosmic–social order. Yet the emperor had lost the monopoly on divine knowledge. The authority to define the 'Way of Heaven' through reading omens thus became the capital of the scholars who compiled, interpreted, and transmitted texts.

Along with the prominence of this cosmological discourse of omens, we see the rise of scholars as a social force, becoming living components of the centralized empire and the bureaucratic system. They were the 'natural enemy' of other political forces: the religious experts serving the emperor's person, the military generals,

[33] ibid 2699.

[34] According to *Shiji*, Emperor Gao was said to dislike Confucian scholars. Once he took off the scholars' ritual caps and urinated in them. He often scolded them, and could not stand a conversation with them (ibid 2693).

[35] ibid 2492.

[36] ibid 1402.

the consort families who influenced the emperor through their women, the legalist clerks who had been controlling the bureaucracy since Qin, and the royal brothers of the emperor, who had been a critical force for maintaining control of the vast territory of the Han and whose power depended on political pluralism. I will illustrate the competition between one pair of these opposing forces, that between the scholars controlling the central bureaucracy of the State and the royal nobility controlling two-thirds of the territory and population. Both parties had to persuade the emperor in order to eliminate their rivals and implement their own blueprints for the empire, that is, centralization versus pluralism.

The competition between two models of rulership and two visions of world order is best illustrated by the diametric opposition between Dong Zhongshu (179–104 BC) and the Han emperor's uncle, the King of Huainan, Liu An (d.122 BC). Dong Zhongshu, living in the capital, influenced the emperor by being called in for consultation and submitting memorials to him. Kings of distant kingdoms did not have such direct channels of influence, but the King of Huainan communicated to the same emperor by submitting to him a book that the king and his circle of consultants had written collectively, which was later entitled *Huainanzi*.

Dong Zhongshu, promoting centralization, developed a moral cosmology and omen theory in the first of his three memorials presented to Emperor Wu:[37]

> The subject of your Majesty [i.e. Dong himself] prudently investigated [the cases in] the *Spring and Autumn* (*Chunqiu*), observing the affairs of the former dynasties; accordingly I see the Heaven and Man connection, which is extremely awe-inspiring. Whenever a state will decline due to the loss of *Dao*, Heaven will first give catastrophes to warn [the ruler]. If [the ruler] fails to realize and introspect, [Heaven] will further show strange phenomena to scare the ruler. If the ruler still does not change [his conduct], then damage and decline will follow. From this one sees that the heart of Heaven kindly loves the human ruler; he intends to stop the chaos for the ruler.

Dong here revives the idea of Heaven as an anthropomorphic deity from Zhou theology, attributing to it a heart, intention, and love. Heaven manifests his will in omens, warning the ruler of the human world. Dong thus defines omens as Heaven's speech, the expression of his moral consciousness. Translating this divine speech into human knowledge is the key to authority in the human world. Dong argues that the only human being who could comprehend the divine messages is the sage Confucius, who converted the meaning of the omens into a sacred text, the *Spring and Autumn*:[38]

> Confucius compiled the *Spring and Autumn*, examining the *Dao* of Heaven above and inquiring into the human sentiment below, referring to the ancient and investigating the present. That is why what the *Spring and Autumn* criticizes is what catastrophes are imposed upon, what the *Spring and Autumn* dislikes is what strange phenomena are given for. It writes about the mistakes of States and families, and the changes of catastrophes and strange phenomena, in order to show that what Man does and the extremities of good and evil resonate back and forth and communicate with Heaven and Earth.

[37] Ban Gu, *Hanshu* (Zhonghua Shuju 1987) 2498. [38] ibid 2515.

Since the authority for translating Heaven's speech lies solely in the sage Confucius and his texts, the scholars who have mastered the sage's writings are the only living men with the authority to interpret omens as Heaven's intention.

The King of Huainan, in contrast, advocated a cosmology of natural law, directly opposing Dong's theology. He views the same cosmological phenomena as the result of resonance (*ganying*), that is, phenomena of the same category and sharing the same *qi* affecting one another spontaneously, free from human intentions:[39]

When the *Yang qi* prevails, it scatters to make dew;
When the *Yin qi* prevails, it freezes to make frost and snow.
Creatures with feathers make up the category of flying things, and are subject to *Yang*.
Creatures with shells and scales make up the category of creeping and hiding things, and are subject to *Yin*.
[...]
Fire flies upward, water flows downward; thus
The flight of birds is aloft, the movement of fishes is downward.
Things within the same category mutually move each other.

*Huainanzi* hereby rejects Dong's moral cosmology of Heaven with a natural cosmology of resonance—'resonance within the same category' or 'resonance with the same *qi*'.[40] This natural cosmology also challenges Confucian scholars' monopolization of sacred knowledge and authority. It argues that the resonance of things cannot be subject to moral judgement or knowledge: 'The resonance of things belonging to the same category is darkly mysterious and extremely subtle. Knowledge cannot explain it, nor discussion unravel it.'[41]

The two opposing theories of 'resonance' are instrumental of the two models of rulership—the active sovereign of centralized power versus the non-active sovereign of a pluralistic world. Dong Zhongshu constructs the absolute authority of the moral ruler with the concept of the resonance between Heaven and Man. He re-establishes the centrality of the sovereign in the cosmos: 'To be at the centre of Heaven, Earth, and Man, and thus to connect the three and put them in communication, is the responsibility of the sovereign, and nobody else can bear such responsibility.'[42] Therefore, 'Heaven and Man resonance' (*tianren ganying*) is the function exclusively of the sovereign. Being the only human agent connecting Heaven and Man, Dong Zhongshu argues, the Son of Heaven should be the active (*youwei*) moral agent, actively realizing Heaven's will in the human world. The emperor must be able to 'receive the action of Heaven from above, and to correct his own actions below'.[43] Being the sole connection of Heaven and Man, the emperor is the single

[39] Liu An, *Huainanzi*; references are to Liu Wendian, *Huainan honglie jijie* (repr, Taiwan Shangwu yinshuguan 1969) ch 3, 2a–3a.

[40] ibid ch 6, 4b. [41] ibid ch 6, 3a.

[42] Dong interprets the very graphic of the character for king—*wang*—by saying that the three horizontal strokes symbolize the three realms of Heaven, Man, and Earth, with the central vertical stroke connecting the three to symbolize the sovereign. Dong Zhongshu, *Chunqiu fanlu*; references are to Su Yu, *Chunqiu fanlu yizheng* (repr in facsimile, Heluo tushu chubanshe 1974)ch 11, 'Wangdao tongsan 44' 9a.

[43] Ban Gu (n 37) 2502.

human agent who makes things happen: 'The human sovereign stands in the position of deciding to let live or to kill, sharing with Heaven the control of power over change and transformation.'[44]

*Huainanzi* resists such cosmological centrality of the emperor using a pluralist model of resonance. It states that resonance has nothing to do with the status or authority of the sovereign, but can be achieved by anyone who unites with *Dao*. The authors present seven people who have achieved resonance with Heaven, Earth, Man, and animals; they are a blind musician, a commoner's daughter, King Wu of Zhou, a high official of Chu, a Chu music master, a renowned archer, and a famous angler. These people have achieved resonance with the universe not through their high status, or through moral knowledge or purposeful effort, but through perfect sincerity (*jingcheng*). Resonance, furthermore, has nothing to do with social hierarchy or authority:[45]

> Take this blind music master and commoner's daughter; their rank was lower than that of the Director of Hemp, their authority lighter than floating feathers. Yet by concentrating their essences (*jing*) and disciplining their thoughts, discarding all concerns and gathering together their spirits (*shen*), they merged above with the Nine Heavens and stimulated their most subtle essences (*zhijing*).

With this decentralized pluralistic mode of resonance with the cosmos, *Huainanzi* promotes a 'non-action' model of rulership. As if written word by word in response to Dong's active model of emperorship, the authors of *Huainanzi* declare:[46]

> Does the ruler of all under Heaven have to possess the power, control the situation, hold the power of deciding to let live or to kill, so that his order shall be followed?! What I [we] mean by the sovereign of all under Heaven is not this kind, but rather the kind that fulfills one's own nature . . . and to do so means to unite with *Dao*.

The ruler, according to *Huainanzi*, is not taking action to dominate and control, but rather uniting with *Dao* through non-action.

The two models for rulership were at the centre of the political struggle over the world order—centralization (*dayitong*) versus pluralism. Dong's model of an active ruler supported Emperor Wu, whose reign saw wholesale centralization in cultural, ideological, political, and economical domains. He also launched massive and prolonged military campaigns expanding the territory in all directions, which earned him his actual ruling title: Wudi-Emperor Martial. For his centralization and expansion, history has always paired Emperor Wu with the First Emperor of Qin as the twin examples of 'active rulership'. In the domain of ideology and culture, Dong claims that the Confucian canon, *Spring and Autumn*, is the supreme authority for ideological unification, and he proposes that Emperor Wu take action to prohibit all other schools of thought: 'Only when depraved theories are exterminated and have disappeared can the universal norms be unified, the rules and standards become clear, and people know what to follow.'[47]

[44] Dong Zhongshu (n 42) ch 11, 'Wangdao tongsan 44' 11b.
[45] Liu An (n 39) ch 6, 1a–b. [46] ibid ch 1, 22b. [47] Ban Gu (n 37) 2523.

The ideological unification was essential for building an authoritarian and centralized imperial order. By suppressing different cultural and philosophical traditions, it established universal rules and standards that were themselves the web of the centralized empire. It also subjected divergent factions of power to a single system of doctrines, moral values, and social norms. Accepting Dong's suggestion, Emperor Wu took the famous step of dismissing the hundred schools and establishing Confucianism as the State orthodoxy. In 136 BC, Emperor Wu established the imperial academy (*taixue*) and increased the number of academicians. He then accepted Dong's suggestion of appointing chairs of academicians exclusively for the five Confucian classics.[48] Beginning in 124 BC, students were placed under the charge of each academician, receiving payment from the government and serving as a pool for the recruitment of civil officials. The number of students increased from fifty for each academician to 3,000 during the reign of Emperor Cheng (23–7 BC). The recruitment of civil servants mainly depended on the recommendations of provincial or central government officials, based on the quality of the man's moral and literary education.[49] Emperor Wu also adopted the advice of Gong Sunhong to appoint scholars of Confucian texts for important civil service jobs, replacing clerks. After that, the offices of the government, ranging from the highest (*gong* and *qing*) to the lowest (*shi* and *li*) were occupied mostly by 'refined and sophisticated literary scholars'.[50] The advocate of this policy, Gong Sunhong himself, was promoted to the highest office of the central government, chancellor (*chengxiang*).[51]

*Huainanzi* protests against such ideological unification, asserting that the hundred schools all had the right to engage in government: 'The hundred rivers have different sources, but they all flow to the ocean. The hundred schools have different achievements, but they are all devoted to good government.'[52] Actually, within this pluralistic view, the authors of *Huainanzi* devalued the teaching of Confucian classics in particular: 'It was only when the *Dao* was damaged that the *Book of Poetry* was compiled. It was only when the house of Zhou decayed and the rites and righteousness collapsed that the *Spring and Autumn* was written. Therefore what the learning of the *Book of Poetry* and *Spring and Autumn* praises are the inventions of a decaying era.'[53] Using the cosmology of *Dao*, which produced 10,000 things without possessing or dominating them, *Huainanzi*'s vision of the empire was one that allowed space for all cultural traditions and ideas to participate, one that embraced rather than suppressed the great variety of cultural and philosophical traditions, just as nature embraced the great variety of beings.

In the actual political realm, the elimination of pluralism had its more visible and tangible manifestation in the bloodshed by the local kings who were defeated in the process of centralization. While the battle was fought with weapons and human lives, both sides employed symbolic weapons as well—omens as Heaven's speech

[48] ibid 159.

[49] For imperial academy and the scholars' role in government, see Hans Bielenstein, *The Bureaucracy of Han Times* (CUP 1980).

[50] Ban Gu (n 37) 3593–96. [51] ibid 2613–23. [52] Liu An (n 39) ch 13, 4b.

[53] ibid ch 13, 4b–5a.

that also had the power to kill. It was through interpreting omens that Dong persuaded the emperor to execute the noble kings. The most extensive record of Dong's use of omens in politics is his memorial of 140 BC. According to the 'Wuxing' chapter in the *History of Han*, the temple and the garden dedicated to the founding emperor Gao caught fire. Dong Zhongshu wrote a memorial to Emperor Wu using an analogy to the four catastrophes of fire recorded in *Spring and Autumn*, saying that these fires were all messages that Heaven intended to execute the evil powers, that is, the royal nobility:[54]

In the past, Qin inherited the malady of the declined Zhou, and failed to cure it. Then Han inherited the malady of Qin and again failed to cure it ... On top of that, Han has yet the problem of [the royal] brothers and relatives, who are overbearing, arrogant, extravagant and indulgent, many of whom are unbridled. That is why we say this is the 'time of deep crisis'.

Speaking in Heaven's voice, Dong explicitly demanded the emperor to execute his royal brothers:[55]

Heaven descends catastrophes as if speaking to your majesty, saying that 'facing the present situation, which is full of evil and deep crisis, you cannot govern except by using great justice and supreme public [standards] (*tai ping zhi gong*). Search among the royal relatives and in the kingdoms outside the capital, for the ones who have most deviated from the standards, and harden your heart to execute them! Just as I burned down the Temple for Ancestor Gao.'

Dong attributes the concept of justice (*ping*) and a public standard (*gong*) to Heaven's will, using them to compete with the private family relations of the emperor. Dong's proposal was not adopted at the time.[56] But eighteen years later, when the King of Huainan was accused of plotting an armed rebellion, Emperor Wu remembered the advice of Dong Zhongshu; he appointed Dong's disciple Lü Bushu to take charge of the case of Huainan. Lü Bushu used the very Confucian canon of *Spring and Autumn* as the law code, executing the criminals first and reporting to the emperor afterward, and the emperor always granted his permission. The King of Huainan, Liu An, committed suicide, and his family, followers, and the people involved with him were killed by the tens of thousands.[57]

*Huainanzi*, which survived as part of Emperor Wu's collection, protested against centralization and persecution of the noble kings. It was a bitter protest against the Confucian scholars, condemning them for using rites and righteousness to 'cause the conflicts between the ruler and the subjects, and to generate hatred between flesh and blood'.[58] Disguising their criticism under the cap of the late Xia Dynasty, the authors of *Huainanzi* attribute the contemporary social conflict to evil scholar-officials in the capital who have manipulated the emperor:[59]

The virtuous ruler presides over the throne but does not have peace; the ministers do not speak for *Dao*, and the crowds of subjects please the emperor at the price of corrupting the principles, distancing the emperor's flesh and blood for their self-interests. The evil people gather to plot in secret, getting in between the ruler and subject and between the father and

[54] Ban Gu (n 37) 1331–33. [55] ibid. [56] Ban Gu (n 37) 2524.
[57] ibid 1425. [58] Liu An (n 39) ch 11, 1a. [59] ibid ch 6, 12b–13a.

son, competing to please the arrogant ruler and to follow his intentions, causing dissension among people in order to achieve their goals. That is why the ruler and subject are in conflict and do not feel close, and the flesh and blood are distanced and detached from one another.

This protest also uses cosmological omens to speak to the emperor. According to the text, the social evil resulted in a series of catastrophes and strange phenomena, including the cracking of temples, the collapse of altars, strange behaviour and phenomena in all kinds of animals, the anger of gods, natural catastrophes, and warfare in the human world. After the long list of catastrophes, *Huainanzi* speaks to Emperor Wu, advising him to distance himself from the evil scholar-officials, to abandon harsh laws and excessive affairs, and to unite with Dao through non-action.[60] Ironically, *Huainanzi*, the swansong of Daoist philosophy and a voice of protest against centralization, was presented to Emperor Wu, during whose reign the King of Huainan and his circle of writers of *Huainanzi* lost their lives, Daoism and other non-Confucian schools were banned, and the power of the kingdoms was finally eliminated. Their models of a non-active ruler and a pluralistic world lost out.

## 7. The First and Only Confucian 'Moral Ruler'

If Confucianism rose during Emperor Wu's centralization, it took another century to see its completion in establishing a moralized rulership at the centre of a moralized cosmology. This completion is evident in the downfall of the Former Han and the rise (and fall) of the first and only Confucian moral ruler, Wang Mang. Wang Mang set up a model of rulership opposite to that based on military conquest and rule by law, as represented by the Qin Emperor and Emperor Wu. Wang Mang was one of the most learned Confucian scholars of his time and a practitioner who spent his life realizing Confucian ideals. He came into power through his reputation as a moral exemplar of Confucian ethics, being known for his filial piety and promotion of 'rule by ritual' in opposition to 'rule by law' and by coercion. Replacing the Han Dynasty with his New Dynasty (Xin) in AD 8, he tearfully accepted the throne that had been abdicated by a 5-year-old boy, the fourteenth emperor of the Former Han. This was the only time in Chinese history a scholar replaced a dynasty, involving no military conquest or the killing of the former ruler. After becoming an emperor, Wang Mang finally put the Confucian ideal of following the Zhou and restoring Zhou ritual order into political practice, implementing a series of economic and ritual reforms, actualizing what Confucian scholars had dreamed about for centuries.

Wang Mang's enthroning edict illustrates how he put the cosmological theory of Heaven's Mandate into practice.[61] In this edict, he listed the following proofs

[60] 'Support the capable, and demote the slanderers and flatterers, silence clever arguments, abandon harsh laws, rid the numerous and excessive affairs, block the channel of rumors, close the door to factionalism, abolish knowledge and techniques … therefore to unite with the undivided darkness (*hunming*, the original state of *Dao*), remove the intentions and release the mind, so that the ten thousand things could return to their own roots' (ibid 16b–17b).

[61] Ban Gu (n 37) 4095–96.

of receiving the Mandate of Heaven. First, he claimed to be the descendent of the mythical Yellow Emperor, and like him, to represent the Phase of Earth. According to the birth cycle of the Five Phases, Earth is the son of Fire, the symbol of the Han Dynasty. In this claim, the conquest cycle that had justified the founding of Qin and Han is replaced by a cycle of birth and nurturing from mother to son, which is an analogy of transmitting the throne by abdicating it to a moral successor, a myth from the antiquity of the sage kings and the ideal found in Confucian canons. Second, Wang Mang claimed Heaven had shifted its Mandate to himself by descending hundreds of auspicious omens as verification, firmly establishing Heaven as the supreme moral authority and omens as verifications of Heaven's Mandate. Third, he claimed to have found a decree from the spirit of the deceased founding Emperor of Han, announcing the abdication of the Han throne.

Wang Mang hereby transformed the concept of sovereignty through a Confucian moralized cosmology. His ritual complex best illustrates this Confucian concept of rulership based on ritual rather than coercion. He reconstructed the highest ritual hall of antiquity, named *piyong*, an archaic temple form found in Confucian texts. The centre of the compound was a hall composed of a central room and four side chambers, which together symbolized the Five Phases. This ritual complex represented a moralized Five Phases, with a generation cycle of birth and nurturing replacing the conquest cycle of force and violence. Each of the side chambers represented one of the Five Phases and one season, while the central room symbolized the phase of Earth and the middle of the year. In his ritual practice, the Son of Heaven, Wang Mang, would dress in the proper colour and perform the proper ritual in the proper chamber in accordance with the season. His movement acted out the generation cycle in a temporal sequence, symbolizing Heaven's nurturing of the people through the Son of Heaven.

Not only did the generation cycle of the Five Phases, symbolizing birth and nurturing, replace the conquest cycle in imperial ideology, but the entire system of Five Phases was subjected to the moral authority of Heaven. The five-chamber ritual hall was built on a round platform 60m in diameter, which was placed in a large square courtyard composed of four walls (235m long each). Surrounding the square courtyard, again, was a large circle 360m in diameter formed by a ditch of water.[62] In the Han symbolic structure, the circle symbolized Heaven and the square symbolized earth. By locating the ritual hall on a round circle, and then a square, then a circle again, Wang Mang reproduced the cosmological structure of Earth, Human, and Heaven in a material form, and positioned himself at the centre of the cosmos, acting out the Confucian moral cosmology through his rituals. The emperor's body became a microcosm, moving in a generation cycle, and connecting Heaven and earth. The construction of this ritual complex was one of the great achievements demonstrating the moral superiority that had led him to the throne. Building upon two centuries of

[62] For the reconstruction of the ritual complex, see Wang Zhongshu, *Han Civilization* (Yale UP 1982) fig 30.

discursive transformation of the concept of sovereignty, Wang Mang now actualized it in political practice.

## 8. Conclusion

The founding emperors of Qin and Han had been military conquerors who established their dynasties on the warhorse, as did all founding emperors of the other twenty-three dynasties in the following two thousand years. Wang Mang, in contrast, received his throne through abdication (*shanrang*), the only case in Chinese history that actualized the Confucian ideal of peaceful transmission of Heaven's Mandate to a moral ruler. Wang Mang's dynasty lasted fourteen years, one year shorter than the Qin. Ironically, he has been the most condemned emperor of all. The twenty-five dynastic histories exclude his Xin dynasty and unanimously call Wang Mang a usurper. Emperor Xuan (the grandson of Emperor Wu) had warned his heir apparent against his whole-hearted favouring of Confucianism, saying that the Han Dynasty had always been ruling by mixing the way of hegemons (legalist) and the way of the kings (the Confucian). He predicted that his son's inclination of using Confucianism exclusively would doom the dynasty. His prediction, alas, came true.

The first emperor of Qin and Wang Mang exemplify two competing models of the Son of Heaven, one based on coercive power (rule by law) and one based on moral power (rule by morality). The Chinese dynasties after them, inherited their institutions and practices, and also learned lessons from their doomed fate. Emperor Xuan would be happy to see that all later dynasties continued to mix the two models. All founding emperors of the twenty-five dynasties were military conquerors, and all their succeeding heirs were hereditary princelings, appointed based on birthright rather than morality. All emperors wished the same wish of the first emperor that the throne would be handed down to his descendants for thousands of generations, and none considered abdicating it to a more moral person. Great emperors of each dynasty had strong militaries and expanded territory, a legal system similar to that of Qin, and a centralized economy. At the same time, all dynasties also continued Wang Mang's cosmology of the generation cycle of Five Phases, adopting a symbol from it that was the 'son' of the previous dynasty, even though they actually conquered the 'mother' through military campaigns.

All later dynasties also adopted Confucianism as imperial ideology, and used the scholars as teachers of the heir, advisers of the government, and civil servants. These loyal servants helped the emperors eliminate social forces that could potentially challenge the autocracy. The emperors also periodically purged Confucian scholars for their criticism of the government, from Qin's burying them alive, to Ming and Qing literary prisons. Yet Confucian scholars, in turn, have never become a social force truly independent of the authoritarian ruler, and their umbilical cord to the centralized State was never cut.[63] They served as active components of the State bureaucracy, as well as the most vocal critics and reformers of it. When, at the end of the nineteenth century, Kang Youwei attempted a constitutional reform and a modern world order based on Confucianism, his social position remained, as that of Jia Yi and Dong Zhongshu, an adviser of the emperor.

The struggle between the two models of rulership continued beyond the empires. Chairman Mao acknowledged that 'power comes from the gun', yet Mao Zedong thought became the highest moral authority, the spiritual 'nuclear bomb' (in Liu Shaoqi's words). He used intellectuals to convey his moral authority to mass movements, from land revolution to Cultural Revolution, eliminating enemy classes one after another. Yet he purged intellectuals periodically as well for their criticisms. Today, the struggle of the two models of rule has continued into a struggle between the 'rule of law' and the 'rule of man'. It seems to be perfect timing to re-enact Confucianism, now that Western democracies are in crisis and Chinese economic, military, and political powers are rising miraculously. But the trouble is, now that Heaven is dead, from where does the Son of Heaven derive his moral authority? Even if he could stand alone without Heaven, how could his morality be measured and who has the authority to measure it? How would the moral ruler rise, if not from the hereditary princelings holding guns? Confucianism has been instrumental for hierarchical societies and authoritarian States. When we engage the Confucian concept of a moral ruler of All Under Heaven, we must assess its social and institutional bases and political implications upon China's immediate future. Maoist China claimed to bypass capitalism by a great leap forward armed with Mao Zedong thought; will post-Mao China bypass democracy and rule of law armed with Confucian autocracy as an alternative? Or, alternatively, could ancient Chinese thought be revived as a critical force challenging the corruption and abuse of power within China and the Eurocentric world order outside? Will Confucianism promote a neo-authoritarianism of one kind or another in the twenty-first century, or could it reconcile with democracy and rule of law to construct a better China and a better world? All these should be taken into account in our reconstruction of ancient Chinese thought.

[63] P Bol argues that Neo-Confucianism in the southern Song started to move away from serving the emperor and the central government to build and represent the local communities. Nevertheless, its leading figure Zhu Xi still demanded that the government restrict private landholdings to curb the rising land wealth. See Bol, *Neo-Confucianism in History* (Harvard University Asia Center–Harvard UP 2008) 143.

# 12

# 'Humane Governance' as the Moral Responsibility of Rulers in East Asian Confucian Political Philosophy

*Chun-chieh Huang**

## 1. Introduction

This chapter explores the East Asian Confucian political thoughts centred on Humane Governance, and their internally imbedded theoretical issues. Humane Governance is a critical core value in East Asian Confucian political thoughts. Evoking Humane Governance, Confucians stipulated moral responsibilities for political rulers. The latter were expected to rule by the order of Heaven, to treat the subjects as children and to be compassionate towards the suffering of the people as if they were family members.[1] Confucians also emphasized the importance of Humane Governance by claiming it had been practised during the Three Dynasties—Xia (夏, 2070–1600 BCE), Shang (商, 1600–1046 BCE), Zhou (周, 1046–256 BCE)—when it served as the essence of 'former kings' way' or 'the kingly way'.[2]

In the thoughts of Confucius (孔子, 551–479 BCE) and Mencius (孟子, 371–289 BCE), Humane Governance was originally meant for imposing moral responsibilities onto political rulers, and therefore emphasized whether a ruler had a 'humane heart'. The concept of a 'humane heart' was considered inseparable from Humane Governance. In the context of the time in which Confucius and Mencius lived, the political discussions about Humane Governance reflected the Confucian criticism of the politics during the Spring–Autumn and Warring-state periods (722–222 BCE). Therefore, they were political thoughts that contained counter-factual implications. Nevertheless, the following discussions by Confucians in

* Translated by Zhang Longyi.

[1] We stated elsewhere that the ideal type of government according to Mencius was a populist government of familial empathy. See Chun-chieh Huang, *Mencian Hermeneutics: A History of Interpretations in China* (Transaction 2011) ch 3, 80–102.

[2] Mencius said, 'The Three Dynasties won the Empire through benevolence and lost it through cruelty' (*Mencius* (DC Lau tr, Chinese UP 2003) Bk IV, Pt A, ch 3, 153).

China, Japan, and Korea have been learning the implementation of actual political policies, instead of simply being an exploration of the theoretical issues within the original thoughts. Their discussions focused on political management instead of political principles.[3]

As Xiao Gongquan (蕭公權, 1897–1981) stated, Chinese traditional political thought of which Confucianism is the most representative—mostly fall into the category of Art of Politics (Politics), while few fall into the category of Political Philosophy (Staatslehre; Political Science).[4] Under the traditional East Asian authoritarian politics, the Confucian discourse on Humane Governance has become 'eternal nostalgia' of the intellectuals and therefore an 'unfinished project'.

Section 2 discusses how the Pre-Qin Confucian discourse on Humane Governance was proposed. It also discusses the development of Benevolence in the history of Confucian thoughts. Section 3 is a narrative on the development of Humane Governance in Joseon Korea (1392–1910) and Tokugawa Japan (1603–1868). Section 4 examines two theoretical issues within the Confucian discussions on Humane Governance. Section 5 concludes the chapter.

## 2. The Classical Confucian Discourses on Humane Governance and the Essence of Benevolence

### 2.1. Discussions on Humane Governance by Confucius and Mencius

Confucius and Mencius ignited discussions on Humane Governance in East Asian Confucians. Confucius was the first to propose the essence of Humane Governance. He particularly emphasized Benevolence. The word 'Benevolence' (仁 ren, Humanity, Humaneness) occurred in the *Analects* of Confucius 105 times. This concept bridges the inner and external worlds, helping to build connections between the self and others. In this way, human emotions would become integrated with objective political policies. As Xiao Gongquan stated, 'In terms of personal cultivation, *jen* is a matter of one's individual ethics. But in terms of practice, *jen* is additionally both social ethics and political principle. When Confucius spoke

[3] The notions of 'Principle of Legitimation' and 'Principle of Governance' were first proposed by Mou Zongsan (牟宗三, 1905–95). Mou argued that China only had 'principle of governance' but no 'principle of legitimation'. The former refers to the right to govern, while the latter refers to the right to rule. He also pointed out that the functional presentation of the rationale behind Chinese culture was a moralized principle of governance, which shows a relationship of subordination instead of coordination. Confucianism based the legitimacy of political rule on the myth about wise emperors and capable officials, thus giving priority to the individual morality of the ruler instead of objective political institutions, a fact that enabled revolutions in which rulers were overthrown. See Mou Zongsan, *Zhengdao yu Zhidao* 政道與治道 [*Principle of Legitimation and Principle of Governance*] (Guangwenshuju 1961) 1, 48, 52, 134–40. Lee Ming-huei (李明輝, 1953–) recently introduced new translations: 'zhengdao' as 'principle of legitimation' and 'Zhidao' as 'principle of governance'. We believe these translations are the closest possible to Mou's original ideas. See Ming-huei Lee, translated by Hong Tzu-ki, 'Building Democracy: The Theory and Practice of New Confucianism' (to be published).

[4] Xiao Gongquan 蕭公權, *Zhongguo Zhengzhi sixiang shi* 中國政治思想史 [*A History of Chinese Political Thought*] (Lianjing chuban shiye gongsi 1982), vol 2, 946.

about *jen* he was in fact smelting the one of ethics, social relationships, and politics together in one crucible; he was bringing others, the self, the family, and the state into alignment through the development of "one all-pervading" concept'.[5] Confucius's discussions on Benevolence stressed that it 'helps others to take their stand in that he himself wishes to take his stand, and gets others there in that he himself wishes to get there'.[6] He also emphasized that 'Government (cheng, 政) is being correct (cheng,正)' (*Analects*, 12.17), a statement that implies politics is 'a great mechanism for nurturing people's characters'.[7] Politics in Confucius's discourses—which took Benevolence as the core value—gave priority to the educational purposes of political measures and policies. According to Confucius, the purpose of politics was to guide the people towards the supreme standards of morality. In that sense, the ideal politics pursued by Confucius could be categorized as a form of ethocracy.

Benevolence was the core political value in Confucius's thoughts but was better explicated by Mencius. Mencius coined the concept 'Humane Governance', which was mentioned in *Mencius* eight times. Humane Governance, according to Mencius, was based on Humane Heart. He encouraged rulers to rule 'With such a sensitive heart behind compassionate government' (*Mencius*, 2A6).[8] The essence of Humane Heart is 'a heart sensitive to the suffering of others'.[9] Therefore, we could conclude that Mencius's philosophy tended to be based on personal idealism. Regarding his other statements, particularly that everybody has 'a heart sensitive to the suffering of others', we could find Mencius's discussions appearing to involve characteristics integral to social idealism.

Mencius's thoughts on Humane Governance also emphasized the implementation of policies. He argued that a ruler should hold 'a heart sensitive to the suffering of others' and extend his bounty in policymaking, which should eventually be realized through specific measures. Such measures include: (1) economic and political land demarcation (*Jingtianzhi*, 井田制);[10] (2) decreasing the people's taxation burdens;[11] (3) ensuring abundant material resources to sustain the people's quality of life.[12] His discussions touched on both 'a heart sensitive to the suffering of others' and 'compassionate government', which are inseparable. According to Mencius,

[5] Xiao Gongquan (Kung-chuan Hsiao), *A History of Chinese Political Thought* (FW Mote tr, Princeton UP 1979), vol 1, 103.

[6] See *The Analects* (DC Lau tr, Chinese UP 1992) Bk VI, ch 30, 55.

[7] Xiao Gongquan (n 4), vol 1, 66.

[8] See *Mencius* (n 2) Bk II, Pt A, ch 6, 73. Sa Meng-wu (薩孟武, 1897–1984) reviewed the essence of Mencius's Humane Governance and his suggestions for political policies. See Sa Meng-wu, *Rujia zhenglun yianyi: Xianqin rujia zhengzhi sisiang de tixi jiqi yianbian* 儒家政論衍義——先秦儒家政治思想的體系及其演變 [Interpretation of Confucian Political Theory: The System of Pre-Qin Confucian Political Thought and Its Development] (Dongda tushu gongsi 1982) 376–84.

[9] Kang Youwei (康有為, 1858–1927) once commented that 'when externalized, this sensitive heart would result in compassionate politics. If the generations to come as well as sages lose such a heart, we would stop having sages, nor would we have compassionate politics. Therefore, it is obvious that compassionate politics fundamentally stem from such a heart as sensitive to the suffering of the people' (*Mengzi wei* [*A Study of the Mencius*] (Taiwan shangwu yinshuguan 1970), vol 1, 2 (lower part)).

[10] See *Mencius* (n 2) Bk III, Pt A, ch 3, 109.

[11] ibid Bk II, Pt A, ch 5, 71.

[12] ibid Bk I, Pt A, ch 3, 7.

such an ideal form of Humane Governance had been realized during the Three Dynasties and therefore could be termed 'the Kingly way' or 'the way of the Former Kings' (*Mencius*, 4A1).[13] He also encouraged political rulers to 'become a true King by tending the people' (*Mencius*, 1A7)[14] and go further to 'be father and mother to the people' (*Mencius*, 1A4).[15]

Two points in Mencius's thoughts on Humane Governance deserve special attention. First, like the thoughts of Confucius, those of Mencius were counterfactual and critical of the world in their time. In his historical comparisons, Confucius often idealized the history of the Three Dynasties articulating his ideals on 'antiquity' and referring to 'today' as the decay of his times.[16] Mencius followed Confucius's tendency of stating the 'ought to be' for 'today' and by idealizing the 'to be' of 'antiquity'. Therefore, Humane Governance as discussed by Mencius was fundamentally counterfactual.[17]

Second, Mencius emphasized that a government that practises Humane Governance must be 'one who is father and mother to the people' (*Mencius*, 1A4).[18] However, Mencius's 'moral politics' lay outside the scope of the 'strict father model' proposed by George Lakoff (1941–); we should categorize them as a 'nurturing parent model' instead.[19] Mencius emphasized that a ruler had to ensure the ability of his people to be 'in the support of their parents when alive and in the mourning of them when dead, they will be able to have no regrets over anything left undone' (*Mencius*, 1A3).[20] He argued that 'no man is devoid of a heart sensitive to the suffering of others', by analogy: 'seeing a young child on the verge of falling into a well' (*Mencius*, 2A6).[21] Mencius also argued that rulers should 'share their enjoyments with the people' (*Mencius*, 1A2).[22] All these facts indicate that Mencius's Humane Governance essentially falls into the 'nurturant parent model' for moralistic political thoughts. It employs sharing, tolerance, compassion, and responsibility as its core values and displays a distinctive maternal character.[23]

[13] ibid Bk IV, Pt A, ch 1, 149; cf Chun-chieh Huang, 'Historical Thinking in Classical Confucianism: Historical Argumentation from the Three Dynasties' in Chun-chieh Huang and Erik Zürcher (eds), *Time and Space in Chinese Culture* (Brill 1995) 72–88.

[14] See *Mencius* (n 2) Bk I, Pt A, ch 7, 15. [15] ibid ch 4, 11.

[16] Confucius said, 'Men of antiquity studied to improve themselves; men today study to impress others' (*The Analects* (n 6) Bk XIV, ch 24, 141). And 'In antiquity, the common people had three weaknesses, but today they cannot be counted on even to have these ... In antiquity, in being foolish, men were straight; today, in being foolish, they are simply crafty' (ibid Bk XVII, ch 16, 177).

[17] For 'counterfactual' argumentation in traditional Chinese thoughts, see Kuang-ming Wu, 'Counterfactuals, Universals, and Chinese Thinking' (1989) 19(2) Tsing Hua Journal of Chinese Studies 1–43.

[18] See *Mencius* (n 2) Bk I, Pt A, ch 4, 11.

[19] George Lakoff, *Moral Politics: How Liberals and Conservatives Think* (University of Chicago Press 1996) 35; George Lakoff, 'Metaphor, Morality, and Politics, or, Why Conservatives Have Left Liberals in the Dust', http://www.wwcd.org/issues/Lakoff.html

[20] See *Mencius* (n 2) Bk I, Pt A, ch 3, 7. [21] ibid Bk II, Pt A, ch 6, 73.

[22] ibid Bk I, Pt A, para 2, p 5.

[23] Joanne D Birdwhistell, *Mencius and Masculinities: Dynamics of Power, Morality, and Maternal Thinking* (State University of New York Press 2007) 89–109.

## 2.2. Essence of Benevolence in the history of traditional Chinese thoughts

Ren 仁 (Benevolence, Humanity, Humaneness) is the core value of Confucius and Mencius's discussions about Humane Governance. Therefore, we must typologically categorize it as a critical concept in Chinese Confucian thoughts and analyse its theoretical focus.

Confucian thinkers have offered a variety of interpretations of Benevolence in the intellectual history of Chinese Confucianism. The majority of these interpretations fall into one of four categories: (1) Benevolence interpreted as a place for humankind's soul and being; (2) Benevolence as the persistent capability of making value judgements; (3) Benevolence as a social principle; (4) Benevolence as a political cause. The first two categories fall into the internal sphere of Benevolence, while the last two belong to its external sphere. The former realm can be controlled by one's mind while the latter realm is beyond one's mind and has much to do with socio-political structure. Confucianism insists that the two spheres of Benevolence must be connected and that Humane Governance must be based on Humane Heart. The following section will elaborate on the four connotations.

First, Confucius interpreted Benevolence as a place where one can rest his mind and soul, and wander therein. He said, 'Of neighbourhoods benevolence is the most beautiful. How can the man be considered wise who, when he has the choice, does not settle in benevolence?' (*Analects*, 4.1).[24] He also said, 'The benevolent man is attracted to benevolence because he feels at home in it. The wise man is attracted to benevolence because he finds it to his advantage' (*Analects*, 4.2).[25] By arguing so, he was comparing Benevolence to a space in which people can settle down, depart, and return. Confucius argued that 'A young man should be a good son at home and an obedient young man abroad, sparing of speech but trustworthy in what he says, and should love the multitude at large but cultivate the friendship of his fellow men' (*Analects*, 1.6).[26] Human beings can learn about concepts such as dedication to family (filial piety) and obedience in society from the homes in which they lived, according to Confucius. This idea serves as the starting point for developing this view of Benevolence. Confucius's disciple Youzi (有子, 518–458 BCE) said, 'Being good as a son and obedient as a young man is, perhaps, the root of a man's character' (*Analects*, 1.2).[27]

Both Confucius and Mencius applied 'ontological metaphors'—a term proposed by Mark Johnson—to their explanations of the meanings of Benevolence.[28] After citing Confucius's 'Of neighbourhoods benevolence is the most beautiful', Mencius went further by arguing that 'Benevolence is the high honour bestowed by Heaven

[24] See *The Analects* (n 6) Bk IV, ch 1, 29.

[25] ibid ch 2, 29.

[26] See *The Analects* (n 6) Bk I, ch 6, 3.

[27] ibid ch 2, 3. Zhu Xi (朱熹, 1130–1200) later explained this argument by saying, 'filial piety and social obedience do serve as the starting point of benevolent behaviours, and make up one aspect of Benevolence. However, they are the root for benevolent behaviours only, instead of Benevolence itself.' This is an inspiring explanation.

[28] George Lakoff and Mark Johnson, *Metaphors We Live By* (University of Chicago Press 1980) 25–32.

and the peaceful abode of man' (*Mencius*, 2A7).[29] He compared Benevolence to a concrete house, thus concretizing Benevolence as a concept and fully defining Benevolence as a means by which a human being can settle down, wander about, and break away from the fences between the self and others so that the individual is completely free within his private world.[30] Wang Fuzhi (王夫之, 1619–92) accurately explained Confucius's belief in 'the benevolent man being attracted to benevolence'. Wang said, 'When the heart has become home to Benevolence, all seen in the world will appear to be benevolent deeds, and there will be no repulsion or fear.'[31]

Second, Benevolence is the human capability of making value judgements based on endless internal élan. Youzi, a pupil of Confucius, said, 'The gentleman devotes his efforts to the roots, for once the roots are established, the Way will grow therefrom. Being good as a son and obedient as a young man is, perhaps, the root of a man's character' (*Analects*, 1.2).[32] 'The Way will grow therefrom' implies that persisting values are fundamentally generated inside the human mind. When annotating this expression, Zhuzi (朱熹, Huian 晦庵, 1130–1200) cited Cheng Yi's (程頤, 1033–1107) statement, 'Virtues has roots. Once the roots are in place, the Way will be illuminated.'[33] However, this interpretation deviates from the original meaning of 'the Way will grow therefrom', as it misses 'grow', which indicates continuation and vitality, as Qian Mu (錢穆, 1895–1990) mentioned.[34] This everlasting heart originates from 'the heart of compassion' as explained by Mencius.[35]

In the Han Dynasty (206 BCE–220 CE), thoughts emphasizing interactions between heaven and humankind gradually gained popularity. In the context of his time, Dong Zhongshu (董仲舒, 179–104 BCE) believed that Benevolence originates in nature. He wrote, 'The beauty of Benevolence is determined by heaven. Heaven is embodied by Benevolence. It nurtures all living creatures, by both giving birth to them and raising them up, in an endless circle.'[36] Dong Zhongshu thus built a connection between Benevolence, which is supposedly full of implications for value judgements, and the natural Heaven, which is free from value judgements. However, such an attempt jeopardized the subjectivity of humankind towards morality.

[29] See *Mencius* (n 2) Bk II, Pt A, ch 7, 75; Yang Xiong 揚雄 (53 BCE–18 CE) also metaphorized Benevolence as a house. See Wang Rongbao 汪榮寶 (1878–1933), *Fa yian yi shu* 法言義疏 [*Commentaries and Sub-commentaries of* Fa yian] (Zhonghua shuju 1987, 1997) 92.

[30] Mencius said, 'Where is one's dwelling? In benevolence' (*Mencius* (n 2) Bk VII, Pt A, ch 33, 301).

[31] Wang Fuzhi 王夫之, *Lunyu xunyi* 論語訓義 [*Interpretation of the* Analects] in *Sishu xunyi* 四書訓義 [*Interpretation of the* Four Books], *Wuqiobeizhai Lunyu jicheng* 無求備齋論語集成 [*Wuqiobeizhai Collection of the* Analects] (Yiwen yinshuguan, 1966), vol 2, juan 8, Bk 4, 2.

[32] See *The Analects* (n 6) Bk I, ch 2, 3.

[33] Zhu Xi 朱熹, *Lunyu jizhu* 論語集注 [*Collected Commentaries on the* Analects], in his *Sishu zhangju jizhu* 四書章句集注 [Four Books *in Chapter and Verse with Collected Commentaries*] (Zhonghua shuju 1983) 48.

[34] Qian Mu 錢穆, *Kongzi yu Lunyu* 孔子與論語 [*Confucius and the* Analects], in *Qian Binsi Xiangsheng quanji* 錢賓四先生全集 [*Complete Work of Mr Qian Mu*] (Lianjing chuban gongsi 1998), vol 4, esp 272.

[35] See *Mencius* (n 2) Bk II, Pt A, ch 6, 73.

[36] Su Yu 蘇輿 (1874–1914), *Chunqiu fanlu yizheng* 春秋繁露義證 [*Commentaries on the Luxuriant Gems of the Spring and Autumn Annals*] (Zhonghua shuju 2007) 392.

In the eleventh century, Cheng Hao (程顥, 1032–85) argued that 'Benevolence does not discriminate among all creatures under heaven'.[37] Cheng Yi held that 'the human heart is just like a millet grain, and Benevolence is the nature human beings are born with'.[38] When Zhu Xi wrote his famous treatise on Benevolence, he started with Cheng Yi's words 'the mind of Heaven and Earth is to produce things', and followed that with 'in the production of man and things, they receive the mind of Heaven and Earth as their mind'.[39] By saying so, Zhu Xi elevated the importance of human life to the height of cosmology and ontology. He explained Benevolence as 'the virtue of mind-heart and the principle of love',[40] which helps transforming the essence of Benevolence into the principle that connects the individual with the universe itself. Following Zhu Xi, Wang Yangming (王陽明, 1472–1529) argued that 'Benevolence is the principle behind the circle of life'.[41]

The previous two interpretations of Benevolence allude to the development of human beings' tenacity. The former is the essential meaning of Benevolence, while the latter is a derivative meaning. Regardless of their differences, all Chinese Confucians after Confucius and Mencius have held the belief that Humane Heart must be reflected in Humane Governance. In other words, the internalization of Benevolence must be carried out in its externalization.

Benevolence can also be interpreted as a social principle. This third connotation of Benevolence is centred on the relationship between the self and others. It takes 'love your fellow men' as its core value. Confucius's pupil Fan Chi (樊遲, 514–? BCE) once asked about the meaning of Benevolence, and Confucius answered with 'love your fellow men' (*Analects*, 12.22).[42] When answering Zhong Gong (仲弓, 522–? BCE) about the latter's question on Benevolence, Confucius stated, 'do not impose on others what you yourself do not desire' (*Analects*, 12.2).[43] He answered Zi Gong (子貢, 520–? BCE) with Benevolence 'helps others to take their stand in that he himself wishes to take his stand, and gets others there in that he himself wishes to get there' (*Analects*, 6.30).[44] All these answers indicate that Benevolence serves as a social principle in Confucius's thoughts. Mencius said, 'If others do not respond to your love with love, look into your own benevolence' (*Mencius*, 4A4)[45] and that 'A benevolent man never harbours anger or nurses a grudge against a brother. All he does is to love him' (*Mencius*, 5A3).[46] He believed that 'feeling is intimate concern for his parent. To feel this is benevolence' (*Mencius*, 6B3),[47] and that 'a benevolent man

[37] Cheng Yi and Cheng Hao, *Er Cheng ji* 二程集 [*Complete Works of the Two Chengs*] (Zhonghua shuju 1981, 2004) upper vol, juan 2, 15.

[38] ibid juan 18, 184.

[39] See Wing-tsit Chan, tr and ed, *A Source Book in Chinese Philosophy* (Princeton UP 1973) ch 34, 593.

[40] Zhu Xi noted, 'Benevolence is the virtue of mind-heart and the principle of love'. *Lunyu jizhu* 論語集註 [*Collected Commentaries on the* Analects], vol 1, in his *Sishu zhangju jizhu*, 48. See Zhu Xi, *Lunyu jizhu*, in *Sishu zhangju jizhu*, 48.

[41] Wang Yangming, *Yulu* 語錄.一 [*Conversation, I*], in Wang Yangming quanji 王陽明全集 [*Collected Works of Wang Yangming*] (Shanghai guji chubanshe, 1992), upper vol, 26.

[42] See *The Analects* (n 6) Bk XII, ch 22, 117.

[43] ibid, ch 2, 109.

[44] See *The Analects* (n 6) Bk VI, ch 30, 55.

[45] See *Mencius* (n 2) Bk IV, Pt A, ch 4, 153.

[46] ibid Bk V, Pt A, ch 3, 199.

[47] ibid Bk VI, Pt B, ch 3, 267.

loves everyone' (*Mencius*, 7A46).[48] All these statements help to explain Benevolence as 'love'. Liao Ming-chun (廖名春, 1956–) referenced the latest unearthed archaeological archives to verify the belief that the ancient meaning of Benevolence was just 'love your fellow men'.[49]

Moreover, the *Book of Rites* stated that 'Benevolence is the affection between the above and the below' [50] and affirmed 'the supreme principle for a benevolent person to love the others'.[51] Both passages interpreted Benevolence as a social principle. Confucians in the Han Dynasty also tended to explain Benevolence as love. Jia Yi (賈誼, 200–168 BCE) wrote, 'Benevolence is to love the people with one's heart'.[52] *The Outer Commentary to the* Book of Odes recorded, 'Benevolence is the reflection of love through emotions'.[53] Gongsun Hong (公孫弘, 200–121 BCE) wrote, 'Benevolence is love. Righteousness is appropriateness.'[54] Dong Zhongshu said, 'the principle of Benevolence is to love the others, instead of one's very self'.[55] Xun Yue (荀悅, 148–209) in the later-Han Dynasty said, 'Benevolence is found in kindness'.[56] When the Han Confucians discussed Benevolence with love, they were essentially referring to Benevolence as a social principle.

The last of the connotations of Benevolence is that of a political cause, or Humane Governance as proposed by Mencius. Zilu (子路, 542–480 BCE) once asked about the meaning of a 'gentleman' (*Junzi*, 君子), and Confucius answered with '[a man who] cultivates himself and thereby achieves reverence', with 'cultivates himself and thereby brings peace and security to his fellow men', and with 'cultivates himself and thereby brings peace and security to the people'.[57] He implied a process that resembles concentric circles going through the self, one's family, the State, and heaven, in that order, inside to out. Another of Confucius's pupils, Zizhang (子張, 503–? BCE), once asked about Benevolence, and Confucius answered with 'There are five things and whoever is capable of putting them into practice in the Empire is certainly "benevolent".' The five things here are 'respectfulness, tolerance, trustworthiness in word, quickness, and generosity' (*Analects*, 17.6)[58] According to Confucius, the supreme goal of a human being is to 'give extensively to the common people and

[48] ibid Bk VII, Pt A, ch 46, 309.

[49] Liao Ming-chun 廖名春, '"Ren" zi tanyuan「仁」字探源 [An Inquiry into the Origin of "Ren"]' *Zhongguo xueshu* 中國學術 [*Chinese Scholarship*] 8 (April 2001) 123–39.

[50] See Sun Xidan 孫希旦 (1736–84), *Liji jijie* 禮記集解 [*Collected Commentaries of the* Book of Rites] (Zhongwha shuju 1989), vol 3, 1256.

[51] See Wang Pinzhen 王聘珍, *Dadai liji jiegu* 大戴禮記解詁 (Zhonghua shuju 1983, 2004) 8.

[52] Jia Yi 賈誼, Yian Zhenyi 閻振益 and Zhong Xia 鍾夏 (ed), *Xinshu jiaozhu* 新書校注 [*Commentaries of Mew Discourses*] (Zhonghua shuju 2000) 303.

[53] Han Ying 韓嬰 (200–130 BCE), *Hanshi waizhuan* 韓詩外傳 [*The Outer Commentary to the* Book of Odes *by Master Han*], see Han Ying 韓嬰, Qu Shouyuan 屈守元 (1913–2001) (ed), *Hanshi waizhuan jianshu* 韓詩外傳箋疏 [Commentaries and Sub-commentaries of The Outer Commentary to the *Book of Odes* by Master Han] (Bashu shushe 1996), vol 4, 411.

[54] Ban Gu 班固 (32–92), 'Gongsun Hong zhuan 公孫弘傳 [Biography of Gongsun Hong]' in *Hanshu* 漢書 [*History of the Former Han*], see *Ershiwu shi* 二十五史 [*The 25 Histories*] (Yiwen yinshuguan 1956), vol 4*Hanshu*, juan 58, 1019.

[55] Su Yu 蘇輿, Zhong Zhe 鍾哲 (ed), *Chunqiu fanlu yizheng* 春秋繁露義證 *[Commentaries on the Luxuriant Gems of the Spring and Autumn Annals*] (Zhonghua shuju 2010) 250.

[56] Xun Yue 荀悅, *Shenjian* 申鑒 [*Extended Remarks*] (Taiwan zhonghua shuju 1970) 1.

[57] See *The Analects* (n 6) Bk XIV, ch 42, 147.

[58] ibid Bk XVII, ch 6, 173.

bring help to the multitude' (*Analects*, 6.30), a statement in resonance with the thought of 'having Benevolence to tend the people'.[59] Mencius encouraged kings in the Warring-state period to hold 'a heart sensitive to the suffering of others' and therefore 'extend their bounty'. In this way, a king would eventually 'become a true king by tending the people' and 'be a father and mother to the people'. He emphasized that Humane Heart must be implemented politically in Humane Governance. This idea was fully adopted, clarified, and practised under Emperor Wu of Han (156–87 BCE) when China had achieved nationwide unity. When Dong Zhongshu proposed the thought of 'placating the people with Benevolence', he was also referring to Benevolence as a political cause. Towards the end of the nineteenth century, amid a severe invasion of Western Powers, Tan Sitong (譚嗣同, 1865–98) advocated a series of political concepts, including 'liberty' and 'equality'. He argued that the Chinese people should leave behind the traditional principles and rules as well as completely abandon the 'three principles and five virtues' to redefine the relations between the monarch and his subjects.[60] His book *Renxue* (仁學) stood out as the most straightforward elaboration of the political connotation of Benevolence in Chinese intellectual history.[61]

Despite all the interpretations of Benevolence that emerged in the history of Chinese Confucianism, Confucians from different generations all agreed that the relationship between Humane Heart and Humane Governance is like the relationship between the two wheels of a cart or the two wings of a bird—neither is disposable. Nevertheless, the development of the Confucian discussions on Benevolence has been focused on concrete political measures, instead of the exploration of Humane Heart. According to Confucius, the government has the moral responsibility of educating and nurturing the people. When discussing Humane Governance, Mencius attached a special importance to educational practices, such as 'exercise due care over the education provided by village schools'.[62] In addition, he also offered administrative measures, such as 'the mulberry is planted in every homestead of five *mu* of land'.[63] After pragmatism gained prevalence in the Song Dynasty, Ouyang Xiu (歐陽修, 1007–72), Li Gou (李覯, 1009–59), Wang Anshi (王安石, 1021–86), Chen Liang (陳亮, 1143–94), and Ye Shi (葉適, 1150–1223) all analysed various Humane Governance-related policies that were supposed to help to boost the capacity of the State.[64] By the end of the nineteenth century, the new study on Benevolence, led by Tan Sitong, introduced a variety of Western political institutions and thoughts. However, it is not far-fetched to say that the focus of the Confucian thoughts on Benevolence has been centred on political management instead of the analysis of the principles

[59] ibid Bk VI, ch 30, 55, and Shanghai shifan daxue guji zhengli zu 上海師範大學古籍整理組 (ed), *Guoyu* 國語 [*Discourse of the States*] (Liren shuju 1981), juan 2, 'Zhoyu zhong 周語中 [Discourse of Zhou Dynasty]' 45.

[60] See Xiao Gongquan, *Zhongguo Zhengzhi sixiang shi*, vol 2, 760–3.

[61] Tan Sitong 譚嗣同, *Renxue* 仁學 [*Discourse on Humaneness*], in Tan Sitong chuanji 譚嗣同全集 [*Complete works of Tan Sitong*] (Shenghuo, dushu, xinzhi sanlian shuju 1954) 3–90.

[62] See *Mencius* (n 2) Bk I, Pt A, ch 3, 9.

[63] ibid 7–9.

[64] Xiao Gongquan, *Zhongguo Zhengzhi sixiang shi*, vol 1, 479–514.

of legitimation.[65] Hence, a series of theoretical issues remains unsolved. We will discuss these issues further in section 4.

## 3. Development of the Confucian Discourse on Humane Governance in Japan and Korea

Before discussing the reception and appropriation of the Chinese Confucian conception of 'Humane Governance' in Joseon Korea and Tokugawa Japan, we have to consider the relationships among China, Korea, and Japan since the eighteenth century as well as Confucian scholars' comments on those relationships.

In the eighteenth century, people in East Asia enjoyed a calm and peaceful century. However serene on the surface, the East Asian countries were experiencing what might be called 'the awakening of subjectivity in the world of thought'. This growing awakening in the spiritual realm set Korea and Japan apart from China in the psychological sense. The best barometer with which to measure the changes of intellectual ambiance in East Asia was the appropriation and new interpretation of the concept of Zhongguo (中國, Middle Kingdom, China).

At that time, the term Zhongguo had already appeared in Chinese classics such as the *Book of Documents* and *Book of Odes*. In ancient China, the term Zhongguo was formed and used in the political context of 'Sinocentrism'[66] in the 'Sinocentric World Order'.[67] A running theme in the numerous occurrences of the term Zhongguo in imperial China was the merging of political identity and cultural identity.

As we have illustrated elsewhere,[68] when the Chinese people used the term Zhongguo, the 'political China' and 'cultural China' were intimately united into a harmonious whole. The most representative fully-fledged treatise on Zhongguo was written by the eleventh-century Northern Song scholar-official Shijie (石介, 1005–45). In his essay titled 'On Zhongguo' (中國論, Zhongguo lun), Shijie proclaimed powerfully and ardently that China occupied the centre of the universe. In his assertion, China was the inner realm, while the 'four barbarians' (四夷, siyi) were the outer realms.[69]

Shijie's assertions did not stop at simple geography. Shijie indicated further that culture and morality stemmed from China.[70] Moreover, Shijie argued that the geographical layout and political establishment of China were in conformity with that of the cosmos.[71] Apparently, the theoretical foundation of Shijie's argumentation of the concept Zhongguo was a binary world view and its corollary ethical and moral duality.

[65] ibid vol 2, 946.

[66] John K Fairbank (ed), *The Chinese World Order* (Harvard UP 1968) 1.

[67] Lien-sheng Yang, 'Historical Notes on the Chinese World Order' (ibid 20–33, esp 20).

[68] Chun-chieh Huang, *East Asian Confucianisms: Texts in Contexts* (V&R Unipress and National Taiwan UP 2015) Appendix 2.

[69] Shijie, 'Zhongguo lun' in his Culai Xiansheng ji 徂徠先生集 [*Corpus of Mr Culai*] (Zhonghua Shuju 2009), vol 10, 116.

[70] ibid. [71] ibid.

However, since the seventeenth century when the concept of Zhongguo was disseminated to Korea and Japan, it underwent appropriation and reinterpretation. As early as the seventeenth century, the Japanese Confucian scholar Hayashi Razan (林羅山, 1583–1657) announced that Japan was the 'country of gentlemen',[72] which indicated its equality with China. Yamaga Sokō (山鹿素行, 1622–85) insisted that Japan had comprehended the principle of equilibrium (中, zhong)[73] and therefore was more qualified to be referred to as Zhongguo.[74]

The eighteenth-century Japanese Confucian scholar Asami Kēisai (淺見絅齋, 1652–1711) composed an essay entitled 'Distinguishing Chugoku' (中國辨) to offer a counter-argument against the time-honoured Sino-centric view of Zhongguo. Asami criticized the Japanese Confucians' acceptance of the Chinese demarcation between Chinese and the barbarians, insisting that Japan was equal to China. He indicated that Japan comprehended the true teachings of Confucius and therefore was more suitable to be referred to as Zhongguo, where the principle of Confucius's *Spring and Autumn Annals* prevailed.[75]

In a similar vein, the Korean Confucian scholar Hong Daeyong (洪大容 홍대용, 1731–83) also strove to dismantle the Chinese conceptualization of the distinction between the Chinese and the barbarians.[76]

In sync with the rise of the Korean and Japanese subjectivities in the eighteenth century, the Koreans and Japanese began to sense a type of 'distanciation' from imperial China. However, although the Korean and Japanese intellectuals and scholar-officials refused to accept the Chinese concept of Zhongguo, as we will see, they still agreed that 'Humane Governance' was the most important moral responsibility of their rulers. It was on the basis of this universal assent that the Chinese Confucian concept of 'Humane Governance' embarked on its odyssey in Korea and Japan.

## 3.1. Discussions on Humane Governance in the Tokugawa Japan

After the Chinese Confucian discourses on Humane Governance were introduced into Japan and Korea, the concept was further transformed by the local pragmatism in the two countries. As a result, it grew to lean even more on the aspect of the concrete policy of Humane Governance, while its attention to Humane Heart was further reduced. We begin this section with a discussion on the discourse on Humane Governance by Japanese Confucians.

[72] Hayashi Razan 林羅山, *Hayashi Razan bunshū* 林羅山文集 [*Literary Corpus of Hayashi Razan*] (Perikan-sha 1979), vol 73, 914–15.

[73] Yamaga Sokō 山鹿素行, *Chūchō jijitsu* 中朝事実 [*Facts of Japan*] in Hirose Yutaka 広瀬豊 (ed), *Yamaga Sokō zenshū* 山鹿素行全集 [*Complete Works of Yamaga Sokō*] (Iwanami shoten 1942) ch 13, vol 1, 234.

[74] Ibid.

[75] Asami Kēisai 淺見絅齋, *Chūgoku Ben* 中国辨 [On 'Zhongguo'], in *Yamazaki Ansai Gakuha* 山崎闇齋学派 [*The School of Yamazaki Ansai*] (Iwanami shoten 1982) 418.

[76] Park Hee-byoung, 'Asami Keisai and Hong Daeyoung: Dismantling the Chinese Theory of the "Civilized" and "Uncivilized"' (2004) 17 Seoul Journal of Korean Studies 67–113.

This discussion is not complete without an understanding of the context of Japanese Confucians during the Tokugawa era (1603–1868). During this time, they re-explained the classic concept of Humane Governance, introducing the permeation of pragmatism (*Shixue, jitsugaku*, 実学) with heavy Japanese characteristics. According to Minamoto Ryōen (源了圓, 1920–), the pragmatism in the mind of Confucians in Tokugawa Japan meant both 'real' and 'true'—referring to the 'practical' and 'empirical' dimensions, respectively. The 'practical' *jitsugaku* included 'practical *jitsugaku* based on individualized morality', '*jitsugaku* pursuing the truth of human nature', and 'practical *jitsugaku* for politics'.[77] Minamoto also considered Kumazawa Banzan (熊澤蕃山, 1619–91) and Yokoi Shōnan (横井小楠, 1809–69) to be the representatives for 'practical *jitsugaku*' and Ogyū Sorai (荻生徂徠, 1666–1728) to be the representative for 'empirical *jitsugaku*'.[78] Itō Jinsai (伊藤仁齋, 1627–1705) summarized the spirit embedded in the Japanese Confucian pragmatism, stating, 'The works by our sages shed light upon truth with empiricism, therefore the meaning of core concepts—such as filial piety, social obedience, manners and virtue—are automatically revealed.'[79]

As discussed in section 2, the centre of Confucian discourse on Humane Governance rests on Benevolence as a core value. Therefore, we can attempt to build an understanding by first examining the Japanese Confucians' approach to Benevolence. In *Four Books in Chapter and Verse with Collected Commentaries*, Zhu Xi redefined Benevolence as 'the morality for heart, the principle for love' based on his *Li-Qi* (理氣, binary) binary theoretical framework, which was discussed and criticized in Korea and Japan. As we have discussed elsewhere, the reflection by Japanese Tokugawa Confucians on Zhu Xi's thoughts were mainly diverted into two ways of thinking.

The first way of thinking included the destruction of metaphysics. When discussing Benevolence, Japanese Confucians rarely adopted Zhu Xi's *Li* framework. Itō Jinsai's latter works, such as *Gomō jigi* (語孟字義) and *Dōjimon* (童子問), had completely broken away from Zhu Xi's influence and adopted the approach of explaining Benevolence with love, with an emphasis on the idea of practising Benevolence in concrete daily life. Ogyū Sorai, in contrast, explained Benevolence as the 'virtue for allowing the people to settle down'. Supporting or opposing Zhu Xi, Japanese Tokugawa Confucians were all dedicated to destroying the metaphysical basis of Zhu Xi's theories. Explained in a traditional manner, they were all opposed to the *Li* thoughts by Zhu Xi, while building a base on the *Qi* thoughts.

The second thread of thinking was in the creation of new definitions for Benevolence in the context of the social–political life. They both rejected Zhu Xi's *Li* concept for interpreting Benevolence, instead arguing that Benevolence could

[77] Minamoto Ryōen 源了圓, *Kinsē shoki jitsugaku shisō no kenkyū* 近世初期実学思想の研究 [*A Study of Practical Learning in Early Modern Japan*] (Sōbunsha 1980) 64–65.

[78] ibid 66.

[79] Itō Jinsai 伊藤仁齋, 'Dōshikai hikki 同志會筆記 [Notes of the Companion Society]' in *Kogaku sensē shibunshū* 古学先生詩文集 [*Collection of Poems and Essays from Masters of the Ancient School*], in Sagara Tōru 相良亨 (1921–2000) et al (eds), *Kinsē juka bunshū shūsei* 近世儒家文集集成 [*Complete Works of the Literary Corpus of Early Modern Confucians*] (Perikan-sha 1985), vol 5, 11.

only be carried out with love. Itō Jinsai discussed Benevolence amid interpersonal interactions, while Ogyū Sorai discussed Benevolence amid the development of politics.[80]

Among all Tokugawa Confucian discussions on Humane Governance, Ogyū Sorai's thoughts were the most representative. In Japanese intellectual history, his thoughts have stirred the most controversies and created the most debates.[81] Such divisions were even referred to as 'incidents' by Koyasu Nobukuni (子安宣邦, 1933–).[82] We previously mentioned that Ogyū Sorai's study of *Analects* was mainly based on 'the Way' (*Tao*), 'Sage' and 'the *Six Classics*' (*Liu Jing*).[83] Among these, his redefinition of 'the Way' was the most distinctive. In *Rongo Chō*, Sorai argued that:

> The way advocated by Confucius was the way practiced by the ancient kings. Such a way was established in order to make the people settle down ... Therefore, since the way of the ancient kings had its focus on settling the people, such a way symbolized Benevolence which was the main virtue practiced by the ancient kings. Thus Benevolence is the approach to pass on their way.[84]

Sorai's definition of the 'The Way' is a political path for settling the people and emphasizes various political measures ranging from social manners and rituals to punishment. He also argued:

> The way is a comprehensive name. It refers to everything that the early kings established, especially the rites, music, penal laws and administrative institutions. The way embraces and designates them all. There is not something called 'the way' apart from their rites, music, penal laws and administrative systems of government.[85]

His interpretation of 'the Way' in Confucius's thoughts stresses political implications, therefore narrowing its transcendental aspects outside politics—such as private morality—and missing out the ethical and cosmological connotations of the Way. In Sorai's understanding, 'the Way' is externalized and reflected in political measures. He said:

> For the most part, the way of the early kings is external to the self. This means that the rites and ritual principles of the early kings' way are administered to people ... For this reason,

[80] See Huang Chun-chieh, 'Zhuzi 'renshuo' zai dechuan riben de huixiang 朱子〈仁說〉在德川日本的迴響 [Zhu Xi's "Discourse in Humanity" and Its Reinterpretation in Tokugawa Japan]' in Zhong Caijun 鍾彩鈞 (ed), *Dongya shiyu zhong de ruxue: chuantong de chuanzhi* 東亞視域中的儒學:傳統的詮釋(第四屆國際漢學會議論文集)[*Confucianism in East Asian Perspective: Traditional Interpretation (Collection of Essays of the Fourth Conference on Sinology)*] (Academia Sinica 2013) 409–29.

[81] Iwahashi Junsei 岩橋遵成, *Sorai kenkyū* 徂徠研究 [*A Study of Ogyū Sorai*] (Seki Shoin 1934) 1.

[82] Koyasu Nobukuni 子安宣邦, *Jiken to shite no Soraigaku* 事件としての徂徠学 [*The Learning of Sorai as an Event*] (Seudosha 1990).

[83] Huang Chun-chieh, *Dechuan riben 'Lunyu' quanshishi lun* 德川日本《論語》詮釋史論 [*A History of Interpretations of the* Analects *in Tokugawa Japan*] (Taiwan UP 2006) 145–78

[84] Ogyū Sorai 荻生徂徠, *Rongo Chō* 論語徵 [*Comments on the* Analects], in Seki Giichirō 関儀一郎 (ed), *Nihon meika shisho chūshaku zensho* 日本名家四書註釋全書 [*Complete Works of the Annotations of the Renowned Japanese Scholars*] (Ōtori Shuppan 1973), vol 7, 83–84.

[85] See John A Tucker, tr and ed, *Ogyū Sorai's Philosophical Masterworks: The Bendō and Benmei* (Association for Asian Studies and University of Hawai'i Press 2006) 140.

the teachings of the early kings include nothing other than the rites to regulate the mind. Apart from that, techniques of mind control are absurd fabrications. How can they not also be deemed confining?[86]

Sorai argued that the government can apply these externalized institutions and measures to educate the people and motivate them with rituals.[87]

Having reinterpreted the Confucian 'Way' by referring to the former kings' way, Sorai then redefined Benevolence:

Of the Confucian teachings, humaneness is the greatest. Why? [This is so because] humaneness well upholds the early kings' way and gives it substance. The way of the early kings is the way that brings peace to the realm below heaven. Although there are many aspects to this way, essentially they all return to [the project of] bringing peace to the realm below the heaven through [humaneness].

The foundation of the way resides in revering the decree of heaven. Heaven decrees that [in some cases] we be the son of heaven, a form of lord, or a grandee. Accordingly, there are ministers and common people among us. As [heaven decrees that we] be scholar-knights, there are also families, wives, and children among us. All of these [positions] depend upon us so that thereafter there will be peace. Moreover, all scholar-knights and grandees, along with their rulers, have heaven [-decreed] occupations. Therefore, the way of the prince *(junzi/kunshi)* deems humaneness alone as the great [virtue] of all.

Moreover, the human nature of humanity naturally tends toward mutual kinship, mutual love, mutual livelihood, mutual completion, mutual assistance, mutual nourishment, mutual protection, and mutual help. Therefore, Mencius said, 'In acting humanely *(ren/jin)*, we are [fully] human *(ren/jin)*'. When we combine all of these [attributes of humaneness], we refer to them as the way.[88]

Sorai also emphasized that Benevolence should not merely stay at the level of 'loving the others', but must be applied to benefit the welfare of the people. He said:

If they can realize that the early kings' way basically returns to bringing peace to the realm below heaven, and then apply their strength toward humaneness, thereupon each person [in the realm] will follow what is close to their human nature and realize aspects of the way. As with You's [Zilu] courage, Si's [Zigong] achievements, and Qiu's [Ran Qiu] arts, everyone will complete their particular talents. This will be sufficient to make them followers of humane men so that they can join in bringing peace to the realm below heaven. In completing their virtues, they will be like Bo Yi and Shu Qi who completed their purity, Hui in attaining harmony and Yi in completing his responsibilities. None will have to transform their human natures, nor will they impair the efforts of the humane man in this. Some people might not realize how to apply their strength toward humaneness. If not, then none of their talents or virtues can be completed. Rather, the various philosophers and hundreds of schools will arise. This is why the Confucian school teaches humaneness.

Mencius discussed humaneness in terms of love with his notion of 'compassion' [as the beginning of humaneness]. His comments were part of his explanation of the goodness of human nature, which he necessarily rooted in the human mind. Thus, he could not avoid discussing humaneness in terms of love. Although we possess a mind that loves people, if its blessings do not extend to everything, then how is it sufficient to be considered humane?

[86] ibid 237–38. [87] Ogyū Sorai (n 85) 304. [88] See Tucker (n 86) 145–46.

Therefore, although Mencius indeed offered an account of humane government, later Confucians did not understand that Mencius was actually trying to encourage the world [away from heterodoxies] with his words. [Thus, later Confucians] declared that no one had ever surpassed Mencius in applying themselves to humaneness. Their suggestion that we expand this mind of compassion to complete the humaneness of a sage was indeed a far-fetched idea revealing how extremely little [its proponents] understood their own measure, and that is all.[89]

In the above, Sorai emphasized the necessity of the objectification of the subjectivity of Benevolence. In his mind, a political leader must practise Benevolence. He argued, 'Benevolence should be used for settling the people. If the emperor fails to take responsibility for the world (*Tianxia, tenka*, 天下), an aristocrat fails to take responsibility for his State, an official fails to take responsibility for his family, then Benevolent politics would be impossible.'[90] Therefore, he believed that the deed of the ancient kings *Yao* 堯 and *Shun* 舜 abdicating and handing over the throne to someone else and that of *Tang* 湯 and *Wu* 武 resorting to forcefully overthrowing the incumbent rulers were actions representative of 'taking benevolence as their burden'.[91]

Sorai's emphasis on embedding Benevolence in concrete political measures reflects a belief that principles are only relevant when reflected within concrete matters. This thought is in accordance with the theories of Hayashi Razan, a *Bakufu* Confucian from the sixteenth century. Hayashi argued that the essence of Benevolence is in filial piety and social obedience, while its application should be in tending to the people and nurturing resources.[92] Generally speaking, Japanese Tokugawa Confucians rejected the belief of Chinese Song Confucians that principles are above concrete matters.

Under the influence of Tokugawan pragmatism, Japanese Confucians adopted a stance of 'utilitarian ethics' for evaluating Humane Governance or benevolent people, thus rejecting the stance of 'ethics of intention'.[93] The most intellectually indicative example was the debate among Japanese Confucians about whether Guan Zhong (管仲, 730–645 BCE) was benevolent.

The Japanese also interpreted the Benevolence of Guan Zhong differently. Regarding the Japanese Confucians' view of Guan Zhong, we previously cited that mainstream Japanese Confucians found it difficult to accept Mencius's contempt for Guan Zhong. The majority of them did recognize the Guan Zhong as benevolent. Nevertheless, though it seems that Japanese Confucians followed Confucius's comment on Guan Zhong that 'Such was his benevolence', they were

[89] ibid 146–47.

[90] Ogyū Sorai, *ken'en rokuhitsu* 護園六筆 [*Sixth Corpus of Kenen*], *Nihon jurin sōsho* 日本儒林叢書 [*Series on Japanese Confucianism*] (Ōtori shuppan 1978), vol 7, 117.

[91] ibid.

[92] Hayashi Razan, *Hayashi Razan bunshū* 林羅山文集 [*Literary Corpus of Hayashi Razan*] (Perikansha 1979), vol 67, 832, upper half.

[93] See Lee Ming-hui, 'Mengzi wangba zhi bian chongtan 孟子王霸之辨重探 [Reinterpretation of Mencius's Distinction between King and Hegemon]' in his *Mengzi chongtan* 孟子重探 [Revisiting Mencius] (Lianjing chuban gongsi 2001) 47.

in reality interpreting Benevolence differently, heavily tinged with characteristics from Japanese pragmatism. Japanese Confucians tended to connote Benevolence with love. They rejected Zhu Xi's theory of connoting Benevolence with *Li*. They were opposed to the thought of grounding ethics—as mainly covering concrete daily life—on metaphysics or cosmology. Redefining the meaning of Confucian Benevolence within the net of politics, society, and economy, Japanese Confucians believed that Guan Zhong was benevolent. To support this idea, they cited his political endeavours as beneficial to the people, such as by citing Confucius's comment that 'the people are still benefiting today'. They therefore argued that despite Guan Zhong's flaw—his deviation from martyrdom—in individual moral regard, this imperfect 'process' did not nullify his 'result' as beneficial to the people and the State.[94]

## 3.2. Confucian discourse on Humane Governance in the Joseon Korea

Now let's turn to discussing the debates among Korean Confucians on Humane Governance in the Joseon era (1392–1910).

Starting in the fifteenth century, the focus of Korean Confucians' discussions on Humane Governance had been placed on institution building—especially the conduction of economic–administrative policies (such as land demarcation policies)—instead of the theoretical analysis of legitimation. In other words, Korean Confucians paid more attention to the externalization of Humane Governance, instead of its internal theoretical issues.

To examine the Korean Confucians' discussions on Humane Governance, we look at their memorials to the throne. A memorial submitted by Song Hyon (成俔 성현, 1449–1504)—the Guanchashi (觀察使 관찰사) of Pyeongan-do (平安道 평안도) on 8 October 1486, stated that in his area 'the culture is far different from that further inland, and the people have been suffering from heavy labour service and are in need of comfort and compensation',[95] because 'the farm measuring has just began while the forced labour service for constructing the city fence has not finished, the local people are over distracted by these and barely capable of harvesting'.[96] He therefore requested that 'the farm measuring should be cancelled for this year given the grievances with the farm work'.[97] The most important citation in this memorial was that Mencius's 'benevolent government must begin with land demarcation. When boundaries are not properly drawn, the division of land according to

[94] Huang chun-chieh, 'Riben yu Chaoxian ruje de guanzhong lun ji qi xiangguan wenti 日本與朝鮮儒者的管仲論及其相關問題 [Japanese and Korean Confucian's Comments on Guan Zhong and Its Related Problems]' in *Quanqiu yu bentu zhijian de zhexue tansuo: Liu Shuxian xiansheng bazhi shoqing lunwen ji* 全球與本土之間的哲學探索:劉述先先生八秩壽慶論文集 [*Philosophical Inquiry between the Global and the Indigenous: Essays in Honour of Mr Liu Shu-hsien*] (Xuesheng shuju 2014) 407–36.

[95] *Seongjong-sillok* 성종실록 成宗實錄 [*Veritable Record of King Seongjong*], in Guksapyeonchan Wiwonhoe국사편찬위원회國史編纂委員會 (ed), *Joseonwangjosillok*조선왕조실록 朝鮮王朝實錄 [*Veritable Record of Korean Dynasties*] (Dongguknunhwasa 東國文化社 1956), vol 11, Bk 196, 148.

[96] ibid 147–48. [97] ibid 147.

the well-field system and the yield of grain used for paying officials cannot be equitable' (*Mencius*, 3A3).[98] After citing *Mencius*, Song Hyon requested the cancellation of a specific policy due to a poor harvest in his area.

An intellectual from the mid-Joseon era in the sixteenth century—Yi Eon-jeok (李彥迪이언적, 1491–1553)—authored *Jinsupalgyu* (進修八規 진수팔규).[99] The sixth item in it was about 'conducting Humane Governance'. In this memorial to the king Joseon Injong (仁宗 인종, 1515–45), Yi sang highly of Injong's benevolence reflected in his decision not to execute bisexual people. Yi stressed that 'Benevolence is in absolute sincerity and kindness. With such a benevolent heart, a ruler will be able to conduct effective ruling. Without the heart, however, law alone does not suffice to regulate the people.'[100] Most importantly, he insisted that to transmute Humane Heart into Humane Governance, the political rulings must be based on an institution that de-emphasizes punishment or taxation. He wrote:

> In history there have been two misdeeds by virtuous people who originally attempted to practice Humane Governance: one is that when there is excessive punishment, the people would have too many grievances for them to recognize the governance. The other is that when there is excessive taxation, the people would suffer too much from the burden for them to recognize the governance. Therefore, Mencius believed that the foundation for Humane Governance should be light punishment and taxation. Otherwise, the people would not be able to benefit from politics regardless of how much benevolence the ruler had.[101]

In the words of the philosopher Isaiah Berlin (1909–97) from the twentieth century, Yi Eon-jeok's emphasis in the sixteenth century was that of 'negative liberty' instead of 'positive liberty'. Yi valued economic institutions that could secure basic welfare for the people and allow the people to be free from heavy taxation. He valued the 'freedom from' more than the 'freedom of'.[102]

The king of Korea and his subjects arrived at a consensus: Human Governance is a responsibility of the government. The record of 22 September 1719, in the *Sukjong-sillok* (肅宗實錄 숙종실록), contained a debate over the legitimacy of land demarcation in the royal court. The king at the time quoted Mencius's 'benevolent government must begin with land demarcation' and declared that 'land demarcation is the top priority of politics',[103] thus supporting its necessity.

In the dialogue between the Korean king and his subjects lay a tacit assumption that Humane Governance was a legitimate proposition that both sides had accepted, and yet both agreed that Humane Governance should not be discussed as

[98] See *Mencius* (n 2) Bk 3, Pt A, ch 3, 109.

[99] The *Jinsupalgyu* was composed in 1550, when Yi Eon-jeok was 60 years old. See 'Munwongong Hoejae-seonsaeng Yeonbo문원공회재선생연보 文元公晦齋先生年譜 [Chronological Biography of Mr Hoejae]' in Minjokmunhwa Chujinhoe 민족문화추진회 民族文化推進會 (ed), *Han-guk munjip chonggan* 한국문집총간 韓國文集叢刊 [*Series of Literary Corpus of Korea*] (Minjokmunhwa Chujinhoe 1988), series 24, *Hoejaejip* 회재집 晦齋集 [*Collection of Essays by Mr Hoejae*], vol 13, 487a–496c.

[100] Yi Eon-jeok 이언적 李彥迪, 'So.Jinsupalgyu소.진수팔규 疏.進修八規 [Eight Principles of Cultivation]' (ibid vol 8, 437a–438b).

[101] ibid. [102] Isaiah Berlin, *Four Essays on Liberty* (OUP 1969, 1977) 121–54.

[103] *Sukjong-sillok* 숙종실록 肅宗實錄 [*Veritable Record of King Sukjong*], in Guksapyeonchan Wiwonhoe (n 96), vol 40, Bk 60, 677.

an abstract theoretical deduction but as a way of introducing concrete policies. On 23 February 1741, Yang Deuk-jung (梁得中 양득중, 1665–1742)—a Confucian advocating pragmatism that focused on pursuing the truth—submitted a memorial to the throne, expressing his opposition to permitting lectures on the *Classified Conversations of Master Zhu* (朱子語類, Zhuzi Yulei) in the royal court. He argued, 'What needs redressing today is not a lack of lecturing, but the problem of merely lecturing without practicing.'[104] He therefore insisted that Humane Governance had to be practised through concrete and objective political measures, such as land measuring, which promised the people property.

Amid the admiration of pragmatism in the Joseon era, Jeong Yak-yong (丁若鏞정약용, 1762–1836) argued that Humane Governance was actually referring to the ancient Chinese institution of land demarcation. He wrote:

> Mencius considered Jingtian (井田) as Humane Governance. Humane Governance, therefore, is Jingtianzhi (井田制). According to Mencius, without conducting this institution, even Yao and Shun would fail to rule the state.[105]

Jeong Yak-yong was a pragmatist Confucian, and his equation of Humane Governance with land demarcation was fundamentally focused on the belief that Humane Governance as an obligation by the government should not be reflected only in words but also be based on solid land policies.

In conclusion, the Korean Confucians' discussions on Humane Governance were deeply rooted in the spirit of pragmatism. They attached special significance to the construction of institutions, as inspired by Mencius's thought of paralleling the importance of Humane Heart and Humane Governance.

## 4. Theoretical Issues in the East Asian Confucian Discourse on Humane Governance

The foregoing discussions make possible a thorough analysis of the underlying theoretical issues within the East Asian Confucian political thoughts on Humane Governance. Among all the issues, the following two merit the most attention.

First, what is the relationship between the internal and external spheres of Humane Governance? From Mencius onward, Confucians have been holding the belief that 'a heart sensitive to the suffering of others' could be transformed into a 'compassionate government'. However, a gap between the *modus operandi* of Humane Heart and that of Humane Governance still exists. The former stems from willpower, as Confucius put it 'No sooner do I desire it [benevolence] than it is here' (*Analects*,

[104] *Yeongjo-sillok* 영조실록 英祖實錄 [*Veritable Record of King Yeongjo*] (ibid vol 43, Bk 53, 6).

[105] Jeong Yak-yong 丁若鏞, 'Jigwansuje Jeonje (9).Jeongjeonui (1) 지관수제전제구 . 정전의일 地官修制田制九 . 井田議一 [On Regulation of the System of Fields]' in Minjokmunhwa Chujinhoe (ed), *Han-guk munjip chonggan*, series 284, *Yeoyudang jeonseo* 與猶堂全書 [*Complete works of the Yeoyudang*], vol 7, *Gyeongse Yupyo* 경세유표 經世遺表 [*Essays of Statecraft*] (Minjokmunhwa Chujinhoe 2002) 137a.

7.30).[106] By contrast, the latter always involves the interactions among the self, and the world and the operations of the structure of political power. The individual cannot dominate the operation of power structures.

In response to this question, East Asian Confucians would probably answer: the process through which individuals, families, society, the State, and the world develops resembles the unfolding of a set of concentric circles. Confucius told his pupil Zilu that a person 'cultivates himself and thereby achieves reverence', 'cultivates himself and thereby brings peace and security to his fellow men', and 'cultivates himself and thereby brings peace and security to the people' (*Analects*, 14.42).[107] By saying so, he was indicating a Confucian world view that comprehends the world as a continuum, aimed at pursuing 'the Confucian project', as Yu Yingshi (余英時, 1930–) put it.[108]

Nevertheless, 'the Confucian project' is in reality based on certain assumptions. The so-called 'external sphere' (Humane Governance) is a mere extension and expansion of the 'internal sphere' (Humane Heart). Therefore, the external sphere is controlled by the internal sphere. Based on this assumption, Mencius stated that 'there is a common expression, "The Empire, the state, the family"'. The empire has its basis in the State, the State in the family, and the family in one's own self' (*Mencius*, 4A5).[109] The 'self', here, refers to individuals—in particular the 'heart' of an individual. Therefore, the Confucian concept of 'self-cultivation' (*Xiushen*, 修身) essentially means 'nurturing one's heart'. Similarly, the 'state', 'family', and 'one's own self', according to Mencius, are the expansions of value-loaded concepts (such as 'a heart sensitive to the suffering of others') instead of concrete spaces or territories.[110]

Does this theoretical assumption hold? If Confucians insist on the necessity of a path from the awakening and stretching of Humane Heart to the conduction of Humane Governance, a question remains: is such a necessity a logical necessity or a historical necessity? In other words, the question is to ask whether the necessity is theoretical or practical? In response to such questions, most East Asian Confucians have advocated the unity of 'virtue' and 'achievement', considering the former to be the foundation of the latter. The *Doctrine of the Mean* states, 'Only those who are absolutely sincere can order and adjust the great relation of mankind, establish the great foundations of humanity, and know the transforming and nourishing operations of heaven and earth.'[111] However, the East Asian discourse on Humane Governance we have examined in this chapter indicates that Confucian scholars have failed to conduct an in-depth substantiation of the theoretical necessity of the

106 See *The Analects* (n 6) Bk VII, ch 30, 65.

107 ibid Bk XIV, ch 42, 147.

108 Yu Yingshi 余英時, 'Shisho rujia de zhengti guihua 試說儒家的整體規劃 [On the Confucian Project]' in his *Song Ming Lixue yu zhengzhi wenhua* 宋明理學與政治文化 [*Song Ming Neo-Confucianism and Political Culture*] (Yunchen wenhua shiye gufen youxian gongsi 2004) 388–407.

109 See *Mencius* (n 2) Bk 4, Pt A, ch 5, 155.

110 See Ishida Hidemi石田秀實, *Kakujū suru seishin—Chugoku Kodai niokeru seishin do shindai nomondai* 擴充する精神——中國古代における精神と身體の問題 [The Spirit of Extension: Problems of Spirit and Body in Ancient China] in *Tōhōgaku* 東方学 63 (1982) 1–15.

111 See Wing-tsit Chan (n 39) 112.

development from Humane Heart to Humane Governance. Therefore, this 'missing link' has rendered their discourse on Humane Governance an unfinished project.

The second question crucial for a comprehensive understanding of this issue is what should the people do when the government has failed to fully accept the moral responsibilities of a political ruler? Put another way, what if the political ruler fails to be benevolent? As this question involves the issue of legitimacy of domination, it merits a detailed discussion.

Based on the historical experiences of Europe, Max Weber (1864–1920) defined three types of domination: traditional domination, rational–legal domination, and charismatic domination.[112] Although these three types of domination all existed to varying degrees in Chinese history in terms of the legitimacy of political leadership, the most persistent type of domination was actually 'monarchy domination', which could also be called 'cosmic legitimation'. Chinese emperors were considered 'sons of Heaven', who were appointed by Heaven to rule the people. Mencius often quoted the *Book of Documents* and said, 'Heaven sees with the eyes of its people; Heaven hears with the ears of its people' (*Mencius*, 5A5),[113] arguing that the government's insurance that they 'win their [the people's] hearts' (*Mencius*, 4A9)[114] is the supreme condition for securing control of the entire world. The discussions on Humane Governance by both Mencius and other East Asian Confucians emphasized the necessity for governance to be based on the people. Throughout East Asian history, however, the authoritarian regimes in different East Asian countries still gave priority to their political leaders. As Liang Qichao (梁啟超, 1873–1929) wrote, 'Over 2,000 years, Confucianism has been prevailing in China. There have, however, been few kings and emperors that chose to follow the thoughts of Confucius and practiced Humane Governance for the people.'[115] As a result, a 'conflict of dual-subjectivity', a term proposed by Xu Fuguan (徐復觀, 1904–82), has emerged, creating differences between the subjectivity of the head of State and the subjectivity of the people.[116] With this a conflict between the ideal and reality, the East Asian Confucian discourse on Humane Governance has become the 'nostalgia' of intellectuals under authoritarian regimes. Xiao Gongquan wrote:

Mencius' theory of the importance of the people differed from modern democracy; the two should not be confused. In simplest terms, democratic thought must contain all the three

[112] M Weber, *The Theory of Social and Economic Organization* (AM Henderson and Talcott Parsons tr, Free Press 1964) 324–29.

[113] See *Mencius* (n 2) Bk 5, Pt A, ch 5, 205–07.

[114] Mencius said, 'There is a way to win the Empire; win the people and you will win the Empire. There is a way to win the people; win their hearts and you will win the people' (ibid Bk 4, Pt A, ch 9, 159).

[115] Liang Qichao 梁啟超, 'Ruxue tongyi shidai 儒學統一時代 [Era of Unification of Confucianism]' in *Lun Zhongguo xueshu sixian bianqian zhi dashi*論中國學術思想變遷之大勢 [*On the Major Trends of China's Academic Thinking*] (Taiwan guji chubanyouxian gongsi 2005) ch 4, 90.

[116] Xu Fuguan 徐復觀, 'Zhongguo de chidao 中國的治道 [Principle of Governance in China]' in his *Rujia zhengzhi sixiang yu minzhu ziyou renquan* 儒家政治思想與民主自由人權 [*Confucian Political Thoughts and Democracy, Liberty, Human Rights*] (Bashi niandai chubanshe 1979) 218–19; cf Huang Chun-chieh, *Dongya ruxue shiyu zhong de Xu Fuguan ji qi sixiang* 東亞儒學視域中的徐復觀及其思想 [*Xu Fuguan and His Thought in East Asian Confucian Perspective*] (Taiwan UP 2011) ch 3, 41–120.

concepts of 'for the people', 'of the people', and 'by the people'. For, not only must the people be the objective toward which government is directed, and the chief element of the state, but they must also necessarily have the right voluntarily to participate in the authority of government. Weighed in this balance, Mencius' 'importance of the people' merely commences with the idea of 'for the people', and proceeds toward that of 'of the people'. Both the principle of 'by the people', and the institutions necessary to it, were things of which he had never heard.[117]

Due to such historical limitations on the theory, East Asian rulers could easily escape from the moral responsibilities imposed by the Confucian discourse on Humane Governance.

## 5. Conclusion

This chapter examined the Chinese, Japanese, and Korean Confucians' discourses on Humane Governance, employing analyses of their political thoughts and the theoretical dilemmas embedded therein. We arrived at the following two conclusions.

First, the East Asian Confucian discourses on Humane Governance assumed that Humane Governance should be based on a Humane Heart and that the development of Humane Governance unfolded from individuals, families, society, and the State; at the centre of the set of circles is 'a heart sensitive to the suffering of others' of the ruler. All the East Asian Confucian discussions on Humane Governance assumed that all kinds of political operation were 'mind-correlated' (or 'mind-correlative') to various degrees. Mencius's notions of 'the world', 'the state', 'family', and 'one's own self' were not referring to concrete spaces or territories but to the spheres of the development of core values. This assumption of East Asian Confucians led to their dedication to 'rectifying the evils in the prince's heart' (*Mencius*, 4A20)[118] and their expectation that political leaders would act as 'moral guardians'. East Asian Confucians hence gave more prominence to the 'ethic of intention' than the 'ethic of responsibility'.[119] When discussing Humane Governance, they paid more attention to political techniques than to political principles. However, the reality of East Asian authoritarian rule was that the rulers always possessed 'ultimate power', while Confucians only had 'derived power'. Consequently, in spite of all the moral responsibilities imposed on political rulers, the Confucian 'Humane Governance' could by no means avoid becoming 'eternal nostalgia' for Confucians under their authoritarian political realities.

Second, East Asian Confucian discourses on Humane Governance were, to different extents, developed from the perspective of the political rulers. They demanded the rulers to treat their subjects as children and rule in a 'nurturing parent model', forming a 'compassionate government' based on 'a heart sensitive to the suffering of others'. Therefore, Confucians in East Asian countries laid the focus of their

[117] Xiao Gongquan (n 5), vol 1, 161. [118] See *Mencius* (n 2) Bk 4, Pt A, ch 20, 167.

[119] M Weber, 'Politics as a Vocation' in WG Runciman (ed) and E Matthews (tr), *Max Weber: Selections in Translation* (CUP 1978) 212–25.

discussions of Humane Governance on the promotion of concrete political measures, thus failing to think from the perspective of the ruled. As a result, in these discussions, the relationship between the ruler and the ruled was a 'relationship of subordination'; it was not until Huang Zongxi (黃宗羲, 1610–95) in the sixteenth century and Tan Sitong in the nineteenth century that Confucians started emphasizing a 'relationship of coordination' between the ruler and the ruled—finally permitting the thinking of Humane Governance with a notion of 'mutual subjectivity' between the two.

# 13

# Bridging the Western and Eastern Traditions

## A Comparative Study of the Legal Thoughts of Hugo Grotius and Lao Zi

*Henan Hu*

## 1. Introduction

The encounter of the Western and Eastern world order has been a fundamental challenge to international law since the nineteenth. Although China has been admitted into the modern States system originated in Europe and the principle of sovereignty has been applied to it, the legacy of ideological clash between the two civilizations remains.

This chapter examines the issue of the compatibility between the Western and Eastern ideas of international order. It first examines two major Western conceptions of international order, known as the Grotian and Vattelian traditions. Second, it examines the traditional Chinese conception of international order, widely considered as the Confucian tradition. The chapter considers that the continued Vattelian tradition in the contemporary world order is impossible to reconcile territorial or national interests and that the Confucian conception is also unlikely to be accepted as universal. As a result, the chapter opens a new perspective by comparing two lost 'peace forces' in the Western and Eastern civilizations—Grotius and Lao Zi—so as to analyse their ideological convergences. This could possibly serve as a universal legal ground for the conception of international order. It highlights the importance for both civilizations to return to their original international theories that not only fit well into a State-centred system but also possess the essential characteristic of universalism.

## 2. The West–East Controversy

### 2.1 Two conceptions of Western international order

Since the beginning of the twentieth century, there have been two major international legal theories on the conception of international society. According to

Hedley Bull,[1] the first is the Grotian or solidarist conception, which was mainly underpinned by two important studies of Cornelius van Vollenhoven[2] and Sir Hersch Lauterpacht[3] who are known as the neo-Grotians. The second is the pluralist conception, the representative of which is Lassa Oppenheim, who wrote in 1905 and 1906 the two volumes of *International Law*.[4] The Grotian conception, as upholding the foundation of Grotius, makes the central proposition that solidarity exists in the States which comprise an international society and there is superior objective law to judge the conduct of States. On the contrary, the pluralist conception which could be traced back to the late eighteenth century theorist Emmer de Vattel holds that such a solidarity as assumed by the Grotians does not exist and States are only capable of agreeing on limited matters for certain minimum purposes, which is lack of an enforcement mechanism.[5] Although recognizing the similarities between these two theories for their affirmation of the existence of an international society and opposition to realism which excludes the role that law could play, Bull commented that the Grotian conception was still too unrealistic and premature in the twentieth century.[6]

Contrary to Bull, Randall Lesaffer has argued for a return of the Grotian tradition in the twentieth century and its continuity throughout the history of the early-modern law of nations.[7] Lesaffer argued that there was a paradigm shift generally in the twentieth century back to the Grotian tradition as opposed to the Hobbesian tradition, in the sense that the extreme sovereign State system had gradually evolved into a more moderate society of States that accepts legally binding rules.[8] In the Grotian tradition, he gave credit to Vitoria for many contemporary international legal patterns.[9] In his analysis, Lesaffer took the Hobbesian tradition as being in opposition to the Grotian. These two opposing traditions may be described as 'anti-legal' and 'legal'. Contemporary international order is definitely not a system under the conception of the Hobbesian tradition which denies international cooperation and common rules. Various international cooperations achieved so far have testified to this. The nineteenth-century positivist scepticism of John Austin on the legal character of international law is obsolete. When we compare the Grotian and Hobbesian traditions, we compare a legal and political tradition; but within legal traditions, the Grotian and the Vattelian are the two most critical founding theories of international law. Therefore, when discussing international legal foundation or legal traditions, it is a necessity to examine the Vattelian tradition.

[1] H Bull, 'The Grotian Conception of International Society' in H Butterfield and M Wight (eds), *Diplomatic Investigations: Essays in the Theory of International Politics* (Allen & Unwin 1966) 51–73.

[2] C van Vollenhoven, *The Three Stages in the Evolution of the Law of Nations* (Martinus Nijhoff 1919).

[3] H Lauterpacht, 'The Grotian Tradition in International Law' (1946) 23 British Yearbook of International Law 1–53.

[4] L Oppenheim, *International law: A Treatise* (Longmans, Green, & Co 1905).

[5] Bull (n 2) 52. [6] ibid 73.

[7] R Lesaffer, 'The Grotian Tradition Revisited: Change and Continuity in the Theory of International Law' (2002) 73 British Yearbook of International Law 103–39.

[8] ibid 108. [9] ibid 138.

As a major founder of the early-modern law of nations, Vattel should be regarded as fundamentally contrary to Grotius in the theorizing of what is a State and what is the law among States. He was the first person to treat the State as a totally independent moral being, irrespective of any social or anthropological basis within it. Although both Grotius and Vattel accepted the dichotomy between natural–necessary and volitional–voluntary law of nations, they differ in an important point. Grotius regarded natural law as the source of volitional law and both self and others were subordinate to these two laws as an integral body, whereas Vattel regarded necessary law and voluntary law as separate laws regulating respectively the self and relations with others.[10] Vattel's invention that voluntary law rather than natural law being the sole law for relations between States provides the theoretical soil for the establishment of international legal positivism in the late nineteenth century. International legal positivism only recognizes what States will as the only law among States.

Contemporary international legal order is based more on the Vattelian than the Grotian tradition. Contemporary international legal order is based upon a reality that the world is separated by territorially defined States. The State is legally entitled to a distinctive 'international legal personality', independent of human personality. The State is considered as a corporate being, able to make a decision, and has a will of its own which is irrespective of the will of its citizens. There is no vertically higher authority that could impose an external restraint on an independent State. It is a legal system primarily underpinned by State consent. Although there are 'general principles' and '*jus cogens*' which are claimed to be peremptory, the universal abidance and enforcement of the 'peremptory norms' remain controversial due to the absolute liberty to which the international legal framework entitles States. States basically do not submit to any objective criteria but each is able to freely choose whether to be bound by a particular rule. Unlike in civil societies where people are bound by social, political, and cultural solidarity, the so-called international society is conditional and merely weakly underpinned by international agreements in some limited areas where States could have common interests. Even though international law nowadays is said to be functioning virtually everywhere in international relations, the universal rule of law is hardly achieved. The theory of realism remains sensible in explaining the failure of law in many areas, due to the existence of irreconcilable national interests.[11] The fundamental obstacle for a comprehensive rule

[10] For Vattel, while necessary law of nations is the natural law applied to States which is pursued only when a State fulfils its duty to itself, 'when there is question of what it can demand from other States, it must consult the *voluntary law*' (E de Vattel, *The Law of Nations or the Principles of Natural Law Applied to the Conduct and to the Affairs of Nations and of Sovereigns*, CG Fenwick tr, 1758 edn, Introduction by A de Lapradelle (Carnegie Institute of Washington 1916)); J Brown Scott (ed), *The Classics of International Law* (Carnegie Endowment for International Peace 1911–50) 4 and 9. For Grotius's distinction between natural and volitional law, see H Grotius, *De Jure Belli Ac Pacis Libri Tres*, vol II, Book I, FW Kelsey tr, with collaboration of Arthur ER Boak, HA Sanders, JS Reeves, and HF Wright, and Introduction by J Brown Scott (Clarendon Press 1925), J Brown Scott (ed), *Classics of International Law* 38. Grotius said: 'Law of nature serves as the common ground for nations and States, through their own will and consent, to reach norms that are mutually binding for them, those resulted norms are the volitional law of nations.'

[11] For classical works of realism, see H Morgenthau, *Politics among Nations: The Struggle for Power and Peace* (Knopf 1948); K Waltz, *Theory of International Politics* (McGraw-Hill 1979).

of law is caused by the Vattelian endorsement of absolute freedom of States. Within such a theoretical framework, territorial matters which are inherently associated with sovereignty are absolute in character as well and become the biggest obstacle to achieving consensus. From a perspective of legal foundation, one has to acknowledge that contemporary international legal order is built on the Vattelian conception. The Grotian conception of a metaphysical order above sovereign States is in fact barely adopted in existing approaches to international law.[12]

Therefore, Bull is persuasive in saying that the application of the Grotian tradition into contemporary world has a weakness of being over optimistic about the underlying *realpolitik*. This chapter proceeds on the basis that contemporary international legal order is founded on the Vattelian conception upon which States are merely able to agree with each other in limited areas. It is a brutal fact that a universal legal order remains far from being achieved. This is particularly the case in legal issues of a territorial nature.

## 2.2 The Confucian conception of world order

With the penetration of China by Western powers since the late Qing dynasty, the issue of Chinese international order has consistently commanded scholarly attention. There are three dimensions in the existing discussions.

The first dimension is a search for Western-style international law in ancient China. In the late Qing dynasty, WAP Martin, who translated Henry Wheaton's *Elements of International Law* into Chinese for the first time wrote an article on the evidences of the existence of international law in ancient China.[13] He maintained that a Western-style international law can also be found in the classics of ancient China, in particular the *Book of Rites* of the Zhou dynasty, while the *Spring and Autumn Annals* edited by Confucius could be considered as an international code.[14] Hu Wei-yuan, a provincial official in Sichuan, wrote a book called *The Source of International Law* which also used Confucian thoughts to explain Western international law.[15] He concluded that the similarity between Chinese and Western international law is the pursuit of national interests.[16] He attributed the emergence of international law in both the Western world and ancient China to the splits and

[12] For a summative account of existing approaches to international law, see A Carty, 'International Law' in D Bell (ed), *Ethics and World Politics* (OUP 2010) 274–91.

[13] See WAP Martin, 'Traces of International Law in Ancient China' (1883) 14 International Review 63–77. The Chinese version was translated by his student and published by Tung-wen College in 1884. See WAP Martin, 'International Law in Ancient China' reprinted in Wang Jian (ed), *The Eastward Transmission of Western Laws: Foreigners and the Modern Transformation of Chinese Laws* (China University of Political Science and Law Press 2001) 31–39.

[14] Martin, 'Traces of International Law' (n 13) 66 and 77.

[15] Xu Xing-wu, 'Confucian Thoughts and "Geyi" of Modern International Law: The Reading of W. A. P. Martin's *International Law in Ancient China* and Hu Wei-yuan's *The Source of International Law* (in Chinese)', Paper for the Fifth Meeting of Chinese Harvard-Yenching Scholar Association, 11 March 2010, available at http://aiwk.sysu.edu.cn/A/?C-1-65-1.Html (accessed 10 April 2011), section 3. 'Geyi' means an elucidatory way of ancient China for interpreting foreign culture. I rely on Xu Xing-wu's paper for the analysis of Hu Wei-yuan's work, because the original book is not available to me.

[16] ibid section 4.

conflicts in the world. He insisted that international law was not a long-term rationality, and the right way for China was to be self-strengthening.[17] In both the early and late twentieth century, there emerged a number of works which focused on a Chinese code of international law.[18]

The second dimension is the analysis of Chinese traditional world order and its uniqueness. John King Fairbank edited a book on traditional Chinese world order, in particular the tributary system. He regarded the Chinese world order was from the first hierarchic and anti-egalitarian, and in which Confucianism was the orthodoxy.[19] The foreign relations of China were basically an outward extension of its domestic order.[20] He highlighted the incompatibility of the Chinese order with a Western one.[21]

The third dimension is the attempt to reconstruct world order for a new international law. After the first Sino-Japanese War, the Hundred Day reformists as led by Kang You-wei in critique of Martin argued that the world order and international law should be reconstructed by Confucianism. Kang attempted to incorporate China into the international system but with its imperial structure intact.[22] In contemporary times, Chinese philosopher Zhao Ting-yang sought a world philosophy in the Chinese civilization as a whole. He put forward the concept of 'all-under-heaven' as the political philosophical basis of a world institution and aimed to eliminate the internal and external dichotomy in the Western world view.[23] He proposed

[17] ibid.

[18] See for example Chen Gu-yuan, *The Traces of International Law in China* (Commercial Press 1931) (in Chinese); Xu Chuan-bao, *The Traces of International Law in Pre-Qin China* (China Science Company 1931) (in Chinese); Hong Pei-jun, *Public International Law in the Spring and Autumn Period* (Zhonghua Book Company 1939) (in Chinese); Sun Yu-rong, *Studies on International Law in Ancient China* (China University of Political Science and Law Press 1999) (in Chinese); Zhao Yan-chang, 'A Study on International Law in the Spring and Autumn Period' (master's dissertation, Jilin University 2004) (in Chinese). These works mechanically applied the normative framework of Western international law and argued for the existence of a similar normative system in ancient China. Professor Wang Tie-ya however considered that there existed some rules and customs in the interstate relations in ancient China but they differed from Western international law and cannot be said to have any correlations with the latter (Wang Tie-ya, 'International Law in China: History and Contemporary Perspectives' (1990) 221 Collected Courses of The Hague Academy of International Law 203–356, 213). Chinese scholar Wang Hui also argued that the *Book of Rites* and *Spring and Autumn Annals* did deal with the war and peace affairs among the Dukedoms, but they did not have any common legal foundation with the so-called Western international law (Wang Hui, *The Rise of Modern Chinese Thought*, vol I, pt II: Empire and State (SDX Joint Publishing Company 2004) (in Chinese) 721).

[19] J King Fairbank (ed), *The Chinese World Order: Traditional China's Foreign Relations* (Harvard UP 1968) 5–6.

[20] ibid 11.

[21] For analysis of traditional Chinese world order, also see F Tse-Shyang Chen, 'The Confucian View of World Order' in MW Janis and C Evans (eds), *Religion and International Law* (Martinus Nijhoff 1999) 27–49; Li Zhao-jie, 'Traditional Chinese World Order' (2002) 1 Chinese Journal of International Law 20–55.

[22] For relevant discussion of K You-wei, see R Svarverud, *International Law as World Order in Late Imperial China: Translation, Reception and Discourse 1847–1911* (Brill 2007) 190; Wang (n 18) 734–36.

[23] Zhao Ting-yang, 'Rethinking Empire from a Chinese Concept "All-under-Heaven" (Tian-xia)' (2006) 12 Social Identities 29–41; Zhao Ting-yang, 'A Political World Philosophy in Terms of All-under-heaven (Tian-xia)' (2009) 221 Diogenes 5–18; Zhao Ting-yang, *The Tian-xia System: An Introduction to the Philosophy of World Institution* (2nd edn, Renmin University of China Press, 2011) (in Chinese).

the world per se as a new political unit for the analysis of world order, instead of the nation State in the Western tradition. Zhao Ting-yang's theory however was criticized by some Western scholars as imposing Chinese values over the world views of others.[24]

As can be seen, scholars in establishing a Chinese system or theory of international order mostly focus on the Confucian conception. The traditional Chinese world order based on the Confucian conception has the following key characteristics. First, it is a universal empire that is all-embracing and indivisible, with neither rivalry nor equality; second, China is considered as the centre of the world and vassal States voluntarily submitted to Sinocentrism on the basis of its natural greatness; third, it is a system of hierarchy, in which the emperor or 'Son of Heaven' in the post-Qin China situated himself at the top of the world order; fourth, it is a culturally and ethically based system rather than political and legal. In the Confucian conception of world order in which there is a superior political being, there is a question of how to situate oneself, as the subordinate vassal States or the superior emperor. A traditional Confucian conception also seems to be one that advocates the hegemony of a single vassal State who could be powerful enough to unify all China so as to restore the world order of the West Zhou dynasty. There is a practical weakness of Confucianism in becoming a universal international ideology in that the Confucian conception is sharply incompatible with the dominant Western Hobbesian and Vattelian tradition of absolute States and it receives continued Western criticism for seeking hierarchy and hegemony.

## 3. Two Peace Figures in a World of Cultural Replacement

In the light of the incompatibility between the dominant ideologies in the West and East, what I aim to propose in this chapter is the possibility of bridging the Western and Eastern traditions by finding the key ideological—rather than normative—convergence in the history of political and legal thoughts in both traditions. A good way for proceeding is to adopt an evolutionary perspective in the two world orders. The international order in Western and Eastern civilization underwent similar political regimes of feudalism, empire, and sovereign States, albeit in different chronological orders.

From a perspective of macro history, the Eastern world is in no sense unique in developing the conception of the State and international order. It has undergone almost all the patterns of State and international order that Europe has undergone. The Chinese Confucian Empire was a similar universal international order as the Roman Empire in terms of political unification, in which the modern meaning of international law was largely absent. The Spring–Autumn and Warring-States period on the contrary was an international order of divided political communities

[24] WA Callahan, 'Chinese Visions of World Order: Post-hegemonic or a New Hegemony?' (2008) 10 International Studies Review 749–61.

much closer to early-modern Europe, in which philosophers like Lao Zi and Grotius envisaged a metaphysical order above independent States. With the advent of modernity, either through ways natural or coercive, both Western and Eastern international order were replaced by the Vattelian tradition of absolutism and statism. It is notable that Western and Eastern international order underwent two diverging paths of evolution: one from unity to division, the other from division to unity. Nonetheless, these two patterns were merely of historical significance, and when it came to modernity in the nineteenth century both worlds entered into an increasingly strengthened Vattelian tradition under the tremendous driving force of imperialism and expansionism. From a civilizational point of view, one can say that the Western tradition is mainly a kind of exclusion and expansion, while the Eastern counterpart is mainly a kind of inclusion and absorption. Once an evolutionary perspective of human history is adopted, it is easier to suppose that the conceptions of international order in the Western and Eastern world may not always conflict with each other. The way to proceed could perhaps be a search for the theories in the two worlds that could converge with each other, in particular to restore what the human societies had lost on the way to modernity.

This chapter aims to achieve a much easier task than Zhao Ting-yang's: it does not aim to philosophize 'world-ness' (which is genius but far too advanced for our contemporary and realistic world of nation States), but rather to propose some common universal elements in human history for a territorialized or State-centred world. Thus, the purpose of the remainder of this chapter is to carry out a preliminary search for a means by which both Western and Eastern conceptions of the State, international order, and territory could converge. In order to do that, a comparative approach in a civilizational sense is adopted. Two 'peace figures' from each tradition are selected for comparison: Grotius as representative of the peace force in the West and Lao Zi as the same in the East.

It is necessary for me to justify the selection of the two figures for comparison. I make the justification in two aspects: first, the significance of Grotius and Lao Zi in a world of cultural replacement; second, the feasibility for comparing them. The world we live in nowadays is a world of cultural replacement. This is to say, the international political and legal cultures underpinning the contemporary world, namely the Vattelian tradition in the West as well as the Western-influenced region (eg Japan and ASEAN) and the Confucian legacy in China are either not indigenous or not original but rather imposed or evolved products towards modernity or empire through history. In such circumstances of cultural replacement, the Western (including the Western-influenced region) and Eastern worlds were on a diverging path to different international cultures. As a result, this rendered a clash of civilizations, particularly in territorial outlooks.

Despite the cultural replacement, Grotius was the first person in the Western world to provide a natural law theory of the law of nations around the time when the Westphalian States came into being. Although Grotius's predecessors—the school of Salamanca, in particular Vitoria—envisaged a secular universal order based on human reason earlier than Grotius, they did not theorize the law of nations and had not dealt specifically and systematically with the non-Christian world in a legal language yet. Grotius was the first to provide a legal foundation for territorial States and moreover he recognized all the nations on the earth under a legal mechanism of universalism and equality. Although it used to be controversial, Chinese historians and archaeologists have proved that Lao Zi, the founder of philosophical Daoism in the Spring–Autumn period, was born earlier than Confucius. As a predecessor of Confucius, it is said that Confucius was taught by Lao Zi. Lao Zi is now widely recognized as the first person in Chinese history to create a primitive theory of natural law and dialectics. Unlike Confucius who called for the restoration of the unified political order of the West Zhou dynasty under the system of *Li*, Lao Zi was critical of continuous wars caused by the ambitions of great powers to annex and unify, and was in favour of a divided status quo of peaceful coexistence between great and small powers. In this regard, he created a Daoist natural law theory, particularly in relation to the rulers of the Dukedoms.

The significance of studying Grotius and Lao Zi is that both of their theories are the original 'international' theory in the two worlds for a State-centred world. Their replacement by the Vattelian and Confucian traditions and loss of preceding influence enhance the value in studying them. The feasibility of comparing Grotius and Lao Zi lies first in the originality and theoretical significance of the two figures, in particular their natural law theory of the State or the ruler in which overarching, objective, and universal legal standards were created; it then lies second in the ultimate purpose of their political theories, aiming at achieving social peace and elimination of conflicts in a divided world. By offering an account of the convergence between the Grotian and Daoist conceptions of international order, this chapter opens the possibility for a common legal foundation of a universal international order.

This chapter aims to construct an ideological convergence between the theories of Grotius and Lao Zi. It argues that only by retrieving these two long-lost peace traditions of international order in the Western and Eastern worlds can the two worlds be possibly connected under a universal conception of international order.

## 4. Western International Order in Grotius

This section examines the first major founder of the early-modern law of nations—Hugo Grotius—'major' in the sense that international law was for the first time treated systematically and distinctively by him, and that his works determined the key normative elements of international law as a legal existence; 'founder' in the sense that Grotius was the first to establish a philosophical foundation of the law of nations based on human nature. The State in his view is morally no different from biological persons. He treated the State as an aggregate of individuals and of identical nature to the latter. Based on this essential premise, he was able to envisage a greater international society which is humanist and ethically identical to national societies, though not politically in that Grotius accepted no superior political body above States. The social contract of individuals on which civil society is based also serves as the basis of the international society.

## 4.1 Balance of twofold human nature

### *4.1.1 Self-interest as the first principle of nature*

Grotius premised his entire discussion of the law of nations on his account of human nature. His interpretation of human nature was twofold. Grotius mentioned the two aspects as one's own good and the good of all in his *De Iure Praedae Commentarius* and expediency and sociability in his *De Jure Belli Ac Pacis Libri Tres*. In *De Iure Praedae Commentarius*, he regarded the individual's own good or self-interest as the first principle of nature. He pointed out that:

> [L]ove, whose primary force and action are directed to self-interest, is the first principle of the whole natural order ... Horace should not be censured for saying ... that expediency might perhaps be called the mother of justice and equity. For all things in nature, as Cicero repeatedly insists, are tenderly regardful of self, and seek their own happiness and security.[25]

In *De Jure Belli Ac Pacis Libri Tres*, although it treated the desire for society as more impelling, Grotius acknowledged that: '[t]he law of nature nevertheless has the reinforcement of expediency ... expediency afforded an opportunity also for municipal law, since that kind of association of which we have spoken, and subjection to authority, have their roots in expediency'.[26] Evidences of Grotius's focus on 'self' are contained in *De Iure Praedae Commentarius*.[27] He not only held that 'in human affairs the first principle of a man's duty relates to himself'[28] but also further developed such a nature as 'desire': '[l]ove, then, is twofold: love for oneself, and love for others. In the former aspect, it is known as "desire"; in the latter, as "friendliness" '.[29]

Based on the first aspect of human nature, Grotius derived his first and second fundamental laws. He quoted Plato, saying that: 'justice is concerned ... with the care of the body and the possession of property'[30] and that 'two precepts of law of nature emerge: first, that It shall be permissible to defend [one's own] life and to shun that which threatens to prove injurious; second, that It shall be permissible to acquire for oneself, and to retain, those things which are useful for life'.[31] It is clear that Grotius treated two rights as fundamental—the right to life and the right to property—the sole basis of which is self-interest. Desire for things that are useful in life is one of the most important fundamentals of Grotius's natural law theory. Such a nature could be best reflected by the following statement of Grotius:

> God created man 'free and *sui iuris*', so that the actions of each individual and the use of his possessions were made subject not to another's will but to his own. Moreover, this view

[25] H Grotius, *De Iure Praedae Commentarius*, vol I, GL Williams tr of original 1604 MS, with collaboration of WH Zeydel (Hein & Co 1995); Scott (ed) (n 18) 9.

[26] Grotius (n 10); Scott (ed) (n 18) 15.

[27] There is a slight difference between *De Iure Praedae Commentarius* and *De Jure Belli Ac Pacis Libri Tres* in approaching human nature: Grotius in his first book devoted much discussion to the priority of self over others; in the second book, he minimized the role of expediency and put the central position to the role of sociability.

[28] Grotius (n 25) 9. [29] ibid 11. [30] ibid 10. [31] ibid.

is sanctioned by the consent of all nations. For what is that well-known concept, 'natural liberty', other than the power of the individual to act in accordance with his own will? And liberty in regard to actions is equivalent to ownership in regard to property.[32]

Based on such a natural liberty, Grotius derived the rule of good faith that '[w]hat each individual has indicated to be his will, that is law with respect to him'.[33]

### *4.1.2 Common good as more compelling*

To Grotius, the State is a product of the collective agreement of each individual, indicative of their will for the sake of 'self-protection through mutual aid and for equal acquisition of the necessities of life', in other words, for the sake of 'common good'.[34] Such a unity is a 'commonwealth' and the individuals making up the commonwealth are 'citizens'.[35] According to Grotius, 'nothing achieved on earth is more acceptable than those associations and assemblies of men which are known as States'.[36] These indicate the second aspect of human nature that Grotius put forward: the good of all, or sociability. In *De Jure Belli Ac Pacis Libri Tres*, he began his discussion by refuting Carneades's statement about human nature seeking advantage for itself and Carneades's denial of justice:

> Man is, to be sure, an animal, but an animal of a superior kind ... among the traits characteristic of man is an impelling desire for society, that is, the social life ... therefore, the assertion that every animal is impelled by nature to seek only its own good cannot be conceded.[37]

He further pointed out that even in children, before their training has begun, there is a disposition to do good for others.[38] While mature man has a special faculty of knowing, he has knowledge to act in accordance with general principles. It is from such human intelligence that man has the desire for the maintenance of social order which Grotius considered as the source of law.[39] Meanwhile, man has another power of judgement which 'enables him to decide what things are agreeable or harmful' and is also part of law.[40] In *De Iure Praedae Commentarius*, Grotius attributed such a second nature to a peculiar faculty that human race has—reason.[41] He said that men commonly agree to care for the welfare of others.[42] It is because there is a certain kinship established among mankind by nature so that it would be sinful to injure a fellow man.[43] Grotius expressed the same kind of statement in *De Jure Belli Ac Pacis Libri Tres*.[44] Justice, to him, has an intermediate aspect that is concerned with the good of others.[45] Based on the second human nature, Grotius derived his two further laws: '[l]et no one inflict injury upon his fellow ... Let no one seize possession of that which has been taken into the possession of another. The former is the law of inoffensiveness; the latter is the law of abstinence.'[46]

[32] ibid 18. [33] ibid. [34] ibid 20. [35] ibid. [36] ibid.
[37] Grotius (n 10) 11. [38] ibid. [39] ibid. [40] ibid 13.
[41] Grotius (n 25) 11–12. [42] ibid 12. [43] ibid 13. [44] Grotius (n 10) 14.
[45] Grotius (n 25) 13. [46] ibid.

With respect to these two aspects of human nature which are also the two underpinnings of his international legal theory, Grotius meant to say that there could be a perfect balance between them. He said: 'it is to the advantage of the whole that the individual parts be preserved, even so mankind will show forbearance toward individuals because we are born for a life of fellowship'.[47] 'That social impulse was the source of ... reciprocal acts and sentiments, and of the intermingling of one's own goods and ills with the goods and ills of others'.[48] In his comparison between one's own good and the good of all, Grotius's endeavour to balance becomes more evident:

> [T]he first set of laws and of those following immediately thereafter has indicated that one's own good takes precedence over the good of another person ... it indicates that by nature's ordinance each individual should be desirous of his own good fortune in preference to that of another ... nevertheless, in questions involving a comparison between the good of single individuals and the good of all, the more general concept should take precedence on the ground that it includes the good of individuals as well. In other words, the cargo cannot be saved unless the ship is preserved.[49]

To judge from Grotius's wording, he favourably opted for the good of all as more impelling in his balance of human nature. He thought that when faced with the good of another person, one's own good prevails. However, when faced with the good of all, one's own good yields to the good of all. Such an observation could be further reinforced by his citation of Pericles to clarify 'why and to what extent private well-being is subordinate to public well-being':

> [P]rivate citizens, too, derive more benefit from a state which is successful as a whole, than from one where individual interests flourish but where the state itself, as an entity, is falling into ruin. For even he whose personal fortunes are well invested, must nevertheless perish if his country is destroyed; while on the other hand, if some individual within a prosperous state is not particularly fortunate, he is still far more likely to be preserved unharmed through the latter.[50]

Based on his argument that the good of individuals is subordinate to the good of all for the reason that individuals have consented to this arrangement, 'the will of all, when applied to all, is called *lex* [statutory law] ... *lex* resets upon the mutual agreement and the will of individuals ... Demosthenes and Plato sometimes refer to it as "the common pact of the state"'.[51] Hence, the following rule was developed: '[w]hatever the commonwealth has indicated to be its will, that is law in regard to the whole body of citizens'.[52] This rule was regarded by Grotius as the source of municipal law.

It is noteworthy that the discussion of Grotius so far had been categorized by him as 'municipal' and 'domestic'.[53] The 'public well-being' meant by him is confined to the border of a State. The rationale behind Grotius's theory of municipal law is that the existence of mutual agreement between individuals (common good) is prior to

[47] ibid. [48] ibid 14. [49] ibid 21.
[50] The speech of Pericles cited by Grotius (ibid 22). [51] ibid 22–23. [52] ibid 23.
[53] ibid.

the existence of a State. In other words, Grotius's argument that common good is inclusive of individuals' good makes sense at municipal level in that a State is created by individuals who desire the same good and long for a superior protection. Just as Grotius himself put it: 'it is the will involved that constitutes the measure of a good'.[54]

## 4.2 Identical nature of individuals and States

The major aim of Grotius is to extend such a foundation of municipal law to that at the international level. When proceeding to the law of nations, Grotius made a homogenization of the nature of individuals and States by which he established the law of a greater society among nations:

> [T]he laws of each state have in view the advantage of that state, so by mutual consent it has become possible that certain laws should originate as between all States, or a great many States; and it is apparent that the laws thus originating had in view the advantage ... of the great society of States. And this is what is called the law of nations, whenever we distinguish that term from the law of nature.[55]

In *De Iure Praedae Commentarius*, Grotius pointed out that the love for others, as the rational faculty of man, is especially manifest in the mutual accord of nations.[56] He regarded the accord as the secondary law of nature and the primary law of nations.[57] The existence of common good among nations is regarded as the secondary law of nations: '[f]or just as the common good of private persons gave rise to the precepts above set forth, so also, owing to the existence of a common good of an international nature, the various peoples who had established States for themselves entered into agreements concerning that international good'.[58]

It is clear that it is based on the same human nature that Grotius made his analogy of the municipal and international system with an emphasis on the greater role of common good. The existence of the natural law of nations is justified by Grotius on the ground that States are of identical nature as individuals: '[w]hatever all States have indicated to be their will, that is law in regard to all of them'.[59] Based on such a homogenization, it follows that 'on any matter, the consensus of all nations should be regarded as a precept of the natural law' and '[w]hat the common consent of mankind has shown to be the will of all, that is law'.[60] To Grotius, there is no essential difference between voluntary law of nations and natural law. Voluntary law of nations will always follow natural law through the inherent tendency towards common good within States. Grotius thus created an international legal framework that is identical to a municipal legal framework based on human nature.

Under this international legal framework, we may see that the very source of the law of nations is the nature of individual men. Thus, the two sets of fundamental

[54] ibid 22. [55] Grotius (n 10) 15. [56] Grotius (n 25) 11–12. [57] ibid 12.
[58] ibid 26. [59] ibid. [60] ibid 12.

laws applicable to individuals that Grotius derived from nature are also applicable to States:

> [F]irst, Individual citizens should not only refrain from injuring other citizens, but should furthermore protect them, both *as a whole* and as individuals; secondly, Citizens should not only refrain from seizing one another's possessions, whether these be held privately or *in common*, but should furthermore contribute individually both that which is necessary to other individuals and that which is necessary to *the whole*. [emphasis mine][61]

In addition, even though Grotius accepted a superior and objective standard of sociability or common good as the source of the law of nations, he did not accept any superior political institutions above States:

> For citizens [are subject] to their respective States, and therefore, both in disputes with one another and in disputes with the state, they rightly submit to the judgement of the latter; whereas one state ... that is to say, it is not in subjection but in contraposition—to another state, and citizens of the one are likewise contraposed to citizens of the other ... there is no greater sovereign power set over the power of the state and superior to it, since the state is a self-sufficient aggregation.[62]

Thus, the international order in Grotius is neither constitutional (no world government) nor realist. Instead, it is regulated under moral and ethical standards in which humans are seen as the fundamental underpinnings of the international society and this society only exists in the state of nature in that Grotius accepted no world State.

## 5. Eastern International Order in Lao Zi

To understand the international theory of Lao Zi, it is necessary to understand the path of Lao Zi's philosophical reasoning. The Daoist path flows from ontology, cosmology, law of nature, view of human life, and ultimately to political theory. With lots of foreshadowing of the theory of *Dao* and *De*, the major target of Lao Zi, as a governmental official, was to establish a theory of State governance.[63] Lao Zi lived in the Spring–Autumn period of the East Zhou dynasty in which the Zhou King had virtually lost his power. Wars were waged frequently among great Dukedoms for hegemony and in the annexation of small Dukedoms by those great. The poorest victims of war were ordinary people who longed for a simple and safe life. In the light of such eager popular demands for peace, Lao Zi who was more concerned for the welfare of ordinary people created the philosophy of Daoism. It is important to note that unlike Confucianism which starts from an imposed political order and advocates the benevolence of the ruler, the standpoint of philosophical Daoism is the ruled or the disadvantaged group. Such a spirit of philosophical Daoism makes it more compatible with contemporary international values of fairness, equality, and peace.

[61] ibid 21. [62] ibid 27–28.

[63] According to the classic book *Historical Records*, Lao Zi used to work as historiographer for the Zhou royal house.

## 5.1 The Daoist ontology

All things that 'lie within shapes and features' have their names. That is the actual and objective world that we could see. When people see actual things, they have no difficulty in expressing them so that they use names for things. In this sense, Heaven, Earth, and all the creatures which we could see are 'the Nameables'. Lao Zi however put forward a contrary concept 'the Unnameable': that is '*Dao*' which lies beyond shapes and features. In the first chapter of his book, Lao Zi stated: 'the *Dao* that can be comprised in words is not the eternal *Dao*; the name that can be named is not the abiding name. The Unnameable is the beginning of Heaven and Earth; the Nameable is the mother of all things.'[64] A similar distinction in the Daoist thoughts is 'Being' and 'Non-being'. They are other ways of expressing the distinction between 'the Nameable' and 'the Unnameable'. For example, Lao Zi stated: 'all things in the world come into being from "Being"; and "Being" comes into being from "Non-being"'.[65] Therefore, the first paragraph cited above could be understood as: *Dao* as 'the Unnameable' or 'Non-being' is the beginning of Heaven and Earth. Heaven and Earth refer to 'the Nameable' or 'Being' in general. As a result, *Dao* is the beginning of 'Being' while 'Being' is the mother of all things. The punctuation added in Fung Yu-lan's translation of the Chinese text is understandable. However, another way of punctuation seems even more understandable: '"Non-being" is to name the beginning of Heaven and Earth; "Being" is to name the mother of all things'.[66]

Lao Zi in other chapters elaborated on *Dao*. He stated: '*Dao* is eternal, nameless, and the uncarved block [simplicity]';[67] '*Dao*, lying hid, is nameless.'[68] *Dao*, as described, is the most primitive state. However, in order to speak about it, the name '*Dao*' was forced on it. Hence, the name of *Dao* is really not a name at all. Lao Zi stated this clearly: 'there is an integral whole before the coming into being of Heaven and Earth. It is inaudible and invisible; it is independent and invariable; it circulates forever; it is the origin of the world. I do not know its name, but I give it a forced name called *Dao*.'[69]

Such a concept of *Dao* is merely a formal one rather than a positive one.[70] It indicates nothing regarding fact or actuality. *Dao* per se is not a thing, not a being, and it

[64] Chapter 1, The Book of *Lao Zi*, also known as *Dao De Jing*. A large part of the English translations of the Book of *Lao Zi* quoted in this chapter is from Fung Yu-Lan, *A Short History of Chinese Philosophy*, Derk Bodde (ed) (Free Press 1948) 94–95. See also the Chinese version, Fung Yu-Lan, *A Short History of Chinese Philosophy* (Tu You-guang tr, Peking UP 2010). Since the book of Fung Yu-Lan does not give a full translation of the original text of the Book of *Lao Zi*, and the translation of other sources are not all satisfactory, some parts of the translation were done by myself based on a synthetic consideration of the interpretation and translation of the Book of *Lao Zi* in the following works: Chen Gu-ying, *The Annotation and Review of Lao Zi* (Zhonghua Book Company 1984) (in Chinese); *A Taoist Classic: The Book of Lao Zi* (He Guang-hu, Gao Shi-ning, Song Li-dao, and Xu Jun-yao trs, Foreign Languages Press 1993), based on Ren Ji-yu, *Book of Lao Zi: A Modern Chinese Translation* (Shanghai Chinese Classics Publishing House 1985); Ren Ji-yu, *Lao Zi: An Interpretation and Commentary*, Ren Yuan (tr), K Leyton-Brown (ed) (Commercial Press 2009).

[65] Chapter 40, translation from Fung (n 64) 96.

[66] See Chen (n 64) 225, my translation.

[67] Chapter 32, translation from Fung (n 64) 95.

[68] Chapter 41, translation ibid.

[69] Chapter 25, my own translation.

[70] Fung (n 64) 95.

cannot be described. *Dao* only refers to a metaphysical 'that' which all things come to be. All things coming into being from 'Being' indicates that there first needs to be 'Being'. Such a sequence of 'first' has nothing to do with time but rather a concept of inclusiveness in logic. 'Being' refers to the general state of all things and is a superior concept to things as beings. There must be 'Being' before there could be things as beings. By the same token, 'Being' coming into being from 'Non-being' does not mean that there had ever been the existence of 'Non-being' before 'Being' in terms of time. Rather, it is to say that there must be 'Non-being' before 'Being' in terms of logic. This is the metaphysics of Daoism. It has nothing to do with time and the actual world, because in time and the actual world there are only things as beings. There is only one 'Being' as a superior concept, and there are many beings as the actual things. This is the Daoist ontology.

## 5.2 The Daoist cosmology

Lao Zi stated that 'from *Dao* there comes one, from one there comes two, from two there comes three, from three comes all things'.[71] This is Lao Zi's description of how things come into being. The concepts of 'one, two, and three' do not refer to anything particular but only to signify the process from 'Non-being' to many beings.[72]

There were various interpretations of 'one, two, and three' in the annotation history of the book of *Lao Zi*. To echo the citations in the last section, the following explanation might be more understandable: 'one' refers to 'Being' so that 'from *Dao* there comes one' means from *Dao* there comes 'Being'; 'two' refers to Heaven and Earth which symbolizes the world in general. Lao Zi further stated that 'all things bear *Yin* (the negative) and harbour *Yang* (the positive), the two essences communicate into *He* (harmony)'.[73] According to this, the annotator in the Han dynasty interpreted 'two' as the two essences of *Yin* and *Yang*.[74] Heaven and Earth respectively represent the essences of *Yin* and *Yang*; 'three' represents *Yin*, *Yang*, and the outcome *He* of their communication.[75] Then, all the matters come into being from *He*. This is the Daoist cosmology.

## 5.3 The Daoist law of nature

The concept of *Dao* has different carriers throughout the whole book of *Lao Zi*. The aforementioned *Dao* in the ontology and cosmology of Daoism is the metaphysical *Dao*. We have seen that Lao Zi also called *Dao* 'Non-being'. However, in talking about the law of nature, Lao Zi conveyed *Dao* a dialectical meaning: another core concept 'the Invariable'. For example, Lao Zi stated:

> To know the Invariables is called enlightenment. Not to know the Invariables and to act blindly is to go to disaster. He who knows the Invariable is liberal. Being liberal, he is without prejudice. Being without prejudice, he is comprehensive. Being comprehensive, he is

[71] Chapter 42, translation ibid 96–97.
[72] Chen (n 64) 225.
[73] Chapter 42, my own translation.
[74] Chen (n 64) 226.
[75] ibid 228.

vast. Being vast, he is with the truth. Being with the truth, he lasts forever and will not fail throughout his lifetime.[76]

According to Lao Zi, things are changing but the law that governs the change of things is not changeable. The fundamental reflection of such an 'invariable' law of the change of things is the statement: 'reversing is the movement of *Dao*'.[77] Some annotator noted that the statement could also be translated as 'circulation is the movement of *Dao*'. These two interpretations are both fine and they are in fact both included in the book of *Lao Zi*. According to the Daoist cosmology, everything comes into being through the communication of two opposite essences *Yin* and *Yang*. Therefore, everything has its opposite. The two essences of things stay in harmony because of their balance. If some qualities of things develop into certain extremity, their opposites will revert. There are the famous sayings of Lao Zi: 'it is upon calamity that blessing leans, upon blessing that calamity rests';[78] 'diminish a thing and it will increase, increase a thing and it will diminish'.[79] This is the Daoist law of nature which derives from *Dao*—the ontology of the cosmos.

## 5.4 The Daoist view of human life

Lao Zi taught us that human conduct should follow the law of nature (to know the Invariables). In other words, human conduct should follow the movement of *Dao*. However, if *Dao* is nameless and shapeless and cannot be seen and perceived, then on what basis could humans know *Dao* or the law of nature? Lao Zi said:

From *Dao* all things come into being and from the nourishing of *De* they get their own nature, all things take on their individual forms, they develop and complete under different circumstances. Therefore, all things respect *Dao* and value *De*. The reason why *Dao* is respected and *De* is valued is that *Dao* and *De* never intervene so that all things can transform and complete in their spontaneous ways ... To give all things being but never seek to own them, to complete all things but never seek to give credits to themselves, to nourish all things but never seek to control them, this is called the profound *De*.[80]

*Dao* is that by which all things come to be. According to Lao Zi, in the process of coming into being, each individual thing obtains something from the eternal *Dao* which is called *De* (ethics).[81] After all things come into being from *Dao, Dao* has become an inherency and nature of all things. *De* is the transformation of *Dao* into all things and is the empirical reflection of *Dao*.[82] *De* is that by which things are what they are.[83] This is the Daoist nature of all things, including human nature.

Therefore, to follow *De* is the ethical standard of human conduct. To follow *De* means to follow everything as it is without any arbitrariness. The Daoist law of nature indicates that 'when a thing reaches one extreme, it reverts from it'.[84] A man

[76] Chapter 16, translation from Fung (n 64) 98–99.
[77] Chapter 40, translation ibid 97. [78] Chapter 58, translation ibid.
[79] Chapter 42, translation ibid. [80] Chapter 51, my own translation.
[81] Fung (n 64) 100. [82] Chen (n 64) 258. [83] Fung (n 64) 100.
[84] ibid 97.

should make his conduct according to the nature and spontaneity of things and do things as necessary. He should never overdo, otherwise he will reach the opposite of his purpose. If he wants to achieve something, he should start with its opposite. For example, Lao Zi stated:

> Be twisted and one shall be whole. Be crooked and one shall be straight. Be hollow and one shall be filled. Be tattered and one shall be renewed. Have little and one shall obtain. But have much and one shall be perplexed ... He does not show himself; therefore he is seen everywhere. He does not define himself; therefore he is distinct. He does not assert himself; therefore he succeeds. He does not boast of his work; therefore he endures. He does not contend, and for that reason no one in the world can contend with him.[85]

*De*, according to Lao Zi, is beyond the distinction of good and evil: 'if all people of the world know that beauty is beauty, there is then already ugliness. If all people of the world know that good is good, there is then already evil.'[86] People lost their *De* because they have known too much and have too many desires. People have desires because of their increasing knowledge. Desire is the root of social conflicts. When people try to satisfy too many desires, they get the opposite results: 'there is no disaster greater than not knowing contentment with what one has; no greater sin than having desire for acquisition'.[87]

Therefore, according to Lao Zi, the ethics of humans is to have few desires and to have less knowledge. Lao Zi believed people should retain innocence and simplicity like children as far as they possibly can: 'not to part from the invariable *De* is to return to the state of infancy';[88] 'he who holds *De* in all its solidity may be likened to an infant'.[89] However, to ask people to have less knowledge and to be innocent and simple does not mean that people should not learn and be educated. The Daoist innocence means to reach a similar yet heterogenetic state to that of children. The Daoist innocence is gained after the process of a conscious cultivation.[90] It is beyond and superior to knowledge. It is great wisdom and an achievement of spirit.[91] A man who has achieved the Daoist innocence is a sage: 'the sage, therefore, discards the excessive, the extravagant, and the extreme'.[92]

## 5.5 The Daoist political theory

The ultimate aim of Lao Zi was to provide a political philosophy to the rulers of Dukedoms during the East Zhou dynasty so as to eliminate the conflicts between divided political communities and achieve peace. As a result, Daoism has in fact great significance in international affairs. The Daoist view of human life is ultimately applied to the theory of the ruler or the State. Lao Zi maintained that an ideal State is one ruled by a sage who has achieved the greatest wisdom of innocence and simplicity. The responsibility of a ruler to his State is to allow all things to develop and

[85] Chapter 22, translations ibid 99.
[86] Chapter 2, translations ibid 101.
[87] Chapter 46, translations ibid.
[88] Chapter 28, translations ibid 103.
[89] Chapter 55, translations ibid.
[90] ibid.
[91] ibid.
[92] Chapter 29, translation ibid 100.

complete in their own spontaneous ways and he then rules with 'non-action': 'I act not and the people of themselves are transformed. I love quiescence and the people of themselves go straight. I concern myself with nothing, and the people of themselves are prosperous. I am without desire, and the people of themselves are simple.'[93]

To rule with non-action does not mean to do nothing at all. It means not overdoing. The activities that a State carries out ought to be necessary, non-excessive, and follow the spontaneity of all things. In such a way, it looks as though nothing is done yet everything is accomplished: '*Dao* invariably does nothing and yet there is nothing that is not done.'[94] *Dao* is invisible, nameless, and it never acts or intervenes. Yet all things come into being from *Dao* through their nature and spontaneity. The ruler or the State should allow everything that it can do rather than impose artificiality. The world is in disorder not because something has not been done but rather too much has been done. As a result, the rulers of States should refrain from occupying and contending with each other: 'therefore the sage promotes all things but does not think the effort as his own, achieves merit but does not claim credit for himself, and does not wish to parade his wisdom and ability'.[95]

As analysed earlier, Lao Zi saw *Dao* as the nature of all things and the very source of law of human societies. Ontologically speaking, the Daoist world order is cosmological. Socially speaking, the Daoist world order is ethical. It accepts only a metaphysical and objective standard. It does not accept tyrannical political institutions, even the ruler in the State was merely seen as the assistance of people. Both the ruler or the State and the people were regarded as the incarnation of *Dao*, and they are in nature identical to each other.

## 6. Grotius and Lao Zi: Bridging the West and East in a State-centred World

After the overall examination of the theories of Grotius and Lao Zi, the key issue left is in what way the two theories converge with each other and how could they provide a universal legal foundation of international order in a territorialized world. In this section, I will analyse the issue from three aspects: first, the metaphysics of Grotius and Lao Zi; second, their law of nature; third, their ethical theory of the State.

### 6.1 Sociability and *Dao*: overarching, objective, and universal standards

As shown in the earlier two sections, both Grotius and Lao Zi accepted a metaphysical order above the secular States. While Grotius attributed such a superiority to a natural tendency towards sociability based on human nature of common good, Lao Zi argued for an eternal and invisible *Dao* which generates humans and their

[93] Chapter 57, translation ibid 102–03. [94] Chapter 37, translation ibid 103.
[95] Chapter 77, translation from *A Taoist Classic* (n 64) 98.

societies. The universal law applicable to different human societies derived from this kind of overarching, objective, and universal standards. In this regard, Grotius and Lao Zi departed from a similar point of view that human societies were subordinate to a certain intrinsic force, of which humans were inevitably the constituents.

Grotius was a transitional figure from medieval to early-modern times in Europe. This historical background is reflected in his unique thoughts of semi-antiquity and semi-modernity. Grotius belongs to the early-modern camp as the political organization in him was already non-divine. He remains medieval, as compared to other figures such as Hobbes and Vattel, in that he accepted superior moral standards over human societies but only replaced the medieval Christendom with an international society based on sociability. Lao Zi lived in one of the earliest dynasties in Chinese history and his theory appeared more than two thousand years earlier than Grotius. Nonetheless, the particular social and political circumstances during his time—the fall of the power of the East Zhou King, the division of power among Dukedoms, and the protracted wars for hegemony and annexation—made the East Zhou dynasty of Chinese antiquity a period no less violent than the Middle Ages and the early-modern eve of Europe. Both Grotius and Lao Zi were realistic about the territorial divisions of the world and accepted no superior political institution above the sovereign. They in the meantime aimed to morally and legally justify such a division of power.

Both Grotius and Lao Zi possessed the classical thinking in which humans were envisaged to live in a natural and unrestrained way. Yet this freedom is not absolute in that it is subject to higher supernatural orders. The theory of Lao Zi is not explicit in putting forward that human nature is free but his consistent stress on the non-action of the ruler indicates that the State institution is not justified in suppressing or restraining the spontaneous development of people. This spontaneity is close to the Grotian natural liberty of men. Although men submitted to the ruler or the State in both Grotius and Lao Zi, this human institution nonetheless was only seen as providing protection to people rather than an arbitrary force that could go against the popular will. The State was seen in nature identical in Grotius with man and in Lao Zi with all other beings in conformity with *Dao*. For Grotius, the submission of men to a State is a natural way to protect public security and their common good. For Lao Zi, he emphasized many times that the submission of people to the ruler is natural and the movement of *Dao*. For example, 'if the kings and princes could preserve it [the *Dao*], all things will submit to them spontaneously'.[96]

What an overarching and objective superiority of nature generates is the universality in legal application. In the Western tradition, the universalist school of natural law—notably Vitoria and Grotius—treated the non-Christian world as having common human nature as the Christians. The corresponding international legal system as first formulated by Vitoria and theorized by Grotius was inclusive of the non-Christian world. In the Eastern tradition, although not yet knowing of the existence of the Western counterpart, Lao Zi made an all-embracing argument that

[96] Chapter 37, translation ibid 55.

all matters in the world are generated by the eternal *Dao* and as a result bear the same nature. Such a Daoist metaphysics is far-reaching, inclusive of all human societies, and even matters beyond that. The relationship between the metaphysics of Grotius and Lao Zi could be seen in a way that the latter is so all-embracing as to be able to include the former.

The metaphysics of Grotius and Lao Zi in particular implies the spirit of non-hegemony and peaceful coexistence of States, regardless of imbalance of power. They accepted superior objective standards rather than superior political institutions. It is particularly important to understand Lao Zi's attitude in this regard. The philosophical Daoism preferred to keep the status quo of political divisions in the Spring–Autumn period and criticizes hugely the disaster caused by wars for hegemony. The fundamental concern of Lao Zi is the welfare of ordinary people so that he aimed to achieve peace through a way contrary to military annexation for unification. Lao Zi's sympathy to small powers poses an essential difference to Confucius who favoured a unified world order under a superiority. Lao Zi made this point clearly:

> The great powers should lie in the lower reaches, to which all things under Heaven come together [like all streams run into the sea], and situate themselves in a feminine position under Heaven. The feminine always surpasses the masculine by tranquillity, because she is calm and willing to lie lower. Therefore, if great powers may treat small powers in modesty, they can unite small powers. If small powers may be modest towards great powers, they can win trust from the latter. Thus, being lower and humble in order to unite, or being lower and humble so as to be united. For great powers, what they need is no more than to unite and conserve small powers; for small powers, what they need is no more than to be embraced by the great. In this way, both of them could fulfil their wishes, the great powers should especially be humble.[97]

Lao Zi's central political theory of non-contention reflects such a principle of non-hegemony and peaceful coexistence in international relations.[98]

## 6.2 'Force of nature' and spontaneity: universal legal foundation of a territorialized world

In Grotius's theory of property, all things were common and undivided possession of all men in their primitive state.[99] It is the gaining of knowledge by men that changed this primitive state. Driven by the desires for the advantage of life, this primitive common ownership was then abandoned, and men began the process of 'occupation' to include things in their private ownerships.[100] This process is also described by Grotius as the force of nature.[101] The use of things, to Grotius, is the foundation of private ownership.[102] To situate such a force of nature in Grotius's

[97] Chapter 61, my translation. [98] See (n 95). [99] Grotius (n 10) 186.

[100] ibid 189–90.

[101] See H Grotius, *Mare Libervm*, R Van Deman Magoffin (tr), with revision of the 1633 Latin text, J Brown Scott (ed), with introductory note (OUP 1916); Carnegie Endowment for International Peace, 25.

[102] Grotius (n 101) 24–25.

theory of natural law, it could be seen that the force of nature in humans to occupy land belongs to the first aspect of human nature—self-interest. Grotius had pointed out that natural liberty in regard to actions is equivalent to ownership in regard to property.[103] In the meantime, he used the greater place of common good to restrain the self-interests of individuals: the natural liberty as possessed by one should be under the restraint of the other, and one should refrain from occupying the possessions of others.

Nonetheless, Grotius did not apply such natural liberty to that of the State. To Grotius, nature only conveys the force to humans for their acquisition of things for life, but such nature does not necessarily have anything to do with the political organization of States. In other words, States do not have a distinctive nature of their own but are simply aggregates of private persons.[104] As a result, public ownership of the State was seen as arising in the same process of private ownership.[105] This is the very legal foundation of a territorialized world on which the original land of a State is based. It is particularly important to note that Grotius did not regard the State as having natural liberty and could occupy things, but only that the ownership of the State is the public and collective manifestation of the private ownerships of all the citizens.

The 'force of nature' is vital in understanding Grotius's theory of a territorialized world. It is primordial and exists before politics. It belongs to an anthropological rather than political dimension. The key point in understanding Grotius's legal framework is that the constituent parts of his international system remain private persons rather than States. Territorial possession of a State was viewed not as a priori. It has to rely on physical persons and their enclosure of land as premise. When men became political beings during a certain stage of their anthropological development and were able to envisage public matters, their possession of land began to obtain political characteristic so that territorial divisions came into being.

Lao Zi did not have a specific theory of property as such. However, from his various reasoning on spontaneous and natural development of people in social and political issues and non-action as just behaviour of rulers, it is not difficult to perceive his attitude towards the possession of land: 'the sage manages affairs by non-action, teaches by non-speech. He leaves all things to grow and change without interference, raises all things but claims for no ownership, manages all things but claims for no credit';[106] 'to love the people and govern the State, is it possible to have no action? . . . Raise and nourish all things; to raise but claim for no ownership, to manage but claim for no credit, to lead but not dominate. This is the profound *De*.'[107]

As can be clearly seen from the above quotations, the sage or the ruler raises and nourishes all things but he does not claim ownership. When the ruler does not interfere, the people become prosperous. This indicates lucidly enough that

[103] Grotius (n 25) 18; see also (n 32).

[104] Vattel in this regard differs fundamentally from Grotius in that he made an analogy between the nature of individuals and States and argued that the State has the same natural liberty as man.

[105] Grotius (n 101) 26.

[106] Chapter 2, translation from Ren, *Lao Zi* (n 64) 51 and 53, with my own revisions.

[107] Chapter 10, translation ibid 87, with my own revisions.

things should be possessed by people rather than the ruler. Lao Zi used a very rustic concept of *De* to signify ethics of the ruler. Lao Zi praised *Dao* and *De* for their non-intervention in the human affairs, namely to let people and societies complete in themselves. It is not difficult to read from Lao Zi's words that the ruler should practise non-action so as to assist and nourish the natural or spontaneous development of the individual's life. The main natural activities of people during the Spring–Autumn period as primitive agrarian societies were agriculture. Therefore, it is under the spontaneous force of *Dao* and *De* that humans do agriculture and enclose lands for their own necessary uses. It is under the spontaneous force that civil and political societies develop in themselves. The ruler of a State should never impose any arbitrary power upon its citizens and their society. At the international level, the great powers should be humble and not interfere with the small powers so that States form and develop by themselves and they do not depend on any external force. Lao Zi's image of undisturbed folk life is very close to the Grotian image of state of nature.

It is evident that Grotius and Lao Zi had two distinctive interpretations of human nature. Lao Zi adopted a cosmological view of all matters and saw human beings as no different from any other matters, while Grotius rooted his theory exclusively in the human society in which human centrism is the central pillar. Although Lao Zi had a broader metaphysics, the humanism in Lao Zi is also remarkable.[108] Despite the distinctiveness, these two theories converge at how 'the State' should be understood, founding it on humanism rather than statism. To find the 'person' in the State is critical in understanding how a territorially divided world was founded.

The thoughts of Grotius and Lao Zi converge in following spontaneous (at the cosmic level) and anthropological (at the societal level) movements of people and treating these as the real foundation of law. The humanism found in their thoughts was indigenous in both the West and East and is thus truly universal.

## 6.3 Ethical theory of the State and critique of external acquisitions

To Grotius, the law of nature is not only a set of principles that binds the just conduct of individual men. It is also in the sense of law of war and peace applicable to the public being—the State and its ruler. The essential homogenization of ethical and legal principles of individuals and States, while keeping the conceptual difference between the two, is the essential foundation of Grotius's political theory. Such a homogenization is also evident in the Daoist approach which applies principles of human life to the political life. Under this reasoning, both Grotius and Lao Zi advocated an ethical theory of the State.

However, the prima facie difference between the Grotian and Daoist foundation of the law of nature is also sharp. Grotius regarded the knowledge of good and evil as the driving force of humans to develop and desire is the origin of the law of nature. Lao Zi however treated knowledge and desire as the source of conflicts and

[108] See Chen Gu-ying, *The Humanism of Philosophical Daoism* (Zhonghua Book Company 2012) (in Chinese).

the root of social disorder. Despite that, one must note that that Lao Zi did not deny the natural process of humans to gain knowledge and possess desires, while getting rid of knowledge and desire is only a perfect condition that Lao Zi thought a sage would finally achieve. What he was critical of is the excessive possession of desires. For Grotius, the law of nature is more the obligation that men bear so as to preserve social peace and the principal requirement of that is to respect one another's rights.[109] Natural desires in Grotius's eyes are not limitless, and they should be subordinate to the more impelling obligation for the good of others. Therefore, the prima facie difference between Grotius and Lao Zi is actually caused by their different perspectives in reasoning.

The essential convergence between Grotius and Lao Zi should be viewed at the level of their political theories which aim ultimately the justice of the conduct of States and their demands for peace. In particular, Lao Zi's critique of the rulers' desires to occupy and expand echoes Grotius's theoretical end that Christian sovereignties and territories should not be extended to the non-Christian World. Grotius stated that while vacant land could be occupied by foreigners for the cultivation of nature, sovereignty of the original people over that land should not be impaired:

> [I]f within the territory of a people there is any deserted and unproductive soil, this also ought to be granted to foreigners if they ask for it. Or it is right for foreigners even to take possession of such ground, for the reason that uncultivated land ought not to be considered as occupied except in respect to sovereignty, which remains unimpaired in favour of the original people.[110]

Grotius also explicitly recognized the sovereign Status of East Indies.[111] This is to say, the natural rights possess by men to occupy vacant land should not be automatically applied to the State. Territorial sovereignty of a State over a portion of land could only be based on an accumulated process of private ownerships that when a community of people occupy a large portion of land without previous private owners could their territorial sovereignty be established. In other words, external forces do not lead to the shift of sovereignty and sovereignty only arises from within.

Lao Zi in a similar spirit criticized external acquisitions of rulers. He said:

> He who desires to acquire/govern all under heaven and accordingly acts on it, I assert that he will not succeed. 'All-under-heaven' are holy things and cannot be handled by force. He who acts forcefully will fall, he who holds on to it will lose . . . therefore, the sage discards the excessive, the extravagant, and the extreme.[112]

Lao Zi's critique of external acquisition is also reflected by his anti-war attitude. He regarded that wars were caused by the excessive desires of rulers for others' land and property, and the exertion of military power to acquisition and annexation will eventually result in disasters:

[109] R Tuck, *Natural Rights Theories: Their Origin and Development* (CUP 1979) 73.
[110] Grotius (n 10) 202. [111] Grotius (n 101) 21.
[112] Chapter 29, my own translation.

When State affairs are on the right track, war horses are used in farming. When State affairs are off track, even the [pregnant mares have to be used and] foals are born on the battlefield. There is no calamity greater than discontentment, there is no guilty greater than desires of acquisition. Therefore, to be satisfied with contentment is the eternal contentment.[113]

## 7. Concluding Remarks

This chapter analyses the convergences between the natural law theories of Grotius and Lao Zi though the two thoughts diverge in some respects. It endorses their prima facie distinction in viewing human nature and the derived rules for the regulation of individuals' life. Nevertheless, it in a more important place emphasizes their sharing of a metaphysical order above human societies and an ethical theory of the State for the implication of international law. It points out that the key point for the conception of international order is how 'the State' is understood. Humanism rather than statism is the essential convergence between the two theories and the fundamental way to eliminate the West–East controversy. A Grotian and Daoist conception will say that States are divided or territorialized due to their own natural or spontaneous civil and political development in history. States ought to be rooted in humans rather than being morally independent.

This chapter does not argue that Western and Eastern conceptions of international order are fundamentally incompatible. Nor does it attempt to establish a normative system of Chinese international law. Rather, it endeavours to explore the possible connections in international theories of the two civilizations, in particular in understanding the concept of the State. It argues that these two traditions could adapt to each other by recognizing or restoring the essential elements of humanism in their political and legal cultures, notably the Grotian and the Daoist. In particular, Daoism is more compatible with the Western tradition of equality and division between States compared to Confucian hierarchy and unification.

113 Chapter 46, translation from *A Taoist Classic* (n 64) 66, with my own revisions.

# 14

# The Hazards of Translating Wheaton's *Elements of International Law* into Chinese

## Cultures of World Order Lost in Translation

*Emily Cheung and Maranatha Fung*

### 1. Background

Translation of Henry Wheaton's *Elements of International Law*[1] is the first systematic legal text translation in China. It was translated by WAP Martin, an American missionary, with the assistance of several Chinese translators at the School of Combined Learning (同文館).

Due to a minimal understanding of Western conceptions and a different Chinese comprehension of international order, when Wheaton's book was translated there was an absence of a semantic reference scheme. Western civilization was still foreign to the Chinese and it was an early period for China to implement Western knowledge. For example, when Prince Gong was presented the manuscripts of *Wanguo Gongfa*, he complained that the language in it was confusing and incomprehensible without further oral explanation.[2]

In this chapter, we, first, investigate the translatability of Wheaton's *Elements of International Law*. We argue that Wheaton's book was not accurately translated and the translation was heavily affected by the traditional Chinese culture and Chinese ways of thinking. International law concepts contained in Wheaton's book were hence altered and even distorted. Second, by investigating the reception of the translation by Chinese officials in the late Qing period, we argue that the Chinese perception of international community was not altered by the introduction of Wheaton's book and remained fundamentally different from their Western counterparts. We further argue that the unique Chinese conception of international community remains vibrant in today's China.

[1] H Wheaton, *Elements of International Law* (Little, Brown 1866).
[2] *Chouban yiwu shimo* 籌辦夷務始末, 27:26.

## 2. Methodology

This research conducts a close analysis of the Chinese translation of Wheaton's book. A collection of important words or phrases is selected from the Chinese translation and a comparison is drawn with Wheaton's text. The eighth edition of Wheaton's book is used as it is the last revision. References are made to ancient Chinese texts to find out the meaning of the Chinese characters at the time. We wish to deduce the Chinese comprehension of the neologisms and novel translations in *Wanguo Gongfa*. Chinese legal/philosophical traditions are referred to investigate how the deep-rooted concepts might have affected the reception of the translation.

Relevant parts of Hajime Nakamura's *Ways of Thinking of Eastern Peoples: India, China, Tibet, Japan* are taken as the framework for our analysis.[3] Nakamura's observations of the traditional Chinese ways of thinking are based on an in-depth comparison between the Chinese translations and original texts of Indian Buddhist scriptures.

Nakamura observes that there is an obvious element of concreteness in the Chinese language.[4] Express bodies and shapes are often used in phrases to make a description. He further claims that the 'Chinese thinking has tended to concreteness of expression'.[5] In Chinese, concepts and ideas are also expressed in a highly concrete form. It is evident that the goal is to express things by individualization and specification rather than by analysis.[6]

Nakamura also claims that there is a non-development of abstract thought since the Chinese are 'little interested in universals which comprehend or transcend individual or particular instances'.[7] Complex multiplicity is expressed in a concrete form and the Chinese are 'especially sensitive to the complex variety of phenomena instead of the laws and abstractly conceived unity of things'.[8]

It is rare for the Chinese to explore regulation of the multiplicity by the universal validity of laws. This lack of abstract thought is also manifested in the grammatical ambiguity.[9] For expressing abstract thoughts, Chinese is an awkward medium and ancient Chinese philosophies were usually expressed in a figurative and intuitive way.[10] The Chinese tradition was weak in the formation of objective laws since the Chinese were not interested in canonical formulae.

According to Nakamura, the Chinese tended to adopt an anthropocentric attitude towards all things and understand abstract ideas in relation to man.[11] As a result, most of the Chinese people were pragmatic and utilitarian. Traditional Chinese philosophical studies also focused on subjects which were related to everyday

[3] Nakamura, Hajime, *Ways of Thinking of Eastern Peoples: India, China, Tibet, Japan* (University of Hawaii Press 1971).

[4] ibid ch 15 'Emphasis on the Perception of the Concrete' 177. [5] ibid.

[6] ibid 178. [7] ibid ch 16 'Non-Development of Abstract Thought' 185.

[8] ibid ch 19 'Fondness for Complex Multiplicity Expressed in Concrete Form' 217.

[9] ibid ch 16 'Non-Development of Abstract Thought' 186. [10] ibid 188.

[11] ibid ch 21 'The Tendency Towards Practicality' 232.

life, eg morals, politics, and worldly ways of living which would lead to success.[12] Metaphysics was underdeveloped in China.

Nakamura has provided various insights into the traditional Chinese ways of thinking, however, due to the different ideological emphasis and exegetical skills used in religious and legal texts, we only refer to his observations that are relevant to our research.

## 3. Close Textual Analysis of Selected Translated Words

Several Chinese translations of the concepts which we consider are elementary and fundamental in the Western system of international law are selected and listed in Table 14.1. We have identified inaccuracies and inadequacies in the Chinese translation, which, in our opinion, demonstrate that Wheaton's *Elements of International Law* is, to a large extent, untranslatable.

### 3.1 Elements of international law as *Wanguo gongfa* 萬國公法

International law is defined in Wheaton's book, 'International law, as understood among civilized nations, may be defined as consisting of those rules of conduct which reason deduces, as consonant to justice, from the nature of the society existing among independent nations; with such definitions and modifications as may be established by general consent.'[13] This definition is a shift from the classical concept of international law originating from natural law to a more positive view of law 'established by general consent'.[14] The emphasis is less on moral being or reciprocal obligations but more on consent. The mid-nineteenth century went through a transition period from international law based on natural law to positive law,[15] and such is apparent in Wheaton's work.

*Wanguo gongfa* 萬國公法, the translation of *Elements of International Law*, literally means public law for ten thousand nations. *Wanguo* 萬國 means the world (*tianxia* 天下) and various countries (*geguo* 各國);[16] and *gongfa* 公法 means state law (*guofa* 國法).[17] The character *gong* 公 also carries multiple meanings, including common (*gongtong* 共同),[18] public or collective as opposed to private,[19] and belonging to the ruler (*gongjia de* 公家的).[20] Although *gongfa* can mean public law (a modern Chinese reader is likely to have such an understanding), we believe that a Qing reader would have no concepts of public and private. This does not only refer

[12] ibid 233. [13] Wheaton (n 1) 23.

[14] L He Liu, *The Clash of Empires: The Invention of China in Modern World Making* (Harvard UP 2004) 135.

[15] B Fassbender, A Peters, S Peter, D Högger, *The Oxford Handbook of the History of International Law* (OUP 2012) 460.

[16] *Yi qian* 易▪乾 (Zhou dynasty); *Shiji: Dongyue liezhuan* 史記▪東越列傳 (Western Han dynasty).

[17] Book 6 'Youdu' in *Han Feiz i*韓非子▪有度 (Warring States period).

[18] Huang Zongxi 黄宗羲, 'Yuanjun' in *Mingyi daifanglu* 明夷待訪錄▪原君 (1663, Qing dynasty).

[19] 'Lunji zhushu' in *Hanshu: Shihuo zhi* 漢書▪食貨志▪論積貯疏 (Western Han dynasty).

[20] *Shijing youfeng Qiyue* 詩經幽風七月 (Western Zhou dynasty).

**Table 14.1** Presenting the selected translated words

| Original English Text | Chinese translation in *Wanguo gongfa* (with Pinyin) | Meaning in English[1] |
|---|---|---|
| Elements of International Law | 萬國公法 *Wan guo gong fa* | Public law for ten thousand nations |
| Law | 法 *Fa* | Punishment and/or prohibitions |
| Natural law | 性法 *Xìng fa*/埋法 *Li fa* | Natural instincts; life; reasons; principle and discipline of life; emotions and reasons; humanity and justice |
| Right(s) | 權利 *Quan li* | Power and wealth |
| Sovereignty | 主權 *Zhu quan* | Power of self-direction |
| Sovereign States | 自主之國 *Zi zhu zhi guo* | Self-directed States |
| Independent/Independence | 自主 *Zi zhu* | Self-direct |
| Absolute | 自然 *Zi ran*/自有 *Zi you* | Being itself as it is |
| Self-defence/Self-preservation | 自護 *Zi hu* | Self-protection |
| Equality | 同 *Tong*<br>平行 *Ping xing*<br>均權 *Jun quan* | Same<br>Parallel<br>Even power |
| Authority | 君 *Jun* | Sovereign; ruler; emperor |
| Individual | 人人 *Ren ren* | Human beings; people |
| Added general values in *Wanguo gongfa* | | |
| — | 天理 *Tian li* | Natural rules |
| — | 情 *Qing* | Passion and feeling; natural qualities; a person's character |
| — | 理 *Li* | Reasons |
| — | 公義之大道 *Gong yi zhi da dao* | Natural rules of justice |

[1] The *Collins Mandarin Chinese Dictionary* (HarperCollins 2016) was used to translate the Chinese characters, taking into account the contextual background.

to public and private law, but also the public and private realms in the Western sense. There was no protection of the private realm by the law or other mechanisms. What was allowed in private was that granted by the emperor. There was no idea of the private individuals being protected by the law as against the government, and there was definitely no notion of a limited government. Further, law would mean state law to the people, and it was difficult to comprehend a difference between private and public law. This ambiguity of *gong* was noted but not addressed by Martin and his collaborators, as they considered the compound appropriate for rendering all of the three terms: 'the law of nations', 'positive law', and 'public international law'.[21]

*Gongfa* is divided into two kinds one which conforms to nature and reasons, the other derived from general consent between the States. Due to the ambiguous nature

[21] Liu (n 14) 134.

of *gongfa*, a Qing reader might have viewed the general consent between States as being part of natural law.[22] The translation's vagueness fails to bring out the positive element. Further, *gong* is derived from a specific thinking in China, *Xingli* thinking (性理思想) (explained below), which is more similar to the natural law concept. Hence the compound *gongfa* may produce a less positive image of international law, failing to bring out Wheaton's intended meaning.

The ambiguity and multiple possible meanings of *gong* is problematic. In the translation, the distinction between *gongfa* and *xingfa* 性法 (translation for natural law) is not clearly made. There is also not a new term created to represent 'positive law'. As there was no commensurability of the concept of positive law, *gongfa* might have been viewed as natural law, given the strong natural law flavour in Martin's translation.[23] Some have argued that *Wanguo gongfa* strictly speaking only reflects the notion of 'law of nations' in Chapter 1 but not the semantics of the later term 'international law'.[24] Perhaps due to the ambiguous and unneutral nature of *gongfa*, such term is no longer in use in modern Chinese legal writings. Rather, a new term, *guojifa* 國際法, was brought into China in the early twentieth century after Wheaton's book was translated in Japan.[25]

## 3.2 Law as *fa* 法

'Law' was translated as *fa* 法. A modern Chinese reader, who is accustomed to the Western meaning of 'law', may not find this translation problematic. However, such translation was likely to be confusing to a Qing reader.

Yan Fu, a late Qing scholar and translator, commented in the translator's note of *Fayi* 法意, the translation of Montesquieu's *The Spirit of the Laws*:

> In Chinese, right and wrong of things is called *li* 理, prohibitions of a state is called *fa* 法, whereas Westerners name both concepts as *fa* 法. *Fa* 法 in Western language can be translated into four different words *li* 理 (reasons),[26] *li* 禮 (rites),[27] *fa* 法 (law meaning punishment), *zhi* 制 (system and regulation).[28, 29]

[22] Lam Hok Chung 林學忠, *Cong Wanguo gongfa dao gongfa waijiao-wan Qing guojifa de chuanru quanshi yu yingyong* 從萬國公法到公法外交-晚清國際法的傳入、詮釋與應用 (Shanghai guji chubanshe 2009).

[23] Yin, Z also argues generally that there is an undue emphasis on natural law in Martin's translation of *Wheaton's Elements of International Law*, Heavenly principles? The translation of *international law in 19th century China and the constitution of universality* EJIL vol 27.4 (2016) 1005–23.

[24] Rune Svarverud, *International Law as World Order in Late Imperial China: Translation, Reception and Discourse, 1847–1911* (Brill 2007) 107.

[25] Qiu Hongda 丘宏達, 'Zhongguo guojifa mingci de fazhan ji qi fanyi wenti' 中國國際法名詞的發展及其翻譯問題, in *Haiwai xueren zhuzuo xuankan diyiji* 海外學人著作選刊第一集, Xue Guangqian 薛光前, Guoli bianyiguan 國立編譯館 (Zhengzhong 1976) 81.

[26] 'Ruxiao' in *Xunzi* 荀子▪儒效 (Warring States Period); Qiu Chi 丘遲, *Yu Chenbo zhi shu* 與陳伯之書 (Liang of Southern dynasty); Liu Zong Yuan 柳宗元, *Song Xuecun Yixu* 送薛存義序 (Tang dynasty); 'Qiushui' in *Zhuangzi* 莊子▪秋水 (Warring States period).

[27] 'Qu Li (part one)' in *Liji* 禮記·曲禮上 (Warring States period, Qin and Han). According to *The Book of Rites*, 'rites' is the moral standard of human behaviour, which is to define closeness of relations, decide doubts, distinguish similarities and differences, and demonstrate rights and wrongs.

[28] 'Lishu' in *Shiji* 史記▪禮書; 'Sunquan Zhuan' in *Sanguo Zhi* 三國志▪孫權傳 (Western Jin dynasty). In the *Kangxi* Dictionary 康熙字典'制:又成法曰制。'

[29] Yan Fu 嚴復, Translator's Note 按語, in *Fayi* 法意(1909, Late Qing).

Yan Fu pointed out that the concept of 'law' in the Western legal culture actually includes four different Chinese legal–political concepts, whereas in the Chinese tradition, *fa* 法 would only mean punishment and/or prohibitions. Chinese classics define *fa* 法 as punishments or prohibitions inflicted by the state.[30] As *Shuowen Jiezi*, an authoritative ancient Chinese dictionary, explained, *fa* 法 was equated to punishment.[31]

The Western concept of 'law' was entirely foreign to the Chinese in the nineteenth and early twentieth centuries. Its meaning could not be equated to any single Chinese character and it is obvious that China had a very different legal tradition comparing to its Western counterparts and law was only the ruler's tool for punishment. By translating 'law' as *fa* which traditionally meant punishment and/or prohibition, a Qing reader might have perceived international law primarily as imposition of restrictions when States deal with each other.

## 3.3 Natural law as *xingfa* 性法

Natural law has a strong Christian basis and is a philosophical concept derived from classical thinkers, eg Vitoria and Grotius. Grotius claims that men are moral and accountable beings which live in a social state independent of positive human institutions, ie the state of nature. The law of God is prescribed by God to His rational creatures and revealed by the light of reason. The idea of justice thus has the metaphysics of the independent God.

Natural law is translated as *xingfa* 性法. Because of a lack of direct equivalence of natural law, the translators aimed to build commensurability by fusing natural law with two Chinese lines of thought: the Taoist *Tiandao* thinking (天道思想) and Neo-Confucianist *Xingli* thinking (性理思想). This move was strongly reminiscent of the seventeenth-century Jesuit strategies of reconciliating Confucianism and Christianity. As the Chinese were not interested in the theological explanations of Christianity, the missionaries camouflaged the religious doctrines with secular knowledge that was already inculcated into the Chinese culture.[32] A common technique was to 'internalize' the text to adapt to the Chinese mindset so that Western norms could be transmitted more easily.[33] In the English preface to *Wanguo gongfa*, Martin argued for cultural commensurability on the basis of natural law, 'The Chinese mind is prepared to yield a ready assent. In their state ritual as well as their canonical books, they acknowledge a supreme arbiter of human destiny, to whom kings and princes are responsible for their exercise of delegated power; and in theory, no people are more ready to admit that His law is inscribed

[30] 'Meng Qiu Ji' in *Lushi Chunqiu* 呂氏春秋▪孟秋記 (Warring States period); 'Yue Ling' in *Liji* 禮記▪月令 (Warring States period to Qin and Han); 'Ding Fa' in *Han Feizi* 韓非子.定法 (Warring States period).

[31] *Shuowen Jiezi* 說文解字 (Eastern Han dynasty).

[32] Liu (n 14) 116.

[33] Lu Mingyu 盧明玉, Wang Kefei 王克非, 'Lun wan Qing chuanjiaoshi Lin Lezhi zhuyi de bentuhua quxiang' 論晚清傳教士林樂知著譯的本土化取向, *Jiangxi shehui kexue* 江西社會科學1 (2007).

on the human heart. The relations of nations, considered as moral persons, and their reciprocal obligations as deduced from this maxim, they are thoroughly able to comprehend.'[34]

In *Tiandao* thinking, the occurrence and development of nature are natural. There is no other institution which dominates the nature. As seen from the outset, *Tiandao* thinking is similar to natural law, except that the transcendent God is absent. Neo-Confucianism, conversely, is a combination of Confucianism and Buddhism/Taoism. On the one hand, it consists of the self-consciousness of Confucianism; on the other, it incorporates the enlightenment of Buddhism and Taoism. Through self-reflection, one develops innovative thinking. This fusion of Confucianism and Buddhism/Taoism is Neo-Confucianism and it had been very popular since the Song dynasty. Neo-Confucianism consisted of two important concepts: *xing* 性 and *li* 理. These two concepts are used interchangeably but each of them has distinct meanings. *Xing* has a meaning of natural instincts (*benxing* 本性),[35] life (*sheng* 生),[36] and true nature from Buddhism; while *li* means reasons.[37] Together, *xingli* also means the principle and discipline of life (*shengming zhi yuanli* 生命之原理),[38] emotions and reasons (*qingxu he lizhi* 情緒和理智),[39] and humanity and justice (*renxing yu tianli* 人性與天理).[40] It is the last meaning which is the crux of the Neo-Confucian idea of *xingli* and Qing readers were likely to equate *xing* and *li* in Martin's translation with Neo-Confucian thinking. As seen from this philosophical context, *xingli* has a very different cultural background, which was created by a fusion of multiple philosophies. *Xingfa* as read in light of Neo-Confucianism may have an altered nature as well as added meaning to natural law, which has a totally different religious tradition.

Hence some argue that Martin's translation has transmitted the meanings of both *gongfa* (translation for international/positive law) and *xingfa* (translation for natural law) to somewhere in between the traditional meanings of the two languages. The neologistic use of the two compounds takes *xing* and *gong* out of their philosophical context. At the same time, it also takes 'natural law' and 'public law' out of the traditional Western legal discourses.[41] Arguably, the translation created a textual and cultural 'limbo'.

## 3.4 Added general values

A more general comment building on the observation above is that general values are often inserted in the translation. Besides *xing* being used in the context of

[34] W Martin, Translator's Preface to *Wanguo gongfa*, 1:1.

[35] Confucius, Book 17 'Yang Huo' in *Confucius Quotes* 論語▪陽貨 (Spring–Autumn and Warring States periods).

[36] Book 40 'Nanshi' in *Han Feizi* 韓非子▪難勢 (Warring States period).

[37] Xunzi, Book 8 'Yuxiao' in *Xunzi* 荀子▪儒效 (Warring States period).

[38] Si Maguang, *Chujian baifa kairan ganhuai* 初見白發慨然感懷詩 (Northern Song dynasty).

[39] 'Xieshuzhuan' in *Songshu* 宋書▪謝述傳(Liang of Southern dynasty).

[40] Chen Shan, *Menshi Xinhua: Benchao wenzhang yi sanbian* 捫虱新話▪本朝文章亦三變 (Song dynasty).

[41] Liu (n 14) 133.

*xingfa* (natural law), words of similar nature are added, including *tianli* 天理, from *Tiandao* thinking, which means natural rules.[42] This again creates a much stronger flavour of natural law, tilting away from Wheaton's position.

One particular example which strongly influences the nature of the text is in paragraph 1 of Part 1 of Wheaton's book. Wheaton states that since there is no authority recognized by all nations to determine the law regulating relations of States, the origin of the law must be sought in the principles of justice. He then poses the question what are the principles of justice.[43] In Martin's translation, this question is answered directly in the translation. The text reads that the origin of law comes from the general values: *qing* 情 meaning passion and feeling,[44] natural qualities or a person's character,[45] and reasons;[46] *li* 理 meaning reasons; and *gongyi zhi dadao* 公義之大道 meaning natural rules of justice.[47] This immediate answer is prominent as these general values carry strong elements of natural law, so that a Qing reader might immediately believe that the origin of international law is natural law. Contrastingly, in Wheaton's text, the answer is left open until his definition of international law in paragraph 14.

Translation, as Yin argues, is to build a bridge between two linguistic cultures through an interaction between subjectivity and objectivity.[48] Translation does not only bring out the ideology of the original writer but also that of the translator. Hence it is clear that the missionaries' culture had a huge influence on the translated text. Translation was used as a tool for religious infiltration,[49] as a sacred mission of social reform, as well as creation of a humanitarian social order.[50] Martin was known as a natural lawyer and his translations definitely offer a 'higher' purpose. His emphasis on natural law does not only tilt away from Wheaton's original intent, but may also have influenced the Chinese understanding of the origin of international law.

## 3.5 Rights as *quanli* 權利

Although legal philosophers propose different conceptions/definitions of rights, it is undoubted that the concept of rights is fundamental to the Western legal system. In general, the concept of rights defines the content of Western laws, recognizing certain actions and institutions as just and proper. The concept is also important in international law, for instance, in Grotius's theory, the only justification for war is the enforcement of rights.

The Chinese translation of 'right(s)' as *quanli* 權利 is an invention by Martin. To translate 'right(s)', Martin has used a compound of two Chinese characters, *quan* and *li*. The Chinese meaning of *quan* is power (權勢) and the meaning of *li* is wealth (貨財).[51]

[42] 'Tianyun' in *Zhuangzi* 莊子▪天運 (Warring States period).
[43] Wheaton (n 1) 13. [44] 'Liyun' in *Liji* 禮記▪禮運 (Warring States period).
[45] 'Shangde' in *Lushi Chunqiu* 呂氏春秋▪上德 (Spring–Autumn period).
[46] Book 11 'Jiudi' in *Sunzi* 孫子▪九地 (Spring–Autumn period).
[47] 'Tianxia' in *Zhuangzi* 莊子▪天下 (Warring States period).
[48] YinYanan 尹延安, 'Chuanjiaoshi faxue fanyi de lishi wenhua yujing ji qi bianqian' 傳教士法學翻譯的歷史文化語境及其變遷, Lilun yuekan 理論月刊 9 (2008): 85.
[49] ibid. [50] ibid 86.
[51] 'Quanxue' in *Xunzi* 荀子▪勸學 (Warring States Period); Fan Ye, 'Dongzhuo Zhuan' in *Hou Hanshu* 後漢書▪董卓傳 (Liu Song of Southern Dynasties).

It is clear that translating 'right(s)' as 'power and wealth' departs greatly from the original concept, which has the background of restricting the powerful and wealthy. It was indeed very difficult to translate 'right(s)' into Chinese, as there were no Chinese concepts or words which could be equated to 'rights'. Ancient China did not have the Western concept of 'right(s)' or 'duties'. The Chinese only had the Confucian concept of *ming* 名(*name*) and *fen* 分 (*shares*).[52] *The Book of Rites* stated that 'according to the different *ming, li* is different'.[53] In short, the identity (*ming*) of a person would affect his behaviour and code of conduct (*li* 禮). It is clear that *ming* and *fen* cannot be equated to the concepts of 'right' and 'duties' in the Western culture. Another example showing the Confucian concept of *ming* is that, *jun* 君 (*emperor*) having the identity (*mingfen*) as an emperor, could instruct his subordinates to die as well as claim all the land in the ancient Chinese world as his own land. Everyone living within the emperor's land would be subordinate to the absolute power of the emperor,[54] whereas the emperor's corresponding responsibility would be to treat his subjects in accordance with the rites.[55] However, such a responsibility was only one of a moral nature and was in no way sanctioned by any laws or rules.[56]

The Western concept of rights is also in conflict with the Chinese traditional ideal of 'no conflict' (無訟).[57] It is obvious that the concept of rights would create many conflicts among different stakeholders and hence it was difficult for the late Qing Chinese to understand or accept the concept of 'rights'.

Martin's choice of the characters *quan* 權 (power) and *li* 利 (wealth) might be influenced by the natural law tradition. It might be his attempt to convey the meaning that 'right' is 'a moral quality of a person, making it possible to have or to do something correctly … a capacity or power possessed by the agent … a "faculty" or an "aptitude" of the person'.[58] The choice of *li* 利 (wealth) might be an attempt to convey that 'rights' can bring benefits to the relevant right-bearers. However, as mentioned above, due to the existing meaning of *quan* and *li* as 'power' and 'wealth', as well as a total lack of conception of rights in the Chinese history and culture, Martin's translation would likely confuse a Qing reader who would not be able to distinguish 'rights' from 'power'.

[52] Fan Zhongxin 范忠信, Zheng Ding 鄭定, and Zhan Xuenong 詹學農, *Qinglifa yu Zhongguoren-Zhongguo chuantong falu wenhua tanwei* 情理法與中國人-中國傳統法律文化探微 (China Renmin UP 1992) 204.

[53] 'Zhuanggong shibanian' in *Zuozhuan* 左傳▪莊公十八年 (Spring–Autumn period): '名位不同,禮亦異數。'.

[54] Chinese proverb: '君要臣死臣不得不死。'; *Bei shan, Gu feng zhi shi, Xiao ya* in *Shi jing* 詩經▪小雅▪谷風之什▪北山 (Xian Qin period): '普天之下莫非王土,率土之濱莫非王臣。'.

[55] 'Shiyi' in *Liji* 禮記▪十義(Warring States period): '君禮臣忠。'.

[56] Fan, Zheng, and Zhan (n 52) 205.

[57] Huang Yuansheng 黃源盛, *Zhongguo fashi daolun* 中國法史導論 (Yuanzhao chuban, 2012), 109. Wang pointed out that when 'civil' disputes arose, the most important thing to the Chinese officials was not to define the 'rights' and 'duties' of the parties, but to dissuade the parties from pursuing their claims.

[58] H Grotius, Chapter 1.4 of Book 1, in *The Law of War and Peace in Three Books* (AC Campbell tr, W Dunne, 1901).

## 3.6 Sovereignty as *zhuquan* 主權 and Sovereign States as *zizhu zhiguo* 自主之國

'Sovereignty' is an essential concept in international law. Historically, the international community was seen as a system of sovereign States and this view was confirmed at the Peace of Westphalia. Philosophically, international law jurists such as Grotius and Vattel affirmed that sovereignty is fundamental to States and the system of international law. For example, Vattel wrote:

> [A] nation or a state is . . . a body politic . . . it is necessary that there should be established a Public Authority, to order and direct what is to be done by each in relation to the end of the association. This political authority is the Sovereignty; and he or they who are invested with it are the Sovereign.[59]

Sovereignty is translated by the neology *zhuquan* 主權. In the ancient Chinese language, *zhuquan* had two meanings: (1) authority of the ruler;[60] and (2) officials who control certain authorities/power.[61] When looking at the two characters, *zhu* 主 literally means lord or master, while *quan* 權 means power. When the two characters are read together, it can mean *zizhu zhiquan* 自主之權 (the power of self-direction). On the other hand, 'sovereign States'[62] is translated as *zizhu zhiguo* 自主之國 (self-directed state). Sovereignty was undoubtedly a foreign concept to the Chinese, as the renowned Chinese historian Cho-yun Hsu observes:

> The old Chinese world was a conglomerated cultural system and international actions were regulated by cultural values, but it was not an international community involving many sovereign States . . . This was an order of *li* 禮 (*rites*), not an order of *fa* 法 (*law*).[63]

Martin's translation of *zhuquan* seems to be a decent translation which is able to capture the core meaning of 'sovereignty' that it is a supreme and independent political authority. According to Vattel, a sovereign state is a 'nation that governs itself, under what form soever, without dependence on any foreign power . . . Its rights are naturally the same as those of any other state . . . To give a nation a right to make an immediate figure in this grand society, it is sufficient that it be really sovereign and independent, that is, that it govern itself by its own authority and laws.'[64] *Zhuquan* (the power of self-direction) or *zizhu* (self-direct) are descriptions of the core quality of 'sovereignty' described by Vattel. However, 'sovereignty' being an abstract concept, when translated into Chinese, is expressed in a more concrete and anthropocentric way.

[59] Emmerich de Vattel, Chapter 1 'Of Nations or Sovereign States' of Book I: Of Nations Considered in Themselves, in *The Law of Nations or the Principles* (T & JW Johnson 1853) para 1.

[60] 'Zapian san' in *Guanzi* 管子▪七臣七主第五十二▪雜篇三 (Spring–Autumn period to Qin, Han period): '藏竭則主權衰。'.

[61] *Zizhitongjian* 資治通鑿▪唐穆宗長慶三年(Northern Song dynasty): '凡中外主權,多納弘貨。胡三省注:主權,謂中外官之有事權者。'.

[62] Wheaton (n 1) 89, para 60.

[63] Cho-yun Hsu 許倬雲, Preface in *Wanguo gongfa* 萬國公法 (Taipei: Zhongguo guojifa xuehui, 1998).

[64] Vattel, 'Of Nations or Sovereign States' (n 59) para 4 'What are sovereign States'.

## 3.7 Independent and independence as *zizhu* 自主

According to Vattel, independence is an essential quality of a sovereign State.[65] Interestingly, 'independence' in the title of Chapter 1 'Right of Self-Preservation and Independence' in the second part of Wheaton's book is also translated as *zizhu* 自主 (self-direct),[66] which is the same translation as 'sovereign' (in the compound 'sovereign States'). It is obvious that the concept of 'sovereignty' cannot be simply equated to 'independence' and vice versa. Hence, such translation is absolutely inaccurate.

In paragraph 60 under the same title, 'an independent moral being' is not properly translated.[67] The original text is '[e]very State has certain sovereign rights, to which it is entitled as an independent moral being; in other words, because it is a state'. The corresponding translation is '夫國之所以為國者,即因其為自主而有義之當守,有權之可行也', meaning that a state is a state because it is independent, and it has righteousness to be observed and power to be used. To be more accurate, 'an independent moral being' is translated as '其為自主而有義之當守', in English literally, [the State] is self-directed and has righteousness to be observed. Again, 'independent' is translated as *zizhu* 自主 (self-direct). Moreover, interestingly, 'moral being' as a body politic capable of enjoying rights is not directly translated. Rather, it is stated that a sovereign State has righteousness or moral duties to be observed. This shows that the Chinese translation fails to translate highly abstract concepts deriving from the Western metaphysics such as 'moral being', and hence resort to concrete and anthropocentric expressions.

As mentioned above, while *zizhu* 自主 (self-direct) is indeed the core quality of sovereignty/a sovereign state, such translation is a concrete and anthropocentric description of the actions that a sovereign state can take. Such incapacity to translate the word in an abstract way may not be a problem when we only look at the translation of 'sovereignty'/'sovereign States'. However, when looking at the translations of 'sovereignty'/'sovereign States' and 'independence' together, we can see that the non-development (or absence) of the Western abstract thought in Chinese culture, as described by Nakamura, blurs the delicate but necessary distinction between different abstract legal concepts. This is unfavourable to the development of legal analysis, as capability in differentiating abstract legal concepts is absolutely essential.

## 3.8 Absolute as *ziran* 自然 or *ziyou* 自有

The word 'absolute' is constantly used in Wheaton's book to describe or qualify 'rights'. The word 'absolute' is important because Wheaton distinguishes absolute rights, which are defined as the inherent sovereign rights of States (such as the right of self-preservation which includes the right of increasing a state's national dominion by all innocent and lawful means limited only by the equal correspondent rights of other States growing out of the same primeval right of self-preservation), from conditional international rights arising from international relations existing in peace or in war.[68]

65 ibid. 66 The title of Chapter 1, Second Part of *Wanguo gongfa* is '論其自護自主之權'.
67 Wheaton (n 1) 89, para 60. 68 ibid paras 60–61, 65.

The title of the second part of Wheaton's book, 'Absolute International Rights of States', is translated into '論諸國自然之權', in English literally, On the Natural Rights of States. 'Absolute' is translated into *ziran* 自然. The word *ziran* in modern Chinese language means 'the (mother) nature'. However, this was not the meaning in ancient Chinese language.[69] According to Laozi, *ziran* means 自己如此, in English 'itself as it is'. Ziran (itself as it is) does not have any fixed state or mode. It is a phenomenon that things exist according to its own existence and form without any distortion or external coercion.[70] Hence *ziran* is the state of letting a thing be itself as it is.[71] On the other hand, the phrase 'primitive or absolute rights'[72] is translated as 自有之原權 (in English literally, the primitive rights that a state itself has or is). Such translation only includes the meaning of 'primitive' but omits the meaning of 'absolute'. It is quite clear that the concept of 'absolute' was not easily translatable.

We are of the view that the best translation of the word 'absolute' in *Wanguo gongfa* is *ziyou* 自有 ([it] itself has or is) in paragraph 62 of the second part of Chapter 1 of Wheaton's book. *Ziyou* 自有 is an extended concept of *zirani* 自然, which means that things in a state of *ziran* will have what it itself has, or will be what it itself becomes. Nevertheless, the ideas *to be itself as it is* and *as it itself has or is* have gone beyond the discussion of the concepts of rights being absolute or conditional.[73] Therefore, it is hard to conclude whether *ziran* or *ziyou* itself contains the meaning of 'absolute', or whether these two compounds convey, at least, an extended/associated meaning of 'absolute'. Since the paradigm of the concept *ziran* is so different from the Western concept 'absolute', it is very likely that the compounds *ziran* (itself as it is) and *ziyou* ([it] itself has or is) were unable to convey the meaning of 'absolute (rights)' (as opposed to 'conditional rights') to the Qing readers. In any event, 'absolute' and *ziran or ziyou* are definitely not equivalent concepts. Due to this inability to convey the meaning of 'absolute'/'absolute right', the inviolable and inconvertible nature of absolute international rights such as the right of self-preservation is not adequately translated.

## 3.9 Self-defence and self-preservation as *zihu* 自護

Both 'self-preservation'[74] and 'self-defence'[75] are translated into the same compound, *zihu* 自護, in English literally *self-protection*. It is evident that there is a distinction between self-preservation and self-defence. According to Wheaton, the

[69] *Shuowen Jiezi* 說文解字 explained that *zi* 自 means nose. Since the ancient Chinese thought that formation of a foetus started from the nose, *zi* meaning nose had an extending meaning of *the beginning* 本始, *the original point* 本初, and *the original nature* 本性。 In the *Guangya* Dictionary 廣雅▪釋詁 *ran* is defined as *formation*, in Chinese '然,成也。'.

[70] Book 17 'Daodejing gongcheng shisui' in *Laozi* 老子▪道德經▪功成事遂 (Spring–Autumn period and Warring States period): '悠兮,其貴言。功成事遂,百姓皆謂: "我自然"。'; Book 51 'Daosheng zhi, dexu zhi, wuxing zhi, shicheng zhi' 道德經; Book 25: '人法地,地法天,天法道,道法自然。'

[71] A philosopher in the Three Kingdoms period, Wang Bi 王弼, annotated 'Daodejing' in *Laozi*:'道不違自然,乃得其性。法自然者,在方而法方,在圓而法圓,於自然無所違也。'; '天道任自然,無為無造,萬物自相治理。'

[72] Wheaton (n 1) 89, para 60.

[73] Book 2 'Youwu xiangsheng' in *Laozi* 老子▪有無相生.

[74] Wheaton (n 1) 89, para 61.

[75] ibid 90, para 62.

right of self-preservation is one of the most essential absolute international rights of States. It 'involves all other incidental rights, which are essential as means to give effect to the principal end. Among these is the right of self-defence.'[76] In short, the right of self-defence is incidental to the right of self-preservation.

Translating both 'self-preservation'[77] and 'self-defence'[78] as *zihu* 自護 (self-protection) shows the incapacity of the Chinese translation to differentiate similar but unequal abstract concepts. The incorrect equation of 'self-preservation' and 'self-defence' might have misled the Qing readers to think that the foundational right of self-preservation is limited to the right of self-defence (ie fighting against foreign aggressors) only. They would unlikely have understood that the right of self-preservation is actually much wider than the right of self-defence, and can give rise to many other incidental rights enjoyed by sovereign States.

## 3.10 Equal and equality as *tong* 同 or *pingxing junquan* 平行均權

The heading of paragraph 62 'Right of self-defence modified by the equal rights of other States, or by treaty'[79] is omitted in the Chinese version and this paragraph is put under the heading of paragraph 61, 'Right of self-preservation'.[80] Therefore, the word 'equal' in the heading is not translated.

In *Wanguo gongfa*, 'these absolute sovereign rights can be controlled only by the equal correspondent rights of other States, or by special compacts freely entered into with others, to modify the exercise of these rights'[81] is translated into '故此等自有之原權別無他限,然若使他國有危,則他國亦可執其自護之權而扼其行,或該國自甘立約而改革之可也'. In English literally, 'therefore, these inherent primitive rights are without limits, however, if other States are endangered, ***the endangered state can also use its right of self-defence*** to restrict the relevant act, or the state can voluntarily sign a compact to reform the right'. The highlighted part is the corresponding translation of 'the equal correspondent rights of other States'. The word 'equal' is actually quite important in this sentence as it conveys the meaning that States are equal and hence the rights of self-defence enjoyed by a state would be limited by other States' correspondent rights. However, the word 'equal' is not translated here.

Paragraph 63 of the second part of Chapter 1 of Wheaton's book, '[i]t can be limited in its exercise only by the *equal* correspondent rights of other States, growing out of the same primeval right of self-preservation' is translated to '他國同此原權者或可扼之以自護也'. In English literally, 'other States having the *same* primeval right can restrict it for self-preservation'. Here, 'equal' was translated as '*tong*' (同, same). While 'equal' was actually translated here, the abstract concept of equality was simplified and expressed in a more anthropocentric and concrete way, ie States having the *same* right (of self-defence).

Interestingly, although Martin and his assistant translators were unable to produce a satisfactory translation of 'equal(-ity)' in the above instances, they were able

[76] ibid 89–90. [77] ibid 89, para 61. [78] ibid 90.
[79] ibid para 62. [80] ibid 89, para 61. [81] ibid 89.

to produce better translations in other parts of the book. 'Equal(-ity)' is translated as *pingxing* 平行 (meaning parallel) and *junquan* 均權 (meaning even power) in other parts of *Wanguo gongfa*. The title of Chapter 3 of the second part, 'Right of Equality', is translated as '論諸國平行之權'. In particular, 'equality' is translated as *pingxing* 平行 (parallel). Further, '[t]he natural equality of Sovereign States'[82] is translated as '自主之國本皆平行均權', in English literally, 'self-directed States are originally parallel and have even power'.

*Pingxing* 平行 is an existing compound in the ancient Chinese language, literally meaning parallel. More accurately, *pingxing* means treating others equally,[83] or that the parties have the same status and are not subordinate to each other.[84] The use of *junquan* 均權 meaning 'even power' has the same problem as the translation of 'right' as *quanli*. As explained above, *quan* means 'power' in ancient Chinese, for example, in the *Biography of Shen Tu-gang in the History of Later Han*,[85] *junquan* means even powers were given to the subordinates.

*Pingxing* (parallel) and *junquan* (even power) seem to be decent translations of 'equality'/'equal' as they express the meaning of States sharing equivalent status and powers, and not subordinating to each other. Nevertheless, it can be observed that the translations are concrete and anthropocentric expressions. 'Equal(-ity)' is an abstract concept, whereas, the Chinese translations meaning 'parallel' and 'even power' are descriptions of substantive relations between men, ie certain men have parallel status and certain men share even power among themselves. Further, the fact that 'equal(-ity)' was sometimes not translated, and sometimes translated into different words (ie *tong* meaning same, *pingxing* meaning parallel, and *junquan* meaning even power) demonstrates that it was a foreign and unprecedented concept which was not easily translatable in late Qing.

## 3.11 Authority as *jun* 君 meaning emperor

Authority is translated into *jun* 君 which means sovereign, ruler, and emperor.[86] In paragraph 1 of Chapter 1 of Wheaton's book, 'legislative authority', 'judicial authority', 'legislative power' were all translated to emperor. We believe that this is because there was not an equivalent concept of authority in the Chinese mindset. Up until the Qing dynasty, the emperor had taken absolute control. There was no concept of the legislative or judicial power in the Western sense, since all was under the emperor's rule. The branches which made law and adjudicated cases were seen more as being parts of the central government. They were governmental departments and tools to effect the government's administration, rather than separate branches limiting the emperor's power. Due to this concept of equating emperor to authority, when the

[82] ibid 232, para 152.
[83] Xin Wenfang, 'Liu Yuxi' in *Tangcaizi zhuan* 唐才子傳▪劉禹錫 (Yuan dynasty).
[84] Wu Qiao, Book 2 *Weilu shihua* 圍爐詩話卷二 (Qing dynasty).
[85] 'Shentugang zhuan' in *Hou Hanshu* 後漢書▪申屠剛傳.
[86] 'Lilun' in *Xunzi* 荀子▪禮論; 'Luxing' in *Zhou Shu of Shang Shu* 尚書▪周書▪呂刑 (Western Zhou dynasty).

Qing emperor abducted at the time the West took control over China, many Chinese people saw China as ceasing to exist as an entity. They considered that they lost their authority totally. Although Martin introduced concepts of legislature and judiciary by neologisms in the later chapters, because of the mistranslation in Chapter 1 and inconsistency of the translated terms throughout the text, the translation would be confusing to a Qing reader. Without offering any explanation to the neologisms, the translation failed to introduce the fundamental Western governmental concepts of legislature and judiciary. A Qing reader would also easily think that the emperor's power without any limitation is a valid and legal concept in international law.[87]

## 3.12 Individual as *renren* 人人 meaning human/people

Individual in the Western culture is a concept opposed to the public. An individual has private rights protected by the law. This is the core concept of Vattel. Human lives are equally natural and free, and laws that regulate States are seen on the same basis as law regulating individuals. This law that regulates States operates just like a social contract. Individual is a fundamental concept in the Unequal Treaties signed by China. The basis of the West attacking China was that China should treat all States equally and China had no reason to refuse to trade with the West. Hence in the treaties, China had to agree to treat each state equally on the basis that one should treat each individual in the same manner.

Individual is translated to *renren* 人人. *Ren* 人 traditionally means human being or person,[88] and *renren* 人人 means people or everyone.[89] *Ren* can also mean the common people.[90] *Ren* is an example showing the Chinese anthropocentric mentality. However, it does not carry the same meaning and tradition as 'individual' in the West. In the Chinese culture, *ren* only has the meaning of human, as opposed to animals; or common people as opposed to the ruler, but it does not bear the meaning of private persons. There is no conveying of the concept of individual rights. Although individual right is translated by a neologism, *siquan* 私權, in English literally private power, this would not make any sense to a Qing reader since he had no idea of the distinction of public and private spheres but only that of the emperor and his subjects. Subjects were bound to obey any rule made by the emperor and there was no notion of possessing something in private unless allowed by the emperor. The law was not to protect individuals but a tool for the emperor to maintain sociopolitical order and to effectively rule the country.

The lack of the concept of 'individual' means that the Chinese would not understand the reasons that the West offered for imposing the Unequal Treaties on China. All they would know was that because they lost in the war, the winning States could

[87] He Qinhua 何勤華, 'Falu fanyi zai Zhongguo jindai de diyici wanzheng shijian - Yi 1864 nian *Wanguo gongfa* de fanyi wei zhongxin' 法律翻譯在中國近代的第一次完整實踐—以 1864 年萬國公法的翻譯為中心, *Bijiaofa yanjiu* 比較研究法 2 (2014): 196.

[88] *Shuowen Jiezi* (n 69).

[89] 'Li Lou (part one)' in *Mencius* 孟子▪離婁上 (Warring States period):"人人親其親,長其長,而天下太平。".

[90] Lin Juemin 林覺民, *Yuqishu* 與妻書 (1911, Qing dynasty).

do whatever they wanted. Such was the Chinese belief of losing a war. This probably also underlies the Chinese government's thinking until the present day that nothing is more important than building a powerful country.

## 4. Reception by Late Qing Chinese Officials

In this part, we briefly present how *Wanguo gongfa* was understood by the late Qing Chinese officials. By examining their reception of the book, we would be able to understand whether the late Qing Chinese indeed accurately understood or internalized the legal concepts in *Wanguo gongfa.*

Although the Qing government supported the publication of the translation, it did not intend to integrate itself into the system of Western international law nor did it fully understand its nature or normative foundations. In Prince Gong's (奕訢) letter to the emperor, he expressly stated that China was not willing to comply with Western international law as he considered that China had its own laws.[91] This showed that the Qing government had no intention in being westernized in the legal aspect. The government supported the publication of *Wanguo gongfa* only because Prince Gong treated it as a useful tool for dealing with the Westerners. Such attitude was obvious in the same letter by Prince Gong, who said that the translation of Wheaton's book could provide 'examples' to argue against the eloquent foreigners.[92] He also highlighted the successful experience of some officials making arguments using Wheaton's book when a Danish ship was captured by Prussia outside Tianjin.[93] Therefore, copies of *Wanguo gongfa* were sent to treaty ports as a tool for the Chinese officials to deal with the foreign consuls.[94]

On the other hand, Prince Gong said that he was afraid that the foreigners might keep Wheaton's book confidential. This demonstrates that, to him, international law was just a sword to fight against the Westerners in times of coercion. While Prince Gong's letter illustrates an active desire of the Qing government to learn and use Western international law, the motive was clearly not one of appreciation of international law's value or normative foundations. There was no internalization and/or intention to be internalized by international law.

Apart from treating international law as a matter of expediency, Prince Gong misunderstood Wheaton's book as a Western version of the Qing Code, the domestic law of Qing China. This was a result of Martin's wilful misrepresentation. In answering Prince Gong's doubts that China might be forced to observe Wheaton's book, Martin said 'although the Great Qing code has now been translated by foreign countries, China has never compelled foreign countries to act by it. It cannot be that when a foreign book is translated into Chinese, China should be forced to follow it.'[95] Martin's misrepresentation was twofold. First, Martin claimed that Wheaton's book was just another domestic legal text like the Qing Code, omitting that Wheaton's book was

[91] *China's Response to the West: A Documentary Survey 1839–1923* (Harvard UP 1965) 97–99.
[92] ibid. [93] ibid. [94] ibid. [95] ibid.

meant to have international legal significance. The Qing Code was a code of punishments to consolidate imperial administration, whereas international law explained in Wheaton's book undoubtedly did not share the same objective or normative foundation. Therefore, equating international law with the Qing Code was conceptually wrong. Second, the translation of the book was an effort to integrate China into the Western international legal system but Martin concealed this purpose.

In Prince Gong's brief summary of the content of Wheaton's book, he said 'Upon examination, the book seems to deal generally with treaties, laws of war ... Particularly there are laws that govern the mutual controls and restrictions imposed on each of the belligerent parties at the outbreak of hostilities'.[96] The Prince only referred to the substantive rules in relation to treaties and wars, whereas the fundamental normative notions such as sovereignty, independence, and equality were not mentioned at all. Such normative notions were, in fact, highly relevant to the Qing government's situation. If China was to raise any right-based claim against the Western powers, eg to invalidate any treaty clause which violated the fundamental principles of international law, it must rely on these normative notions. The silence of China in making any substantial right-based argument illustrates Prince Gong's ignorance of international law's normative structure and he was unlikely to have truly understood Western international law.

Li Yumin, a contemporary Chinese historian, holds a positive view towards the Qing government's reception of international law. He concludes that its attitude can be divided into three phases: (1) doubt, (2) passive acceptance, and (3) upholding international law as a guiding principle.[97] While Li adduced certain historical evidence to support his argument, we cannot agree with his interpretation of those historical facts. In particular, Li argues that the late Qing government had fundamentally changed its conception regarding international treaties and relations. He argues that 'international treaty' was accepted and its nature was well understood after numerous diplomatic dealings. He points out that the Chinese political culture did not encompass a widespread use of international treaties. Usage of 'international treaties' (*mengshi* 盟誓, literally meaning covenants and promises) could be traced back to the Spring–Autumn period, when China was divided into small warring States. At that time, there were divided understandings of 'international treaties'. Some thought that treaties should be strictly observed as a manifestation of the virtues of righteousness 義 (*yi*) and faithfulness 信 (*xin*); others thought it was not necessary to observe the treaties as they could be easily breached at will (whether the treaties were entered by coercion or consent).[98]

Li suggests that the fundamental change occurred after China's humiliating defeat at the Boxer Rebellion (1900–01) where the Qing government was forced to accept the Western legal conception of 'international treaty' and many important governmental figures then demonstrated deeper understandings of 'international treaty'.[99] However,

[96] ibid.

[97] Li Yumin 李育民, 'Wan Qing shiqi tiaoyue guanxi guannian de yanbian' 晚清時期條約關係觀念的演變, Li shi yan jiu 歷史研究, 5 (2013): 91.

[98] ibid 84. [99] ibid 86.

his contention does not seem to be supported by proof, and the quotes that he presents as evidence actually tell a conflicting story. It is undoubted that Chinese officials showed unprecedented feelings that international treaties were important in international politics. However, the evidence hardly shows any deeper understanding or internalization of the concepts of international treaties or international law. For example, Li quoted Yuan Shikai 袁世凱, the Viceroy of Zhili 直隸總督, who was of the view that Chinese scholars should study international law because:

> As the world changes so fast, substantive works of building and training military forces, together with *the language of faithfulness and peacekeeping* are the internal and external measures [that a State should take].[100]

Yuan did not demonstrate any understanding of the essential concepts of international law, eg sovereignty, independence, and equality. Rather, he called international law and/or treaty 'the language of faithfulness and peacekeeping'. Faithfulness is not the foundation of Western international law, but a distinct Chinese moral concept. Peacekeeping might be the outcome of international law in some circumstances, but it is not a part of its fundamental normative structure. The essential normative idea that sovereign States are equal and independent and hence bear certain natural rights was not understood by Yuan, as he reduced international law to a tool for peacekeeping and a way to express faithfulness.

Li further argues that China's gradual internalization of international law was demonstrated by its pursuit of treaty amendments. The traditional Chinese understanding was that treaties were meant to be perpetually valid (or at least as long as a certain dynasty lasted). For example, when the Treaty of Nanking was signed, both Emperor Daoguang 道光帝 and Qi Ying 耆英, the Governor of Guangdong and Guangxi, thought that the Treaty was a peace treaty for millions of years to come (萬年和約). They believed that the Treaty should be observed continually and it would be able to eliminate the possibility of any further military conflicts between China and Britain.[101] As seen from this, from the very beginning of international politics, the Qing government did not understand that a treaty is only a negotiation and settlement between States, which would be valid only for the period stated therein and is subject to amendment upon agreement of the signatories.

Li argues that since around 1874, due to the spread of knowledge of international law, the Qing government started to realize the unequal nature of the treaties with the Western powers and actively pursued amendments of them. In particular, after the Sino-Japanese War (1894–95), the Qing government attempted to amend the unequal treaty clauses in relation to customs and consular jurisdiction. He also argues that after the Boxer Rebellion, the Chinese officials became well aware of the concepts of sovereignty, independence, sovereign rights, and the rights to amend treaties.[102]

He quoted Qian Xun 錢恂, the Qing government's ambassador in Italy, who said that 'every state has the right of independence and sovereignty . . . [China] can not

100 ibid, original Chinese quote: '世變日極,詰戎練武之實與講信修睦之文,二者相為表裏'.
101 ibid 95.
102 ibid 96–97.

enjoy sovereignty . . . [the customs arrangement] are extremely unfair'. But Qian also believed that if '[China] carries on with perseverance, the day of amending the treaties will come'.[103] From the outset, it seems that Qian understood that the customs arrangements made in the unequal treaties were unfair and were against China's sovereignty and independence. However, he did not seem to understand the concept of rights (ie the right to protest against unequal treaties which seriously violate a state's sovereignty and independence). International rights would not be acquired by a state's perseverance, rather, such rights are inherent in every sovereign state.

Further, all the other quotes that Li presents demonstrate that most of the important Chinese officials did not accurately understand Western international law. For example, Liu Kunyi 劉坤一, the Governor of Liang Jiang 兩江總督, wrote:

> [We should] declare a substantive plan for internal policy reform, and let all the other countries know that we have the hope of self-strengthening and the determination to eliminate bad practices. Then, when we negotiate for amendments of treaties, [they would] at least allow us to say something.[104]

It is obvious that Liu Kunyi's basis for China's future requests of treaty amendments was by reforming China to become a stronger and more 'civilized' state (in the Western sense). But he was not relying on the concept that China, as a sovereign state, was entitled to rights and should be treated equally.

The historical fact that the Qing government did actively seek amendments of the unequal treaties is not to be ignored. However, compliance with the treaties and the desire to amend the unequal clauses were not due to a real understanding of Western international law and its normative foundations. We argue that the Qing government's reception of international law was only a pragmatic adaptation to pressure and coercion. It is doubtful whether there was any true internalization of international law concepts. The translation of Wheaton's *Elements of International law* was unable to convert the Qing government into a true believer of international law.

The Chinese officials' reception of *Wanguo gongfa* proves that the inaccuracies and inadequacies in the translation is not a pure theoretical argument. It is clear that Qing readers were indeed influenced by the inadequate Chinese translation. Xu and Fu argue that in order for a legal translation to be deemed successfully 'transmitted', there must be internalization in the receiving country, ie the foreign legal concepts should become an integral part of the local legal system, and be used by the local people as local law.[105] Legal texts are cultural in nature, hence legal translation must also be cultural. Without the necessary culture and linguistic environment, the original meaning will be lost in the translation.[106] Therefore, local circumstances, including the social, economic, and legal culture, have to be reformed for the legal translation to be understood, implanted, and implemented in the local society.[107] This is the

[103] ibid 98.

[104] ibid, original Chinese quote: '即行宣示整頓內政切實辦法,使各國咸知我有發奮自強之望、力除積弊之心,則籌議修約時尚可容我置詞'.

[105] Xu Wenbin 徐文彬, Fu Xiao 傅曉, 'Faluyizhishiyuxiadefanyicelue' 法律移植視域下的翻譯策略 (2004) 31(4) Dongjiang Journal 東疆學刊48.

[106] ibid. [107] ibid 49.

'cultural fill',[108] or 'thick translation' as proposed by Appiah.[109] It is believed that the large cultural gap between the Western and Chinese cultures was the major obstacle when Wheaton's text was translated into Chinese. At that time, the West already had more than 2,000 years of legal development, whereas China had been immersed in 2,000 years of autocratic politics.[110] The historical background, culture, and legal–political tradition of China and the West were so different that Martin's translation of Wheaton's book was incapable of bridging the cultural gap or facilitating any internalization of Western international law in China.

## 5. Conclusion

Nakamura observes that many meanings in the original Buddhist scriptures were altered and even distorted in its Chinese translation and such discrepancies reveal the unique Chinese ways of thinking. We are of the view that the same phenomenon can be found in Martin's Chinese translation of Wheaton's *Elements of International Law*.

Our research demonstrates that, due to the lack of a semantic reference system of Western international law in late Qing China, Wheaton's book was neither accurately nor adequately translated. Basic notions in the Western legal culture such as individuals, rights, and sovereignty were totally foreign and had no equivalences in the Chinese culture in late Qing China. Martin and his fellow Chinese translators attempted to bridge the gap of huge incommensurability between the two cultures by drawing references to Confucian thinking and creating neologisms from existing Chinese characters. However, the Chinese translation and neologisms were incapable of accurately transmitting the concepts of Western international law embedded in Wheaton's book. Many concepts and notions of Western international law were altered or even distorted during the translation process.

While it seems to be true that, as Nakamura suggests, the Chinese prefer concrete expressions, the incommensurability seems to have gone beyond language. Abstract thoughts are essential in the Western legal culture and the Chinese preference for concrete expressions affected their attempts to understand Western international law concepts. It seems that the Chinese could not understand the concept of 'absolute', nor realize the distinction between 'self-preservation' and 'self-defence'. However, although the Chinese did not develop metaphysics similar to that of the West, they did have abstract thoughts such as the Confucian and Mencius ideas of *ren* 仁 (benevolence), *yi* 義 (righteousness and justice), and *li* 禮 (rites) etc. Hence it seems that the crux of the incommensurability is not related to the incapacity of Chinese readers to understand abstract concepts. Rather, it is the incomparability of the Chinese and Western approaches to (international) social order, which cannot easily be shaken. Therefore, the incommensurability of languages is only at the

[108] Ma Li 馬莉, *Falu yuyan fanyi de wenhua zhiyue* 法律語言翻譯的文化制約 (Falu chubanshe 2009).

[109] KA Appiah, 'Thick Translation' (1993) 16(4) Callaloo 808–19.

[110] He Qinhua (n 87) 190.

surface of the problem, its root actually goes way down to the clashes of the two different and even conflicting cultures.

As Xu and Fu argue, there is a cultural abyss standing in the way of legal translation to be internalized. This argument also corroborates Bozeman's proposition that Asian and African countries have borrowed and repeated the legal language of the West without internalization as they do not share the same legal–cultural background and there is no true belief of the idea of law.[111] Bozeman's thesis is that international law derives from the conceptual and social premises of Western culture and there is poor translatability of Western categories cross-culturally.[112] In the West, law forms a natural point for the maintenance of internal and external stability; law also derived from the respect for individual rights as well as rights and duties of citizenship. However, law is not a dominant reference in every culture and as discussed above, many basic Western legal notions were absent in ancient China. Therefore, international law, which is based on Western cultural values, is not easily translatable.[113] Even though late Qing China was forced to engage in many Unequal Treaties,[114] it is believed that the Chinese government did not truly understand or internalize the underlying concepts, premises, or cultural background of Western international law.

One and a half century has passed since *Wanguo gongfa* was published, many may be of the view that today's China is no longer the imperial China which was incapable of understanding Western international law. In the recent years, China seems to have integrated into the Western-oriented international community. It has signed international treaties on an equal footing with other States and it is actively involved in international affairs. International jargons (some were retained since Martin's translation) are frequently employed. However, while modern China may appear to have integrated into the international legal system, whether it truly understands or internalizes international law is a separate matter. We are sceptical about any deep reception of the normative structure of international law. Further, modern China's distinctive approach in dealing with the international community urges us to think that perhaps there is something which has not been eroded by the modern Chinese history of Westernization since the late Qing period, nor has it been assimilated by imperialism or globalization. Indeed, it cannot be excluded that the traditional Confucian view of the Celestial Empire and Tributary System remain and still play a role today.

In this chapter, we have identified that there is a traditional Chinese conception of international order which is very different from the West, and we believe that this influence is still present. Due to the traditional influence of the Confucian empire and Tributary System, China views the world as a family. In the past, States were distinguished according to their proximity with the emperor, just like the feudal States,

[111] Adda Bozeman, *The Future of Law in a Multicultural World* (Princeton UP 1971).

[112] Milton Altschuler, 'The Future of Law in a Multicultural World (Book Review)' (1975) 77(1) American Anthropologist 102–03.

[113] Bozeman (n 111) 182.

[114] Zewei Yang, 'Western International Law and China's Confucianism in the 19th Century: Collision and Integration' (2011) 13 Journal of the History of International Law 305.

and treating the whole world as one family (天下一家) was always the foreign policy of ancient China. This fundamentally different conception of international community arguably still affects Chinese foreign affairs and acts as a challenge to the Western view of the world today.

An example supporting this argument is the case of the Asian Infrastructure Investment Bank. At the Boao Forum for Asia Annual Conference in 2015, although President Xi used terms of Western international law (such as 'we need to make sure that all countries respect one another and treat each other as equals'), his speech carries strong and distinct Chinese characteristics which suggests a different Chinese conception of international order. He says: 'On matters that involve us all, we should discuss and look for a solution together ... Being a big country means shouldering greater responsibilities for regional and world peace and development.' He also says:

> Facing the fast changing international and regional landscapes, we must see the whole picture, follow the trend of our times and jointly build a regional order that is more favorable to Asia and the world. We should, through efforts towards such a community for Asia, promote a community of common interest for all mankind ... The old mindset of zero-sum game should give way to a new approach of win-win and all-win cooperation ... This way, we could turn the seas of Asia into seas of peace, friendship and cooperation for Asian countries ... As people of all countries share common destiny and become increasingly interdependent, no country could have its own security ensured without the security of other countries or of the wider world. The Cold War mentality should truly be discarded and new security concepts be nurtured as we explore a path for Asia that ensures security for all, by all and of all.[115]

This speech of President Xi presents much of the Chinese conception of international order, ie treating the whole world as a family. Underlying this seems to be the idea that the world is an international community. Disputes should be solved by collaboration and there is not the idea of a 'zero-sum game' but cooperation and friendship. States should not be seen as separate entities, but they should be united. Introduction of these Chinese concepts and leading in this new international order can be seen as a challenge to the dominant Western or American thinking. This Chinese approach of international order has been advanced since the leadership of Hu Jintao, when 'peaceful development' was an official foreign policy of China.[116] The idea was that nations should increase their security through diplomatic and economic interaction, and the Western Cold War mentality of antagonistic power blocs is outdated. Rather than building alliances, China's foreign policy more resembles family partnerships. Thus, this Chinese notion of international order, which seems to trace its origin back to the Tributary System, has a very different cultural background from the Western development of international law since the times of Grotius and Vattel. The two cultures' fundamental divergence still has a great impact on the countries' foreign policies today.

[115] 'Full Text of Chinese President's Speech at Boao Forum for Asia' available at http://www.globaltimes.cn/content/914349.shtml (accessed 23 May 2015).

[116] Congyan Cai, 'New Great Powers and International Law in the 21st Century' (2013) 24(3) European Journal of International Law 785.

To conclude this chapter, Martin's translation of Wheaton's *Elements of International Law* was neither accurate nor adequate. It also failed to internalize Western international law in Qing China due to the incommensurability between the Western and Chinese cultures. The Chinese understanding of international order remains vibrant, and with China's continuous rise in the twenty-first century, the Chinese conception of international community is acting as an alternative or challenge to the traditional Western perception of international law.

# 15

# Chinese Intellectuals' Discourse of International Law in the Late Nineteenth and Early Twentieth Centuries

*Tian Tao*

Although China's contact with international law can be traced back to an earlier time,[1] the concept that there existed a certain legal order among countries had not been accepted in China until H Wheaton's *Elements of International Law* was introduced into China by WAP Martin.[2] Thereafter, during his tenure in Tongwen Guan, the earliest official new-style school in China, Martin translated some other international law works.[3] In addition, the versions of international law works translated by John Fryer, while working for Jiangnan Arsenal of Shang Hai, were printed in 1894–95.[4] These translations were the first batch of international law literature known by the officials and intellectuals in the late Qing Empire.

Western international law first drew attention from some senior officials and intellectuals who were interested in current affairs in coastal areas. Their understanding and commentary of international law can be found in their books, the prefaces they wrote for the Chinese versions of international law works, the reports, and suggestions to the royal court as well as in their private letters and diaries. With the worsening Chinese situation at the end of the nineteenth and early twentieth

[1] Researchers usually think that Western international law in some degree was applied in the negotiation of the first boundary treaty between China and Russia in 1689 with the influence of Jesuits, Jean-Francois Gerbillon and Thomas Pereira. Before the outbreak of war in 1840 between China and Britain, Lin Zexu being sent to Guangzhou to deal with opium-smuggling problems, commissioned his private translator Yuan Dehui and American medical missionary, Peter Parker to translate some chapters of Emmerich de Vattel's *The Law of Nations, or Principles of the Law of Nature, Applied to the Conduct and Affairs of Nations and Sovereigns.*

[2] The Chinese translation of this book is Wanguo Gongfa, which means public law of nations.

[3] These great works include Charles de Martens, *Guide Diplomatique* (in Chinese: Xingyao Zhizhang) (Brockhaus 1866); TD Woolsey, *Introduction to the Study of International Law* (Scribner 1872/1891), JC Bluntschli, *Le droit international codifié* (Guillaumin 1874); Institut de Droit international, *Manual of the Law of War on Land* (OUP 1880).

[4] Including Gongfa Zonglun (being translated according to the entry of international law 9th edn of *Encyclopaedia Britannica* A & C Black 1889), Geguo Jiaoshe Gongfa Lun, Geguo Jiaoshe Bianfa Lun (respectively being the first three volumes and the fourth volume of Robert Phillimore, *Commentaries upon International Law* (T and J.W. Johnson 1854)).

*Chinese Intellectuals' Discourse of International Law in the Late Nineteenth and Early Twentieth Centuries.* Tian Tao.  Published 2018 by Oxford University Press.

centuries, international law received more attention, reflecting the Chinese intelligentsia's comprehension of Western international law, and their views of the world order, rules, and even the direction of movement of human society.

## 1. Public Law in Spring–Autumn: Re-establishment of Confucian World Order

With the introduction of Western modern knowledge into China in the mid-nineteenth century, some scholar-officials (Shi-dafu) accepted that such views as Western scientific knowledge and principles, including practical techniques and inventions could also be traced in Chinese ancient books. Even the Western democratic system and spirit could be found to have its roots in ancient Chinese sages' remarks. Some officials who visited Western countries also thought that the West was very similar to the immemorial time of China—in the history of Chinese ideology. This was generally accepted as an ideal time, but it became worse due to deviating from the sages' spiritual insight that the world should be shared openly by all..

In their book calling for reformation, written in the 1890s in Hong Kong, He Qi who studied law in Britain and his friend Hu Liyuan explained that Confucian goals—knowing the will of heaven and giving peace to people—seemed to have no difference from the pursuit of rational nature in the West. Similarly, Mencius did not use such a concept as civil rights, but also his idea of freedom appeared to have much in common with that of Western thinkers. As incontrovertible axiom, Confucius and Mencius's thought was not about to fade away after two thousand-odd years.[5] In 1898, Pi Xirui, a scholar in Hunan who was famous for studying Confucian classics, claimed that Western respect for *caritas*, ie charities such as the Red Cross, foundling houses, and hospitals, all embodied the Confucian *Ren* (benevolence); probing general law and international law showed the concept of Yi (righteousness); international alliance and diplomatic intercourse reflected the Li (manners); skilful manufacturing contained the Zhi (wisdom); and their credit transactions symbolized the Xin (faith). All of these were examples of the existence of Confucian ethics in the Western world.[6]

Such analogies resulted in Chinese scholar-officials' misreading Western culture and society, but it provided an effective approach for communicating and mutually verifying Chinese and Western learning. At the end of the nineteenth century, a remarkable phenomenon about the Chinese intelligentsia's understanding of international law was to compare Western international law with the Confucian classic *Spring and Autumn.* The latter is the state Lu's history from 722 to 481 BC. Although it is not certain whether Confucius was the author, for Confucius scholars, this book was not so much a true historical account as a strong implication of or argument

[5] He Qi and Hu Liyuan, *Xinzheng Zhenquan* (*The True Interpretation of New Policies*) (Scientific Review Publishing House 1901) 6.

[6] Pi Lumen, *Xuezhang Nanxuehui Dijiuci Jiangyi* (*Ninth Lecture of South Society* by Senior Pi Xirui), Xiang Bao (*Hunan Daily*, 1898) [Changsha] no 57.

for political ethics. In his epoch, the competition for power among emperors, vassals, as well as their officials and retainers, plunged China into a state of confusion. Confucius wrote this book to express cautiously his moral principles in concise words; he praised the well-doing and blamed the ill-doing by using the very words and sentences which were aimed at showing his political ideal, elucidating morality and the benevolent policies, deterring the rebels, and building rules and orders for the world. In this regard, *Spring and Autumn* could be seen as a great and fundamental code for State governance.

Reinterpretation of the Confusion classics was an important model of the Chinese academic tradition. Since Confucianism became the official ideology, almost all the political revolutions in Chinese history sought support from Confucian classics. Ideologists at different times always explained those classics in line with their needs to support their own political views. Chinese defeat by Japan in 1895 was regarded as a burning shame by intellectuals and resulted in political reform. As the most famous leader of the movement, Kang Youwei, a scholar from Guangdong, also followed this tradition. He did not believe that the so-called three generations of sage governance actually existed, given the lack of evidence. While respected by the Chinese through the ages, the idea of three-stage sage governance was sheer invention on the part of Confucius to express his view of political reform. Kang believed *Spring and Autumn*, the most respected Confucian classic, which elaborated the axiom of human society, created fundamental rules forever, and best presented the Confucian reform ideal. According to Kang's explanation, his outstanding students Liang Qichao, Hunan scholars Tang Caichang and Tan Citong who were deeply influenced by Kang's thought, began to link this book to international law. They repeated Kang's views on *Spring and Autumn*, and considered Confucius as 'an uncrowned King'—owning regal virtue and status while not being the true emperor or prince. They believed that while *Spring and Autumn* was an eternal instructive general law, international law equated to the common norms abided by all the countries; Confucius, as the 'uncrowned king', created the axiom for instructing society, whereas Huge Grotius, as a civilian, developed the spirit and principles of natural law and then compiled a body of international law for all countries to observe. Moreover, the nature and rationality which were emphasized in international law reflected exactly Confucius's original will, and international law's upholding justice in a troubled world had nearly the same role as Confucianism's revitalizing the country and comforting the common people in troubled times. So, *Spring and Autumn* could be confirmed by international law and compensate for defects in international law. The former was the root of Chinese academic thinking on politics, while the latter acted out the same role in the Western world.

Song Yuren, a Sichuan scholar with the title of Jinshi and also a counsellor in an embassy, had a similar viewpoint. He proposed perfecting international law with Confucian classics such as *Spring and Autumn*. He said that Grotius used international law to curb the violent and assist the weak which fundamentally depended on human conscience. In Grotius's view, international law was derived from God's commandment which was the truest knowledge of the West. Because international law has no power to forbid wars, it's hard to avoid its being broken, but it still, to some extent, constrained countries. In Song's eyes, European countries were Christian nations. Their original meaning in creating international law was to stop the Christian nations from violating each other. However, international law became the tool used by powerful European countries to threaten the pagan countries. What's more, nowadays European international law was full of ambiguities, and its principles could not be clearly and accurately interpreted. Nevertheless, *Spring and Autumn*, Confucius's framework for social affairs, was the general law abided by nations through all ages, and its complete norms and exalted principles could supplement Western international law's weaknesses and solve its controversial issues. Song Yuren also cited Confucian argumentation to criticize and correct the rules of international law.[7] Tang Caichang also suggested improving international law according to the moral principle interpreted by *Spring and Autumn*, and make Confucian thought the guide for the contemporary world, because Confucian thought was totally based on a public spirit, beyond the confines of time and space.[8]

The ways in which Chinese intellectuals compare international law with *Spring and Autumn* might have been (but may also have inspired) inspired by WAP Martin. Martin set out his thesis about Chinese ancient international law when he attended the Congress of Orientalists in September 1881 in Berlin. Later, this paper was printed in French and English, and its Chinese version was published in 1884. In this book, Martin tried to explore the historical events of the Spring–Autumn and the Warring States period of China to show that some principles in international law could find their traces in Chinese history. His study caught the attention of Chinese scholars. Tang Caichang inferred that Martin spent much of his time in China and knew the consistency in spirit between international law and Confucian classics, which enabled him to write this book. Although the content and style of it still needed to be perfected, 'it still marks the very beginning of interlinking international law with *Spring and Autumn*'.[9]

Some scholars like Kang threaded Spring and Autumn and international law together not only because Confucius and Grotius had in common their mode of behaviour and their spiritual pursuits, but also because international law and *Spring and Autumn* had the same internal basis—both carrying the idea of axiom and general law.[10] Tan Sitong even borrowed the words of the famous scholar of Song dynasty, Lu Jiuyuan:

> By axiom, it meant that it is available everywhere whether it is in the east sea or the west sea or the south sea or the north sea. There is a sage in each sea who has the same thought with others, therefore, has same principles. Like international law, not knowing its creator, all

[7] Song Yuren, *Caifeng Ji* (*Miscellaneous Notes on World Customs*) (Chengdu 1897), vol 5, 1–6.

[8] Philosophy and Social Science Institution of Hunan Province Tang (ed), *Caichang Ji* (Collection of Tang Cai Chang) (Zhonghua Book Company 1980) 45.

[9] ibid 96.

[10] After the name of Wheaton's work was translated into '*Wanguo Gongfa*' (public law of all nations), in the late nineteenth century, international law's Chinese names became Wanguo Gongfa and Gongfa. But in the last years of the nineteenth century, when Kang Youwei and others used the word Gongfa, not only did it mean international law, it also usually referred to public and universal principles.

nations followed it, not because they are able to obey to it but because they have to, which is the meaning of an axiom.[11]

The word Gongli (axiom) appeared in Chinese books very early, but the intellectuals' concept of axiom in the late nineteenth century was inspired also by Western natural science. The scientific knowledge introduced into China through missionaries opened up an amazing world for such scholar-officials as Kang Youwei, and helped them have a new understanding of nature, universe, and human society. Before the war with Japan broke out in 1894, Kang attempted to interpret his knowledge about human life with Euclid's geometrical axioms, for example, such ideas as human equality, parents, and children having their own autonomy—all these belonged to geometrical axioms. In the following reform movement, Kang's followers stressed that the universal knowledge and laws uncovered by natural science were also the bases of human social development, and were also called axioms. Axioms were the ultimate norms of world evolution and the essential standard of judging social politics. They considered that Western progress in society and politics was owed to their axiom-oriented conduct, while the decline of Chinese politics and academic life was the result of ignoring the axioms. As the value core of a new knowledge and academic system—called new learning—sprang up at the end of the nineteenth century, the axiom not only embodied these scholar-officials' new understanding of nature and the universe but also became the theoretical basis of their political arguments.

In Chinese scholar-officials' observation of international politics in the 1870s and 1880s, Li (morality) was a common concept. One of the popular views was that power and morality were the two decisive factors for establishing international order, that is, the relationship among nations was constrained by the powerhouse's will as well as having to adhere to moral principle. The former was called Shi (power) and the latter was Li (morality). The scholar Feng Guifen from Jiangsu, a Jinshi, had realized this viewpoint in his book written in the 1860s in Shanghai and published in 1876 after he passed away. He compared the world of the nineteenth century to the Chinese Spring–Autumn period when the societies presented a disordered situation of contests for supremacy, with nations' fighting, yet still following certain 'manners' and 'faith'.[12] Guo Songtao, also a Jinshi, and Chinese first minister to Britain and France in 1875, expressed a similar feeling in his diary during his missions. He claimed the reason that Western countries remained strong and prosperous was their intellectual elites' and State managers' pursuit of ethics and justice, which they regarded as norms of ruling and leading society. Moreover, Western countries' study and improvement of politics were not just out of their private interests, but for the target of realizing world justice. Western nations' setting up international law was to embody such a pursuit. Their praise of faith and manners was in a larger degree than

[11] Cai Shangsi and Fang Xing (eds), *Tan Sitong Quanji* [Complete collection of Tan Sitong] (available with) (Zhonghua Book Company 1984) 264.

[12] Feng Guifen (commentary and notes by Dai Yangben). *Xiaobinlou Kangyi* [Straightforward words of Xiaobin Studio] Zhengzhou: Zhongzhou Guji Chubanshe (Central Plains Ancient Books Publishing House 2014).

the Chinese *Spring and Autumn*'s.[13] Zheng Guanying also showed in his special expositions of international law that while some Western countries adopted monarchy, some democracy, and some 'rule by the monarchy and the people' (constitutional monarchy), they all take morality as their code of conduct.[14]

Obviously, these scholar-officials acknowledged international power politics, but still believed that moral principle was the basic foundation. The famous scholar Wang Tao, once travelling around Europe, fiercely condemned power politics. But in his opinion, the most powerful country could not exist relying on its power unless it also followed morality, the ultimate promise for the existence of one's country, because the country owning the advantage in morality naturally could gain assistance from others, without considering its lack of troops. In contrast, if a country focused only on developing its troops, violated others, and cruelly enforced obedience, it was bound to fail in the end.[15]

As an important concept in Chinese intellectual history, Li could be understood as everything's natural, lasting, and universal principle, essence, and norm. Since the Song dynasty, Lixue (Cheng-Zhu School) had been Confucianism's new form of expression. The most famous scholar in the Song dynasty, Zhu Xi thought that Li was the origin of the universe, the lasting entity; and everything derived from Li and natural ethics were its manifestation. As to politics, Li was the universal moral principle and following it or not determined whether the political power was legal or not. A reasonable social system and order should comply with Li. With morality as its core, Li was transcendental, governing, authoritative, and embodied the fundamental order of the world. This theory produced far-reaching effects, and Li became a basic ideological belief of Chinese scholar-officials. During the process of translating the books of international law, Martin borrowed some concepts and items from the Cheng-Zhu school. For example, natural law was translated as Xingfa (law from natural instinct). Rules originating from international exchanges in practice were called Lifa (conventional law). Those translations claimed that although international law had many sources, fundamentally it accorded with the natural law. It conveyed scholar-officials such information that international law was generally acknowledged as the embodiment of natural law. Evidently, this enlightened the Chinese scholar-officials' understanding of the world order in the nineteenth century.

Advocating moral principle in international law also aroused the scholar-officials' memory of the aspiration of Wangdao (kingly-way-politics). As Chinese classical political philosophy, kingly-way-politics was an ideal political model constructed by Confucianism, based on the legendary three generations of sage governing as the prototype, which was the opposite of tyrannical politics ruling by force. It was symbolized by the rule of virtue and the policy of benevolence. The kingly-way-politics

[13] Guo Songtao, *Guo Songtao Riji* (Guo Songtao Dairy) vol 3 (Hunan People Publication 1982) 136, 452, 518.

[14] Xia Dongyuan (ed), *Zheng Guanying Ji* [Collection of Zheng Guanying] (Shanghai People Publication 1982) 65.

[15] Wang Tao, *Pu fa Zhanji* [A record of Franco-Prussian War] (1882) epilogue, 8–9.

showed natural law was just an ideal impossible of realization because practical politics were Machiavellian. Yet as a weapon of criticism, its moral advantage still could restrict and overawe political practice. And scholar-officials always regarded whether the kingly-way-politics was adhered to as the standard by which to judge political value. For such reasons, the scholar-officials in the late Qing dynasty especially paid attention to the value of international law for the weak and small countries, and often emphasized that the law was an effective tool for protecting those weak and small countries. In the beginning of the 1880s, when China negotiated around the problem of Vietnam with France, some officials required that France be blamed according to both international law and moral principles, and they suggested that the government should proclaim France's action to the world. They believed that other countries would discourage France's plots and even send troops to stop France's violations, based on the principle of justice and the need to maintain the international legal order. This proposal revealed their superficial understanding of international politics, but showed their deep impression of international law, by their praise of the moral spirit of international law.

In this respect, intellectuals' elucidations of morality in international politics in the last years of the nineteenth century continued the tradition of explaining the world with 'Li', as advocated by the scholar-officials in late Qing dynasty. Although 'axiom' was widely adopted in different social and political issues, the main purpose of Kang elucidating this conception was to elucidate and enlighten the developing direction of human society and guide the world into the situation of so-called Datong (great harmony). The actual crisis in China meant intellectuals had to acknowledge international political cruelty, for which reason, the Confucian axioms could not be amply reflected in international law. At the same time, the Chinese intellectuals saw that it was the Western countries, such as France, which did not completely obey international law. Tan Sitong called Wanguo Gongfa 'the book of western people's extreme love and kindness', and he asked, since there were so many small countries such as Switzerland whose land was not large, but had enjoyed 600 years' peace under the joint protection of nations, could not also the heyday of three generations in China surpass Switzerland? What's more, it could after all participate in an international alliance, which showed the power of international law, did it not?[16] Liang Qichao and Tang Caichang thought that international law was limited, but to an extent still maintained world order and avoided war and disaster. Despite that, nowadays the world remains in a troubled state, the principle of the axiom is all the same the highest authority. As the axiom manifested itself more and more, the world would attain a great harmony at last.

According to the early Confucian classic *Liji* (the book of rites), by harmony in society was meant harmonious and peaceful times, where everyone was equal, the talents could be chosen and endorsed, there were appeals for faith and harmony, a fullness of friendship and goodwill, voluntarily sharing of property without any cupidity, pilferages, or wars. In later Chinese history, this great harmony was at all

[16] *The Complete Collection of Tan Si Tong* (additional version), 225.

times Confucians' ultimate ideal of society. After a long time composing and modifying it, in 1903 or so, Kang Youwei at last finished his great work *Datong Shu* (book of great harmony). In this book, he described his plan for the future of society where there existed one single world government with no national or racial discrimination, even no family itself; everyone was a world civilian and the economy belonged to a State-owned system, so that no one owned private property, but, still, unprecedentedly there would be abundant material wealth. Despite Kang's drawing inspiration from Buddhism and utopian socialism, the most important basis of his ideal was Confucian great harmony.[17]

Kang's vision of a great harmonious world based on human beings as equal could be regarded as Chinese traditional culture's response to the modern world order at the end of the nineteenth century. Relying on inherent Chinese thought resources, Kang tried to relieve the challenges and tension caused by Western cultural expansion by going to exclusively Chinese perspectives. And in his interpretation of Confucianism, Confucius was thought of as a great human maker of social norms. The cardinal principles of righteousness, proclaimed by the *Spring and Autumn* were seen as the code of conduct in the present world, and Confucian ideals of great harmony became humankind's end goal. From this, Kang bridged the two thought worlds of China and the West with the axiom and universal law, in which process ancient Confucianism was given a new colour, accepting the value of modernity and universality and viewed as the highest pursuit of humankind. Apparently, Kang's visualization displayed the late Qing dynasty' scholar-officials' idealist vision of world order, as well as showing his endeavour to continue the Chinese cultural bloodline.

Yearning for an ideal world order led to the unparalleled interests of the intellectuals of the late nineteenth century in international law. In 1898, Bi Yongnian in Hunan started an international law study group—Public Law Society, which organized lectures and discussion in Changsha.[18] In the same year, in the Current-Affairs School, a new-style school in Changsha, Liang Qichao made 'public law' one of its special courses,[19] and assigned international law as a topic of study for its students. Some of the best papers advocating reformation were published in the local newspapers. The British missionary Timothy Richard and the American missionary Young John Allen's article on the introduction of universal peace congresses, which translated as *Mibing hui* (Society for the Abolition of Armaments), was reprinted many times.[20] The intellectuals showed their great interest in The Hague Peace Conference

[17] Kang Youwei (commented and noted by Li Sizhen), *Datong Shu (Book of Great Harmony)*, Zhengzhou: Zhongzhou Guji Chubanshe (Central Plains Ancient Books Publishing House 1998).

[18] Bi Yongnian. *Gongfa Xuehui Zhangcheng* [Constitution of Public Law Society] Xiang Bao (*Hunan Daily* 1898) no 48.

[19] Liang Qichao, Shiwu Xuetang Gongke Xiangxi Zhangcheng [Detailed courses of current-affairs school] Xiang Bao (*Hunan Daily* 1898) no 102. Liang called the constitution, civil law, and criminal law 'internal public laws', while negotiation and international treaty law were 'external public laws'. The students studying this discipline needed to read the materials on European and Chinese history, law books and Chinese commercial treaties with other nations as well as to study international law books.

[20] In 546 AD Song statesmen Xiangxu, Jin, Chu, and others proposed that more than ten States attend a peace meeting to make a non-aggression pact, which was called Xiangxu's Mibing (abolishing war). At the end of nineteenth century, the word Mibing hui (Society for the Abolition of Armaments)

of 1899. Kang Youwei named this conference 'the starting point of nations connecting together' and 'the foundation of nations' great harmony'. He declared that this conference was the first step towards ideal times, and from this point human society was bound to enter ultimately the great world harmony.[21]

## 2. Might Makes Right: The International Law in the Era of Imperialism

Kang Youwei's ambition to establish an ideal new-world order in accordance with Confucianism, with international law as evidence in support, did not seem to gain recognition. And when Kang praised The Hague Conference as the first step towards great harmony, Liang Qichao who was then in his exile in Japan, expressed another viewpoint. He asserted in his article written in late 1901, that The Hague Congress was actually the preparation of the European powers to relieve their internal contradictions so as to expand outward. Its main purposes were 'protecting the peace in Europe', 'and then joining together to dominate the nations beyond Europe'. The conference did not mean that China would gain equal rights on the international plane, but meant, instead, that danger was approaching.[22] This difference in ideas from Kang was not a coincidence, but presented the intellectuals' new understanding of the world order in the early twentieth century.

After the failure of the Sino-Japanese War in 1895, and in order to study the experience of Japan rising, some Chinese officials began to advocate sending students to Japan. In the early years of the twentieth century, studying in Japan formed a trend against the background of the Qing dynasty launching large-scale reformation, especially the abolition of the imperial examinations system. Among the students in Japan, some of them were political exiles who could not stay at home, some were students sent by the authorities to study new-style education, politics, law and the military, and others were studying in Japan at their own expense for personal gain. Anyway, large numbers of the returned students replaced the previous Western missionaries as the main medium of introducing Western science into China. With their efforts, a batch of international law books translated from Japanese became popular. As far as we know, there were about fifty translations before the Qing Empire was replaced by the Republic of China. Most of them were the lecture notes of Japanese scholars, several were edited from various Japanese books, and one or two were translated from Japanese versions of the European scholars. The versions translated by these overseas students, which included international law, strictly speaking could not be seen as academic works. They were criticized by scholars such

was used to refer to any kind of meeting for peace, civil peace groups, and their activities in Europe and America.

[21] Kang Youwei (n 17) 107, 111.

[22] Liang Qichao, 'Benbao Yibaice Zhuci bing Lun Baoguan zhi Zeren ji Benbao zhi Jingli' [Congratulations on memorizing 100 volumes and statements of the responsibility and experience of this magazine], *Qingyi Bao Quanbian* [Whole China discussion] (Wenhai Publication 1986) vol 1, 12.

Yan Fu, who deeply understood Western thought. At least, in these students' view, the new translated versions of international law were much more practical than the previous 'pedantic' translations by missionaries. In reality, many Chinese terms in international law came to be determined by these translated versions.

When Japanese international law books were translated and edited into Chinese, rapidly developing new-style periodicals and newspapers also became the main media of spreading international law. The students in Japan brought out many publications in Tokyo in which they often published articles about international law, most of which were translated and edited from Japanese presses; some were international law books in serial form, others were interviews with Japanese scholars of international law. Some other articles were on discussions around Chinese diplomacy and international relations with an international law aspect, such as, the Japan–Russia war of 1904–05, the foreigner's legal status in China, leased territories, consular jurisdiction, and the laws of war. Similar content could also be found in the domestic official as well as non-official presses. *Diplomatic Review*, the first diplomatic publication, began being published in Shanghai from 1902, and reported continuously much international law learning, most of which was the exposition of Japanese scholars. The journal also published a large number of articles on the status of China in international society and its diplomatic problems in the light of international law, mostly written by Chinese students studying law in Japan. The first issues of the famous *Eastern Miscellanies* published in 1904, discussed the problem of neutrality, and the following issues introduced the Red Cross convention and the international conventions for radio and postal services. These new-style publications effectively and widely promoted the spreading of international law knowledge.

During the last years when the imperial examination still existed, international law was brought into the test content. In the 1880s, some Chinese officials called for placing international law into the literati's area of study and used for selecting the talents, but they failed. After the Sino-Japanese War, the imperial examinations system became the major object of criticism by the intellectuals supporting reformation, and the officials taking charge of exams made international law and Western scientific knowledge the subject of examination questions in some provinces in order to encourage the literati to gain useful knowledge and current affairs. This boosted the sales of new Western books, including translations of versions of international law. In 1901, the Qing government announced its reform of the imperial examinations system which officially brought Western science into the content of examinations. In the following years, questions related to international law appeared in the different grades of imperial examinations. Some of the exams asked examinees to answer with some basic knowledge of international law, some demanded comparative exposition of international law and Chinese classics, and others required candidates to propose a variety of advice for Chinese diplomacy in the light of international law. Such a situation forced the literati into studying international law, further promoting its spreading and popularization. After the imperial examinations system was abolished in 1905, a batch of medium or above-medium new-style schools introduced law and politics, and international law became one of the official disciplines; the institutions training candidate officials in each province also added international law to the syllabus. Zhang Zhidong even invited Martin to teach international law to officials in Hubei province.[23]

Unlike the scholar-officials in the nineteenth century, the new intellectuals represented by the returned students in the beginning of the twentieth century had no interest in exploring the ethical meaning of international law, but stressed its value as a tool. Some of the students involved in translating Japanese books on international law, declared that the reason China's situation and diplomacy in the international world went from bad to worse was the fact that the study of international law had been neglected. And the purpose of translating international law was to introduce the new knowledge to Chinese people, helping them to know their national rights and duties, assisting Chinese diplomacy, protecting Chinese interests, and improving its situation within international law. What they all agreed on was that the efficacy of international law depended on China's actual strength. Western powers never treated China according to the law, and China could never gain any actual benefits from the law, but it did not mean that the law was totally meaningless to China. The fact that Japan abrogated unequal treaties and ranked among powers successfully impressed these overseas students. They appealed to Chinese nationals to value and study private international law so as to abolish Western countries' consular jurisdiction in China and the unequal treaties between China and the West.

The movement of the students in Japan spreading international law was an epitome of their introducing the new knowledge to China. During the final ten years of the Qing dynasty, these students introduced into China all kinds of new knowledge, new theories, and conceptions that they had acquired in Japan. New terms from Japanese pervaded the newspapers and magazines, which led young literati to pursue and imitate such trends. Thus, a new space of knowledge and thought came into being and modern Western terms, by way of Japan, rapidly sprang up around China. Under the conditions of national crisis, the great shock of new ideas stimulated the intellectuals to ponder the country and nation's status and to re-evaluate China's civilization value. During this process, Chinese intellectuals' values, modes of thinking, and spiritual orientation began to be converted, causing a subversive change in the traditional thought world and urging Chinese intellectuals to respond anew to the world order.

After 1840, China was defeated by Western powers many times, but Chinese scholar-officials had not acknowledged for a long time that China had been a laggard. However, the failure in the war with Japan in 1895 insulted them grossly, and in the following years, the powers forcibly occupied leased territories, divided up their sphere of influences, and formed a 'partition' of China. In 1900, an eight-nation allied force occupied Beijing again. This series of blows made the intellectuals feel further Chinese deterioration, but, most importantly, the cultural reflection initiated by these events caused the collapse of the intellectuals' confidence in developing a self-culture. They had to acknowledge that the traditional China-centric order had collapsed, and now there was a Western-countries-centric world. Such a

[23] WAP Martin, *The Awaking of China* (Doubleday, Page, & Co 1907) 229, 273.

view was mentioned and stressed time and again in the expositions by Liang Qichao, Yan Fu, and others. At this time, China was an unimportant peripheral country and was being faced with the crises of national subjugation and genocide which terrified the whole Chinese intellectual world. In this worried state, the new intellectuals soon accepted nationalism as their weapon. In their opinion, the root of the crisis was that the Chinese lacked a concept of a modern national State. Only by shifting into a Western-style national State and fostering the sense of competition with other nations, could China be able to stand up in the world and realize national prosperity. This made the last years of the nineteenth century and first decade of the twentieth century the early period of the rise of Chinese nationalism.

Those intellectuals who first accepted and advocated nationalism paid particular attention to interpreting the concept of national competition, which was related to the introduction of Darwin's theory of evolution by Yan Fu, the thinker who had studied the navy in Britain and later been a teacher in a naval school in Tianjin for a long time. He translated the first half of *Evolution and Ethics and Other Essays* by Thomas Henry Huxley into Chinese and named it *On Evolution*. In this book, he emphasized the theory of 'the survival of the fittest', simply put, a view of human society as a process whereby different nations compete with one another, to establish which is the best and strongest, weeding out the weaker in the process. This translation was regarded as the most important intellectual contribution of Yan Fu, who was viewed as the best-known enlightenment thinker. But his view of evolution was not immediately recognized, partly because it was inherently contradictory to Kang Youwei's ideal of great harmony, and partly because Kang had won a high reputation through his appeal for political reformation. At the very beginning of the twentieth century, this book had become popular in intellectual cycles and produced great effects. Thus, as it became more difficult for the traditional theory to deal with the real pressures from the West, the theory of evolution proved to be a new basis for understanding the world situation for the intellectuals.

In fact, Kang Youwei interpreted the world order in an idealistically passionate way, but his attempt could not relieve the Qing officials and intellectuals' mental tension which resulted from the current situation of China. An influential official in the late Qing Empire, Zhang Zhidong published his famous book *Quan Xue Pian* (Exhortation to Study) in 1898—it was quickly translated into English and French by the missionaries in China—the name in the English version was *China's Only Hope*—in which he argued that Western countries did not treat China justly by their use of international law, so that the law was meaningless for the Chinese.[24] Kang's view was unconvincing even for his followers. For example, Liang Qichao, an advocator of the role of the axiom in the late nineteenth century, was also influenced by the theory of competing evolution, and described the evolution of the world as a process of continuing competition in his series of articles calling for reformation. He thought that the survival of the fittest was human society's axiom and the weaker races were destined to be conquered by the best ones, a development which even the

[24] Zhang Zhidong, *Quanxue Pian* [Exhortation to study], Changsha: Lianghu Shuyuan (Hunan-Hubei Academy of Learning 1898) 49.

sage could not change.[25] After the reform of 1898 failed, Liang denied Kang's view of the axiom publicly in his series of articles written in Japan. In his eyes, the so-called axiom and great harmony was an ideal for cosmopolitanism and the human future, but it could not to be applied to the real world, full of fierce competition. In order to keep a foothold in such circumstances, statism and nationalism should be advocated and carried forward. In his famous work *Theory of New People* written from 1902, Liang Qichao argued that ideas such as great harmony, universal love, and cosmopolitanism could not be realized 'in a thousand years'. Even in the great harmony society, competition was inevitable from the perspective of humanity. Therefore, the axiom and the great harmony spirit were merely a spiritual ideal which could not be turned into reality.[26]

Despite the inspiration of Yan Fu' translations, Liang Qichao's publications on the theory of national competition in the early twentieth century, like the work of many other overseas students, were directly under the influence of Japanese intellectuals. A clear example was that expositions about evolution and competition not only borrowed a large number of terms from Japanese, but also these terms were often merely translations from Japanese periodicals and newspapers. So, they were just playing a role of conveyer or translator, which included Liang Qichao. When explaining the world order, these students abroad adopted concepts such as the survival of the fittest in natural selection, nationalism, imperialism, and so on. A periodical published by students of Hubei in Japan claimed that the contemporary world was imperialist and China confronted a dreadful situation facing cruel competition:

> What times are today? They are the times when China is firmly the centre of competition in the world. During the nineteenth century, European countries further progressed to national imperialism from nationalism. But who are the imperialists? It is the imperialists who have said barbarians have no ability to develop natural resources of land and the civilized will do so instead; and that the best races are abusing the weaker races is being taken for granted. With such ideas, these nations hunt everywhere like greedy wolves and hungry tigers, regardless of natural justice and universal laws, kill people cruelly without any hesitation but for the only purpose of great power competition, which is the true nature and capacity of imperialism.[27]

Competition led to conflict which undoubtedly resulted in the best and the strongest knocking out the bad and the weak. Might makes right in the competition of nations and races. Chinese intellectuals condemned such subjugation and wars with no morality at all behind them, but in the atmosphere of imperialist threats and competing evolution, these new intellectuals tended to accept the concept that competition makes right, might makes right, and might makes justice. Liang Qichao declared that there existed competition in the natural world and human society from the earliest evolution, and, as long as it existed, competition was either good or bad, and was

[25] Liang Qichao, *Lun Bianfa bi zi Ping Man Han zhi Jie Shi* (The start of reformation is abolishing the difference between Hans and Manchus), *Yinbingshi Zhuanji* [Collected essays of the ice-drinker's studio] pt 1 (Zhonghua Book Company 1936) 77.

[26] 3 Liang Qichao, *Xinmin Shuo* [Theory of new people] *Yinbingshi Zhuanji* (n 25) pt 4, 17–18.

[27] *Lun Zhongguo zhi Qiantu ji Guomin Yingjin zhi Zeren* [Prospect of China and national responsibilities] Hubei Xueshengjie (Hubei Students 1903) no 3.

successful or failed; 'thus, the principle of might had to become truth even though it was not'.[28] Liang believed that imperialists conquering the small and weaker nations and countries satisfied the theory of evolution, and the rights of inferior races were doomed to be seized by superior races, which was 'the new law of eliminating countries'. He said that hundreds of countries had been eliminated in the world. Thus, so-called civilization, so-called international law, and maxims such as the so-called loving others like love of self and viewing enemies as friends could not find their place in the real world. He cited the words of a 'western philosopher', that reason existed nowhere but among the countries having the same level of power and did not exist between the strong and the weak, because it is power that makes right. In his view, European countries' power was balanced so they had to obey reason, but towards the countries outside of Europe, these European countries thought power was right, a fact which was determined by the law of human social evolution.[29]

Based on observation of the imperialist political phenomena, as well as the influence of Japanese intellectuals, the scholars like Liang Qichao tended to believe that world politics were dominated by power, not by morality and universal truth. In the cruel competition for existence, the backward countries were faced with the danger of being destroyed. But their portrayal of Western imperialist crudity alongside the evolution theory also carried some strategic meaning, that is, they aimed at initiating in the Chinese the sense of danger so as to promote Chinese self-reformation. They thought, for those backward countries like China, the only way to find its own standing place in the imperialist era was to acknowledge the reality of might making right, while at the same time work hard to realize self-improvement. Only then could the Chinese avoid being wiped out by the thread of world evolution. This threat proved that the competition among countries was the necessary road to the development of human society, and, with no competition, no progress. In imperialist times, international law was produced by power, so it just was 'the convention of reciprocity of the powers', but not the weaker side's amulet. If the backward countries and weak nations could realize this reality, and reformed energetically to reach self-improvement, then competing with the powers, finally the common development of human society could come true. Evidently, repeating might making right again and again did not mean that they acknowledged the rationality of imperialist logic from the bottom of their heart.

However, the coming of the imperialist era still impacted strongly on Chinese intellectuals and began to destroy their ideal vision of world order. In 1903, a Chinese student in Japan said emotionally that one of the most important reasons why China was reduced to being bullied by the powers was because Chinese still talked about idealistic great harmony and were reluctant to admit the reality of might making right.[30] This reflected the intellectuals' deep anxiety about China's

[28] Liang Qichao, *Guojia Sixiang Bianqian Yitong Lun* [Similarities and differences in the development of national thought] *Yinbingshi Wenji* (n 25) pt 6, 20.

[29] Liang Qichao, 'Mieguo Xinfa Lun' [New method to eliminate countries] *Qingyi Bao Quanbian* (n 22), vol 7, 9.

[30] Diexuesheng, China's Open, Zhejiang Chao (*Zhejiang Tide*, May 1903) no 6.

future. Yang Tingdong, studying in Waseda University, claimed the fundamental way out lay in self-reformation. We could not enjoy the right set by international law unless we become strong enough to be one member with equal footing with Western powers in the international world. Even if common people could recite international law, we had no ability to stop the country from being destroyed.[31] An article published in the magazine *Juemin* (Awakening People) in Jiangsu, discussed the problem of great harmony and evolution by the way of debate. One part thought that 'survival of the fittest in natural selection' was the dynamic of human civilization's development; the other insisted that whereas 'all humans were equal and love was towards everyone', and one nation could not be classified as the superior or the inferior, nevertheless among them competition brought nothing but trouble. The author of this article strove to seek a balance between the two sides; on the one hand, he declared the great harmony ideal was the undoubted 'axiom', while evolution and competition were the indispensable 'universal conventions', and human beings had to follow the law of evolution so as to realize the 'axiom' of great harmony in the end; on the other hand, he indicated that even if future human civilization could reach a high degree, even when the great harmony ideal came true, competition could not be eliminated completely. Therefore, he concluded that great harmony should not be today's topic.[32]

Clearly, during the process of intellectuals accepting Western words like nationalism and competing evolution in the early twentieth century, what they revealed thereby was their helpless mood. The reality of imperialist power politics wore down the moral spirit of international law and made their great harmony ideal remain a dream forever. All those thoughts inevitably brought troubles into their spirits. In fact, new intellectuals all agreed that China could keep its foothold in the imperialist era only if it became a strong Western-style modern country, but they still clung to the axiom and the great harmony. In the following history, this complex situation would be presented in different forms and played different roles.

## 3. International Law as the Standard of Civilization

When the theory of evolution was accepted by Chinese intellectuals, *Wenming* (civilization) as a new concept began to be popular. Although this word appeared in Chinese ancient books very early, it was gradually identified as the Chinese name for 'civilization' after the opium war and became a modern term. From the last years of the nineteenth century, 'civilization' and its opposite 'barbarians' were used to describe and evaluate all kinds of phenomena and things, from national systems to

[31] Yang Tingdong, *Gongfa Lungang* [Outline of international law] (1902) preface.

[32] Jun Ping, 'Tianyan Datong Bian' [Controversies between evolution and great harmony] Zhang Nan and Wang Renzhi (eds), *Xinhai geming qian shinian jian shilun xuanji* [Selections from opinions expressed in periodicals and newspapers during the decade before the 1911 revolution] vol 1 (Joint Publishing Co 1960) 872–84.

personal behaviour, and became an important standard for Chinese intellectuals to evaluate the degree of social development and evolution.

The acceptance of the concept of civilization by intellectuals at the same time meant the breaking up of the traditional Huayi idea. As a Chinese scholar indicated, if the concept of civilization was the symbol of European cultural approval and self-praising, the rise of this concept in China was the result of Chinese cultural crisis and self-reflection.[33] According to the traditional idea of scholar-officials, the reason why China was called Hua (native) while smaller countries surrounding were called Yi (foreigner/barbarian), the difference of Hua and Yi, did not just lie in the geographical difference of centre and periphery, but in the cultural difference of progress and backwardness. However, after the knowledge of the earth/world was introduced into China, China lost its place in the geographical centre, and advanced Western military technique also broke down the superiority of the scholar-officials' culture. Some officials and intellectuals began to criticize Chinese self-centredness and realized that Western countries were not barbarians in the traditional meaning of the term. During a long time after the opium war, scholar-officials had pointed out some places which were more backward than the West, but they generally maintained confidence in Chinese culture. After the failure of the war of 1895, intellectuals started to turn around the Huayi idea, changing from saying 'western European were not barbarians' to 'China was not better than barbarians'. In 1898, Liang Qichao said that civilization or barbarism depended on a matter of contrast, and today's China naturally was barbaric compared with Western countries; while China was viewed as a civilization compared with the peripheral tribal nations, such as African black slaves, the American red race, and brown race from Malaya. Despite the fact that the differences could not be unalterable in the future, Western countries' superior status was undoubted. He noted critically that China had been so weak and backward, but still called itself a civilized nation and viewed others as barbarians, 'No wonder the westerners regarded us as a third grade barbarous country and said that the world could not allow such people to exist.'[34] His acceptance of a modern civilization concept and Western civilizing grades showed that the traditional order of civilization and barbarian was overturned.

With the building of the new idea of the West as civilization and China as barbarian, for the new intellectuals whose sense of cultural reflection became stronger and stronger, following international law or not became the standard to distinguish civilization and barbarian. Their reflection on the Boxer Uprising proved this point. For intellectuals, the Boxers believed in magic, fought against all the Western things, and killed indiscriminately missionaries and those civilians who were believers. They even killed the German minister in China, Clemens Freiherr von Ketteler and Tsugiyama Akira, the secretary at the Japanese embassy. These actions could be characterized by the word 'barbarian'. When the Boxers failed, Laing Qichao

[33] Fang Weigui, 'Lun Jinxiandai Zhongguo "Wenming" "Wenhua" Guan de Yanbian' [The changing of conceptions of civilization and culture in modern China] (1999) 4 Historical Review [Shanghai].

[34] Liang Qichao, 'Lun Zhongguo yi Jiangqiu Falv zhi Xue' [China should study legal learning] *Xiang Bao* (*Hunan Daily*, 1898) no 5.

published the views of a student of Kang Youwei, Mai Menghua's series of comments on current events in the famous magazine, *China Discussion* published in Japan. In these reviews, Mai blamed the Boxers because they did not abide by international law. It was for this reason the Westerners regarded China as barbaric, needing to be conquered and devastated. So, this led China to lose its right to autonomy. He wrote that having 'civilized thought' or not was the difference between 'the righteous civilian and the mob', and having it or not lay in obeying international law or not. He praised the leaders in the southern provinces as 'honest patriots' who kept peace in Yangze River Valley with other nations and remained in their behaviour civilized during the Boxer movement. Mai argued that resisting foreign forces was the proper right for any countries, but the methods should be differentiated as barbarian and civilization. The boxers did not know the difference. Their behaviour offended against the international law and brought a disaster to China.[35]

The criticism of the Boxers was one part of the intellectuals' self-cultural reflection in the early twentieth century. Liang Qichao said that the fundamental reason the Boxers violated the norms of civilization lay in Chinese social thinking, 'the idea of being conservative and arrogant and disliking the outsiders' which obviously went against the idea of 'the world axiom', and was also at the root of Chinese decline.[36] Li Shucheng, a Hubei student in Japan, claimed that common Chinese lacked knowledge, let alone patriotism. Such nationals in China were unable to compete with other countries' 'civilized nationals'.[37] *Dagong Daily*, a quite influential newspaper in Tianjin, published an article in 1903, in which it was said that after the Boxers killed the German minister, China had still a chance to realize peace with the West, out of the nation's compassion. 'Would we Chinese behave brutally like this forever, or upgrade into the civilized ranks? Would we spinelessly stay in an ignorant and stubborn circle, be excluded and despised as slaves forever?'[38] While the intellectuals condemned Chinese backwardness and barbarism, they emphasized that civilization was destined to replace barbarism during the process of evolution, all of which further established the highest status for 'civilization'.

However, the intellectuals expressed another mood when they exclaimed that the criticism of the boxers as 'barbarians' was in essence the logic of Western powers and the irony of 'civilization'. In 1901, an article defending the Boxers appeared in the magazine *kaizhilue* (Wisdom Guide, published in Tokyo by Chinese students in Japan). It declared, 'The most startling, confusing, disgusting, and hateful one was not others but what are called civilized countries.' In the eyes of the author, those new traffic techniques such as ships, railways, and electric wire relatively reduced

35 Mai Menghua, 'Lun Yihe' [On peace negotiation]; 'Lun Zhongguo Minqi zhi Keyong' [Chinese popular morale]; 'Paiwai Pingyi' [Fair comment on anti-foreign] *Qingyi Bao Quanbian* (n 22), vol 4, 6; vol 4, 5; vol 2, 5 respectively.

36 Liang Qichao 'Lun Jinri Geguo dai Zhongguo zhi Shanfa' [Clever method of other countries for dealing with China] *Yinbingshi Wenji* (n 25) pt 5, 52.

37 Li Shucheng, 'Xuesheng zhi Jingzheng' [Students' competition] Hubei Xueshengjie (Hubei Students, 1903) no 2.

38 'Zhongguo Tuzhi zhi San Yaoce' [Three key measures for China's self-improvement] *Dagong Daily* (7 April 1903, Tianjin).

the earth, drew the nations closer to each other, promoted the progress of social fashion, the flourishing of culture, and opened up an unprecedented developing picture of human society. In such a period, each nation should pursue peace out of humanity, obey common rules, love each other, be honest, show kindness, jointly promote world civilization, and let all peoples enjoy 'world universal right', but the Western powers' enormities in China were actually not civilized at all. According to this article, the encouragement and spirit presented by the Boxers was the symbol of emerging Chinese modern national thought and the hope for China to get away from the powers' violations and oppression.[39]

Actually, in the last years of the nineteenth century, the intellectuals had revealed they shared the Boxer mood. Liang Qichao even said that the Western newspapers loudly claimed the Chinese a barbaric nation, ignorant people, but this was merely a hypocritical religious critique which was the way to destroy and enslave China.[40] Another influential politician, Wang Kangnian also thought the motive for which Western countries slandered China as a barbaric nation was that they needed an excuse for annexing and behaving barbarically towards China.[41] Mai Menghua, who criticized strongly the Boxers, also exclaimed that the West often defamed China as an inferior race, and even called the Chinese 'barbarian aborigines' merely as an excuse for eliminating China. In his opinion, it was the Chinese who were 'the best' race.[42] All these opinions showed that the intellectuals remained alert to the true nature of Western civilized values which they accepted. In 1903, an article in the magazine *Continent* in Shanghai said it was unacceptable that China was equated to a 'barbarian', when China itself looked down on countries such as Egypt, India, and Turkey. These could not match the value of Chinese civilization, which the West must know.[43] One of the articles of *Gagong Daily* in 1905 also said, being a 'civilization' or not was really measured by the West in terms of power. Western countries called themselves a civilization, but took it for granted that they bullied so-called semi-civilized nations without any sense of guilt. This showed a terrible hegemonic mentality.[44]

The modern Western idea of civilization established in the colonial conquering age and tied to an obvious colour of European superiority in civilization, aroused in Chinese intellectuals complex feelings about modern civilization, while they were still in the process of accepting the concept. On one hand, they respected European countries and America as the tutor of civilization and took being among the civilized countries as a Chinese target; on the other hand, it was the power of the 'civilized

[39] Yihetuan 'Yougong yu Zhongguo Shuo' [Yihetuan's contribution to China] *Xinhai Geming Qian Shinian Jian Shilun Xuanji* (n 32), vol 1, 58, 59.

[40] Liang Qichao, 'Zhongguo zhi Jiang Qiang' [China will be strong] *Yinbingshi Wenji* (n 25) pt 2, 12.

[41] Wang Kangnian, 'Lun Jianglai Bi Zhi Zhi Shi' [On destined future age] *Shiwu Bao* [Chinese progress] Shanghai, no 65 (1898).

[42] Mai Menghua, 'Lun Zhongguo zhi Cunwang Jueding yu Jinri' [China's survival depends on today] *Qingyi Bao Quanbian* (n 22), vol 1, 100.

[43] 'Zhongguo zhi Gaizao' [China's rebuilding] *Xinhai Geming Qian Shinian Jian Shilun Xuanji* (n 32), vol 1, 420.

[44] Wang Shushan, 'Lun Shijie Weiyou Qiangquan' [Nothing but power in the world] *Dagong Daily* (25 January 1905).

countries', their impact upon China, that led China into the reality of itself as being 'the third-grade barbarous country'. This mental contradiction and tension made the intellectuals identify with the value of modern civilization and pursue it as a goal, but remain, simultaneously, dissatisfied with its discrimination of civilizations. This sense of tension and contradiction was a common mood in the discourse of civilization in the late Qing dynasty.

However, this mood did not become the mainstream of current intellectual opinion. With the rise of nationalism in the early twentieth century, the word 'anti-foreign' became very popular as slogans connected exclusively with 'civilization'. Even if the revolutionary intellectuals advocated getting away from Western powers' oppression by force, all the same they stressed the idea of an anti-foreign civilization, that is, to realize national independence by following international law, a part of the same civilization. In 1903, Zou Rong, a radical revolutionist from Sichuan, claimed in his *Revolutionary Army*—one of the most widespread books advocating revolution—that there were two kinds of revolution, ie barbaric and civilized, the former was thoroughly bad as an expression of social terror, and the Boxers were a proper example.[45] In 1904, a revolutionary, Chen Tianhua who came from Hunan, argued in his popular book *Menghuitou* (Wake up!) that the Boxers' purpose of resisting the 'foreign' was right, but its superstition and fighting indiscriminately in its war against the Western countries could not be accepted. He especially criticized the Boxers' ignorant actions of besieging embassies and burning churches, and thought Chinese revolution 'must resist the foreign with civilized means, but not with barbarian tactics'.[46] In the views of these two writers, the Boxers' uncivilized, fanatical anti-foreign agitation was turned into an excuse for the West to oppress China. Rational, orderly, and civilized anti-foreign behaviour, that is following international law to expose anti-foreign failure, was the only way to realize national independence. The revolutionists who studied in Japan pointed out that a country's place in the international order should be on condition of obeying the principles of international law to then be acknowledged by the world. Therefore, 'International law should be known if China wants to reform in the twentieth century. Going even further, if we want to found a new China, knowing international law is necessary.'[47]

Thus, for revolutionary intellectuals, following international law was regarded as the essential way to realize national independence, recapture, and assert national sovereignty. In 1906, a long exposition *Anti-foreign and the International Law*, by Hu Hanmin, one of the revolutionary leaders, serialized in the *Minpao Magazine*—published in Japan by the Chinese Revolutionary League led by Sun Zhongshan—expressed the Chinese revolutionary intellectuals' basic opinion on international law. This article expounded a series of problems, including the anti-foreign, sphere of influence, leased territory, national equality, independent, and self-defending

[45] Selected and noted by Zhizhi, *Menghuitou: Chen Tianhua Zou Rong Ji* [Wake up! Collection of Chen Tianhua and Zou Rong] (Liaoning People Publishing House 1994) 202.

[46] ibid 6, 70.

[47] Qianshou, 'Guojifa Shang zhi Guojia' [Nation in international law] *Ershishiji zhi Zhina* [Tokyo] [China in the twentieth century] (June 1905) no 1.

rights, treaties, and international interference. Hu pointed out that previous forms of anti-foreign action against civilization embodied Chinese egocentrism; however, the anti-foreign in the modern sense was to assert national sovereignty. The problem was that the Chinese did not know the difference between 'legitimate' and 'illegitimate' anti-foreign action. On the one hand, China could not protect its rights by proper diplomatic means, and was rejected and oppressed by Western powers; on the other hand, China resisted the West in the ways unacceptable to international society, which finally gave the big powers excuses, and conversely left China trapped. He thought the standard to judge whether the ways were proper was whether one abided by international law.[48] So, following international law to resist the powers was confirmed as one of the basic principles in the revolutionary canon, and an indispensable mark of a new civilized country. In 1912, when Sun Zhongshan became the interim president of the Republic of China, he declared 'as soon as the interim government is established, China should perform the obligation of a civilized country so as to share equal rights. The behaviour of a shameful nation and anti-foreign thoughts existing during the Qing dynasty must be eliminated. Besides, we should keep harmonious relations with friendly nations and maintain pacifism, to make for China an important part in international society, and then promote a great harmony in the world.'[49] This ideal of ascending to the 'civilized countries' showed that the pursuit of modern civilization as a primary value had been set up as a basic belief of the new country.

For those new intellectuals in the early twentieth century, civilization was the label of Western countries, while barbarism was the characteristic of China. Being converted to and believing in Western civilization, the intellectuals criticized radically the value of China's culture and social reality and developed a bitter hatred towards it. Actually, an identity crisis in Chinese culture hid behind the appeal of the intellectual elites and revolutionary people to set up new principles based on international law. Afterwards, Sun evaluated:

> The Boxers in 1900 were the last confident Chinese thoughts and capabilities to counter new western culture. And that defeat taught Chinese that the old-style bows and swords could not combat with the foreign guns and cannons any more, and that the new western cultures were far better than Chinese ... Hence, after that defeat, the Chinese who were good at thinking had got to know that we should imitate the foreign countries in every aspect, not only in materials and science but also anything to do with politics and society, if we were eager to be strong and to eliminate the grave humiliation of the unequal Boxer protocol in Beijing. From then on, the Chinese lost their confidence totally, and the sentiment of worship of foreign countries grew day by day ... which was the biggest change of Chinese political ideology.[50]

[48] Hanmin (Hu Hanmin), 'Paiwai yu Guojifa' [Anti-foreign and international law] *Minpao Magazine* [Tokyo] (1906–07) no 4, 6–10, 13.

[49] Academy of Chinese Social Science etc, Sun Zhongshan Quanji (ed) *The History Study Division of the Republic of China, Modern Chinese History Institution* (Complete collection of Sun Zhongshan), vol 2 (Zhuohua Book Company 1982) 2.

[50] ibid vol 9, 316–17.

As international law became the criterion of civilization, the law itself in the modern sense also marked the victory of the Western discourse of power.

The end of the nineteenth century and the early twentieth centuries witnessed a radical change in Chinese traditional culture. Kang Youwei and other Chinese scholars, by building a bridge between *Spring and Autumn* and the international law, found the common points between their imaginings about the ideal world order, which represented an attempt to sustain Chinese traditional culture. With the emergence of some new terms, such as nationalism, evolution, and civilization, China began a process of replacing the traditional ideology with the Western value system. When Western discourse power gradually established itself by relying on its advantage of practical position, the Chinese intelligentsia's understanding of international law and the world order tended in general to be close to the Western understanding. Nevertheless, it was destined to be an intricate process full of contradictory thoughts and mental entanglement: realism prevails but idealism never vanishes.

# 16

# The Crisis of the Ryukyus (1877–82)

## Confucian World Order Challenged and Defeated by Western/Japanese Imperial International Law

*Patrick Sze-lok Leung and Anthony Carty*

### 1. Introduction

The Japanese integration of Ryukyu in 1879 has been differently narrated by Chinese and Japanese historians. China sees the Japanese action as seizure of a Chinese vassal State, while Japan emphasizes that Ryukyu had been dominated by Japan since the seventeenth century and was finally integrated. From the perspective of international law, it is important to identify whether Ryukyu was an independent State in order to understand the nature of this political crisis. The Meiji government of Japan did not admit the independence of Ryukyu, and therefore regarded the integration as an entirely internal matter for Japan. Instead of 'integration', the Japanese word 'shobun' 処分, which means disposal or punishment, was therefore used to describe the incident. This argument was later confirmed by George H Kerr, an American post-war diplomat who argued that Ryukyu had lost its independence since the seventeenth century.[1] A century after the integration of Ryukyu, problems arising from American base in Okinawa put the historical incident on the agenda again. In the Diet, Abe Shinzō 安倍晋三, the Japanese Prime Minister, refused to define the historical status of the Ryukyu Kingdom.[2] The problem remains controversial among politicians and historians.

Besides the legitimacy of the integration, Wang Hui 汪暉, a Chinese historian, argues like a Marxist that the Japanese action was a modernist march of history whereby international law relaxed the tributary system and led to the formation of

[1] GH Kerr, *Okinawa: The History of an Island People* (Tuttle 2000) 166.

[2] Shinzō Abe, 'A Written Response to Congressman Suzuki Muneo's Further Questions on the Status of the Ryukyu Kingdom' published by Japanese House of Representatives, 11 November 2006, http://www.shugiin.go.jp/internet/itdb_shitsumon.nsf/html/shitsumon/b165131.htm. The legality of Japanese governance of Okinawa continues to be challenged. For example, some Japanese scholars argue that Ryukyu was annexed unilaterally, forcibly and illegally into Japan. The Japanese government however refuses to recognize Ryukyu to be its colony. The indigenous status of the Ryukyan people is thus not respected in Japan. See H Uemura, 'The Colonial Annexation of Okinawa and the Logic of International Law: The Formation of an "Indigenous People" in East Asia' (2003) 23(2) Japanese Studies 107.

*The Crisis of the Ryukyus (1877–82): Confucian World Order Challenged and Defeated by Western/Japanese Imperial International Law.* Patrick Sze-lok Leung and Anthony Carty.  Published 2018 by Oxford University Press.

imperialism and nationalism. He sees the crisis as 'a conflict between nation-state relations on the Western model of international law, and the traditional regional order based on the "tribute system"'. When China tried to preserve the tributary system, Japan took 'European international law as its basic conceptual framework' and eventually constructed a new order in East Asia.[3]

This chapter tries to draw a different picture of the Japanese seizure of Ryukyu. During the late nineteenth century, international law was manipulated by imperialists as a set of rules for legitimating colonialism and expansionism. Survival of weak States like Ryukyu was not guaranteed. Meanwhile, although the Chinese tributary system was inadequate and seemed unequal, it was closer to the absolute ethical values which were violated by Japan. On the other hand, China, which had 'no force but argument', was unable to restore the Ryukyu Kingdom. Rather than 'modernity', or whatever we call it, the political crisis only showed the absence of morality in international order.

## 2. The American Treaty with Ryukyu (July 1874): the Nature of International Law in the Late Nineteenth Century

There is a basic need to understand the character of international law in comparison with the tributary system. The former is described, as a mark of modernity in relation to the latter, for example, by Wang Hui. This creates a picture of the inevitability of the eclipse of the premodern in the face of the modern. The reality of Western international law is better seen in the pragmatic attitude of Admiral (Captain) Matthew Perry in his negotiation of the 1854 Treaty with Ryukyu (Liu Chee). Unlike the tributary system, this Western legal system did not afford a comprehensive or systematic view of world order. Even within Europe it was little more than a series of treaties, some general, others bilateral, which together made up a so-called public law of Europe. The only context in which this treaty system produced a semblance of general order was where there was a general peace treaty, such as Westphalia, Utrecht, Vienna, Versailles, and, most recently the 1990 Four Power Agreement in Europe with respect to Germany and especially its eastern borders.

In particular, the question of the existence of a State in international law was resolved in a very limited way at Westphalia. It meant that a prince or even lesser ranking rulers had freedom from any superior to conclude treaties and declare wars. It meant nothing more in terms of guarantees of existence. The international legal personality of princes was tied to or linked to family and inheritance laws of dynastic lineages. Most importantly this 'legal order' had no theory or philosophy of security. Princes were free to quarrel with one another over their dynastic inheritances. European thinkers therefore approached the question of international order in a bifurcated way, in which the role of law or international law, as such, was not exhaustive. It was supplemented by doctrines of balance of power, most fundamentally. Attached to such doctrines were views about the need to pre-emptively attack in the event that

[3] Wang Hui, *The Politics of Imagining Asia* (Harvard UP 2011) 229–30.

the growth of a country beyond a certain size could disturb the balance. At the same time, States constantly strove to increase their relative power, in the absence of any global normative order. This would mean concretely that the disappearance of one very small or even a medium-sized country would not matter as long as it did not appear to upset the balance too much. Hence, as will be seen, there was no reaction from the Western powers to the Ryukyu incident, but there was a firm Triple Intervention against Japan over the first terms of settlement it tried to impose on China with respect to Korea in 1895. The West realized this could lead to the wholescale penetration of China by Japan and the collapse of the Treaty order which had been built up in China.

This is not to say that ignoring the weak as insignificant is morally feasible. Our narrative will be that injustice comes back to haunt. The San Francisco Treaty of 1951 does not adequately resolve the outcome of the collapse of the Qing Dynasty and China, because it does not even include China and questions related to it. There is a huge *non liquet*, or legal as well as moral void here. The historical research into the field is complicated by the retrospective reversal of values presented by the Cairo Declaration of 1943.

More concretely by way of illustration, to focus on Perry, we may first describe his approach and then extrapolate from it, to a theory of the legal order. Perry set out in memoranda to his political masters, a very full account of American goals. These related to further trade and economic expansion in East Asia, either through treaties opening otherwise closed boundaries or territorial annexation—whichever the situation required, regardless of morality. Russia and especially Great Britain were regarded as rivals to American interests. Perry pointed out how both Singapore and Hong Kong being firmly under British control, Britain had virtually closed the South China Sea. In a despatch to the US Secretary of the Navy of 14 December 1852, Perry writes of the necessity of territorial expansion:

> The honor of the Nation calls for it, and the interest of commerce demands it. When we look at the possessions in the East of our great maritime rival England, and of the constant and rapid increase of their fortified ports, we should be admonished of the necessity of prompt measures on our part.
>
> By reference to the maps of the world, it will be seen that Great Britain is already in possession of the most important points in the East India and China Seas, and especially with reference to the China Seas.
>
> Singapore commanding the South Western, while Hong Kong covers the North Eastern Entrance, with the Island of Labuan on the Eastern, she will have the power of shutting up at will, and controlling, the enormous trade of those seas ... not under 15,000,000 Sterling.
>
> Fortunately the Japanese and many other islands of the Pacific are still left untouched by this unconscionable (or annexing) Government, and as some of them lay in a route of commerce, which is destined to become of great importance to the United States, no time should be lost in adopting active measures to secure a sufficient number of ports of refuge.[4]

The US objective should be, in the alternative to the South China Sea, to keep open the East China Sea, preferably through open frontiers to trade and movement of persons, but, if necessary, through territorial annexation. There could be in American

[4] 6 UST 743 1942 Document 166, 758–59.

or Western eyes, no restraining legal influence on the objectives of treaties to be concluded. This could only mean that any resistance to the conclusion of an 'opening up treaty' could be met with whatever pressure or force was necessary, leading ultimately to annexation through war and conquest. These were not primarily a matter of opening up to trade but rather, concerned hospitality and a recuperation and shelter for American shipping, offering them minimum facilities of a naval port and/or base. Perry recognized the absolute unwillingness of the Ryukyuans and his response was his estimate that it would not be necessary to go beyond the exertion of pressure so far as to have to use force. He could get what he wanted through a visible readiness to pressurize. The so-called treaty involved no measure of mutual negotiation, but was merely a list of demands by Perry which reflected what he thought were American needs. So again the same despatch states the 'normative dimension' in the following brutal terms:

> Now it strikes me, that the occupation of the principal ports of those Islands, for the accommodation of our ships of war, and for the safe resort of merchant vessels of whatever nation, would be a measure, not only justified by the laws of state necessity, the argument may be further strengthened by the certain consequence of the amelioration of the condition of the Natives, although the vices attendant upon civilization may be entailed upon them.[5]

The first instrument to achieve this would be the conclusion of treaties. For this purpose, it was necessary to ascertain who were the persons or entities capable of providing valid signatures to conclude agreements to facilitate the hospitality for shipping and trade. This is partially why it can appear misleading and confusing that the United States appeared to recognize Ryukyu as a State in 1854 and then abandoned it in 1879–82. In fact the Perry record shows clearly the context. He started from the assumption that Ryukyu was a dependency of Japan and tried to have it 'opened' in negotiation with Japan.[6] It was only when the Japanese did not agree that it was to be included among the Japanese ports he wished to open, that he decided that Ryukyu must itself have the capacity to conclude treaties. The capacity to conclude treaties had to lie somewhere in relation to any territory and population. Since Japan would not include Naha as one of the Treaty Ports in its Treaty of 31 March 1854, Perry had to go elsewhere:

> Lew Chew it appears, is in a measure an independent sovereignty, holding only slight allegiance either to Japan or China, but preferring rather its relationship to the later Empire; that the Islands stretching from Formosa to Kiusiu are all under its sovereignty, and are in such intercourse with the parent Island Great Lew Chew, as the imperfect character of their means of navigation will allow.[7]

Once he reached this conclusion, Perry was still faced with an extreme reluctance on the part of Ryukyuans to conclude any agreement with him on any matter at all, no matter how small the detail. He was met, inter alia, with the concern of the Ryukyuans, especially, that they could not conclude an agreement on their own, without the consent of China. They denied their own treaty-making capacity, but

[5] ibid 758. [6] ibid 753. [7] ibid.

without any mention of their Satsuma dependency. They insisted on their vassalage in relation to China. Perry could see no substance in these arguments and paid no attention to them. The tone of the negotiation can be gathered from these extracts from Perry's secretary:

> We must have a free trade in the market, and the right to purchase articles for the ships . . .
>
> Let the mayor clearly understand that this port is to be one of rendezvous, probably for years, and that the authorities had better come to an understanding at once . . .[8]
>
> The Commodore, however, was not to be balked of his purpose by any of the shames and devices of Lew Chew policy, and went straight on to the end proposed, without allowing himself to be diverted from a broad, honest course of fair dealing, into any of the bye-ways of the oriental hide-and-go-seek diplomacy. As to resorting to force, which had been threatened at the close of the conference with the regent, the necessity of violent measures was never seriously contemplated by the Commodore, as it was rightly judged that a resolute attitude would answer all the purposes of a blow.[9]

So, some preliminary concluding remarks about the nature of international law and statehood may be made. International law, under the Westphalia system does not guarantee the independence of States. They have to be capable of maintaining their own independence. It reasons from established and stable facts. If a prince, under the 1648 Westphalia system, has the capacity to maintain his independence of any outside power, he will have, actually, the capacity to conclude treaties. If the Prince loses the territory to another prince it will be the new Prince who has the capacity. So the United States was simply interested in where the treaty capacity actually lay, with Japan or Ryukyu. International legal persons are those who are addressed by treaty norms. What matters is that there is an entity which is in effective control of territory and population. In other words, this 'legal order' has no ethical purpose and no concept of human welfare. It is an instrument of the goals which States set themselves, a purely formal instrument. It is not even a matter of law being subverted by power. Cassese, a leading authority on the contemporary meaning of statehood, always subordinates the possible principle of the self-determination of peoples to the principles of territorial integrity of already existing States. He says:

> New situations are not recognised as legally valid unless they could be seen to rest on a firm and durable display of authority. No new situation could claim international legitimacy so long as the 'new men' failed to demonstrate that they had firmly supplanted the former authority. Force was the principal source of legitimation.[10]

So, when Japan chose to seize Ryukyu and China objected in terms of the welfare of the population, this could not mean anything to the United States in legal terms. If its goals could be guaranteed by Japan, it would only get what it wanted by resort to the route which Perry had originally chosen—inclusion of Ryukyu in the ports the Japanese were to open.

So, the American record shows that by a note of 5 November 1872 Japan declared that as Ryukyu was an 'integral portion of the Japanese Empire it is natural that the

[8] ibid 766. [9] ibid 768–69.

[10] Quoted in A Carty, *Philosophy of International Law* (Edinburgh UP 2007) 82.

provisions of a compact entered into between the Lew Chew and the United States on the 11th July 1854, will be observed by this government'.[11] This course was acquiesced in by the United States by instruction from Secretary of State Fish. When informed of the incorporation, the American minister to Japan had merely asked whether the 1854 Compact would be observed by Japan, and assurance was given. Fish then conveyed his approval:

> It is supposed that the absorption or incorporation of one State by another does not discharge or release within the limits of the absorbed or incorporated State the obligation which it may be under to a third power at the time of such absorption or incorporation.[12]

## 3. The Ryukyu Question from the Perspective of the Japanese and Chinese Archives

### 3.1 An overview of Ryukyu's international identity (to the 1870s)

Before the introduction of international law in the nineteenth century, the East Asian world did not have the Western notions of 'sovereignty' and 'independence'. Instead of treaties, the Chinese world order had been developed in the form of 'tributary system'. Vassal States were required to send regular tributes to China, in return for investiture and commercial interests. Despite some similarities, it might be dangerous to equate the Chinese vassal States and the Western protectorate without taking the historical context of East Asia into account. According to Western international law, protectorates or subordinate States could not make treaties without permission from their superior. On the other hand, the Chinese tributary system was different in nature. It did not imply Chinese dominance over internal and external affairs of its vassal States. As JK Fairbank and SY Teng suggest, the tributary system 'came to be used by the rulers of China for political ends of self-defense', and 'in practice it had a very fundamental and important commercial basis'.[13] In other words, it could be compatible with the Western concept of independence.

Ryukyu had been a Chinese tributary state since the Ming Dynasty. On the other hand, after being invaded by the Shimazu clan of Satsuma, one of the Japanese feudal domains, its status was complicated. Ryukyu agreed to become Satsuma's subordinate, and was then regulated by '15 Articles', mainly on social and economic aspects. Satsuma commissioners were appointed to Ryukyu to supervise its economic and even political affairs. After the invasion, Ryukyu became dually subordinate to China and Japan. Before international law had been introduced, the legitimacy of this relationship was determined by Confucianism. Confucian intellectuals believed that political ethics were derived from interpersonal relationships. The relationship between the father and the son, between the emperor and the servant, and between the superior State and the subordinate State, should be theoretically similar. A son

[11] UST Document 166 (n 4) 784. [12] ibid.

[13] JK Fairbank and SY Têng, 'On the Ch'ing Tributary System' (1941) 6(2) Harvard Journal of Asiatic Studies 137.

could not have two fathers, while a servant could not serve two masters at the same time. In order to moderate its embarrassment and legitimate its foreign relationship, Ryukyu claimed China and Japan as its father and mother. More importantly, the dual subordination was approved by China tacitly. Satsuma, which aimed to use Ryukyu as the medium for foreign trade rather than dominate the kingdom, should be happy to see that.[14] Although no treaty was signed between China and Japan, the status was accepted by both States. Consequently, Ryukyu still enjoyed virtual independence during the period of dual subordination.

As emphasized above, the notion of 'vassal state' in East Asia was different from that in the West. Ryukyu was treated as a subordinate State by China and Japan, but not by the Western powers. By looking into the history of the 1850s, it is quite clear that the West saw Ryukyu as an independent State. Like other East Asian States, Ryukyu had no official communication with the West before the nineteenth century. In 1852, Perry started his expedition to the Far East. Before landing in Japan, he arrived at Ryukyu and reached a treaty with the kingdom. Perry was then followed by the French and the Dutch, who signed treaties with Ryukyu in 1855 and 1859 respectively. It can be argued that each move of the negotiation with France was, as Kerr mentioned, directed from behind the scenes by Satsuma with its full consent.[15] However, strictly speaking, this fact only showed Satsuma could influence Ryukyu's diplomatic policies to a certain extent. It might also be suggested that Japan, compared with China, was more influential in Ryukyu at that period. However, it did not imply Ryukyu could be understood as a protectorate in the sense of Western jurisprudence. At least, the Western powers, which negotiated directly with Ryukyu, recognized the kingdom as an independent State.

These historical facts merely shows the complexity of the international relationship at that time. Although the tributary system had been in place for hundreds of years, it seems to be unclear in international law. Although China and Japan were respected as superiors, Chinese vassal States could make policies on their own and enjoy virtual independence. Treaties signed with Western powers further confirmed the international identity of Ryukyu. Later in 1881–82, when the United States negotiated with China and Korea for the making of the United States–Korea Treaty, the Americans also refused to admit Korea as a Chinese protectorate.[16] This showed the weakness and ambiguity of the tributary system, caused by the difference between the Chinese concept of world order and Western jurisprudence. The impact brought by international law, which came along with the Western powers, thus caused a gradual collapse of the Eastern world order. It also created an ambiguity of the situation, and a chance for the Japanese, who were learning Western

[14] Kerr (n 1) 156–69, 179–82. [15] ibid 344.

[16] Kuo Ting-yee 郭廷以, 'China and the First U.S.–Korean Treaty' (Zhongguo yu diyi ci Mei Han Tiaoyue 中國與第一次美韓條約) in Huang Tsen-ming 黃正銘 et al (eds), *Collected Papers on Chinese Diplomatic History* (*Zhongguo waijiao shi lunji* 中國外交史論集) (Zhonghua wenhua chuban shiye weiyuan hui 1957), vol 1, 1–18; Lin Min-te 林明德, *Yuan Shih-k'ai and Korea* (袁世凱與朝鮮) (Institute of Modern History, Academia Sinica 1984); Song Pyŏng-gi 宋炳基, *The 1882 Korean–American Treaty and Ch'ing China*, Yang Xiu-zhi 楊秀芝 tr (Lexis Book 2006).

culture and international law rapidly, to take over the Chinese vassal State Ryukyu—and even Korea.

### 3.2 Integration of Ryukyu: process and justification (1871–79)

Ryukyu's status of dual subordination had remained stable for 200 years with the tacit consent from both China and Japan, but its stability was weakened by the arrival of the Western powers. While China was making efforts to preserve the tradition, Japan was more sensitive and more willing to adapt itself to the changing situation. They tried to replace the East Asian world order with the Western international legal order, and this finally led to the integration of Ryukyu into Japan.

The idea of integration of Ryukyu can be traced back to the 1840s, when Britain and France sent warships to Ryukyu, requesting diplomatic relations and the rights of trade and preaching. Threatened by the possibility of a Western seizure of Ryukyu and the arrival of Perry, some Japanese suggested taking over Ryukyu for self-defence.[17] The plan was not immediately put into action because of the political disorder during the Bakumatsu period. Nevertheless, the beginning of the Meiji Restoration brought an opportunity for change. Following the abolishment of the *han* (feudal domain) system and the establishment of a centralized government in 1871, the vice-minister of Finance Inoue Kaoru 井上馨 recommended integrating Ryukyu into the Japanese Empire. He attempted to justify his idea by emphasizing the relationship between Ryukyu and Japan. He claimed that King Shuntin 舜天, the ancestor of the Ryukyu Kingdom, came from Japan. Ryukyu's language, social customs, and political system were also similar to those of the Japanese. Geographically, Ryukyu was close to the Japanese mainland, together with other outlying islands. In Inoue's words, Ryukyu was actually Japanese mountains floating on the Southern Sea.[18]

While regarding Ryukyu as a dependency of Satsuma in the past, Inoue claimed, by using the Confucian theory introduced above, that Ryukyu should only be loyal to one superior State, that is, Japan. He criticized Ryukyu for being disloyal to Japan as it was a Japanese dependency which used the Chinese calendar and received investiture from Chinese emperors.. The government should therefore change the relationship by calling the Ryukyu king to Tokyo, exposing his disloyalty, and giving him reasons for integration.[19]

While claiming Ryukyu should only be subordinate to Japan, the Japanese government was indeed clear that Ryukyu was also subordinate to China at the same time. Inoue's memorial seemed to be a political claim without any international legal justification, rather than a workable plan with a diplomatic strategy towards China. Instead of adopting Inoue's suggestion, the Japanese government in 1872

[17] Yoshida Shōin 吉田松陰, *Record from Prison* (*Yūshūroku* 幽囚録) (Yoshikawa Hanshichi 1891) 12.

[18] Shinomura Fujio 下村富士男 (ed), *Series on Cultural Materials of the Meiji Era* (*Meiji bunka shiryō sōsho* 明治文化資料叢書) (Kazama Shobo 1987), vol 4, 8.

[19] ibid.

took a first step towards strengthening its legal status in Ryukyu by calling the king's representative to Tokyo to celebrate the restoration. Aimed at demonstrating the legal relationship between Japan and Ryukyu to the international community, Emperor Meiji of Japan granted the king the title of 'King of Ryukyu Domain'.[20] Furthermore, Ryukyu's foreign affairs, including matters concerning the treaties signed with the Western States before, were then dominated by the ministry of foreign affairs of Japan.[21] Later in 1874, the responsibility for Ryukyu affairs was transferred to the home ministry to implicitly show that Ryukyu was a part of Japan instead of an independent State.[22] The purpose of these actions was to demonstrate Japanese suzerainty over Ryukyu. Here, the suzerainty had the meaning of both East Asian style (investiture) and Western style (dominance of foreign policies). Before 1874, Japan's attitude towards Ryukyu had never been aggressive.

The Taiwan Expedition in 1874 was obviously a turning point of Japan's policy on Ryukyu. The cause of the expedition was the Mudan Incident of 1871, in which Ryukyu people were killed by Taiwanese savages. The Kagoshima Prefecture reported the incident and suggested taking revenge for Ryukyu. On this occasion, Yamagata Aritomo 山縣有朋, the deputy minister of war, advocated the idea of changing Ryukyu's dual-subordination system. He pointed out that the dual-subordination system of Ryukyu had never been clearly defined by international agreements. In the context of colonialism, Ryukyu was at risk of falling into Western domination because of its ambiguous status. Therefore, the dual-subordination system should be rectified by international law and replaced by a legally clarified relationship with either China or Japan only.[23]

Yamagata attempted to define the subordinate relationship according to the Western standard and contended that China's suzerainty over Ryukyu was in name only. He explained that Ryukyu, which lacked resources, only pretended to be obedient to China, by adopting the Chinese calendar given by the Chinese emperors, in return for Sino-Ryukyuan trade. As Yamagata argued, Ryukyu was deceiving the Chinese people. On the contrary, the Ryukyu people had been governed by Japanese officials sent by Satsuma for a long time. More importantly, Yamagata added that the Ryukyu people, who reported their misfortune in Taiwan to the Japanese government, had shown their admiration and reliance on Japan. He therefore suggested using his justification to negotiate with China in order to get control of Ryukyu. However, just like Inoue, Yamagata failed to provide any decisive international legal justification for Japanese dominance over Ryukyu.[24] Although he mentioned the term 'international law' in his memorial, his understanding of Western jurisprudence might be insufficient.

The Japanese expedition to Taiwan in 1874 created an argument for Japan to claim its suzerainty over Ryukyu. The expedition was claimed as a punitive action in

[20] ibid 19. [21] ibid 21. [22] ibid 72.

[23] Yasuoka Akio 安岡昭男, *A Study on the Sino-Japanese Diplomatic History during the Early Meiji Era* (*Meiji zenki Nisshin kōshōshi kenkyū* 明治前期日清交渉史研究) (Gannandō Shoten 1995) 65.

[24] ibid 66.

response to the Mudan Incident of 1871. After the expedition, China, in the engagement signed with Japan, admitted that

> The present proceedings having been undertaken by the Government of Japan for the humane object of affording security to its own subjects, the Government of China will not therefor impute blame to it.[25]

The words 'own subjects' were later interpreted by Gustave Boissonade, a French legal scholar working for Japan, to justify the Japanese legitimacy of dominating Ryukyu.

Boissonade was appointed as a legal adviser for the negotiation with China. After returning to Tokyo, Boissonade drafted a plan for further steps towards Ryukyu to answer enquiries from the Japanese government.[26] He regarded Ryukyu as a semi-independent State, but the situation was changing for two reasons. The first one was the Meiji Restoration which abolished the rights of the feudal lords and established a centralized government. As a result, the Tokyo government succeeded the privileges of Satsuma's status as the superior of Ryukyu. The second factor was the Mudan Incident. Boissonade claimed that because Japan, which invaded Taiwan in response to protect its people, was indeed exercising the sovereignty of the king, its power in Ryukyu would be further expanded. Moreover, based on the words 'own subjects', Boissonade claimed that China had recognized that Ryukyu people were subjects of Japan.[27]

However, Boissonade's justification has not been accepted by Chinese and Ryukyu people. First of all, there is no evidence showing that the Ryukyu king had asked the Japanese to invade Taiwan on its behalf. Shō Tukukō 向德宏 (also known as Kōchi ueekata Chōjō 幸地親方朝常), who was the king's brother-in-law, later declared that the Ryukyu people had never been happy with the Japanese invasion. Besides, he insisted that Japan was just invading Taiwan for its own interests.[28] Therefore, based on Ryukyu's attitude, it might be hard to show Ryukyu was a Japanese protectorate by using the expedition as an example. Second, Boissonade's interpretation on the Engagement of Beijing was more difficult to persuade the Chinese. Before the invasion, Japan claimed that several Japanese were plundered in Taiwan in 1873 and used this as another excuse, besides the Mudan Incident, for the expedition. Therefore, Chang Chi-hsiung 張啟雄 argued that 'subjects of Japan' might refer to those Japanese but not the Ryukyu people. From the perspective of international law, Chang added that the engagement could not be unitarily and arbitrarily interpreted by the Japanese government, while the Chinese had never admitted the Ryukyu people were 'subjects of Japan' in any other situation.

[25] *British and Foreign State Papers*, vol LXVI, 425.

[26] Ōkubo Toshimichi, *Diary of Ōkubo Toshimichi* (*Ōkubo Toshimichi Nikki* 大久保利通日記) (Hokusensha 1997) 384.

[27] Itō Hirobumi 伊藤博文 (ed), *A Collection of Secret Documents (Diplomatic Volume)* (*Hisho ruisan gaikō hen* 秘書類纂•外交篇) (Hisho ruisan kankōkai 1936), vol 3, 282–84.

[28] Li Hongzhang, *The Complete Works of Li Hongzhang* (*Li Hongzhang quanji* 李鴻章全集) (Anhui Educational Publishing House 2008), vol 32, 460.

Therefore, he concluded that the engagement provided no legal foundation for the sovereignty of Ryukyu.[29]

Rather than proving Ryukyu had already completely become a Japanese dependency, Boissonade stated this was ambiguous because Ryukyu still had some features of an independent State. Therefore, he suggested to Ōkubo Toshimichi 大久保利通, the Japanese home minister, ways to demonstrate Japan's suzerainty over Ryukyu. He recommended sending a Japanese official to Ryukyu to inspect the land and carry out reforms to prepare for future actions. Cruel laws in Ryukyu should be abolished to win people's support. To show Ryukyu was part of Japan, Boissonade suggested adding Ryukyu to the Japanese map and also changing Ryukyu's 'tributes' to 'taxation' in name because tributes were voluntary, whereas taxation was obligatory. The king should also be called to Tokyo to acknowledge the Japanese expedition.[30]

As a legal expert, Boissonade recognized that it was unsuitable to make agreements between Japan and Ryukyu without the participation of China. Before the invasion of Taiwan, he had argued that it was essential to get an agreement from China for the expedition. Similarly, after the invasion, he warned the Japanese government that without getting Chinese consent, stopping Ryukyu from sending tributes to China would damage the friendship between Japan and China. Instead of doing so, Japan should negotiate with the Chinese government to terminate Ryukyu's diplomatic relationship with China, although diplomatic obstacles could be expected.[31] Boissonade implicitly meant that China still had the right to maintain its relationship with Ryukyu. Although the Taiwan expedition and the Engagement of Beijing could be used as Japanese arguments or excuses, the international legal justification was still insufficient without Chinese consent.

Despite Boissonade's proposal, the Japanese government decided to send Matsuda Michiyuki 松田道之 as the representative to Ryukyu, instead of dealing with China directly. The main mission of Matsuda was to stop the king from sending tributes to China and receiving investiture from the Chinese emperor. In addition, he also requested that the king use the Japanese calendar, replace its legal system with that of the Japanese, make reforms to the political system, send students to study in Japan, remove Ryukyu's manor in Fuzhou, go to Tokyo to appreciate the Taiwan Expedition, and allow Japanese forces to station on the islands.[32] On 5 August, the king agreed to some of the requests, but he refused to terminate the relationship with China. Seeing China and Japan as Ryukyu's 'parents', he added that the State did not want to cut off its relationship with its father and became unfaithful.[33]

Three days later, Matsuda replied that because of the Meiji Restoration and the diplomatic relationship with the foreign States, Japan had to develop itself according

[29] Chang Chi-hsiung, 'Was the Suzerainty of Ryukyu Decided by the Engagement between Japan and China? Evaluating the Sino-Japanese Negotiation on the 1874 Taiwan Incident' (Nisshin Gokan Jōyaku ni oite Ryūkyū no kizoku wa kettei saretaka: 1874 nen no Taiwan jiken ni kansuru nisshin kōshō ni saikentō 日清互換條約において琉球の帰屬は決定されたか——一八七四年の台湾事件に関する日清交渉の再検討——), *Okinawa bunka kenky ū*沖縄文化研究 (September 1992) 19, 95–129.

[30] Itō (n 27), vol 3, 284–86.

[31] ibid 285–86.

[32] Shinomura (n 18), vol 4, 104–07.

[33] ibid 117–18.

to international law and legitimacy. If Ryukyu, which he claimed as a Japanese domain, was still allowed to send tributes to China, it would be contradicting international law. The Japanese government would have difficulty in facing the international opinion, and the survival of Ryukyu would also be threatened because of its ambiguous status. Besides emphasizing the geographical situation and ethnic, cultural similarities between Ryukyu and Japan, he also argued that China had given up its suzerainty over Ryukyu because it had done nothing for the Mudan Incident, while the Japanese suzerainty had been admitted by China in the Engagement of Beijing. Although in 1874 the Japanese minister for foreign affairs Soejima Taneomi 副島種臣 promised that the system and governmental organization of Ryukyu would not be altered, Matsuda explained the promise was impossible to be kept forever because the environment had changed a lot.[34] Both sides continued to repeat and elaborate on these arguments. Matsuda added that Ryukyu was just using the Chinese calendar and receiving investiture from China while actually being protected by Japan.[35] Against the Ryukyu ministers who claimed China and Japan as Ryukyu's parents, Matsuda argued that according to international law Ryukyu could not be subordinate to both States because a person (or a State) could not serve two States, although he could be grateful to his father and mother at the same time.[36] Matsuda finally agreed to let the king send his representative to negotiate with the Tokyo government,[37] but no consensus was reached in discussions which lasted a year.

When the Ryukyu representatives were staying in Tokyo, the Japanese government was stimulated by the Ryukyu king who complained to China and to the foreign ambassadors in Japan.[38] Moreover, after the first Chinese ambassador He Ruzhang 何如璋 arrived at Tokyo in 1877, Japan could no longer prevent direct negotiation with China. Becoming more and more anxious, the Japanese government chose a more aggressive policy. On 6 January 1879, Matsuda was assigned to go to request that the king terminate the relationship with China for the second time. He was instructed to give the king one week and warn him that there would be 'serious punishment' if the requests were not accepted.[39] As the king refused again, Matsuda received another assignment on 11 March to abolish the Ryukyu Domain and replace it with the Okinawa Prefecture. The king had to go to Tokyo and become a Japanese noble.[40] On 27 March, the king accepted Japan's offer and handed over the capital Shuri to Matsuda.[41]

By reviewing the historical facts, we that Japanese integration could neither be justified by East Asian traditions, nor by Western international law. As mentioned, Ryukyu was an independent State whose dual subordination was allowed by its superior States China and Japan for hundreds of years. Japan's intention was to protect Ryukyu from Western invasion to prevent further invasion towards Japan. However, the East Asian traditional relationship of suzerainty and subordination did not work as shown by the Western States which signed treaties directly with

[34] ibid 121–23. [35] ibid 139. [36] ibid 143. [37] ibid 149.
[38] ibid 173–74, 179–80. [39] ibid 186. [40] ibid 217–18. [41] ibid 222.

Ryukyu. In order to demonstrate its dominance of Ryukyu in terms of the Western standard to the Western powers, Japan made attempts such as changing the kingdom to a domain in name and controlling Ryukyu's diplomacy. At the very beginning, there was no evidence showing that the majority of Japanese ministers were aiming at integrating Ryukyu. Otherwise, they could coerce the king to give up his throne immediately. Instead, they preferred a moderate way to strengthen Japanese dominance. The Taiwan Expedition, although it was also a result of the coup in 1873, was also aimed at Japanese dominance over Ryukyu. However, after the Taiwan Expedition, Japan became too confident and thus adopted a rapid move towards Ryukyu, rather than negotiating with the Chinese government. When the Ryukyu king complained to China and the Western States and created a difficult situation for Japan, Japan chose a more aggressive way, that is, replacing the domain with the prefecture, to achieve its objective.

While attempting to adopt the Western international order for East Asia, Japan was unable to provide any persuasive international legal justification for such integration. Although the Japanese ministers insisted on the importance of modifying their relationship with Ryukyu according to international legitimacy, they could only justify the Japanese claims by emphasizing the geographical and culture features of Ryukyu. They even used Confucianism during the negotiation with Ryukyu, such as claiming a State could not serve two superiors at the same time. Indeed, there was no such international legislation. The States could have many different kinds of relationship with the others, such as the Balkan States' subordination relationship with both Turkey and Russia. In other words, Ryukyu's dual subordination did not violate international law. This shows the Japanese had not been familiar with international law yet. The investiture in 1871 was also a replica of Chinese-style suzerainty, rather than Western style.

Instead of obeying international law, Japan used political tricks and administrative measures to prove to the international community that it, rather than China, was the suzerain State of Ryukyu. At the same time, significant factors in international legal practice, such as Ryukyu people's will and the Chinese participation, were omitted. In fact, it was clear that the Ryukyu king did not want to terminate the relationship with China and integrate with Japan. As Boissonade suggested, China, as a State claiming suzerainty over Ryukyu, should not be excluded during the negotiation with Ryukyu. The king finally consented to the integration because he was too weak to resist the Japanese aggression. In other words, Japan used the unequal position to force the king to agree. While the desire of China and Ryukyu was ignored, the unfair settlement and coerced agreement should not have been justified by international law and thus led to unresolved problems in the future.

## 3.3 Sino-Japanese negotiations (1878–1880s)

As shown in the last section, the Japanese integration of Ryukyu, which was completed in 1879, can be traced back to 1871 when the Ryukyu Kingdom was replaced by the Ryukyu Domain. China, being one of Ryukyu's suzerains, was excluded in this process for years simply because it had not received any notification from Japan, which was not eager to face Chinese intervention. Sino-Japanese negotiations did not begin until 1878, after China received complaints from Ryukyu. However, it had already become impossible for Japan to withdraw the political decision which had been set in train.

Ryukyu, which might have been frightened of complicating matters, had not reported its situation to China for years. In late 1876, when Japanese pressure intensified, the Ryukyu king sent his brother-in-law Shō Tukukō and other representatives to China. After arriving at Fujian in early 1877, the representatives made complaints to the Chinese government. The governor-general of Fujian and Zhejiang suggested that the Empress Dowager send He Ruzhang, who had just been appointed first Chinese ambassador to Japan, to discuss the matter with Western ambassadors in Japan by using international law.[42] In 1878 when He arrived in Japan, Ryukyu had not yet been integrated as the Okinawa Prefecture. He firstly collected information about Japan and Ryukyu, and then submitted his plan to the Chinese government.

He was realistic about ways to deal with Japan. Although he aimed at keeping Chinese suzerainty, he might also know that it was difficult to reverse the situation to what it had been before 1871. So, he suggested, at least, preserving the relationship with Ryukyu in another way, that is, giving up the right of either granting investiture or receiving tributes. Alternatively, China could invite Western ambassadors to force Japan to promise maintaining Ryukyu's independence forever.[43] At the same time, He critically noted that international law could not be relied on. Among the three plans he proposed, the first one was to send warships to Ryukyu. The action would be justifiable because China could claim tributes from Ryukyu. The aim was to show Japan that China would definitely fight for its tributary state. He regarded this plan as the best, as Japan, having just suppressed the Satsuma Rebellion, would be wary of a and immediate war with China. The second-best way was to debate with Japan by using international law, while at the same time forging military alliance with Ryukyu against Japanese aggression. Negotiation by means of international law without any other action was the worst plan.[44] If we review these three plans by looking at the final result of the negotiation, He was logical and sensible because he understood international law was meaningless, unless supported by power. However, the majority of Chinese officials, including Li Hongzhang 李鴻章, disagreed. Placing too much confidence in international law and the chance to get Western powers' support, they thought He was just exaggerating the problem and making it more serious. As a result, they chose He's 'worst plan' and ordered him to start negotiations. Moreover, He was instructed to tell Japan that all of his information had been collected from Ryukyu officials in Japan. He was warned not to mention the official

[42] National Palace Museum Library 故宮博物院文獻館 (ed), *Archives of the Sino-Japanese Diplomatic History during the Guangxu Era* (*Qing Guangxu chao Zhong Ri jiaoshe shiliao* 清光緒朝中日交涉史料) (National Palace Museum Library 1932), *juan* 1, 22.

[43] Wen Tingjing 溫廷敬 (ed), *Works of Three Authors from Chayang* (*Chayang Sanjia Wenchao* 茶陽三家文鈔) (Wenhai Chubanshe 文海出版社 1966) 51–52.

[44] ibid 50–51.

complaints made by Ryukyu to the Chinese government, and that he was ordered by the government to negotiate. This instruction significantly weakened He's status in the negotiations.

After a brief conversation with Terashima Munenori 寺島宗則, the Japanese foreign minister, He sent him a diplomatic note on 7 October 1878.[45] He claimed that Ryukyu, which was a weak State without rich resources, did not merit foreign integration. The kingdom had been subordinate to China since the Ming Dynasty and had received mercy from the Qing. The subordinated State had been recognized by China and Japan for a long time, and Chinese characters were used in Ryukyu's treaties with the Western powers. He regarded the Japanese as unreasonable and not faithful for having stopped Ryukyu from sending tributes to China; that it was actually persecuting a weak State. Moreover, he pointed out the Japanese action violated the first article of the Sino-Japanese Friendship Treaty signed in 1871, which stated territories of both States should be respected. He concluded that both persecuting a weak State and violating the treaty were not accepted under international law.[46] Terashima's reply, on 21 November, was later than He expected. The reply was also simple, merely stating that Ryukyu had been part of Japan for hundreds of years, and had been placed under the administration of the home ministry. Furthermore, Terashima criticized He for damaging the Sino-Japanese friendship by using aggressive words, such as 'unreasonable' and 'not faithful' based on 'imagination' without understanding the real situation of Ryukyu.[47] Terashima was urged by He to continue the discussion, but he refused to explain anything more on 'our Ryukyu domain, saying that all he could tell had been written in the letter on 21 November.[48]

After the establishment of the Okinawa Prefecture in 1879, Terashima, in response to He's further request for explanation, emphasized that the replacement of Japan's Ryukyu Domain was just a matter of Japanese internal affairs unrelated to China.[49] He, who did not accept Terashima's statement, claimed that Ryukyu had been a State rather than part of Japan, and asked Terashima to clarify when the Ryukyu Kingdom had been turned into a domain.[50] Terashima argued that the Sino-Ryukyu relationship in the past had been only a trading relationship under Satsuma's permission, and it was the time to alter this ambiguous situation. Again, he reminded the Chinese ambassador that any statement based on imagination would harm the Sino-Japanese friendship.[51] Prior to negotiations with Japan, He had contacted other foreign ambassadors in Japan, but he did not receive meaningful help from them. Later, China found out that the British ambassador Harry Smith Parkes actually supported Japan. Parkes even disclosed the information, which he collected from He, of the Chinese side to the Japanese foreign ministry, aiming at creating Sino-Japanese tension for British interests.[52] The reason for Terashima's lack of cooperation might be because he knew, from Parkes, that the Chinese government did not want to be seen

[45] Ministry of Foreign Affairs of Japan 外務省 (ed), *Documents on Japanese Foreign Policy* 日本外交文書 (United Nations Association of Japan 1936–63), vol 11, 269–71.
[46] ibid 272. [47] ibid. [48] ibid 272–73. [49] ibid vol 12, 179–80.
[50] ibid 180. [51] ibid 181. [52] Li (n 28), vol 32, 455.

as too unyielding. In other words, the Chinese ministers, who believed the international community would help, were over-optimistic.

At the same time, the central government of China was searching for a solution to this serious problem, which might lead to a collapse of the whole tributary system. Guo Songtao 郭嵩燾 recommended making some concessions, such as recognizing Ryukyu as an independent State subordinate to neither China nor Japan, in order to win support from Western powers which followed international law and respected the independence of States. Also, it would be easy for Japan, which was learning from the West, to concede. Although China would lose a tributary state as a result, at least the Ryukyu Kingdom could be saved.[53] Taking Guo's advice, Li Hongzhang attempted discussions with the foreign ministers, but he was disappointed by the powers. As the translator of the German ambassador told Li in April 1879, the Ryukyu matter was just treated as a Chinese affair, unrelated to the European powers. The German and Italian ambassadors were not interested and did not want to intervene. They even justified Japan because it took the Western model of self-strengthening, and disapproved of China which was still unwilling to abandon the tributary system and make changes. After speaking to the ambassadors, Li felt that China could hardly win support from the Western powers. He also thought that it would be difficult to achieve the restoration of the Ryukyu State, unless the Ryukyu people revolted against the Japanese government before the newly appointed governor of the Okinawa Prefecture arrived.[54]

The new Japanese ambassador Shishido Tamaki 宍戸璣 was instructed by Terashima not to negotiate with the Chinese government, as he had no authority to do so.[55] At the same time, Terashima also sent a statement to the Chinese government. The statement first mentioned that it was impossible for Japan to withdraw its political decision, and urged China, in order to preserve the friendship between both States, not to take it seriously. It then quoted different historical texts claiming that Ryukyu was part of the Japanese southern islands dominated by Satsuma, and that its language, writing system, religion, and customs were all Japanese. It also traced Japanese domination of Ryukyu to 735 during the Tang Dynasty in China, when the Japanese built a stele there. Moreover, King Shuntin of Ryukyu also came from Japan. Two hundred years later, Ryukyu was granted to Satsuma by the shogun. Since the invasion of Ryukyu in 1609, the king and his officials sent pledges to admit Satsuma as their superior, and even obeyed fifteen articles together with other political orders issued by Satsuma. When Ryukyu suffered from disasters, it was helped by Japan. Therefore, it was legitimate to change Ryukyu to a prefecture, as its superior Satsuma was also changed to the Kagoshima Prefecture. Thus, Japan refused to admit that Ryukyu was a State, or a State dually subordinated to both China and Japan. It also denied that the integration violated the Sino-Japanese Friendship Treaty, because China had already admitted that Japan was legitimately protecting the Ryukyu people in the Engagement of Beijing.[56]

[53] ibid 416. [54] ibid 419–20.
[55] Ministry of Foreign Affairs of Japan (n 45), vol 12, 182. [56] ibid 182–84.

At the same time, Shō Tukukō, the Ryukyu representative, sailed from Fujian to Tianjin to seek China's help.[57] He mentioned that the Ryukyu king was forced to abandon his city because Ryukyu was weak and did not have sufficient military force.[58] He also drafted his opinion in response to Terashima's statement, arguing that Ryukyu had never sent a diplomatic mission to Japan until the sixteenth century, while the history during the Tang Dynasty claimed by Japan was fabricated. Geographically, Ryukyu was not only close to Satsuma, but also close to Taiwan and Fujian, without evidence that it had been a part of Satsuma. Although King Shuntin came from Japan, his dynasty had already finished, while the king of the current dynasty, who received his surname from the Ming Dynasty, was not a descendent of the Japanese. Even if the fabricated history was real, Britain could not claim the United States as its territory just because the Americans came from Britain. The pledges written by the king and his officials to Satsuma were real, but they were coerced. Shō admitted the similarities in religion, language, and customs between Ryukyu and Japan, but he explained the similarities were a result of communication between both States. If these similarities could be used to justify the Japanese integration, Ryukyu could also use them to integrate Japan into itself. Furthermore, he argued that Japan had invaded Taiwan for its own and not for Ryukyu's interests. He concluded that Ryukyu, which was not dominated by Japan, only obeyed Chinese leadership.[59] Although the king consented to the Japanese integration, Shō, as his representative, clearly showed that the king was not willing to accept the integration. Although the independence of Ryukyu, which had been recognized by Western powers since 1854, implied that the Japanese integration by coercion was not justifiable, the self-interested European powers did not react nor put pressure on Japan.

The early Sino-Japanese negotiations achieved nothing: Japan's attitude was uncooperative and neither power made concessions to the other. The situation remained unchanged until 1879 when the former US President Ulysses Grant's visit to China and Japan created a chance to motivate negotiations. During his visit, a conversation took place in Tianjin between Grant and Li Hongzhang on 12 June. After getting the background information from Li, Grant asked whether China was eager to preserve the tributary relationship with Ryukyu. As a westerner, Grant might not be interested in helping China maintain its traditional order. Instead of claiming the tributary relationship, Li emphasized that Japan had violated international law. Just like European States such as Belgium and Denmark, the Ryukyu Kingdom which had already signed treaties with other powers should not be arbitrarily abolished. He also hinted that a possible Sino-Japanese war would affect the Pacific trade route from Yokohama to Shanghai and harm the US commercial opportunities. During the conversation, the assistant US ambassador Pethick William, who later became Li's adviser, helped Li by providing legal justification for US action. He quoted the first article of the Treaty of Tianjin, signed between the United States and China in 1858, which stated that 'if any other nation should act unjustly or oppressively, the United States will ... bring about an amicable arrangement of the question'. He

[57] Li (n 28), vol 32, 464. [58] ibid 444. [59] ibid 459–61.

also mentioned that it was a pity that it did not clearly state Korea and Ryukyu in the treaty, and that China was concerned about the territory instead of the tributary relationship. Grant finally agreed that the Japanese integration was 'unjust' and 'oppressive', and US mediation would be legitimate under the Treaty of Tianjin.

Concerning the Ryukyu issue, Grant made a big effort to help China. In a discussion with the Japanese ministers, Grant expressed his idea that Japan, which had already established its diplomatic relationship with China, should discuss the important issue of Ryukyu with the Chinese government, having recourse to international law. Without negotiation, this kind of problem would definitely cause a war in the West. At the same time, John Pope Hennessy, the Governor of Hong Kong who disagreed with the British ambassador Parkes's idea, also helped China to persuade the Japanese government. At first, the Japanese ministers pretended to be surprised when hearing that China saw Ryukyu as its subordinate State, and replied that Ryukyu had been subordinate to Japan while its tributes to China was just a way to obtain trading privileges. They further claimed the establishment of the Okinawa Prefecture was just like abolishing the Japanese feudal domains in the past. They also explained that they did not want to discuss the matter because of He Ruzhang's insulting words.[60] Being warned about the possibility of a war by Grant, Itō Hirobumi 伊藤博文, the new home minister, became quite worried and promised to report to the cabinet.[61] Later, Grant's follower John Russell Young notified Li Hongzhang that the Japanese Emperor Meiji was willing to keep his friendship with China forever.[62] As He Ruzhang reported, Grant, before going back to the United States, had made a proposal with the US ambassador John Armor Bingham which suggested splitting Ryukyu into three parts. The central part would still be governed by the Ryukyu king, the Okinawa prefecture would be moved to the northern part, while the southern part would be ruled by China.[63]

As a result of US mediation, China and Japan restarted negotiations in December 1879. Because both States did not wish to send officials to the other State to discuss the matter, the negotiation was mainly carried out in Tianjin by Li Hongzhang and Itō Hirobumi's friend Takezoe Shinichirō 竹添進一郎 in an informal way secretly.[64] Takezoe first explained Japan's intention of integrating Ryukyu was to prevent Russian or German expansion. He mentioned that the westerners always used international law as an excuse, and according to international law, there could be a ruler dominating two States, but not a State controlled by two rulers—like a wife who had two husbands. If Ryukyu was to be subordinated to both China and Japan, the Western States could use that as an excuse to force Ryukyu to subordinate to a third State. Therefore, Japan was rectifying Ryukyu's situation to avoid foreign invasion. In addition, Takezoe again argued that Ryukyu was publicly subordinate to Japan and only privately sending tributes to China—like a wife, committing adultery with her neighbour. China, being an adulterer, was not legitimate to argue with Japan.[65] In another conversation, he regarded the Chinese investiture as similar

[60] ibid 453–55. [61] ibid 466. [62] ibid 476. [63] ibid 477.
[64] ibid 500. [65] ibid 498.

to that granted by the Pope to the European kings in the past, while the tributes by Ryukyu only expressed its respect for a strong power. This kind of relationship was not significant enough to be used as legal arguments.[66] When Li quoted Shō Tukukō's statement claiming the pledges to Satsuma had been coerced, Takezoe ended the conversation and returned to Japan.[67] At this time, the plan of splitting Ryukyu was not mentioned.

After Li's first conversation with Takezoe, He Ruzhang also continued the negotiation in Japan. In early 1880, he reported that the new Japanese foreign minister Inoue Kaoru agreed to give China the southern part of Ryukyu, while keeping the central part under Japan. Later in March, Takezoe returned to Tianjin.[68] In this second negotiation, Li showed Takezoe the letter by He Ruzhang which mentioned Grant's proposal of splitting Ryukyu into three parts.[69] Takezoe replied that Grant's proposal was not reasonable because the northern part of Ryukyu had already been ceded to Satsuma after the invasion in 1609. Furthermore, regarding Ryukyu as one of the feudal domains in the past, Takezoe refused the idea of returning the central part to Ryukyu since all the feudal domains had been abolished. He also pointed out that it was impossible for the Ryukyu people to maintain their kingdom with only the central part of the State. He then returned to Tokyo and reported to the government.[70] Li understood that it would be impossible to get anything more from Japan by negotiation.[71] In addition, he was worried about Russian pressure on Xinjiang. In late August, he suggested accepting the Japanese concession to prevent Japan became its new enemy.[72] He then recommended that the government choose a new king to rule the southern part of Ryukyu because the former king was unlikely to be released by Japan.[73]

After Prince Gong 恭親王 of China and the Japanese ambassador Shishido Tamaki were appointed as plenipotentiary representatives, formal discussion took place in Beijing, starting in August 1880. On 22 October, Shishido reported that negotiations were complete and a treaty had been drafted.[74] Dramatically, in November, the Chinese side notified Japan that they would not sign the treaty.[75] It was because Shō Tukukō, who was proposed by China to be the new Ryukyu king, thought that the southern part of Ryukyu was too poor to support the kingdom. He expressed his objection to the treaty by crying, prostrate on the ground. In addition, Li Hongzhang was also worried that the southern Ryukyu would finally be seized by Japan because it would be difficult to survive with two islands only.[76]

Later in early 1882, the Japanese ministers Iwakura Tomomi 岩倉具視 and Inoue Kaoru invited He Ruzhang to discuss the matter, while Takezoe visited Li to negotiate again. However, China insisted that Japan had to hand over the central and southern parts of Ryukyu and no concession could be offered.[77] In March, Takezoe stated that even if Japan were to return only the southern part or the whole territory to Ryukyu, the kingdom would still be too weak to survive. Li told Takezoe

[66] ibid 499. [67] ibid. [68] ibid 525. [69] ibid 529. [70] ibid 535–56.
[71] ibid 525. [72] ibid 586. [73] ibid 589.
[74] Ministry of Foreign Affairs of Japan (n 45), vol 13, 376–79. [75] ibid 379–80.
[76] Li (n 28), vol 32, 621. [77] ibid 621.

that the temple of the Ryukyu king's ancestors was located in the capital Shuri. He thus offered another option which required Japan to return the southern islands together with Shuri to Ryukyu. Nevertheless, Takezoe rejected his idea as he thought this option was too similar to returning the whole territory.[78]

In 1883, Li Shuchang 黎庶昌, the new Chinese ambassador to Japan, proposed another solution with the Japanese minister Matsukata Masayoshi 松方正義. He suggested Japan permit China to recognize Ryukyu as a tributary state and continue giving investiture. The former king would only be granted the title of prefecture governor, but his descendants would succeed him as the governor forever. Matsukata replied that this seemed feasible, but Japan wanted to declare Ryukyu would be subordinate exclusively to Japan. However, Li Hongzhang thought that the title of prefecture governor did not correspond to the reality. More importantly, he was aware that once Ryukyu was declared Japan's subordinate State or prefecture, Japan would ultimately use this as an excuse to terminate Ryukyu's relationship with China. Also, he thought the plan was not feasible because Japan which had already controlled Ryukyu would not easily withdraw all its officials and forces.[79] As Japan had been attempting to control Korea since 1884, the Chinese ambassador made two other plans in relation with Korea. The first plan was to abandon Ryukyu in return for Japan's promise not to intervene in Korean affairs. The second was to concede some Chinese rights and privileges in Korea to Japan, in return for the Japanese consent to restoration of the Ryukyu Kingdom. However, both plans were not adopted by the Chinese government.[80]

## 4. British Perspectives on the Japanese Intervention in Ryukyu

Western international law did not guarantee or even concern itself with the integrity of communities, least of all non-Western ones. So, it is important when one moves to the next stage of the Ryukyuan story, China's intervention on its behalf from 1879 onwards, to see whether there is any Western reaction to the normative arguments used by China. The tributary system was concerned with the well-being of its circle of influence, whereas Western 'protectorates', in the colonial context, were manifestly merely stages to annexation—first, exclusion of other Western States; then, second, rapidly increasing Western control of the internal affairs of its victim, up to final annexation.

The reason for placing Britain in the centre of the picture, as evidence of Western international law and balance of power, was that it was the dominant power in the world and also the principal power in China until the end of the Manchu Dynasty in 1912. As will be seen, three-quarters of the Western interests in China were British. The basic British perspective can be seen in the exchanges between the British

[78] ibid, vol 33, 130. [79] ibid 207.

[80] See Dai Dongyang 戴東陽, 'Li Shuchang's Strategies with Regard to the Liuqiu (Ryukyu) Question before and after the December Incident of 1884 in Seoul' 甲申事變前後黎庶昌的琉球策略 *Historical Research* 歷史研究 (April 2007) 2, 98–107.

minister in Beijing and the ambassador in Tokyo, and the Foreign Secretary, Lord Salisbury. The British were concerned that the disagreement between China and Japan could break out into all-out war. This could destabilize China, with serious consequences for British commercial interests in China.[81] Perhaps the most representative despatch showing the British perspective is from Sir T Wade (minister in Peking) to the Marquis of Salisbury Peking, 18 August 1879, received in London, 18 October.[82]

The Chinese are in an awkward dilemma, because they have shown sufficient feeling about the treatment of Loochoo by Japan to make it difficult for them to retire without a word more; and if, on the other hand, they assert themselves with excess of warmth, they are certainly not as ready to strike a damaging blow as the Japanese are believed to be . . .

My colleagues, M de Butzow and M von Brandt (Germany) deplored my intervention, the latter emphatically. It was in our interest, he contended, to let the two semi-barbarous Powers, with whom negotiation is practically impossible, tear each other to pieces. All question of sympathy apart, I do not hold this opinion. A struggle between China and Japan carried on, as it can scarcely fail to be with the aid of adventurers of all flags, our own included, must for certain act prejudicially upon our trade.

I think Russian annexation of parts of Corea at the same time not impossible, and although no immediate consequence to us need be apprehended from such a proceeding, we shall be unable, I fear, to dispense with an augmentation of our squadron in these seas.

We can expect nothing at present from China herself. She is too massive to be annexed by Japan, but she is as little prepared against a *coup de main* as she was in 1874. She has vast resources, but no one fit to employ them, and all difficulties are aggravated by the corruption and incapacity of the Empress Regency.

Perhaps the next most useful comparison to draw is between how the Chinese were seen to regard their quarrel with Japan and how they knew Europeans would regard the same matter. It should not be a *casus belli.* It is clear from the despatch of Sir T Wade to the Marquis of Salisbury of 20 November 1879 that there was division within the Chinese elite as to the nature of the conflict with Japan over Loochoo. Li Hongzhang, the Grand Secretary in Tienstin, thought the Japanese could wage war, while Grand Secretary Shen in the Tsungli Yamen did not. Wade nonetheless reported Shen's lengthy views about the nature and prospect of China's dispute, with the comment that the apparent *sangfroid* 'proves nothing':

That although such issues as that between China and Japan, in western countries, do lead to wars, China, as I was aware, preferred to dispose of them by discussion. In fact, she 'owns no force but argument'.[83]

The difficulty was that the Chinese government was too confused and divided for any productive intervention on Britain's part, even although its interest in favour

[81] The primary reference point is a Confidential Print, called Loochoo (Ryukyu), 1879 FO 405/26 and I Nash (ed), *British Documents on Foreign Affairs Part I Series E Asia volume 22 Chefoo Convention and Its Aftermath 1876–1885* (University Publications of America 1994).

[82] FO 405/26 (n 81) 24; *British Documents on Foreign Affairs* (n 81), vol 22, 157

[83] FO 405/26 (n 81) 65; *British Documents on Foreign Affairs* (n 81), vol 22, 195.

of peace was extremely strong. In fact, Wade's exasperation with China was evident in the following two despatches. Li Hongzhang was indiscreetly expressing anxiety, listening to aggressive, petty advisers. Instead, he should see that China ought to 'apply herself somewhat more seriously to preparation than she has been doing'. Wade was not in favour of appeals for mediation, whether to General Grant or himself or anyone else, 'China being, in my opinion, competent to hold her own if she tries'. Still if Li 'had anything like a reasonable proposition to make that might secure adjustment of the misunderstanding with Japan, I should be happy to see what could be brought about'. The fundamental difficulty was also that while Li had devised a scheme of defence, he was overborne by his great rival, Shen 'which may be regarded as a chief among the chiefs of the reactionary majority, which unhappily governs the country'.[84]

This is not to say Britain had no interest in the matter, but rather it had no practicable way of realizing it. Another proposal coming from Germany was 'the expediency of obtaining the neutralization of the seas of China and Japan, so that in the event of a war between Western States, neither Chinese nor Japanese should be enabled to play one Power against another out here'. While Wade thought the prospect of cooperating with von Brandt, of Germany, unpromising, he did conclude that 'all foreign interests in China and especially our own, which are three-fourths of the whole, would be greatly advantaged by a common understanding of the kind I assume to be contemplated'.[85]

In the event the Chinese proposed a Joint Japanese Chinese Commission, which broke up acrimoniously with Japanese allegations that the Chinese were prevaricating, while the Chinese merely said the conclusions of the Commission were with their Throne for consideration. As to the substance of the proposals for discussion, Sir H Parkes, the British minister in Tokyo calls a halt the British correspondence in the Confidential Print, with his letters to Wade (7 March 1882) and Earl Granville (8 March 1882). He felt that the Chinese proposal to leave the Northern Islands to Japan and keep the Central and Southern for Loochoo was unrealistic, as the former were already recognized to be Japanese. He comments:

> If such a proposal be seriously contemplated by the Chinese Government, it signifies that they intend to demand that Japan shall entirely reverse all her past action and return to the *status quo*, as her right to the small northern group has, I believe, never been contested by China...
>
> According to the Foreign Minster (of Japan) ... the material condition of the people of Loochoo has been greatly improved by the change of administration, as new channels of trade have been opened up to them and they have been relieved of the burden of maintaining a large and non-productive aristocratic class.[86]

[84] FO 405/26 (n 81) 68–69; *British Documents on Foreign Affairs* (n 81), vol 22, 198–99.
[85] FO 405/26 (n 81) 69; *British Documents on Foreign Affairs* (n 81), vol 22, 199.
[86] FO 405/26 (n 81) 90; *British Documents on Foreign Affairs* (n 81), vol 2, 80–81.

Wade is not only referring to the Loochoo aristocracy, but also to the feudal Satsuma class of Japan, to which they had been subject.

While it may be fair to say that the British were never clear how, on whose behalf, or at whose request, they might have intervened in the conflict, it is also a fact that they were faced with a fait accompli by the time they became aware of the issue of Loochoo. They were not approached directly by the Loochoo authorities and, as can be seen, did not know how they could have cooperated with China. They were, finally, led to acquiesce in the prospect that modernization, through integration of Loochoo into a post-feudal Japan, was generally unproblematic, at least from the perspective of order generally in East Asia.

However, this is not to say that the British were not aware of the issues of law and ethics involved. Sir T Wade, probably also informed by the British diplomat and Japanologist Ernest Satow, discounts any Japanese attempt to argue that as a matter of modern international law Japan had a better claim to Loochoo than China. The reference point for facts on the ground was primarily Ernest Satow and he was very disparaging of the Japanese attempt to manipulate international law against China on this matter. It was clear that Ryukyu was an independent kingdom, for which the so-called vassalage system simply meant Ryukyu would look to China for support when under pressure from Japan.[87]

As already seen, the British minister's view was that there was nothing to do by 1879. He quotes Seward, the US Secretary of State considering 'the Japanese to have gone too far at Loochoo to recede, no matter who mediates. He is also persuaded that the Japanese are going no farther.'[88] Nonetheless, how the British perceived Japanese international law arguments specifically addressed to them is important for an understanding of the nature of their acquiescence in Japanese behaviour. At no point did the British think that the Japanese were the country of progress, which had international law on their side. Instead they clearly understood the injustice done to Loochoo, but could see no avenue through which to intervene. At the same time, there was no immediate or obvious geopolitical factor to drive them to reverse Japanese actions.

The Japanese tried to represent to the international community that the Chinese claimed, as a matter of international law, that Loochoo, as indeed the whole world, belonged to them. Commenting on the undoubted fact that China did receive tribute from Loochoo, the Japanese government launched a general attack on what it took to be the Chinese world view, also as applied to Loochoo. It is clear that the Japanese government was not only interested in the question of Loochoo, but also wished to challenge a Sinocentric view of the world which it represents, threatens all countries.

> We have always known (and all foreign countries now know) that it has from time immemorial been the custom of the Chinese Empire to declare all the countries of the earth to be its vassals . . .

[87] It is not intended here to consider the merits of the Chinese, Japanese, and Ryukyu arguments on Ryukyu's status.

[88] See (n 11).

Verily, the Empire of China is universal, and it behoves all nations to act guardedly, lest in dealing with their own country or other countries they are offending against the paramount claim of that Empire ... Will the Chinese Government claim to exercise its sovereign authority over Japan? It has invested our Shoguns; shall our Emperor do homage to the Emperor of China? Shall Italy and England and other Powers tremble, lest, in something they shall do, they shall infringe the paramount rights of their great overlord of China? ... The claim of the Government of China to interfere in Riu Kiu is no better founded than all these.[89]

Instead, the criterion of sovereign title to territory, argues Japan, is by 'the constant and approved practice of nations ... the uninterrupted possession of territory "whereby" one State excludes the claim of every other'. The supposition is that 'every nation will, as individuals do, seek to enjoy that which belongs to itself'. Such an acquisition of title to territory is necessary for peace's sake, among nations as among individuals. Japan concludes that 'long and firm possession, especially if practically undisputed by force, is sufficient to create a Sovereign title'.[90]

In his despatch to the Marquis of Salisbury, Sir T Wade adds the comment he had made to the Japanese minister in Peking:

I said that I had not heard such a claim as this advanced on the part of China. All that I had been told of the question was that Loochoo had been deprived of an autonomy which she had possessed for centuries, which had of course distressed the Loochooans ... he (the Japanese Minister) reminded me that China asserted dominion over all the countries named in her political geography as having brought, at any time, tribute. This is not strictly true, although all States that ever sent Missions were, as a fact, set down as tributaries. We, the English, figure in the list.[91]

Satow himself disagreed with the Japanese narrative in a memorandum that Mr Kennedy sent the Marquis of Salisbury on 13 February 1880. He points to the subjugation of Ryukyu by the Satsuma and that the Loochoo language is virtually the same as Japanese. However, the early seventeenth-century invasion and annexation still did not prevent the Loochoos from maintaining themselves on a more independent footing as regards their neighbours, as central power in Japan declined and they had only the Satsuma to deal with. The connection with Japan was always concealed from China, while the Chinese investiture system was always well known to the Japanese.[92]

Satow explains in detail the propaganda war which was going on, making it appear that the Chinese Empire was making unsubstantiated claims to territory for which it was willing to use force, while Japan was merely prepared to use self-defence to uphold its incontestable rights to territory:

It seems worthwhile to observe that the attitude of China in this question has been constantly misunderstood and misrepresented. She is frequently spoken of as laying a claim to sovereignty over Loochoo, and as disputing with Japan about proprietary rights. To exhibit

[89] FO 405/26 (n 81) 57–58; *British Documents on Foreign Affairs* (n 81), vol 22, 188–89.
[90] FO 405/26 (n 81) 59–60; *British Documents on Foreign Affairs* (n 81), vol 22, 190–91.
[91] FO 405/26 (n 81) 65–66; *British Documents on Foreign Affairs* (n 81), vol 22, 195.
[92] FO 405/26 (n 81) 84–85; *British Documents on Foreign Affairs* (n 81), vol 2, 70.

the matter in this light is no doubt of great service to Japan, as the Chinese Government, which has never exercised any authority over the islands, can thus be easily made to appear in the wrong. The real position is that the Loochooans, finding their autonomy threatened by Japan, turned to China as their nearest friend and besought her to use her influence to preserve them from being deprived of their independence. The justification for China's interference was the peculiar paternal relationship in which she had stood to Loochoo for several centuries past, while the weak and defenceless position of the petitioner, and the point of honour involved, rendered the appeal irresistible. The Loochooans have from the commencement urged their desire to remain as they were before, threatened by no one, and enjoying the friendship of their two powerful neighbours, and China has simply supported their claim . . . ..

In conclusion, I venture to submit my opinion that it suits the convenience of journalists and certain other interested persons to attribute to China claims which she has never dreamt of setting up, and to circulate rumours that she intends to support these alleged claims by an appeal to force. On the other hand, they assure the world that Japan will not relinquish her hold of the islands, which is doubtless the fact, and that she is prepared in defence of her rights, to carry the war, if necessary, into the enemy's country.[93]

## 5. Conclusion

Although a number of attempts had been made, no consensus was reached between China and Japan. The reason seemed to be simple, but it was indeed based on the cultural differences between China and the West. Compared with Japan, during the late Qing period, China was aiming at preserving the tributary system, instead of expanding its territory. Its aim was actually affected by the Confucian teaching of 'restore States that have been annexed'.[94] On the other hand, the Western powers were not interested in helping China to maintain its traditional tributary system, which might have been incomprehensible for them, and did not care about Ryukyu. Under these circumstances, it was difficult for China, without sufficient support from the Western powers, to persuade Japan to hand over the main island of Ryukyu. From an objective point of view, as the Japanese scholar Ueda Toshio suggested, it was unfortunate for both States which missed a chance of reaching the settlement based on a treaty.[95] After the First Sino-Japanese War in 1894–95, China, as a defeated State, became too weak to bargain with Japan. Possibly because Japan regarded the integration of Ryukyu as its internal affairs, the Ryukyu issue was not mentioned in the Treaty of Shimonoseki in 1895. In other words, there turned out to be no international legally binding agreement setting out Ryukyu's situation. However, based on the discussions in this chapter, Japan had indeed never presented any justification to demonstrate its legitimacy of the integration. The result of the crisis was determined by power and forces rather than legal arguments.

[93] FO 405/26 (n 81) 85; *British Documents on Foreign Affairs* (n 81), vol 2, 73–74.

[94] DC Lau tr, *Confucius* (Penguin 1979) 158–59.

[95] Ueda Toshio 植田捷雄, 'Sino-Japanese Negotiations over the suzerainty of Ryukyu' (Ryukyu no kizoku wo meguru Nisshin koushou 琉球の歸屬を繞る日清交渉), *The Memoirs of the Institute of Oriental Culture* 東洋文化研究所紀要 (September 1951) 2 200.

It did not lead to any improvement in the international order. On the contrary, it only exposed the manipulation of international law by imperialists. Restoration of the situation required the independence of Ryukyu, which was excluded from the post-war settlements. As long as the Pacific powers involved do not sit down and discuss the future of Ryukyu or Okinawa, the current status of the region will remain questionable.

# 17

# Lost in Translation in the Sino-French War in Vietnam

## From Western International Law to Confucian Semantics: A Comparative–Critical Analysis of the Chinese, French, and American Archives

*Anna Irene Baka and Qi Fei*

### 1. Introduction

This chapter deals with the Sino-French War of 1883–85 in Tonkin, an area in modern Vietnam that was colonized by the French, with an eye to shedding light as to how cultural and semantic factors interfered with the way the French and Chinese administrations perceived, interpreted, and reacted to the diplomatic and military events that led to the Tonkin War.

There were, of course, several geostrategic reasons that caused the war, such as the colonial aspirations of the Ferry government that aimed to circumvent, and thus openly clashed with, the Chinese interests in the area. We suggest, however, that the conflict was significantly exacerbated by two foundationally pervasive patterns that undermined diplomatic communication: (a) semantic contradictions due to the profound and cultural–ethical differences in the philosophies of the two administrations, as well as (b) diplomatic doubletalk due to the ideological incoherence of the French administration and the atypical organization and functioning of the Qing Empire and particularly the Tsungli Yamen.

*Administrative bilingualism:* the Third French Republic was marked with profound ideological contradictions and political instability. French nationalism and the post-revolution ideals of the French Enlightenment were clashing. Due to the ensuing ideological chasm, it appeared inevitable that the French administration would exhibit serious signs of incoherence in its external affairs. Besides, Ferry was constantly scrutinized by the French parliament which was prone to dethroning its premiers within short periods of time.

For the expansionist policy in French Indochina a considerable amount of responsibility was borne by Ferry's subordinates who were avid nationalists, such as

*Lost in Translation in the Sino-French War in Vietnam: From Western International Law to Confucian Semantics: A Comparative–Critical Analysis of the Chinese, French, and American Archives.* Anna Irene Baka and Qi Fei.  Published 2018 by Oxford University Press.

Albert Billot and French Commander Henri. After the conclusion of the Treaty of Saigon, Rivière was sent with a small military unit to Hanoi to chase the pirates from the Red River, and there he defied his instructions and captured Hanoi.[1] On the other hand, there were French officials such as Burée who adopted a pro-republican, conciliatory approach in Tonkin. The latter, after imperialist M Challemell Lacour came to power as head of the French foreign office, was disavowed and recalled. The ideological bilingualism in the French administration was a source of a series of misunderstandings with the Chinese administration; it caused significant confusion and increased suspicion among the Chinese, who had already been feeling uncomfortable as they had to deal with Western international law concepts.

Neither had the political circumstances within the Qing Empire been favourable. The Chinese administration was torn and essentially divided into two camps: the nationalists-traditional Confucianists, and the pacifists-modernists. The conflicting ideologies landed on fertile ground inasmuch as there was already a communication gap among high-ranking and low-ranking Chinese officials. Chinese rulers were almost entirely remote from the Chinese administrative process. High-ranking Chinese officials controlled sizable bulks of Chinese bureaucracy, whereas middle and low-ranking officials essentially acted as 'the conscience of the Confucian state'.[2]

There were also anthropological examples such as Li Hung-Chang. Li, was a modernist and played a central role in the Sino-Chinese controversy in Tonkin. Despite being a politically pre-eminent figure in the Qing dynasty, Li appeared indifferent to arguments based on Confucian ethics. He exercised control over the military forces in North China and enjoyed the support and loyalty of other officials. This granted him the necessary political leverage, which eventually won him the favour of the throne. Li acquired power also within the Tsungli Yamen, namely the office of foreign affairs of the Qing dynasty, which had been established in 1861, largely because other Chinese officials eschewed from taking over diplomatic intercourse with Western nations, and because of his perceptiveness of Western logic and international legal arguments. For apparent reasons, both the Tsungli Yamen and foreign States welcomed the appointment of Li in a high-ranking position in Chinese foreign affairs.

Li was a pragmatist and favoured a conciliatory policy in the Tonkin War, which ran against the militant policy of other officials in the Tsungli Yamen. Such militant policy was connected to Chinese nationalism and the dominance of Confucian morality. It is interesting to note that, despite the pre-eminent role of Confucianism in the Chinese administration and government, Confucian ideology did not create any poles but was actually diffused in all ranks, though particularly in low and middle-ranking official circles. Those who promoted the Confucian dogma were normally promoted to higher ranks, whereas disrespecting Confucian ethics essentially amounted to disrespecting the emperor.[3] This policy of favouring Confucian

[1] TF Power, *Jules Ferry and the Renaissance of French Imperialism* (Octagon Books 1977) 159.

[2] LE Eastman, *Throne and Mandarins: China's Search for a Policy During the Sino-French Controversy 1880–1885* (Harvard UP 1967) 10.

[3] ibid 17–18.

ethics within the administration must be traced back to the latter Han dynasty, where government officials were selected on the basis of strictly moral criteria, and the Chinese government encouraged moral discourse and scrutiny of the behaviour of office holders.[4] This was the so-called 'ch'ing-i', ie the 'pure criticism' or the literati of each dynasty who gradually became a type of political opposition. The purpose of the class of literati was to preserve social and political morality in the empire. Moreover, during the Qing Empire, the ch'ing-i's political opposition was mainly directed against modernization and Western-style policies. During the Sino-French War in Tonkin, the ch'ing-i became virtually identical with Chinese nationalism.[5]

*From a double language to another language:* due to the ensuing incoherence in the ethnic policies of the French and Chinese administrations, ideological bilingualism inevitably encumbered the already problematic communication between the French and the Chinese. It favoured misunderstandings and diplomatic flubs and thus overshadowed the bilateral relations of France and China before and during the Tonkin War. Ideological bilingualism was one of the main reasons for the breaking down of diplomatic talks at critical points in the conflict.

That being said, the communication chasm proved even deeper than that. Rivière's actions in Tonkin alarmed the Chinese who, for the first time, formally protested against and challenged the Treaty of Saigon on the basis of their own distinctive, Confucian understanding of their relationship with Tonkin as one of a parent state towards a 'vassal state', whereas France responded with Western-style arguments, formulated in the language of international law (France argued that what it did was only to enforce its treaty rights). It was therefore not only a matter that the two administrations used a double language, but to a certain extent, that they used *an entirely different language.*

In practical terms, all the above created paralleled semantic–legal universes expanding in the militarily heated geographical region of Tonkin. Different perceptions and understandings of the same interstate relations, of the respective rights and duties of the two States towards each other and towards Tonkin, became a time bomb set to explode once the first semantic conflict would be proven serious enough to transform into a military conflict—as indeed happened in Bac-Lê due to the radically different interpretation of the Li–Fournier Convention. France was, generally, utterly indifferent and degrading towards the Chinese and generally chose to turn a blind eye to Chinese political characteristics. The Chinese, on the other hand, were very suspicious towards the French. Chinese officials had barely begun to understand the language of international law. Some of them largely regarded the latter to be a foreign imperialist construct.

The purpose of the chapter is precisely to demonstrate and attempt to explain how the recurring breakdown of diplomatic talks between the two States was largely the product of administrative bilingualism and semantic confusion due to conflicting interpretations of such legal concepts as 'law', 'justice', 'reasonableness', 'right', 'duty', 'treaty', 'protectorate', 'vassal state', or even such pragmatic concepts as

[4] ibid 21. [5] ibid 25.

'time' and 'timely withdrawal'. How all this misunderstanding paralyzed diplomatic talks is particularly evident in the diplomatic context of international legal agreements made between France and the Court of Hué as well as France and China, and particularly the Burée and Li–Fournier/Tientsin Agreements which intended to delimit, among others, the international legal rights and jurisdiction of the two States in Cochinchina, Annam, and Tonkin. The profound confusion surrounding the rights and duties of the two nations led to the escalation of the conflict and caused two serious military incidents: the Bac-Lê ambush and the Langson incident.

The method employed in the chapter is primarily archival. It is based on French, Chinese, American Archives, and secondary sources.

## 2. Double Language in the Four Circles of Peace Negotiations

As early as the seventeenth century, France had been exerting influence in Indochina. Missionaries were sent to Vietnam and trade activities started to grow with the establishment of the French East India Company. The nineteenth century saw French expansion in Indochina accelerated. In 1862 France signed a treaty with the Vietnamese court and acquired three provinces known as Cochinchina. It is remarkable that French interests in Indochina were largely commercial with a view to opening trade roads to southern China via Tonkin. One has to take note of four international legal texts that were pivotal to the diplomatic and military Sino-French controversy: the Treaty of Saigon in 1874, the Burée Agreement in 1880, the Treaty of Hué in 1883, and the Convention of Tien-Tsin in 1884.

The Treaty of Saigon or 'le traité Philastre' for the French, was signed in 1874 between by the French delegate Paul-Louis-Félix Philastre and Nguyên Van Tuong, who represented the last precolonial Emperor of Nguyen, Tự Đức. The Treaty of Saigon provided for lasting peace, and alliance between France and the Kingdom of Annam, recognized that the whole region of Cochinchina was under French rule, and opened the commercial route to the Red River, two ports, and Hanoi, while the Kingdom of Annam became a virtual protectorate of France.[6] Although the treaty practically ended (in the eyes of France) Annam's vassalage to China, the term 'protectorate' was not explicitly used in the text. According to article 2, France recognized 'la souveraineté du roi d'Annam et son entière independence vis-à-vis de toute puissance étrangère' while promising help and protection.[7]

French ideological bilingualism made its first appearance upon the signature of the treaty. The conservative French government of that time was not particularly favourable to French expeditions in Indochina. It therefore adopted a very restrictive interpretation of the Treaty of Saigon, while the French envoy in Cochinchina adopted the same conservative line.[8] In 1877, Decazes, the French minister of foreign affairs noted that French policy towards Annam amounted to a renouncement

[6] C Fourniau, *Vietnam: Domination colonial et résistance nationale 1858–1914* (Les Indes Savantes 2002) 273.

[7] ibid. [8] ibid 282.

of the French legal right of protectorship over Annam: 'Cette politique [vis-à-vis de l'Annam] a été traversée dès l'origine par des considérations diverses qui s'imposaient à notre prudence. Sous l'empire de ces préoccupations nous avons renoncé à exercer ouvertement un protectorat qui était sans doute originairement dans les vues du négotiateur français.'[9]

In the meantime, China had not formally reacted to the Treaty of Saigon. The Chinese had not realized the profound incompatibility between their Confucian worldview, their traditional reading of interstate relations and the Western international law system 'in which all sovereign States are legally equal'.[10] What is notable is that the Vietnamese were also in the dark; they did not consider that the Eastern tradition of vassalage, as well as the Confucian tributary system applying to their relations to China, had been replaced by the Treaty of Saigon. Vietnamese kept sending their missions to Beijing on schedule, and even more so, it appears that the French conservative approach to Annam presumably encouraged a certain expansion of the diplomatic mobility between China and the Court of Hué: the latter sent an ambassador to Beijing, thus upgrading the diplomatic relations between the two States.[11] In 1879, when irregular Chinese bandits (Black Flags) began to ravage Sino-Vietnamese borders under the commander Liu Yung-fu, Tự Đức did not ask for the help of the French but, in accordance with the Confucian dogma of vassalage, he appealed to Beijing. Liu, who was practically a Chinese outlaw, essentially became 'legitimate' when Tự Đức offered him official rank for his help against the Miao tribesmen—bandits regarded as a principal threat to the stability of the area. The Chinese responded by sending troops to Vietnam, in violation of the Treaty of Saigon. For the Chinese, the Franco-Vietnamese treaty did not annul the traditional vassalage system.

The French government was at that time anti-imperialist and politically introverted. This changed in 1879 and 1880 when the President of the Third Republic, Marie de MacMahon retired and the republicans came into power under the Premiership of Jules Ferry who was an avid colonialist. This ideological shift introduced a radical change in the French policy in Vietnam. The ideological shift reflected acutely after 1881, when the French chamber decided to finance an armed expedition in Tonkin with the purpose of restoring the prestige of French authority or, pragmatically, to annex northern Vietnam. Nonetheless, there were still conservative voices within the French administration who advised against 'rushing into the adventures of a military conquest'.[12]

[9] In the same spirit, Albert Billot noted in his memoires that before 1879 France did not exercise its rights in Annam: 'Durant plusieurs années, nous n'avions manifesté par aucun acte la volonté de retenir et d'exercer le protectorat. C'est en 1879 seulement que nos intentions s'étaient affirmées ouvertement mais le malentendu était déjà complet, et l'Annam ne pouvait être ramené par de simples pourparlers à notre manière de voir. Depuis lors, pas un des Ministres, qui s'étaient succédé aux départements des Affaires étrangères et de la Marine, n'avait méconnu la nécessité d'affirmer les droits de la France, et de les mettre à l'abri des contestations, soit par un nouveau traité avec la cour de Hué, soit par d'autres mesures' (*L'affaire du Tonkin: histoire diplomatique de l'établissement de notre protectorat sur l'Annam et de notre conflit avec la Chine 1882–1885 par un diplomate*, J Hetzel (ed) (Gauthier-Villars et fils 1888) 3).

[10] Eastman (n 2) 30. [11] Fourniau (n 6) 282. [12] Eastman (n 2) 46.

The encroachment of French influence alerted Chinese officials. The Yamen realized that some form of response should have been articulated but it was unable to formulate a common policy. From 1880 onwards, the Chinese ambassador to France Zeng Jize was engaged in rounds of conversations with French high officials, although hardly any common ground could be reached. There were four important circles of diplomatic negotiations that exposed the problem of ideological bilingualism and the communication gaps between the two administrations. These were the Bourée–Li negotiations, the Fournier–Li negotiations, the Li–Tricou negotiations and the Tseng–Patenôtre negotiations.

## 2.1. The Burée–Li negotiations

In April 1882, France occupied Hanoi and the French government took a hard line on Tonkin. In late 1882, Li Hung-Chang negotiated with the French envoy, Frédéric Albert Bourée, the status of Vietnam in relation to China and France. Burée was basically an independent diplomat and a presumably conservative figure in so far as his personal initiative in Tonkin was not in line with the pro-colonial sentiments of Ferry's government. His persona and diplomatic manoeuvres produced serious confusion among the Chinese regarding the French intentions in Tonkin.

Burée exhibited apprehension, openness, and was very conciliatory. He was determined to reach a peaceful solution in Tonkin and suggested the controversy in Vietnam be resolved on the basis of a geostrategic plan that would set up a buffer zone in northern Tonkin, which would then be placed under Chinese administration. He essentially suggested, by means of a trade-off, that northern Tonkin become a Chinese protectorate in the Western sense.[13] For the Yamen this translated into French acquiescence or willingness to accept the Chinese vassalage tradition of Tonkin and, as one would have expected, Burée's proposal (known as Burée's Convention) was welcomed by the Yamen.

Burée's Convention consisted of three articles. In the first article, it was provided that the Chinese troops would be withdrawn from Tonkin and, in return, the French would declare to the Yamen that they would not conquest Vietnam or otherwise diminish its sovereignty. The second article stipulated that France would be allowed to maintain trading facilities in the south of Yunnan province, while the third article would set up a buffer zone, the northern part of which would practically become a Chinese protectorate, with the southern part being brought under French colonial administration. There was a strong indication that the Chinese would accept the Convention. In a discussion between Bourée and Li Hung-Chang, the latter asserted that he strongly believed that the provisions would be acceptable to the Yamen: 'Le Tsong-Li-Yamen ne peut encore se prononcer formellement à cet égard, mais, à première vue, ces propositions lui paraissent fort acceptables.'[14] The

[13] ibid 58.

[14] Procès-Verbal d'une entrevue de M. Bourée, Ministre de France en Chine, avec le Vice-Roi Li-Hung-Chang au palais da Vice-Roi à Tien-Tsin, le 2 Décembre 1882. Livres Jaunes, Documents Diplomatiques, Affaires du Tonkin, 2me Partie, Décembre 1882–83.

Yamen, however, did not reply immediately. The most likely explanation for this appears to have been the slow, ponderous, and ideologically fragmented Chinese bureaucratic machine. The Yamen informed the throne, which, as explained above, was detached—if not isolated—from the administration, had no knowledge of provincial matters, and it was for the very first time that it took note of Burée's proposed settlement. It is notable that the Yamen submitted the proposal to the throne *nine days after* receiving Li's suggestion.[15] The throne had mixed feelings about the settlement and thus did not react immediately. Although it is questionable whether the throne would have ultimately approved the Burée Convention, Chinese inefficiency and procrastination (no definite answer was given until March) was received very badly by the French who considered that the prolongation was unjustified, unsustainable, and even a pretext for the Chinese to gain time in order to strengthen their position in Tonkin.

In any case, the question how the throne would have ultimately reacted remains an academic question, as the French essentially withdrew their settlement proposal. This did not occur *de jure* but *de facto* because of two major events in the history of the conflict: first, because of the death of French officer Rivière; second, because Ferry came to power and placed M Challemell Lacour as the head of the French foreign office. Bourée's proposal was formally rejected on 5 March 1883 when Lacour sent a telegram to Burée informing him that his terms were not acceptable to the new government: 'Cet arrangement consacrait au profit de la Chine des concessions auxquelles il ne nous appartient pas de souscrire.'[16] M. Bourée was subsequently disavowed and recalled 'under circumstances which he regarded as a humiliation'.[17] Ferry's coming to power signalled a radical shift in French colonial policy. In a speech Ferry declared that '[i]t would be anti-French to forbid the Republic to have a colonial policy' whereas, when discussing the relations between France and China he said that 'the negotiations that we have begun with China have not succeeded because China has no interest in outstripping accomplished facts ... faced with accomplished facts, Asiatic good sense bows and accepts them'.[18] The radical change in French policy produced disastrous diplomatic equivocation that had an impact on how the Chinese administration received subsequent French proposals for a settlement of the dispute in

[15] Eastman (n 2) 64.

[16] Fourniau (n 6) 318. Télégramme de M. Lacour, Ministre des Affaires étrangères, à M. Bourée, Ministre de France en Chine, Paris, le 5 Mars 1883, Livres Jaunes, Documents Diplomatiques, Affaires du Tonkin, 2me Partie, Décembre 1882–83, No 166. 'Il n'est pas tenu, dans l'arrangement dont vous avez pris l'initiative au sujet du Tonkin, un compte suffisant de notre situation conventionnelle. Cet arrangement, consacrerait, au profit de la Chine, des concessions auxquelles il ne nous appartient pas de souscrire. Pour bien marquer notre sentiment à cet égard, je me vois, à regret, dans la nécessité de mettre fin à votre mission. En attendant vos lettres de rappel, vous vous appliquerez à établir que notre décision n'implique aucune pensée d'hostilité contre la Chine, notre seul but étant d'assurer l'ordre au Tonkin dans les conditions du Traité de 1874.'

[17] J Davids (ed), *American Diplomatic and Public Papers: The United States and China, 1861–1893* (Scholarly Resources Inc 1979); Young to Frelinghuysen, 8.8.1883, Peking: Ministers' Dispatches, China: Dispatch 230, Roll 66.

[18] Power (n 1) 169.

Tonkin. Burée's reaction to Lacour's telegram was a desperate last appeal to China for the avoidance of war.[19]

## 2.2 The Li–Tricou negotiations

In May 1883, Tricou was ordered to take the place of Burée in the negotiations with Li Hung-Chang, the envoy of China. The French rejection of the Burée Convention created a wave of mistrust both to the throne and the Yamen. Confucian ideas became prominent in Chinese administration because the nationalistic influence of the literati scaled up. In this new ideological context, Beijing ordered Li Hung-Chang to continue talks with the French with a view to 'restoring the prestige of the military' despite the latter's reservations. Li was anxious to avoid a fight with the French and, despite advancing several reasons against his appointment, he had no choice but to assume command. He actually regarded his appointment as a direct threat to his career, political suicide, and in fact 'a plot of his enemies to ruin him'.[20] Li, being very percipient and astute, was fully aware of the administrative and military difficulties faced by China, and most significantly the ideological and operational fragmentation in both the Chinese administration and the military. He knew that the only safe way to either peace or victory was unity of action and thought, and this philosophy of his he projected on the negotiations with Tricou.

The negotiation process could only be described as confrontational. The Chinese were particularly alarmed because of the radical shift in French colonial policy. This led to diplomatic escalation. When Li, who had become suspicious, asked Tricou how the Chinese were supposed to know when and whether in fact they were dealing with France, Tricou presumably responded by saying that 'M. Bourée was not a good minister. His country repudiated and recalled him.'[21] Tricou repelled Li's criticism of France's bilingual tactics and his subsequent insistence that, in order to be trustworthy, French policy should be consistent and unitary, by responding that the French Assembly never had the necessary unanimity for this.[22] For Li, however, it was unjust to hold China responsible 'for acts which only a few months ago were done with the sanction of the French minister, and presumably with the knowledge and approval of the French Government'.[23] Li asserted that China had translated

[19] Télégramme de M. Bourée, Ministre de France en Chine à M. Lacour, Ministre des Affaires étrangères, Shanghaï, le 7 mars 1883, Livres Jaunes, Documents Diplomatiques, Affaires du Tonkin, 2me Partie, Décembre 1882–83, No 167. 'J'allais vous mander qu'une Ambassade annamite, partie de Canton le 4, se dirige vers Pékin pour adresser un appel désespéré à la Chine, au moment où j'ai reçu votre télégramme du 5. Votre refus de souscrire aux arrangements dont le Département avait, à deux reprises, admis le principe, nous rejette dans l'inconnu le plus inquiétant; votre éclatant désaveu réduit, d'ailleurs, ici mon rôle à néant, je doute que l'on ait pu peser à Paris toutes les conséquences de la détermination que vous me notifiez et dans laquelle je fais abstraction des considérations qui me sont personnelles.'

[20] Eastman (n 2) 75.

[21] Davids (n 17) 25–163, no 6, 8.8.1883; Dispatch 230, Young to Frelinghuysen, Peking: Ministers' Dispatches, China: Roll 66.

[22] ibid. [23] ibid.

the French reversal of tactics as a conspiracy of Western nations against it, and confirmation that it had no friends.[24]

Li's case exhibits how the element of fear and his personal inability to strike a balance between the then prominent nationalistic ideology of the literati and his own patriotic ideology and awareness that a military encounter would be catastrophic for China, determined the outcome of diplomatic talks with Tricou. It is interesting to note, though, that Li was sincere with Tricou as to how difficult his position was and how the shadow of Beijing constricted him: 'What can I say to the Yamen? Now can I make face with my government? They expect me to fight France, and how can I satisfy them?'[25] Li's fears were not without reason. According to Chinese archives he had been harassed by the literati and other pro-war Chinese officials: 'I am plagued by the irresponsible talk of officials not in positions of authority ... They discuss matters of policy, and after matters of policy they discuss men. Most engage in bullying.'[26] The *coup de grâce* to the diplomatic round of talks between Li and Tricou was given when the former was informed of the content of a telegraph which essentially confirmed that the French policy in Vietnam lacked the necessary legitimacy because 'the Vietnamese affair is being run according to the dictates of political parties without unanimous approval of the people', that the French political parties were composed entirely of opportunists, and would just continue to advance unless the Chinese rendered them a setback.[27] Even so, Li was not convinced that military involvement in hostilities with France would be the right answer to the puzzle. A day after the telegram, Li sent a memorial to Beijing advising the throne against going to war with France. He, however, had to wait for imperial orders that never arrived.

Li played this out by asserting to Tricou that China did not and would not recognize the Treaty of Saigon and that diplomatic points of controversy had to be referred directly to Beijing because his mandate was limited and he did not possess the necessary plenipotentiary powers: 'Je n'ai plus de pouvoirs; ils sont aujourd'hui entre les mains du Marquis de Zeng Jize. Tout ce que je peux dire, c'est que nous n'avons jamais reconnu et que nous ne reconnaîtrons jamais le traité (franco-annamite) de 1874'.[28] Tricou, who has already been complaining that the negotiations with Li never advanced, was outraged. Despite Tricou's attempts to resume talks with Li, the latter was negative and unreceptive. Again, the French thought that the Chinese procrastination tactics were deliberate.

## 2.3 The Li–Fournier negotiations

The collapse of the Li–Tricou talks signalled military escalation and enhanced mobility in both camps. The French army began to expand northward in Vietnam, while the Chinese army responded by constructing defence in the area and engaging the French military forces in a series of battles. Billot had changed his avid pro-colonialist policy and observed that, due to the situation in Europe, it would

[24] ibid. [25] ibid. [26] Quoted in Eastman (n 2) 82. [27] ibid 80.
[28] Billot (n 9) 60; Eastman (n 2) 77.

have been imprudent to enter full-scale war with China and disregard the possibility of a settlement. For this reason, soon after the Li–Tricou negotiations had failed, the French minister of foreign affairs, Chameller-Lacour, proposed to the Marquis Zeng Jize in Paris the drafting of a memorandum, known as the 'September 15 Memorandum' in 1883 which basically replicated the Burée Convention, only this time it explicitly provided for a buffer zone between Northern Vietnam, under Chinese administration, and Southern Vietnam, under French occupation. The new proposal was rejected by Zeng. There are two possible explanations for that. First, due to the French offensive, Chinese levels of intolerance were scaled up. The literati nationalistic movement had at that time become very powerful—presumably exercising renewed pressures upon Chinese diplomats.[29] Second, the rejection could have been (also) connected to Zeng's foresight that under the new memorandum, the buffer zone would not have been in reality neutral but controlled by Annamists and thus, essentially, by the French. For Zeng, who was a Confucian, rapprochement between two great powers should have been avoided because it could become a source of misunderstandings.[30] The Chinese tradition of vassalage meant that a great power must use small neighbouring States as buffer zones.

As the rapprochement failed, the hostilities between the two armies resumed. In August 1883, the French forced the Vietnamese to sign a new treaty, the Treaty of Hué that broadened the scope of the treaty of Saigon by explicitly and equivocally reducing Vietnam to a French protectorate. The signing of the Treaty of Hué as well as the renewed French offensive increased the pro-war sentiment of the Chinese administration. The rising literati movement had an impact on Chinese imperial policy. On 16 November, the Yamen issued a formal declaration to France that if for any reason imperial troops met any French troops in Tonkin that would be a *casus belli*.[31]

In December 1883, France gained a victory in Son-Tay, a city long guarded by the Chinese army, and caused the Chinese army to retreat. After the fall of Son-Tay came the fall of Bac-Ninh, Hung-Hoa and Thai-Nyuyen. The French military victory lifted the morale of the French army. Beijing's declaration that a French attack against imperial forces would signal a war with China never materialized. The throne hesitated, wishing to avoid open hostilities, although powerful ch'ing-i officials kept desiring war and a French defeat. However, because the military situation had deteriorated significantly for the Chinese, the throne had no choice but to reconsider the path of diplomacy. In May 1884, French envoy Fournier began talks with Li Hung-Chang.

[29] Eastman (n 2) 89.

[30] 'Dans l'entretien qu'il avait eu le 21 juin avec M. Ferry, le représentant de la Chine avait longuement développé ce qu'on a, depuis lors, appelé la théorie des tampons. D'après lui, le contact de deux Puissances, de mœurs et de civilisations différentes, pourrait devenir une cause de mésintelligence. Entre deux grands États comme la France et la Chine, il fallait interposer des tampons. Si la France étendait sa souveraineté ou son protectorat sur tout l'Annam, il y aurait contact et froissement. Au contraire, si la France consentait à laisser une partie de l'Annam, contiguë à la Chine, en dehors de son protectorat, le tampon existerait: partant, plus de froissements ni motifs de rupture' (Billot (n 9) 91).

[31] Eastman (n 2) 96.

The Li–Fournier negotiations exposed, more than in any previous diplomatic rapprochement, the distorting effect the literati had on Chinese administration, diplomats, and even the throne itself. It also revealed French ignorance and, most fundamentally, the chasm in communication between the two administrations. Li was in a very difficult position, for he had to manage and reconcile two opposing and equally hostile poles of pressure: the French and the rising ch'ing-i. He knew in advance that due to France's militarily favourable position he would have to make significant concessions, which would be anathema to the literati. For this reason, he requested assertions and backing from the throne as well as precise instructions as to the uppermost limits of his mandate, ie what type of concessions he could never make to Fournier. After a convocation of the Grand Council, the prevalent sentiment was pro-war, but many higher-ranking officials feared that the forthcoming negotiations would be another trick—another Burée fiasco. Moreover, there was a vicious attack by the ch'ing-i against Li Hung-Chang. He was bullied, charged of weakness and credulity. He was believed to be easily deluded by the enemy, was accused of corruption, and it was even requested that he be put to death.[32] Despite the vitriolic attacks, the throne disregarded the ch'ing-i and preserved its trust in Li who was given the necessary instructions—a set of four principles that were not to be compromised: (a) the vassalage with Vietnam; (b) the prohibition of trade by the French in Yunnan province; (c) that Black Flags should not be eradicated; and (d) that China must not pay an indemnity.[33]

The pourparlers were obscure and controversial. Fournier suggested, and Li ultimately accepted, the violation of two of the Chinese principles: first, the attack against the Black Flags; second, the *immediate* withdrawal of the imperial troops from Tonkin and their return to the Chinese frontier, ie an open admission that the Chinese had no right over Vietnam. It has been documented that Li understood the content of this agreement and purposely distorted the conversation and the clauses to the Yamen, in order to escape reaction from the ch'ing-i and be able to conclude the agreement with the French. To this effect, he informed the Yamen that there would be no violation of the four principles and that the imperial troops would remain in their current locations.[34] A possible explanation of Li's controversial behaviour is that he maintained two different communication channels: one with the Yamen and one, directly, with the throne.[35] It appears that he attempted to avoid the Yamen by withholding information that would have placed him in a difficult position. He risked making this commitment as he also miscalculated the position of the imperial troops: his impression was that the imperial troops had already retreated to Lang-Son and Lao-Kay, two Vietnamese cities very close to the Chinese frontier.[36] In other words, Li succeeded in setting up a temporary 'reconciliation' between the two States, by effectively circumventing the Yamen and by concealing from

[32] ibid 117–18. [33] ibid 119. [34] ibid 121.

[35] This can be derived from the fact that, although the Yamen was never formally informed of the true content of the Li–Fournier Convention, the throne does not appear to have reacted as viciously to the final document (ibid 124).

[36] ibid 121.

the French such important information as the true intentions of the Yamen, the ideological struggle within the Chinese administration, and the tense relation between himself, the Yamen, and the throne. By silencing all these powerful pro-war voices, the agreement was therefore, from the very beginning, fundamentally distorted yet seemingly valid from the perspective of international law.

The Li–Fournier Convention explicitly provided that the Celestial Empire was obliged to (a) withdraw its forces from Tonkin to its own frontiers; (b) respect in the future all treaties directly concluded between France and Vietnam; and (c) allow the free traffic of goods among France, Vietnam, and China over the whole extent of the latter's southern frontiers, thus practically allowing France to have trade access to Yunnan. The trade-off was in article III, where France renounced its right to ask for an indemnity from China. The convention would be provisional to the extent that, once signed, the plenipotentiaries of the two governments would have to meet in three months' time to work out the details of a definite treaty that would also settle the commercial details of the agreement. After receiving the final document, the throne expressed suspicion by noting that the French were filled with 'treacherous schemes' and the final treaty must be 'drafted with the utmost care to deprive the crafty barbarians of loopholes'.[37] This was a landslide victory for France.

The Li–Fournier Convention was killed by the Bac-Lê incident. Ambiguous treaty terms such as the absence of a concrete withdrawal date led to an unexpected fight in Bac-Lê where France was hit by an ambush and suffered a defeat.[38] One of the Convention's most prominent ambiguities was the determination of the time of withdrawal of the imperial forces from Vietnam. The definition of 'immediacy' gave rise to heated diplomatic exchanges after the Bac-Lê incident.

After the signature of the Convention, Fournier appeared to have suspected that the withdrawal provision was not incontestably clear and so he feared that the lack of exactness might give rise to subsequent controversial interpretations. He thus (argued to have) proposed to Li the conclusion, on 17 May 1884, of an additional memo that would provide for specific dates for the withdrawal of the Chinese army from Tonkin and the subsequent taking over by the French. According to French archives, the memo stipulated that, twenty days after the signature of the Li–Fournier Convention, the Chinese would have withdrawn from Tonkin and the French would be able to occupy Lang-Son, Cao-Bang, Chat-Khé, and all those areas of Tonkin adjacent to the frontiers of Kouang-Tong and Kouang-Si during which time the French would be able to establish naval stations along the whole coast of Tonkin. Forty days after the signature of the Li–Fournier Convention, the French would be able to occupy Lao-Kaï and all the territories of Tonkin adjacent to Yunnan. After the expiration of these dates, the French would have the right to expel Chinese forces from Tonkin.[39]

[37] ibid 125.

[38] It has been documented that the Chinese troops in Bac-Lê never received an official order to withdraw (Fourniau (n 6) 336).

[39] 'Après un délai de vingt jours, c'est-à-dire le 6 juin, nous pourrons occuper Lang-Son, Cao-Bang, Chat-Khé et toutes les places du territoire tonkinois adossées aux frontières du Koùang-Tong et du Kouang-Si; à la même date, nous pourrons établir des stations navales sur toute l'étendue des côtes

The existence of the memo was questioned by the Yamen, which insisted that the only legal text regulating the withdrawal of the imperial forces was the Li–Fournier Convention. There is diplomatic correspondence involving both the French ambassador in Beijing, Vicomte de Sémalle, and the Chinese ambassador to Paris, Li Fong-Pao, on the Yamen's alleged ignorance of the memo, but at the same time its willingness to abide by the second article of the Tien-Tsin/Li–Fournier Convention regarding the eventual withdrawal of the imperial forces.[40] It is remarkable that according to French archives, Li Hung-Chang did not deny that Fournier had indeed suggested the conclusion of such memo, but he asserted that he never gave his consent to the dates proposed by the French envoy.[41] This was also subsequently confirmed by the Yamen, which officially denied the existence of such a document.[42] Another argument put forth by the Yamen was that the concept of 'immediacy' was not self-evident because the Li–Fournier Convention did not stipulate exact dates for the withdrawal of the Chinese forces, which were to be eventually defined in the final treaty that would settle the details of the arrangement between France and China three months after the provisional Li–Fournier Convention.[43]

Based on the archives, one cannot tell with absolute certainty whether something was really agreed between Li and Fournier on 17 May 1884. What is obvious is that

du Tonkin. Après un délai de quarante jours, c'est-à-dire le 26 juin, nous pourrons occuper Lao-Kaï et toutes les places du territoire du Tonkin adossées au territoire du Yunnan. Ces délais expirés, nous procéderions sommairement à l'expulsion des garnisons chinoises attardées sur le territoire du Tonkin' (Livres Jaunes 1884, Documents Diplomatiques, Affaires du Tonkin, Convention de Tien-Tsin du 11 mai 1884, Incident de Lang-son, Remise par le Commandant Fournier à Li Hung-Chang, le 17 Mai 1884, No 17, p 17).

40 'Le Tsong li-Yamén ne songe pas à nier que les troupes impérials dussent être rappelées sans délai et déclare qu'il se mettait en devoir d'exécuter l'article 2 de la Convention de Tien-Tsin, lorsqu' est survenu le fâcheux incident de Lang-Son ... Le départ de ces troupes, comme le fait observer le Tsong-li-Yamen, oblige en outre à des dispositions qui ne pouvaient être prises dans le trop court laps de temps proposé par M. le Commandant Fournier. Il résulte bien de ces explications que le Gouvernement impérial n'a jamais eu l'intention de se soustraire à l'exécution de la Convention de Tien-Tsin, et j'espère que Votre Excellence trouvera dans cette dépêche les assurances qu'elle a réclamées dans sa lettre du 4 Juillet' (Livres Jaunes 1884 (n 38) M. Li Fong-Pao, Ministre de Chine à Paris, à M. Jules Ferry, Président du Conseil, Ministre des Affaires étrangères, Paris le 10 Juillet 1884, No 40, p 35).

41 'Je me permets d'appeler vôtre attention sur cette déclaration que Son Exc. le Gouverneur général du Tçhëli n'avait pas cru pouvoir donner son assentiment à la demande que lui avait adressée le Commandant Fournier, au moment de son départ, de fixer des datés précises et rapprochées pour le retrait des troupes chinoises du Tonkin, et qu'il n'existe aucun document servant à prouver qu'un arrangement avait été conclu à ce sujet' (Livres Jaunes 1884 (n 38) M. Li Fong-Pao, Ministre de Chine à Paris, à M. Jules Ferry, Président du Conseil, Ministre des Affaires étrangères, Paris le 10 Juillet 1884, No 40, p 35).

42 Livres Jaunes 1884 (n 38) Télégramme, Le Tsong-li Yamen à M. Li Fong-Pao, Ministre de Chine à Paris, Pékin, le 8 Juillet 1884, No 40, Annex No 1, p 37.

43 'Ils prétendent qu'aucun passage du Traité de Tien-Tsin ne stipule l'évacuation dé Lang-Son et ne fixe une date pour l'évacuation d'aucun point du Tonkin. J'ai invoqué l'article 2 du Traité, et comme on a soutenu que le texte chinois n'était pas conforme au texte français, j'ai invoqué l'article final, aux termes duquel ce dernier texte fera seul foi. Malgré cela, les membres du Tsong-li-Yamen déclarant que l'évacuation, dans leur pensée, n'a jamais dû avoir lieu avant la signature de l'arrangement définitif' (Livres Jaunes 1884 (n 38) M. le Vicomte de Sémalle, Chargé d'Affaires de France à Pékin, à M. Jules Ferry, Président du Conseil, Ministre des Affaires étrangères, Pékin, le 29 Juin 1884, No 27, p 23).

Li was torn, for he knew that should he dare to transmit the memo to the Yamen he would be committing political suicide. On the other hand, one can hardly imagine that he denied discussing the memo without giving it a second thought, since the recently concluded peace agreement would be jeopardized. It appears, however, that Li had indeed agreed, in principle, to the troop evacuations on the basis of the time schedule provided in the memo.[44] Fournier reported in his memoires that Li informed Fournier that he would undertake the dispatch of the necessary orders himself without involving the Yamen. This is why Fournier presumably used a pencil and crossed out from the memo the contentious article referring to the evacuation of Chinese troops from Tonkin (because that part of the memo would not be transmitted to the Yamen). Although Fournier performed his part of the agreement by informing General Charles Millot about the dates, Li apparently did not, presumably because he did not expect that the French army would be able to occupy Tonkin any time soon. This was a gamble that did not end well, since Li was unaware that there were Chinese troops several kilometres further south than where he initially thought. When he was informed that French troops were approaching, he reportedly sent a telegram to the Yamen about the memo. Although that occurred five days before the Bac-Lê incident, the throne instructed the troops to stand fast, as immediate withdrawal would be a display of weakness.[45] Possibly because of ch'ing-i reactions, the Chinese position hardened and fighting broke out. According to this scenario, the literati, whose influence in the Chinese administration had strengthened, were determined to kill the Li–Fournier Convention, which they regarded as unsatisfactory. Indeed, it seems that Li attempted, to the knowledge of the throne, to circumvent the pro-war advocates. However, their influence was overwhelming and the ch'ing-i succeeded in overshadowing Li Hung-Chang and his supporters. Needless to add that the ambiguities surrounding the Li–Fournier Convention as well as the controversies regarding the 17 May memo, such as the fact that there was no duplicate, that the only copy was allowed to remain in the hands of the Chinese signatory plus the (intentional?) crossing out of the most crucial passage, were aggravating elements against the successful implementation of the Li–Fournier Convention.

## 2.4 The Tseng–Patenôtre negotiations

After the Bac-Lê incident the French government became enraged and subsequently issued an ultimatum demanding an indemnity. It also became clear to the French that there was a serious problem of diplomatic communication with the Chinese, which Fournier had described as 'Les fourberies chinoises' (ie Chinese double-dealings).[46] Despite ill feelings from both sides the peace negotiations did not cease. Only this time, the Chinese through Tseng Kuo-ch'iian who was governor general of the Liang- Kiang provinces, would have to negotiate with Jules Patenôtre

[44] It is claimed that Li had indicated to the Kwangsi troops that the French would advance on the specific dates of the memo (Eastman (n 2) 127).

[45] ibid 130. [46] ibid 131.

who was also the nephew of Jules Ferry. Patenôtre's mandate was to ask Beijing to conform to the Li–Fournier Convention, particularly the second article relating to the immediate withdrawal of the imperial forces from Tonkin, and also demand a heavy indemnity from the Chinese for bad faith because of the Bac-Lê incident. Beijing acquiesced in the first demand, by clarifying, however, that the withdrawal of the imperial forces was made in accordance with the three-month limit that was set out in the Li–Fournier Convention (clearly contradicting previous interpretations of the second article by the Chinese).[47] The Yamen protested to France against the second demand for an indemnity. It moreover argued that, since the two States are not at war, the question of indemnity was unlawful according to international law.[48]

The Tseng–Patenôtre negotiations were marked with another serious controversy. The Chinese initially informed Paris that Tseng only had the mandate to negotiate questions related to the specification of the Li–Fournier/Tien-Tsin Convention, ie the final peace treaty, and not the indemnity question, which was 'specifically reserved for the throne'.[49] Either because the Yamen had started becoming familiar with international law arguments, or due to its own ideological struggles, it appears to have changed this position twice.[50] The change of policy resulted into two contradicting telegrams that confused Ferry and terrified Li Fong-Pao who, being aware of the ch'ing-i bullying practices, begged Ferry to dispatch to him written affirmation that he made no alterations to the two telegrams.[51]

The Sino-French War broke out in the end. The French navy attacked Fujian and destroyed Fuzhou shipyard. Then it moved on and attacked Tamsui and Keelung in Taiwan. In land battles, the Chinese and French armies continued to fight in Tonkin. In January 1884, Robert Hart, a British official working at the Chinese Imperial Customs, sent his subordinate Campbell to Paris. Campbell got in contact with Jules Ferry, President of the Council and Minister of Foreign Affairs, and

[47] 'Conformément à la Convention du 11 mai, on doit dans le délai de trois mois discuter un Traité définitif sur les bases contenues dans les quatre premiers articles. Comme ce délai va expirer, il est nécessaire d'exécuter aujourd'hui l'article 2' (Livres Jaunes 1884 (n 38) Incident de Lang-son, M. Patenôtre, Ministre de France en Chine à M. Jules Ferry, Président du Conseil, Ministre des Affaires étrangères, No 54, p 53).

[48] Livres Jaunes 1884 (n 38) Son Exc. Li Hung-Chang à M. Li Fong-Pao, Tien-Tsin, le 20 Juillet 1884, No 61, p 60. 'Comme il n'y a pas guerre entre la France et la Chine, une demande indemnité lui paraît contraire aux lois internationales. En cas de conflit, la Chine décline toute responsabilité en ce qui concerne la protection des sujets étrangers, des marchands, des chrétiens, etc. dans les ports ouverts, quelles que soient les pertes éprouvées par eux. Le devoir des Puissances est, d'après lois internationales, de nous refuser armes, munitions, vivres, approvisionnements de toutes sortes. Les Représentants étrangers sont priés d'informer leurs Gouvernements par le télégraphe' (Livres Jaunes 1884 (n 38) M. Patenôtre, Ministre de France en Chine à M. Jules Ferry, Président du Conseil, Ministre des Affaires étrangères, Shanghai, le 21 Juillet 1884, No 60, p 59).

[49] Eastman (n 2) 141.

[50] Livres Jaunes 1884 (n 38) Télégramme, Son Exc. Li Hung-Chang à M. Li Fong-Pao, Ministre de Chine à Paris, à M. Jules Ferry, Président du Conseil, Ministre des Affaires étrangères, Tien-Tsin, le 20 Juillet 1884, No 61, p 60; Télégramme, M. Patenôtre, Ministre de France en Chine à M. Jules Ferry, Président du Conseil, Ministre des Affaires étrangères, Shanghai, le 25 Juillet 1884, No 65, p 63.

[51] Livres Jaunes 1884 (n 38) Télégramme, M. Li Fong-Pao, Ministre de Chine à Paris, à M. Jules Ferry, Président du Conseil, Ministre des Affaires étrangères, Paris, le 27 Juillet 1884, No 68 p 66.

negotiated a peace treaty directly with him. The peace treaty was finally signed in 1885 in which China agreed to recognize the Li–Fournier Convention.[52]

## 3. From a Double Language to Another Language: the Confucian Response to Western Legal Semantics

We have so far examined how conflicting political ideologies within the French and Chinese administrations produced polyphonies, semantic inconsistencies—essentially a doubletalk that undermined the four diplomatic rounds of the Sino-French negotiations. One has to add to this equation certain translation problems,[53] and a series of intentional, and unintentional, reversal of tactics, such as the initial communication that France did not intend to conquer Tonkin but only improve its administration and assist the latter's police against the Black Flags.[54] The legal and diplomatic misunderstandings that ensued subverted confidence in both camps, and, inevitably, poisoned bilateral talks, filling them with suspicion and distrust.[55] The question is whether all these misunderstandings were the result of personal mischief and failures of the particular negotiators, or whether they expressed a deeper chasm of communication: a more profound inability of the two administrations to understand the political and administrative idiosyncrasy of the other side. In other words, one has to wonder whether the war could have been avoided.

The answer to this is not straightforward. As much as it follows from the French archives that the French had some knowledge of the influence of the literati in the process of Chinese decision-making,[56] their diplomatic choices do not reveal that this knowledge was somehow absorbed and transformed into policy. It also appears that the Chinese, particularly the circle of the literati and the Chinese ambassadors, were becoming familiar with Western semantics and the language of international

[52] Fourniau (n 6) 344.

[53] Huan-Lai Cho, *Les origines du conflit Franco-Chinois à propos du Tonkin jusqu'en 1883* (Jouve & cie 1936); Livres Jaunes, Documents Diplomatiques, Affaires du Tonkin, Deuxième Partie, Décembre 1882–83, Annexe I à la Dépêche de Shanghai du 20 Décembre 1882, Procès-Verbal d'un entretien entre M. Bourée, Ministre de France en Chine, et le Vice-Roi Li-Hung-Chang, au Consulat de France a Tien-Tsin, le 27 novembre 1882, p 34: 'Le Ministre explique que, par la faute de son interprète, sans doute, le Marquis Zeng a envoyé au Ministère des Affaires étrangères des communications officielles fort inconvenantes, tout au moins dans la forme.'

[54] 'Comme je m'y attendais, on s'en est montré très satisfait; un passage notamment a été particulièrement, agréable, c'est celui dans lequel j'insiste sur notre intention formelle de ne pas conquérir le Tonkin, mais seulement d'en améliorer l'administration et d'en assurer la police dans notre intérêt comme dans celui de tout le monde, la Chine comprise' (Livres Jaunes (n 53) M. Bourée, Ministre de France en Chine, à M. Duclerc, Ministre des Affaires étrangères, Pékin, le 3 Novembre 1882, No 150, p 6).

[55] 'Les fonctionnaires chinois ne croient pas que nous puissions agir loyalement dans nos rapports avec eux, et ils cherchent toujours dans nos déclarations les plus simples et les plus droites des arrière-pensées du genre de celles qu'ils garderaient eux mêmes vis-à-vis de nous, si les rôles étaient renversés' (Livres Jaunes (n 53) M. Bourée, Ministre de France en Chine, à M. Duclerc, Ministre des Affaires étrangères, Pékin, le 3 Novembre 1882, No 150, p 5).

[56] ibid 22.

law, which, interestingly enough, they did not all regard as a foreign imperialist construct.

It is remarkable, for instance, how Marquis Zeng Jize, the Chinese ambassador to Paris before the Li–Fournier talks, rather skilfully used international law arguments, which is also probably one reason why he irritated the French who asked for his removal as precondition for starting the Li–Fournier talks in Tien-Tsin. Zeng Jize was not a typical example of ch'ing-i. His skilfulness and independent thinking was related to his education and unique personality. Zeng Jize's early education included extensive reading of the classics such as the Four Books and the Five Classics, Records of the Grand Historian, Book of Han, Zhuangzi, and Han Yu's essays, which constituted typical elite- Confucian education for literati. His father, however, left him enough room to develop hobbies of his own. Zeng Jize grew up not very interested in the imperial exam (the entry exam for higher officials, the ruling class of the Qing dynasty), degrees, or positions like the other literati. He was said to be fond of learning foreign languages and to have a special eye for Western learning. He was under the influence of Guo Songtao, a close friend of his father and a fellow Hunanese and had frequent contact with WAP Martin, a missionary keen to spread the knowledge of international law in China. During his term as minister to Britain, France and Russia (1880–81), he successfully renegotiated the 1879 Treaty of Livadia with Russia; also the Treaty of Saint Petersburg 1881 which minimized China's loss to Russia. Zeng's efforts in the Sino-Russian dispute were regarded as a diplomatic victory—a rarity in late Qing diplomacy.

Despite (or even because of) Zeng Jize's and Li's cases which brought about a certain semantic rapprochement with Western legal thought, it became evident that the communication chasm with France was considerable and paved the way to the undeclared Sino-French War. There were profound philosophical differences between the two States, which could not have been easily bridged. It is revealing that in one diplomatic correspondence reported in the American archives, M Challemel Lacour appeared extremely confused.[57] The two States had fundamental differences in their respective philosophies and theories of international relations. Their approaches to international law induced very different understandings of the international legal order; the protectorship system; the element of silence and acquiescence; time and historic titles; justice and reasonableness. Although for China and Zeng Jize these semantic universes could have existed in parallel, for France that was hardly the case. Burée was the only French diplomat who considered that there was not necessarily a contradiction between the two legal philosophies and that they could in fact coexist: 'Votre Altesse me dit aujourd'hui que la Chine a des droits de suzeraineté sur l'Annam; mais c'est là un point qui n'est nullement mis en cause, et je ne vois pas quel intérêt il y aurait à le discuter, puisque rien dans notre conduit n'implique la négation du principe que vous voulez rappeler. Pourquoi, dès lors, nous placer sur un terrain où l'accord serait difficile à

[57] Davids (n 17) 283–355, no 27, 24.12.1883; Dispatch 308, Young to Frelinghuysen, Peking: Ministers' Dispatches, China: Roll 68.

établir entre nous plutôt que de rechercher ce qui nous rapproche, en confondant nos intérêts?'[58]

## 3.1 Law and reasonableness

Against the Western, legal positivist dissociation between law and morality, Confucianists cannot fathom how any system of law can be either unethical or unreasonable. Law and reasonableness are interrelated. According to the traditional Confucian philosophy, one should use reasonableness to make decisions. Where reason rests, people are indomitable and cannot be defeated by force.[59] Zeng Jize stressed reasonableness and attached great importance to its role in foreign affairs. He believed that even though the cultural gap between East and West is vast, there is a shared common ability to perceive, understand, and judge things and relations. If Chinese reason appeals to Western common senses, a strong argument could be made to China's advantage. He was quite optimistic about reasonableness in that it cannot be defeated by force. But what is this 'reason' Zeng Jize advocated so passionately? There is no answer from Zeng Jize's writings to the question, but if we look to the writings of Guo Songtao, one of his major intellectual influences, we make some interesting discoveries.

Guo's understanding of the relationship between reason and power shares a striking similarity with Zeng Jize's. In his diary, he described the relationship as follows:

> Everything I say is backed by reason. For three generations, to console and defend ourselves from the barbarians, despite the passage of time and the differing responses, it has been fair to use reason as a standard of judgement. Since the Zhou Dynasty there have been border problems, there's something we cannot fight against. That is power. There is also something thousands of generations cannot transcend. That is reason. The foreigners harass China for their own motives. That is exactly why China should hold on to its power and reason. At the centre of the affairs under heaven lies reason. After reason we would take special circumstances and power into consideration, then there is no difficulty in solving problems under heaven. .... The foreigners come with excuses. We should seek common grounds and refrain from taking military measures. Even if we end up fighting, we should have reason on our side. Then either losing or winning, there would be no regret. .... For Saints, war is the last resort.[60]

To understand how reasonableness is inherent, according to Confucian dogma, to any system of law, one must first attempt conceptualizing the traditional Chinese worldview, which is centred around the idea of Sino-centrism. The Chinese concept of 'Tian Xia', ie the Empire under Heaven has two aspects. On the one hand, it presupposes the universal kingship, which is unique only when it is linked with the Confucian criteria of higher culture and moral order. The expression of this moral

[58] Livres Jaunes (n 53) Annexe V à la dépêche de Shanghai du 20 Décembre 1882, Télégramme, M. Bourée, Ministre de France en Chine, au Prince Kong, Président du Tsong-Li-Yamen, Tien-Tsin, le 2 Décembre 1882, p 45.

[59] Zhong Fa Yuenan Jiao She Dang, vol II (Zhong Yang Yan Jiu Yuan Jin Dai Shi Yan Jiu Suo 1962) 618.

[60] *Guo Songtao Ri Ji*, vol I (1st edn, Hunan Ren Min Chu Ban She 1981–83) 401.

order is mostly found in li, an all-inclusive term for ceremonies, rituals, and rules of proper conduct. On the other hand, 'Tian Xia' refers to the Chinese Empire as well as China's known world. In the latter aspect, 'Tian Xia' is a dynamic concept as it changes with the expansion of the Chinese Empire and of the world to the knowledge of China. When facing new systems of law, and particularly the idea of international law, the Empire under Heaven draws instant analogies and simply assumes that, since Heaven is dominated by reason, international law as the law of Heaven must, by definition, be dominated by reason, too. This interpretation is also confirmed by Guo Songtao: 'Heaven is reason. This is penetrating . . . .. Heaven is dominated by reason . . . .. Before dealing with matters and judging people, we should first understand reason and then observe the workings of the matter to know ups and downs in course of events. When the heart is free of doubt, it can be translated into language. This is to establish honesty in rhetoric.'[61]

On another occasion, he explained the relationship between reason, the human heart, and the art of ruling:

> I therefore reckon the ancients' rule appeals because it appeals to justice resting in the human heart. Although the human heart changes and takes different forms, the essence of the love of good and hate of evil applies to a common state of mind. The rulers instruct people based on the commonality of the human heart, which is extended and generalized into the common good. The ruling is ever-successful if it appeals to the justice of the human heart. Ming Fu runs local militia in the western river bank of Shan Hua. Whenever there is a matter of persuasion or punishment, he relies on the justice in the human heart, and says: Justice in the human heart is reason. If I cannot follow human emotion or reason, it will be the end.[62]

Interestingly, Guo described law as an advocating process which could be manipulated to maintain order under Heaven. There is no other way to maintain order than advocating goodness among people and suppressing evil. The law holds Tian Xia hostage. If one advocates goodness among people, the law becomes advantageous. If one advocates suppression of evil among people, the law prevails. The law declines when it is used to advocate evil and suppress good, which leads to the emergence of crisis and unrest.[63]

Most of Guo's arguments are beautifully written and seem very convincing. However, Guo was a scholar official with very limited practical experience. He was not engaged in high-class diplomatic negotiations during his term in London as was Zeng Jize. So, what did happen when China raised 'reason' against Western States to defend itself? In a discussion with Travers Twiss in 1870s, Zeng Jize, then Chinese ambassador in London, argued:

> Zongli Yamen has selected and translated crucial parts of the *Elements of International Law*, which are frequently quoted whenever foreign affairs are involved. Yet this matter should proceed progressively and at the moment not every detail could fit into the system. The

[61] 朱子曰,天即理也。此语至精 。 ... 天者,所以主宰乎理者也。 ... 处事论人,先明理而后究观乎事之本末始终,以知其曲折,沛然无疑于心矣,而后文之以言,所谓修辞立其诚也。(ibid 508).

[62] ibid vol II, 695.

[63] ibid vol III, 903.

origin of the law of nations rests with criminal law. Books on the law of nations are written by lawyers. Criminal law varies in different States, therefore it is not unusual to hold different opinions. The most important in the law of nations is the word 'reasonableness'. Everything should be judged with a peaceful heart, and naturally the law of nations will not be violated. As for how China treats small neighbouring States and vassal States, the profound benevolence and generosity from the sages outrank those written in *Elements of International Law*. If westerners ask people from Annam, Ryukyu, Korea, Siam, and Burma, they understand.[64]

## 3.2 International law and the Confucian world order

From September 1881 to March 1882, the demarche of Marquis Zeng Jize to the French government referred to the question of Chinese sovereignty, China's 'historic title' over the land of Tonkin, and the denial of the Treaty of 1874.[65] He construed his arguments by drawing from both international law and traditional Confucian dogma. International law started appearing in Chinese diplomatic documents with minor but slowly growing effect.

The concept of 'international law' was used very frequently in the Chinese archives, although from the Western perspective the use was not really accurate. From the Confucian perspective, it is interesting to note that international law was understood as a form of natural law order while the law of nations was conceptualized as a nexus of higher moral rules applying to a family of States which had to act reasonably in respect of one another in order to be legitimate under the mandate of Heaven: 'other States claim they are civilized. To be honest, those States are different from barbarian islanders and ethnic minorities. We should not quote our platitude "to honor Zhou dynasty and drive off barbarians" and despise those States because they have different rites, justice, and education. Even though rites, justice, and education are different, unreasonableness would not be allowed by those States located thousands of miles away.'[66] For the Qing literati, international law, justice, and reasonableness were overlapping concepts.[67]

Apart from Zeng Jize, the Governor of Yunnan and Guizhou Liu Changyou also made comments on Western international law as the idea of international rightness. In his memorial to the Grand Council, he suggested that the throne 'summon foreign ambassadors and consuls stationed in Beijing and hold a public discussion to declare the rightness. He said that they should declare the sage's generosity to move the foreign ambassadors' and consuls' heart; raise international law to break their tricks. In another memorial, he said that, if the public discussion failed, they would know that the French are greedy and hateful, and that other Western States are

[64] *Zeng Jize Ri Ji* (Yue Lu Shu She 1998) 890.

[65] Cho (n 53) 140.

[66] 彼诸邦者。咸自命为礼义教化之国。平心而论。亦诚与岛夷杜番苗猺獠猓情势判然。又安可因其礼义教化之不同而遽援尊周攘夷之陈言以鄙之耶。礼义教化虽有不同。然事之不在情理中者。则虽僻在数万里外之国。亦不能径行而无滞。Zhong Fa Yuenan Jiao She Dang (n 59), vol II, 617.

[67] See eg Qing Guangxu Chao Zhong Fa Jiao She Shi Liao, vol IV (Wen Hai Chu Ban She 1967) 257, 692, 1233.

also treacherous.[68] Here international law was mentioned after the sage's generosity, which seems to indicate that China's foreign policy should be based on traditional values, while international law serves as a defence with secondary importance. The idea of China conducting public discussion over the Vietnam issue failed to win a positive response from France. During his meeting with Li Fong-Pao, French President of the Council Jules Ferry said: 'When there is a dispute between the two countries, public discussion could be helpful. However, the proposal to conduct a public discussion must be agreed by both sides. Now China is planning to invite other States on its own. France would not agree to that.'[69]

In the end, Zeng Jize, a strong supporter of international law in the Chinese context, became disappointed with the role that Western international law played during the Sino-French War. He was no longer convinced that reason could appeal to Western States. This change from an optimistic take of international law to a sceptical one is also remarked upon by WAP Martin. In his letter to Moynier from the Association for the Reform and Codification of the Law of Nations, Martin wrote:

> The Chinese who read my translations quickly identify the advantageous side. From their understanding of law, they are able to understand that Western States' aggressive plan could be defeated. However when the advantageous side to European international law is to be followed, certain obligation has to be complied with. This, they cannot understand. They are only starting to learn the concept of obligation, which is a high concept far detached from daily life. About the dispute in Tonkin ... They lost on their claim. Now they are saying public international law is the reason of the strong. At the moment, they are starting to have doubts over the efficacy of international law, but they have progressed so far and there is no turning back.[70]

However, like Zeng Jize, Martin was in the end disheartened at the prospect of introducing international law in China, albeit from a critical legal perspective. There was a difficulty in Chinese modernization according to Yang, another critical legal scholar. What couldn't fit into 'Chinese learning as foundation and Western learning for practice' is, on the one hand, that Chinese learning as foundation, developed over thousands of years, could not accommodate law implanted from the West. Thus the transplant of Western law had to be made by force. Western law is not a singularity but a whole nexus of legal concepts, which is to say one element of Western law will bring another. The former suggests that the forced introduction of Western law compels indigenous Chineseness to make way since the forced introduction of Western law is progressively expansive.[71] Besides, under the treaty system, 'sticking

[68] 宣列圣之宽大。以动其心。举众国之公法。以破其诈。 Zhong Fa Yuenan Jiao She Dang (n 59), vol I, 238.

[69] 两国有不能决之事宜。则请各国公论。然须为两国合请。今中国独请各国。必不答复。 ibid vol IV, 2100.

[70] M Harada, 'Situation over the Introduction of International Law to China: A Study from the Letters of WAP Martin' (16 March 2013) Modern East Asian History 215–31, 221–22.

[71] 与"中学为体,西学为用"不相符合的是,一方面,几千年积累而成的"中体"没有预备一种现成的空间可以容纳借来的西法,是以借来的西法移入中国一定会是锲入;另一方面,西法不是单个的,而是彼此联结的,是以一种西法一定会带来另一种西法。就前一面而言,西法的锲入不能不要求中国原有的物事让路,就后一面而言,西法

to treaty compliance' also means conscious affirmation of vested interests won by Western powers. Foreign interests are realized in the process of impacting upon and devouring Chinese interests. This alien thing gains legitimacy through the aid of treaty law.[72] In other words, transplanting modern international law into ancient China would transcend the traditional idea that only tributes exist, not diplomacy. The historic era yearns for metabolic changes, but the dualism of this era submits the Chinese idea of reasonableness to the restrictions of unreasonableness, through the expansion of Western law.[73]

Yang's idea that international law is transplanted to the Confucian bureaucracy by force is of course challengeable. Positive efforts were made in several occasions by the Chinese government for the adoption of international law. That said, Yang's structure of 'reason suppressed by power', 'law as the aid of power', and the paradox between addressing reason and facing reality captured the essence of the Sino-French War. From this perspective, the Sino-French War is a case where Confucian ethics couldn't serve the purpose for the Chinese side. Between reason and power, the latter prevailed. Between the mandate of heaven and the treaty system, the latter prevailed. Over the course of time and in the face of brutal denial accompanied with gunboat diplomacy from the West, China realized the inefficiency of international law and looked out for other strategies. It still paid lip service to international law in the mere hope that once China was accepted in international society, she could enjoy the privileges enjoyed by all recognized nations. The Sino-French War marks this turning point together with other major events in the late Qing dynasty. Faced with imperialist assertions, Chinese representatives made arguments challenging a Western monopolistic perception of the world, by raising a Chinese equivalent as its parallel.

It is true that the Chinese diplomats were no rival to their Western counterparts in terms of the knowledge of international law. However, they hardly stopped raising international law as a defence, although in most cases their arguments were ineffective. Why would they continue using international law while knowing it was not working to China's advantage? The answer appears to be twofold. We have seen that for some Qing officials, the general principles of international law had roots in a natural law order, and thus were reconcilable with the traditional values of Chinese philosophy. As they regarded international law as a code of ethical and reasonable conduct among Western States, they believed that 'reasons' from the sage's teachings would appeal to the 'reasons' of Western countries, thus the disputes could be resolved. Those who were pragmatists fought for China's position as a suzerain and tasted the bitterness of denial from the West. They hoped, however, that using international law to defend China's position could be of benefit in the future and would secure her place in the international world order.

的锲入不能不节节扩张。Guoqiang Yang, Yi Li Yu Shi Gong Zhi Jian De Huai Huang: Zeng Guofan, Li Hongzhang Ji Qi Shi Dai (Du Shu, Xin Zhi San Lian Shu Dian 2008) 193.

72 ibid 19

73 ibid.

In the eyes of such Qing officials as Zeng Jize, international law was both alien and familiar; both useful and ineffective. Zeng Jize tried to locate some middle ground between French imperialism and the rule of the Qing Empire, which only led to contradictions and denials. These contradictions gradually took root in Zeng Jize's mind and his position changed from an active promoter of international law to a sceptic. Western imperialism changed the way the Qing literati regarded international law and had a tremendous impact on China's traditional relationship with its neighbours.

## 3.3 Vassalage vs protectorship

One could specifically refer to a series of legal anomalies that emerged during the Sino-French controversy and related to fundamentally different legal perceptions and evaluations by the French and the Chinese of the very same factual relationships. These involved the concept of protectorship and the legal evaluation of silence.

France and China had a very different understanding of the concept of international protectorship. From the Western perspective, the concept of protectorship entailed both economic and political benefits. It explicitly involved the administration of the domestic affairs of the protectorate. On the basis of the Western legal definition, France put forth an argument that China's international protectorship over Annam was only nominal to the extent that it was only based on certain economic benefits (tributes) and did not encompass the element of political administration. For the Chinese, on the other hand, Annam had been their vassal state for many years, whereas their understanding of protectorship was conceived as an expression of virtue, moral responsibility, and benevolence, whereby the protector state does not constantly interfere with the life of the protégé but only intervenes as a good 'brother' or 'uncle' when something wrong or hostile occurs to it.

The traditional concept ren (仁), which generally means the virtue of benevolence, was put forward to confirm China's claim to protect Vietnam. Being China's vassal state, Vietnam had to pay respect in the form of tributes to China. Being Annam's suzerain, China showed, in return, benevolence usually by granting generous gifts and conferring titles. The Chinese drew family analogies and tended to think of the empire, and of the world at large, in terms of an extension of the family. In the Confucian world order China should then act as an elder brother or parent.[74]

To understand the relationship between China and its vassals, it is necessary to have some background knowledge about the traditional worldview in China, which, centred around the idea of Sino-centrism, runs against the fundamental international

[74] Yongjin Zhang, *China in the International System, 1918–20: The Middle Kingdom at the Periphery* (Macmillan 1991) 8. Another example of this observation is found in Zeng's metaphor of Vietnam as a nephew and China as an uncle: 'Assume I have a nephew living in my household, who relies on me financially. One day, a friend proposes to help and raise him. It could be allowed. However, I also learn that this friend might bully my niece, then I'm obliged to inquire and see if it is true' 譬如我家有一侄儿。平日恃我抚养。有一朋友帮我抚养。原无不可。忽闻此朋友将有欺凌我侄之事。我不能不问事之真假也。Zhong Fa Yuenan Jiao She Dang (n 59), vol I, 151.

law idea of sovereign equality. According to Confucian dogma, the unequal relationship between the centre (China) and its periphery (vassal States) had existed for centuries. Its historical feature has been remarked on by Yang Guoqiang: 'The Mandate of Heaven system is fossilized with history. It is conditioned by sinocentrism, and therefore the inequality established between Yi and Xia is its natural colour.'[75] Zhang Yongjin illustrated the relationship between the concept of Tian Xia, vassal States and rites:

> The Chinese concept of 'Tian Xia' has two aspects. On the one hand, it presupposes the universal kingship, which, Benjamin Schwartz maintains, is unique only when it is linked with the Confucian criteria of higher culture and moral order. The expression of this moral order is mostly found in li, an all-inclusive term for ceremonies, rituals and rules of proper conduct. On the other hand, 'Tian Xia' refers to the Chinese Empire as well as China's known world. In the latter aspect, 'Tian Xia' is a dynamic concept as it changes with the expansion of the Chinese Empire and of the world to the knowledge of China.[76]

Neighbouring areas were expected to recognize the superiority of the Son of Heaven, ie the Chinese Emperor and pay tributes to the Chinese Empire. The ideological tension between the Western protectorship and Eastern vassalage is vividly depicted in a conversation between Zeng Jize and Jules Ferry:

ZENG: What could be the difference between being a protector and being a ruler of a country? 保护某国与作某国之主何异乎。

FERRY: They are quite different. As ruler of a state, one takes responsibility and administers all political affairs on behalf of the state. While as a protector, one manages general affairs with no duty of administration. The purpose is to take care and protect as a manifestation of preferential treatment. 是大有不同者。即如作某国之主。则该国一切政事吏治皆为之做主。代其治理。至保护某国。则不过总其大纲。不管吏治。而照料保护以示优待之意而已。

ZENG: When China treats its vassal States, it doesn't interfere with its internal affairs and gives its vassal States autonomy. This is like how America treats people living in the frontier, a treatment different from territorial jurisdiction in Western law. If any conflict happens in Vietnam, China will lend a hand to suppress it, and withdraw its army once the turmoil is over. Integrity of the political authority in Vietnam will not be harmed. France claimed it will protect Vietnam. Does it intend to protect Vietnam in the way China does, or to protect Vietnam in the way Britain protects Egypt? 中国之待属国。不预该国内治政事。听其自理。犹如美国之待边部之道。而不似西洋治属地之法也。遇越南有乱。中国代为戡定。事竣即还。不侵其国之政。法国既言保护越南。不识将效中国保护越南之法乎。抑效英国保护埃及之法乎。

ZENG: Your esteemed minister thinks China's non-interference in Vietnam's domestic affairs renders its title fictional. However, when France entered Vietnam, the latter felt threatened. If Vietnam felt threatened, China feels worried. Things fictional and intangible could develop into potential material harm. 不预内治。贵大臣即以为虚事。然法入越南。则越南不安。越南不安。则中国不能无虑。向之所谓虚事者。或恐有实害矣。[77]

[75] Guoqiang Yang (n 71) 17. [76] Zhang (n 74) 8.
[77] Zhong Fa Yuenan Jiao She Dang (n 59), vol II, 1001.

### 3.4 Silence vs acquiescence

The elements of time and inertia appear very frequently in both the French and the Chinese archives. For the French, time can be used in a very deceiving way and thus the Chinese procrastinate on purpose; they use time to their favour to shirk their obligations; avoid the implementation of their international commitments. Contrarily to the French, a 'more recent' people, the Chinese appear more confident with time: they have a longer history and therefore a much broader horizon which enables them to evaluate time in a widely linear and diachronical fashion. China signs treaties that will secure peace for the future and examines whether her actions or inactions, such as the setting of wrong precedents, can affect future Chinese generations. This social phenomenology can be of particular legal value when it comes to the different interpretations of 'immediacy' and 'immediate withdrawal' and even the conceptualization of historic titles.

For the French, silence in international law is acquiescence. In the same vein, the absence of protests by the Chinese when portions of Cochinchina fell into the hands of the French under the treaty of 1874 meant that the Chinese had acquiesced. If there is a right under Western international law, it must be claimed, asserted, declared, otherwise it is lost. In the Confucian order, inaction does not equal acquiescence. The Chinese government never considered that, because of the Franco-Vietnamese treaty, the vassalage system was questioned in anyway. Nor did China consider at that time that a parallel legal system could somehow supersede her traditional relations.[78] China's affinity to her vassal States as well as her strong cultural and racial ties to Vietnam were considered proof enough that China's historic titles were incontestable. According to Zeng: 'Even though France concluded a treaty with Vietnam, China's rights over Vietnam still exist. It is France's good intention to protect Vietnam. Yet China also has her right of protection. Protection established later does not invalidate protection established before.'[79]

If the French had studied the Chinese administration, they would have noticed that inaction was a natural, inherent characteristic of the Confucian system. Emperors were devoted to maintaining the traditional orders of past emperors. Even though a few reforms were implemented occasionally, the reformers claimed that they were only following the paths of their fathers and grandfathers. Action and change in the Confucian system was, by definition, undesirable. For example, the Jiaqing Emperor (1796–1820) doubted his own 'new policy' from the very beginning. This was because he was worried that his new policy would be seen as a reversal of his father's policy.[80] The Confucian system was, accordingly, not tolerant to innovations. If someone wished to innovate, he would have to risk, if not break out of, his old relationships and resources. If the Confucian system did not respond to the innovation positively, he would be condemned to death. The cost of action,

[78] Eastman (n 2) 41. [79] Zhong Fa Yuenan Jiao She Dang (n 59), vol I, 150.
[80] Hongjie Zhang, *The Ten Faces of the Qianlong Emperor* (People's Literature Publishing House 2010) 323.

change, and innovation was therefore too high for one to take within the Confucian administration.

## 4. Conclusions

The archival study of the Sino-French controversy in Vietnam depicted the multi-faceted lack of communication between the French and Chinese administrations. Ideological incoherence in ethnic policies, misunderstandings, and diplomatic flubs were only a few of the reasons for the breaking down of diplomatic talks at critical points of the conflict. Different perceptions and understandings of the same factual events, interstate relations, rights, and duties towards Tonkin, created profound confusion that led to the escalation of the conflict. The problem was that, with some few individual exceptions such as Burée from the French side and Li and Zeng from the Chinese side, neither administration had, at that time, the insight to decipher the communication problem in a timely and efficient manner in order to prevent hostilities.

American archives indicate internal conditions in China were so unique that they could not have been resolved with typical diplomatic mathematics:

> You have the most absolute of monarchies; the most democratic of democracies. You have a most conservative and patient people to whom tradition is a religion, and precedent a commandment, and yet who have maintained within the present generation, the greatest rebellion of the century. You have the most skeptical of men, who believe in nothing but what they see with their own eyes, or read in the books of Confucius; the most credulous of men, who apprehend the fate of a dynasty in the nebula of a star, or the flushing of the sun at sunset.[81]

It finally all comes down to how the facts were understood and evaluated from both sides. To certain questions, there are still no self-evident answers: why, contrary to Chinese literati, most French diplomats did not bother trying to understand the arguments of the enemy? Can the proactive, amoral Western concept of international legal order ever coexist peacefully with the Chinese traditional ideas of justice, reasonableness, and Confucian passivity? Is it, in the end, desirable that China become adapted to Western ways? For an American diplomat:

> [there will be] no regeneration in China, unless the Empire has a violent agitation, and that after all French guns might open the way for French ideas, for a constitution, railways, the gospel, brandy, canals, newspapers, churches, the noblest and as the shadow of following the sun, the most ignoble agencies of Western civilization. I have compared the counsels of these earnest men, to that of some impatient husbandman who because the plough will not turn up his anvil rapidly enough bethinks himself of dynamite. The difficulty with dynamite in nature, and dynamite agency in politics is, that no one knows where they will end ... Of

[81] Davids (n 17) 283–355, no 27, 24.12.1883; Dispatch 308, Young to Frelinghuysen, Peking: Ministers' Dispatches, China: Roll 68.

course a war would make a tremendous impression upon China. It might rend the Empire to its foundations. The dynasty might fall. Revolution might come, and with revolution anarchy. But is there any power in the world, even the mighty power of France, that would care to govern China in anarchy? And is there not more to be feared, in the sudden awakening of China, to the fact that we live in the nineteenth not the ninth century?[82]

[82] ibid.

# 18

# The Sino-Japanese War and the Collapse of the Qing and Confucian World Order in the Face of Japanese Imperialism and European Acquiescence

*Patrick Sze-lok Leung and Bijun Xu*

## 1. Introduction

International law has appeared to be a peacemaking measure for centuries. Before it was introduced to East Asia, the stability of the Far East was supported by the Confucian world order. When international law came to East Asia along with Western aggression, from the mid-nineteenth century, it did not improve international relationships. Instead, it served as a legal foundation for expansionism, created ambiguities and conflicts, and damaged the stability of the region. The Chinese efforts to maintain traditional order together with its superiority was under pressure from the West and also Japan, a rapidly rising Asian power which adopted the Western system. The Sino-Japanese War in 1894–95 not only showed the difference in military strength, but also demonstrated the tension between international law and Confucian doctrines of international relationship. The war was ended by the Japanese victory, and thus sped up the collapse of the Chinese vassal system, and the implementation of international law in East Asia. Neither the intrinsic values of international law nor the legality of the Japanese actions can be implied by the victory through violent means. Meanwhile, just as the Western powers utilized international law to colonize the world, Japan was merely doing the same thing in East Asia. The legitimacy of the Japanese aim, together with its measures, was indeed questionable. Western powers were aware of Japanese aggression and perceived its actions as violation of international law. However, they finally gave up playing a role in preventing the outbreak of this war, which illustrated the defects of international law in the late nineteenth century. The main aim of this chapter, which uses the Sino-Japanese War as a case, is to show how both Chinese Confucianism and Western international law failed to function as restrictions on political expansionism.

## 2. Japan's Hidden Agenda and Its Pretext for the First Sino-Japanese War

The First Sino-Japanese War was officially declared on 1 August 1894. In the text of *Imperial Japanese Rescript Declaring War*, the cause of this war was given as follows:

> Under the guidance of Japan, Korea was introduced into the family of nations and became an independent state; however, China insisted Korea as her dependency and interfered with her domestic affairs openly and secretly. In order to procure for Korea from the calamity of perpetual disturbance and maintain the peace of the East in general, Japan invited China to co-operate on reform of Korea, which was refused by Qing government. Then Japan started to advise Korea to reform her administration on her own and Korea had already consented to undertake the task. But China endeavored to thwart Japan's purpose and even further endeavored to make warlike preparations both on land and at sea. When China was prepared, she not only sent large reinforcements to Korea, but also opened fire upon Japanese ships in Korean waters. Such conduct on the part of China is a direct injury to Korea and also a menace to the peace and tranquility of the Orient. In this situation, Japan found it impossible to avoid a formal declaration of war against China.[1]

China issued a counter-proclamation of war denouncing Japan as invaders of Korea:

> Korea had long been China's tributary for over two hundred years and this was a matter known to the world. Although China had the habit of assisting their tributaries with putting down the rebellion, she never interfered with their internal government. On the contrary, it was Japan, who sent large armies to bully Korea and forced the Korean king to change his system of government. With Japan's increasing number of troops there in Korea, China had to send more troops there to protect the people of Korea and Chinese merchants. On the half way to Korea, a number of Japanese ships suddenly appeared and opened fire upon Chinese unprepared transports. As Japan violated the treaties and not observed international laws, commencing hostilities herself, China determined to hasten with all speed to root the Japanese troops out of their lairs.[2]

It is obvious from these declarations that the conflict over Korea between China and Japan was the direct cause of this war. Japan claimed to bring Korea Western civilization, including Western international law. The West regarded China, including Korea within the tributary system, as barbarism because this system was obviously against the basic principle of Western international law. . However, this chapter argues with solid evidence that Japan was adopting the Western way to colonize Korea by using international law justifying its aggression, and protecting the independence of Korea was only a pretext. Japan's hidden agenda was to establish predominance in Asia.

[1] Takahashi Sakuye, *Cases on International Law During the Chino-Japanese War* (CUP 1899) 165.
[2] ibid 167.

Like China, Japan used to suffer from Western imperialism and unequal treaties. By realizing that foreigners could not be expelled, Japan sought to improve itself by importing Western civilization. Besides westernizing themselves in culture, education, and international law, Japan also followed the imperialist ways, among which, occupying Korea and the First Sino-Japanese War were representative. In the mind of the Japanese leadership, international law was one of the most important institutions in European international society.[3] Accordingly, Japan paid much attention to Western international law and made full use of it for its matters of international diplomacy. International law thus played an important role in whitewashing Japan's aggression towards Korea. By looking at pre-war incidents, Japan's long premeditated plan can be revealed.

The first debate between China and Japan over the status of Korea happened in 1875. A small Japanese warship was dispatched to survey coastal waters without Korean permission and was shot at by the Korean garrison, which triggered conflict between Korea and Japan. Considering China's influence over this peninsula, Japan went to China seeking help in opening Korea, which was refused by the Zongli Yamen. Realizing that there was little hope of cooperating with China in opening Korea, Japan began to use Western public international law to deny the tributary relationship between China and Korea, arguing that Korea was an independent country, and the tributary system was inconsistent with international law. However, when China argued that Japan's action of entering Korean territorial waters without permission violated international law by not respecting the independence of Korea, Japan responded that Korea had no right to be protected by international law because it never concluded treaties with other nations.[4] The double standard application of international law shows clearly that international law was just a tool for achieving Japan's political purpose. In other words, Japan's real intention was not to maintain the independence of Korea, but to wipe out China's influence over this peninsula in order to establish its own control. Having failed in seeking Qing's cooperation, Japan determined to open Korea by itself.

A year later, Japan employed gunboat diplomacy opening up Korea and pressed Korea to sign the Japan–Korea Treaty of Amity in 1876. This treaty is a typical unequal one. Articles 4 and 5 opened Pusan and two other ports for residence and trade by Japanese subjects; Article 7 gave the Japanese mariners the right to freely survey the Korean coasts; and Article 10 granted Japan the right of extraterritoriality, which was a feature of previous Western treaties signed with Asian countries.[5] Japan treated Korea in the same way it has been treated by Western powers. The first two provisions seemed to put Japan and Korea on an equal footing under international law, but it can be seen from Japan's following actions that the main purpose of these

[3] RP Anand, 'Family of "Civilized" States and Japan: A Story of Humiliation, Assimilation, Defiance and Confrontation' (2003) 5(1) Journal of the History of International Law 22.

[4] 'Records of the Negotiations between Li Hongzhang and Mori Arinori at Baoding in 1876' (1876 nian Li Hongzhang yu Sen Youli Baoding huitan jilu 1876 年李鴻章與森有禮保定會談記錄) Wang Yuanchong 王元崇 (ed and tr) *Jindaishi ziliao* 近代史資料 (October 2012) 126, 131.

[5] Matsui Yoshirō, 'Modern Japan, War and International Law' in Ando Nisuke (ed), *Japan and International Law: Past, Present and Future* (Kluwer Law International/Martinus Nijhoff 1999) 13.

articles was to block China from dominating or influencing Korea, not to protect its independence. When both Chinese and Japanese troops were stationed in Korea in the 1890s, Japan referred to Article 1 of this convention forcing Korea to evacuate Chinese troops.

After opening up Korea, Japan continued to strengthen its influence. In 1884, Japan supported the Gapsin coup, aiming to reform Korea. Although the coup failed because of China's dispatching 1,500 soldiers suppressing it, this incident ended with the Convention of Tianjin, Article 3 of which was interpreted by many scholars as putting China and Korea on equal status in terms of Korea by granting Japan the right to send troops when necessary. The different interpretations of this term led to disputes between China and Japan, discussed in section 2 of this chapter.

The conflict over Korea between China and Japan escalated in 1894 and finally led to the outbreak of war. Because of the Tonghak Rebellion, Korea asked China to send troops to suppress the rebellion.[6] In accordance with the convention of Tianjin, 'neither nation would send troops to Korea without prior notification to the other side', China informed Japan of its dispatching troops.[7] After receiving the notification, Japan replied that they also intended to dispatch troops to Korea under the Tianjin Convention.[8] Korea repeatedly requested that Japan delay taking such action, and also tried to prevent the Japanese minister Ōtori Keisuke from entering Seoul accompanied by Japanese soldiers. However, neither succeeded.[9] China was also surprised at the considerable number of soldiers Japan sent to Korea.[10] China explained that its dispatch of troops was at Korea's request and once the insurgents had been put down Chinese forces would be withdrawn immediately.[11] The Japanese military and naval forces were rapidly increased in Inchon and even moved into Seoul.[12] Japan argued that the troops were sent to guard its legation and consulates in Korea, which was a right protected under Article V of the Chemulpo Convention of 1882. However, according to American record, no one was actually menacing them.[13] In fact, Japan would not give up this opportunity, because this affair handed Japan the pretext they had long desired, ie of intervening massively in the Korean peninsula.[14]

When peace was restored after suppressing the disturbances in Seoul and Inchon, Korea proposed that Chinese and Japanese military contingents withdraw from Korea. In response to Korea's request, the Qing government proposed that Japan

[6] Kajima Morinosuke, *The Diplomacy of Japan 1894–1922*, vol 1, Sino-Japanese War and Triple Intervention (Kajima Institute of International Peace 1976) 31; Mutsu Munemitsu, *Kenkenroku: A Diplomatic Record of the Sino-Japanese War, 1894–95*, Gordon Mark Berger (ed and tr) (University of Tokyo Press 1982) 7.

[7] National Palace Museum Library 故宮博物院文獻館 (ed), *Archives on Sino-Japanese Negotiation during the Guangxu Era* (*Qing Guangxu chao Zhong Ri jiaoshe shiliao* 清光緒朝中日交涉史料) (National Palace Museum Library 1932), *juan* 13, no 949, 7.

[8] Mutsu (n 6) 15. [9] Kajima (n 6) 32. [10] ibid. [11] Mutsu (n 6) 15.

[12] Kajima (n 6) 32. See also National Palace Museum Library (n 7) *juan* 13, no 968, 11.

[13] J Davids, *American Diplomatic and Public Papers: The United States and China 1894–1905*, vol 2 (Scholarly Resources 1981) 107.

[14] SCM Paine, *The Sino-Japanese War of 1894–1895: Perceptions, Power, and Primacy* (CUP 2003) 113.

withdraw its troops jointly from Korea.[15] It was obvious that the legal ground claimed by Japan for sending troops no longer existed; however, Japan still neglected entertaining any proposition for the simultaneous removal, arguing that the Korean government would be incapable of preventing a recurrence of disturbances and maintaining peace and order for long. Thus it was an urgent necessity to carry out administrative reform to uproot the causes of the trouble and strive for the maintenance of an endurable peace in the Far East. Therefore, Japan's troops would not retreat until the reform had been carried into effect.[16]

Foreseeing that China was unlikely to agree to this plan, the Japanese government prepared in advance for the countermeasure, which was to force Korea singlehandedly to execute the administrative reform.[17] As expected, after several rounds of negotiations, China and Japan could not conclude an agreement. Afterwards, Japan determined to abandon the quest for Sino-Japanese cooperation in Korea and moved on from the stage of maintaining balanced strength in Korea with China to the stage of making Korea totally under its own control.[18] Japan started to reform the Korean administrative structure singlehandedly and assigned minister Ōtori the responsibility of executing this policy in Korea.[19]

However, the reform did not go smoothly, because the reformist faction in Korea was too weak to confront the opposite party. [20] Relying on the backing of China, Korea hesitated carrying out the reform while pretending to comply with it. At the same time, Korea insisted that Japan's proposal for reform could only be considered after its troops withdrew from Korea.[21] Being stuck with the situation, minister Ōtori proposed besieging the royal palace by force. The internal discussions among Japanese high officials showed that Japan knew well that this action violated international law by infringing the autonomy and independence of Korea and would provoke an unjustifiable war with China.[22] However, without any other superior proposal, Japan finally entered the royal palace on 23 July and replaced the Min Family with Taewon'gun, who promised to cooperate and consult with minister Ōtori on all subsequent reform affairs.[23] These incidents show clearly that Japan on one hand used international law to castigate others' actions, while on the other hand, violated international law when necessary.

After learning of the besiege of the Korea Palace and the naval battle off P'ung Island on 25 July, China finally entered into war with Japan.[24]

Domestically, the emotions of the Japanese people had been running very high before the war. They had grown tired of peace and nothing could be more welcome to them at present than an opportunity to make a difference by winning a war. The Japanese seemed to be so excited that it would be almost impossible for the government to withdraw the troops without bringing back some compensation.[25] Public opinion can be reflected from songs widespread among ordinary people in Japan. In

[15] Mutsu (n 6) 19; National Palace Museum Library (n 7) *juan* 13, no 990, 15–16.
[16] Kajima (n 6) 33. [17] ibid 34. [18] ibid 40; Mutsu (n 6) 26.
[19] Mutsu (n 6) 39. [20] Kajima (n 6) 49. [21] ibid 58. [22] Mutsu (n 6) 81.
[23] ibid; Kajima (n 6) 66; Davids (n 13) 191. [24] Takahashi (n 1) 165–67.
[25] Davids (n 13) 116.

1894, a song of conquest of China was published, and the 'Song of the Rising Sun Flag' stated it was the job of our noble nation to bring aid and progress to a neighbouring land still closed to the world.[26]

At the same time, some of the most influential intellectuals were quite supportive of war with China. Fukuzawa Yukichi had been encouraging Japan in throwing off Asia since the 1880s.[27] In order to avoid China becoming the master of East Asia, he asserted that, Japan should 'unite[d] internally, complete its armament expansion, and bring its political strategy for East Asia to a successful completion'. He flatly stated that 'in culture we should become a leader of enlightenment, and in military arts we should become the leader in Asia'.[28] Fukuzawa was also in favour of the use of force, in his mind:

> A hundred volumes of the public law of all nations will not be equal to the power of a single cannon. Numerous copies of treaties of peace and amity will not be equal to the power of a box of gunpowder. Cannons and gunpowder are not the means for upholding the reason that you already have, but a tool for creating a reason where there is none.[29]

Ariga Nagao, as a leading international law scholar in Japan, regarded war as the means by which States achieved their political aims. He thought that when two countries could not reach agreement, they could use their power to achieve their object and the losing side should obey the winning.[30] All of these ideas prepared Japan for war in ideological and theoretical ways.

On 26 August 1894 during the war, Japan concluded with the Korean government a treaty of alliance, which confirmed that Korea was an independent state and that it had formed an offensive and defensive alliance with Japan against China. Again, Japan justified this treaty by saying that

> The object of the alliance is to maintain the independence of Corea on a firm footing and to promote the respective interests of both Japan and Corea by expelling Chinese soldiers from Corean territory.[31]

However, according to Mutsu's memoir, the real purpose of this treaty was to prevent Korea from turning elsewhere for advice and thus keep the Koreans firmly under Japan's control.[32] In addition, this treaty required Korea to give facility to Japanese warlike operations against China. More importantly, the preamble of the treaty deserves more attention—it stated:

> In view of the fact that on 25th of July 1894, the Corean Government entrusted His Imperial Majesty's Envoy . . . at Seoul . . . with the expulsion, on their behalf, of Chinese soldiers from

[26] Saya Makito, D Noble tr, *The Sino-Japanese War and the Birth of Japanese Nationalism* (International House of Japan 2011) 17–18.

[27] Miwa Kimitada, 'Fukuzawa Yukichi's "Departure from Asia"—A Prelude to the Sino-Japanese War' in E Skrzypczak (ed), *Japan's Modern Century: A Special Issue of Monumenta Nipponica* (Sophia University 1968) 1.

[28] ibid 12–13.

[29] Anand (n 3) 23.

[30] Ariga Nagao 有賀長雄, *Wartime International Law* (*Bankoku Senji Kōhō* 萬國戰時公法) (Army War College 1894) 1–4.

[31] Kajima (n 6) 117–18.

[32] Mutsu (n 6) 93.

the Corean territory, the Governments of Japan and Corea have been placed in a situation to give mutual assistance both offensive and defensive.[33]

The preamble was crucial in achieving at least the following purposes: first, Japan mentioned the 25 July date intentionally, because this could justify Japan's action of expulsion of Chinese soldiers from the Korean territory, and cover up the truth that Japan actually took action before getting official consent from the Korean government.[34] At the same time, this preamble aimed to ensure that the treaty had retroactive force back to the date of 25 July.[35] By bringing the retroactive force back to this date, Japan could claim for the right of visit and search in Korean waters by not breaking the principle of the inviolability of neutral territories, because Korea had been an ally of Japan from 25 July and the territory of Korea was not neutral at all.[36]

Japan's hidden agenda can be seen not only from their pre-war preparations, but also from the terms they asked for during the peace negotiation.

After eight months of fighting, China asked America to mediate for the peace negotiation by offering the recognition of the independence of Korea, which was claimed by both Japan and China as the cause of the war, and some indemnity for Japan's military expenditure as terms for peace.[37] Japan rejected these terms firmly because they thought they deserved more. When determining what terms to ask for, discussions in Japanese naval circles contended that Japan's long-range strategic plans required Japan to annex Liaotung as Japanese territory, which lay at Korea's back and commanded the gateway to Peking, which revealed Japan's intention to occupy Peking later.[38] During the negotiation, Japan asked to obtain southern Fengt'ien, which obviously could be used as a base for land and sea operations, thus posed an immediate and constant threat to the capital of the Chinese Empire.[39] Japan's long-term goal could also be seen in Aoki's proposal on peace terms sent to Mutsu. He explained the necessity of having Fengt'ien by saying that this would comprise a buffer zone of approximately 5,000 square *ri* between China and Korea and would serve as a military base permitting Japan's freedom in the future to establish predominance in Asia.[40] All in all, Japan's aim was not only Korea, but also China and all Asia.

Besides using international law justifying actions during war, Japan was also keen to present their version of this war to the Western world through academic publications, in which it always behaved well in compliance with Western diplomatic etiquette and obeyed international law. Takahashi Sakue, as a Japanese international law scholar, played a big role in presenting the law-abiding spirit of Japan. In his words, Japan was keen to be doing everything in accordance with international law.[41] Both Holland and Westlake spoke highly of Takahashi's work and Japan's

[33] Kajima (n 6) 117–18. [34] Kajima (n 6) 69–70.

[35] Sugimura Fukashi 杉村濬, *Record in Korea, 1894–1895* (*Meiji nijūshichi hachinen zaikan kushinroku* 明治廿七八年在韓苦心録) (Sugimura Yōtarō 1932) 79.

[36] Takahashi (n 1) 48–49. [37] Mutsu (n 6) 138. [38] ibid 144. [39] ibid 184.

[40] ibid 144.

[41] Takahashi Sakue, 'The Application of International Law During the Chino-Japanese War' (1898) 56 Law Quarterly Review 405–07.

behaviour as presented by him. Holland commented that 'Mr. Takahashi's narrative is always clear, and his arguments are, as a rule, convincing'.[42] Though excellent from the perspective of international legal techniques, Takahashi ignored some fundamental questions, including the issue of 'the conflict over Korea', 'who fired the first shot', '*casus belli*', and 'the Port Arthur massacre', which are all important in revealing Japan's hidden agenda and deciding the nature of this war. Ariga Nagao, as a legal adviser to Japan, wrote *The Sino-Japanese War from the Point of View of International Law* in French, in which, he justified the Port Arthur massacre on the grounds of provocation and reciprocity.[43]

Occupying Korea was just the first step for Japan in establishing predominance in Asia. By following the Western way of imperialistic policy in Asia, Japan demonstrated that its civilization was high enough to play a part in its forcible dissemination.[44] International law for Japan was just a tool for winning the Western powers' sympathy and recognition, to serve as pretext for conquering Korea, and wage war against China.

## 3. Who Violated International Law?

As shown in section 2, a crucial Japanese argument for the war was the protection of Korean independence which appeared to be harmed by the Sino-Korean tributary relationship. In addition, the Japanese dispatch of forces in preparation for the forthcoming war seemed to be justified by the 1885 Tianjin Convention. Some may then argue that both the aim and the measure were just. This section tries to illustrate another picture of the story by asking three important questions: (1) were there really contradictions between the concepts of 'independent state' and 'tributary state'? (2) did the 1885 convention authorize Japan's sending troops to Korea even when the Korean government was opposed to same? (3) did Japan really treat Korea as an independent state? These questions need to be clarified by careful study of historical facts and treaties.

The Japanese government justified their military action by arguing that the tributary relationship between China and Korea violated the Japan–Korea Treaty of 1876, in which Korea was recognized as an independent state.[45] In order to see whether there was violation, it is essential to study the meaning of 'independent state' from the perspective of international law. An independent state, or a sovereign State, is an entity which has a central government holding the sovereignty of a geographical area. In contrast, a dependency, also known as dependent state, subordinate state, or protectorate, is a state partly controlled by another state and does not have complete sovereignty, for example, the right to declare wars or sign treaties. The tributary system adopted by East Asian States might be perceived by international lawyers as an

[42] Takahashi (n 1) preface, vi. [43] Paine (n 14) 212.

[44] Suzuki Shogo, *Civilization and Empire: China and Japan's Encounter with European International Society* (Routledge 2009) 2.

[45] C Parry (ed), *The Consolidated Treaty Series*, vol 150 (Oceana 1969–81) 325.

unequal system which contradicted independence. However, it should be noted that tributary system and international law were originally two distinct systems in two different worlds. The former was oriental, while the latter was invented by the West. Therefore, it was dangerous to draw a parallel between 'tributary state' in East Asia and 'dependency' in the West arbitrarily. In order to see whether these two entities were the same, historical review of the tributary system is necessary.

In fact, there have been controversies over the nature of the tributary system. Fairbank saw tributary system as 'the medium for Chinese international relations and diplomacy'. Under the system, the neighbouring States, respecting the Chinese suzerainty and superiority, received investiture and trading profits from China.[46] Hamashita Takeshi argued that the tributary relationship provided a basis for the formation of the East Asian economic circle. Tributes were paid to show nominal loyalty towards China. In return, tributary States usually received gifts which were more valuable than their tributes. At the same time, they were allowed to trade in the Chinese capital and at the frontier. Thus, the activities were virtually exchange of goods forming a trading system, in which China acted as the core member. The tributary States appeared as subordinates, but they still enjoyed sovereignty to a certain extent.[47] On the other hand, scholars have pointed out that the relationship could be perceived in many different ways, for there were so many States and tribes involved in the tributary system.[48]

Meanwhile, Korean contemporary scholars argue that the tributary system was mutually beneficial to both China and Korea. Since the fourteenth century, the Ming Empire accepted Korea as its vassal state to restrain the Mongols. Emperor Chengzu of the Ming, who seized the throne from his nephew, was eager for recognition by foreign States. Meanwhile, the Korean kings also voluntarily paid tributes to the Ming to get authorization to rule their state, and to secure national defence. As long as China received tributes, the emperor would not interfere in Korean affairs.[49]

Though mutually understood by China and Korea, the tributary relationship needed to be clarified when the Western powers signed treaties with Korea. The

[46] JK Fairbank, 'A Preliminary Framework' in JK Fairbank (ed), *The Chinese World Order: Traditional China's Foreign Relations* (Harvard UP 1968) 1–19.

[47] Hamashita Takeshi, *China-centered World Order in Modern Times: Tribute Trade System and Modern Asia* 近代中国の国際的契機：朝貢貿易システムと近代アジア (University of Tokyo Press 1990); *China, East Asia and the Global Economy: Regional and Historical Perspectives* (Routledge 2008).

[48] Lin Hsiao-ting 林孝庭, 'The Tributary System and Historical Imagination: China and Kanjut, 1761–1963' 朝貢制度與歷史想像：兩百年來的中國與坎巨堤（1761–1963）, Bulletin of the Institute of Modern History, Academia Sinica 中央研究院近代史研究所集刊 (December 2011) 74, 44.

[49] Seo Kyoung-yoon 徐耿胤 and Shih Chih-yu 石之瑜, *Restoring the Individuality under the Tributary Relationship* (*Huifu chaogong guanxi zhong de zhuti: Hanguo xuezhe Quan Haizong yu Li Chunzhi de Zhongguo yanjiu* 恢復朝貢關係中的主體——韓國學者全海宗與李春植的中國研究) (Research and Educational Center for China Studies and Cross Taiwan–Strait Relations, Department of Political Science, NTU 2012) 79–83; Fan Wing Chung 范永聰, *Serving the Great and Preserving the State: Sino-Korean Relations During the Yüan-Ming Transition* (*Shida yu baoguo: Yuan Ming zhi ji de Zhong Han guanxi* 事大與保國——元明之際的中韓關係) (Hong Kong Educational Publishing 2009); DC Twitchett and FW Mote (eds), *The Cambridge History of China*, vol 8, The Ming Dynasty, 1368–1644, pt 2 (CUP 1998) 272–300; Chun Hae-jong, 'Sino-Korean Tributary Relations in the Ch'ing Period' in Fairbank (n 46) 90–111.

Japan–Korea Treaty of 1876, which confirmed Korean independence, was followed by the United States–Korea Treaty of 1882. The latter was signed under the influence of China, especially Li Hongzhang.[50] Li intended to mention the Korean subordinate status in the treaty signed with the United States, but the US representative refused by quoting the 1876 treaty. At last, the Korean king sent a note, suggested by the Chinese side, to the US government before signing the treaty. The note clarified that Korea was a subordinate of China, but it enjoyed sovereignty in both internal and external affairs. The Chinese era name Guangxu was adopted by the note to demonstrate Chinese suzerainty. [51] Later, similar notes were also sent to other Western powers which made treaties with Korea.[52] In 1894 when Japan intended using the ambiguity of the Korean international status as an excuse to expel Chinese troops from Korea, the Korean government still responded in the same way.[53] The aim of China and Korea was to maintain the tributary relationship while admitting independence rights of Korea under Western pressure. It is argued that such kind of actions were not successful because the United States neither publicized nor answered the Korean note.[54] However, the Western powers did not raise any objection to stop Korea from sending tributes to China. Accordingly, the tributary relationship was not incompatible with independence. As the Korean government argued, as long as it observed all the obligations required by the 1876 treaty, its relationship with China should not be questioned by Japan.[55] Therefore, Korean independence was not a strong and legitimate reason to terminate the Sino-Korean tributary relationship.

Next, concerning question (2), ie the legality of the Japanese expedition in 1894, the Japanese government justified its action by quoting the third clause of the Sino-Japanese Convention of Tianjin in 1885:

> In case of any disturbance of a grave nature occurring in Corea [Korea], which necessitates the respective countries or either of them to send troops to Corea, it is hereby understood that they shall give, each to the other, previous notice in writing of their intention so to do, and that after the matter is settled, they shall withdraw their troops and not further station them there.[56]

Many historians argued that this convention 'virtually reduced Korea to a co-protectorate of China and Japan, eliminated China's claim to exclusive suzerainty, and confirmed Japan's right to send troops'. [57] As described in section 2, Japan refused to withdraw its troops even at the request of Korea after the rebellion had

[50] Kuo Ting-yee 郭廷以, 'China and the First US–Korean Treaty' (Zhongguo yu diyi ci Mei Han Tiaoyue 中國與第一次美韓條約) in Huang Tsen-ming 黃正銘 et al (eds), *Collected Papers on Chinese Diplomatic History* (*Zhongguo waijiao shi lunji* 中國外交史論集) (Zhonghua wenhua chuban shiye weiyuan hui 1957) vol 1, 1–18; Lin Min-te 林明德, *Yuan Shih-k'ai and Korea* (袁世凱與朝鮮) (Institute of Modern History, Academia Sinica 1984); Song Pyŏng-gi 宋炳基, *The 1882 Korean–American Treaty and Ch'ing China*, Yang Xiu-zhi 楊秀芝 tr (Lexis Book 2006).

[51] Lin (n 50) 90–91.

[52] ibid 92.

[53] National Palace Museum Library (n 7) *juan* 14, no 1063, 2.

[54] Lin (n 50) 91–92.

[55] National Palace Museum Library (n 7) *juan* 14, no 1063, 2.

[56] Parry (n 45), vol 166, 100.

[57] Immanuel CY Hsü, *The Rise of Modern China* (OUP 2000) 337.

been put down. Li Hongzhang was then blamed by historians for consenting to the convention, creating an excuse for the Japanese dispatch and leading to the defeat.[58] However, this chapter intends to review this matter from a different perspective. Did the 1885 convention really authorize Japan's action in sending troops to Korea in 1894?

First, the interpretation of the convention should stick to the wordings, while nothing beyond the words should be implied. The clause quoted above actually imposed two conditions for Chinese or Japanese dispatches of forces in the future: (1) 'disturbance of a grave nature' which needed Chinese and/or Japanese reinforcement; (2) 'previous notice'. Logically speaking, both of these were merely 'necessary conditions'. China and Japan had to ensure that both conditions had already been satisfied before sending their troops to Korea. On the other hand, 'necessary conditions' did not mean 'sufficient conditions'. Even if the two conditions had been satisfied, it did not imply that China and Japan would automatically have the right to dispatch troops. In other words, this term only imposed restrictions to future dispatches.

Second, did the Korean government have the right to accept or refuse Chinese and Japanese reinforcement? Since the clause itself did not directly give an answer, it is meaningful to explore the background and negotiation process of the convention. In 1882, Japan acquired the right to station in Korea from the Japan–Korean Treaty of Chemulpo. Two years later, in the Gapsin coup, the Korean king was captured by the pro-Japanese Enlightenment Party. He was finally saved by the Chinese troops under Yuan Shikai. In the following year, Japan sent Itō Hirobumi as its representative to China to negotiate an agreement for mutual withdrawal of forces. There were six meetings between Itō and Li Hongzhang, in which future dispatch of troops was discussed from the fifth one.

As historians argue, the actual aim of Japan during the negotiation was to gain Sino-Japanese equality in Korea. Itō planned to do so by making China abandon some of its suzerain rights which Japan did not have, or grant Japan the same rights. The right of sending troops to Korea was thus put on the agenda, regardless of which particular right Japan could get, and which condition was required by dispatches of forces.[59] At first, Itō suggested a clause which forbade both China and Japan to send troops to Korea, but it was declined by Li. [60] Itō then modified the suggested clause as the following:

> In case of any disturbance occurring in Korea, when the Korean king requests either of the respective countries to send troops for suppression, the country has the right to send troops to Korea after getting consent from the other country.[61]

[58] Dai Dongyang 戴東陽, 'Xu Chengzu and the Sino-Japanese Tianjin Convention' (Xu Chengzu yu Zhong Ri Tianjin Tiaoyue 徐承祖與中日《天津條約》) in Institute of Modern History, Chinese Academy of Social Sciences (ed), *Academic Forum for the Youth* (*Zhongguo Shehui Kexue Yuan Jindai Shi Yanjiu Suo Qingnian Xueshu Luntan [2005]* 中國社會科學院近代史研究所青年學術論壇〔2005〕) (Social Sciences Academic Press 2006) 110.

[59] Dai (n 58) 109.

[60] Ministry of Foreign Affairs of Japan 外務省 (ed), *Documents on Japanese Foreign Policy* 日本外交文書 (United Nations Association of Japan 1936–63), vol 18, no 160, 276–77.

[61] ibid 289; National Palace Museum Library (n 7), *juan* 8, no 369, 5.

Because this suggestion was refused by Li again, Itō drafted another version which excluded Korean request and mutual consent, in order to get Li's agreement.[62] The process of negotiation clearly showed that Itō saw Korean permission and Chinese consent as essential criteria for Japanese dispatches.

On the other hand, Li simply wanted to maintain the Sino-Korean tributary relationship which had lasted for centuries, and prevent Japanese intervention in Korean affairs. Accepting the final draft of the convention, which did not clearly mention the necessity of Korean authorization for Chinese and Japanese dispatches, did not imply Li's disrespect for the right of Korea. As a matter of fact, Li's concern came from the Gapsin coup in 1884. In this incident, the king captured by the pro-Japanese party was unable to ask for Chinese help. Li was worried about the possibility of a similar incident in the future. If the king was captured again, or even killed, China should still dispatch its troops to help his family.[63] Li's worry of Japanese aggression was repeatedly expressed throughout the meeting.[64] In order to make Japan withdraw its troops from Korea, he finally agreed to the clause suggested by Itō and let Japan appear to achieve the same right which China originally had.

In short, it can be seen that Itō, at least in 1885, understood that Korean consent should be necessary for Japanese intervention in the potential crisis in Korea. Li's concern was only for extreme cases, for instance, when the king was overthrown. During the Tonghak Rebellion in 1894, the Korean king and his government were still properly functioning. The situation was far from the special cases which Li anticipated. The Japanese dispatch of forces, which ignored Korean opposition, undoubtedly violated the intentions of Itō and Li.

Besides, it is important to note that the 1885 convention was only an agreement between China and Japan. Korea, whose independence had been respected by the powers, was not obligated to observe the convention. Moreover, the interpretation of the 1885 convention could not contradict the Japan–Korea Treaty of 1876, which recognized Korean independence. In other words, the independence of Korea, which had already been perceived by Japan and the West, should not be affected by the 1885 convention. Therefore, Japan's dispatching forces into the independent state Korea was obviously against the fundamental principles of international law.

Furthermore, Japan's refusal to withdraw its troops after the suppression of the rebellion also violated the clause of immediate withdrawal stated in the 1885 convention. Japan behaved even more aggressively afterwards. In response to Japan's proposal for Korean reform, Li Hongzhang said that international affairs should follow international law and treaties. Since Japan recognized Korea as an independent state, it should allow Korea to decide whether implementing the reforms.[65] Korea also protested that Japanese intervention in Korean internal affairs was an infringement of Korean independence.[66] Regardless of these voices, Japan still stationed its troops in Korea for purpose of coercion, blamed China for opposing reforms beneficial to

[62] Ministry of Foreign Affairs of Japan (n 60), vol 18, no 160, 290–91. [63] ibid 284.
[64] ibid 282–85.
[65] Ministry of Foreign Affairs of Japan (n 60), vol 27, pt 2, no 564, 220.
[66] ibid pt 1, no 412, 606.

Korea, and made demands which would not be accepted by China.[67] Finally, the war which Japan expected broke out.

It has been pointed out that the Japanese justification for the Sino-Japanese War came from its idea of constructing a 'Greater East Asia', rather than modern nationalism and international law.[68] Based on the discussion in this section and the previous one, it can be further concluded that both the aim and process of starting the war were unjust because they violated international law.

## 4. Confucian and Western Responses to Japanese Aggression

In the contemporary world, even if there are intergovernmental peacekeepers like the United Nations, wars, no matter just or unjust, are not eliminated. It is thus not difficult to imagine that at the time before the First World War and the establishment of the League of Nations, international law was inefficient in preventing military conflicts. Meanwhile, Confucianism, as a world order adopted by East Asia, was too weak to contain colonialism. Therefore, the Japanese aggression could not be stopped.

### 4.1 Confucian response

Confucianism, which oriented in China, had been the ideology of the state since the second century BC. In the Middle Ages, its status was challenged by Buddhism. Nevertheless, the period of Song, founded in the tenth century, was seen as the renaissance era of Confucianism. Confucianism became influential among intellectuals and politicians, because in order to gain high ranks in the government they had to study Confucian classics to pass the civil examination. However, in modern China, scholars suspected that Confucianism was accountable for the weakness of the state. Since the twentieth century, Neo-Confucian scholars suggested reinventing Confucianism by 'conversations' with Western or global values.[69] The Confucian world order is certainly one of the most important value systems. In fact, similarities and differences between Confucianism and international law have been discussed for more than a century.[70] Regardless of the controversies, the purpose of this section is to explore whether Confucianism can serve as a peacemaking philosophy.

[67] National Palace Museum Library (n 7), *juan* 14, no 1173, 41.

[68] Jin Guantao 金觀濤 and Liu Qingfeng 劉青峰, 'The Tianxia Worldview of China, Japan and Korea in the Nineteenth Century and the Outbreak of the Sino-Japanese War' (Shijiu shiji Zhong Ri Han de tianxia guan ji Jiawu Zhancheng de baofa 19 世紀中日韓的天下觀及甲午戰爭的爆發) Reflexion 思想(October 2006) 3, 125.

[69] Tu Weiming 杜維明, *Preliminary Topics on the Third Phase of Development of Confucianism* (Ruxue disan qi fazhan de qianjing wenti: dalu jiangxue, wennan he taolun 儒學第三期發展的前景問題——大陸講學，問難和討論) (Linking Publishing 1989) 315–16; Charles Wei-Hsun Fu 傅偉勳, *The Life of Learning and the Learning of Life* (*Xuewen de Shengming yu shengming de xuewen* 學問的生命與生命的學問) (Cheng Chung Bookstore 1994) 255–58.

[70] Zeng Tao 曾濤, 'Analogical Interpretation for International Law in Modern China' 近代中國的國際法附會論, in Chinese Legal History Society (ed), *Chinese Journal of Legal History* 法史學刊, vol 11 (Social Sciences Academic Press 2008) 217–37.

Before the war began, Li Hongzhang expected that international mediation would solve the conflict. Historians have criticized Li for being too confident with mediation, not understanding the international situation, not actively preparing for the war, which led to China's failure to protect Korea from aggression. Li made his decision possibly because he was insecure about the war, but the Confucian tradition was also an underlying factor in his strategy.

First, it is important to understand that the core of Confucianism is a 'way' (*dao*) which can be followed by a person, a family, a state, and even the world. A sage king can rectify himself, and then his family, his state, and the whole world. In other words, the 'way' of the state is extended from the 'way' of the person and his family. Similarly, the world order is extended from domestic affairs of a state. Therefore, wars between States were the same, in nature, as punishing criminals among individuals within one single state.[71] The aim of war is 'to put an end to violence and to do away with harm, not in order to contend with others for spoil'.[72] On the other hand, Confucianism does not encourage using violence as a solution to disputes. At state level, punishment was not the best way of governing. This idea was elaborated in *The Analects*:

> The rule of virtue can be compared to the Pole Star which commands the homage of the multitude of stars without leaving its place.[73]
>
> Guide them by edicts, keep them in line with punishments, and the common people will stay out of trouble but will have no sense of shame. Guide them by virtue, keep them in line with the rites, and they will, besides having a sense of shame, reform themselves.[74]
>
> To impose the death penalty without first attempting to reform is to be cruel.[75]

Besides, Confucianism encourages mediation, instead of resorting to litigation.[76] It prefers virtue and rites to administrative and legal means as governing measures. This represents a harmonious way of ruling the state. If the king manages to demonstrate his morality, his people will follow. The 'way' of maintaining world order is the same:

> [W]hen distant subjects are unsubmissive one cultivates one's moral quality in order to attract them, and once they have come one makes them content.[77]

Hence, political matters, whether municipal or international, should be dealt with on a morality basis, rather than by administrative measures or punishments. International order can also be considered as a moral order. Accordingly, rulers of States should prevent using force to settle international disputes. Even wars punishing tyrants were criticized as 'perfectly beautiful but not perfectly good'.[78]

[71] Confucian scholars argued that there were five levels of punishments. The highest level was the war against feudal lords who disobeyed the order of the king. See *Discourses of the States* (*Guoyu* 國語) (Shanghai Chinese Classics Publishing House 1978), *juan* 4, 162.

[72] *Hsün Tzu: Basic Writings*, Burton Watson, tr (Columbia UP 1963) 69.

[73] *The Analects*, DC Lau tr (Penguin 1979) 63. [74] ibid. [75] ibid 160.

[76] ibid 115. [77] ibid 139. [78] ibid 71.

Of course, Confucianism does not forbid wars of all kind. On the contrary, Confucian scholars had a strong sense of 'just war'. The main concern is who has the right to war, that is, the authority to implement punishments to States. This is a complicated problem in *jus ad bellum* even nowadays, but Mencius managed to provide a clear answer:

> In the *Spring and Autumn Annals* there were no just wars. There were only cases of one war not being quite as bad as another. A punitive expedition is a war waged by one in authority against his subordinates. It is not for peers to punish one another by war.[79]

In the Zhou Dynasty, there were States ruled by feudal lords who needed to obey the king. If there was any disobedience, the king had the authority to implement punishments. After the power of the king deteriorated, the responsibility was eventually taken by strong feudal lords. However, Confucius was critical:

> When the Way prevails in the Empire, the rites and music and punitive expeditions are initiated by the Emperor. When the Way does not prevail in the Empire, they are initiated by the feudal lords.[80]

If this idea is elaborated in the contemporary world, it can be argued that only supranational organizations like the United Nations have the right to wage war. Otherwise, wars among sovereign States would be considered unjust.

During the Warring States period when the king of Zhou was too weak to maintain world order, there were feudal lords ruling unjustly. When the Qi prepared to launch a war against the Yan which was thought to be unjust, Mencius argued:

> When Shen T'ung asked me, 'Is it all right to march on Yen (Yan)?' I answered, 'Yes'. And they marched on Yen. Had he asked, 'Who has the right to march on Yen?' I would have answered, 'A Heaven-appointed officer has the right to do so'. Suppose a man killed another, and someone were to ask, 'Is it all right to kill the killer?' I would answer, 'Yes'. But if he further asked, 'Who has the right to kill him?' I would answer, 'The Marshal of the Guards has the right to kill him'.[81]

Accordingly, the right to war against the unjust should belong to the superior. Although Mencius mentioned the god and his representative, that is, the 'heaven-appointed officer', his idea was not a mythical theory. He quoted the Confucian classics saying that,

> Heaven sees with the eyes of its people. Heaven hears with the ears of its people.[82]

Instead of praying to the god, Mencius insisted that the will of the heaven could be observed by listening to the people. Therefore, a war would only be just if the forces were welcomed by people of the enemy state.[83]

At the time before the outbreak of the First Sino-Japanese War, there was no intergovernmental authority, such as the League of Nations or International Court

[79] *Mencius*, DC Lau tr (Penguin 1970) 194.
[80] *The Analects* (n 73) 139.
[81] *Mencius* (n 79) 90–91.
[82] ibid 144.
[83] ibid 69.

of Justice, which could provide judgments for international conflicts among sovereign States. Meanwhile, Confucianism could hardly justify a war against Japan as an equal state for China. Li Hongzhang obviously did not want to enter into a war. Because of the absence of international authority, he could only rely on mediation by the international community. Unfortunately, he was finally disappointed by the self-interested Western powers which did not have a strong sense of international order and morality.

Some might doubt Li Hongzhang for not actively preparing for the war. Li's passive attitude towards war might be better understood by looking at another story in *Mencius*. When the Qi threatened the Teng by fortifying the frontier, the duke of Teng asked for Mencius's advice. Mencius answered

> If a man does good deeds, then amongst his descendants in future generations there will rise one who will become a true King. All gentlemen can do in starting an enterprise is to leave behind a tradition which can be carried on. Heaven alone can grant success. What can you do about Ch'i [Qi]? You can only try your best to do good.[84]

Mencius's idea was further clarified in another paragraph. When the duke of Teng asked whether he should please the Qi, Mencius responded as follows:

> 'In antiquity' answered Mencius, 'when T'ai Wang was in Pin, the Ti tribes invaded the place. He tried to buy them off with skins and silks; he tried to buy them off with horses and hounds; he tried to buy them off with pearls and jade; but all to no avail. Then he assembled the elders and announced to them, "What the Ti tribes want is our land. I have heard that a man in authority never turns what is meant for the benefit of men into a source of harm to them. It will not be difficult for you, my friends, to find another lord. I am leaving." And he left Pin, crossed the Liang Mountains and built a city at the foot of Mount Ch'i and settled there. The men of Pin said, "This is a benevolent man. We must not lose him." They flocked after him as if to market.
>
> Others expressed the view, "This is the land of our forbears. It is not a matter for us to decide. Let us defend it to the death."
>
> You will have to choose between these two courses'.[85]

In short, Mencius believed that a state did not have to be frightened of foreign threats. Instead, it should continue good policies as usual. Even if the state was attacked, the ruler and his people could leave the place and live elsewhere. Alternatively, the people could choose to stay in their country and risk death. Mencius's idea was a way to preserve morality, but not sovereignty. As scholars argued, when international law was not sufficient in solving conflicts of interests among States during periods of keen competition, the Chinese mentality might be expected to represent a peaceful world order. However, a reasonable world order could not be formulated merely by morality.[86] It should be noted that the main concern of Confucianism was morality rather than sovereignty. It indeed could not provide a feasibly practical mechanism for containing aggression, expansionism, and colonialism because of the complexity of the modern world.

[84] ibid 71. [85] ibid 71–72. [86] Jin and Liu (n 68) 127.

## 4.2 Western response

In the nineteenth century, the interests of Western countries were deeply affected by the situation in Asia. Many Western countries followed up the development in Asia and took action accordingly.

### *4.2.1 Western perception of Japan's action in Korea*

From the time when Japan sent troops to Korea, its ambition of complete control of Korea and a war with China was noticed by Western countries. In June, the US Naval Force on Asiatic Station reported to US Navy Force that if Japan was not deliberately provoking a war with China, it was difficult to know what its aggression towards Korea meant.[87] In addition, the US perceived Japan's argument that its residents in Korea required protection as a pretext only, because no one was menacing them at all.[88] Also, Mr Sill, the US minister to Korea, in a telegram sent to Mr Uhl stated that while the Chinese were in favour of simultaneous departure, Japan seemed to desire war and Korean integrity was being threatened.[89] A telegram sent from Gresham to Thomas F Bayard clearly shows US perceptions and attitudes towards Japan's action in Korea

> The United States indulge the hope that Korean independence and sovereignty will be respected. You are instructed to say to the Government at Tokio, that the President will be painfully disappointed, should Japan visit upon her feeble and defenseless neighbor the horrors of an unjust war.[90]

This statement shows clearly that the US perceived Japan's action as damaging to Korea's independence and sovereignty and alluded to the possibility of Japan's starting an unjust war. Britain even predicted that Japan would besiege the royal palace by force. In a telegram sent from O'Conor to the Earl of Kimberley on 15 June 1894, he attached a letter sent from Drummond, Her Majesty's Acting Crown Advocate at Shanghai talking about the political forecast of the designs of Japan in regard to Korea, including:

1. The Japanese will seize the King of Corea, if they can, and carry him to Japan.
2. They will assist the rebels at first, but afterwards will try to conquer and retain Corea, which they are determined to possess, if possible.
3. … make a diversion by a sudden dash, with a few ships, upon Chinkiang and Nanking.
4. … make an attack upon a southern port, probably Formosa or Foochow.
5. … conquering and retaining Formosa …[91]

All these records show that Japan's hidden agenda had been known by Western countries and they perceived Japan's action as violating international law.

[87] Davids (n 13) 93–94. [88] ibid. [89] ibid 99. [90] ibid 183.
[91] British Foreign Office, *Confidential Print: China*. FO 405/60, 133.

### *4.2.2 Western responses to Japan's aggression*

Confronting with Japan's aggression, Western powers, especially Britain and Russia, took corresponding actions for mediation.

#### 4.2.2.1 Britain

The British government was keen to maintain peace in Asia and tried to bring China and Japan back to peaceful negotiation. As a mediator, the British government tried to make Japan and China meet halfway. The Chinese government accepted Britain's advice and informed the Japanese government of conditions on which they were willing to reopen the negotiation. However, unfortunately, after several correspondences, these two countries still could not reach an agreement.[92] As a matter of fact, Japan knew that the preconditions they raised for negotiation would not be accepted by China. In order to avoid a violation of diplomatic courtesy by rejecting the new British overtures flatly, Mutsu believed that the only possible course they could follow was to promote a spontaneous cessation of negotiations by offering conditions the Chinese government could never accept.[93]

Perceiving that the Sino-Japanese War was unavoidable in the long run, the British government gave up the mediation and just requested Japan to agree in advance not to take any military action against Shanghai and its line of communications.[94]

Japan's success in refusing Britain's proposal for mediation and finally making the attitude of Britain change was due to its accurate understanding and judgement of Britain's concern and intention. Mutsu explicitly pointed out that Britain's main concern was the enormous impact the hostility between China and Japan might have on its own political and commercial interests and its primary desire was to maintain the peace of the Far East.[95] Accordingly, Japan believed that Britain was not necessarily hostile as long as Japan made sure that Britain's interest would not be damaged. Just as Japan expected, Britain finally gave up the mediation and even changed their attitude dramatically later on with the development of the situation in the battlefield. It seemed that Britain, after realizing that Japan would be the final winner, was standing with Japan and turning its back on China. The change in British attitude can be seen in the case of *Kowshing*.

At the very beginning of hostility between China and Japan, the Japanese navy sank the British steamship *Kowshing*, leased by China transporting troops to Korea. The British foreign secretary believed the Japanese government must be held responsible for loss of life and property sustained by British subjects through the action of the Japanese naval officers at the time;[96] British public opinion and the press in particular held that Britain should make Japan apologize for their navy's insult to the British flag and should provide appropriate compensation to the owners of *Kowshing*. In short, the general view in Britain was that the Japanese navy had violated international law by committing such an outrage prior to the declaration of

[92] Kajima (n 6) 81–83. [93] Mutsu (n 6) 50. [94] Kajima (n 6) 83.
[95] Mutsu (n 6) 52. [96] ibid 86.

war between Japan and China.[97] However, surprisingly, Japan's efforts finally made the British government sanction the legality of Japan's sinking of *SS Kowshing*.[98] What was most striking is that British victims afterwards turned to the Foreign Office for assistance in suing China for compensation.[99]

#### 4.2.2.2 Russia

Russia's mediation underwent a change from a tough approach to a much softer one. At the very beginning, the Russia government exerted its utmost efforts to persuade the Japanese government to withdraw their troops from Korea. Russia warned Japan that if it refused to recall its troops simultaneously with Chinese withdrawal, it would be obliged to bear serious responsibility for the consequences. Japan at this stage, bore enormous risk in refusing Russia's proposal. In Mutsu's mind, compared with the irresolution of Britain, Russia's intention seemed firm and unshakeable, which posed a threat to Japan.[100]

However, nobody could stop Japan's determination to occupy Korea. After thorough consideration, Japan planned to make use of Britain as a counterbalance to Russia, which finally succeeded in letting Russia's retreat.[101] The Russian minister in Japan suggested to his government that once Russia stood beside China, Britain was very likely to be with Japan; and then other powers would be quite happy to see Russia trapped in Asian affairs.[102] Considering that Russia was not well prepared to intervene by force and it would be useless without force to persuade Japan to retreat, Russia softened its attitude and decided not to be involved further in this issue. In response to minister Cassini's telegram, Giers indicated the end of mediation, stating that

> we absolutely do not wish to be involved in the present Korea dispute as Japan and China have been ... It must not be forgotten that in spite of its extreme severity, our demand made to Japan ... was friendly advice in character ... We have reasons to believe that Britain will move in nearly the same direction as ours.[103]

#### 4.2.2.3 United States and Italy

When the situation remained deadlocked, Korea asked the US to intervene. At the same time, Britain also approached the US to see whether it would unite with Great Britain in an intervention to avert war between China and Japan.

[97] ibid 88–89.

[98] Douglas Howland, 'The Sinking of the S.S. Kowshing: International Law, Diplomacy, and the Sino-Japanese War' (2008) 42(4) Modern Asian Studies 688.

[99] ibid 689. [100] Mutsu (n 6) 53.

[101] Lin Min 林敏, 'On the Foreign Policy of Great Britain and Russia in the Far East Before the Sino-Japanese War in 1894' (Shilun Jiawu Zhanzheng qianxi Ying E de Yuandong waijiao 試論甲午戰爭前夕英俄的遠東外交) Journal of Sichuan University (Philosophy and Social Science Edition) 四川大學學報(哲學社會科學版)(May 2002) 120, 96.

[102] *Translations of Selected Documents from Red Archives on Chinese Diplomatic History* (*Hongdang zazhi youguan Zhongguo jiaoshe shiliao xuanyi* 紅檔雜誌有關中國交涉史料選譯) (SDX Joint Publishing 1957) 18.

[103] Kajima (n 6) 93.

US attitude was clear: even though it sympathized with the Korean government and desired to see its sovereignty respected, it maintained towards Korea and the other powers an attitude of impartial neutrality; US influence could be exerted over Japan only in a friendly way; in no event could it intervene jointly with other powers.[104]

The US government's position did not cause Japan to become overly alarmed. In Mutsu's words

> The United States historically had been a most friendly and cordial nation toward Japan, and her own particular foreign policy also militated against her intervening in the Far Eastern situation. Obviously, the Americans were actuated only by a desire for peace which is common to all men, and a feeling that they could not simply ignore Korea's plea for assistance.[105]

Based on this assessment, the Japanese government gave no ear to US mediation. Italy, just before the Sino-Japanese War started, also joined the mediation. In view of the circumstances, Japan believed that Italy joined just to enhance its position in the Far East, therefore it was of no concern to Italy whether mediation succeeded.[106] Japan did not counter-propose, but rejected Italy's plan by sending a letter the day after Japan occupied by force the Korean palace.[107]

After reviewing the perceptions and mediation attempts of Western powers, it is unfortunate to conclude that all the countries chose to retreat or just pretended to play a role for their own interests, despite their knowing that Japan's aggression was in violation of international law. International law in these circumstances was useless in preventing aggression happening.

## 5. Conclusion

The tension between Confucianism and international law created the complexity of the East Asian international relationship during the late nineteenth century. Japanese scholars have argued that the First Sino-Japanese War helped preserving stability and peace in the Far East by implanting the Western international legal order. The traditional Confucian tributary system was claimed to be old-fashioned and uncivilized. This chapter reviews the reformation of world order and international relationship from a different perspective. Before the arrival of the Western powers and the introduction of international law, the tributary system had been successful in preserving world order without substantial problems. Instead of improving the East Asian world order, international law was playing a key role in deconstructing the stability and creating chaos and conflicts. Japan was not building a peaceful East Asian world, but trying to establish its own predominance in Asia by replacing the Chinese superiority and hegemony. The Western way of justifying colonization by means of international law was obviously followed by Japan. By detailed study on the background of the war based on historical sources, it is not difficult to find

104 Davids (n 13) 186–87. 105 Mutsu (n 6) 54. 106 ibid 98.
107 ibid 100.

that Japan actually violated international law and relevant treaties. International law, which had become a set of game rules for colonialism, did not stop Japanese aggression. While the Chinese power was declining, Confucianism could not offer an alternative solution to the crisis. A more reasonable world order which could efficiently prevent aggression and expansionism had yet to be constructed.

# 19

# Confucianism and Western International Law in 1900

## Li Hongzhang and Sir Ernest Satow Compared: A Case Study of the Crisis of Russia in Manchuria (1900–01)

*Anthony Carty and Jing Tan*

### 1. The General Educational Background of Satow and Li

It is perhaps to be expected that China and Britain would represent a confrontation between Confucianism and international law around 1900. English diplomats would be trained in and/or take international law as their benchmark while the Chinese officials are, with fierce rigor, trained in the Chinese classical texts of Confucianism. This study will show that on neither side is this the case exactly, at least in the sense of an educational discipline having a decisive outcome in shaping their professional activity.

The case study of Satow and Li, above all with respect to the Russian proposed acquisition of a Manchurian Rail Concession, affords an opportunity to test the interaction of individual personalities, their cultural backgrounds, the impact of their respective country's internal organization (with their institutional place within it) as well as the structural restraints imposed by the conflictual relations of their States with one another. Out of this should emerge a more nuanced assessment of the nature of the idea of systems of Confucianism and international law.

Generally in his study of the life of Sir Harold Nicholson, Derek Drinkwater points out how the foundation for the education of Oxford (and Cambridge) students, who would go onto government and diplomatic service, was the Greek classics, and in particular Aristotle's *Politics*.[1] Ernest Satow did not go to Oxford but to University College London. In the first chapter of his work *A Diplomat in Japan*[2] he explains the nature of his own education wryly. He had only begun his studies when he responded successfully to an advertisement for an appointment

[1] D Drinkwater, *Sir Harold Nicolson and International Relations: The Practitioner as Theorist* (OUP 2005) especially ch 3.

[2] E Mason Satow, *A Diplomat in Japan* (Seeley Service 1921).

as a student interpreter in Yedo, Japan. While in preparation in Beijing he did the Consul's examination in 1862:

The great fault of the system is that it takes no account of moral qualities. Whether a candidate has the manners or feelings of a gentleman cannot be ascertained from the way in which he will reproduce a proposition of Euclid or translate a passage from a Greek author. It does not test the intellectual powers, for a stupid young man who has been properly coached will almost always beat the real student who has not got the right 'tips'. Nowadays, every candidate for a public examination goes to a crammer, who trains him in a few months for the contest, and enables him to bring forth forced fruit for a moment. Show me a successful examinee, and I will show you a well-coached candidate. In the majority of cases the process disgusts the man who has undergone it, and takes away any inclination he may previously have had for study. And without serious study it is not possible to acquire such languages as Chinese, Siamese or Japanese. The scheme of examination is no test of the linguistic capabilities of the men, and sometimes sends into the service those who can no more learn to speak a foreign language than they can fly. My own success in the examination was due to my having left school more recently than any of the other competitors.[3]

This dryness and narrowness is a little surprising, since Drinkwater points out that the concentration on Aristotle's *Politics* at Oxford was intended to ensure a broad-ranging, flexible understanding of politics as an exercise of reasonableness, prudence, and a sense of proportion in the conduct of public affairs. This may have already been inculcated in Satow while at school.

When Satow was eventually appointed as minister in Beijing in 1900 he was chosen by Lord Salisbury, after a lifetime of experience in Japan and China, as someone 'more circumspect and more aware of the wider significance of China for British diplomacy than MacDonald had been; someone who would put the maintenance of the *status quo* before concession hunting'.[4] Otte explains authoritatively that the tradition in China, unlike Japan, was to leave the British minister on the spot a very free hand to act as he pleased and in the first year that Salisbury remained in charge he received no directions. Satow's experience in Morocco was considered an advantage because he had shown ability in dealing with another decaying monarchy. His own view of China was that it was not a centralized modern State, but 'rather a congeries of semi-autonomous satrapies, a confederacy of territories each possessing a separate financial, military, naval and judicial organization, in fact a sort of "Home rule all round" system, presided over by a central committee'.[5] This profound understanding of the inner workings of the immensely impenetrable Chinese bureaucracy will prove key to the case study which will be undertaken, of the 1900–01 crisis over a proposed Chinese concession to Russian with respect to a Manchurian Railway. However, first something has to be said about 'the wider significance of China for British diplomacy'.

[3] ibid 19.

[4] TG Otte, '"Not Proficient in Table-Thumping": Sir Ernest Satow in Peking, 1900–1906' (2002) 13(2) Diplomacy and Statecraft 161–63.

[5] ibid 165. Otte is drawing on Satow's diaries, deposited in the national archives of the UK government.

At the age of 24 (1847), Li Hongzhang (李鸿章) ranked thirteen in the second class of Jinshi (进士, advanced scholar) in court examination, the last round of imperial examinations. This means only fifteen people were ranked higher than Li Hongzhang in his year of the imperial examinations. He was entitled to Jinshi Background and then started to work in the Hanlin Academy (翰林院). The academy members stood on the top of the social hierarchy who were confined to an elite group of scholars. One of the main duties of Hanlin scholars was to interpret Confucian classics for the court. Li Hongzhang's position in the academy gave him an opportunity of pursuing a promising political future. In comparison with him, his father, Li Wen'an (李文安, 1801–55) ranked the third class in court examination at the age of 37 (1838).

The successful examination candidates of the same year automatically formed a relationship similar to alumni. To be specific, they had to pass the final round of the imperial examinations in the same year and then they would be called the 'same year alumni' (同年). This was the milestone of their interpersonal relationships. This relationship would follow them in their whole life and become the most important resource for their political interests. Among the same year alumni of Li Hongzhang's father, one person became one of the most influential officials in the late Qing period and was given the title of Marquis Yiyong of the First Class (一等毅勇侯). Being recommended by his father, Li Hongzhang became that person's student and his aide later on. That person's name is Zeng Guofan (曾国藩, 1811–72). This was a great opportunity for Li Hongzhang to get close to the centre of Confucian scholars and politicians. This was the biggest contribution his father made to his family. The father's relationships were passed down to Li Hongzhang and became Li Hongzhang's resources in his future political life.

The imperial examination system provided Li Hongzhang with two obvious benefits. The first was the opportunity to secure a position in the government. The second was to establish his interpersonal relationships as his father did. The first benefit was open to qualified people. Because of the movements between classes realized by the imperial examination system, there was no gentry class in China. The social status was based on the result of one's imperial examinations. Whether poor or rich, so long as one could pass all levels of the imperial examinations, one was given this opportunity. To this point, the imperial examination system was a fair system and therefore it provided a hope to the whole nation, especially to the people who wanted to change the fate of their lives and honour their families. The imperial examination system was a State monopoly for ordinary people who did not come from Manchu families. They could not get as many benefits as the imperial examination system provided elsewhere, so they had no choice but to tie their fortunes to the proper running of this system. Li Hongzhang showed his ambition to be a top official when he was only 20.

The second benefit was exclusive, members only. Once people passed the final round of the imperial examinations, they established connections with the ruling class. They became shareholders of the ruling system which was sustained by the imperial examination system and the theories of Confucianism. The Confucian system was a closed system in which independent and liberal people would not grow. People's values and even their lives existed in their relationships. One's relationships in this system were a legacy that could be succeeded by their descendants. Family became an important resource of one's development. Therefore, people were motivated to develop their interpersonal relationships and pursue the perpetuation of their family. The harder people tried to survive in this system, the more stable the system stood. The more stable the system stood, the more difficult it became for people to escaped from it. This resulted in the inertia of the people in this system. If the imperial examination system and the Confucian culture system were destroyed, the shareholders' benefits would also perish. This is a key to understanding why some conservative officials in late Qing strongly opposed China's learning from Western countries and the reason why it was difficult for some Chinese officials to make any changes to the Qing government.

## 2. The Respective Country Contexts of the Two Leading Diplomats

The terms of British diplomacy towards China evolved in the course of events leading up to the Treaty of Beijing of October 1860, which ensured the ratification by China of the 1858 Treaty of Tianjin. The latter had guaranteed the principle of equality of States and exchange of permanent ambassadors. The key provision of the later treaty could be in art III, that the British minister would not be expected 'to perform any ceremony derogatory to him as representing the Sovereign of an independent nation on a footing of equality with that of China'. He would in turn treat China's emperor with all the respect that would be shown by agents of Her Majesty 'towards the Sovereigns of independent and equal European nations'.[6] Nonetheless, the reality was that China was in a very fragile state and Britain was continually concerned that pressure from the foreign powers could lead to its disintegration. So, Britain gave China to understand, in the course of the two-year-long 'ratification process' of the Tianjin Treaty to the Beijing Treaty, that it would regard China in the same protective aspect that it had just adopted towards Russian aggression against the Ottoman Empire, ie the Crimean War and the Peace of Paris 1856.

For instance, in the exchanges between the Qing official Pieu and the British agent, Lay, the former indicated that his government knew the Crimean War had been 'undertaken to prevent the Tsar from appropriating "little Turkey" '. In response Lay asserted categorically 'that a foreign nation could not always commit what acts of aggression it pleased, for if one nation were unreasonable others could interpose to restrain her'.[7] Indeed one of the reasons Lord Elgin, the British plenipotentiary, wished to have a permanent mission in Beijing was that he 'looked forward to the possibility of invigorating the Imperial administration just as Great Britain was hoping to do in Turkey'. 'The Imperial power is to be sustained and among the means of doing so is that which this treaty provides—a sort of diplomatic protectorate at the capital.'[8]

[6] C Parry, *Consolidated Treaty Series 1860–1861*, vol 123 (Oceana 1969) 165.
[7] W Conrad Costin, *Great Britain and China 1833–1860* (Clarendon Press 1937) 266–67.
[8] ibid 269.

This was a far cry from the brutality of the Treaty of Nanking of 1842 and indeed the circumstances preceding the ratification by China of the Treaty of Beijing in 1860. As a punishment for the torture and killing of British envoys during the final stages of compelling the Chinese to ratify the Treaty of Beijing, Lord Elgin, the English commissioner for the negotiations, had quickly imposed a huge indemnity to be paid at very short notice, in default of which he had the Summer Palace burned.[9] This was intended as a punishment for a crime, the killing of envoys.

However, the wider context was the compulsion being used to drive the Chinese Empire into a style of diplomatic relations which it did not want. How this wider context is assessed can hardly be left exclusively to the terms of international law. As Costin says in his epilogue, the 'Son of Heaven' could hardly have denied himself by recognizing the Queen of England as his equal. The collapse of the Qing dynasty 'was inevitable if there was to be a full recognition of that equality of status and common humanity which was the real demand of the British and other foreign Governments'.[10] This judgement contains a Western progress narrative, that the Chinese will finally see that is possible to: 'reach out into the full and free life of a positive common citizenship and a collective partnership with other peoples'.[11]

Costin very astutely points out that such was the paradoxical context in which the British and other Western powers were to lend the Qing regime military and financial support.[12] The first British envoy in Beijing, Bruce wrote back to the Foreign Office on the last day of 1860, describing the great difficulty of substituting for chronic war, peaceful discussion. It is mainly a matter of overcoming the bigotry and arrogance of the Chinese which makes it inevitable that every question depends on force, where the balance of that force is against them. Instead if the British 'are fortunate enough to come into contact with an influential man of reasonable views, I do not despair of proving that our objects are essentially pacific, that our demands are reasonable, and that we are inclined to be moderate and conciliatory, if we are met in a corresponding spirit'.[13] The fundamental question running through the negotiations between Satow and Li is maybe whether the British could be moderate and conciliatory as much as whether Li was an influential man of reasonable views.

How 'reasonable' could Li be, as an influential Han official in the late Qing dynasty? The cultural system of Confucianism had existed in China for over two thousand years, becoming more and more complicated over time. How could westerners understand the Confucian system and its people on their first arrival in China without spending their whole life studying the plethora of works on Confucian classics? While Satow will have come as close to this ideal as could be 'reasonably expected' it is doubtful whether he appreciated fully the extent to which any Chinese is bound into networks of relationships. The nature of interpersonal relationships is a guideline for understanding people's behaviour in the Confucian system. An essential principle of Confucian theories is to educate people to define the interpersonal relationships: the relationship between a ruler and his officials, the relationship between

[9] ibid 332–37. [10] ibid 346. [11] ibid. [12] ibid. [13] ibid.

a father and his sons, and the relationship between a husband and his wife, which require loyalty, filial piety, and chastity. Among the three relationships, the relationship between a ruler and his officials is crucial to understand the behaviour of Li Hongzhang in the Boxer Rebellion period and his relationships with the court and his peers.

The Confucian system was not tolerant of innovation. Even as great a Confucian teacher as Zhu Xi (朱熹, 1130–1200), who had laid the foundation of the imperial examination system since the Southern Song dynasty (1127–1279) and established a school of Confucianism to interpret Confucian classics, created, with his contribution of the interpretation of Confucian classics, a tool to imprison scholars in the imperial examination system. If someone wanted to innovate, he had to break out of his old relationships and existing resources. If the system was not responding to his innovation positively, he and his family would die out. The cost of innovation was too high for insiders to endure. As a result, the insiders had no choice but to make the system strong enough to secure the continuity of their benefits. This was the principle of Li Hongzhang's diplomacy.

Official Confucianism was an autarkic system in the Qing dynasty. There was no need to learn and apply Western theories in order to make this system run. With the support of the imperial examination system, people in the Confucian system would gain security and accomplishments through their relationships with other people in the system. Li Hongzhang was no exception. The imperial examination system was run by the Qing government. Li Hongzhang's achievement was awarded by the Qing government. To protect the Qing government was to maintain the legitimacy of his own benefits. It is hard to say whether Li Hongzhang had an outlook with respect to international relationships. He did not on his own initiative develop any international relationships that would benefit China. He only contributed to stabilizing the rule of the Qing government when it was confronted with foreign problems. During the process of settling the Boxer Crisis, of which the Russia–Manchuria crisis was a small part, he treated the Boxer Rebellion as a domestic riot involving foreigners. He tried to solve the crisis of the Boxer Rebellion through his personal relationships with Russia. When he had no bargaining powers to persuade foreign powers to retreat troops, he refused to go to Beijing because he did not want the foreign powers to be disappointed in him.[14]

In Confucian bureaucracy, officials looked up to the officials on top tiers. The good relationships with top officials brought more benefits to them than caring about people on lower tiers. In the Boxer Rebellion, Li Hongzhang did not show mercy for the loss of the Boxer rebels, Chinese and foreign armies, and ordinary foreigners. He did not care for the exact number of the casualty and loss in the riot. He only cared about the safety of foreign ambassadors. He assumed foreign powers would withdraw troops from Beijing if these ambassadors were safe. Li Hongzhang warned that he would not go to the north until foreign ambassadors were safely

[14] Tinglong Gu and Yalian Ye (eds), *Telegram*, vol 3, *The Collected Works of Li Hongzhang* (Shanghai People's Publishing House 1987) 941.

escorted to Tianjin.[15] The retreat of foreign armies was directly associated with his own benefits, which were connected with the stability of the Qing government.

The Confucian system was not an outgoing system. It developed a complicated inward community which the insiders served with honour. It helped its insiders to recreate the behaviour of ancient sages. It did not require flexibility, diversity, and creativity from the insiders. As an elite insider on the top of the pyramid structure, Li Hongzhang chose to maintain the running of the system. He established a net of interpersonal relationships to hunt his benefits and he himself was also in other shareholders' nets being hunted. The benefits of these shareholders were granted by the imperial examination system in form and the Confucian system in theory. Li Hongzhang's survival in the Confucian system was the ultimate goal. His diplomacy also served this purpose. He was benefited within the system by his dealing with foreign affairs. The interpersonal relationships he established with foreigners helped him never fall out of the mind of the rulers.

Now to come to the rulership itself, how would it relate to an official like Li and how would he respond? This had to be the immensely complex background against which Satow had to contend in his own direct dealings with Li. Manchurian rulers valued Confucianism very highly. Though Manchurian officials did not need to take the imperial examinations as Han officials did, they were also bound by the Confucian theory. Filial piety was the most important requirement on all of the officials. The relationship between rulers and officials seemed like a blood-likeness relationship. The rulers were parents and the officials were sons.

The concentration of power in the hand of a ruler required the system of filial piety. If an emperor could not hold all his ruling power in hand, the system of filial piety would fall apart. This does not mean that officials would then have the opportunity not to obey the emperor. It means instead that officials would have to secure their positions under another powerful ruler. This is where the Emperor party and the Empress Dowager party came into play in the late Qing period.

The nature of the imperial power was traditionally exclusive control.

> The traditional imperial power was to exploit all the power in the society. It was being coveted all the time. Therefore the autocratic monarchy power was high-handed, exclusive, and antagonistic to dissidents. It must be established in a rigorous hierarchy. If the ruler could firmly grasp his power and keep the rigorous sequence of hierarchy in the chain of power and order, he could maintain the long term stabilization of the society. Once the ruler could not hold his power tight, the supreme power would be encroached upon or split. And then the whole country would fall into disorder and different powers would fight against each other.[16]

When it came to the late Qing period, the rulers were not as strong as previous emperors. They could only try to keep the balance between different parties. The Empress Dowager Cixi (慈禧, 1835–1908) and the Guangxu Emperor (光绪,

[15] ibid 1093.

[16] Hongjie Zhang, *The Ten Faces of the Qianlong Emperor* (People's Literature Publishing House 2009) 22.

1875–1908) accentuated this problem. The Guangxu Emperor ascended to the throne at the age of 3. He was inevitably ruling China under the influence of the Regent Empress Dowager Cixi. Though the Guangxu Emperor was the official ruler, the Empress Dowager Cixi was the actual ruler of China. Officials were divided into two major groups: the Emperor party and the Empress Dowager party. These differences were unofficial categories because parties were seen as threats to the power of the ruler. 'The biggest enemy of each dynasty was not rebels, alien races, or natural disasters, but the parties among bureaucrats.'[17] These parties of bureaucrats were not easy to control and rulers often tried to crack down on them before they became too strong to manipulate. This explains why these parties or alliances were undercover and officials were cautious not to be identified with any such party publicly.

There was no room for independence and fairness in Confucian society. The lives and fortunes of officials were under the power of rulers, which meant officials lived under high pressure and uncertainty. Therefore most of the officials tried to make alliance with others. These alliances were loose and unofficial, such as the Manchu officials group, the Han officials group, and the group of officials from the same hometown. Rulers saw these alliances as trouble and took strict precautions against them.

The bureaucratic system had been built by rulers. Intellectuals who passed the final round of the imperial examinations were automatically recruited by the government. Once recruited, they did not have the right to resign from their position.[18] The bureaucracy system was a tool for rulers and also an obstacle for them. Rulers owned everything in the country. The imperial power exploited all aspects of Chinese people's life. If one wanted to gain better social and financial status, one had to survive the imperial examinations and become an official. Otherwise, one had to work in the field all his life and had little chance to be respectable or rich. The paths of possibilities were already set up by the government. When Earl Macartney was travelling in China in 1793, he observed that:

> The influence that, in nations of Europe, is derived from birth, fortune, and character, is of no weight in the Chinese government. The most learned, and I have already explained how far the term extends, provided he be not of notorious bad character, is sure to be employed; though under the present Tartar government, the Chinese complain that they never arrive at the highest rank till they are advanced in years. Learning alone, by the strict maxims of state, leads to office, and office to distinction. Property, without learning, has little weight, and confers no distinction, except in some corrupt provincial governments, where the external marks of office are sold, as in Canton. Hence property is not fo [*sic*] much an object of the laws in China as elsewhere, and consequently has not the same security. In the governments of Europe, property seldom fails to command influence and to force dependence: in China, the man of property is afraid to own it, and all the enjoyments it procures him are stolen.[19]

This means power and fortunes were bound together. The more powerful the officials were, the richer they could be. The desire for fortunes motivated people to

[17] ibid 28. [18] Zhang (n 16) 67.

[19] J Barrow, *Travels in China* (Cadell and Davies 1804) 385.

become officials through the imperial examination system. But nothing was guaranteed. They could easily lose their fortunes or even their lives if they failed to fulfil the requirements of the rulers.

The officials did focus on the long-term interests of the country, but this meant the long-term dominion of the ruling class. That is, the officials cared about their own interests which they gained from their positions. When not being driven by interests, officials carried out policies passively. When they found flaws in policies, they would maximize their own interests by mixing them with the national interests.[20] During the late Qing period, government corruption was endemic. It had become a tremendous net involving all officials and was impossible to break. Before the Qing dynasty:

> Confucianism, on one hand, required its followers to serve rulers at their best; on the other hand, it required them not to give up their own dignity and their pursuit of spiritual values. On the secular level, Confucian followers obeyed the emperors and the order of power; on the spiritual level, they aimed at becoming a sage eventually. Through moral polishing, they wanted to become the perfect human being and surpass emperors and other powerful figures.[21]

However, by the time it came to the Qing dynasty, Confucianism was being selectively promoted by the rulers. The aspect of obedience to the power was promulgated by the government; in the meantime, the rulers tried hard to delete any independent spirit and thought in intellectuals' minds. Through the Qing dynasty, the spiritual cleanliness of Confucian intellectuals and officials was gradually eliminated by the rulers. Qing governments had plenty of capable officials but they were not helping increase the benefits of the country. Officials cared about their own fame and fortune more than the real interests of the country.

Li Hongzhang's telegram about the railway problem in the Boxer Rebellion showed another form of pursuing interests by officials. There were a bunch of officials who favoured criticizing the policies of the government and the behaviour of officials. They were called the Qingyi Group. They pursued the fame of being brave to admonish the policies they thought were problematic, especially those policies that were in conflict with Confucian principles. They sometimes set up obstacles for officials who actually carried out plans to do business for the government. The majority of them were against the Self-strengthening Movement (or the Modernization Movement). For example, Li Hongzhang was often targeted by such officials. 'The Boxer bandits destroyed over one hundred and twenty miles of railways. Who would pay for the mending fee? If other people copy this, the whole railway system may be destroyed. Qingyi did not think the railway was a good idea. They are happy about the current situation.'[22] Li Hongzhang was confronted with a lot of difficulty in constructing and maintaining railways in China because many officials were virulently anti-foreign. Therefore the opinions of Qingyi were often used by conservative officials to attack their political opponents. They did not care about the conflicts caused by their actions between China and other countries.

[20] Zhang (n 18) 29. [21] ibid 172. [22] Gu and Ye (n 14) 924.

## 3. The Boxer Rebellion and Satow–Li Diplomacy over the Russian–Manchurian Crisis[23]

The Russian–Manchuria Railway Concession issue was not central to the Boxer Rebellion but it was an integral part of it. The most offending article in the draft Russia–China Agreement provided: 'It is expedient that a Russian official with general powers of control should be stationed at Mukden for the settlement of all questions affecting the two countries, between the Tartar General, on the one hand and the Governor of the Liaotung Province on the other.'[24] In addition, the whole Agreement gave final say to the 'Russian official' on all questions of the maintenance of order and the Russian version of the Agreement was authoritative.

The British ambassador to St Petersburg, Sir C Scott reported to the Marquess of Lansdowne through the Russian foreign secretary, Count Lamsdorff, that Chinese military authorities in the province of Manchuria had attacked the Russians without warning and, in addition to destroying Russian railways in the province had invaded Russian territory. As for the Russian response 'Russia would have been quite justified in taking the permanent possession of Manchuria by right of conquest'.[25] However, the Russian emperor chose not to regard the Chinese aggression as an act of war of the Chinese State, but merely the behaviour of rebels. Therefore, not being in a state of war, Russia would not claim a right of conquest. Nonetheless, he thought it necessary to obtain assurances from the Chinese State that 'before the final evacuation by her (Russian) troops, (Russia) must obtain some guarantee from China against the recurrence of disturbances and attacks on her frontier and be more adequately secured in the protection of her railway in Manchuria'.[26]

As the crisis of the Boxer Rebellion deepened, Li Hong Zhang was summoned to Beijing from Guangdong, where he had been sent after the disaster of the Sino-Japanese War of 1894–95. Li Hongzhang disobeyed the court's decrees twice before he went to Beijing to solve the crisis of the Boxer Rebellion. He managed to push the court into a corner so that it had no choice but to give whatever he needed. The Boxer Rebellion was a chance for Li Hongzhang to regain what he had lost after the Sino-Japanese War in 1895. Li Hongzhang was certain that the court would not break its relationship with him because no other officials could replace him.

The first decree required Li Hongzhang to go to Beijing. He did not reject this decree publicly and showed his willingness to obey the order. But, in fact, he did not make a move on this order. Li Hongzhang sent two telegrams to local officials

[23] The majority of the materials used to analyse Li Hongzhang's behaviour and views on international relations are the telegrams sent to and by Li Hongzhang with the court and his peers. Limited to the resources of telegraph, most of their correspondence was compact in length with less rhetoric language. This material served as a quality resource for analysing Li Hongzhang's behaviour and thoughts because they were less camouflaged.

[24] 'Ernest Mason Satow's Further Correspondence Respecting Affairs of China Part XXII' FO 405/105 (National Archives of the United Kingdom), Confidential Print, 87–88.

[25] 'Satow's Further Correspondence Part XXII' (n 24) 122, Dispatch No 155 20, February 1901.

[26] ibid.

to inquire whether the roads to Beijing were in good condition on 22 June 1900.[27] Before he got responses, on the second day, in his reply to Yuan Shikai (袁世凯), the governor of Shandong Province, Li Hongzhang revealed his dissatisfaction with the decree. He commented that General Dong, who led the government army to attack foreigners, was terribly wrong and was a disaster for the country. Li Hongzhang then said he did not have any guard so that foreign armies and Boxer rebels might obstruct his trip to the north.[28] On 23 June, Li Hongzhang sent an express telegram to Zongli Yamen in which he said he was ready and eager to set off for Beijing but had no way to get to Beijing due to the destruction of the roads to the north.[29] In his later two telegrams on 24 June to Sheng Xuanhuai (盛宣怀) who was the former aide of Li Hongzhang and the head of the Chinese Railway Company during the Boxer Rebellion, Li Hongzhang said the people of Guangdong and Guangxi provinces urged him to stay, so he had to linger in his place until later orders came.[30] Li Hongzhang also asked whether or not Liu Kunyi (刘坤一) and Zhang Zhidong (张之洞) were sending troops to Beijing in this telegram. Liu Kunyi was the minister of Nanyang and Zhang Zhidong was the viceroy of Hunan and Hubei Provinces. It is obvious that Li Hongzhang refused to go to Beijing and found some excuse to conceal his real opinion. In Li Hongzhang's telegrams to the four parties in three days, the telegrams to local officials and Zongli Yamen were treated like official business; in the telegrams to Yuan Shikai and Sheng Xuanhuai, however, Li Hongzhang carefully revealed his concern and asked about other viceroys' reactions to the court. Li Hongzhang was trying to form an alliance with some powerful local officials.

When Li Hongzhang was asked to go to Beijing to solve the potential military conflicts between China and other countries, he said in his reply telegram to his former co-worker that 'I already asked foreign ambassadors to pay attention to their governments' opinions and let me know their settlements. But General Dong is working with bandits and planning to attack foreign embassies. This would become chaos for sure. Do I have any excuse to stop foreign countries to send more troops? Moreover, the court has not come up with final decisions. I cannot go back on my words to foreigners.'[31] It can be seen that Li Hongzhang kept a close eye on the situation and tried to figure it out by his own efforts. But he would not fully devote himself to solving this problem until the Emperor and the Empress Dowager made up their minds. This is because he would not get the credit of settling down the problem if the court did not agree with his suggestion. In his other telegram to the Chinese ambassador to Russia, he commented that the chaos in the capital (Beijing) was caused by themselves[32] (the Emperor, the Empress Dowager, or the court). In his telegrams, Li Hongzhang seemed unwilling to respond to foreign threats and was not always consistent with the court's policies. Li Hongzhang could stay aloof from the chaos because he was also needed by the foreign countries. His own interest would not be harmed by either the court or the foreign forces.

[27] Gu and Ye (n 14), 934. [28] ibid 935. [29] ibid 936. [30] ibid 937.
[31] ibid 941. [32] ibid 974.

In Confucian bureaucracy, most officials relied on leaders and were reluctant to lead themselves. Li Hongzhang needed an alliance to support him in dealing with foreign affairs. However, most officials did not like to take risks and assume responsibilities. Some officials tried hard to persuade Li Hongzhang to go to Beijing as soon as possible so that they could maintain their benefits in their administrative areas. No one (except those who fought against the foreigners) volunteered to solve this serious problem at risk of failure. When Li Hongzhang was summoned to Beijing, officials from all levels started to persuade him to solve the chaos in the north as soon as possible. These officials included local governors, generals, viceroys, Chinese ambassadors.[33] Foreign governments were also interested in having Li Hongzhang as a Chinese representative.[34] Both Chinese officials and foreign powers firmly believed that Li Hongzhang was the only person capable of settling the situation. Li Hongzhang replied that the road condition stopped him from going to the north. After Li Hongzhang finally arrived in Shanghai and was promoted to the position of the viceroy of Zhili on 9 July 1900, other officials started to persuade him to go to north again.[35] Now his strategy of waiting had worked. But this time, Li Hongzhang had a reasonable excuse that he was sick. Li Hongzhang even asked for sick leave of twenty days.[36]

Soon after he arrived in Shanghai, he was appointed as the plenipotentiary of China on 8 August 1900.[37] Still he insisted upon more conditions. On 3 September, Li Hongzhang sent a 3,675-word memorial to the throne by telegram in which he asked the court to appoint Prince Qing and Grand Scholar Ronglu (荣禄) as the plenipotentiaries of China on behalf of the royal family, punish two generals who advocated a war towards Russia and failed to protect Russian railways in the northeast, and repair the wires in Zhili and Shanxi Provinces.[38] In the end, Prince Qing was appointed as the royal plenipotentiary.[39] As soon as this decree was confirmed, Li Hongzhang decided to go to the north.

Li Hongzhang was pro-Russia in solving the problem of the Boxer Rebellion. An imperial decree by the court had declared a war on foreign powers and required all local governors to raise funds and support the Boxers[40] (the Boxer Rebellion was not considered as a war by foreign powers, which ended up with a protocol instead of a peace treaty). In Li Hongzhang's telegram to Sheng Xuanhuai, he took this decree as a fake one and decided not to obey it. He said this decree was an arbitrary order and also asked Sheng to forward his telegram secretly to Liu Kunyi and Zhang Zhidong.[41] Besides that, Li Hongzhang asked Chinese ambassadors to Britain, France, Germany, Russia, and Japan to find out the attitudes of those governments towards China. He tried to solve the Boxer Rebellion before a war was officially started between China and the foreign powers. At the same time, Li Hongzhang made personal contacts with his friends in Russia. He asked Ukhtomsky and his 'closest friend' Sergei Witte, the Russian minister of finance, to help him if he went

[33] ibid 943–45. [34] ibid 955. [35] ibid 1043. [36] ibid 1063.
[37] ibid 1070.
[38] Tinglong Gu and Yi Dai (eds), *Telegram*, vol 27, *The Collected Works of Li Hongzhang* (Anhui Education Press 2008) 254.
[39] ibid 278. [40] Gu and Ye (n 14) 971. [41] ibid 954

to Beijing.[42] Without court approval, Li Hongzhang started to find solutions for the crisis of Boxer Rebellion in his own way.

In his prevarications over the nature of the decree declaring war, Li Hongzhang was taking a very complex stance on who had power at the court. This is very important for an assessment of the British record because it assumes that power and authority were with the emperor and not the empress dowager. Li Hongzhang stood beside the Empress Dowager Cixi. In two of his telegrams to other officials, he showed his concerns about the attitude of the Empress Dowager Cixi[43] and the reaction of Cixi to the dynamic situation.[44] As a mature and successful politician, Li Hongzhang clearly knew which power was more reliable and when to make his decision accordingly. In a confidential telegram between him and his former co-worker, he commented that the decree declaring war was fake and arbitrary.[45] A dilemma can be found in his statement. A fake decree should not exist in the first place. How could it be arbitrary? Only a real decree could be an arbitrary one. He did not want to obey this decree because he predicted the failure of the Boxer Rebellion. In the meantime, he was not afraid of the investigation from the Empress Dowager Cixi for not obeying this decree in the future because this decree was issued under the name of the Guangxu Emperor. Li Hongzhang was sure that the Empress Dowager Cixi would eventually regret having issued the decree.

The priority of the court was to balance power between different groups of officials other than unite them together to develop international relationships. This is why the foreign policies of Qing government could not stay consistent. When Western powers asked for more than a ruler wanted to surrender, the ruler would use the conflicts between different groups of officials to change its policies. Before the court declared the war against foreign powers, the Empress Dowager Cixi sent officials to disband the organizations of Boxers.[46] She then changed her mind because she thought the foreign powers would like to require her to return all administrative power to the Guangxu Emperor. This was revealed in the telegram from Russia.[47] Li Hongzhang was trying to keep a delicate balance in his relationship with the court. Though as powerful as Li Hongzhang, he had to do what the rulers asked him to do. His illness worsened on his way to Beijing, but the court would not let him rest for long. He died shortly after he signed the Boxer protocol. Li Hongzhang repeatedly gained and lost power and fortune in the process of climbing to higher positions. He took most of the responsibility for the failure of the Sino-Japanese War (1894–95) because of his leading position in the war. He regained during the Boxer Rebellion the prestige and esteem which he had lost over the Sino-Japanese war.

He largely relied on his personal relationships with some important Russia officials. Ukhtomsky and Sergei Witte were Li Hongzhang's old acquaintances. Sergei Witte was the minister of finance in Russia at that time. They got to know each other on Li Hongzhang's trip to Russia to sign the Sino-Russian Secret Treaty in 1896, and became mutually beneficial for each other. Ukhtomsky actively contacted Li Hongzhang through telegram and even in person. When Ukhtomsky heard Li

[42] ibid 953. [43] ibid 928. [44] ibid 940. [45] ibid 954. [46] ibid 925.
[47] ibid 1028.

Hongzhang was summoned to Beijing, he sent a telegram to Li Hongzhang to urge Li Hongzhang to go to the north. He said only Li Hongzhang could settle this disaster and Sergei Witte would love to help China.[48] Ukhtomsky made a trip to China to discuss the solution with Li Hongzhang. Li Hongzhang suggested they did not contact one another directly to avoid suspicion from other countries.[49] Not only to avoid suspicion from other countries, Li Hongzhang also wanted to conceal his relationships with Russia from his peers because he was careful not to be categorized as a member of the Pro-Russia Party.[50]

Although closely working with Russian officials, Li Hongzhang was aware of the threats from Russia. Before he was contacted by Russian officials, he promised to other officials that he would discuss with Russian officials and that Russia would definitely not take the lands of China.[51] He wanted to warn the court about Russia but he did not do so by himself. He forwarded Zongli Yamen the telegrams from Yang Ru (杨儒), the Chinese ambassador to Russia. In these telegrams, ambassador Yang clearly pointed out that the railways in China's north-east provinces were crucial national interests of Russia; if the Qing government could not protect the railways from being destroyed by rebels, the relationship between China and Russia would be destroyed too.[52] When it was confirmed that railways were destroyed, Yang worried that the three north-east provinces would be occupied by Russia in the near future.[53] Li Hongzhang covered his traces in these telegrams. For his own benefit, he intentionally ignored one of Russia's attentions. In Yang's telegram, he mentioned that Russia would like to help China if Guangxu Emperor had the administrative power in his own hands.[54] Li Hongzhang and Yang Ru were in frequent contact during the Boxer Rebellion. Li Hongzhang replied to all of Yang Ru's telegrams except this one. The Empress Dowager Cixi was the actual ruler of the late Qing dynasty. All the relationships of Li Hongzhang with the court were bound with the empress dowager instead of the emperor. Russia's suggestion conflicted with his own interest. Fortunately, this was not mentioned again. Russia was a personal resource of Li Hongzhang. In his longest telegram to the court, 1,714 out of 3,675 words were on Russian affairs.[55] He worked hard at persuading the court to accept every request made by Russia. He could not afford to break his connections with Russia because he had no other relationships with foreign powers. In one of his telegrams to Ambassador Yang, he tried to inform the US, Japan, and Germany that Russia wanted to move troops to Tianjin. He complained that the British government was devious and had no common sense,[56] because it did not acknowledge Li Hongzhang's plenary powers, did not start the negotiation, and did not withdraw troops.[57]

To return to the question of whether the British had now found a reasonable interlocutor, in 1900 the ground for investigating this question is the interaction of Satow and Li concerning primarily the Chinese Russian draft Manchurian Railway Agreement, with respect to which they were both key negotiators. The story is

[48] ibid 951. [49] ibid 1060. [50] Gu and Dai (n 38) 260.
[51] Gu and Ye (n 14) 954. [52] ibid 963. [53] ibid 1005. [54] ibid 1028.
[55] Gu and Dai (n 38) 254. [56] ibid 249. [57] ibid 260.

described below from the British Foreign Office Confidential Prints. The framework set by the British diplomatic historian, Otte is that the draft Chinese Russian Railway Agreement was a facade for the setting up of a Russian protectorate over a large part of Manchuria (Fengti'en, one of the three provinces), with the retention of Chinese sovereignty a pure facade. In Otte's view, Li Hongzhang wished to resist this but did not feel strong enough to do so directly. Satow, in Otte's view, was sufficiently astute to perceive that Li had probably leaked the draft Agreement to provoke a crisis and to drive other foreign powers, especially Britain, to resist Russia. While the other powers suspected Li of pro-Russian sympathy Satow assumed that Li simply felt not strong enough to resist Russia alone. In the face of vacillation by the Chinese in Beijing and their ambassador in London, Satow had resort also to viceroys in the Yangtze region, besides encouraging other powers to express concern. Russia withdrew its proposal and Satow concluded by warning the Chinese of the need to reform Manchurian administration and not give the Russians the excuse to argue that someone in addition was needed to maintain order.[58]

A possible British close reading of the Confidential Print does go a long way to support the view that Li Hongzhang's policy was very self-regarding, having regard to his own interests, while also being pro-Russian. This reading also accepts the apparently impenetrable character of the Qing administration, while allowing that this is attributable to the constantly changing sectional interests within it. That is to say, there was no overall centralized strategy and so each Chinese would feel in danger of being repudiated and taken together Chinese public utterances could appear inconsistent. However, Otte thinks that Satow, with the aid of his consuls and Chinese agents completely understood that apparently labyrinthine administration.[59]

The first stage in the story has already been recounted. The British ambassador to St Petersburg raised the alarm at the draft Chinese Russian Agreement on 20 February 1901.[60] The next stage in the story is that Satow reported to Lansdowne, the British foreign secretary, a memorandum, dated 1 March 1901, of a meeting between Sir W Hillier (an adviser to Satow) and Li Hongzhang. The meeting also concerned the negotiations over the Boxer Protocol. About this aspect of the negotiation the record is revealing. The impact of interpersonal relationships was obvious during the negotiation. In a memorandum of the British diplomat, Walter Hillier, on the interview with Li Hongzhang, he mentioned that 'a great step in advance had been made by the satisfaction of the demands of the Powers in the matter of punishments. If the punishment of certain provincial officials, of whom a list would shortly be sent in, was also carried out as required, I considered that half the difficulties would be over.'[61] These to be punished Chinese officials were taking actions with the approval of the empress dowager in the Boxer Rebellion. Punishing these officials was equal to punishing the empress dowager for her mistake. In Confucian

[58] Otte (n 4) 174–77.

[59] ibid 175. Otte points out how Satow had cultivated secret sources within the Chinese government. 'He even purchased a "safe house" in the Chinese quarter of Peking where the Chinese secretary of the legation could receive native visitors undisturbed.'

[60] See (nn 24–26).

[61] 'Satow's Further Correspondence Part XXII' (n 25) 276.

bureaucracy, rulers could not be judged by others. They could only be punished by themselves, such as issuing a decree to admit their mistakes. In addition, these officials were closely associated with the empress dowager, some of whom were the relatives of the empress dowager. When Li Hongzhang was sent to the most southern part of China, these officials had much closer relationships with the empress dowager than him. It would not add value to Li Hongzhang's relationship with the empress dowager if he eliminated these officials even though they were his political enemies. Although being appointed as a plenipotentiary, Li Hongzhang would not be positively engaged in making the agreement on punishments.

On the contrary, Li Hongzhang did not push hard on five articles in the negotiation of the Boxer Protocol. 'We then proceeded to take the twelve Articles one by one. Their Excellencies agreed that there was nothing on their part to be done with regard to importation of arms, &c. (Article 5), indemnities (Article 6), Legation guards and areas (Article 7), demolition of forts (Article 8), and occupation of lines of communication (Article 9), as on all these matters the foreign Representatives could practically take action without reference to the Chinese Government.'[62] These articles did no harm to Li Hongzhang's interpersonal relationships with the empress dowager, his peers, and his foreign connections.

Finally, with respect to the draft Railway Agreement, Hillier reported that the Russians were pressing the Chinese to sign and he spoke in the following terms to Li Hongzhang:

> I ventured to warn him that he would lay up for his Government an incalculable amount of trouble if he signed the treaty in the face of the opposition offered by other Powers. He said he knew very well that it was a serious matter, but he was in a very tight corner, for Russia claimed Manchuria by right of conquest, and refused to surrender her self-constituted rights except under stringent conditions. It was all very well to warn him [Li] that he must not sign; why did not the foreign Representatives convey a similar warning to M. de Giers.[63] They all attacked China and left Russia alone, and, as far as he could learn from telegraphic reports, no protest had been lodged by the Representatives of other powers at St Petersburg.[64]

The next stage in the story is a direct meeting between Satow and Li on 19 March 1901 in which the main subject was the draft Railway Agreement. The notes of the interview are to be reproduced in full shortly in this chapter. There was some discussion of whether the Chinese were in breach of their understanding with Russia by concluding a railway construction agreement with the British beyond the Great Wall. Li was insistent that Russian allegations of bad faith were unjustified as China had never given any undertaking to Russia not to do this. Then came the terms of the draft Agreement itself. Satow alleged that to sign the Agreement would stultify China and Li responded that 'he was of the same opinion, but found himself in a difficult position' Russia had conquered Manchuria by force of arms but was willing to hand it back for exchange, but China was being pressurized to sign without the details of the agreement having

[62] ibid. [63] The Russian chancellor.

[64] 'Satow's Further Correspondence Part XXII' (n 25) 277; Satow to Lansdowne, 11 March 1901, and accompanying dispatch enclosure No 252, memorandum of interview by Sir W. Hillier with Grand Secretary Li and Chou-fu 1 March 1901.

been fully disclosed. Yet Li also said the terms of the Draft were such as generally neither China nor the powers could object, except for the already mentioned issue of an accusation of bad faith by China. Li continued to say that M. de Gier was exercising the greatest pressure, but he, Li, was kept in the dark by his own government as to what they had conceded in St Petersburg. Russia had imposed a deadline of six days in which to sign and Li wished to know whether Satow could induce his government to make representation to Russia that his (Li's) government 'was being forced to subscribe to a misstatement of facts and that it was obviously unfair to make her do so' (that Russia in fact knew and approved of the British–Chinese contract). Li appeared greatly relieved that Satow said he would telegraph London in this respect.[65]

Further discussion of the terms of the Agreement was difficult because Li said he was not at liberty to disclose them without Russia's approval. Satow asked whether there were any further objectionable clauses, to which Li replied that there were not, except that one or two points in their present form might 'give bad example'. However, Li complained that the Russians were not giving the Chinese enough time to discuss these. Then Satow asked whether it was Russia that was proposing handing Manchuria back. Li affirmed this and then Satow continued that he had heard Manchuria was proving too difficult to govern properly, Russia was anxious to be rid of the province, so that China could hold out against Russia as its threats were empty. Li said 'he was not inclined to share this view'.[66]

Li would not disclose the terms of the Agreement but gave Satow to understand that objectionable terms had been eliminated. Satow made the following general comment on the style of the meeting, and Li's approach to negotiation:

> His Excellency too was anxious to explain that he was not the person who was empowered to sign the Agreement and negotiate the terms thereof. It was assumed that it was *his* Convention, but that assumption was erroneous. The Plenipotentiary for settling the Manchuria question was Yang Ru, the Chinese Minister in St Petersburg, who was instructed by the Court at Hsian. His Excellency himself was only consulted occasionally. A very interesting feature of the interview was the extreme reluctance in the beginning, of the Grand Secretary to discuss the matter at all. He was evidently bearing in mind Russian threats as to what would happen, were he to disclose particulars. But, as the conversation went on, this reluctance gradually disappeared, until towards the end his Excellency discarded it entirely and more or less implored our assistance in the matter. While conscientiously refraining from giving direct information, he hinted that ... most objectionable points in the original draft have been eliminated ... It may be possible in a day or two to find out what it is his Excellency fears other Powers ... will be afforded an opportunity of 'imitating a bad example'.[67]

Satow appeared to have been sceptical of Li Hongzhang's remarks and encouraged his consul-general in Hankou to communicate with the secretary of the viceroy, Mr Liang on 1 April 1901. He informed Mr Fraser that the court had given strict orders that the Manchuria Agreement was not to be signed. The emperor had at one time empowered Li Hongzhang to act on his own discretion if he were sure the Agreement

[65] 'Satow's Further Correspondence Part XXIII', FO 405/ 106, 46–47; Satow to Lansdowne, 21 March 1901, and enclosure No 72.

[66] ibid. [67] ibid.

would not prove dangerous to China. Mr Liang explained that Li Hongzhang had in fact already ordered the Chinese in St Petersburg, Yang Ru to sign, while the Yang-tsze viceroys sent a telegram to Yang Ru, warning that if he did he would be in personal danger, and so he delayed long enough for the viceroys to be able to sway the court. Then the emperor ordered Yang Ru to transmit to the Russian emperor a letter saying that China could not deal alone with Russia while the other powers were conferring in Beijing, a letter the latter refused to receive. Whereupon, to avoid further responsibility, the Chinese minister in St Petersburg declared himself seriously ill.

The emperor then encouraged all the various viceroys opposed to the Agreement to encourage the powers to dissuade Russia from hostile action against China. The court was in danger of panicking over Russian hostility and so the viceroys pressed Britain as to how to avoid this. At the same time while Li was one plenipotentiary, Prince Qing was another who complained that Li spoke in his name without his consent, a division which would greatly weaken Li at the court. The consul-general also said to Liang that he was unable to understand Li's course of action. Liang's response was to remind him:

> of the Viceroy's remarks on Li's pride and self-importance, and suggested that the explanation of his conduct might be found in the fact that, while the other Ministers snubbed Li on his arrival in Peking,[68] the Russian Representative treated him with the utmost consideration and flattery. Li had also reported to the Throne that on his telling Mr de Giers that China would of course expect Russia's support against the pressure of other Powers, the Minister assented as he left.[69]

The next dispatch is from Fraser to Satow describing an interview in Hankou on 4 April 1901 granted by Viceroy Zhang Zhidong, following a letter from Lansdowne. The viceroy explained how Li Hongzhang was warning the throne that Russia would not restore Manchuria if it did not get the Agreement. Then Fraser discussed tactics with the viceroy for getting the issue into the Peace Conference, where Russia would have to compromise. They also discussed how the Manchuria Agreement would completely tie China to Russia in the daily conduct of administration and policy.[70]

In September Sir C Scott (in St Petersburg) reported that Li was continuing to urge the emperor to sign the Agreement with Russia before telling the other powers. The court, while declining this course, was telling Li to endeavour to negotiate favourable terms with the Russian minister. However, with the absence of a Russian minister in Beijing, nothing was happening. At the same time Russia could not hand back Manchuria while China was not capable of keeping order there.[71]

Yet another discussion between Fraser and the viceroy in Hankou on 24 October had the viceroy expressing concern that there were no real improvements in the

[68] 'Peking' is now replaced by 'Beijing', but 'Peking' is kept in its original form in quotations.

[69] 'Satow's Further Correspondence Part XXIII' (n 65) 67–68; Fraser to Lansdowne, copies to dispatches sent to the Minister (Satow) in Peking 5 April 1901 re enclosure 1 in No 81, Hankou 1 April 1901.

[70] ibid 68–69; enclosure No 2 in No 81, Acting Consul General Fraser to Sir E Satow.

[71] 'Satow's Further Correspondence Part XXVII' FO 405/110, 8–9; No 20, Sir C Scott to Lansdowne, 5 September 1901.

terms offered by Russia in the new Manchurian Agreement which Li had pressed the court, vainly as yet, to accept. 'The virtual protectorate remained.' The only improvement was the excision of a clause referring to a railway in the direction of Beijing.

The court had told Li to try for better terms, but it was in extreme apprehension of Russia's making the delay in signing an excuse for absorbing Manchuria where Russian troops were in overwhelming force. England, America, and Japan would all suffer by such absorption. The viceroy from Hankou asked Fraser did he think His Majesty's Government would help China? Fraser's response was:

> I suggested that ... the clauses impairing the Treaty rights of other nations were retained in the new Treaty, China might surely inform Russia that in view of her obligations to other Powers, she could not assent to such clauses without obtaining the consent of other nations affected.
>
> The Viceroy doubted whether the Court would dare to adopt such a step, unless England and the other friendly Powers would first formally warn China against giving differential privileges in Manchuria to a single Power. The Court ... was fully aware that Manchuria must inevitably be absorbed by Russia unless it were thrown open to all the world, and the Court was ready and eager to take this course. But to announce its intention, while Russia was pressing for special privileges and without assurances of support from other nations, would almost certainly irritate Russia into proclaiming the annexation of the three Provinces.[72]

Li Hongzhang died on 7 November 1901. There is a further report of Satow to Lansdowne, a telegram of 7 December, recording a conversation which he had with Prince Qing who had conveyed to him the full details of the Draft Agreement whose negotiation had stopped with the death of Li. The difficulty was that Chinese subjects had damaged Russian railways the previous year and it was not unnatural that they should not want to evacuate without safeguards against a recurrence of disturbances. Nonetheless there were numerous Russian demands which called for privileges and monopoly advantages, which were objectionable to the other powers, as there were numerous restrictions on normal sovereign powers of China, eg concerning building of railways and stationing of troops. Prince Qing agreed that this was the case and would press these points when negotiations resumed. Satow appeared largely satisfied with Prince Qing's assurances, including an undertaking to keep him confidentially informed of further developments.[73]

## 4. Conclusion

Finally, lines of communication appeared to be open and on track, once Li Hongzhang was eliminated from the picture. The British record shows an obsession with blocking Russian advancement, which they displayed as a threat to the

[72] 'Satow's Further Correspondence Part XXX' FO 405/113, 75; Satow to Lansdowne, 6 November 1901, enclosure in No 53, Consul General Fraser to Sir E Satow, 24 October 1901.

[73] ibid 4–5, Satow to Lansdowne, 7 December 1901, No 9. Otte (n 4) 176–77 believes the Russian climbdown came as early as March 1901, but the Further Correspondence appears to indicate otherwise.

territorial integrity of China, but which was simply a fear of any Russian advantage which they did not share. In their struggle against Li Hongzhang, they suspected him of Russian sympathies, but they did not realize that he, in turn, saw the Russians as the soundest protectors of China's integrity, and assurance of the continuance of the Qing dynasty. The British considered the emperor was in charge of the diplomatic process, whereas Li Hongzhang's loyalties were with the empress dowager. Yet because she had favoured the Boxer Rebellion, which he opposed, he could not support her openly. The briefing against Li Hongzhang does not represent 'the truth' but merely a rival faction within China more sympathetic to the emperor. At the same time Li Hongzhang played along with the British, and, while not revealing fully the Chinese–Russian position, or even that he had responsibility for it, he was willing to let the British believe he really did consider there was a Russian threat, against which he welcomed British support.

None of this shows profound cultural difference between the Chinese and the British, as represented by Li and Satow. Both wished to see the Qing dynasty and China preserved, but had differing views as to how to achieve this. Li did not expect any real support from Britain or the other powers except Russia. Both Satow and Li Hongzhang equally opposed the Boxer Rebellion and any major use of force by States. However, Li had to contend with such divisions within the empire and so little real support from the Great Powers, locked in hostility to China also, but only, by the Boxer Rebellion. Yet he could not reveal his reliance on Russia, not only because this would have given internal enemies a clear target, but also because it would have openly intensified rivalries from the foreign powers towards Russia.

On the substance of the specific issue, the security of Russian investment and equipment and personnel in Manchurian railways, Li Hongzhang and Satow were in complete agreement. Li Hongzhang deplored the Boxer-motivated attacks on Russian railways, a popular move at the time also among sections of higher officialdom, he also doubted whether there was the will from the throne to prevent this. So he considered the Russian concerns for control of security in the region reasonable, although he did not say as much to the British. At the same time the British estimated that the Russians had a legitimate grievance against the deprivation they had suffered and were entitled to have more effective protection from the Chinese throne. The British even believed the Russians would have preferred this to having to maintain order in Manchuria themselves.

These very fine points indicate that both Satow and Li Honghzhang, with the knowledge available to them, and with the institutional capacities in their possession, wanted the same thing. They wanted a reasonable settlement of the disorder created by the Boxers and they looked to achieve it through meticulous negotiation, not open and candid, because conditions of diplomacy in the circumstances did not allow for it, but as fairly and reasonably as possible. The cultures of Confucianism and international law did not stand in the way. Nor did the strategic interests of China, Russia, and Britain as powers. The main difference between the countries was the advanced state of institutional decay within China which made Li Hongzhang's task of pursuing a rational policy to maintain China's integrity immensely difficult.

# *Name Index*

# *Subject Index*

The manufacturer's authorised representative in the EU for product safety is Oxford University Press España S.A. of El Parque Empresarial San Fernando de Henares, Avenida de Castilla, 2 – 28830 Madrid (www.oup.es/en or product.safety@oup.com). OUP España S.A. also acts as importer into Spain of products made by the manufacturer.

Printed in the USA/Agawam, MA
July 30, 2026

908341.172